THE IMPERIAL PRESIDENCY AND THE CONSEQUENCES OF 9/11

THE IMPERIAL PRESIDENCY AND THE CONSEQUENCES OF 9/11

Lawyers React to the Global War on Terrorism

VOLUME 1

Edited by James R. Silkenat and Mark R. Shulman

Foreword by Barry Kamins, Bettina B. Plevan,
E. Leo Milonas, and Evan A. Davis

PRAEGER SECURITY INTERNATIONAL
Westport, Connecticut · London

Library of Congress Cataloging-in-Publication Data

The imperial presidency and the consequences of 9/11 : lawyers react to the global war on terrorism / edited by James R. Silkenat and Mark R. Shulman.
v. cm.
Includes bibliographical references and index.
ISBN 0–275–99440–6 (set : alk. paper) — ISBN 0–275–99441–4 (vol 1 : alk. paper) — ISBN 0–275–99442–2 (vol 2 : alk. paper)
1. War and emergency powers—United States. 2. Terrorists—Legal status, laws, etc.—United States. 3. Prisoners of war—Legal status, laws, etc.—United States. 4. Detention of persons—Cuba—Guantánamo Bay Naval Base. 5. Trials (Genocide)—Iraq. 6. War on Terrorism, 2001– 7. Executive power—United States I. Silkenat, James R. II. Shulman, Mark R.
KF5060.I47 2007
342.73'062—dc22 2006100488

British Library Cataloguing in Publication Data is available.

Library of Congress Catalog Card Number: 2006100488
ISBN-10: 0–275–99440–6 (set code) ISBN-13: 978–0–275–99440-2 (set code)
0–275–99441–4 (Vol. 1) 978–0–275–99441-9 (Vol. 1)
0–275–99442–2 (Vol. 2) 978–0–275–99442-6 (Vol. 2)

First published in 2007

Praeger Security International, 88 Post Road West, Westport, CT 06881
An imprint of Greenwood Publishing Group, Inc.
www.praeger.com

Printed in the United States of America

The paper used in this book complies with the Permanent Paper Standard issued by the National Information Standards Organization (Z39.48–1984).

10 9 8 7 6 5 4 3 2 1

Contents

About the Editors and Contributors

EDITORS

JAMES R. SILKENAT is a partner in the firm of Arent Fox PLLC in New York City. He is a former Chair of the 16,000-member ABA Section of International Law and helps coordinate Arent Fox's international practice in New York, where he specializes in international finance, securities, and corporate law. He is also a former Chair of the ABA's Section Officers Conference and a member of the Executive Committee of the ABA Board of Governors. He has served for 15 years as a member of the American Bar Association House of Delegate and Chairs New York's Delegation in the ABA House of Delegates.

From 1980 to 1986, Mr. Silkenat was Legal Counsel for the International Finance Corporation, the private-sector-oriented affiliate of the World Bank in Washington, D.C., where he concentrated on privatization issues (including projects in China, Pakistan, Indonesia, Zimbabwe, and other countries). He has also handled significant privatization efforts in Australia, Peru, and Turkey. He is also the founder and former Chair of the ABA's Privatization Committee.

Mr. Silkenat received his J.D. from the University of Chicago Law School, where he was Editor of the *University of Chicago Law Review*. He also received an L.L.M. in International Law from New York University School of Law.

Mr. Silkenat was formerly Chair of the ABA Committee on the People's Republic of China and was the founder of the *China Law Reporter*. He has led Delegations to China for both the ABA and the Association of the Bar of the City of New York, and to the Common Market and Mexico for the ABA. He has also served as a Fellow of the National Endowment for the Humanities and as a Fellow in the U.S. State Department Scholar/Diplomat Program.

Mr. Silkenat is the Editor of *The Moscow Conference on Law and Bilateral Economic Relations, The Law of International Insolvencies and Debt Restructurings, The ABA Guide to Foreign Law Firms* (1988, 1993, 1999, and 2004 Editions), and *The ABA Guide to International Business Negotiations* (1994 and 2002 Editions). He is also the author of more than 100 articles on international law, finance, and public policy, and he has published articles in the *Harvard Law Review, Business Week,* the *New York Times,* and the *Stanford Law Review,* among other publications. He also served as Adjunct Professor of Law at Georgetown University Law Center, where he taught a graduate seminar on international project financing.

Mr. Silkenat also previously served as Chair of both The Lawyers Committee for Human Rights (now, Human Rights First) and The Council of New York Law Associates (now, The Lawyers Alliance for New York). He is a Life Fellow for the American Bar Foundation, has served as Chair of the Fellows of the American Bar Foundation, and is a member of the Council on Foreign Relations. Mr. Silkenat is also a former Chair of the International Human Rights Committee of the Association of the Bar of the City of New York, the City Bar's Task Force on International Legal Services, and the City Bar's Council on International Affairs.

Mr. Silkenat has particular expertise in the negotiation and drafting of international investment funds and international joint-venture agreements, Eurodollar and other international loan agreements, and related documentation, and he has worked on international mergers and acquisitions (including privatizations and restructurings) in both developing and developed countries.

MARK R. SHULMAN is Assistant Dean for Graduate Programs and International Affiliations and an Adjunct Professor of Law at Pace Law School. Until 2003, he practiced corporate law at the international firm of Debevoise & Plimpton.

Immediately prior to joining Pace, Mr. Shulman directed the Worldwide Security Program at the EastWest Institute. He has previously taught in the History Department at Yale University, at Columbia University's School of International and Public Affairs and at Columbia Law School, as well as the U.S. Air War College.

Mr. Shulman has published widely in the fields of history, law, and international affairs. Along with Sir Michael Howard and Professor George Andreopoulos, he edited *The Laws of War: Constraints on Warfare in the Western World.* He wrote *Navalism and the Emergence of American Sea Power, 1882–1893,* as well as numerous articles and book chapters. Mr. Shulman received his B.A. from Yale, a Masters degree from Oxford, and a Ph.D. in history from the University of California at Berkeley. He received his J.D. from Columbia where he served as Editor-in-Chief of the *Journal of Transnational Law,* on the board of which he continues to sit. He has also enjoyed Postdoctoral Fellowships at Yale and Georgetown and is a Visiting Scholar at Yale's International Security Program. He has also been a Visiting Research Scholar at the Naval War College.

He is currently Chair of the New York City Bar's International Human Rights Committee and a member of the City Bar's Council on International Affairs.

CONTRIBUTORS

JAMES J. BENJAMIN, JR. is a partner at Akin Gump Strauss Hauer & Feld LLP. Before joining Akin Gump, he served for more than five years as a federal prosecutor in the U.S. Attorney's Office for the Southern District of New York and he also served as a law clerk at the U.S. Supreme Court for Justices Lewis F. Powell Jr. and John Paul Stevens. He has published articles extensively in the *New York Law Journal,* his most recent article being titled "Rule 10b5-1 and Criminal Insider Trading Cases" (New York Law Journal, July 2004).

JOSEPH G. DAVIS is a partner in the Litigation Department of Willkie Farr & Gallagher LLP in Washington, D.C. Mr. Davis specializes in complex litigation and corporate compliance matters. Mr. Davis represents corporations and individuals in proceedings before federal and state courts and other tribunals. He is a graduate of Amherst College and the University of California at Berkeley School of Law (Boalt Hall).

NICOLE DELLER is a senior program officer at the World Federalist Movement-Institute for Global Policy and the Chair of the International Security Affairs Committee of the New York City Bar Association. Before joining WFM, Ms. Deller was a research associate and consultant for the Lawyers' Committee on Nuclear Policy and the Institute for Energy and Environmental Research.

MILES P. FISCHER is a lawyer in private practice in New York City. He is currently on the Board of Director-Advisors at the National Institute of Military Justice. He has also served as Chair on the Military Affairs and Justice Committee of the New York City Bar.

MARTIN S. FLAHERTY is Leitner Family Chair in International Human Rights and Professor of Law and Co-Director of the Joseph P. Crowley Program in International Human Rights at Fordham Law School in New York. He is a former Chair of the Committee on International Human Rights of the New York City Bar. He has published widely on constitutional law, foreign affairs, and international human rights in such journals as the *Columbia Law Review,* the *Yale Law Journal,* and the *University of Chicago Law Review.*

THOMAS H. MORELAND is a partner at Kramer Levin Naftalis and & Franklin LLP. He handles a wide variety of complex civil litigation matters in international and domestic arbitration. He has served as Vice President and Chair of the Executive Committee of the New York City Bar. He was also a founding member and currently serves as the Chairman of the Board of Volunteers of Legal Service, Inc., which facilitates pro bono service by lawyers in New York City.

ALAN R. ROTHSTEIN serves as General Counsel of the New York City Bar, where he coordinates the extensive law reform and public policy work of this 22,000-member Association. Prior to his 20 years with the Association, Rothstein was the Associate Director of Citizens Union and also practiced with the firm of Weil, Gotshal & Manges. Prior to earning his J.D. from New York University, Mr. Rothstein worked as an Economist in the environmental consulting field and for the New York City Economic Development Administration. Mr. Rothstein currently serves on the Board of Directors for Volunteers of Legal Service, Inc.

MARGARET L. SATTERTHWAITE is an Assistant Professor of Clinical Law and Faculty Director of the Center for Human Rights and Global Justice at New York University School of Law. She has written extensively in the field of international human rights law, and her most recent publications include "Fate and Whereabouts Unknown: Detainees in the 'War on Terror'" (*Center for Human Rights and Global Justice,* 2005) and "Crossing Borders, Claiming Rights: Using Human Rights Law to Empower Women Migrant Workers" (*Yale Human Rights & Development Law Journal,* 2005).

STEPHEN J. SHAPIRO is a lawyer in private practice in New York City. He is a past Chair of the Committee on Military Affairs and Justice of the New York City Bar.

DANIEL SILVERMAN serves as counsel for the Labor and Employment Group at Skadden Arps, Slate, Meagher & Flom LLP. Prior to joining Skadden, he had a distinguished career at the National Labor Relations Board where he acted in various capacities from trial attorney to the Regional Director at the New York City office. He is the Chairman of the Committee on Labor and Employment Law of the New York City Bar. Mr. Silverman also is as an Adjunct Professor at Cardozo Law School.

CLAUDIA SLOVINSKY has been an immigration and nationality attorney for over 20 years and heads her own law firm in New York City. She serves as the Chair of the Immigration and Nationality Committee of the New York City Bar and is a frequent lecturer on immigration issues both to the immigration bar and lay audiences. She also serves on the Board of the American Friends Service Committee Immigrant Rights Program, and is a member of the American Immigration Lawyers Association and the National Immigration Project of the National Lawyers Guild.

MARIANN SULLIVAN is the Deputy Chief Court Attorney for the New York State Appellate Division, First Department. She is the former Chair of the Committee on Legal Issues Pertaining to Animals of the New York City Bar and a current member of that Committee, as well as of the Special Committee on Animals and the Law of the New York State Bar Association. She co-authored "Foxes in the Henhouse: Animals, Agribusiness and the Law" (*Animal Rights: Current Debates and New Directions,* 2004).

Foreword

BARRY KAMINS, BETTINA B. PLEVAN, E. LEO MILONAS, AND EVAN A. DAVIS

The September 11 attacks profoundly affected the Association of the Bar of the City of New York. We watched the towers burn and then collapse. We lost friends and colleagues. As we dealt with our shock and loss, we immediately began to receive calls from lawyers in New York and around the country asking: how can we help? We coordinated an enormous volunteer effort so that the New York legal community could help families who lost loved ones deal with their loss, and persons who were injured or displaced to rebuild their lives. Every victim's family who wanted a lawyer received free assistance, as thousands of lawyers pitched in with great dedication.

While our attention, and indeed that of the City and nation, was focused on helping individuals and families, we also observed the beginning of the government's response to the attacks. We were alert as to what to anticipate: a strong, rapid reaction by the government, through administrative and legislative actions, to attempt to deal with the terrorist threat. We were aware that the scope of the threat was not clear and that a climate of fear was pervasive. We also were mindful that it is in just those times that individual rights—basic constitutional protections—would be most in jeopardy. Since the founding of the Association in 1870, we had seen it before. We spoke out during the "Red Scare" of 1919 and during the McCarthy period in the early 1950s, and we were often only one of the few establishment organizations to do so.

Of our 160 committees, at least a dozen addressed subject matter that would be implicated by government policy. The first impact of governmental action was felt by immigrants from nations with a substantial Muslim population. Extensive roundups and detention of male immigrants from these countries, and the draconian policies imposed, signaled that there would be a need for a strong response from the legal community. What made our work more difficult is the secrecy with which the government attempted to act, preventing contact between detainees and the outside world (including their attorneys) and barring access to immigration proceedings.

In short order, there followed the USA PATRIOT Act and the President's Military Commission Order. It then became clear that the Executive Branch had embarked upon a strategy of enhancing its power. We were told the purpose was to more effectively engage the terrorist threat. However, as we and the world have since learned, the effort was part of a broader plan to generally empower the Executive Branch to what many felt was an unprecedented level. It further became clear that the exercise of this Presidential power was to be at the expense of individual rights, and of the authority of the Congress and, to a greater extent, the Judiciary.

At times of constitutional crisis, it is particularly essential that the legal community mobilize and make itself heard. Lawyers are the guardians of the Constitution and have the unique perspective to understand how changes in law and government policy will affect constitutional rights and values. We are also equipped to provide direct assistance to those whose rights are deprived, and indeed many Association members have undertaken the direct representation of detainees and others who have legitimate claims that their rights have been abrogated. Lawyers must also serve as strong advocates for the independence of the Judicial Branch. By its very nature, the federal bench cannot defend itself from criticism, however unwarranted, and from attempts to limit the courts' jurisdiction.

This Association zealously undertook these solemn responsibilities. The resulting body of careful analysis, legal exposition and, when appropriate, strong advocacy is on display in these volumes. Each of the materials presented is introduced by a preface that provides the context. You will see that these efforts—all by the dedicated volunteers who staff our committees—were all focused on preserving the rule of law, and our fundamental Constitutional principles and liberties.

Throughout the post-9/11 period, one question continued to be asked: should not the preservation of individual rights and the rule of law be secondary to the cause of national security? National security is a primary concern, but our Constitution was born in a time of great uncertainty and was designed by leaders who had experienced one war and clearly anticipated more. The Constitution and the Bill of Rights were clearly meant to remain in effect through wars and other crises. War-related powers were meticulously meted out between the legislative and executive branches, and there is nothing in Article III to suggest that judges should have different powers during times of crisis.

We have seen too many examples over the years of how the exercise of power in the name of national security—both in the United States and in other nations—has caused the loss of a moral and legal compass. The "war on terrorism" may be uncharted territory, but it is certain to be of long duration, and may well affect the rights of law-abiding Americans in ways that our previous crises have not. Throughout this struggle, it is essential to have an independent bar serving as the protectors of our laws. This Association will continue to serve that function, and to work with others to make sure that the basic character of our free nation is preserved.

The Association will always be indebted to the men and women who volunteered their time and energy to assist those who suffered from the 9/11 attacks. We are also very grateful to the committee members who advocated and continue to advocate for the rule of law.

Barry Kamins, President 2006–2008
The Association of the Bar of the City of New York

Bettina B. Plevan, President 2004–2006
The Association of the Bar of the City of New York

E. Leo Milonas, President 2002–2004
The Association of the Bar of the City of New York

Evan A. Davis, President 2000–2002
The Association of the Bar of the City of New York

Acknowledgments

This massive book owes its existence to the voluntary labors of dozens of talented but busy people. Each chapter is the product of a Committee of the City Bar of New York—a marvelous organization that provides an outlet for the civic-minded members of the nation's most diverse bar. In inviting various attorneys to contribute introductory remarks for these chapters, we tried to reach out to the principal author of the specific report or letter underlying the chapter. When that proved futile for one reason or another, we relied on the Association's general counsel and jack of all trades, Alan R. Rothstein, to provide the appropriate perspective. Alan's resourcefulness and erudition frequently made the difference between a compilation of reports and a book that would remain useful as a guide and resource for years to come.

A debt of gratitude is also owed to the outstanding members of the American Bar Association whose leadership on human rights and Constitutional issues have helped shape the work evidenced in this book. In particular, Michael S. Greco, Jerome J. Shestack, Neal R. Sonnett, Mark D. Agrast, Steven D. Walther, Robert A. Stein, and Robert F. Drinan have each provided the moral, intellectual, and personal standards that have guided this effort.

Likewise, this book could not have been published without the careful assistance of future lawyers Edward Quilice and Galit Waysglas. For over a year, these fine young people managed the complex tasks of identifying and locating reports and letters, overseeing the preface-writing process, and ensuring timely submission to the publisher. Likewise, Mark's assistant, Deborah Zipf, did much of the heavy lifting for this project.

To Alan, Edward, Galit, and Deborah, thank you. To the many lawyers who participated in the writing of the reports and letters that follow, thanks would be inappropriate: you were serving your profession with great energy, probity, and intelligence. This book is evidence of your dedication.

Introduction

MARK R. SHULMAN AND JAMES R. SILKENAT

Over the past five years, members of the Association of the Bar of the City of New York have produced an impressive variety of hard-hitting reports, letters, and briefs addressing issues arising out of the so-called "global war on terror." For the most part, these publications have taken positions critical of the U.S. government's conduct and of the legal justifications offered by the Administration of President George W. Bush. These critiques are nonpartisan. Lawyers from many political orientations—members of both major parties—have drafted and signed them. Rather, the authors of these materials represent the independent voice of the nation's largest and most influential municipal bar.

Lawyers are frequently maligned as being amoral guns-for-hire, willing to take any position that pays. And with America's adversarial legal system, we are thankful to have lawyers willing to take unpopular cases. Without them, freedom of expression and freedom of choice would be far narrower. Without them, many more innocent people would be imprisoned or even executed. Someone must defend unpopular or marginalized people or rights are diminished for each of us. Many lawyers represent the unpopular at their standard billing rates. Many defend those who cannot pay on a *pro bono* basis. Even beyond that, lawyers frequently dedicate their time to protecting the legal system as the embodiment of our republic's values. What lawyer jokes invariably ignore is the tremendous amount of work lawyers do on principle.

Bar associations around the country (indeed around the world) perform critical roles in channeling the creative and honorable impulses of lawyers. The City Bar is one of the largest and oldest in the nation, established in 1870. For a century and a quarter, its members have worked to channel the efforts of a diverse group of individuals into improving the law and its implementation. For much of its history, however, the City Bar worked without much recognition outside the somewhat rarified circles of its membership. As with many venerable and important institutions, that low profile was raised considerably during the tumultuous events of the late 1960s and early 1970s when its President, the distinguished corporate lawyer Francis T.P. Plimpton, asked, "Are our unobtrusive, calmly analytical committee reports adequate for our stormy present?"[1] Plimpton was wondering if the stately organization was effective at promoting the role of law in ways that would help the United States address the day's raging debates.

Plimpton answered his own question with a charge. "I submit that our expert committees should continue their hard working expert ways, but that they should be infused and all our membership infused, with a new sense of urgent and deeply felt concern at the crisis that confronts our legal institutions and law itself, and a new determination, in the long and high tradition of this Association, to seek out and steadfastly fight for the changes that can and should be made to meet the just demands of today and tomorrow. Let us be militant activists, militant activists for the constructive reform of the law we were founded to promote."[2] And this new activism did infuse the City Bar with a spirit of reform and justice. A few short months later, that spirit was put to the test.

In the spring of 1970 President Richard M. Nixon ordered U.S. troops to move from Vietnam into Cambodia to attack Communist sanctuaries. "The invasion of Cambodia set up a galvanic shock in the New York legal community," wrote Mr. Plimpton in a City Bar report. "Does the President of the United States have the right to start a new war? There had been no consultation with Congress," he noted.[3] Standing up for the rule of law and, in particular, the separation of powers that protects this Republic from descending into autocracy, Plimpton told lawyers gathered in the Association's Great Hall that when "the President ordered American troops to invade Cambodia, he was acting on his own, in blithe and unilateral disregard of the Congress, which under the Constitution has the sole right to declare war."[4]

Plimpton decried this act as a threat to the Constitutional order. The "fact remains that the result of the President's action was a new war, war in another country, war by unilateral Presidential fiat, war without Congressional consultation, without Congressional authorization and without Congressional support."[5]

And with that conclusion, Plimpton (a Republican who embodied the legal establishment) led a "march on Washington," but not just any march on Washington. On May 20, 1970, some 1,200 lawyers from leading New York firms—many on chartered cars on the 6:30 train—invaded the nation's capital. Dividing into some 150 teams of six or seven people dressed in their corporate finest, the lawyers met with lawmakers and other high-ranking officials. Plimpton's first appointment, Senator Sam J. Ervin, Jr. (D–NC), stood him up. But after meeting with a full house of Washington lawyers, Plimpton called on the U.S. Solicitor General, his old friend Erwin Griswold. Griswold in turn arranged for Plimpton to discuss the legality of the war with U.S. Attorney General John M. Mitchell and then with Under Secretary of State Elliott Richardson.[6] With this sort of lobbying, the leading members of the preeminent bar were deploying their reputations, their time, and their wits in order to promote greater adherence to the spirit and the letter of the law.

Over the quarter of a century that followed, hundreds of lawyers have worked to live up to Francis Plimpton's spirit of reform and justice. When planes crashed into the Twin Towers of New York's World Trade Center on September 11, 2001, members of the Association sprang into action—not chasing ambulances as the cynic might suggest but running in advance of them to rescue the wounded and distraught. In the months that followed, the Association also served as a clearinghouse for assistance both to lawyers and to those who needed lawyers.

Equally as important, members of the Association have continued to devote countless hours to research and write the kind of "expert reports" that Plimpton spoke of two decades before. Such work has been done both by the City Bar on its own and in cooperation with the American Bar Association House of Delegates, particularly through the ABA Sections of Criminal Law, International Law, and Individual Rights and Responsibilities. The Association's Committee on Military Affairs issued the first of these reports within a few months after 9/11. This report decried the impact of President George W. Bush's Military Order of November 13, 2001, regarding "Detention, Treatment, and Trial of Certain Non-Citizens in the War Against

Terrorism." This report contained a timely and prescient analysis of an issue that continues to plague us years later. The Association's interest in ensuring that the Administration (the United States) not carve out areas beyond the law has subsequently resulted in several other significant publications by the Association, including two amicus briefs to the U.S. Supreme Court, letters to the General Counsel and the Inspector General of the Department of Defense, and three important committee reports. The most recent of these reports broke the story nationally about how the U.S. is engaged in "Torture by Proxy" by removing detainees to other jurisdictions in order to facilitate inhumane interrogations. International media picked up and ran with this information, but the practice may still continue, despite the remarkable work of the Association and a strongly worded letter from the President of the Association to Congress seeking to end U.S. involvement in these abhorrent practices.

By the summer of 2002, the Association's Committee on International Security Affairs found itself facing another of Plimpton's issues: whether the President has the authority to order the invasion of a sovereign state without an act of Congress? Just as the Association had concluded in 1970, the Committee argued persuasively that he has not.

More recently the Association has also been working to ensure that lawyers who have counseled the government poorly be held accountable for their advice. These efforts are reflected in the letter to the leaders of the Senate Judiciary Committee in connection with the nomination of the General Counsel of the Defense Department for a seat on a U.S. Court of Appeals.

The Association's vigilance on rule of law issues after 9/11 has drawn its members into some unpredictable areas. One traditional role for the Association is to comment on legislation proposed either by the U.S. Congress or by the state legislatures. One recent bill proposed using antiterrorism laws to deter (or punish) protestors against the inhumane treatment of animals in a slaughterhouse. This may sound far-fetched, but similar laws have actually been enacted in California and Oklahoma.

The important work of the Association continues on terrorism and rule of law issues, but after five years, it seems like an appropriate time to collect its contributions to this important work into one book. If the reports were an early draft of history, this work may be considered a second draft and useful resource for the history of the years following 9/11. Over the course of American history, wartime administrations have frequently overstepped the legal boundaries. During the Quasi War with France, President John Adams sponsored the notorious Alien and Sedition Acts. Facing all out Civil War, Abraham Lincoln suspended the writ of *habeas corpus*. Managing the United States' efforts during the catastrophic First World War, Woodrow Wilson jailed dissenters for speaking out, including one man who had received nearly a million votes in the 1912 Presidential election. In the panic of the Second World War, Franklin Roosevelt's Administration was responsible for the odious internment of tens of thousands of Americans of Japanese descent. And Vietnam era Presidents had their intelligence agencies collect information on U.S. citizens who were opposing the wars in Southeast Asia.

And yet, from each of these missteps, the nation's legal system rebounded after the war ended. By the time of the Presidential campaign of 1800, boisterous dissent had returned to American politics. Immediately after the Civil War, the Supreme Court ruled that Lincoln was wrong to suspend the most essential writ. President Warren G. Harding had ordered Eugene V. Debs released from prison early. The United States apologized to its *Issei* and *Nisei* brethren and offered reparations. And the intelligence community was ordered not to conduct surveillance of U.S. persons. Unlike previous wars, however, the struggle to defeat global terrorism is one that may not end soon or neatly. Therefore, our legal system cannot wait until the danger has completely passed before righting some of its wrongs. And these historical lessons seem oddly relevant as dissent is squashed, ethnic minorities interned, and domestic surveillance once is again in the government's toolkit.

The pendulum may already have swung back. Two weeks after the Association's Committee on International Security Affairs released its war powers report, President Bush did an about-face and sought Congressional authorization to invade Iraq. In 2004 the Supreme Court found, with the Association's *amici* brief, that the detainees at Guantanamo Bay were not beyond the reach of the law. Two years later, the Court found the President's military tribunal to be unconstitutional. And New York will not use a "terrorism statute" to jail animal rights protestors for photographing poultry factories.

We hope that this book proves useful in explaining how the rule of law fosters the national interest in stability and security, while helping to maintain a sphere of individual liberty. We also hope that this book illustrates the constructive role that civilian lawyers can play in the political process, helping to explicate the law—its objectives and its implications. And in the end, we hope that this book will encourage young lawyers to follow in Francis Plimpton's footsteps, using their skills to serve their neighbors, their country, and their world, as well as their paying clients.

NOTES

1. Francis T.P. Plimpton, "Centennial Convocation of the Association of the Bar of the City of New York" (February 17, 1970) reprinted in Pauline Ames Plimpton ed., The Plimpton Papers: Law and Diplomacy (1985) 75 at 77.
2. *Id.*
3. Report cited in Pauline Ames Plimpton ed., The Plimpton Papers: Law and Diplomacy (1985) 85.
4. "Meeting on Military Action in Southeast Asia at the House of the Association—May 19, 1970" quoted at length in Pauline Ames Plimpton ed., The Plimpton Papers: Law and Diplomacy (1985) 85 at 86.
5. *Id.* at 86–87.
6. *Id.* at 88–89. The fact that he was a registered Republican opposing the actions of a President from the same party gave ome considerable credibility to Plimpton. To many, Plimpton embodied the Establishment. Born to a wealthy publisher who had descended from very early English settlers in Massachusetts, Plimpton had been educated at Exeter, Amherst and Harvard Law School. Along with Eli Whitney Debevoise and William E. Stevenson, in 1933 he founded the firm that eventually became Debevoise & Plimpton LLP. Over the decades, he built and maintained an extensive network of leaders. His old friend Solicitor General Griswold had been Dean at Harvard Law School, and Under Secretary (later Attorney General) Richardson served with Plimpton on Harvard's governing Board of Overseers.

CHAPTER 1

Inter Arma Silent Leges: *In Times of Armed Conflict,* Should *the Laws be Silent? A Report on the President's Military Order of November 13, 2001, Regarding "Detention, Treatment, and Trial of Certain Non-Citizens in the War Against Terrorism"*

PREFACE BY MILES P. FISCHER AND STEPHEN J. SHAPIRO

Since 1946 the Association's Committee on Military Affairs and Justice has reported on the intersection of the law and the military. Our report, *Inter Arma Silent Leges,* was a timely continuation of that tradition, being the first response of its kind to the President's Military Order of November 13, 2001. The first internal draft of the Report was dated November 15, 2001; the Report came out just one month later.

Between the date the Military Order was issued and the date our Report was released, the three principal authors[1] of the Report attended the annual program of the American Bar Association's Standing Committee on Law and National Security on November 29–30, 2001, in Washington, D.C. There, we had an opportunity to interact directly with the senior Administration lawyers responsible for the production and ultimate implementation of the Military Order.[2] Their answers heightened our concern about the procedures authorized by the Military Order and significantly influenced the Report, as did views expressed by other attendees (many in uniform) who were strongly supportive of national security interests but stunned by the Military Order.

The Military Order raised profound questions of constitutional law, statutory law, international law, and national policy. Our early analysis of these issues proved to be a seminal one when the American Bar Association (ABA) adopted a Resolution[3] along the lines of the recommendations in our Report over those appearing in the ABA's own report, and it was even the subject of other legal commentary.

The implementing orders for U.S. military commissions, issued over the course of several years, responded to many of the criticisms we raised in our Report, as well as in follow-on documents, including the Committee's letter dated March 21, 2003 (published herein), but nonetheless so far leaving the Military Order on the books with a legacy of controversy over the precepts of constitutional, statutory, and international law on which we reported in 2001. It is striking that the

Administration immediately drew back from its effort to block *habeas corpus* proceedings through the text of the Military Order, which we had so strongly criticized. It sought instead to avoid prisoner recourse to the courts through *habeas corpus* by locating both the prisoners and the military commissions outside the continental United States at Guantanamo Bay—a gambit blocked by the United States Supreme Court in its *Rasul* decision.

The most dramatic subsequent development is the decision of the Supreme Court in *Hamdan v. Rumsfeld*[4] on June 29, 2006, holding that the military commissions created under the Military Order lack the power to proceed because their structure and procedures violate both the Uniform Code of Military Justice (UCMJ) and Common Article 3 of the four Geneva Conventions. The plurality opinion reflects as to the Military Order, as implemented by subsequent regulations, many of the concerns we expressed as to the Military Order itself. However, that decision is not the end of the story. The Court's interpretation of treaty and statutory law is subject to Congressional action. In October 2006, as this publication was going to press, Congress passed the Military Commissions Act of 2006 which sought to undo the impact of the Hamdan decision by eliminating detainees' right to *habeas corpus* proceedings and recourse to claims arising under the Geneva Conventions.[5]

Throughout, we have regretted that policy makers did not use established procedures for courts martial under the UCMJ, to the extent constitutionally applicable to *enemy combatants* charged with *offenses against the law of war,* and the body of military law established by the well-respected Court of Appeals for the Armed Forces. We continue to urge consideration of that alternative in a manner consistent with international law and, more broadly, the rule of law in the tradition of our nation and its Armed Forces.

INTRODUCTION[6]

On November 13, 2001, President Bush issued a "Military Order" (the "Order") regarding "Detention, Treatment, and Trial of Certain Non-Citizens in the War Against Terrorism."[7] The Order would apply to all non-citizens determined by the President (1) to be members of the international organization known as al Qaeda,[8] or (2) to have engaged in, aided or abetted or conspired to commit, acts of international terrorism or acts in preparation therefore that have caused, threaten to cause or have as their aim to cause injury or adverse affects on the United States, its citizens, national security, foreign policy or economy; or (3) to have intentionally harbored such persons.[9] Such individuals are to be "detained at an appropriate location designated by the Secretary of Defense outside or within the United States."[10] There is no time period set forth with respect to such detention; nor is there any sunset provision, for that matter, for the Order itself.

The Order authorizes the creation of military commissions to try such persons, when and if they are to be subject to prosecution.[11] Further, such individuals, whether detained or tried under the Order, are not permitted under its terms to seek "any remedy" or "maintain any proceeding" in any U.S. federal or state court, any foreign court or any international tribunal.[12] Presumably, this very broad prohibition on *any* proceeding or remedy is an attempt, when read with the detention provisions of the order, to deny the detainees the privilege of the writ of habeas corpus and thereby prolong their detention as a matter of public safety when necessary, as determined by the President. Further still, although military commissions bear certain similarities to courts martial under the Uniform Code of Military Justice[13] (including, for example, by providing trial by appointed judges—rather than a jury—of both fact and law), the similarity is misleading. Courts martial follow procedural rules closely parallel to those of the federal criminal courts, while the commissions to be established under the Order are very different and may function *without regard to "principles of law and the rules of evidence generally recognized in the trial of criminal cases."*[14] Further, they are not subject even to the *procedural* rules governing courts martial, which include the right of appeal to a higher court and, ultimately, to the Supreme Court of the United States.

The "privilege of habeas corpus" is a fundamental Constitutional right. The Order's literal terms suspend it by preventing subject persons from pursuing *any judicial remedy in any court* whatsoever. When combined with the provisions for unlimited detention (including the recent rule-making announced by the Attorney General providing for virtually unlimited detention of certain aliens before INS [Immigration and Naturalization Service] courts), it seems plain that this is a use to which the Order may be put, despite only recent public statements by the Administration to the contrary.[15] If so, such use would be an extreme measure, not used since the time of the Civil War rebellion. Moreover, suspension of the privilege of habeas corpus is permitted only in the two crisis circumstances of rebellion or invasion. Even then, the power to suspend habeas corpus is vested by Constitution only with the Congress and not to the President.[16]

In both the area of the President's authority to create military commissions for the trial of the persons subject to the Order and his authority to detain persons without charge and to suspend habeas corpus, the issuance of the Order raises serious questions of both constitutional law and statutory interpretation, in addition to important international and domestic policy considerations.

This report considers, therefore, whether (1) if the Order were employed for detention or trial of alleged al Qaeda members or supporters, whether in the U.S. or abroad, it would be found to be constitutional; (2) if so, whether it complies with statute; (3) whether its use would be effective as a matter of policy and, (4) if not, what alternatives exist.

Based on the legal and policy analysis and conclusions below, we urge that with respect to this or any similar military order that is issued, Congress and the President should assure that the order will:

1. Not be applicable to persons lawfully present in the United States, including United States citizens and lawful resident aliens;
2. Not be applicable to persons apprehended or to be tried in the United States, except for persons subject to the settled and traditional law of war who engage in conduct alleged to be in violation of such law of war;
3. Not be applicable to cases in which violations of Federal or state criminal laws, as opposed to violations of such law of war, are alleged;
4. Not permit indefinite detention of persons subject to the order;
5. Require that its proceedings be governed by the Uniform Code of Military Justice and provide the rights afforded in courts-martial thereunder, including but not limited to the right of appellate review by the judicial branch and the privilege of the writ of habeas corpus.

The American Bar Association should address these issues promptly. As the voice of the nation's organized bar, it must speak out to protect the rights afforded in the Constitution and the delicate balance of power the Constitution provides among the branches of our government during times when it may seem popular or expedient to flaunt basic constitutional values. The Military Order should not be allowed to encroach on these values, which underlie the country's power, its role in the world scheme, and its democratic way of life.

THE CONTEXT OF THE ORDER

The Order was issued two months after the September 11, 2001 terrorist attacks against the World Trade Center and the Pentagon ("9/11 attacks") by 18 foreign nationals believed by the U.S. Government to have been associated with the al Qaeda organization based primarily in Afghanistan.[17] Al Qaeda has been accused of providing the inspiration, training, financing and control of the 9/11 attacks, as well as assaults on two U.S. embassies in Africa, and on the *U. S.S. Cole* in Yemeni waters. In response to the 9/11 attacks, the Congress on September 18 authorized military action[18] but did not declare war. The United States' decision to use force was supported generally by resolutions of the United Nations Security Council[19] and specifically by the North Atlantic Treaty Organization, as well as by many national governments. On September 21, the President declared that a National Emergency had been in existence since September 11.[20] After the Islamic fundamentalist Taliban "government" of Afghanistan refused to surrender the al Qaeda leaders, U.S. and U.K. armed forces launched a military campaign against Taliban forces in Afghanistan.

Almost simultaneously with issuance of the Military Order on November 13, Afghan units opposing the Taliban and assisted by U.S. air support expelled the Taliban from the country's major cities, including from its capital Kabul. Although the course of the conflict remains uncertain due to its ongoing nature, it is, as this is written, within the realm of possibility that some al Qaeda leaders (as opposed to soldiers or leaders from the Taliban's armed forces) may be captured and come within the control of U.S. armed forces, at which time it would have to be determined when, where and how they might be tried.

These acts occurred against the domestic backdrop of the discovery of a number of intentionally-inflicted cases of anthrax infection in Florida, Washington, D.C., New York City and Connecticut. Some anthrax-tainted letters were discovered in the mail, including ones delivered to government officers. As of this writing there have been 5 deaths from 18 confirmed cases of anthrax infection.[21] No evidence has been disclosed as of now to indicate that these incidents are related in any way to the 9/11 attacks or even to al Qaeda, but their occurrence —and their undiscovered source—nonetheless informs the public debate about terrorist activities at this time.

Moreover, a large number of foreign nationals have been detained within the U.S.—according to Justice Department officials exceeding 1,000 in number but whose actual number remains undisclosed—many of whom are still in custody. It appears that some if not all of these detainees may be transferred from the control and custody of the Department of Justice (*i.e.,* Immigration and Naturalization Service) to the control and custody of the Department of Defense, as such transfer is directed by the Order.

It should be noted that events with respect to the Order—including its interpretation and possible application—are fast-moving and may be evolving even as this Report is being prepared.[22] In view of the importance of the matter, the Committee has opted to work primarily from the text of the Order and the powers asserted by the President therein, giving consideration to the discussions and interviews referred to and the material published in the press by members of the Administration, but with the awareness that such views are not only not binding on the President but could again be revised at any time. Indeed, if the powers asserted by the President in the Order were upheld, this President or a future President could use the Order as precedent to exercise those powers in a different context and without the gloss now presented by his representatives.

THE PRESIDENT'S AUTHORITY TO ORDER TRIAL BY MILITARY COMMISSION AND TO ESTABLISH AD HOC RULES FOR THEIR USE

Authority Cited by the Order.

The Order states that it is issued under three sources of authority:

1. The President's authority as Commander-in-chief of the Armed Forces[23];
2. The Authorization for Use of Military Force Joint Resolution (Public Law 107-40, 115 Stat. 224); and
3. Sections 821 and 836 of Title 10, United States Code (the Uniform Code of Military Justice).

Although civilian lawyers are unfamiliar with military commissions, they are nevertheless not unknown in American history. Such commissions have been upheld by the U.S. Supreme Court, and, despite disuse for nearly one-half century during which time the U.S. has participated in several major armed conflicts, they are in fact contemplated by existing law.[24] U.S. military commissions convicted British Major Andre of espionage in the Revolutionary War, tried those accused of the assassination of President Lincoln, imposed the death penalty on German saboteurs who landed on Long Island during World War II (including one who claimed U.S. citizenship), and tried some 1,200 German war crimes defendants (more than eight times the number tried by the international Nuremberg tribunal) and many Japanese defendants.

Judicial Authority—The *Quirin* Case

U.S. Supreme Court cases have clearly established the constitutionality of military commissions within at least the prototypical declared war between nations involving members of the armed forces of an enemy state. Less clear is the support for military commissions in the context of an act of mass murder by 18 individuals neither members of the armed forces of any nation state nor, even, organized in a conventional military or even para-military formation.

In *Ex parte Quirin,*[25] impliedly relied upon by President Bush (and explicitly by officials in his Administration) as a precedent for the Order,[26] the Supreme Court upheld during a declared war a military commission's jurisdiction over German military saboteurs who had landed in the U.S. from a German submarine and then operated in civilian clothing and, therefore, in violation of the laws of war. The prosecution, in opposing the defendants' application for a writ of habeas corpus in *Quirin,* asserted that no federal court had jurisdiction to hear the case because the military commission's authority was exempt from habeas corpus under the terms of its constitutive order.[27] The Court rejected that contention, holding that even alien members of enemy armed forces were entitled to the writ when found within the U.S. Having found jurisdiction, the Court went on to consider the merits of the military commission's authority notwithstanding the absence of Fifth and Sixth Amendment protections in the conduct of the trial before the commission, such as the right to trial by jury and other procedural rights that are normal in criminal cases. The Court upheld the authority of the commission, grounded on the time-honored practice of trying unlawful, enemy-state combatants in a declared war by military commission, which the Court found to be exempt from the constitutional right to trial by jury. That exemption exists, the Court said, because the practice of such military proceedings was recognized by the law of war prior to the adoption of the Constitution and was consistently followed in subsequent wars between the U.S. and other countries, as well as during the Civil War.[28]

The *Quirin* decision addressed a case arising within the territory of the U.S. during declared war, and, accordingly in view of other cases addressing the distinctive rights of citizens and aliens, its constitutional holding must be limited to that situation. With respect to aliens outside the

U.S., the authority to convene military commissions to try law of war violations is subject only to statutory and international law limitations.[29]

Legislative Authority—the UCMJ

Although the *Quirin* Court did not find it necessary to determine whether the President had independent authority as Commander-in-Chief to create such commissions,[30] we believe that although the President may have implied authority to do so absent Congressional action, when Congress acts, Congress has the exclusive authority to define the use of military commissions by exercise of its powers "to constitute tribunals inferior to the Supreme Court,"[31] "to define offenses against the law of nations,"[32] and "to make rules for the government and regulation of the land and naval forces."[33] In a manner that appears to be consistent with the constitutionally permitted exclusion from the domestic right to trial by jury of proceedings before traditional military commissions, Congress has specifically authorized military commissions to act under the laws of war.[34] As will be discussed, however, use of such commissions—as *Quirin* found—requires a war, at the least *de facto,* if not declared.

Substantively, Article 21 of the UCMJ,[35] among the statutory provisions cited in the Order as authority for its issuance,[36] provides that the UCMJ does not deprive military commissions "of concurrent jurisdiction with respect to *offenders* or *offenses* that by statute or by the law of war may be tried by military commissions, provost courts or other military tribunals."[37] The classic case where both the *offender* and the *offense* are covered is when Japanese General Yamashita was tried for war crimes committed against U.S. personnel during the then recently ended World War II. Either the defendant's whereabouts (Yamashita was in custody, taken during battle) or the predicate offense (traditional war crimes) could serve as a basis for jurisdiction in that case. As an example of jurisdiction over the offender, the U.S., as an occupying power, could use military commissions to try persons within occupied territory pending establishment of civil government, as it did extensively in the post-war occupation of Germany and Japan. This was so whether or not the offense related to the war, generally applying local law then in effect.[38] Article 21, and therefore, statutory support for military commissions (and constitutional authority within the U.S. under *Quirin*), reaches its limits as to persons who are neither offenders, nor charged with offenses, traditionally tried under the law of war by such military commissions.

Offenses—The Law of War

With respect to the offense, it is not at all clear that at the time of the 9/11 attack the U.S. was engaged in a war or even armed conflict to which the law of war[39] could be applied. International treaty law has black letter rules defining when the law of war (or as now often termed, the law of armed conflict) applies. Common Article 2 of the Geneva Conventions[40] provides that "the present Convention shall apply to all cases of declared war or of any other armed conflict which may arise between two or more of the High Contracting Parties, even if the state of war is not recognized by one of them."

Thus, for a state of war to exist under the classic definition of war, the conflict must be between states. "The law of war has been conceived primarily for armed conflicts between States or groups of States, that is, for international armed conflicts."[41] This international law requirement is unfulfilled with respect to the persons covered by the Order. It is fulfilled for international law purposes with respect to Afghanistan, with whose *de facto* Taliban government the United States is engaged in armed conflict (albeit an undeclared war under US domestic laws).

Conflicts *not* between states are covered by the laws of war to a lesser degree, as made more precise in the 1977 Protocols. Protocol II for "non-international conflicts", that is, non-state conflicts, applies to those conflicts which "take place in the territory of a High Contracting Party between its armed forces and dissident armed forces or other organized armed groups which, under responsible command, exercise such control over a part of its territory as to enable them to carry out sustained and concerted military operations and to implement this Protocol."[42] Clearly this definition—also—does not apply to al Qaeda, as it does not exercise control over any part of U.S. territory.[43]

Illustrative of the need for a predicate war is the 1865 opinion of Attorney General James Speed issued with respect to whether military tribunals (by which he meant the courts for military justice generally) could be used to try the civilian assassins of President Lincoln, whom he found to be serving the war aims of the enemy. He found that such persons were subject to the laws of war and trial by military tribunal because—*in times of war:*

> A bushwacker, a jayhawker, a bandit, a war rebel, an assassin, being public enemies, may be tried, condemned and executed as offenders against the laws of war.... The civil courts have no more right to prevent the military, *in time of war,* from trying an offender against the laws of war than they have a right to interfere with and prevent a battle.[44]

Some have argued, including officials in the Bush Administration, that this is a "new kind of war," one in which state participants are not required for a determination of war because of the amorphous nature of international terrorism. Others have argued that while a "war" is required for the Order to be lawful, the armed conflict of the United States with Afghanistan's Taliban puts the country at war for some if not all domestic law purposes, the existence of the conflict would, thus, allow the Order's actions toward the non-citizen residents to whom it is directed by virtue of their nexus with international terrorism generally, even if they have no relationship to Afghanistan or the Taliban. Still others have refined this latter argument by "imputing" the al Qaeda to the Taliban, or, even, vice-versa, noting that recent evidence indicates that al Qaeda may have in fact been controlling the Taliban.[45]

Although the United States has not declared war and the President, in fact, said that he was not seeking a declaration of war, it is not difficult to find that for *international* law purposes the United States is at war in Afghanistan.[46] However, in this regard, it is important to note that the Order is not limited to the "enemy aliens" with whom we are at war, i.e., all Afghans, much less to the Taliban and not even to al Qaeda. It goes to all non-citizens, U.S. resident or not, alleged to commit the acts set forth in it. In contrast, had the Order been limited to enemy aliens, members of an armed body, they would be classic "offenders" subject to the law of war, including the Geneva Protocols. Had the Order been directed to the al Qaeda and the Taliban as a *combined entity,* it might arguably be easier to characterize that joint force as an enemy subject to the laws of war during a time of war with them. Separating al Qaeda from the state elements of territory, governance and organized troops makes it that much more difficult to view as a military, as distinguished from a criminal (though terrorist) organization.

The 1942 Order, which served as the basis for the military commission in *Quirin,* stated the specific, objective and wholly traditional standard. It applied to:

> all persons who are subjects, citizens or residents of any nation at war with the United States or who give obedience to or act under the direction of any such nation....

It is doubtful whether the constitutional logic behind the Court's opinion in *Quirin* upholding that order could be stretched to apply instead to the current Order's novel application to "any individual who is not a United States citizen with respect to whom I determine...there is reason to believe that such individual...has engaged in, aided or abetted, or conspired to commit, acts of international terrorism, or acts in preparation therefore, that have caused, threaten to cause, or have as their aim to cause, injury to or adverse effects on the United States, its citizens, national security, foreign policy, or economy. . ."[47]

This point, it should be emphasized, does not diminish the right of the US armed forces fighting in Afghanistan to both capture and try by military commission abroad members of either the Taliban or al Qaeda who are participating in the combat. Abroad, many of the constitutional guarantees under the Fourth, Fifth and Sixth Amendments do not apply to non-citizens,[48] and certainly not to persons captured during hostilities conducted by the US armed forces.[49]

Offenders—In the U.S. and Abroad

With respect to determining the offender status of persons subject to the Order, civilians residing in the U.S. and not in or near a theater of military operations or engaged as combatants are examples of offenders who have never been subject to the jurisdiction of military commissions under our laws. For example in the Civil War *Ex parte Milligan*[50] case, "Milligan, a citizen twenty years resident in Indiana, who had never been a resident of any of the states in rebellion, was found not to be subject to trial by a military commission because he was not an enemy belligerent either entitled to the status of a prisoner of war or subject to the penalties imposed upon unlawful belligerents." *Quirin, supra,* at 45. Yet, non-citizen, U.S. residents accused of the crimes set forth in the Order relating to 9/11, such as aiding, abetting and harboring al Qaeda, but who may fall far short of violating the laws of war applicable to saboteurs and the like, are among the direct targets of the Order (compare this to Mr. Milligan, who was accused of rebellion).

The application for domestic statutory and constitutional purposes of the laws of war should be distinguished from the international law regarding the existence of a state of war or the right of the U.S. to take military action in self-defense against an attack or against a country that harbors the attackers. As indicated above, the latter action has been affirmed internationally by the Security Council of the United Nations and by the North Atlantic Treaty Organization and domestically by Congress. Moreover, as also indicated above, there is no substantive issue as to the statutory or constitutional authority of a military commission to try aliens outside the U.S.

The issue of greatest importance is whether the present circumstances permit the application of the laws of war under domestic law to deny the application of constitutional rights otherwise available to persons within the U.S. That question is most acute as to a circumstance in which armed members of the Taliban, with whom we are engaged in an undeclared war, say, or of al Qaeda, the specific subjects of the Order and whose personal status is less clear, are found entering or already in the United States to commit hostile acts.

For these persons (at least unlawful, Taliban combatants), the subject matter authority for the President to utilize a military commission to try such persons based on their acts seems clear under the Constitution as interpreted by *Quirin.* With respect to the individual status of such captured "combatants," the Taliban members would almost certainly qualify as combatants under the law of armed conflict (although potentially unlawful, depending on such factors as their uniforms and behavior) whose prosecution is subject to the provisions of the international law of armed conflict.[51] The al Qaeda members are more difficult to characterize, depending on the evidence linking them to being controlled by, or controlling, the Taliban, a state-like entity, leaving some doubt as to the legality of the use of a commission to try them in the United States without a jury trial.

On the other hand, the persons charged only with "aiding", "abetting", "conspiracy" or simply "harboring" the other persons subject to the Order, that is, people who have committed traditionally civilian criminal acts rather than the "commission" of military-like terrorist acts themselves may not be tried in a military commission as the Order contemplates. Such persons are guaranteed by the Bill of Rights, as interpreted by the Supreme Court in *Milligan* and *Quirin,* a trial by jury. The aliens detained by the U.S. and charged with crimes were accused of subsidiary offenses, such as immigration violations, money laundering, credit card fraud or other money-raising crimes. Persons charged with civil crimes are exceedingly unlikely to come within the class of persons traditionally tried by the law of war, and, to such extent, the Order must be facially invalid.

SUBSTANTIVE OVERREACH—PERVASIVE DEATH PENALTY AND UNRELATED TERRORISM

A corollary of the jurisdictional application of the laws of war is the resulting substantive penalty. The traditional laws of war are draconian in applying the death penalty to irregular combatants out of uniform and not carrying arms openly. Mere presence in the enemy force constitutes the offense without more. Thus, if the laws of war apply to such irregulars, the death penalty follows. If the laws of war do not apply, a military commission has no jurisdiction. This extreme black and white result should require the greatest caution in extending the laws of war to situations not traditionally contemplated.

Moreover, the Order by its terms may be applied to the commission of acts of international terrorism whether or not related to al Qaeda or the 9/11 attacks. It could, for example, be applied to prosecute aliens in the U.S. supporting terrorism in Northern Ireland having "adverse effects on . . . [U.S.] foreign policy", a legitimate government measure but far removed from a U.S. war. This broad jurisdictional reach is consistent with the concept of a "war on terrorism" but inconsistent with any definable "war" in the sense known to U.S. jurisprudence.[52]

As these principles are therefore applied to the Order, the Order does not confine its scope to either offenders or offenses traditionally tried by the law of war, as provided by law, implied in the Constitution and required by the *Quirin* Court. Absent Congressional action, we cannot see how the President in the current situation has authority permitting him to convene military commissions to proceed inside the U.S. without providing grand jury indictment, jury trials or the right to confront witnesses, among other exceptions from constitutionally guaranteed rights.[53]

We must, therefore, conclude that the Order substantively violates both Article 21 of the UCMJ and, as to persons within the U.S., the Constitution, as well, to the extent that it covers offenses and offenders not covered by the law of war as historically described in *Quirin.* That possible legal infirmity and, at the very least, uncertainty, severely undercuts the policy objectives of the Order as more fully discussed below.

PROCEDURAL CONCERNS UNDER THE UCMJ

In addition to the substantive issue, there is a procedural concern. The Order cited as additional authority Section 36 of the UCMJ,[54] which provides that in cases under the UCMJ the President may prescribe by regulation the procedures for military commissions subject to two qualifications. First, the procedures "shall, so far as he considers practicable, apply the principles of law and the rules of evidence generally recognized in the trial of criminal cases in the United States district courts." In the Order, President Bush declares *in haec verba* that such principles and rules are not practicable to apply under the order. That extraordinary finding is presumably his prerogative, whether or not it is a wise exercise thereof.

Secondly, and more importantly for present purposes, Article 36 specifies that the procedures "may not be contrary to or inconsistent with this chapter [the UCMJ]." The Order only outlines the parameters for procedures to be implemented by orders and regulations of the Secretary of Defense.[55] However, the framework of the Order is already inconsistent with the essential elements of due process provided for in the UCMJ in numerous respects.[56] Accordingly, if Section 36 is indeed necessary authority for the Order, then the Order appears to be procedurally defective.

Exclusive Jurisdiction to Military Commissions

Finally, the Order states that "with respect to any individual subject to this order...military tribunals shall have exclusive jurisdiction with respect to offenses by the individual...."[57] This grant of exclusive jurisdiction to military commissions appears to conflict with the Congressional intent set forth in Article 18 of the UCMJ, which provides that for purposes of prosecutions for violations of the law of war, general courts martial shall have jurisdiction concurrent with military tribunals:

> General courts-martial also have jurisdiction to try any person who by the law of war is subject to trial by a military tribunal and may adjudge any punishment permitted by the law of war.

Inasmuch as the UCMJ by its terms applies to prisoners of war,[58] we conclude that Order conflicts with Congress' determination that courts martial and military tribunals (commissions) should have concurrent jurisdiction with respect to prosecution of POWs for violations of the laws of war.

PREVENTIVE ARREST, INDEFINITE DETENTION AND THE SUSPENSION OF HABEAS CORPUS

The provisions of the Order regarding detention of persons subject to it permit seemingly indefinite detention without charges, trial,[59] or the right to seek a remedy in federal or state courts. Thus, they provide for 'preventive arrests,' unlimited detention and literally suspends the privilege of the writ of habeas corpus, notwithstanding statements by Administration officials to the contrary. These provisions are clearly unconstitutional as to the writ of habeas corpus and extremely controversial as to detention.

Preventive arrests are anathema to American values. It is bedrock in American constitutional law that the deprivation of liberty may only occur pursuant to the principles and mechanisms of due process enshrined in the Bill of Rights. To determine whether liberty has, in fact, been properly deprived, the Framers maintained the privilege of the writ of habeas corpus.

Habeas Corpus

The privilege of the writ of habeas corpus is considered a "*magna carta* of the kingdom."[60] Justice Story said of it:

> It is...justly esteemed the great bulwark of personal liberty; since it is the appropriate remedy to ascertain, whether any person is rightfully in confinement or not, and the cause of his confinement; and if no sufficient ground of detention appears, the party is entitled to his immediate discharge. This writ is most beneficially construed; and is applied to every case of illegal restraint, whatever it may; for every restraint upon a man's liberty is, in the eye of the law, an imprisonment, wherever may be the place, or whatever may be the manner, in which the restraint is effected.[61]

Chief Justice Rehnquist has praised the privilege: "It has been rightly regarded as a safeguard against executive tyranny, and an essential safeguard to individual liberty."[62]

Beginning in the nineteenth century and continuing without exception through to the present day, the Supreme Court has consistently held that non-citizens within the jurisdiction of the United States are "persons" within the meaning of the Fifth Amendment and are thus entitled to the protections of the due process clause.[63] In fact, it was recognized by the Supreme Court in the wartime cases *Quirin* and *Yamashita* as available even to members of the German military and to the Japanese command within the U.S. (or in Yamashita's case, in the Philippines, under U.S. rule) to test the authority of a military commission to detain and try them.[64] It is also available to persons charged under the UCMJ and held for court martial under that statute.[65]

As noted, the President's Order states that the authority for its issuance is (1) the President's authority as Commander-in-chief of the Armed Forces, (2) the Authorization for Use of Military Force Joint Resolution (Public Law 107-40, 115 Stat. 224) and (3) Sections 821 and 836 of the UCMJ.

The Constitution states in Article I (the enumeration of Congress' powers), Section 9 (a list of limitations on those Congressional powers):

> Clause 2: The Privilege of the Writ of Habeas Corpus shall not be suspended, unless when in Cases of Rebellion or Invasion the public Safety may require it.

It seems plain from the text of the Constitution that only the Congress, not the President—whether as Commander-in-chief or otherwise—has the authority to suspend habeas corpus, and then only in the two circumstances mentioned. The Supreme Court has upheld that principle and the most prominent of commentators on the Constitution have agreed.[66]

The other bases cited in the Order for the President's authority to detain the subject persons indefinitely without recourse offer no support either. The text of Congress' Resolution Authorizing Use of Military Force—the second cited basis—does nothing to alter habeas corpus whatsoever, much less authorize the President to do so. In fact, it plainly refers specifically and solely to the use of *military force,* hence its title. Section 2, the substantive section of the Resolution, is titled "Authorization For Use Of United States Armed Forces" and provides simply: "That the President is authorized to use all necessary and appropriate force...,"[67] with nothing said about arrests, detentions, habeas corpus or the like. It therefore appears clear that the Use of Force Resolution cited by the President as a basis for his authority in issuing the Order also does not, in fact, provide such authority.

Finally, the Order refers for authority to Sections 821 and 836 of the UCMJ, both of which go to the issue of military commissions, as discussed, *supra.* Neither provide Congressional suspension of the privilege of habeas corpus or have anything to do with that subject but are cited, apparently, for authority regarding the Order's establishment of military commissions, discussed *supra,* and, thus, too, offer no authority for the detention provisions of the Order.

It appears clear, therefore, that the three bases cited in the Order by the President do not in fact provide the legal authority necessary to validate these provisions of the Order effectively suspending habeas corpus. The conclusion is that the power to suspend the privilege of the writ of habeas corpus is given to the Congress and that the President may not exercise it.

Congress, in fact, *has* acted with respect to the events of September 11, 2001 specifically in connection with habeas corpus. On October 26, 2001, it adopted legislation sought by the Administration; the USA Patriot Act of 2001,[68] whose full name is "Uniting and Strengthening America by Providing Appropriate Tools Required to Intercept and Obstruct Terrorism (USA Patriot Act) Act [sic] of 2001." The Act was intended, as its name indicates, to provide a comprehensive set of "tools" to the federal government in the service of law enforcement and intelligence gathering.

The USA Patriot Act specifically addresses habeas corpus in Section 412 (Mandatory Detention Of Suspected Terrorists; Habeas Corpus; Judicial Review).[69] That Section amends Section 236 of the Immigration and Nationality Act to provide that aliens subject to the Act who are detained must be criminally charged or placed in removal proceedings within seven days following commencement of detention unless release of the alien will result in activity that endangers the national security of the United States. In that case, the Attorney General must so certify and recertify every 6 months thereafter, if the alien is to continue in detention. Importantly, habeas corpus proceedings to review decisions made under the Section are available to the suspect alien on application to the Supreme Court, any Justice of the Supreme Court, any circuit judge of the D.C. Circuit Court of Appeals, or any district court with jurisdiction. Further still, determinations by district courts or circuit court judges are subject to appeal to the D.C. Circuit Court of Appeals.[70]

This provision of the Congressional act differs profoundly from the President's Order with respect to the application of habeas corpus to aliens arrested within the United States and suspected of connection to terrorism, which provides no release process, no certification process, no right to a petition of habeas corpus and no right to appeal adverse decisions. The analogy to the Steel Seizure Case is apparent. There, the President—by seizing strike-bound steel mills in order to continue production of steel to supply the armed forces then engaged in Korea—acted contrary to the will of Congress expressed through various statutory schemes in an area the power over which belonged to Congress. Of such extreme and far reaching Presidential behavior contrary to the expressed will of Congress, Justice Jackson wrote in his concurring opinion:

> When the President takes measures incompatible with the expressed or implied will of Congress, his power is at its lowest ebb, for then he can rely only upon his own constitutional powers minus any constitutional powers of Congress over the matter. Courts can sustain exclusive presidential control in such a case only by disabling the Congress from acting upon the subject. Presidential claim to a power at once so conclusive and preclusive must be scrutinized with caution, for what is at stake is the equilibrium established by our constitutional system.... In short, we can sustain the President only by holding that seizure of such strike-bound industries is within his domain and beyond control by Congress. Thus, this Court's first review of such seizures occurs under circumstances which leave presidential power most vulnerable to attack and in the least favorable of possible constitutional postures.

Id., at 637–638. Justice Jackson continued his analysis by finding that neither the President's Constitutional 'Executive' powers, nor his Commander-in-Chief authority (whether in time of war *de facto* or war *de jure*), nor his obligation to faithfully execute the laws could trump the Constitutions' plain grant of authority to Congress to raise and support armies and to provide and maintain a navy.[71]

Here, as noted, the power to suspend habeas corpus is granted to the Congress by Article I of the Constitution, and the USA Patriot Act—which fails to suspend the privilege—is the act of Congress on the subject. It is, therefore, our conclusion that the Order, which effectively seeks to suspend the privilege of habeas corpus for those aliens subject to it and detained under it, impermissibly seeks to exercise a power not only reserved to the Congress but one already exercised by the Congress in this specific area in a contrary manner. As such, determinations under the Order will likely be subject to successful Constitutional attack on this ground, leading to a significant amount of litigation at a time when efficiency and speed of process is the desired result. The Order in this regard, therefore, not only appears to be illegal, but unwise.

In response to questioning from various sources, including members of this Committee, Administration officers stated that the Administration had no intention of opposing the right of detained persons to seek the writ of habeas corpus, and that the Order was not intended to do so despite the language of Section 7. They acknowledged that the *nearly identical* provisions of the 1942 Order in question in *Quirin* did seek to suspend habeas corpus and had been ruled unconstitutional.[72] Such informal statements about the true meaning of the Order or the President's intent in issuing it, without amendment of the Order or Congressional legislation, are less than satisfactory.[73]

SEVERABILITY

If a provision of the Order, such as suspending habeas corpus, were to be found unconstitutional, it is unclear what effect that finding would have on the remainder of the Order, since the Order lacks a severability provision. In *Quirin, supra,* the 1942 Order lacked a severability provision and its attempt to suspend habeas corpus was found to be invalid without affecting the substance of the military commission's authority set forth in the remaining portion of that order. The Court in *Quirin* did not discuss severability.

Although it used virtually the same language for the suspension of habeas corpus which appears in the Order (and which was found invalid), the 1942 order expressly provided for the possibility of correction by the regulations to follow:

> [S]uch persons shall not be privileged to seek any remedy or maintain any proceeding directly or indirectly, or to have any such remedy or proceeding sought on their behalf, in the courts of the United States, or of its States, territories, and possessions, *except under such regulations as the Attorney General, with the approval of the Secretary of War, may from time to time prescribe.*[74]

The Order provides no such opportunity for subsequent correction and, thus, the courts may take a different view of the absence of a severability provision than did the *Quirin* court.

DETENTION OF ENEMY ALIENS

Congress has also acted, albeit not recently, in the form of the Alien Enemies Act, 50 U.S.C. 21, permitting the detention or expulsion of aliens over age 14 within the US who are citizens of a foreign government or state with which the US is in a declared war or subject to "any invasion or predatory incursion. . .perpetrated, attempted or threatened against the territory of the United States."[75] While the 9/11 attacks may have constituted a "predatory incursion against the territory of the United States", they were not perpetrated by a "foreign nation or government" as required by Section 21 and, thus, the Alien Enemies Act does not apply to the 9/11 attacks.

These provisions—including this statute, its predecessors and those like it (*e.g.*, those establishing military areas within the United States during World War II, serving as the basis for Executive Order 9066 in 1942), were classically applied, if at all, in declared war against the entire class of enemy aliens, all citizens of the enemy state, along with the expropriation of enemy property.[76] In World War II, they were also put into effect ruthlessly against Japanese nationals found in the United States, in an operation now viewed as a national disgrace. Similar steps were taken against U.S. citizens of Japanese descent.[77] It is noted that the Commission on Wartime Relocation and Internment of Civilians, established in 1980 by Congress to review the 1942 Executive Order providing for the internment found there was "no justification in military necessity for the exclusion,. . .there was no basis for the detention."[78]

Broad, class-based detention or expulsion, when confined to enemy aliens, may have made sense in the context of traditional war between national states against persons owing allegiance to the enemy and reasonably be expected to act on its behalf, but such actions have little relevance to the contemporary crisis involving a cross-border, multinational extremist *culture* and not an enemy state or states. Such a culture has no "citizens," and, thus, determining who to detain or expel as the Order aggressively does—other than based on their individual *actions*—is nearly impossible without casting a net so broad as to be pernicious. Consequently it is not surprising that the Order failed to cite 50 U.S.C. 21 or indeed any statutory authority for its unlimited detention provisions.

The Administration has sought to portray the Order as applying only to enemy combatants. The White House Counsel said recently that "The order covers only foreign enemy war criminals"[79]—and even then only for "violations of the laws of war."[80] The Order itself, however, does *not* in fact specify either the claimed limitation on the class of subject persons or the claimed limitation on the activities by which they become subject to the Order.

The detention provisions of the Order are, therefore, surprising, both in view of the U.S. acknowledgment of its egregious error in World War II—oft cited as precedent—and of the present acquiescence by Congress (through the USA Patriot Act) in expanding the detention powers over aliens suspected of terrorist connections and the specific provision of the right of habeas corpus with appeals from decisions when doing so.

No act of Congress has been found that provides for either the detention provisions referred to in the Order or for authority for the President to act in the area. Simply, the Order purports to give the President this power by fiat. That claim will most certainly be tested by habeas corpus proceedings within the U.S. to determine whether the Order trumps the Constitution's award of authority in this area to Congress, which has acted through Section 412 of the USA Patriot Act.

With respect to indefinite detention without remedy, on the one hand, we have no doubt that regarding aliens in the United States during time of declared war, the federal government could create a scheme substantially restricting the rights they were previously provided that would be upheld by the courts. Much, however, would depend on the factual circumstances. In World War II, the internment of Japanese nationals (as distinct from the internment of U.S. citizens of Japanese descent) occurred at a time of very substantial and genuine threats to the security of the nation as a whole. In fact, Chief Justice Rehnquist, in perhaps a prescient speech reviewing this history in May of 2000 provided this conclusion: "The authority of the government to deal with enemy aliens in time of war, according to established case law from our Court, is virtually plenary."[81] In the present circumstances, however, absent any enemy nation, it is impossible to identify the nationals or citizens of the "enemy." Consequently, the term "enemy alien" has no determinable meaning.

We conclude that the Order's provision of indefinite detention of aliens suspected of terrorist connections or harboring those who have them—particularly given the denial of *all remedy*—is improper since the President does not have the Constitutional authority to issue an order applicable to aliens in the U.S., and Congress has already provided a different scheme with respect to such persons.[82] As a practical matter, we believe that these provisions of the Order, if utilized, will not only lead to widespread litigation testing both the President's authority to issue it and as it may be applied to the individual detainee, which litigation is likely to be successful at least with respect to the question of the Order's suspension of habeas corpus.[83]

Even if the President has the authority to detain persons within the classes targeted by the Order, it would remain to be determined whether a particular detainee within the U.S. is within one of those classes. Therefore, such habeas corpus proceedings might extend not only to determination of a commission's substantive and procedural authority, but also to whether as a matter of fact the detainee came within the jurisdictional predicate of the Order, namely, membership in al Qaeda or commission or certain kinds of involvement in acts of international terrorism or harboring of persons under the prior categories. While the Order purports to give the President authority to define such persons, the corresponding findings may themselves be subject to finding in habeas corpus proceedings, equivalent to challenging probable cause for arrest.[84] This would have the result of placing before the federal District Courts the very issues—whether an individual is an al Qaeda member—the Administration is seeking to keep from those courts.

INTERNATIONAL LAW

International law may also have a bearing on the Order. Common Article 3 of the four Geneva Conventions of 1949, which establishes minimal standards even in armed conflicts not of an international nature, and *a fortiori* in international conflicts, in paragraph 1(d) prohibits persons who have laid down their arms from being subjected to "the passing of sentences and the carrying out of executions without previous judgment pronounced by a regularly constituted court, affording all of the judicial guarantees which are recognized as indispensable by civilized peoples."

The U.S. is a party to, and has ratified, the Geneva Conventions and in 1997, violations of Common Article 3 were added to the definition of "war crimes" for the purposes of the War Crimes Act of 1996.[85] Compliance with such international laws of armed conflict is specifically required of the U.S. Armed Forces pursuant to Department of Defense's Law of War Program.[86]

It follows that the international standard has become binding U.S. law. It would be unlawful for the President to authorize a procedure that resulted in the passing of sentences or carrying out executions without such a regularly constituted court affording the judicial guarantees required by the Common Article 3.[87]

Pending issuance of the regulations for commissions, it would be premature to speculate whether they would violate the applicable international standards, which it should be noted do not require trial by jury, U.S. rules of evidence or habeas corpus. In fact, it is has been reported that a Swiss military court has tried at least one war crime defendant from the former Yugoslavia and one from Rwanda, although on request a case was remanded to the International Court for the Former Yugoslavia.[88] It would, however, be highly questionable if the regulations did not require proof beyond a reasonable doubt (or an internationally acceptable alternative standard), public trials, defense right to choice of counsel or independent judges.

Moreover, the United States certainly desires to avoid adverse effects on its international prestige and foreign policy effectiveness which would potentially result from any erroneous convictions or, worse, executions in haste of persons possibly misidentified or otherwise misjudged. Thus, in addition to legal and ethical concerns, this practical factor should urge upon the United States a scrupulous regard for the rule of law, including by establishing fair procedures as the Order promises to do.

Should the definitive procedures for such a fair trial as issued by the Secretary of Defense fall short of accepted international standards, and, until they are defined, it can be expected that many countries will decline to permit extradition of defendants for trial by military tribunals. This issue is separate from the death penalty issue, which already blocks or conditions extradition to the regular U.S. courts. Military commissions would, however, aggravate that issue to the extent that every irregular combatant becomes vulnerable to the death penalty by participation in a non-uniformed force.

The U.S. has vigorously objected to incidents in which it believes that U.S. citizens have not been accorded minimal judicial rights. Recent examples include a secret trial for espionage in Russia, an execution by order of a special military court in Nigeria and a terrorism conviction by a hooded military court in Peru. Obviously, it would not be productive in future incidents for the U.S. to be tarnished with a repudiation of the very civil rights for foreign nationals it seeks to affirm for its own nationals abroad.

U.S. POLICY SHOULD BE TO PROMOTE RESPECT FOR THE RULE OF LAW, EVEN WHEN PROSECUTING THOSE WHO LACK SUCH RESPECT

The principal justification of the Order is the paramount national security interest in public safety and national security. In pursuit of that, it relies on mechanisms such as indefinite detention and secrecy (intended, it is said, to permit removal from the public realm persons suspected of terrorist connections) and potentially secret trials (designed, it is said, to protect classified, or even classifiable, information).

To the extent, however, that the Order seeks to 'stack the deck' against defendants, it betrays uncertainty about the ability to obtain a conviction even in a secret, non-jury trial under existing civilian or military law,[89] and, we believe, does a disservice to the entire process. It would permit indefinite detention without charges, much less trial, a tack likely to be used when is there is insufficient evidence to convict even by loose standards; and all without the possibility of judicial review. We do not believe that the full range of such procedures contemplated by the Order are necessary and, as a result, hope that the procedural regulations now being crafted do not take full advantage of the overbroad provisions of the Order.

Further, as a practical matter, such overbroad provisions may well hamper the very swiftness with which the government understandably seeks to act in this crisis. Given the constitutional and statutory questions about the validity of the Order with respect to persons placed in custody within the United States, the availability to them of habeas corpus proceedings (including the likelihood that the courts hearing the petitions will go on to determine the validity of the substantive characterization of defendants by the President as members of al Qaeda or another class of persons covered by the Order), and the likely appeals therefrom (notwithstanding the Order's attempt to close them off), it is probable that the Administration will not achieve the quick and final resolution of cases against alleged terrorists that it seeks. Indeed, the defects in the Order—unless they are corrected by the procedures to come or otherwise—make it particularly vulnerable to attack.[90]

Further still, the Order suffers from a lack of a sunset mechanism. Examples of presidential use of military commissions—such as for the Lincoln assassins and the Quirin saboteurs—were pursuant to either one-time operations, as with the Lincoln assassination, or were issued with respect to a declared war that had a visible victory marker, *i.e.*, the defeat of the enemy nation, and thus a clear end date.[91] Here, in an undeclared war with the allies professing that the 'new war on terrorism' could last 50 years against an undefined enemy beyond al Qaeda,[92] the almost total curtailment of liberties previously available to foreign nationals living in or visiting this country has no natural end in sight.[93]

It is of utmost regret that the 9/11 crisis has led the executive branch to give the impression that it would deny as to any class of persons almost the entirety of the procedural rights that have characterized this Republic since 1789, apparently without any effort to find a workable alternative. Even if the Order is never used in practice, or if wiser heads prevail and it is used in a more reasonable manner than its language permits, the Order stands as an historic repudiation of the legal ideals on which the Nation was founded, potentially permitting a reversion to the worst practices of the Star Chamber, Inquisition and other notorious tribunals that put the interests of State or Church ahead of individual rights. Protestations that the Order is but "one tool available, and hasn't been used yet"[94] ring hollow when matched with the Order's stunning scope, exclusive jurisdiction and total absence of review.

These national domestic ideals should be reason enough either to temper the Order in order to avoid a court finding it (or portions of it) unconstitutional, unlawful or unsupportable. Such tempering might be accomplished by its amendment, by Congressional action or, at the least and as has now apparently been promised,[95] by issuing balanced procedures to put it into effect. After reaching out to the entire world to embrace the American cause against terrorism as a fight for civilization on behalf of all nations, including such former adversaries as Iran and Syria in need of rule-of-law models, the Order effectively declares the second class status of foreign nationals under our laws by asserting our right to make preventive arrests of such persons on the determination of one person, detain them indefinitely without charge, prosecute them in secret and based on *ad hoc* rules, and then apply the death penalty when even less than all judges find them guilty of crimes not yet specified. After the nation's demonstration of strength, resolve and resilience in the face of the unprecedented attack of 9/11, the Order threatens to becomes a confession of weakness, of the inability of the United States to utilize established means of prosecution and to marshal sufficient evidence to prove the complicity of al Qaeda in the attacks of 9/11.

We believe that national security must be preserved, and that it must be done while giving as much respect as possible in a time of national emergency to the great American values—embodied in our laws of due process—which make this nation both a target and worth defending. Justice Rehnquist has acknowledged that in times of great national security, the laws, while "muted," are not, in fact, silent—even during war.[96] We acknowledge that the balance is difficult, but also that the national will to seek such balance—not a clear tip of the scale—is not only essential but is the greatest show of strength the United States can offer.

RECOMMENDATIONS AND ALTERNATIVES

Validating the Order

With respect to validating the Order, a Congressional declaration of war would most certainly put the full powers of the national government at work in the anti-terrorism war. Justice Jackson said famously in the *Steel Seizure Case* that when the President acts "pursuant to an express or implied authorization of Congress, his authority is at its maximum, for it includes all that he possess in his own right plus all that Congress can delegate...[and acts so taken] would be supported by the strongest of presumptions and the widest latitude of judicial interpretation..."[97]

Directed certainly against the Taliban government of Afghanistan, conceivably the declaration of war could also include (but should not be limited to) those named international terrorist *organizations,* notably al Qaeda, to whom that enemy state gave aid and comfort and even vice-versa. President Jefferson, for example, was authorized by Congress in 1802 (following skirmishes with the Barbary pirates in the Mediterranean) "to cause to be done all such other acts of precaution or hostility as the state of war will justify, and, may, in his opinion require," finding, in fact, that a "state of war now exists."[98] Al Qaeda may be analogous to pirates of old.[99] Such a Congressional declaration would lay to rest legal concerns with respect to both the President's authority to establish military commissions in a time of undeclared war, since it would now be declared, and also to the status of those persons related to such enemy organizations, since an enemy will have been defined.

However, a declaration of war carries with it enormous implications for the conduct of daily life in the United States. To declare war solely, or even primarily, to rectify the legal problems with the underpinnings of the President's desire to utilize military commissions to try without traditional due process alien civilians arrested in the United States seems to us too radical a solution. Nor would a declaration of war resolve the constitutional issues relating to *domestic* use of commissions in a war for crimes not uniquely violative of the law of war, issues that arose in the Civil War in the context of the *Milligan* case.

Alternatives to Military Commissions for Prosecution

The analysis above demonstrates that the Constitution requires that due process—including jury trials—be given to defendants arrested or tried in the United States for civilian-style crimes that are not violations of the laws of war. Thus, for these defendants, whether they be al Qaeda conspirators or merely harborers, Article 3 federal District Courts must be the forum for their prosecution.

However, with respect to those persons captured abroad in combat or for otherwise violating the traditional laws of war, the Order's proposition of military commissions is not preferred choice. The better approach is to use an alternative means of prosecution.

A menu of alternatives is available to the national government to permit effective prosecution of alleged terrorists and their supporters found in the United States, and thereby avoid the substantive and procedural defects in the Order. The choices include trials in federal district courts, international tribunals, or even UCMJ courts martial. Each has its advantages and its disadvantages with respect to the goal of swift and fair prosecution within the rule of law.

Other goals which some commentators now suggest are paramount and thus argue for the practical use of commissions—e.g., the need to avoid the requirement that US troops in combat give Miranda warnings to captured al Qaeda or Taliban,[100] courthouse, judge and juror protection, revelations of intelligence through open trials, the slow pace of trials, and the ability to admit into evidence under loose rules material that otherwise could not be admitted in federal District Court or even courts martial trials, such as hearsay—seem to us important but far less so (particularly since to a large extent they can be addressed) than the larger goal referred to above. One need only consider the impact on the development of international humanitarian law that the conduct and decisions of the Nuremberg Tribunal had—laying the ground work for the principle of individual responsibility for wrongful state acts—through its process of open trials, uniform procedures modeled primarily on the British and American systems and careful, written decisions to understand that while obtaining a guilty verdict is important, it is not all-important.

International Tribunals

The use of international tribunals, perhaps one created for the purpose of this prosecution, is possible. Nuremberg was certainly a precedent. Such a tribunal, however, presents problems of international representation on the bench, not least because of the divergence of views with our allies over the death penalty, and would, in all likelihood, be the only courts to which certain countries would transfer defendants within their custody given the political and cultural realities.[101]

Further, to avoid the spectacle of Judeo-Christian civilization sitting combined in judgment on the Muslim civilization—an image some say Bin Laden seeks to foster—participation by Islamic judges would be necessary. At that point, developing rules of procedure gets complicated. Further still, experience with recent international tribunals shows these entities to be truly slow in action, as well as expensive. In such tribunals, juries would not be a concern, but, even given the good faith of most judges, the protection of classified information would have to be assumed to be impossible.

The International Criminal Court ("ICC"), were it in effect, would be a likely tribunal for cases involving foreign defendants accused of violating either the international law of armed conflict or crimes against humanity.[102]

Significantly, crimes against humanity under Article 7 of the Rome Statute are not premised upon the existence of an "armed conflict" within the meaning of the Geneva Conventions and

Protocols but instead is premised on the occurrence of any of the listed acts directed toward a civilian population provided they are "widespread and systematic." Thus, this section would include within its subject matter jurisdiction the terrorist acts of 9/11 and others being discovered in the course of the anti-terror campaign. The ICC would be especially useful to try defendants in the custody of countries that might refuse to extradite defendants to the United States, whether for their own domestic political reasons or based on objections to capital punishment or to the procedures of military commissions. The ICC is not an option at this time because the Court is not yet established, due in large part to opposition to the statute by the United States.

Federal District Courts

Time-honored criminal proceedings in the Federal District Courts would be the tried and true solution, not least because it has been proven to work with respect to prosecuting terrorists, including members of al Qaeda. In fact, the federal government has already determined to take the first steps toward prosecuting Bin Laden in Federal District Court by seeking—and obtaining—his indictment in the Southern District of New York. It also will be prosecuting Zacarias Moussaoui, the so-called "20th hijacker", in Federal District Court in Virginia. However, the Federal District Courts may be less adapted to trying enemy combatants (lawful or unlawful) detained in armed conflict.

The idea that such trials are slow, that jurors would refuse to serve or that there would be so many defendants that the work would never be done does not strike us as persuasive. These courts are, in fact, contemplated for use in these circumstances. They have not only convicted al Qaeda members but also have successfully tried and convicted a plethora of serious spies in the service of foreign powers at both the CIA and FBI in recent years.

It should be recalled that the Constitution itself was conceived and drafted in a time of great concern regarding national security, and these issues were never far from the minds of the Framers. "American courts have tried international criminals who have violated the law of nations—including pirates and slave traders—since the beginning of the nation. We have convicted hijackers, terrorists and drug smugglers (including Panama's Manuel Noriega, who surrendered to American soldiers after extended military operations)."[103]

However, the circumstances of the 9/11 attacks would admittedly present exceptional difficulties in administering a fair jury trial where hardly any American citizen has not been touched by the events in controversy. Further, despite established procedures to control confidential information,[104] such procedures relate primarily to pre-trial procedures and are not impenetrable for determined wrongdoers. Nonetheless, while we believe these impediments could be overcome for the purposes of providing the required civilian trials in U.S. District Courts, they are more difficult to overcome for purposes of providing a law of war trial of a foreign combatant.

Courts Martial Under the UCMJ

For use abroad, the alternative we find most acceptable to the commissions proposed by the Order combines most of the benefits sought with fewest of the potential risks: court martial under the UCMJ. White House Counsel Alberto Gonzales described the long, successful and professional history of the American military justice this way: "The American military justice system is the finest in the world, with longstanding traditions of forbidding command influence on proceedings, of providing zealous advocacy by competent defense counsel, and of procedural fairness,"[105] (unfortunately, Judge Gonzales improperly ascribed these attributes to *military commissions* when they apply instead to *military courts martial,* a very different kind of tribunal).

Military courts martial, as described above, combine an essentially non-jury trial in a secure environment—a naval vessel or military base—pursuant to established rules of procedure, evidence and appeal based on written records. The due process provided in these courts is genuine, despite the old adage about military justice and military music, even while the trial process is made more efficient than in civilian courts. A criminal trial in a court martial setting is far quicker than a comparable one in a federal District Court, and not only are there provisions for presenting secret material in camera, the setting on a protected military installation would make such information all the more secure.[106] In any case, a public trial—as was given even to the worst members of the Third Reich—is desirable to demonstrate both the fairness of our system and our confidence that using it is not a sign of weakness but of strength.

A general court martial of persons arrested in the United States would, however, require statutory amendment to confer upon such a court clear jurisdiction to try cases not only under the present UCMJ, but also—to the extent that there is any doubt—under the international law of armed conflict, as well as such other laws as Congress may determine to apply. Absent Congressional action, such a court could be assured of constitutional validity for trials of alien defendants only outside the U.S. or of offenders within the United States for offenses within the traditional law of war.

Military Commissions

For the reasons explained in this Report, we do not recommend the use of military commissions, particularly as described in the Order, to prosecute persons arrested in the United States for acts not traditional violations of the laws of war. They are, however, a potential means of dealing with aliens arrested and tried abroad, but only, in our view, with procedures consistent with the rule of law.

One possible variation on the commissions contemplated by the Order would be military commissions under U.S. law and administration but including foreign jurists on the model of the post World War II war crimes commissions, using procedures consistent with international standards (though not necessarily the same as UCMJ courts martial). This would make them somewhat akin to purely international tribunals but under greater U.S. control as they would still be U.S. military commissions. However, lack of the right to a jury trial alone would prevent such hybrid commissions from adjudicating cases involving (i) aliens in the U.S. or (ii) U.S. citizens anywhere not tried for law of war offenses.

It is recommended in any case that at the appropriate time—which we note is not during a period of national emergency and armed conflict—the Congress examine the use of military commissions for the purpose of clarifying statutory authority therefore. The various Articles of the UCMJ that contemplate commissions could be supplemented by one which provides clear authority for their use and the circumstances in which the President may so establish them. Importantly, Congress could at that time provide the guidelines and framework for the ultimate procedures—e.g., standards of proof, nature of evidence—the President would issue as Commander-in-Chief for trials under such commissions.

IN SUMMATION

Viewing these alternatives on a spectrum of their qualities would show the military commission at the top with respect to U.S. control of confidential information and correspondingly at the bottom with respect to international credibility and procedural fairness, while an international tribunal would be at the reverse end of that spectrum, at least with respect to international credibility. Federal District Courts and UCMJ courts martial would be somewhere in the middle, with the District Courts having relatively higher credibility, lower control of confidential information, a slow pace and a high level of due process, and UCMJ courts martial in a somewhat reverse position.

Given the most likely circumstances here—prosecuting members and supporters of international terrorist organizations found and arrested *outside* the United States for offenses against the laws of war—we believe the choice of courts martial under the Uniform Code of Military Justice is a reasonable one and certainly preferable to military commissions where national security considerations truly require extraordinary measures while basic rights of due process still demand respect. With respect to persons arrested within the United States, Article III courts *must* constitutionally be used for offenders and offenses not involving the laws of war.

Moreover, UCMJ courts martial substantially meet the security needs that are most acute for the type of defendants likely to be apprehended abroad in a shooting war, including the foreign based command and control of al Qaeda. The domestic courts are, or can be made, sufficiently secure for the civilian type of defendants likely to be apprehended in the U.S. whether for committing acts of violence or for various supporting activities (*e.g.*, "harboring" or even stealing in order to raise cash) which are only questionably subject to the laws of war and in any case pose less severe security issues. In order to avoid the uncertainty inherent in applying the traditional definitions of the laws of war to contemporary circumstances, Congress should consider enacting a statutory definition appropriate to these circumstances.

In the last analysis, it is the behavior of a nation in a time of crisis that determines its greatness. Utilizing the historically fair, widely admired military justice system to prosecute abroad law of war offenses at this point in time where and when it is most appropriate—complete as this system is with rights and remedies available to defendants—while using Article III courts domestically, reflects a confidence in this nation's unique ability to balance the necessary expediency required at this moment with the deliberate fairness expected of it always.

APPENDIX A
NOVEMBER 13, 2001 MILITARY ORDER ISSUED BY PRESIDENT GEORGE W. BUSH

Detention, Treatment, and Trial of Certain Non-Citizens in the War Against Terrorism

By the authority vested in me as President and as Commander in Chief of the Armed Forces of the United States by the Constitution and the laws of the United States of America, including the Authorization for Use of Military Force Joint Resolution (Public Law 107-40, 115 Stat. 224) and sections 821 and 836 of title 10, United States Code, it is hereby ordered as follows:

Section 1. Findings.

(a) International terrorists, including members of al Qaida, have carried out attacks on United States diplomatic and military personnel and facilities abroad and on citizens and property within the United States on a scale that has created a state of armed conflict that requires the use of the United States Armed Forces.

(b) In light of grave acts of terrorism and threats of terrorism, including the terrorist attacks on September 11, 2001, on the headquarters of the United States Department of Defense in the

national capital region, on the World Trade Center in New York, and on civilian aircraft such as in Pennsylvania, I proclaimed a national emergency on September 14, 2001 (Proc. 7463, Declaration of National Emergency by Reason of Certain Terrorist Attacks).
(c) Individuals acting alone and in concert involved in international terrorism possess both the capability and the intention to undertake further terrorist attacks against the United States that, if not detected and prevented, will cause mass deaths, mass injuries, and massive destruction of property, and may place at risk the continuity of the operations of the United States Government.
(d) The ability of the United States to protect the United States and its citizens, and to help its allies and other cooperating nations protect their nations and their citizens, from such further terrorist attacks depends in significant part upon using the United States Armed Forces to identify terrorists and those who support them, to disrupt their activities, and to eliminate their ability to conduct or support such attacks.
(e) To protect the United States and its citizens, and for the effective conduct of military operations and prevention of terrorist attacks, it is necessary for individuals subject to this order pursuant to section 2 hereof to be detained, and, when tried, to be tried for violations of the laws of war and other applicable laws by military tribunals.
(f) Given the danger to the safety of the United States and the nature of international terrorism, and to the extent provided by and under this order, I find consistent with section 836 of title 10, United States Code, that it is not practicable to apply in military commissions under this order the principles of law and the rules of evidence generally recognized in the trial of criminal cases in the United States district courts.
(g) Having fully considered the magnitude of the potential deaths, injuries, and property destruction that would result from potential acts of terrorism against the United States, and the probability that such acts will occur, I have determined that an extraordinary emergency exists for national defense purposes, that this emergency constitutes an urgent and compelling government interest, and that issuance of this order is necessary to meet the emergency.

Sec. 2. Definition and Policy.

(a) The term "individual subject to this order" shall mean any individual who is not a United States citizen with respect to whom I determine from time to time in writing that:
(1) there is reason to believe that such individual, at the relevant times,
(i) is or was a member of the organization known as al Qaida;
(ii) has engaged in, aided or abetted, or conspired to commit, acts of international terrorism, or acts in preparation therefor, that have caused, threaten to cause, or have as their aim to cause, injury to or adverse effects on the United States, its citizens, national security, foreign policy, or economy; or
(iii) has knowingly harbored one or more individuals described in subparagraphs (i) or (ii) of subsection 2(a)(1) of this order; and
(2) it is in the interest of the United States that such individual be subject to this order.
(b) It is the policy of the United States that the Secretary of Defense shall take all necessary measures to ensure that any individual subject to this order is detained in accordance with section 3, and, if the individual is to be tried, that such individual is tried only in accordance with section 4.
(c) It is further the policy of the United States that any individual subject to this order who is not already under the control of the Secretary of Defense but who is under the control of any other officer or agent of the United States or any State shall, upon delivery of a copy of such written

determination to such officer or agent, forthwith be placed under the control of the Secretary of Defense.

Sec. 3. Detention Authority of the Secretary of Defense.

Any individual subject to this order shall be—
(a) detained at an appropriate location designated by the Secretary of Defense outside or within the United States;
(b) treated humanely, without any adverse distinction based on race, color, religion, gender, birth, wealth, or any similar criteria;
(c) afforded adequate food, drinking water, shelter, clothing, and medical treatment;
(d) allowed the free exercise of religion consistent with the requirements of such detention; and
(e) detained in accordance with such other conditions as the Secretary of Defense may prescribe.

Sec. 4. Authority of the Secretary of Defense Regarding Trials of Individuals Subject to this Order.

(a) Any individual subject to this order shall, when tried, be tried by military commission for any and all offenses triable by military commission that such individual is alleged to have committed, and may be punished in accordance with the penalties provided under applicable law, including life imprisonment or death.
(b) As a military function and in light of the findings in section 1, including subsection (f) thereof, the Secretary of Defense shall issue such orders and regulations, including orders for the appointment of one or more military commissions, as may be necessary to carry out subsection (a) of this section.
(c) Orders and regulations issued under subsection (b) of this section shall include, but not be limited to, rules for the conduct of the proceedings of military commissions, including pretrial, trial, and post-trial procedures, modes of proof, issuance of process, and qualifications of attorneys, which shall at a minimum provide for—
(1) military commissions to sit at any time and any place, consistent with such guidance regarding time and place as the Secretary of Defense may provide;
(2) a full and fair trial, with the military commission sitting as the triers of both fact and law;
(3) admission of such evidence as would, in the opinion of the presiding officer of the military commission (or instead, if any other member of the commission so requests at the time the presiding officer renders that opinion, the opinion of the commission rendered at that time by a majority of the commission), have probative value to a reasonable person;
(4) in a manner consistent with the protection of information classified or classifiable under Executive Order 12958 of April 17, 1995, as amended, or any successor Executive Order, protected by statute or rule from unauthorized disclosure, or otherwise protected by law,
(A) the handling of, admission into evidence of, and access to materials and information, and
(B) the conduct, closure of, and access to proceedings;
(5) conduct of the prosecution by one or more attorneys designated by the Secretary of Defense and conduct of the defense by attorneys for the individual subject to this order;
(6) conviction only upon the concurrence of two-thirds of the members of the commission present at the time of the vote, a majority being present;
(7) sentencing only upon the concurrence of two-thirds of the members of the commission present at the time of the vote, a majority being present; and

(8) submission of the record of the trial, including any conviction or sentence, for review and final decision by me or by the Secretary of Defense if so designated by me for that purpose.

Sec. 5. Obligation of Other Agencies to Assist the Secretary of Defense.

Departments, agencies, entities, and officers of the United States shall, to the maximum extent permitted by law, provide to the Secretary of Defense such assistance as he may request to implement this order.

Sec. 6. Additional Authorities of the Secretary of Defense.

(a) As a military function and in light of the findings in section 1, the Secretary of Defense shall issue such orders and regulations as may be necessary to carry out any of the provisions of this order.
(b) The Secretary of Defense may perform any of his functions or duties, and may exercise any of the powers provided to him under this order (other than under section 4(c)(8) hereof) in accordance with section 113(d) of title 10, United States Code.

Sec. 7. Relationship to Other Law and Forums.

(a) Nothing in this order shall be construed to—
(1) authorize the disclosure of state secrets to any person not otherwise authorized to have access to them;
(2) limit the authority of the President as Commander in Chief of the Armed Forces or the power of the President to grant reprieves and pardons; or
(3) limit the lawful authority of the Secretary of Defense, any military commander, or any other officer or agent of the United States or of any State to detain or try any person who is not an individual subject to this order.
(b) With respect to any individual subject to this order-
(1) military tribunals shall have exclusive jurisdiction with respect to offenses by the individual; and
(2) the individual shall not be privileged to seek any remedy or maintain any proceeding, directly or indirectly, or to have any such remedy or proceeding sought on the individual's behalf, in (i) any court of the United States, or any State thereof, (ii) any court of any foreign nation, or (iii) any international tribunal.
(c) This order is not intended to and does not create any right, benefit, or privilege, substantive or procedural, enforceable at law or equity by any party, against the United States, its departments, agencies, or other entities, its officers or employees, or any other person.
(d) For purposes of this order, the term "State" includes any State, district, territory, or possession of the United States.
(e) I reserve the authority to direct the Secretary of Defense, at any time hereafter, to transfer to a governmental authority control of any individual subject to this order. Nothing in this order shall be construed to limit the authority of any such governmental authority to prosecute any individual for whom control is transferred.

Sec. 8. Publication.

This order shall be published in the Federal Register.
GEORGE W. BUSH
THE WHITE HOUSE,
November 13, 2001

APPENDIX B
1942 ROOSEVELT ORDER

Proc. No. 2561, July 2, 1942, 7 F.R. 5101, 56 Stat. 1964

WHEREAS the safety of the United States demands that all enemies who have entered upon the territory of the United States as part of an invasion or predatory incursion, or who have entered in order to commit sabotage, espionage or other hostile or warlike acts, should be promptly tried in accordance with the law of war;
NOW, THEREFORE, I, Franklin D. Roosevelt, President of the United States of America and Commander in Chief of the Army and Navy of the United States, by virtue of the authority vested in me by the Constitution and the statutes of the United States, do hereby proclaim that all persons who are subjects, citizens or residents of any nation at war with the United States or who give obedience to or act under the direction of any such nation, and who during time of war enter or attempt to enter the United States or any territory or possession thereof, through coastal or boundary defenses, and are charged with committing or attempting or preparing to commit sabotage, espionage, hostile or warlike acts, or violations of the law of war, shall be subject to the law of war and to the jurisdiction of military tribunals; and that such persons shall not be privileged to seek any remedy or maintain any proceeding directly or indirectly, or to have any such remedy or proceeding sought on their behalf, in the courts of the United States, or of its States, territories, and possessions, except under such regulations as the Attorney General, with the approval of the Secretary of War, may from time to time prescribe.

APPENDIX C
CONGRESSIONAL RESOLUTION AUTHORIZATION FOR USE OF MILITARY FORCE

One Hundred Seventh Congress
of the United States of America
AT THE FIRST SESSION
Begun and held at the City of Washington on Wednesday,
the third day of January, two thousand and one
Joint Resolution
To authorize the use of United States Armed Forces against those responsible for the recent attacks launched against the United States.
Whereas, on September 11, 2001, acts of treacherous violence were committed against the United States and its citizens; and
Whereas, such acts render it both necessary and appropriate that the United States exercise its rights to self-defense and to protect United States citizens both at home and abroad; and
Whereas, in light of the threat to the national security and foreign policy of the United States posed by these grave acts of violence; and
Whereas, such acts continue to pose an unusual and extraordinary threat to the national security and foreign policy of the United States; and
Whereas, the President has authority under the Constitution to take action to deter and prevent acts of international terrorism against the United States: Now, therefore, be it

Resolved by the Senate and House of Representatives of the United States of America in Congress assembled,

Section 1. Short Title

This joint resolution may be cited as the 'Authorization for Use of Military Force'.

Sec. 2. Authorization for Use of United States Armed Forces.

(a) IN GENERAL— That the President is authorized to use all necessary and appropriate force against those nations, organizations, or persons he determines planned, authorized, committed, or aided the terrorist attacks that occurred on September 11, 2001, or harbored such organizations or persons, in order to prevent any future acts of international terrorism against the United States by such nations, organizations or persons.

(b) War Powers Resolution Requirements—

(1) SPECIFIC STATUTORY AUTHORIZATION— Consistent with section 8(a)(1) of the War Powers Resolution, the Congress declares that this section is intended to constitute specific statutory authorization within the meaning of section 5(b) of the War Powers Resolution.

(2) APPLICABILITY OF OTHER REQUIREMENTS— Nothing in this resolution supercedes any requirement of the War Powers Resolution.

Speaker of the House of Representatives.

Vice President of the United States and

President of the Senate.

APPENDIX D
USA PATRIOT ACT OF 2001 (IN PART)

Public Law No: 107-56, October 26, 2001.

SEC. 412. MANDATORY DETENTION OF SUSPECTED TERRORISTS; HABEAS CORPUS; JUDICIAL REVIEW.

(a) IN GENERAL— The Immigration and Nationality Act (8 U.S.C. 1101 et seq.) is amended by inserting after section 236 the following:

"SEC. 236A. (a) DETENTION OF TERRORIST ALIENS—

'(1) CUSTODY— The Attorney General shall take into custody any alien who is certified under paragraph (3).

'(2) RELEASE— Except as provided in paragraphs (5) and (6), the Attorney General shall maintain custody of such an alien until the alien is removed from the United States. Except as provided in paragraph (6), such custody shall be maintained irrespective of any relief from removal for which the alien may be eligible, or any relief from removal granted the alien, until the Attorney General determines that the alien is no longer an alien who may be certified under paragraph (3). If the alien is finally determined not to be removable, detention pursuant to this subsection shall terminate.

'(3) CERTIFICATION— The Attorney General may certify an alien under this paragraph if the Attorney General has reasonable grounds to believe that the alien—

'(A) is described in section 212(a)(3)(A)(i), 212(a)(3)(A)(iii), 212(a)(3)(B), 237(a)(4)(A)(i), 237(a)(4)(A)(iii), or 237(a)(4)(B); or

'(B) is engaged in any other activity that endangers the national security of the United States.

'(4) NONDELEGATION— The Attorney General may delegate the authority provided under paragraph (3) only to the Deputy Attorney General. The Deputy Attorney General may not delegate such authority.

'(5) COMMENCEMENT OF PROCEEDINGS— The Attorney General shall place an alien detained under paragraph (1) in removal proceedings, or shall charge the alien with a criminal offense, not later than 7 days after the commencement of such detention. If the requirement of the preceding sentence is not satisfied, the Attorney General shall release the alien.

'(6) LIMITATION ON INDEFINITE DETENTION— An alien detained solely under paragraph (1) who has not been removed under section 241(a)(1)(A), and whose removal is unlikely in the reasonably foreseeable future, may be detained for additional periods of up to six months only if the release of the alien will threaten the national security of the United States or the safety of the community or any person.

'(7) REVIEW OF CERTIFICATION— The Attorney General shall review the certification made under paragraph (3) every 6 months. If the Attorney General determines, in the Attorney General's discretion, that the certification should be revoked, the alien may be released on such conditions as the Attorney General deems appropriate, unless such release is otherwise prohibited by law. The alien may request each 6 months in writing that the Attorney General reconsider the certification and may submit documents or other evidence in support of that request.

'(b) HABEAS CORPUS AND JUDICIAL REVIEW—

'(1) IN GENERAL— Judicial review of any action or decision relating to this section (including judicial review of the merits of a determination made under subsection (a)(3) or (a)(6)) is available exclusively in habeas corpus proceedings consistent with this subsection. Except as provided in the preceding sentence, no court shall have jurisdiction to review, by habeas corpus petition or otherwise, any such action or decision.

'(2) APPLICATION—

'(A) IN GENERAL- Notwithstanding any other provision of law, including section 2241(a) of title 28, United States Code, habeas corpus proceedings described in paragraph (1) may be initiated only by an application filed with—

'(i) the Supreme Court;

'(ii) any justice of the Supreme Court;

'(iii) any circuit judge of the United States Court of Appeals for the District of Columbia Circuit; or

'(iv) any district court otherwise having jurisdiction to entertain it.

'(B) APPLICATION TRANSFER— Section 2241(b) of title 28, United States Code, shall apply to an application for a writ of habeas corpus described in subparagraph (A).

'(3) APPEALS— Notwithstanding any other provision of law, including section 2253 of title 28, in habeas corpus proceedings described in paragraph (1) before a circuit or district judge, the final order shall be subject to review, on appeal, by the United States Court of Appeals for the District of Columbia Circuit. There shall be no right of appeal in such proceedings to any other circuit court of appeals.

'(4) RULE OF DECISION— The law applied by the Supreme Court and the United States Court of Appeals for the District of Columbia Circuit shall be regarded as the rule of decision in habeas corpus proceedings described in paragraph (1)."

APPENDIX E
WAR CRIMES ACT: 18 U.S.C. 2441(SEC. 2441, WAR CRIMES)

(a) Offense.—Whoever, whether inside or outside the United States, commits a war crime, in any of the circumstances described in subsection (b), shall be fined under this title or imprisoned

for life or any term of years, or both, and if death results to the victim, shall also be subject to the penalty of death.
(b) Circumstances.—The circumstances referred to in subsection (a) are that the person committing such war crime or the victim of such war crime is a member of the Armed Forces of the United States or a national of the United States (as defined in section 101 of the Immigration and Nationality Act).
(c) Definition.—As used in this section the term "war crime" means any conduct—

(1) defined as a grave breach in any of the international conventions signed at Geneva 12 August 1949, or any protocol to such convention to which the United States is a party;

(2) prohibited by Article 23, 25, 27, or 28 of the Annex to the Hague Convention IV, Respecting the Laws and Customs of War on Land, signed 18 October 1907;

(3) which constitutes a violation of common Article 3 of the international conventions signed at Geneva, 12 August 1949, or any protocol to such convention to which the United States is a party and which deals with non-international armed conflict; or

(4) of a person who, in relation to an armed conflict and contrary to the provisions of the Protocol on Prohibitions or Restrictions on the Use of Mines, Booby-Traps and Other Devices as amended at Geneva on 3 May 1996 (Protocol II as amended on 3 May 1996), when the United States is a party to such Protocol, willfully kills or causes serious injury to civilians.

NOTES

1. The undersigned Chairs and Committee Member, Richard Hartzman.
2. Our Report named the following: White House Counsel, Albert R. Gonzalez; William Haynes, DOD General Counsel; and Legal Adviser to the National Security Council, Richard B. Bellinger, among the presenters in that informative program, who had been involved in the drafting and issuance of the Military Order. It is notable that legislative counsel (who spoke in other parts of the seminar) had not participated in the origins of the Military Order, since Congress had not been consulted. Equally worrying was that the Military Order had been rushed past the expert JAG [Judge Advocate General] attorneys without regard for their views.
3. See letter from Robert E. Hirshon, President, American Bar Association, to William J. Haynes II, General Counsel, U.S. Department of Defense enclosing resolution of the House of Delegates, available at http://www.abanet.org/poladv/letters/107th/militarytrib8c.pdf.
4. Hamdan v. Rumsfeld, 548 U.S. __(2006).
5. Pub. L. No. 109-366, 120 Stat. 2600 (Oct. 17, 2006).
6. This report was prepared by the Committee on Military Affairs and Justice, which was established by the Association of the Bar of the City of New York in 1946. Since that time, it has engaged in study and comment on the military justice system and other legal aspects of military affairs, including the use and regulation of the armed forces. The Committee was involved in the drafting of the Uniform Code of Military Justice.
7. The Order is reproduced in Appendix A.
8. The organization known as al Qaeda is widely believed to be the propagator of many terrorist acts directed toward the United States, including the horrific ones of September 11, 2001 in New York City and Washington, D.C.
9. Military Order, at §2(a).
10. Military Order, at §3(a).
11. Military Order, at §7(b)(2).
12. Military Order, at §3(a).
13. 10 U.S.C. §§801–946 (hereinafter, the "UCMJ").
14. Military Order, at §1(f).
15. As will be explained, events are fast moving and in the course of preparing this Report, it appears as if the Administration may have changed, or may be changing, its position with respect to this issue.

16. U.S. Constitution, Article 1, Section 9, Clause 2.

17. The President has said that al Qaeda operates in no less than 60 nations, including the United States, but because it is believed that Osama bin-Laden, its head, is in Afghanistan, it is that country which is the organization's base. On September 20, 2001, President Bush spoke to Congress: "This group and its leader —a person named Osama bin Laden—are linked to many other organizations in different countries, including the Egyptian Islamic Jihad and the Islamic Movement of Uzbekistan. There are thousands of these terrorists in more than 60 countries. They are recruited from their own nations and neighborhoods and brought to camps in places like Afghanistan, where they are trained in the tactics of terror. They are sent back to their homes or sent to hide in countries around the world to plot evil and destruction. The leadership of al Qaeda has great influence in Afghanistan and supports the Taliban regime in controlling most of that country. In Afghanistan, we see al Qaeda's vision for the world." Quoted on White House Web Site, subsection *America Responds, visited* November 24, 2001.

18. S.J.Res.23, September 18, 2001 (Public Law No: 107-40).

19. United Nations Security Council Resolutions 1368 (September 12, 2001) and 1373 (September 28, 2001).

20. In a proclamation of that date, the President declared that "by virtue of the authority vested in me as President by the Constitution and the laws of the United States, I hereby declare that the national emergency has existed since September 11, 2001, and pursuant to the National Emergencies Act (50 U.S.C. 1601 et seq.), I intend to utilize the following statutes: sections 123, 123a, 527, 2201(c) 12006, and 12302 of title 10, United States Code, and sections 331, 359, and 367 of title 14, United States Code." The President reported this declaration to Congress in a letter dated September 24, 2001: "Pursuant to section 204(b) of the International Emergency Economic Powers Act, 50 U.S.C. 1703(b) (IEEPA), and section 301 of the National Emergencies Act, 50 U.S.C. 1631, I hereby report that I have exercised my statutory authority to declare a national emergency in response to the unusual and extraordinary threat posed to the national security, foreign policy, and economy of the United States by grave acts of terrorism and threats of terrorism committed by foreign terrorists, including the September 11, 2001, terrorist attacks at the World Trade Center, New York, at the Pentagon, and in Pennsylvania."

21. CNN website, http://www.cnn.com/2001/HEALTH/conditions/11/24/connecticut.anthrax/index.html, *visited* November 24, 2001.

22. This report was informed by statements made at a meeting of the ABA Standing Committee on Law and National Security—held in Washington, D.C. on November 29 and 30, 2001. Persons with whom the authors spoke included the White House Counsel, the General Counsel of the Department of Defense, the Legal Adviser to the National Security Counsel, Counsel to the Chairman of the Joint Chiefs of Staff and others in similar capacities. (Hereinafter, references to this event will be to "ABA Meeting.")

23. It has been suggested that the Order may have been issued by the President under his "Executive Powers," such as they are, but its specific designation as a "military order" seems clearly intended to invoke his power as Commander-in-Chief and not as the chief executive officer.

24. *See, e.g.,* 10 U.S.C. §826.

25. 317 U.S. 1 (1942) ("Quirin").

26. President Bush said on November 19: "These are extraordinary times. And I would remind those who don't understand the decision I made [regarding using a military tribunal] that Franklin Roosevelt made the same decision in World War Two. Those were extraordinary times as well." *Bush Defends Military Court Option in U.S. Attacks,* Reuters, Monday, November 19, 2001, 6:06 PM ET, *reprinted at* http://dailynews.yahoo.com/h/nm/20011119/pl/attack_bush_courts_dc_6.html, *viewed* November 26, 2001.

27. The 1942 order is set forth in Appendix B ("1942 Order").

28. See historical examples from the Revolution, the Mexican War and the Civil War cited in *Quirin, supra,* at notes 9 and 10.

29. "[A]t least since 1886, we have extended to the person and property of resident aliens important constitutional guaranties—such as the due process of law of the Fourteenth Amendment. *Yick Wo v. Hopkins,* 118 U.S. 356. But, in extending constitutional protections beyond the citizenry, the Court has been at pains to point out that it was the alien's presence within its territorial jurisdiction that gave the Judiciary power to act." *Johnson v. Eisentrager,* 339 U.S. 763, 770 (1950). Even in U.S. possessions the right to trial

by jury was not guaranteed and only extended when so provided by Congress. *See e.g., Dorr v. U.S.,* 195 U.S. 138 (1904). Citizens are, however, entitled to trial by jury, even abroad, except in time of war. *See, Reid v. Covert,* consolidated with *Kinsella v. Krueger,* 354 US 1 (1957); *Kinsella v. Singleton,* 361 US 234 (1960); *Grisham v. Hagan,* 361 US 278 (1960); and *McElroy v. Guargliardo,* 361 U.S. 281(1960), which overrule prior UCMJ court martial/commission jurisdiction over US citizen spouses accompanying US forces abroad, invalidating inconsistent provisions of the UCMJ. This is the background for Pub. L. 106-523, 18 U.S.C. 3261 *et seq.,* which creates Article III jurisdiction in such cases to fill the gap. In *Reid v. Covert* the Court allowed court-martial jurisdiction to continue over such persons in time of war, but the Court of Military Appeals limited that jurisdiction to declared war; *U.S. v. Averette,* 19 C.M.A. 363 (1970). *See also, The Military Extraterritorial Jurisdiction Act of 2000: Closing the Gap,* 95 Am. J. Intl. L. 446 (2001).

30. *Id.,* at 29.

31. U.S. Constitution, Article I, Section 8, Clause 9.

32. U.S. Constitution, Article I, Section 8, Clause 10.

33. U.S. Constitution, Article I, Section 8, Clause 14.

34. In addition to more direct authority, Congress has recognized military commissions in passing. The legislative history of the War Crimes Act of 1996 includes the statement by the House Judiciary Committee that such statute "is not intended to affect in any way the jurisdiction of any court martial, military commission, or other military tribunal under any article of the Uniform Code of Military Justice or under the law of war or the law of nations." H.R. Rep. No. 104-698 at 12 (1996).

35. 10 U.S.C. 821.

36. Despite the President's assertion of Section 21 as authority, some commentators argue that such Section allows the President's authority without creating it. The distinction is metaphysical if Congress has the authority, as we believe, to provide preemptively for the rules and regulations of the armed forces and compliance with the laws of nations, including the laws of war, if it chooses to do so. Consequently the terms under which Congress permits the President to act concurrently are equivalent to rules authorizing the President to act. *Compare Youngstown Sheet & Tube Co. v. Sawyer,* 343 U.S. 579 (1952) (the "Steel Seizure Case") where the President was found to have acted directly contrary to the specific intent of Congress in a matter subject to Congressional power.

37. Emphasis supplied.

38. Not long before the adoption of the Constitution, Americans were on the receiving end of the military justice of an occupying power when, during the Revolutionary War, British military tribunals became the default criminal justice system successively in Boston, Newport, New York, Philadelphia and Charleston, some of whose judgments continued to be respected by American authorities after the war. *See generally,* F.B. Wiener, *Civilians under Military Justice,* (Chicago, 1967) at 134.

39. The Department of Defense defines the law of war as follows:

> 3.1. Law of War. That part of international law that regulates the conduct of armed hostilities. It is often called the law of armed conflict. The law of war encompasses all international law for the conduct of hostilities binding on the United States or its individual citizens, including treaties and international agreements to which the United States is a party, and applicable customary international law.

Department of Defense Directive Number 5100.77, December 9, 1998, viewed November 25, 2001 on the Defense Department web site at http://www.dtic.mil/whs/directives/corres/pdf/d510077_120998/d510077p.pdf (emphasis supplied). The law of war is not, however, coextensive with the broader field of international law or law of nations. For example, money laundering and drug trafficking are the subject of international treaties, but do not relate to the conduct of hostilities.

40. For example, Convention Relative to the Treatment of Prisoners of War, Article 2, opened for signature Aug. 12, 1949, 6 U.S.T. 3316, 75 U.N.T.S. 135.

41. Frederic de Mulinen, *International Committee on The Red of the Red Cross Handbook on the Law of War for Armed Forces* (ICRC 1987), at 3.

42. Part I, Art. 1(1), Protocol Additional to the Geneva Conventions of 12 August 1949, and Relating to the Protection of Victims of Non-International Armed Conflicts (Protocol II), *opened for signature* Dec. 2, 1977, 1125 U.N.T.S. 609.

43. It has been suggested that the limitations on the international law of armed conflict tending to exclude most violence not between nations was deliberately intended to deny belligerent status to dissidents so that national authorities a freer hand in suppressing them. *See generally* George H. Aldrich, *The Law of War on Land,* 94 Am. J. Intl. L. 42 (2000). "Perversely, the application of Protocol II is far too narrow. . . . It is perhaps cynical, but undoubtedly true, that this narrow applicability of Protocol II explains why there are now 147 states party to it." *Id.* at 60.

44. A.G. James Speed, *Opinion on the Constitutional Power of the Military to Try and Execute the Assassins of the President,* Attorney General's Office (Washington, July, 1865). Emphasis supplied.

45. *See, e.g.,* Bob Woodward, *Bin Laden Said to "Own" the Taliban,* The Washington Post, October 11, 2001, at A1.

46. The conceptual difficulty of characterizing this conflict is typified by the fact that although the U.S. may be at war "in Afghanistan", it is not at war "with Afghanistan." Nationals of Afghanistan are not per se "enemy aliens" and may even be allies, without any reliable mechanism, legal or otherwise, to distinguish friend from foe. It is an ambiguous environment in which to apply the black and white distinctions of the classic law of war.

47. Order, at Sec. 2.

48. *See e.g., United States v. Verdugo-Urquidez,* 494 U.S. 259 (1990).

49. *See e.g., Johnson v. Eisentrager,* 339 U.S. 763 (1950).

50. 71 U.S. 2 (4 Wall.) (1866).

51. Whether the Taliban is recognized as the *de jure* government of Afghanistan (which is doubtful considering that that government has been recognized neither by the United Nations nor most of the international community) or as a dissident force being fought by the lawful government, their status for law of war purposes is the same. In the first case, there would be a conflict between states subject to the 1949 Geneva Conventions. In the second, under 1977 Geneva Protocol II, as noted *supra,* they could be deemed dissidents in control of territory of a High Contracting Party and also subject to the protection of that treaty.

52. The Justice Department recently released a partial list of those persons arrested in connection with the anti-terrorist campaign (although not necessarily pursuant to the Order), including, for some of them, the crimes of which they are accused. It is reported that some of the crimes alleged are civilian in nature, even if the larger purpose is to raise money for an organization like al Qaeda. For example: "Three more men on the list were indicted in New Jersey for conspiracy to embezzle, according to Michael Drewniak, a spokesman for the United States Attorney's office in Newark. The men, Hussein and Nasser Abduali and Rabi Ahmed, were charged with conspiring to buy, receive and possess $43,270 worth of stolen corn flakes. All three have been released pending trial." Lewin, *Accusations Against 93 Vary Widely,* New York Times on the Web, November 28, 2001.

53. In his concurring opinion in *Hirayabashi v. U.S.,* 320 U.S. 81 (1943), Justice Murphy said, "We give great deference to the judgment of the Congress and of the military authorities as to what is necessary in the effective prosecution of the war, but we can never forget that there are constitutional boundaries which it is our duty to uphold. It would not be supposed, for instance, that public elections could be suspended or that the prerogatives of the courts could be set aside, or that persons not charged with offenses against the law of war (see Ex parte Quirin, 317 U.S. 1, 63 S.Ct. 2, 87 L.Ed. 3) could be deprived of due process of law and the benefits of trial by jury, in the absence of a valid declaration of martial law." *Id.* at 110.

54. 10 U.S.C. 836.

55. Such procedures had not yet been issued at the time this Report was prepared.

56. Differences between the procedures required by the Order and those assured by the UCMJ include the following:

- Proof beyond reasonable doubt (10 U.S.C. Sec.851(c)), whereas the Order does not specify a standard of proof, which could under minimum standards of the laws of war be less than proof beyond reasonable doubt.
- The right of the defendant to be present at proceedings (10 U.S.C. Sec. 839), whereas the Order allows for the possibility of secret ex parte proceedings (Sec. 4(c)(4)(b).
- Defense role in selection of the court-martial panel, whereas the members of a military commission convened under the Order would not be subject to challenge by the defense.
- Defense right to choose counsel (10 U.S.C. Sec. 838(b)) whereas the Order limits defense counsel to attorneys "subject to this order" (Sec. 4(c)(5).
- Unanimity in applying death sentence (10 U.S.C. Sec. 852(a)), whereas the Order provides for "conviction only upon the concurrence of two-thirds of the members of the commission" (Sec. 4(c) (6).
- - Appellate review of decisions (10 U.S.C. Sec. 866, 867, 867(a), 869), whereas the Order precludes any appellate review by the courts (Sec. 7(b)), and allows review only insofar as the regulations promulgated under the Order may provide as a matter of administration.

57. Military Order, §7(b)(1).

58. UCMJ, §802 (a)(9).

59. The Order provides only that the detainees be treated humanely; given adequate food, water, shelter and medicine, allowed the free exercise of religion, and otherwise be subject to rules to be made by the Secretary of Defense. It even provides that detention may be outside the borders of the United States. Order, at §3. We assume that circumvention of the rights of aliens within the U.S. by arrest and forced removal from the country for delivery to a remote trial location as literally permitted by this section of the Order (*i.e.,* kidnapping) would violate those rights.

60. William Blackstone, *Commentaries,* 3:129–37 (1768), *reprinted in* The Founders' Constitution, Vol. 1, at 324–327 (University of Chicago Press 1987).

61. Joseph Story, *Commentaries on the Constitution,* 3:§§1333-36 (1883), *reprinted in*The Founders' Constitution, supra (hereinafter " Story, *Commentaries on the Constitution*"), at 342.

62. Remarks of Chief Justice William H. Rehnquist, 100th Anniversary Celebration Of the Norfolk and Portsmouth Bar Association, Norfolk, Virginia, May 3, 2000 *available at* http://www.supremecourtus.gov/publicinfo/speeches/sp_05-03-00.html (hereinafter "Rehnquist Remarks").

63. *See, e.g., Wong Wing v. United States,* 163 U.S. 228, 238 (1886) (resident aliens entitled to Fifth Amendment rights); *Kwong Hai Chew v. Colding,* 344 U.S. 590, 596 (1953) (resident alien is a "person" within the meaning of the Fifth Amendment); *Mathews v. Diaz,* 426 U.S. 69, 77 (1976) ("There are literally millions of aliens within the jurisdiction of the United States. The Fifth Amendment, as well as the Fourteenth Amendment, protects every one of these persons from deprivation of life, liberty, or property without due process of law. Even one whose presence in this country is unlawful, involuntary, or transitory is entitled to that constitutional protection.") (citations omitted); *United States v. Verdugo-Urquidez,* 494 U.S. 259 (1990) (distinguishing reach of Fourth Amendment to cover only "the people"—as in "we the people"—from Fifth Amendment's protection of "any person"). *See also United States v. bin Laden,* 132 F.Supp.2d 168, 181 (2001) (a non-citizen whose only connections to the United States are his alleged violations of U.S. law and his subsequent U.S. prosecution is entitled to due process of law under the Fifth Amendment).

64. "In Ex parte Quirin, 317 U.S. 1, we held that status as an enemy alien did not foreclose "consideration by the courts of petitioners' contentions that the Constitution and laws of the United States constitutionally enacted forbid their trial by military commission." Id. at 25. This we did in the face of a presidential proclamation denying such prisoners access to our courts.... [I]n Yamashita v. United States, 327 U.S. 1, we held that courts could inquire whether a military commission, promptly after hostilities had ceased, had lawful authority to try and condemn a Japanese general charged with violating the law of war before hostilities had ceased. There we stated: "[T]he Executive branch of the Government could not, unless there was suspension of the writ, withdraw from the courts the duty and power to make such inquiry

into the authority of the commission as may be made by habeas corpus." Id. at 9." Black, J. dissenting in *Johnson v. Eisentrager,* 339 U.S. 763, 794 (1950).

65. *See, e.g.,* 28 USC 2241(c).

66. *See Ex parte Merryman,* 17 Fed. Cas. 144 (No. 9487), (C.C.D. Md. 1861) (Chief Justice Taney, sitting as a circuit judge, wrote: "I had supposed it to be one of those points in constitutional law upon which there was no difference of opinion,. . .that the privilege of the writ could not be suspended, except by act of Congress." *Id.* at 148.) After Lincoln ignored the decision and kept Merryman in prison, Congress acted to authorize the suspension of the writ of habeas corpus. *See also,* St. George Tucker, *Blackstone's Commentaries* 1:App.290-92 (1803), *reprinted in* The Founders' Constitution, supra, at 329: "In the United States, [the writ] can be suspended, only, by the authority of congress; but not whenever congress may think proper; for it cannot be suspended, unless in cases of actual rebellion, or invasion." *Accord,* Story, *Commentaries on the Constitution, supra,* at 342 ("It would seem, as the power is given to congress to suspend the writ of habeas corpus in cases of rebellion or invasion, that the right to judge, whether exigency had arisen, must exclusively belong to that body.")

67. The Resolution is set forth in Appendix C.

68. Public Law 107-56. Interestingly, Senator Patrick Leahy, Chairman of the Senate Judiciary Committee, which took the Administration's urgent request for the Act and reported it out rapidly, albeit without significant modification, expressed surprise that the Administration should have requested this Act on an urgent basis, failed to act under it and then issued—without any prior notice to Congress, much less authority from it—the Military Order, which contains very different provisions. Comments by Senator Patrick Leahy made on the television news show *Meet the Press,* November 25, 2001. Perhaps the President's action is not so surprising considering the refusal of Congress to approve the full range of powers sought by the Administration. Having failed to get the desired statutory authority, the President acted as if he did not need it.

69. Section 412 of the USA Patriot Act is reproduced in Appendix D.

70. It should be noted that the USA Patriot Act is viewed by many civil liberties lawyers as "dangerous" in its expansion of the definition of what constitutes terrorism, the basis for an alien's detention and the like. *See, e.g.,* New York Times, November 25, 2001, A1, B4.

71. Nor, for that matter, did "inherent powers never expressly granted but said to have accrued to the office from the customs and claims of preceding administrations" provide the President authority to seize private industry to aid the war effort, *id.,* at 645.

72. *See,* Comments by Assistant Attorney General Michael Chertoff and White House Counsel Alberto Gonzales, ABA Meeting.

73. They may also be less than accurate. It is reported that Attorney General Ashcroft did try to get Congress to suspend the privilege of the writ of habeas corpus when it adopted the USA Patriot Act. Newsweek, Dec. 10, 2001, at 48, reports that the secret first draft of the anti-terrorism bill presented by the Justice Department had a section entitled "suspension of the Writ of Habeas Corpus." Rep. Sensenbrenner (Chairman of the House Judiciary Committee said: "that stuck out like a sore thumb. It was the first thing I [crossed] out." Other claims made by Administration officers likewise do not flow from the text of the Order, *e.g.,* that the Order can provide justice "close to where our forces are fighting," Alberto R. Gonzales, *Martial Justice, Full and Fair,* New York Times, November 30, 2001 ("Gonzales Op-Ed"), whereas the Order can plainly be used for trial in the United States and even provides that the Department of Justice transfer to the Department of Defense subject persons it is detaining; it cannot be imagined that Judge Gonzales is proposing that persons of that group who might be tried under the Order would be shipped to Afghanistan to be close to the combat during their trial. Judge Gonzales also writes that "The order preserves judicial review in civilian courts," whereas Section 7 specifically precludes *any* proceeding or *any*-remedy in *any* court, and when asked at the ABA meeting whether this Section meant denial of the writ of habeas corpus, the Assistant Attorney General for the Criminal Division Michael Chertoff said it did not but was intended to "prevent injunctions *and appeals* from military courts," thus at odds with Judge Gonzales' assertions published the next day.

74. 1942 Order.

75. Section 21 provides:

> Whenever there is a declared war between the United States and any foreign nation or government, or any invasion or predatory incursion is perpetrated, attempted or threatened against the territory of the United States by any foreign nation or government, and the President makes public proclamation of the event, all natives, citizens, denizens, or subjects of the hostile nation or government, being of the age of fourteen years and upward, who shall be within the United States and not actually naturalized, shall be liable to be apprehended, restrained, secured, and removed as alien enemies. The President is authorized in any such event, by his proclamation thereof, or other public act, to direct the conduct to be observed on the part of the United States, toward the aliens who become so liable; the manner and degree of the restraint to which they shall be subject and in what cases, and upon what security their residence shall be permitted, and to provide for the removal of those who, not being permitted to reside within the United States, refuse or neglect to depart therefrom; and to establish any other regulations which are found necessary in the premises and for the public safety.

76. "The resident enemy alien is constitutionally subject to summary arrest, internment and deportation whenever a "declared war" exists. Courts will entertain his plea for freedom from Executive custody only to ascertain the existence of a state of war and whether he is an alien enemy and so subject to the Alien Enemy Act. Once these jurisdictional elements have been determined, courts will not inquire into any other issue as to his internment. Ludecke v. Watkins, 335 U.S. 160." *Johnson v. Eisentrager,* supra at 775.

77. President Gerald Ford issued a national apology in 1976, calling the actions against Americans of Japanese descent a "setback to fundamental American principles." Presidential Proclamation No. 4417, 41 Fed. Reg. 7741 (1976). The Proclamation formally rescinded Executive Order No. 9066, issued in 1942. Subsequently, compensation was paid to U.S.-citizen detainees.

78. Commission on Wartime Relocation and Internment of Civilians, *Personal Justice Denied* (1982), at 3, 10, cited in Dycus, et. al, eds. *National Security Law,* (2d Ed. 1997), at 572–573.

79. Gonzales Op-Ed, *supra.*

80. ABA Meeting, November 30, 2001.

81. Rehnquist Remarks, *supra.*

82. Because of this conclusion, it is not necessary to determine whether the circumstances permitting suspension of the privilege of the writ of habeas corpus—rebellion or invasion—have occurred and have been found to have occurred by the Congress, although it seems plain that the former event has not and the latter is dubious.

83. It is interesting to note that the delays associated with such challenges do not seem to concern the Administration. The Department of Defense General Counsel, William Haynes, when asked by the Committee at the ABA Meeting whether Section 7 was being interpreted as a prohibition on habeas corpus proceedings responded: "I am sure that this will be challenged when and if this [Order] is employed," concluding that he believed the courts would upheld the President's authority.

84. By comparison in the *Quirin* case, the defendants were acknowledged members of the German military and consequently, without dispute, subject to the claimed jurisdiction of the 1942 commission.

85. 18 USC 2441, set forth in Appendix E.

86. Department of Defense Directive 5100.77, DOD Law of War Program (Dec. 9, 1998).

87. It is not within the purview of this Report to determine or analyze the crimes and/or violations of law, whether they are international or domestic, for which defendants subject to the Order may be tried.

88. *Re G.G.,* unpublished, Military Court of Cassation, Sept. 5, 1997, and *Re N.,* unpublished, Military Court of Appeal, May 26, 2000, http://www.icrc.org/ihl-nat.nsf (visited Dec. 3, 2001). The trial court and intermediate appellate courts were composed of military personnel. The defendants had civilian counsel.

89. It has been argued widely that the use of commissions is necessary to ensure convictions which may not be obtainable in other for a. *See, e.g., Terrorists on Trial—II,* Wall Street Journal Review and Outlook, December 4, 2001: "As recently as 1996, the Clinton Administration rejected Sudan's offer to turn over Osama bin Laden because it didn't think it had enough evidence to convict him in a criminal court. A military tribunal would certainly have come in handy then."

90. Another reason for concern is recognition of terrorists as potentially lawful belligerents. If, for example, some al Qaeda members wearing a uniform and bearing arms were captured while attacking a U.S. military installation (such as U.S.S. Cole or a Marine barracks or the Pentagon), they would be

entitled to treatment as prisoners of war and not criminals once the U.S. government had declared the laws of war to be applicable. Most countries insist on treating terrorists as common criminals and go to great lengths to avoid application of the laws of war. *See,* discussion of the Geneva definitions of armed conflict, *infra.*

91. An end date has been recognized by the Supreme Court as important. *See, e.g., Duncan v. Kahanamoku,* 327 U.S. 304 (1946), which struck down martial law in Hawaii so long after the invasion. There, the defendant had violated a military order covering some of the aspects of daily life, which order remained in place and whose violations were punishable only in military tribunals. In a concurring opinion, Chief Justice Stone noted that the bars and restaurants had reopened, and so the alleged crimes in question (essentially civilian ones), should have been referred to civil courts.

92. *See, War on Terror 'May Last 50 Years,'* BBCi, October 27, 2001, available at http://news.bbc.co.uk/hi/english/uk/newsid_1623000/1623036.stm, *visited* December 4, 2001.

93. *See,* Robinson O. Everett, *Military Justice in the Armed Forces of the United States* (Military Service Publishing Co. 1956): "If an undeclared war suffices to permit trial of a spy by court-martial or by military commission, a subsidiary issue is when that jurisdiction comes to an end. Had there been a declared war, military jurisdiction would continue until there was some formal proclamation of peace." *Id.,* at 30.

94. *See, e.g.,* remarks by the General Counsel of the Department of Defense at the ABA Meeting.

95. *See, e.g.,* the remarks at the ABA Meeting of DoD General Counsel William Haynes; Senior Associate Counsel and Legal Advisor to the National Security Council John B. Bellinger III; and White House Counsel Alberto Gonzales.

96. Rehnquist said:

> The courts, for their part, have largely reserved the decisions favoring civil liberties in wartime to be handed down after the war was over. Again, we see the truth in the maxim Inter Arma Silent Leges—time of war the laws are silent. To lawyers and judges, this may seem a thoroughly undesirable state of affairs, but in the greater scheme of things it may be best for all concerned. The fact that judges are loath to strike down wartime measures while the war is going on is demonstrated both by our experience in the Civil War and in World War II. This fact represents something more than some sort of patriotic hysteria that holds the judiciary in its grip; it has been felt and even embraced by members of the Supreme Court who have championed civil liberty in peacetime. Witness Justice Hugo Black: he wrote the opinion for the Court upholding the forced relocation of Japanese Americans in 1944, but he also wrote the Court's opinion striking down martial law in Hawaii two years later. While we would not want to subscribe to the full sweep of the Latin maxim—*Inter Arma Silent Leges*—in time of war the laws are silent, perhaps we can accept the proposition that though the laws are not silent in wartime, they speak with a muted voice.

Rehnquist Remarks, *supra.*

97. *Steel Seizure Case, supra,* at 635 (1952) (Jackson, J., concurring).

98. *Quoted in* Abraham Sofaer, *War, Foreign Affairs and Constitutional Power: The Origins* (Ballinger 1976), at 215.

99. *See, e.g.,* 33 U.S.C. §381: "The President is authorized to employ so many of the public armed vessels as in his judgment the service may require, with suitable instructions to the commanders thereof, in protecting the merchant vessels of the United States and their crews from piratical aggressions and depredations."

100. This is a particularly specious criticism, since there is no assertion that the Fifth Amendment applies in war to foreign combatants captured and tried abroad.

101. Spain—apparently holding important members of al Qaeda who, the investigating judge there claims, had prior knowledge of the 9/11 attacks—has already said it will not extradite to the US because of the possibility of application of the death penalty here. "The European Union already has a policy stating that no member nation must extradite a suspect to a country unless it gets believable assurances that the death penalty will not be asked for or applied." *Spain Sets Hurdle for Extraditions,* New York Times on the Web, November 24, 2001.

102. Rome Statute Of the International Criminal Court, July 17 1998, UN Doc.A/CONF.183/9* (1998) (opened for signature July 17, 1998).

103. Harold Koh, *We Have the Right Courts for Bin Laden,* New York Times, November 23, 2001.

104. *See* the Classified Information Procedures Act of 1980, 18 U.S.C. App §§1–16.

105. Gonzales Op-Ed, *supra.*

106. The concern with respect to the issue that a civilian lawyer who is not cleared to see such information might be hampered in preparing a defense may be addressed either by the clearance of civilian counsel or by the provision of cleared military counsel in those cases where such sensitive material is required to be introduced.

CHAPTER 2

*The Legality and Constitutionality of the President's Authority to Initiate an Invasion of Iraq**

PREFACE BY MARK R. SHULMAN

By the spring of 2002, it had become increasingly clear that the Presidential Administration of George W. Bush had decided to topple the Iraqi Ba'athist regime of Saddam Hussein, even at the expense of an all-out war. Rumblings about war had started almost immediately after the attacks of September 11, 2001. Indeed, we now know that President Bush sought to blame Saddam Hussein in the days following 9/11, notwithstanding convincing evidence that the attacks were planned, financed, and conducted by Osama bin Laden's al Qaeda organization without any assistance or support from the Iraqi government. By late December 2001, the Commander of U.S. Central Command, General Tommy Franks, was briefing President Bush on current war plans. Bob Woodward, *Plan of Attack,* 52 (2005). A month later, the President labeled Iraq part of an "axis of evil" suggesting a transnational conspiracy. By the Spring of 2002, rumors of war had grown too loud to ignore, and the Association's Committee on International Security Affairs decided to look into the President's authority to initiate such a war.

The resulting Report took a fresh look at several significant Constitutional issues, some of which have been the subject of vigorous debate for over a century. The delicate balance of power between Congress and the Executive is nowhere more acute than in questions related to the decision to go to war. The addition of the United Nations into the mix has only complicated the issue. Over the decades, the predominant view of jurists has remained that the U.S. Constitution demands Congressional authorization for war, except to repel actual or imminent invasion. However, Presidents had never explicitly accepted this position.

Recently, the U.C. Berkeley law professor John Yoo argued ardently that the Executive has authority to initiate war without seeking Congressional (or UN Security Council) support. Yoo's voluble writings on the topic deployed history, logic, and precedent to find a vast residual authority inherent in the "Unitary Executive." When U.S. Attorney General John Ashcroft appointed Yoo as Deputy Assistant Attorney General in the Justice Department's Office of Legal Counsel, he was better positioned to advocate this position. And he found a willing client in the Bush

Administration. The Committee, therefore, had to consider Yoo's arguments carefully. In the end, as the Report makes clear, the Committee found Yoo's arguments unpersuasive. Instead, the Committee concluded that under U.S. law, absent an actual or imminent attack, explicit Congressional authorization was required before the United States could invade Iraq. At the same time, international law probably required express UN Security Council authorization.

A few weeks after the Committee issued this Report, President Bush did request Congressional authorization. After only cursory debate, Congress issued its unprecedented Joint Resolution to Authorize the Use of Armed Forces Against Iraq on October 2, 2002. At virtually the same time, the Administration launched its campaign for UN support. In the end, the Bush Administration decided not to wait for express UN authorization. And on March 19, the President declared the opening of armed hostilities.

I. INTRODUCTION

The Committee on International Security Affairs of the Association of the Bar of the City of New York ("the Committee") has considered the legal and constitutional aspects of the President's authority to order an invasion of Iraq without Congressional approval, focusing on the scenario of a large-scale invasion proposed by the Bush Administration for the purpose of regime change, without either a prior attack by Iraq on the United States, an imminent threat of such an attack or evidence that Iraq aided in the perpetration of the terrorist attacks of September 11, 2001. Our examination of the Constitution leads us to conclude that an invasion of this nature would constitute a war within the contemplation of the Founders and would thus require prior Congressional authorization. We believe that such an invasion solely on the President's orders would deny Congress its Constitutionally-granted powers and could be justified only by an excessively expansive notion of Presidential authority, one unsupported by the plain text of the U.S. Constitution.

This report addresses the issue of the legality of a Presidentially-initiated, large-scale invasion of Iraq in three steps:

(1) An examination of the Administration's stated rationale for undertaking a large-scale invasion of Iraq;

(2) An analysis of the U.S. Constitution and other relevant law underpinning the respective authority of the Congress and the President to initiate such an invasion; and

(3) The conclusion of the Committee, based upon the foregoing analysis, that such an invasion of Iraq requires prior Congressional authorization.

II. THE WHITE HOUSE IS LAYING THE GROUNDWORK FOR AN INVASION OF IRAQ

Since 9/11, the Administration has taken an increasingly assertive, proactive stance toward Iraq. In October 2001, the White House noted that evidence linked Iraq and the al Qaeda organization which was responsible for the attacks of September 11, 2001, but found nothing specifically linking Iraq to the attacks on the United States.[1] In the State of the Union Address on January 29, 2002, President Bush included Iraq in the "axis of evil," a list of those countries that sponsored terrorists and possessed or were trying to acquire weapons of mass destruction (biological, chemical, or nuclear weapons).[2] He suggested that the United States needed to act quickly against these nations but proposed no specific actions.[3] In March, Vice President Richard B. Cheney made somewhat clearer the Administration's concerns regarding Iraq, a "possible marriage...between the terrorist organizations...and weapons of mass destruction capability, the kind of devastating materials that Saddam used against his own people in "88," although no link to al Qaeda or other terrorist organizations has yet been publicly shown or even claimed by the Administration.[4] Recently, in a speech at West Point, the President made clear that the United States could no longer "wait for threats to fully materialize" but instead "must take battle to the enemy, disrupt his plans, and confront the worst threats before they emerge."[5]

By late January, newspapers had reported that the White House was planning an invasion involving over 200,000 ground troops.[6] By May, the Joint Chiefs of Staff had apparently convinced the Administration, which seemed to regard an offensive as "all but inevitable,"[7] to postpone the proposed invasion of Iraq at least until after the brutal Iraqi summer.

The Administration has also made pronouncements that the invasion of Iraq is designed to replace that country's leadership with one more amenable to the United States' current international goals. Secretary of State Colin Powell said in recent testimony before the House International Relations Committee: "Regime change is something the United States might have to do alone."[8] Defense Secretary Donald Rumsfeld is quoted in June, 2002, in a Defense Department Report document describing his thoughts that the world "would be a safer place if there were a regime change" in Iraq. He pointed out that the United States and a number of its allies, backed by President Bush and the U.S. Congress, have expressed agreement on this because every new day means another opportunity for Iraqi weapons programs to mature further. "To the extent they become more mature,' he said, "obviously, the capabilities both for weapons of mass destruction themselves, as well as the ability to deliver them, evolve as well.'"[9] Finally, in what has been called "one of the strongest and most detailed explanations by a senior U.S. official of the need to oust Hussein,"[10] National Security Advisor Condoleeza Rice made a "moral case" for the invasion of Iraq:

> This is an evil man [Saddam Hussein] who, left to his own devices, will wreak havoc again on his own population, his neighbors and, if he gets weapons of mass destruction and the means to deliver them, on all of us. It is a very powerful moral case for regime change...We certainly do not have the luxury of doing nothing...if Saddam Hussein is left in power, doing the things that he's doing now, this is a threat that will emerge, and emerge in a very big way.[11]

Thus, the Administration has made abundantly clear that such an attack is based on long-term foreign policy, if not moral reasons, and not on any concept of defending the United States from an imminent military threat. Regardless of the validity of the rationale set forth by the Administration, a massive campaign against Iraq does not appear to the Committee to be the type of emergency defensive action that is within the exclusive authority of the President to undertake.

III. THE PRESIDENT DOES NOT HAVE THE AUTHORITY TO ACT UNILATERALLY TO UNDERTAKE THE LARGE-SCALE INVASION CONTEMPLATED

A. War Powers Clause

The text is simple: Only Congress has the authority to declare war under Article I, Section 8, Clause 11 of the Constitution: "The Congress shall have Power...To declare War...." On this there is no question. Furthermore,

The Founding Fathers drew a distinction between offensive and defensive hostilities.—The records of the convention indicate that this was done to preserve for the executive the power to repel sudden attacks and to avoid the possible implication that Congress was expected to conduct war. . .[12]

As Louis Fisher notes, the Founders' decision to use the word "declare" instead of "make" left the President the limited and clearly delineated power to "repel sudden attacks" against the United States.[13] The difference between the respective war power authority of the two branches can be explained as the difference between "defensive" military action against actual or imminent attack; and all other military action which constitutes "war" under the Constitution, the former being within the authority of the President as Executive and Commander in Chief, the latter within the exclusive authority of the Congress.[14] The proposed invasion does not come close to the exigent defense against imminent or sudden attack contemplated by the Founders as within the Presidential authority.

B. War Powers Resolution[15]

In response to perceived excesses by Presidents Lyndon B. Johnson and Richard Nixon in initiating and expanding the war in South-East Asia, Congress resolved in 1973 to clarify its sole authority to declare war. The War Powers Resolution (the "WPR") requires the President to report to and regularly consult with Congress after unilaterally choosing to deploy U.S. armed forces.[16] Unless Congress otherwise authorizes the military action, the WPR seeks to require the President to withdraw armed forces within sixty days of deploying them. A Congressional declaration of war or enabling resolution waives these requirements and gives the President the full power to conduct a war. Some argue that the WPR is ineffective or even unconstitutional as it seeks to alter the Constitutional war powers framework and note that no President has recognized its constitutionality. However, in large-scale conflicts, Presidents have sought Congressional authorization, most notably in the most closely analogous military action when President George H. W. Bush sought support of Congress for the Gulf War of 1991.

C. Arguments for Executive Authority to Initiate War

Some writers have argued that the Founders reserved for the President the power to initiate wars and gave Congress the power merely to ratify them, i.e., decide the legal status of the conflict initiated by the President.[17] These writers deny the authority expressly granted to Congress under the Constitution and argue in support of the President's authority to undertake unilateral action by positing that the President has the "inherent executive authority" to initiate wars, as Commander-in-Chief under Article II, Section 2[18] and as part of his generic powers as President.[19] This argument, if accepted, gives the President wide-ranging powers to use force —not just to repel a sudden attack but also to initiate full-scale offensives as part of the war against terrorism.[20] According to this view, Congress has also waived its authority over the years by acquiescing to numerous wars initiated by the President.[21]

These arguments deny or miscast the plain text of the Constitution granting Congress the sole authority to declare war. Conversely, no text gives the President the discretion to deploy U.S. forces without Congressional approval in the absence of a sudden danger to national security, not even for the "moral" reasons or concerns of "emerging" threats cited by the Administration.[22]

Advocates of unilateral executive authority over war powers also claim to bring an originalist understanding to the War Powers clause that contradicts both the text and the clear (originalist) evidence that the Founders wished to prevent the President from having strong war powers.[23] Advocates of inherent executive authority to initiate wars argue that the American conception of executive war powers was largely shaped by Britain, even though the colonies revolted from Britain in part, as a reaction to the excess of British executive power they had experienced.[24] The President's role as Commander-in-Chief emphasizes civilian control over the military and, absent an immediate threat to the nation requiring defense, only gives him the power to execute Congress' decision to commence a war.[25] Many Founders believed war declarations were simply not an executive function.[26]

D. UN or NATO Authorization

Some scholars argue that the President may undertake a military action without Congressional authorization if the UN or NATO has authorized such an action.[27] By this view, the purpose of the "declare war" clause is to ensure that the decision to initiate war does not rest with just one person. UN authorization avoids this problem, perhaps even more effectively than does Congress' authorization, because the Security Council "is far less likely to be stampeded by combat fever than is Congress."[28] As examples, proponents of this view observe that Presidents, on two previous occasions, have deployed U.S. forces pursuant to Security Council authorizations: the Korean War[29] and the 1991 Gulf War.[30]

UN or NATO authorization does not absolve the President of his Constitutional duty to obtain Congress' approval. Whether the Security Council approves of an invasion of Iraq or not,[31] the Constitution requires Congressional authorization for war. Treaty obligations, such as those under the UN Charter or NATO Treaty, are equivalent to federal statutory law[32] and, as such, never trump the Constitution.[33]

Arguments relying on the Korean and Gulf Wars as examples are unconvincing. President Harry S. Truman's order sending U.S. forces to Korea might be viewed as repelling a sudden attack—the North Korean invasion had nearly overrun South Korea, threatening irreparable harm to U.S. security interests.[34] In any case, it appears that President Truman sought UN approval as a fig leaf for acting without Congress; he[35] had already ordered American forces to defend South Korea before obtaining UN authorization[36] and would have done so without receiving it.[37] Likewise President George H.W. Bush, despite obtaining UN authorization, sought and received Congressional approval for the Gulf War.[38]

1. *Security Council Resolution 678*

The Administration may argue that not only does UN authorization give the President authority to act without Congress, but that specifically, President Bush already has a UN mandate to invade Iraq. This 1990 Resolution states:

> The Security Council...Acting under Chapter VII of the Charter...Authorizes Member States co-operating with the Government of Kuwait, unless Iraq on or before 15 January 1991 fully implements Resolution 660 (1990) [calling for Iraq to withdraw from Kuwait] and all subsequent relevant resolutions, to use all necessary means...to restore international peace and security in the area.[39]

Congress stated in PL 102-*1* that the President was "authorized to use United States Armed Forces pursuant to United Nations Security Council Resolution 678,"[40] and the subsequent relevant Security Council resolutions referred to in Resolution 660 and thus incorporated into Resolution 678 (including those establishing the Iraq weapons inspection regime), thereby extending Congressional authorization to such subsequent Security Council resolutions. That this is so is indicated by the President's continued reporting to Congress under PL 102-*1*'s reporting requirements regarding the United States' efforts to enforce those subsequent Security Council Resolutions and Congress' acceptance of such reports.[41]

Nonetheless, while it appears that Resolution 678 may still be in effect, and, further, a purely textual analysis of the Resolution may support a broad interpretation of purpose extending even to authorization of force for "regime change,"[42] nonetheless, a review of that and the subsequent resolutions from the Security Council—along with a reading of the debate surrounding the adoption of the Authorization for Use of Force Against Iraq Joint Resolution—suggest that it did not authorize, intend or even contemplate the use of force against Iraq for "moral" reasons or purposes of "regime change." The Committee concludes, therefore, that Resolution 678 does not provide authorization for the invasion contemplated by the Bush Administration.

2. *Security Council Resolution 1373*

Even if UN authorization allowed the President to order American forces into hostilities without Congress' approval, Resolution 1373 passed in response to the events of September 11, does not appear to the Committee to authorize the United States to invade Iraq for the purpose of regime change or even moral reasons.[43] In contrast, nothing in the plain, operative text of Resolution 1373 authorizes any state to invade Iraq absent a connection with 9/11.[44] There are also other flaws with citing Resolution 1373 as a blank check (e.g., the phrase "combat by all means" appears in the preamble and is not binding). All this points to the fact that the Resolution 1373 does not authorize the proposed war against Iraq.

E. 1991 and 2001 Joint Resolutions of Congress

Congress has twice issued resolutions that might be used to support a contention that Congress has already authorized a future war against Iraq; yet, neither resolution currently applies. As noted above, President George H.W. Bush sought and received Congressional authorization for undertaking the Persian Gulf War's Operation Desert Storm in January 1991 pursuant to Security Council Resolution 678 in the form of PL 102-*1* ("Authorization for Use of Military Force Against Iraq Resolution").[45] While, as explained above, from 1991 to the present three Presidents have continued to report to Congress under PL 102-*1* regarding the United States' efforts pursuant to Security Council Resolution 678, and both the U.S. and the British governments take the position that Resolution 678 continues in effect, neither the 1991 Authorization for Use of Military Force Against Iraq Resolution nor Resolution 678 were designed to authorize conquest of Iraq to achieve a change in regime.

More recently, in the immediate wake of 9/11, Congress authorized the President to use armed force against "those nations, organizations or persons he determines planned, authorized, committed, or aided the terrorist attacks on September 11, 2001."[46] This sweeping resolution requires a connection with 9/11 and would only authorize war against Iraq if the President had determined that Iraq had "aided" in perpetrating the attacks. To date, the President has not made such a determination. It is important to note that the United States has not announced any causal link between the events of 9/11 and Iraq; Vice President Cheney has acknowledged as much explicitly.[47] It is thus clear the 2001 Joint Resolution To Authorize The Use Of U.S. Armed Forces Against Those Responsible For The Recent Attacks Launched Against The United States does not extend to authorize war against Iraq for the stated purpose.

F. Congress' Powers of Appropriation Are Insufficient

Some scholars argue that appropriations are a sufficient check, and the primary one intended by the Founders, against the executive authority to initiate war—Congress may simply refuse funding for further military operations.[48] However, this check will often be useless against the President. Under this theory, Congress may stop military actions once troops have been committed. The action may end, damage may be done, and lives (U.S. and foreign) may be lost well before the withdrawal of funding is effective.[49] It may also be dangerous to withdraw funding once a large ground force has been committed.[50] This view of war powers is backwards. Congress should not be in a position to decide merely how many casualties the United States will accept but rather whether losses need be incurred at all.

G. Under the Constitution, the Proposed Invasion Is a War

Under the Constitution, President Bush would have the unilateral authority to commit U.S. troops to Iraq if he could show that such an action constituted repelling a sudden or imminent attack or its modern day equivalent. Under the scenario addressed herein, however, the Committee believes he must seek Congressional approval. There are three reasons for this conclusion, which must be read cumulatively:

(1) The scale of the endeavor strongly suggests the action is a "war" under Constitution (although scale alone is insufficient to put the matter into the legislative domain as the type of war requiring Congressional authorization). The United States District Court for the District of Columbia had "no hesitation in concluding that an offensive entry into Iraq by several hundred thousand United States servicemen...could be described as a 'war' within the meaning of [the War Powers Clause]."[51] (Congress is more likely to acquiesce to unilateral executive decisions to deploy relatively small forces, [52] but despite any such acquiescence, Congress cannot waive its Constitutional war powers.)

The deployment of 200,000 or more troops (or, indeed, even a "smaller" invasion in conjunction with massive air attack) is practically and qualitatively different from the scale of other recent U.S. military interventions, except for the Vietnam and Gulf Wars; in each of these two conflicts, the President specifically sought and received Congressional authorization. The Tonkin Gulf Resolution, while passed by Congress as a reaction to largely fabricated events, shows that even President Johnson believed he was Constitutionally compelled to attempt to obtain Congress' authorization before beginning a full-fledged war in Vietnam. President Johnson likely abused his authority to send troops to Vietnam. More important, in the context of this discussion on the separation of war powers, is how he might have abused his authority. President Johnson's actions, if anything, affirmed the legitimacy of the War Powers clause because he actively sought Congressional authorization for the Vietnam War.[53]

(2) The invasion of Iraq for the purpose of regime change is plainly not for the purpose of repelling a sudden or imminent attack, as discussed above. Iraq has not, since the end of the 1991 Gulf War, used force against or directly threatened the United States (aside from attacks on allied airplanes in the no-fly zones). According to the National Security Advisor, any threat that Iraq poses is not of an immediate nature; if it were, the President would have proposed an immediate action, or, already acted on his own authority. To deem an invasion of Iraq repelling a sudden or imminent attack under these circumstances dangerously distorts the intent of the Founders.

(3) In the case of repelling a "sudden attack," or even the modern day equivalent such as disrupting a terrorist operation about to commence, time limitations help to provide an understanding of the boundary between executive and legislative war powers. The President has the authority and obligation to repel sudden attacks because the unitary Executive can react more quickly than Congress. In such cases there is time to deliberate. Perhaps a President who fears that his war plans will be rejected would not want to subject them to Congressional scrutiny. It is in precisely this situation, however, that the decision is not the President's to make alone; he must convince Congress[54] not only of the justness of the cause but the legitimacy of the means.

IV. CONCLUSION

The Committee has set forth its reasoning and conclusion that the President needs Congressional authorization to launch a large-scale invasion of Iraq for the purpose of regime change or on "moral" grounds set forth.[55] Some may disagree with this conclusion. However, when the President seeks to take the nation from a state of peace to a state of war for reasons other than defense against actual or imminent attack, however valid those reasons may be, the Republic deserves—and the Constitution requires—a Congressional debate over whether to authorize such a war. Swift action in defense of the nation and enforcement of legislation are the President's obligations; decision-making from reasoned deliberation and determining America's long-term security interests is Congress'.

Administration officials, former White House officials, members of Congress, and scholars have argued for and against removing Saddam Hussein, and even those who agree he must be ousted, disagree as to whether using ground troops and a massive air assault in a large scale endeavor is the best means.[56] As such, the prudence of offensive military action—from the perspective of U.S. national security—is far from self-evident. This controversy necessarily requires open and public debate about the merits of a war against Iraq to effect regime change. Such deliberation in Congress and amongst citizens—before using force—is the hallmark of a democratic republic, as conceived of by the Founders and written in the Constitution. The President can best facilitate this necessary debate and honor the Constitutional separation of powers by requesting authorization from Congress for his proposed military action before acting.

August 22, 2002

NOTES

* **Committee On International Security Affairs:** Raenu Barod (chair), Igou M. Allbray, John R. Burroughs, John C. Ericson, William V.O. Gnichtel, Kerry J. Houghton, Thomas E. Miotke, Lisa A. Munoz, John V.H. Pierce, Mark R. Shulman.

Mr. Shulman and Lawrence J. Lee, a student at New York University School of Law who will be joining the Committee in September 2002, are the principal authors of this report. Eleven members of the Committee have approved this report. Five members have recused themselves due to conflicts of interest: Nicholas Rostow, Paul W. Butler, Steven C. Krane, Robert J. Cosgrove and Samrat S. Khichi. The Committee is grateful for the considerable input of Stephen J. Shapiro and Miles P. Fischer of the Standing Committee on Military Affairs and Justice.

1. *See* Interview with Richard B. Cheney, Meet the Press, Mar. 24, 2002. With respect to the connection between Iraq and al Qaeda, "We haven't been able to pin down any connection there... We discovered, and it's since been public, the allegation that one of the lead hijackers, Mohamed Atta, had, in fact, met with Iraqi intelligence in Prague, but we've not been able yet from our perspective to nail down a close tie between the al Qaeda organization and Saddam Hussein. We'll continue to look for it."

2. President George W. Bush, State of the Union Address, Jan. 29, 2002, available at http://www.whitehouse.gov/news/releases/2002/01/20020129-11.html. "States like these [North Korea, Iran, Iraq], and their terrorist allies, constitute an axis of evil, arming to threaten the peace of the world. By seeking weapons of mass destruction, these regimes pose a grave and growing danger. They could provide these arms to terrorists, giving them the means to match their hatred. They could attack our allies or attempt to blackmail the United States."

3. *Id.* "Time is not on our side. I will not wait on events while dangers gather. I will not stand by, as peril draws closer and closer. The United States of America will not permit the world's most dangerous regimes to threaten us with the world's most destructive weapons."

4. *See* Interview with Richard B. Cheney, *supra* note 1.

5. President George W. Bush, United States Military Academy Graduation Speech, June 2, 2002.

6. *See generally* Peter Ford, *'Evil axis' and others talk back,* Christian Sci. Monitor, Jan. 31, 2002, at 01, (describing U.S. invasion plans); Ian Bruce, *Pentagon draws up plans for invasion of Iraq,* HERALD (Glasgow), Jan. 31, 2002, at 11 (explaining Pentagon plans to use ground troops to expel Hussein); William Rees-Mogg, *The countdown starts for Operation Saddam,* TIMES (London), Feb. 18, 2002, Features (criticizing White House plans); Eric Schmitt, Cheney, at Marine Base, *Reinforces Bush's Stand On War Against Terror*, N.Y. TIMES, Feb. 19, 2002, at A10 (reporting Cheney's efforts to garner support in the United States for action against Iraq).

7. *See* Scott Ritter, Commentary: *Behind 'Plot' on Hussein, a Secret Agenda: Killing weapons inspections would clear way for war,* L.A. TIMES, June 19, 2002, at B13.

8. *State Department Report: Powell says U.S. is Examining Full Range of Options on Iraq,* Feb. 6, 2002, issued by U.S. Department of State International Information Programs, viewed at http://usinfo.state.gov/topical/pol/arms/02020605.htm.

9. *Defense Department Report: Afghanistan; Iraq, June 17, 2002,* issued by U.S. Department of State International Information Programs, viewed at http://usinfo.state.gov/regional/nea/sasia/afghan/text/0617dodrpt.htm.

10. "Rice Lays Out Case for War In Iraq Bush; Adviser Cites 'Moral' Reasons," WASH POST, Aug. 16, 2002, at 1, reported at http://www.washingtonpost.com/wp-dyn/articles/A21333-2002Aug15.html.

11. Rice interview with BBC, reported at http://news.bbc.co.uk/1/hi/world/americas /2193426.stm, Aug. 15, 2002. Brackets in original; emphasis added.

12. R. Turner, THE WAR POWERS RESOLUTION: ITS IMPLEMENTATION IN THEORY AND PRACTICE, (1983), at 17 [emphasis in original].

13. Messrs. Madison and Gerry jointly introduced the amendment to substitute "declare" for "make." They noted the change would "leave to the Executive the power to repel sudden attacks." M. Farrand, The Records of the Federal Convention of 1787 (rev. ed. 1937), at 318, cited in THE CONSTITUTION OF THE UNITED STATES OF AMERICA: ANALYSIS AND INTERPRETATION, Congressional Research Service (1992), at 308, note 1420.

See Louis Fisher, *Sidestepping Congress: Presidents Acting Under the UN and NATO,* 47 Case W. Res. L. Rev. 1237 (1997) (arguing that the constitutional structure adopted by the Framers is "remarkably clear in its basic principles. The authority to initiate war lay with Congress. The President could act unilaterally only in one area: to repel sudden attacks."). A number of leading commentators support this view. *See generally* John H. Ely, WAR AND RESPONSIBILITY: CONSTITUTIONAL LESSONS OF VIETNAM AND ITS AFTERMATH (1993); Louis Henkin, CONSTITUTIONALISM, DEMOCRACY, AND FOREIGN AFFAIRS (1990); Harold H. Koh, THE NATIONAL SECURITY CONSTITUTION: SHARING POWER AFTER THE IRAN-CONTRA AFFAIR (1990); Michael J. Glennon, CONSTITUTIONAL DIPLOMACY (1990); Lori Fisler Damrosch, *Constitutional Control Over War Powers: A Common Core of Accountability in Democratic Societies?,* 50 U. Miami L. Rev. 181 (1995) (arguing that "the body of experience of the mature democracies in their war-and-peace decisions reflects a common core of commitment to democratic accountability."). *See also* S. Con. Res. 133, 107th Cong. (2002) referred to Senate Foreign Relations Committee (expressing "the sense of Congress that the United States should not use force against Iraq, outside of the existing Rules of Engagement, without specific statutory authorization or a declaration of war under Article I, Section 8, Clause 11 of the Constitution of the United States").

14. *See,* e.g., William Whiting, WAR POWERS UNDER THE CONSTITUTION OF THE UNITED STATES (1871), at 38–40: "Congress has the sole power, under the constitution, to make [a] declaration [of war], and to sanction or authorize the commencement of offensive war...But this is quite a different case from a defensive...war. The constitution establishes the mode in which this government shall commence wars, the authority which may authorize, and the declarations which shall precede, any act of hostility; but it has no power to prescribe the manner in which others should begin war against us."

15. *See* 50 U.S.C. 1541–1548.

16. The WPR seeks to prevent the President from abusing both his authority as Commander-in-Chief and his ability to respond more quickly than Congress, as the President may deploy troops and undertake a military action that does not constitute a response to a sudden or imminent attack before Congress can act at all, or he may deploy a sufficient number of troops quickly enough to create a self-fulfilling

prophecy—(that to remove U.S. forces immediately after deploying them would be irresponsible and dangerous). If the President can commit troops offensively and only consult Congress when hostilities become inevitable (i.e., shoot and ask questions later), then Congress has no real war powers. *See* Lori Fisler Damrosch, *The Constitutional Responsibility of Congress for Military Engagements,* 89 Am. J. Int'l L. 58 (1994) (arguing that in the post-Cold War era, it is more important than ever to have "robust parliamentary debate and genuine deliberation" before military action, as required by WPR and the War Powers Clause). *See also* infra Part II.F (arguing that Congressional appropriations or other measures after military deployment are insufficient checks against unilateral action by the President).

17. *See generally* John C. Yoo, *The Continuation of Politics by Other Means: The Original Understanding of War Powers,* 84 Calif. L. Rev. 167 (1996). Yoo argues that the Founders understood declarations of war not as legislative authorization to initiate war but as a mere acknowledgement by Congress that the legal status had changed, from peace to war, between the United States and a hostile state. It alerted all nations that violence committed against hostile states was official and public, not the work of pirates or rebels, and alerts U.S. citizens about the identity of the new enemy. Yoo calls this a Congressional exercise of judicial powers. *See id.* at 205.

18. Some argue that the President has more explicit and unchecked authority to use the armed forces under Article II, Section 2 ("President shall be Commander in Chief of the Army and Navy of the United States, and of the militia of the several states, when called into actual Service of the United States."). *See generally* Robert J. Delahunty & John C. Yoo, *The President's Constitutional Authority to Conduct Military Operations Against Terrorist Organizations and the Nations That Harbor or Support Them,* 25 Harv. J.L. & Pub. Pol'y 487 (2002).

19. *See* Yoo, *supra* note 17, at 252–56 (arguing that President's war powers were continuation of British and colonial traditions and that 18th Century citizens expected a "paternal figure vested with the duty of protecting his fellow citizens.").

20. *See* Delahunty & Yoo, *supra* note 18, at 487 ("The President had the innate power not only to retaliate against any person, organization, or state suspected of involvement in terrorist attacks on the United States, but also against foreign states suspected of harboring or supporting such organizations."). Authors are in the Office of Legal Counsel of the Department of Justice (but do not claim to state official views of the Justice Department).

21. *See* John Yoo, *Clio at War: The Misuse of History in the War Powers Debate*, 70 U. Colo. L. Rev. 1169, 1179 (1999) (arguing that Congress has allowed the President to assume the initiative in war).

22. *See* D.A. Jeremy Telman, *A Truism That Isn't True? The Tenth Amendment and Executive War Power*, 51 Cath. U. L. Rev. 135, 189 (responding to Yoo and others who argue for increased executive war powers by arguing that such powers can only come from a theory of inherent authority because "there is no basis, in the constitutional text, in the writings of the Framers, in political theory, or in the constitutional history of the United States for transferring powers invested in the Legislature to the Executive."). Critics like Yoo read "declare war" out of context, separating from neighboring clauses that clearly enumerate the power to raise, support, and regulate the armed forces (Cl. 12–16), all part and parcel of control when and how the United States goes to war.

23. James Madison said that the Constitution "supposes. . .that the Executive is the branch of power most interested in war, and most prone to it. It has accordingly, with studied care, vested the question of war in the Legislature." James Madison, Letter From James Madison to Thomas Jefferson, Apr. 2, 1798, in 6 THE WRITINGS OF JAMES MADISON, 311, 312 (Gaillard Hunt Ed., 1906) (cited by Telman, supra note 22, at 152). Furthermore, during the Constitutional Convention, no one even seconded a motion to give the President the power to initiate wars. See 2 RECORDS OF THE FEDERAL CONVENTION OF 1787, (Max Farrand ed., 1937) (cited by Telman, supra note 22, at 152). Finally, Madison argued that the system of checks and balances required that Congress control the decision to initiate war: "Those who are to conduct a war cannot in the nature of things, be proper or safe judges, whether a war ought to be commenced, continued, or concluded." James Madison, *Helvidius No. 1,* in 6 THE WRITINGS OF JAMES MADISON 145 (Gaillard Hunt ed., 1906).

24. *See* Telman, *supra* note 22, at 180 ("Yoo's theory ignores the great efforts expended in the Revolutionary Era to free the United States from the problems associated with the excesses of executive power experienced when the American states had the status of English colonies."). Even Alexander

Hamilton, once an advocate of constitutional monarchy, conceded that the powers granted the President were much inferior to those granted the King of Great Britain, who could declare war and raise and regulate armies. *Id.* at 182.

25. Hamilton argued at the Constitutional Convention that the executive's war time functions were "to have the direction of war when authorized or begun"; nothing in his statement to the Convention indicated that the President should also have the power to decide whether to start a war. 5 DEBATES IN THE SEVERAL STATE CONVENTIONS, ON THE ADOPTION OF THE FEDERAL CONSTITUTION, AS RECOMMEND BY THE GENERAL CONVENTION AT PHILADELPHIA, In 1787, at 205 (Jonathan Elliot ed., 2d ed. 1996).

This paper takes no position with respect to the authority the President may have to employ the armed forces in military operations other than war, such as peacekeeping, disaster relief, peacetime garrisons in foreign bases, training of U.S. and allied forces abroad and the like.

26. Madison, *Helvidius No. 1, supra* note 23, at 148. "A declaration that there shall be war is not an execution of laws: it does not suppose pre-existing laws to be executed: it is not, in any respect, an act merely executive."

27. *See generally* Thomas M. Franck & Faiza Patel, *UN Police Action in Lieu of War: "The Old Order Changeth,"* 85 Am. J. Int'l L. 63 (1991).

28. *Id.* at 74. "The purpose of the war-declaring clause was to ensure that this fateful decision did not rest with a single person. The new system vests that responsibility in the Security Council, a body where the most divergent interests and perspectives of humanity are represented and where five of fifteen members have a veto power." *Id.* As a practical matter of restraining the President, it may be true that the Security Council, made up of different member states with different and often conflicting political interests, is less likely to authorize the use of American force than Congress. Such support seems unlikely under the circumstances.

29. Delahunty & Yoo, *supra* note 18, at 504 ("Perhaps the most significant operation exercised on the President's sole authority occurred during the Korean War, when President Truman ordered United States troops to fight a war that lasted for over three years and resulted in over 142,000 American casualties.").

30. *See* Fisher, *supra* note 13, at 1266 (observing that during the Gulf War, Richard B. Cheney, the Secretary of Defense, argued that Congressional authorization was not necessary for UN-approved actions).

31. Recent history suggests that three of five permanent members (Russia, China, France) of the Security Council would oppose an invasion of Iraq. Richard Butler, THE GREATEST THREAT: IRAQ, WEAPONS OF MASS DESTRUCTION, AND THE GROWING CRISIS OF GLOBAL SECURITY 91, 220–21 (2000) (describing Russian, French, and Chinese support for ending sanctions against Iraq, despite the lack of Iraqi compliance with UN weapons inspection regime, and self-interested political motives for this support).

32. *See* U.S. Const., Art. VI, cl. 2 ("This Constitution, and the Laws of the United States which shall be made in Pursuance thereof; and all Treaties made, or which shall be made, under the Authority of the United States, shall be the supreme Law of the Land").

33. RESTATEMENT (THIRD) OF FOREIGN RELATIONS LAW 111, Comment (a) ("In their character as law of the United States, rules of international law and provisions of international agreements of the United States are subject to the Bill of Rights and other prohibitions, restrictions, and requirements of the Constitution, and cannot be given effect in violation of them.").

34. Truman's advisers believed that the sudden North Korean attack required an immediate U.S. response: "To sit by while Korea is overrun by unprovoked armed attack would start a disastrous chain of events leading most probably to world war." John Foster Dulles & John M. Allison, Telegram to Dean Acheson and Dean Rusk, June 25, 1950 (one day after the North Korean invasion began), *available at* http://www.trumanlibrary.org/whistlestop/study collections/korea/large/week1/elsy 3 1.htm. Truman regarded the Korean invasion as the beginning of general Soviet aggression and expansion in the Far East. See generally Philip C. Jessup, Memorandum of Conversation, June 25, 1950, *available at* http://www.trumanlibrary.org/whistlestop/study collections/korea/large/week1/kw 4 1.htm (summarizing discussion between Truman and his advisers about the Korean situation, its implications for China, Formosa, and Southeast Asia, and plans to strike at Soviet airbases and ships in the Pacific Ocean).

35. Truman, before the Korean War, had agreed that he must seek Congressional authorization before committing U.S. troops to UN or NATO military actions. *See* Fisher, *supra* note 13, at 1245–46 ("After Roosevelt's death, President Truman sent a cable from Potsdam stating that all agreements involving U.S. troop commitments to the United Nations would first have to be approved by both Houses of Congress.). *See also id.* at 1255–56 ("In 1951, during Senate hearings on NATO, [Under Secretary of State Dean] Acheson. . .acknowledged that the treaty does not compel any nation "to take steps contrary to its convictions, and none is obligated to ignore its national interests.").

36. *Id.* at 1261 (indicating that Truman had ordered American support of South Korean forces, in the form of military supplies and air and sea cover, before the Security Council authorized states to repel the invasion by North Korea).

37. *Id.* ("After he left the presidency, Truman was asked whether he had been willing to use military force in Korea without UN backing. He replied, with customary bluntness: "No question about it.'").

38. PL 102-1 (1991).

"Section 2. Authorization for use of United States Armed Forces

(a) Authorization. — The President is authorized, subject to subsection (b), to use United States Armed Forces pursuant to United Nations Security Council Resolution 678 (1990) in order to achieve implementation of Security Council Resolutions 660, 661, 662, 664, 665, 666, 667, 669, 670, 674, and 677."

39. S.C. Res. 678, U.N. Doc. S/RES/0678 (1990).

40. *Id.* [emphasis supplied].

41. *See* e.g., Letter from the President to the Speaker of the House of Representatives and the President Pro Tempore of the Senate January 23, 2002, Office of the White House Press Secretary, January 24, 2002:

> Dear Mr. Speaker: (Dear Mr. President:)
>
> Consistent with the Authorization for Use of Military Force Against Iraq Resolution (Public Law 102-1) and as part of my effort to keep the Congress fully informed, I am providing a report prepared by my Administration on the status of efforts to obtain Iraq's compliance with the resolutions adopted by the United Nations Security Council. The last report, consistent with Public Law 102-1, was transmitted on October 11, 2001.
>
> Sincerely,
>
> GEORGE W. BUSH

42. "From a purely textual perspective, that authorization seems to have few, if any, limits. "Area" is undefined and could mean Iraq or the entire Middle East. "Restoring international peace and security' could mean occupying Iraq, removing Saddam Hussein from power, or bombing Iraq's military/industrial capacity." Jules Lobel & Michael Ratner, *Bypassing the Security Council: Ambiguous Authorizations to Use Force, Cease-Fires and the Iraqi Inspection Regime,* 93 Am. J. Int'l. L. 124 (1999), *printed at* http://www.asil.org /ajil/lobel.htm93, at text accompanying footnotes 59 and 60.

43. *Id.*

44. *See* S.C. Res. 1373 resolving (that states shall suppress the financing of terrorist acts (P1), deny other support to terrorists or terrorist groups (P2), cooperate with other states to exchange information, become parties to relevant anti-terrorism treaties, and prevent abuse of asylum laws by terrorists (P3). No part of the text of the resolution urges or condones states to invade other states to prevent terrorism), S.C. Res. 1373, U.N. Doc. S/RES/1373 (2001).

45. Public Law 102 - 1, 2(b) (Joint Resolution to authorize use of military force against Iraq) Jan. 14, 1991. "The President is authorized. . .to use United States Armed Forces pursuant to United Nations Security Council Resolution 678 (1990). . . ."

46. United States Public Law 107-40, 2(a) (Joint Resolution to authorize the use of U.S. Armed Forces against those responsible for the recent attacks launched against the United States) Sept. 18, 2001.

47. *See* note 1.

48. *See* Yoo, *supra* note 17 at 297 ("Recent events [i.e. United States-led military operations in Bosnia] confirm that Congress fully understands that its appropriations power may be used to check executive military operations.").

49. For instance, the Office of the Legal Counsel of the Department of Justice advised President George H.W. Bush that he could send U.S. troops to Somalia on his own authority. 16 Op. Off. Legal Counsel 9

(1992) (cited by Delahunty & Yoo, *supra* note 18, at 500 n.51). After a series of dramatic American setbacks, Congress directed the President to withdraw forces from Somalia pursuant to its authority clarified by the War Powers Resolution. See H.R. Con. Res. 170, 103d Cong., 139 Cong. Rec. 9039 (1993). One might imagine that Congress could have ended the operation in Somalia (a military action far smaller than that contemplated in Iraq) by withdrawing funding instead. Either way, this example suggests that if the power to initiate war lies with the President, Congress has no effective check—it can only limit casualties once hostilities have begun because it cannot stop them from taking place.

50. Yoo concedes that Congress may be reluctant to deny appropriations because of the risk of "creating the impression that they are leaving American troops at the front defenseless," but that "a failure of political will should not be confused with a constitutional defect." Yoo, *supra* note 17, at 299. He assumes that the risk of withdrawing funding as largely a perceptual or political danger, rather than one that may, in fact, involve the lives of deployed troops.

51. *See* Dellums v. Bush, 752 F. Supp. 1141, 1146 (D.D.C. 1990). *See also* Bruce Ackerman, *Commentary: Bush Must Avoid Shortcuts on Road to War: President should not try to sidestep Congress in any action against Iraq,* L.A. Times, May 31, 2002, at B15.

52. Telman, *supra* note 24, at 168. "Although Congress has generally acquiesced in the President's unilateral power to commit the Armed Forces to actions of limited scope, that acquiescence in individual cases, no matter how numerous, cannot result in a transfer of war powers from one branch of the federal government to another."

53. Johnson's failing was that he was willing to use false information (allowing the Pentagon to fabricate incidents suggesting North Vietnamese provocation) to get such authorization. The President has an obligation to be truthful when exercising his Executive and Commander-in-Chief war powers.

54. If the reasons for a ground invasion depend on top secret intelligence, and public disclosure will compromise intelligence sources, then the President may provide this information to Congress behind closed doors. *See,* e.g., the current Congressional investigation of possible intelligence breakdowns before 9/11, which remained largely closed to the public. Protecting intelligence sources may be a good reason not to reveal secrets but does not justify the President acting without Congress' authorization.

55. The Committee takes no position regarding the validity of those stated reasons.

56. These debates are not a matter of partisan politics. In addition to many Democrats, former senior Republican officials who served during the Gulf War in the Administration of G.H.W. Bush argue against a ground invasion of Iraq. *See* interviews with James Baker and Brent Scowcroft, *Frontline: Gunning For Saddam,* Nov. 8, 2001 (arguing that Saddam Hussein is not the greatest threat to U.S. security and arguing against a ground invasion).

CHAPTER 3

Letter to President Bush re: United Nations Charter Obligations Regarding Iraq

PREFACE BY ALAN R. ROTHSTEIN

In the fall of 2002, with the United States seemingly on the path to war with Iraq, there was substantial debate as to whether the United States was justified in pursuing this course given the role of the United Nations and the United Nations Charter, which the United States ratified. The United States was attempting to work within the UN structure while making it clear that it was prepared to go to war without UN participation, and that such action was consistent with the UN Charter.

The Association's Council on International Affairs drafted a letter for the Association's President, E. Leo Milonas, to send to President Bush, urging that the United States abide by its international obligations under the Charter. The letter argued that the United States had not made the requisite showing of self-defense that would justify its going to war absent authorization by the United Nations Security Council, under Article 51 of the Charter. It therefore urged that the U.S. government obtain authorization from the Security Council before commencing any military action in Iraq.

October 15, 2002

The Honorable George W. Bush
The White House
Washington, DC 20500

Re: ***United Nations Charter Obligations Regarding Iraq***

Dear President Bush:

On behalf of The Association of the Bar of the City of New York, I write regarding the international law issues that underlie a possible large-scale military action by the United States in Iraq. We assume that the purpose of such action would be to enforce Iraqi compliance with several United Nations Resolutions and, in particular, to ensure the disarmament of Iraq's weapons of mass destruction.

The Association does not take a position on the issue of whether, as a policy matter, Iraq's violations of these resolutions are most wisely responded to by military action, or by a rigorous policy of containment and inspections. The purpose of this letter is to urge, respectfully, that the United States abide by its international obligations and act in accordance with the United Nations Charter.

Security Council authorization of the use of military force is required under Chapter VII of the UN Charter absent circumstances triggering a nation's inherent right of self-defense, as preserved by Article 51 of the Charter. By its terms, Article 51 permits the use of force in self-defense only in response to an "armed attack." It is generally accepted, however, that this right encompasses traditional definitions of self-defense permitting the use of force against the threat of imminent attack, where, as succinctly stated by Secretary of State Daniel Webster in 1837, the "necessity of that self-defense is instant, overwhelming, and leaving no choice of means, and no moment for deliberation."

We recognize that what constitutes an imminent threat today cannot be limited to what constituted an imminent threat in Secretary Webster's day. We do not presume to pass judgments regarding the significance of any military threat. Nor do we address at this time the broader issues under applicable international legal principles of the standards articulated under the new and recently-released National Security Strategy.

Nevertheless, with regard to Iraq, we believe that the United States, through the information so far made publicly available, has itself not appeared to present the case of an actual or imminent Iraqi attack. In our view, the distinction is not simply a question of uncertainty as to "the time and place of an attack." More fundamentally, the United States has so far not publicly made a claim of any certainty or even probability of an Iraqi attack against the United States that rises to a level of imminence justifying unilateral action at the present time. If there exists information of such a threat, we respectfully urge the administration to demonstrate this case to the international community in connection with any unilateral military action, in order that the United States may proceed within the parameters of international law.

We do not question the grave danger posed by an Iraqi weapons development program, and its threat to international peace and security, particularly in the Middle East. In the absence of an imminent threat, however, it is the Security Council under Chapter VII of the UN Charter that must address this grave danger, not the United States under a claim of unilateral self-defense.

The Security Council expressly found in Resolution 707 that Iraq was in "material breach" of the disarmament Resolution 687 as early as April 18, 1991—only 15 days after Iraq accepted the Resolution. Some could argue that as a result of this "material breach," Resolution 678, which authorized the use of military force in the Gulf War, remains in effect and continues to authorize the use of military force against Iraq.

Nevertheless, existing Security Council resolutions with regard to Iraq do not authorize the use of force by nations to enforce those resolutions. In November 1990, the Security Council adopted Resolution 678 to authorize the use of force against Iraq in response to the invasion of Kuwait. Resolution 678 expressly authorized member states to "use all necessary means to uphold and implement Resolution 660 and all subsequent relevant resolutions and to restore international peace and security in the area." After the coalition forces and Iraq entered into a provisional cease-fire, the Security Council by Resolution 687 declared a formal cease-fire to be effective upon acceptance of the terms of such Resolution by Iraq. The Security Council affirmed prior resolutions, including Resolution 678, subject to this significant limitation: "except as expressly changed below [in this Resolution] to achieve the goals of this Resolution, including a formal cease-fire."

It remains the province of the Security Council to determine what enforcement action is necessary. Under Resolution 687, the Security Council "remain[s] seized of the matter" and may determine "such further steps as may be required for the implementation of the present resolution and to secure peace and security in the area." Subsequent resolutions have condemned Iraq's non-compliance and have imposed additional enforcement measures, but the Security Council has not reauthorized the use of military force under Chapter VII.

The United States helped create the current legal framework governing the use of force by substantially designing, and by signing and ratifying, the United Nations Charter. Under Article 103, the Charter is the cornerstone of international relations, superseding "obligations under any other international agreement." The United States and the member states of the United Nations sought to secure a stable international system based on legal principles. In deference to these principles, President George H.W. Bush revitalized the role of the Security Council when he sought UN authorization to attack Iraq in 1990, in the wake of Iraq's invasion and occupation of Kuwait. The Security Council was finally charged with performing the task signified by its very name—ensuring international peace and security.

To sidestep the Security Council's responsibility at this time would be a setback to the international legal system painstakingly developed since the Second World War. In a conflict to enforce Iraqi compliance with international law, the United States should avoid the risk of being perceived as itself violating generally accepted international legal principles. Moreover, we are concerned that a loose application of these principles by the United States will set a bad precedent for other nations to exploit elsewhere.

The Association supports the Administration's current efforts to work within the United Nations system by seeking adoption of a Security Council resolution to ensure the effective disarmament of Iraq. We agree with your statement to the General Assembly:

> The United States helped found the United Nations. We want the United Nations to be effective and respect[ed] and successful. We want the resolutions of the world's most important multilateral body to be enforced. And right now those resolutions are being unilaterally subverted by the Iraqi regime.

In the absence of further facts justifying the use of force in self-defense under Article 51 of the United Nations Charter, the Association of the Bar of the City of New York respectfully urges the government of the United States to obtain authorization of the United Nations Security Council prior to the commencement of any military action in Iraq.

Very truly yours,
E. Leo Milonas

CHAPTER 4

Letter from the Association President to President George W. Bush re Human Rights and Security of Women and Girls in Afghanistan

PREFACE BY ALAN R. ROTHSTEIN

When the United States and coalition forces invaded Afghanistan in November 2001, one of the hoped-for by-products of deposing the Taliban government was the improvement in the condition of women and girls in that country. Females had been deprived of rights by the Taliban government and treated harshly when they sought to exercise those rights. In the aftermath of the overthrow of the Taliban government, however, hope turned to disillusionment. The international community and the central government of Afghanistan were unable to provide the support for a rebirth of women's rights. Several human rights organizations, including Human Rights Watch, issued reports that criticized the United Nations, the United States, and other countries involved in Afghanistan with failing to improve the plight of women and girls.

The Association of the Bar, in a letter to President Bush dated March 10, 2003, sought to focus on specific recommendations for what the President could do to improve the plight of Afghan women and girls. In making these recommendations, the Association was mindful of the deteriorating security situation, particularly outside the capital of Kabul, and the dominance of warlords in many areas of the country, who exercised effective control over wide swaths of territory and over its people. The letter stressed the importance of providing security as an underpinning for achieving success in expanding women's rights.

March 10, 2003

The Honorable George W. Bush
The White House
Washington, DC 20500

Re: Human Rights and Security of Women and Girls in Afghanistan

Dear President Bush:

I am writing on behalf of the Association of the Bar of the City of New York. The Association is an independent non-governmental organization with more than 22,000 members in over

40 countries. Founded in 1870, the Association has a long history of dedication to human rights, notably through its Committee on International Human Rights, which investigates and reports on human rights conditions around the world. The Association, as an organization of lawyers, is particularly interested in the current situation in Afghanistan.

When the United States undertook its mission in Afghanistan, we raised great hopes among all of its citizens—including women and girls—that we would assist them in regaining basic human rights. Indeed, you have spoken out many times in support of the new freedom of Afghanistan's women and girls, and even stressed the importance of this freedom in your recent State of the Union address. We are writing today to express our deep concern about the safety and rights of these women and girls, who are eager to participate as equals in the reconstruction and governance of their country. The dire threat to the security of women and girls in Afghanistan has been made abundantly clear by many recent, independent and reliable sources, including the August 2002 report by the UN Special Rapporteur on Afghanistan, the November and December 2002 reports by Human Rights Watch, and the analysis of the Harvard Program on Humanitarian Policy and Conflict Research, dated January 2003. We urge you to take immediate, strategic and robust action to ensure women's safety and human rights are fully protected.

There is no doubt that the situation for most women and girls in Afghanistan has improved since the fall of the Taliban. However, there are disturbing signs that Taliban-era restrictions are again being promulgated and enforced in several parts of the country—most prominently in districts near Kabul and Kandahar, and in the western province of Herat. In addition, reports indicate that a gravely insufficient number of human rights monitors have been deployed in the countryside, and that women rarely have access to urgently needed services and assistance.

There are credible reports that in Herat, the local governor, Ismail Khan, has censored women's groups, intimidated outspoken women leaders, and sidelined women from his administration. Further, restrictions have been placed on their right to work, so that many women are not able to use their hard-won education. Perhaps most distressing are the physical restrictions on women and girls. Government-enforced limitations on their freedom of movement—including a prohibition on driving and on their being in the presence of unrelated men—mean that women and girls are confined arbitrarily. There are reports of abuses by police in Herat, who have detained women and girls accused of being accompanied by unrelated men and forced them to undergo medical examinations to determine if they have recently engaged in sexual intercourse.

While the violations reported from Herat are deplorable, the worsening situation for women and girls is not limited to that province. Credible reports from across the country indicate that women and girls are facing increasingly harsh restrictions by local leaders. Many women, especially those outside of Kabul, fear abuse by police, troops, and government officials should they attend school or university. Women interviewed by journalists and international workers are not only fearful but also deeply disillusioned; instead of the anticipated improvements in their lives, they are experiencing deteriorating rights.

All of the abuses cited above amount to grave human rights violations. They are also clear threats to the safety and basic security of women and girls in Afghanistan, the backbone of a renewed country. We urge you to work closely with the United Nations and the Government of Afghanistan to press regional leaders such as Ismail Khan to cease immediately the use of decrees and government policies that violate the human rights of women and girls, including their right to bodily integrity and freedom from torture, their right to freedom of expression and equal participation, their freedom of movement and association, and their right to equal treatment, work, and education.

We also call on you to encourage the United Nations Mission in Afghanistan to increase the number of human rights monitors throughout the country, and to offer funding, materials, or technical assistance as needed to support this effort. Human rights monitors should be charged specifically with monitoring violations of the rights of women and girls, as well as other serious abuses, and with publicly reporting on such violations.

Finally, we gratefully acknowledge your support for the Ministry of Women's Affairs and the Independent Human Rights Commission, which will be funded through the Afghan Freedom Support Act. Both the Ministry of Women's Affairs and the Human Rights Commission are in dire need of increased technical and financial assistance, and the promised US funds will go a long way toward ensuring their effectiveness. Money is not enough, however; basic political assistance should be extended to these institutions, and arrangements for their protection should be made by the government and those supporting government institutions.

The United States will make a genuine and concrete difference in the lives of women and girls in Afghanistan by insisting on an end to abuses against women and girls by regional leaders, working with the United Nations to extend the reach of human rights monitors, and supporting the Ministry of Women's Affairs and the Human Rights Commission. Further, by taking these steps, your celebratory words from the State of the Union address—that "today women are free" in Afghanistan—will be supported by the essential complement to freedom: security. Until women are secure in Afghanistan, their freedom will be incomplete.

Thank you for considering our recommendations and concerns. We look forward to your reply.

Respectfully,
E. Leo Milonas
President

CHAPTER 5

Letter to Honorable William J. Haynes II re Comments on Military Commission Instruction —Crimes and Elements for Trials by Military Commissions

PREFACE BY MILES P. FISCHER

"Instruction No. 2,"[1] on which the Association commented with some actual impact, is one of nine Instructions issued by the Department of Defense (DOD) to implement the President's Military Order of November 13, 2003, creating military commissions (MCs). Apart from being the sole substantive guidance for the MCs, Instruction No. 2 is of interest to students of the law of war as a bold attempt at codification of that body of customary law, although it regrettably lacks any citation or reference to customary authority.

Instruction No. 2, as adopted, reflects changes responsive to comments received, including (we are glad to report) some of ours. For example, on a specific offense we questioned how a foreign national owing no duty to the United States could be prosecuted for "aiding the enemy" and proposed requiring such a duty as an element of the offense. Reflecting our suggestion almost literally, the final Instruction added the requirement that "the accused owe allegiance or some duty to the United States of America or an ally or coalition partner." §6B(5)(b)(3).

We also urged greater clarity that the Instruction is declarative of existing customary law. The final Instruction applied that concept to the retroactivity issue, adding that "no offense is cognizable in a trial by military commission if that offence did not exist prior to the conduct in question" and "(B)ecause this document is declarative of existing law, it does not preclude trial for crimes that occurred prior to its effective date." The door seems to be open to defenses challenging whether Instruction No. 2 correctly defined customary law existing at the time of the offense. §3(A).

This amenability of DOD to comments is exceptional. Instruction No. 2 is the only part of the documentation for MCs made available for public comment before adoption. The Military Order itself, Military Commission Order No. 1 thereunder and the other Instructions were all adopted without public comment. However, despite requesting comments on Instruction No. 2, DOD did not take the additional step of making available the comments it received.[2]

Three years later, rereading Instruction No. 2 and the thoughtful views of other known commentators on many implicit issues, we see that even the combined known comments only touched the surface of the innumerable issues presented by this attempted codification of the law of war without indication of supporting authority. A fuller understanding may emerge only after specific allegations of crimes defined by Instruction No. 2 are charged in MCs and litigated before them.[3]

March 21, 2003

Honorable William J. Haynes II
General Counsel
Department of Defense
1600 Defense Pentagon
Washington, DC 20301-1600

Re: Comments on Military Commission Instruction—Crimes and Elements for Trials by Military Commissions (the "Instruction")

Dear Mr. Haynes,

We commend the General Counsel of the Department of Defense for making the Instruction available for public comment. Considering the brief time made available for comments on a subject encompassing nearly the full range of the law of war, we confine our remarks to the following salient points:

The Instruction "provides guidance" and is "declarative" of provisions of the common law of war, "illustrative of applicable principles" and not "an exclusive enumeration". Nonetheless, it is entitled an "Instruction" and purports to "define" the elements of crimes. It should be made clearer that the Instruction is not intended as binding on the members of commissions or defendants with respect to the definition of crimes to the extent that it is determined that a provision is inconsistent with the common law of war, . Moreover, given the authority reserved to the Congress "to *define* and punish. . .Offenses against the Law of Nations", Article I, Section 8 of the Constitution (emphasis added), language stating that the Instruction "defines" the elements of crimes within the purview of military commissions should be amended in favor of language that characterizes the definitions as reflecting existing common law.

Beyond the classic crimes of the law of war within the traditional jurisdiction of military commissions trying members of an enemy force, the Instructions go on to define "related offenses" of Aiding and Abetting, Solicitation, Accessory after the Fact and Conspiracy. Such offenses are susceptible to expanding the subject matter jurisdiction of military commissions to conduct beyond the established purview of the law of war, especially where the defendant is not a member of an armed enemy. Such expansion would not only exceed the self-limitation of the Military Order to "violations of the law of war and all other offenses triable by military commissions", Military Commission Order No. 1, Section 3B, but, if applied to non-combatant defendants found in the United States, would potentially violate the Constitutional right to trial by jury of civilians not members of an enemy force and triable by the regular courts. See *Ex parte Milligan,* 71 U.S. 2 (1866).

Three provisions are of particular concern with respect to potential overreaching. First, under the Instruction the offense of "terrorism", a relatively new offense to the law of war without substantial customary law, would be committed by causing property damage without regard to conduct causing or threatening loss of life. It is submitted that this offense be limited to the commission of "violent acts or acts dangerous to human life", as in 18 USC §2331. Property damage alone is properly covered by a distinct crime more familiar to the law of war. Secondly, because the offense of "aiding the enemy" would appear to extend to an individual, *e.g.*, a foreign national, owing no duty to the United States; we recommend that there be included a reference to such a duty. Finally, the clause in Paragraph 6.B.6)a(1) of the Instruction referring to persons who "joined an enterprise of persons who shared a common criminal purpose" could improperly extend to ordinary crimes beyond the law of war; it should be deleted or rephrased.

Given the unfamiliar and controversial nature of military commissions, which have not been used in any of America's armed conflicts of the last fifty years, it is respectfully submitted that military commissions will be most effective and attain the greatest legitimacy under the rule of law if they are confined to the trial of defendants who are clearly enemy combatants charged with direct complicity in heinous crimes.

Subject to these comments, we believe that the Instructions will be a useful, and even essential, tool for members of commissions, and prosecutors and defense counsel practicing before them.

Very truly yours,
Miles P. Fischer, Chair
Committee on Military Affairs & Justice
Association of the Bar of the City of New York

NOTES

1. Military Commission Instruction No. 2 Crimes and Elements for Trial by Military Commission, http://www.defenselink.mil/news/May2003/d20030430milcominstno2.pdf; 32 CFR Part 11; 68 Fed Reg 39381, July 1, 2003.

2. The National Institute of Military Justice (NIMJ) published comments made available by commentators, NIMJ, Military Commission Sourcebook (2003), and is suing under the Freedom of Information Act to obtain all comments, NIMJ v. Department of Defense, D.D.C., CA No. 04-0312 (RBW).

3. Whether challenges to charges under Instruction No. 2 can be properly litigated, and if so, publicly known, depends among other things on the limitations posed by the potential secrecy of MC proceedings, restrictions on defense counsel, and the severely limited avenues of appeal characteristic of MCs under the Military Order.

CHAPTER 6

Letter to U.S. Department of Defense Inspector General Joseph E. Schmitz re Enemy Prisoners of War and Other Detainees

PREFACE BY MILES P. FISCHER

Our letter of April 2003 sought (it turned out in vain) the intercession of the Army's Inspector General in enforcing at Guantanamo detainee screening procedures under Army Regulations and the Geneva Conventions. In response, the Inspector General apparently referred the matter to the same civilian General Counsel whose failure to enforce the regulations and treaty inspired our recourse to the Inspector General.

Our letter anticipated a fundamental issue that would be raised in *Hamdan v. Rumsfeld,* 344 F.Supp.2d 152 (D.C.Cir. 2004) and ensuing proceedings up to the appeal to the Supreme Court decided on June 29, 2006. Whether the detainees are entitled to the screening procedures and potentially to status as prisoners of war (POWs) reverberated when some detainees, including Salid Ahmad Hamdan, were charged for trial before military commissions. (POWs can be tried only before the same courts martial as try our own service personnel; any other form of trial would be a grave breach of the Third Geneva Convention where fully applicable and a federal felony under the War Crimes Act.) The Supreme Court found it unnecessary to decide this issue once it held that the present military commissions fail to comply with another provision of the Geneva Conventions, Common Article 3,[1] and the Uniform Code of Military Justice. Thus the POW screening issue and arguable claim to trial by court martial remains undecided.

Our letter did not assume that detainees would, in fact, be entitled to prisoner of war status and thus trial by court martial. Although not discussed in the letter, we found it hard to believe that those accused of membership in al Qaeda could show service in a combatant unit "conducting their operations in accordance with the laws and customs of war,"[2] especially while arguing that they were not combatants at all—all the more reason to hold the required screening proceedings, filter out non-combatants mistakenly brought to Guantanamo, and separate combatants not entitled to POW status (presumably al Qaeda members) from those, if any, entitled to POW status (arguably some Taliban members).

While holding such proceedings would still have left much to criticize at Guantanamo, including the issues decided by the Supreme Court in *Hamdan,* they would certainly have removed a major international complaint against the United States and established a clearer legal basis for the trial of detainees, whether by military commission (if otherwise lawful) or court martial. Unfortunately, the Inspector General, civilian General Counsel, and others in authority did not accept the suggestions of our letter.

April 18, 2003

Inspector General Joseph E. Schmitz
Department of Defense
400 Army Navy Drive
Arlington, VA 22202-4704

Re: Enemy Prisoners of War and Other Detainees

Dear General Schmitz:

The Committee on Military Affairs & Justice of the Association of the Bar of the City of New York is a committee of attorneys, judges and law students engaged on a pro bono basis in matters of policy and law relating to the United States Armed Forces. Our objective is to assist the Association in sharing with its 22,000 members and the general public a balanced view of such matters.

As you know, the legal status of detainees in the custody of the Armed Forces at Guantanamo Bay Naval Station in Cuba is an active concern of bar associations both in this country and in other nations that have ratified the Geneva Convention III Relative to the Treatment of Prisoners of War. The legal status of detainees is also a matter of much public interest and media attention. An article, dated March 24, 2003, in *The New York Times,* reports 21 men detained at Guantanamo Bay were repatriated to Afghanistan by the Armed Forces and 660 others remain in detention at Guantanamo Bay. A subsequent *Times* article of April 8, 2003 reports that officials described detainees as falling loosely into three categories—"people who were probably needlessly detained, a few Qaeda members and a group of people about whom they know little."

It does not appear that those detained by the Armed Forces at Guantanamo Bay have been afforded the right to a formal determination of their status, *if any doubt arises as to their status,* as provided in paragraph (b) of Section 1–6, entitled *Tribunals,* of Army Regulation 190-8 (and identical regulations prescribed by the other services) (the "Regulation") and Article V of such Geneva Convention. In this connection, we have not had a reply to our letter, dated March 7, 2003, to Hon. Steven J. Morello, General Counsel of the Department of the Army, a copy of which is enclosed.

In view of the large number of detainees and the history of releasing some detainees, we believe that it is likely that there remain some detainees concerning whom some doubt exists regarding their legal status. On that basis, the mandate of Section 1-6 (b) is clear: "A competent tribunal shall determine the status of any person...concerning whom any doubt...exists." Moreover, Section 1-6(a) of the Regulation and Article V of such Geneva Convention require that pending such determination, such detainees are to be treated as prisoners of war. This requirement suggests that competent tribunals should be convened at the earliest opportunity in the detention process in order to accord each detainee from the beginning the treatment appropriate to his circumstances.

In making this comment, we do not intend to refer to blanket determinations as to the status of Al Qaeda or the Taliban as entities, but rather to the individual status of detainees as persons who may or may not be "enemy combatants" and members of Al Qaeda or the Taliban. It has been suggested that certain detainees were innocent civilians found on or near the battlefield, exactly the type of person whose status should be considered by a "competent tribunal" under such Geneva Convention and the Regulation.

We are cognizant of the national security considerations affecting the confidentiality of information relevant to the status of detainees and believe that administrative tribunals could function consistently with such considerations.

We appreciate that the Regulation provides for an administrative determination and not for a judicial proceeding, and that administrative proceedings would determine solely the status of detainees and not culpability for any alleged violation of the law of war. We do not express a view as to any possible constitutional requirement of a judicial proceeding to determine the legality of the detention of individuals who may be entitled to constitutional protections based on such factors as citizenship, residence, or place or circumstances of detention.

Accordingly, we wish to call your attention to the apparent violation of the Regulation and such Geneva Convention in the detentions at Guantanamo Bay without the benefit of status determinations by competent tribunals when applicable. On behalf of those detained without the status determinations to which they are entitled, and in the interest of the good repute of the Armed Forces and the rule of law, we ask you to investigate.

Respectfully submitted,
Miles P. Fischer, Committee Chair
Committee on Military Affairs & Justice

NOTES

1. The need for military commissions to comply with international procedural standards under Common Article 3 was argued by the Association in its amicus brief in *Hamdan*.

2. Geneva Convention Relative to Treatment of Prisoners of War, Aug. 12, 1949, 6 USTS 3316, Art. 4, A (2)(d) (setting conditions for POW status of militias and others not forming part of the regular armed forces of a State Party).

CHAPTER 7

Amicus Brief: Jose Padilla v. Donald Rumsfeld

PREFACE BY JOSEPH G. DAVIS

On May 8, 2002, Jose Padilla, an American citizen who was traveling through O'Hare Airport in Chicago on his way back to the United States from Pakistan, was arrested pursuant to a material witness warrant issued by Chief Judge Mukasey of the Southern District of New York. After his arrest, Padilla was transferred to New York and detained there on the basis of the material witness warrant.

On May 15, 2002, Padilla appeared before Chief Judge Mukasey, who appointed Donna R. Newman to represent him. On May 22, Ms. Newman moved to vacate the material witness warrant, raising serious statutory and constitutional challenges to the government's decision to detain Padilla indefinitely without charging him. By June 7, the motion had been submitted for decision. A June 11 conference was scheduled on the motion before Chief Judge Mukasey.

On June 9, 2002, President George W. Bush issued a one-page Order declaring Mr. Padilla an "enemy combatant" and ordering the Secretary of Defense to detain him. In reliance on the President's Order, the United States withdrew the warrant and transferred Padilla from New York to the Consolidated Naval Brig, a high-security military jail in Charleston, South Carolina. One day later, on June 10, 2002, at a news conference called in Moscow, Russia, Attorney General Ashcroft proclaimed that Padilla was a "known terrorist who was exploring a plan to build and explode a radiological dispersion device, or 'dirty bomb,' in the United States."

When Ms. Newman arrived at the June 11 conference with Chief Judge Mukasey, her client had already been transferred to military custody, where the government proposed to hold him indefinitely. Padilla's counsel responded by filing a *habeas corpus* petition as next friend, identifying Secretary of Defense Donald Rumsfeld as Padilla's ultimate custodian, and challenging the legality of the government's continued military detention of Padilla. In opposition to Padilla's *habeas* position, the United States argued that the President had the authority to detain and interrogate Mr. Padilla indefinitely, without access to counsel or any contact outside of his prison.

In a pair of rulings, Chief Judge Mukasey upheld the President's power to detain civilians as enemy combatants, but also held that Padilla had a right under *habeas corpus* to a hearing to challenge his designation as an enemy combatant and his detention by the military. Over the government's objections, the Court also found that Padilla had the right to present facts through counsel. Over Padilla's objection, Chief Judge Mukasey ruled that the President's determination that Mr. Padilla was an enemy combatant was entitled to significant deference and must be upheld as long as the government could provide "some evidence" supporting the Executive's actions. Unwilling to accord Padilla even the minimal procedural protection of access to counsel and to submit its actions even to limited judicial scrutiny under the "some evidence" standard, the United States appealed to the Second Circuit.

ABCNY was closely following the *Padilla* case. All interested Committees were in agreement: The President of the United States did not have the authority to imprison indefinitely an American citizen captured on U.S. soil far from any battlefield without any form of due process. Because Padilla was forcibly removed from the criminal justice system in the Southern District of New York, ABCNY felt a particular obligation to address the far-reaching implications of the Executive's actions.

On July 29, 2003, Willkie Farr & Gallagher LLP filed the brief reproduced below on behalf of ABCNY as *amicus curiae.* ABCNY argued that Padilla had a statutory right to challenge his detention through the writ of *habeas corpus,* that this right necessarily encompassed the right to access to counsel, and that the standard of review of his detention had to be more exacting than the overly deferential "some evidence" standard championed by the government.

On December 18, 2003, the Second Circuit issued a historic ruling declaring that the President did not have inherent Constitutional authority to detain American citizens on American soil outside a zone of combat as an enemy combatant. While this decision was reversed by the United States Supreme Court on the ground that the Southern District of New York did not have statutory jurisdiction over Padilla's custodian after he was transferred to the Naval Brig in South Carolina, the Supreme Court did not rule on the merits of Padilla's detention. With the assistance of Willkie Farr, ABCNY participated as *amicus curiae* in these proceedings and in later proceedings before the Fourth Circuit and Supreme Court, after Padilla's *habeas* petition was re-filed in the District of South Carolina.

When Padilla's case was presented to the Supreme Court for the second time, the government changed tactics. On November 17, 2005, a Grand Jury sitting in the Southern District of Florida indicted Jose Padilla and others for crimes that bore little resemblance to those for which he was detained as an enemy combatant. On November 20, 2005, the President issued an order transferring Padilla to the custody of the Justice Department. Based on these actions, the Supreme Court decided not to review Padilla's South Carolina *habeas* petition. Criminal proceedings against Jose Padilla in Florida continue as of this writing.

What will history recall of the *Padilla* case? Justice Stevens, writing in 2004 for the four members of the Court who dissented from the decision to reverse the Second Circuit on jurisdictional grounds, reasoned that whether Padilla was "entitled to immediate release [was] a question that reasonable jurists may answer in different ways," but that there was "only one possible answer to the question whether he [was] entitled to a hearing on the justification for his detention." He continued:

At stake in this case is nothing less than the essence of a free society. Even more important than the method of selecting the people's rulers and their successors is the character of the constraints imposed on the Executive by the rule of law. Unconstrained Executive detention for the purpose of investigating and preventing subversive activity is the hallmark of the Star Chamber. Access to counsel for the purpose of protecting the citizen from official mistakes and mistreatment is the hallmark of due process.

ABCNY recognized the importance of the *Padilla* case to the rule of law and due process from the outset. Hopefully, the voices of ABCNY and many other members of the Bar who rose up to speak in defense of "the essence of a free society" will be remembered.

United States Court of Appeals for the Second Circuit
Jose Padilla, Donna R. Newman, as Next Friend of Jose Padilla
Petitioner-Appellee-Cross-Appellant,
Against
Donald Rumsfeld,
Respondent-Appellant-Cross-Appellee
On appeal from the United States District Court for the Southern District of New York
Brief for Amicus Curiae Association of the Bar of the City of New York in Support of
Petitioner-Appellee-Cross-Appellant

INTRODUCTION AND ARGUMENT SUMMARY

In this case the Court is asked to decide whether a U.S. citizen apprehended on U.S. soil far from any theatre of war and held by the military as an "enemy combatant" has any meaningful recourse to the courts and access to counsel in defense of his liberty. The government contends that the limited role of an Article III court is to review the Executive's *ex parte* factual determination, confirm that "some evidence" supports the enemy combatant designation and validate the detention. According to the government, neither the detainee's counsel, nor the detainee himself, has any meaningful role to play in that process. The Association of the Bar of the City of New York ("ABCNY") respectfully disagrees, and therefore submits this amicus brief in support of habeas petitioner Jose Padilla.

Never before has the Executive successfully asserted the right to detain indefinitely, without charge or process, someone taken into custody on U.S. soil in a non-combat setting based on the unilateral determination that the detainee is an enemy combatant. Twice in perhaps the darkest moments of this country's history the Executive has made similar attempts. In Ex Parte Milligan and Ex Parte Quirin the Supreme Court twice restrained this overextension of executive power. In no uncertain terms, the Court admonished that the judiciary has the power and the obligation (1) to review *de novo* the Executive's determination that a person detained under those circumstances is an unlawful combatant; and (2) to adjudicate the constitutionality of the detention order and disposition of the detainee. In this amicus brief, ABCNY addresses the first of these two exercises of judicial power and Padilla's right to contest the Executive's determination that he is an enemy combatant.[1]

This is a habeas case. The district court correctly concluded that the writ of habeas corpus demands that Padilla be permitted to present facts in support of his petition and communicate with his counsel. The government concedes Padilla's right to petition for habeas corpus but attempts to eviscerate that right by denying him the ability to present facts and to assist his lawyer and next friend in the presentation of his case. The habeas statutes do not permit such an interpretation of the Great Writ. Rather, they expressly grant petitioner the right to "deny" and "allege" facts, and impose on the court the obligation to "hear and determine" those facts. 28 U.S.C. § 2243. Moreover, and in aid of this right, the district court properly determined that the habeas statutes required the government to grant Padilla access to his counsel for the limited purpose of presenting the petition, and properly invoked the All Writs Act to fulfill its "duty" to "provide the necessary facilities and procedures for an adequate [habeas] inquiry." Harris v. Nelson, 394 U.S. 286, 300 (1969). (See Argument, Part I, infra.)

Though this Court need not invoke it to affirm, the Due Process Clause of the Fifth Amendment also requires that Padilla be given the ability to present facts in aid of his petition and consult with counsel. Padilla's right to communicate with the court and present facts in aid of his petition is the most fundamental of all his Fifth Amendment due process rights. The government's contention that it can hold Padilla incommunicado and that the Court can deny his petition—a petition for his very liberty—while Padilla sits mute in a brig is unprecedented and shocks the conscience. (See Argument, Part II.A, infra.)

Moreover, because the Due Process Clause requires not just access to the courts, but meaningful access, Padilla has the related right to consult with counsel in aid of his petition. The government contends that "[t]here is no basis in historical tradition or practice for recognizing a right of enemy combatants to have counsel for the purpose of challenging their wartime detention." (Gov't Br. at 37.)[2] The government adds that the "Constitution likewise affords no right to counsel...because Padilla is being detained as an enemy combatant and not for any criminal or other punitive purpose." (Id. at 39.) As applied to Padilla and the circumstances of his detention, these contentions are simply false. They are belied by Quirin and Milligan, among other cases, and the well-settled line of authority affording a right to counsel in non-criminal and non-punitive settings when individual liberty and other important interests are at stake. Whatever weight might be given to the Executive's asserted interest in shielding from judicial examination its interrogation of Padilla, its right to continue that interrogation is entirely dependent on the outcome of this proceeding. The Executive's interest therefore must give way to an appropriately defined right to assistance of counsel. (See Part II.B, infra.)

After deciding the procedural issues, the district court also ruled on the standards that would apply to the proceeding. Relying principally on the Fourth Circuit's decisions in Hamdi v. Rumsfeld, the government argued that the courts' power to review the Executive's determination that Padilla is an enemy combatant was limited to a determination of whether "some evidence" supported the designation. The district court, interpreting the government's position to be that Padilla is an unlawful combatant—that is, a combatant not entitled to international law protection as a prisoner of war—essentially agreed.

But Hamdi does not support the district court's ruling, as the Fourth Circuit itself explicitly stated. In Hamdi, unlike here, the petitioner was detained in a foreign theatre of war. According to the Fourth Circuit, this key fact was undisputed and sufficient to support the designation of enemy combatant. While the courts will accord deference to executive decisions concerning the disposition of those already determined to be unlawful combatants, deference does not attach to the unilateral decision to detain a U.S. citizen on U.S. soil far from any active zone of combat. Thus, the "some evidence" standard is incompatible with Milligan and Quirin.

Moreover, the "some evidence" standard has never been applied to test executive jurisdiction on U.S. soil over one who contests that jurisdiction. Rather, as the Supreme Court has held on many occasions, Article III courts should review *de novo* the threshold question of whether executive jurisdiction is appropriate. The Supreme Court consistently has imposed on the government a significant burden to justify restrictions on individual liberty in many and varied contexts. Where, as here, the government seeks to detain a U.S. citizen indefinitely and strip him of his right to due process, even significant concerns of national security cannot justify a burden less substantial than *de novo* review under a clear and convincing evidence standard. The district court thus erred by ruling that it would ratify the Executive's determination if the government could adduce "some evidence" to support it. (See Argument, Part III, infra.)

INTEREST OF AMICUS CURIAE AND SOURCE OF AUTHORITY TO FILE

ABCNY is a professional association of nearly 22,000 attorneys. Founded in 1870, ABCNY has long been committed to studying, addressing, and promoting the rule of law and, when appropriate, law reform. Through its many standing committees, including its Committees on Civil Rights, Federal Courts, Military Affairs and Justice, and Criminal Law, ABCNY educates the bar and public about current issues arising in connection with the "war" on terrorism, the pursuit of suspected terrorists, and the treatment of detainees. While it fully understands the importance of preventing future acts of terrorism, ABCNY believes that the Executive's actions in this and similar cases are dangerously eroding civil liberties and the efficacy of habeas corpus. ABCNY therefore submits this brief in support of Padilla's rights to contest the factual basis for his detention and to meaningful habeas review. All parties have given ABCNY consent to file this brief.

ARGUMENT

I. The District Court Properly Determined That the Habeas Corpus Statutes Give Padilla the Right to Present Facts Through Counsel Challenging His Detention

A. Padilla's Right to Petition for Habeas Review Is Undisputed

The government does not dispute directly Padilla's right to petition for habeas review. See Padilla v. Bush, 233 F. Supp. 2d 564, 599 (S.D.N.Y. 2002) ("Padilla I"); Padilla v. Rumsfeld, 243 F. Supp. 2d 42, 53–54 (S.D.N.Y. 2003) ("Padilla II"). Nor could it. The writ of habeas corpus provides the mechanism for reviewing executive detention, Swain v. Pressley, 430 U.S. 372, 386 (1977) (Burger, C.J., concurring), and is the fundamental safeguard against illegal restraint, INS v. St. Cyr, 533 U.S. 289, 301 (2001). The writ's protections are "strongest" when executive detention is challenged, id., because, without judicial scrutiny, such detention "lacks that assurance of legality which has come to be thought of as integral to government under law," Gerald L. Neuman, Habeas Corpus, Executive Detention, and the Removal of Aliens, 98 Colum. L. Rev. 961, 984 (1998). Where, as here, an American citizen is detained under executive authority as an enemy combatant, without judicial or any other process, habeas review is not only appropriate, it is compulsory. See Hamdi v. Rumsfeld, 316 F.3d 450, 464–65 (4th Cir. 2003) ("Hamdi App. III").

B. The Habeas Corpus Statutes Give Padilla the Right to Present Facts Challenging His Detention as an Enemy Combatant

While the government does not dispute Padilla's right to file a habeas petition, it disputes his right to present facts in support of that petition. It contends that "[tlhe habeas statutes do not afford Padilla a free-standing entitlement to raise a factual challenge to his detention." (Gov't Br. at 40.) The district court, correctly, disagreed. See Padilla I, 233 F. Supp. 2d at 600 (finding that "Padilla's right to present facts is rooted firmly in the statutes that provide the basis for his petition").[3]

Padilla petitioned for review pursuant to 28 U.S.C. §§ 2241, *et. seq.*[4] In concluding that Padilla has a statutory right to present facts *in this case,* the district court relied principally on section 2243, which states that "[t]he applicant or the person detained may, under oath, deny any of the facts set forth in the return or allege any other material facts." 28 U.S.C. § 2243. Section 2243 goes on to state that the habeas court "shall summarily hear and determine the facts, and dispose of the case as law and justice require." These provisions grant Padilla the right to raise and support fact-based arguments and require the district court to resolve factual disputes on habeas review. The district court cannot discharge this duty if it only gets to hear the Executive's evidence. See Walker v. Johnston, 312 U.S. 275, 284–85 (1941) (habeas petition could not be adjudicated based on the government's *ex parte* affidavits without opportunity for rebuttal).

Padilla's right to present facts is not discretionary, as the government suggests. (See Gov't Br. at 9.) As the Supreme Court stated over thirty years ago, the writ mandates an opportunity to present evidence in cases where the facts are in controversy, as they are here:

> It is now established beyond the reach of reasonable dispute that the federal courts not only *may* grant evidentiary hearings to applicants, but *must* do so upon an appropriate showing.

Harris, 394 U.S. at 291 (emphasis supplied). While a full-blown hearing, replete with the traditional panoply of procedural safeguards, may not be required in every case, the opportunity to present facts cannot be denied. Id. at 298–99. This conclusion applies with extra force where, as here, the petitioner has been detained without any pre-detention process, see Brown v. Allen, 344 U.S. 443, 533 (1953) (Jackson, J., concurring) ("[t]he historic purpose of the writ has been to relieve detention by executive authorities without judicial trial"), and the proof upon which the detention is premised consists solely of a vague affidavit, cf. Blackledge v. Allison, 432 U.S. 63, 82 n.25 (1977) (noting that the disposition of habeas petitions on the basis of affidavits alone is likely to be improper when credibility is at issue).

Unlike the typical habeas petitioner, who has received notice of the charges against him and an opportunity to be heard in his defense, Padilla has not been convicted of any crime, nor has his status been adjudicated in any forum. Rather, the Executive simply declared Padilla an enemy combatant and locked him away without ever giving him the chance to contest the factual basis for his detention. Because Padilla received virtually no process at any time before or after his detention, the habeas statutes compel the conclusion that he be given an opportunity to present facts in his defense. Cf. Harris, 394 U.S. at 298 (petitioners are "entitled to careful and plenary processing of their claims including full opportunity for presentation of the relevant facts").[5]

Ex Parte Bollman is particularly instructive. In Bollman, Chief Justice Marshall addressed the habeas petitions of two prisoners who were accused of conspiring with Aaron Burr to commit treason by levying war against the United States. Bollman, 8 U.S. at 75–76. The petitioners were seized in Pennsylvania and removed to Washington, D.C. based on a warrant issued by the District of Columbia district court on an application by the military. Id. at 75–6 & n.2. The Supreme Court first decided, in the more often quoted section of its opinion, that it had the power to issue a writ of habeas corpus to free the petitioners. Id. at 93–101. The Court then went on to examine, in detail, the evidence of treason proffered against the prisoners, "which the court below ought to have done," according to Justice Marshall. Id. at 114, 114–37. While recognizing that the acts supported by the government's evidence may have been unlawful, id. at 136–37, the Court nevertheless concluded that the evidence, including military affidavits, was insufficient to justify a charge of treason by levying war against the United States and ordered the petitioners set free. Id. at 136. Bollman thus demonstrates that a core function of the writ is to adjudicate, on the facts, the contention of one held prisoner on the word of the Executive that the detention is wrongful—even, or especially, when the charge is levying war against the United States.

In an attempt to avoid the district court's conclusion that Padilla has a statutory right to present facts, the government relies on Hamdi App. III. The government maintains that Hamdi App. III stands for the proposition that, under the habeas statutes, an enemy combatant "has no entitlement to present facts to challenge the basis for his detention nor any entitlement to counsel for that purpose. . . ." (Gov't Br. at 43–44.) The government misconstrues Hamdi App. III on several levels.

First, the Fourth Circuit admonished that its decision does not control, or even apply to, Padilla's situation: "we have no occasion, for example, to address the designation as an enemy combatant of an American citizen captured on American soil or the role that counsel might play in such a proceeding." Hamdi App. III, 316 F.3d at 465.

Second, the Fourth Circuit's decision actually confirms that the right to present facts is available in section 2241 proceedings. Id. at 470 (recognizing that "the ordinary § 2241 proceeding naturally contemplates the prospect of factual development").

Third, and of greatest significance, the Fourth Circuit held that Hamdi was not entitled to the opportunity to present evidence because the key jurisdictional fact underlying his detention was not disputed: "we hold that no evidentiary hearing or factual inquiry on our part is necessary or proper, because it is undisputed that Hamdi was captured in a zone of active combat operations in a foreign country and because any inquiry must be circumscribed to avoid encroachment into the military affairs entrusted to the executive branch." Id. at 473. The court most certainly did not hold that enemy combatants *never* have a right to present facts. Instead, the court limited its decision to the case before it and held that, where the jurisdictional facts that justify an individual's designation and detention as an enemy combatant are undisputed or conceded, there is no right to, or need for, further development of the facts. Id. at 476. In marked contrast to Hamdi's case, the facts underlying Padilla's detention as an enemy combatant are in dispute. In light of that dispute, the habeas statutes mandate that Padilla receive at the very least an opportunity to present facts attacking the credibility and accuracy of the Executive's evidence.

C. The District Court Properly Directed the Executive to Provide Padilla Access to Counsel for the Purpose of Presenting Facts in Support of His Petition

1. The appointment of counsel was proper and is not disputed

Notably, the government does not dispute the *appointment* of counsel for Padilla. Rather, the government objects to providing Padilla *access* to counsel, citing concerns about security and the impact that appointed counsel will have on the military's ability to extract information from Padilla. (Gov't Br. at 50–53.) The distinction between appointment of counsel and access to counsel is crucial.

Appointment of counsel in "the interests of justice" was well within the district court's discretion under 18 U.S.C. § 3006A(a)(2)(B). Padilla I, 233 F. Supp. 2d at 600; see also Hodge v. Police Officers, 802 F.2d 58, 60–61 (2d Cir. 1986); Engberg v. Wyoming, 265 F.3d 1109, 1122 (10th Cir. 2001); Winsett v. Washington, 130 F.3d 269, 281 (7th Cir. 1997). The complexity and importance of the statutory and constitutional questions in this case cannot be overstated. The government asserts—and asks this Court to sanction—sweeping authority to hold an American citizen incommunicado for an indefinite period and to interrogate him at length, without criminal charge. The appointment of counsel to represent Padilla would be justified by these circumstances alone. That Padilla is being held incommunicado, with no ability to investigate and present the facts or articulate his legal challenges, intensifies his need for legal representation and buttresses the district court's exercise of discretion. Furthermore, the "public interest" militates in favor of appointment of counsel here. "The public conscience must be satisfied that fairness dominates the administration of justice." Adams v. United States ex rel.

McCann, 317 U.S. 269, 279 (1942). It goes without saying that denying Padilla counsel, and forcing him to advocate on his own behalf, would be neither fair nor just. Indeed, it would be impossible.

2. The district court properly exercised its authority under the all writs act to order access to counsel

Habeas petitioners have a right to "plenary processing of their claims including full opportunity for presentation of the relevant facts." Harris, 394 U.S. at 298. The district court found that Padilla's right to present the relevant facts would be meaningless without access to counsel:

> Padilla's need to consult with a lawyer to help him do what the statute permits him to do is obvious. . . It would frustrate the purpose of the procedure Congress established in habeas corpus cases, and of the remedy itself, to leave Padilla with no practical means whatever for following that procedure.

Padilla I, 233 F. Supp. 2d at 602. Having determined that Padilla's habeas remedy would be lost without access to counsel, the district court properly exercised its discretion under the All Writs Act to order the government to provide such access.

The All Writs Act provides that "all courts established by Act of Congress may issue all writs necessary or appropriate in aid of their respective jurisdictions and agreeable to the usages and principles of law." 28 U.S.C. § 1651(a). The Act "empowers federal courts to fashion extraordinary remedies when the need arises." Pa. Bureau of Corr. v. U.S. Marshals Service, 474 U.S. 34, 43 (1985). The courts should exercise that discretionary power when necessary "to achieve the ends of justice entrusted to [them]." Adams, 317 U.S. at 273. An order issued under the All Writs Act is reviewed for abuse of discretion. Id.

The All Writs Act may be invoked in habeas cases to help the court, *and the petitioner,* investigate and present the facts. Harris, 394 U.S. at 300; United States v. Hayman, 342 U.S. 205, 221 (1952). Indeed, when procedural measures are necessary to ensure that the facts are fully developed and that the habeas proceedings are "fair and meaningful," the Supreme Court has held that "it is the duty of the court to provide the necessary facilities and procedures for an adequate inquiry." Harris, 394 U.S. at 300; see also Hayman, 342 U.S. at 223–24 (holding that the district court erred in conducting an *ex parte* hearing and should have exercised its discretion under the All Writs Act to secure the petitioner's attendance).

Here, the district court appropriately exercised its discretion under the All Writs Act when it commanded the government to afford Padilla access to appointed counsel in aid of his petition. See Padilla I, 233 F. Supp. 2d at 603. The Supreme Court has held that:

> [a]n accused must have the means of presenting his best defense. He must have time and facilities for investigation and for the production of evidence. But evidence and truth are of no avail unless they can be adequately presented. Essential fairness is lacking if an accused cannot put his case effectively in court.

Adams, 317 U.S. at 278–79. The Supreme Court's language aptly describes Padilla's situation. Without access to counsel, Padilla will quite literally have no ability to contest the factual basis for his detention. Recognizing as much, the district court ordered access to counsel to ensure that Padilla can exercise his statutory rights in a fair and meaningful way. This constitutes a proper exercise of the district court's authority under the All Writs Act. See United States v. New York Tel. Co., 434 U.S. 159, 175 n.23 (1977) (the All Writs Act authority to issue orders in aid of the court's jurisdiction encompasses the power to issue orders that enable the parties to protect their legal rights).

In exercising its discretion, the district court properly balanced the competing interests at stake and narrowly tailored its order to the facts of this case. See Price v. Johnston, 334 U.S.

266, 284–85 (1948), overruled on other grounds by McCleskey v. Zant, 499 U.S. 467 (1991) (discretion "is to be exercised with the best interests of both the prisoner and the government in mind"). Padilla's interest in having access to counsel is clear: without such access neither he, nor his appointed counsel, will be able to exercise his statutory right to present facts. The Executive's asserted interests are that providing access to counsel will purportedly undermine interrogation efforts and could give rise to security concerns because Padilla may covertly pass messages to al Qaeda through counsel. (Gov't Br. at 50–53.)

The district court thoroughly evaluated these competing interests in the course of ordering access to counsel. In its initial Opinion and Order, the district court addressed the alleged security risks at length:

> Even giving substantial weight, as I do, to the President's statement in the June 9 Order that Padilla is 'a continuing, present and grave danger to the national security of the United States' and that his detention 'is necessary to prevent him from siding with al Qaeda in its efforts to attack the United States,' there has been no fact presented to me that shows that the source of that danger is the possibility that Padilla will transmit information to others through his lawyers. By contrast, Padilla's statutorily granted right to present facts to the court in connection with his petition will be destroyed utterly if he is not allowed to consult with counsel. On the facts presented in this case, the balance weighs heavily in Padilla's favor.

Padilla I, 233 F. Supp. 2d at 604. On the government's Motion for Reconsideration, the district court also comprehensively addressed and dispatched concerns about the impact that giving Padilla access to counsel might have on the military's interrogation efforts. See Padilla II, 243 F. Supp. 2d at 49–54.

Ultimately, the district court tailored its order to minimize the impact on the Executive's interrogation efforts while still providing Padilla a means to effectuate his right to present facts. Specifically, the district court made clear that:

> access to counsel need be granted only for the purposes of presenting facts to the court in connection with this petition if Padilla wishes to do so; no general right to counsel in connection with questioning has been hypothesized here, and thus the interference with interrogation would be minimal or nonexistent.

Padilla I, 233 F. Supp. 2d at 603. The district court's solution was not only proper, but also necessary to effect a meaningful habeas remedy. It should be affirmed.

II. Padilla Has a Constitutional Right to Present His Case and Consult with Counsel

Although the district court recognized that the Fifth Amendment might provide a constitutional basis for its decision that Padilla is entitled to present facts and consult counsel in support of his habeas petition, it believed that the "nonconstitutional" grounds provided by the habeas statutes and All Writs Act were sufficient to support its ruling. Padilla I, 233 F. Supp. 2d at 601. The court therefore declined to explore an explicitly constitutional basis for its decision. Id. However, should this Court find that the habeas statutes and All Writs Act do not resolve the issue, the Constitution requires that Padilla be permitted both to present facts in aid of his petition and consult with counsel.

No court has ever held that a U.S. citizen detained on U.S. soil outside a theatre of war has no Fifth Amendment right to due process in connection with his habeas petition. On the contrary, as discussed below, the Supreme Court has uniformly granted due process rights to habeas petitioners challenging their status as enemy combatants or military detainees.

The Due Process Clause of the Fifth Amendment gives Padilla the right "to be heard at a meaningful time and in a meaningful manner." Mathews v. Eldridge, 424 U.S. 319, 333 (1976), quoting Armstrong v. Manzo, 380 U.S. 545, 552 (1965). Padilla's due process right to be heard, at a minimum, encompasses the right to present facts in support of his habeas petition.

Moreover, Padilla's right to be heard in a meaningful manner, given the complexity of this case and that his liberty hangs in the balance, encompasses the right to be heard through counsel.

A. *Padilla Has a Fifth Amendment Right to Present Facts in Support of His Habeas Petition*

"The fundamental requisite of due process of law is the opportunity to be heard." Goss v. Lopez, 419 U.S. 565, 579 (1975) (quoting Grannis v. Ordean, 234 U.S. 385, 394 (1914)). Access to the courts is therefore a "fundamental constitutional right." Bounds, 430 U.S. at 828; see also Procunier v. Martinez, 416 U.S. 396, 419 (1974), overruled in part by Thornburgh v. Abbott, 490 U.S. 401 (1989) ("The constitutional guarantee of due process of law has as a corollary the requirement that prisoners be afforded access to the courts in order to challenge unlawful convictions and to seek redress for violations of their constitutional rights"). "Rudimentary due process" requires the right to present arguments and evidence and confront adverse witnesses. Goldberg v. Kelly, 397 U.S. 254, 267–68 (1970). The government's contention that Padilla's habeas petition can be adjudicated without his participation, (Gov't Br. at 14, 40–49), flies in the face of this most basic and fundamental of constitutional tenets.[6]

The government's position is essentially unsupported. The Supreme Court has never accepted the contention that it could adjudicate a habeas petition without giving the petitioner the ability to present facts in support of his case. German saboteurs who landed on Long Island in a submarine wearing German uniforms during World War II were given the right to present facts—undisputed though most of them were—in aid of their habeas petition, through counsel no less. Ex parte Quirin, 317 U.S. 1, 19–20 (1942). Likewise, a Japanese General accused of supervising war crimes in the Philippines was given the right to present facts through counsel. Yamashita v. Styer, 327 U.S. 1, 5 (1946); see also id. at 47 (the Court does not suggest that "it could not ascertain whether conviction is founded upon evidence expressly excluded by Congress or treaty") (Rutledge, J, dissenting). Other detainees were afforded the same ability to present a case. See, e.g., Ludecke v. Watkins, 335 U.S. 160, 173 (1948) (affirming United States ex rel. Ludecke v. Watkins, 163 F.2d 143, 144 (2d Cir. 1947) ("Ludecke, the relator-appellant, made an oral argument and submitted a brief, both of which have been interesting and moving.")); In Re Territo, 156 F.2d 142, 142–3 (1946) (petitioner's case was "tried at the hearing on the order to show cause"); Ex Parte Milligan, 71 U.S. 2, 5–6, 107 (1866); Colepaugh v. Looney, 235 F.2d 429, 431 (10th Cir. 1956) (refusing to "preclude access to the courts for determining the applicability of the laws of war").[7] Padilla, at a minimum, must be afforded those rights.[8]

B. *Padilla's Right to Meaningful Access to the Courts Encompasses the Right to Present His Petition through Counsel*

In determining whether Padilla can receive due process—"the opportunity to be heard at a meaningful time and in a meaningful manner"—without access to his lawyer, the court should examine (1) the private interest that will be affected by official action; (2) the risk of an erroneous deprivation of the interest through the procedures used and the value of additional safeguards; and (3) the government's interest. Mathews, 424 U.S. at 333–35.

1. *Padilla has a fundamental interest in the assistance of counsel*

The Supreme Court has "frequently emphasized" the importance of *provision* of counsel in any case in which an individual may be deprived of his liberty. In Re Gault, 387 U.S. 1, 73 (1967) (Harlan, J, concurring and dissenting in part); see also Gideon v. Wainwright, 372 U.S. 335, 344 (1963), (the "noble ideal" of due process "cannot be realized" absent assistance of counsel); Johnson v. Zerbst, 304 U.S. 458, 462 (1938) (the assistance of counsel is "necessary to insure fundamental human rights of life and liberty"). Indeed, it is well established that the "right to be heard" would be of "little avail if it did not comprehend the right to be heard *by counsel.*" Powell v. Alabama, 287 U.S. 45, 68 (1932) (emphasis added).

The government contends that "because Padilla is being detained under the laws of war rather than under domestic criminal laws, the Constitution affords him no right to counsel." (Gov't Br. at 14.) This is wrong as a matter of constitutional history and theory. First, as noted above, numerous wartime detainees have been afforded the right to counsel.

Second, the right to counsel is not confined to cases arising under the Sixth Amendment in the criminal context. On the contrary, courts have frequently found a due process right to *provision* of counsel under the Fifth Amendment in cases in which the liberty interest in freedom from imprisonment has been implicated. See, e.g., United States v. Perez, 330 F.3d 97 (2d Cir. 2003) (deportation of permanent resident); Haitian Centers Council, Inc. v. McNary, 969 F.2d 1326 (2d Cir. 2000) (repatriation of aliens); Iavorski v. INS, 232 F.3d 124, 128 (2d Cir. 2000) (deportation of aliens); United States v. Budell, 187 F.3d 1 137, 1143 (9th Cir. 1999) (discharge of insanity acquitees); Gault, 387 U.S. at 41 (commitment of juvenile delinquents); Proiect Release v. Prevost, 722 F.2d 960, 976 (2d Cir. 1983) (civil commitment). The Supreme Court has even recognized a due process right to counsel in proceedings where physical liberty is not in issue. See Lassiter v. Dep't of Soc. Servs. of Durham County, 452 U.S. 18, 31–32 (1981) (termination of parental rights) and Goldberg, supra, (termination of welfare benefits).

These cases serve as strong reminders of the critical importance of counsel in proceedings where significant rights are at stake, but the issue here is even more fundamental. The government does not contest appointment of counsel; it contests Padilla's right to consult with counsel. While in some situations there is no right to the *provision* of counsel, see, e.g., Vitek v. Jones, 445 U.S. 480, 482–84 (1980) (plurality opinion) (transfer of prisoner to psychiatric facility), outside the purely administrative contexts of prison and school disciplinary proceedings, cf. Goss, 419 U.S. at 583; Wolff v. McDonnell, 418 U.S. 539, 570 (1974), no case suggests that the government may prevent a detainee from consulting with counsel in connection with a proceeding that may well seal his fate forever.

In fact, the opposite is true. The constitutional requirement of "meaningful access to the courts," Bounds, 430 U.S. at 823, means that reasonable access to appointed or retained counsel (or a surrogate for counsel) cannot be denied:

> The constitutional guarantee of due process of law has as a corollary the requirement that prisoners be afforded access to the courts in order to challenge unlawful convictions and to seek redress for violations of their constitutional rights. This means that inmates must have a reasonable opportunity to seek and receive the assistance of attorneys. Regulations and practices that unjustifiably obstruct the availability of professional representation or other aspects of the right of access to the courts are invalid.

Procunier, 416 U.S. at 419 (citations omitted); see also Shaw v. Murphy, 532 U.S. 223, 231 n.3 (2001) (inmates have a right to receive legal assistance from other inmates when necessary to effectuate right of access to courts); Johnson, 393 U.S. at 490 (invalidating prison regulation that barred inmates from providing legal services to other inmates); Coe v. Bell, 89 F. Supp. 2d 962, 967 (M.D. Tenn.), vacated as moot Coe v. Bell, 230 F.3d 1357 (6th Cir. 2000) (death row inmate had constitutional right of access to counsel).

In short, Padilla has a fundamental interest in being permitted to consult with and present his case through counsel.

2. The risk of error in the absence of consultation with counsel is acute

Perhaps more fundamentally, given the process insisted upon by the Executive here, the risk of error is acute. The government has sought to justify Padilla's detention based on information derived from unspecified "intelligence sources" and "reports of interviews" with unidentified "confidential informants." (JA 44.)[9] While these confidential sources supposedly are "believed" to have been involved with al Qaeda, the Mobbs Declaration nowhere states that they *in fact* are al Qaeda operatives or provides any facts that would indicate that the information they have provided is trustworthy. (Id.) Quite the contrary, by the government's own admission, these sources "have not been completely candid" and some information they have provided "remains uncorroborated" and may be "part of an effort to mislead or confuse U.S. officials." (Id.) It cannot be gainsaid that there is a risk that Padilla may have been wrongfully imprisoned, given that his detention is based on allegations of admittedly suspect informants providing admittedly suspect information, neither of which has been subjected to any kind of judicial review.

3. The executive's interests are insufficient to deny access to counsel

In assessing whether an evidentiary hearing was required prior to termination of disability benefits, the Court in Mathews stated that an examination of "the administrative burden and other societal costs" must be had in order to understand the effect of the procedure. Mathews, 424 U.S. at 347. The ultimate question is "when, under our constitutional system, judicial-type procedures must be imposed upon administrative action to assure fairness[?]" Id. at 348.

The government asserts that denial of access to counsel is required to preserve the Executive's interest in national security by preventing its interrogation process from being jeopardized. The government's affiant states that the military's interrogation techniques "rely in large part on developing and maintaining an atmosphere of trust and dependency." (Gov't Br. at 51 (citing JA 58–59.)) Interposing access to counsel even in a limited manner, the government contends, would jeopardize this relationship and threaten or delay its ability to secure potentially critical intelligence information. (Id. at 51–52.)

Critically, the government's assertions about the need to facilitate the interrogation process assume precisely the fact that Padilla has a right to challenge through habeas—that he is an enemy combatant. If Padilla is not an enemy combatant, any conceivable basis for the government's asserted right to detain and interrogate him as one evaporates.

The assumed force of the government's argument is further blunted by the limited right to counsel granted by the district court. As the district court noted, because no generalized right to counsel and no right to counsel in connection with the interrogation are posited, any interference with the interrogation process would be minimal. Padilla I, 233 F. Supp. 2d at 603. Moreover, the government does not dispute the district court's conclusion that the government's assessment of potential effects on Padilla's interrogation of limited access to counsel "is plausible, it is only plausible." (Gov't Br. at 52–53 (citing Padilla II, 243 F. Supp. 2d at 53).) Indeed, it repeatedly characterizes contact with counsel as a "risk," (id. at 51), that "*could* set back" the interrogation process, (id. at 52 (emphasis supplied)). Even though the Executive's concerns may be speculative, the government asserts they are sufficient to deny access to counsel in light of the assumption it has made that there is no constitutional or other right to counsel. (Id. at 53.) Because, as demonstrated above, its assumption is flawed, the government's conclusion utterly fails.

Padilla's interests in access to counsel are fundamental and undeniable; the Executive's interests, while entitled to due consideration, are at least in part speculative and, therefore, ultimately less convincing. Moreover, Padilla's interests coincide with a broader interest of a lawful society in the legitimacy of executive actions. A principal function of the bar is to provide professional counseling and advocacy to both sides of a dispute. The presence of professional advocates inspires confidence that a court's ruling was made with the benefit of full presentations on each side. The government's plan to denude the process of "adversary argument...embracing conflicting and demanding interests," Flast, 392 U.S. at 97, would undermine the very confidence it should be seeking to engender that the war on terrorism is not incompatible with fundamental protection of individual liberty. The balance of interests favors granting Padilla the right to confer with counsel.

III. Padilla's Petition Should Be Granted Unless the Government Demonstrates by Clear and Convincing Evidence That He Is an Unlawful Combatant

Whether Padilla's right to process arises out of the writ of habeas corpus or the Fifth Amendment, he is entitled to contest the Executive's determination that he is an "enemy combatant." If the Executive or the Federal Government as a whole has the power to detain Padilla, hold him incommunicado and interrogate him without charge, that power is contingent on the jurisdictional fact that the Padilla is an enemy combatant, that is, an unlawful combatant not entitled to prisoner-of-war status.[10] The government contends that the deference owed to the Executive on matters of foreign policy and military affairs reaches so far into the life of a U.S. citizen detained on U.S. soil that the Executive's unilateral determination that the detainee is an enemy combatant can be challenged only under a standard typically used to review hearing decisions of administrative tribunals known as the "some evidence" standard. (Gov't Br. at 44–49.) The district court to a point agreed. See Padilla I, 233 F. Supp. 2d at 605–08. ABCNY respectfully submits that this aspect of the district court's holding was erroneous.

Only two Supreme Court opinions directly address executive power to detain (and try by military commission) as unlawful combatants individuals arrested on U.S. soil in a time of war, but not on a battlefield—Ex Parte Quirin and Ex Parte Milligan. Although the outcome of each case was very different, both decisions recognized that the Great Writ gives a court the power to make a *de novo* factual determination about the initial jurisdictional fact: Is the detainee an unlawful combatant?

In Quirin, the Executive Proclamation pursuant to which the petitioners were detained, tried and convicted by military tribunal expressly "denied access to the courts," and the government contended that the petitioners should have no resort to the courts. 317 U.S. at 23–25. Nevertheless, the Supreme Court held that the Proclamation could not "preclude access to the courts *for determining its applicability to the particular case.*" Id. at 25 (emphasis supplied). The "applicability" of the Proclamation, that is, whether the Quirin petitioners were unlawful combatants, was resolved in the initial per curiam opinion, apparently upon stipulated facts. Id. at 20, 25, 46. Accordingly, the Court stated it had "no occasion now to define with meticulous care the ultimate boundaries of the jurisdiction of military tribunals to try persons according to the laws of war." Id. at 45–46. Nowhere in the opinion does the Court suggest that it would not have had the power to draw those boundaries, or that its power would have been limited to a review of whether "some evidence" supported the Executive's determination that the petitioners were unlawful combatants. On the contrary, the Quirin court recognized that it was precisely those jurisdictional boundaries, drawn by the Milligan court, that distinguished its holding from Milligan:

> We construe the Court's statement as to the inapplicability of the law of war to Milligan's case as having particular reference to the facts before it. From them the Court concluded that Milligan, not being a part of or associated with the armed forces of the enemy, was a non-belligerent, not subject to the law of war save

as—in circumstances found not there to be present and not involved here—martial law might be constitutionally established.

Id. at 45.[11]

In Milligan the Court was asked to answer three certified questions concerning the trial by military commission of a citizen of Indiana in the middle of the Civil War. 71 U.S. at 8–9. Although an Act of Congress had given the President the power to suspend the writ of habeas corpus, the Act also provided that those held by the President "otherwise than as prisoners of war," would have to be indicted or presented to a judge for discharge or other disposition "according to law." Id. at 5. On October 5, 1864, Milligan, an alleged member of a 100,000-strong secessionist organization, was arrested, tried, convicted and sentenced to death by a military tribunal for plotting to overthrow the government, aiding the rebels and violating the laws of war, among other things. Id. at 6–7.

The Milligan Court rejected the Executive's contention that, even if the Act had been violated (Milligan was never indicted or presented to a judge), the trial of Milligan was justified by executive power to impose martial law.[12] The Court asserted judicial knowledge that in Indiana the Federal authority was always unopposed, and its courts always open to hear criminal accusations and redress grievances; and no usage of war could sanction a military trial there for any offence whatever of a citizen in civil life, in no wise connected with the military service." Id. at 121–22. In short, although the Court recognized the power of the Executive to declare martial law under appropriate circumstances, id. at 126, it made a *de novo* factual determination that even in the dark hours of the Civil War martial law was not appropriate and could not be used to justify Milligan's trial by the military rather than the courts.

Despite their divergent outcomes, Quirin and Milligan thus demonstrate that one who is detained on U.S. soil away from a theatre of war has the right to challenge directly and substantively the Executive's factual determination that he is an enemy combatant. As further demonstrated below, the some evidence test is incompatible with that right, and the district court should have required the government to prove by clear and convincing evidence that Padilla is an enemy combatant.

A. *The Executive Must Demonstrate That Padilla Is an Unlawful Combatant*

The district court concluded that "when the President designated Padilla an 'enemy combatant,' he necessarily meant that Padilla was an unlawful combatant." Padilla I, 233 F. Supp. 2d at 593. The government has not objected to this conclusion. For purposes of this brief only, ABCNY assumes that the conflict with al Qaeda is governed by the laws of war, such that an unlawful combatant associated with al Qaeda could be considered an unlawful combatant under the laws of war.[13] With that assumption in mind, in order to demonstrate that Padilla is an unlawful combatant, the Executive must demonstrate (1) that Padilla was actively working on behalf of al Qaeda when he was detained; and (2) that his activities were "unlawful" as that term is used to define one who is not a lawful combatant under the Hague and Geneva Conventions. See Padilla I, 233 F. Supp. 2d at 592–93. The government does not appear to disagree that these are the operative elements of the status they seek to impose on Padilla. (See Gov't Br. at 38.)

B. *The "Some Evidence" Standard Does Not Apply*

The history of the "some evidence" test demonstrates both that it should not be applied to the initial judicial determination whether Padilla is an enemy combatant, and that such determination should be subject to *de novo* review. The test arose in the early part of the 20th century as a standard to be applied to habeas petitions challenging exclusion decisions by immigration officials, principally under the Chinese Exclusion Act. See Gerald L. Neuman, The Constitutional Requirement of 'Some Evidence', 25 San Diego L. Rev. 631, 636–41 (1988). These cases were decided against the background of a long history of judicial deference to congressional and executive authority to regulate aliens not unlike the deference accorded the Executive in military affairs. Accordingly, they are instructive not only because the government has invoked them by contending that the "some evidence" standard applies, but also because they concern the role of the judiciary in reviewing executive determinations regarding significant rights of individuals over whom the Executive has great authority.

Two principles emerge from the "some evidence" cases. First, even those who were conceded to be aliens were entitled to a fair hearing by immigration authorities, and denial of such a hearing would constitute a denial of due process and grounds for issuance of a writ. See, e.g., Kwock Jan Fat v. White, 253 U.S. 454 463–65 (1920). For example, rejecting the petition of an alien named Tisi, the Supreme Court noted:

> There is no suggestion that Tisi was not allowed to prepare for the hearing, by prior examination of the written evidence on which the warrant of arrest was issued, or that he was otherwise restricted in the preparation of his defense. The hearing was conducted orally. Tisi was present and he was represented by counsel. He testified fully, and the many witnesses produced by the government were cross-examined by his counsel.

Tisi v. Tod, 264 U.S. 131, 134 (1924). "Upon a *collateral* review in habeas proceedings," that is, only *after* the alien was afforded a sufficient administrative hearing, the "some evidence" standard was applied. United States v. Vajtauer, 273 U.S. 103, 106 (1927) (emphasis added). Thus, it is not surprising that the district court could find no case applying "the 'some evidence' standard to a record that consists solely of the government's evidence, to which the government's adversary has not been permitted to respond." Padilla II, 243 F. Supp. 2d at 54. Because Padilla has had no process—his petition tests a unilateral executive decision, not the outcome of an administrative hearing process—the "some evidence" test is inapplicable.

Second, the Supreme Court consistently distinguished between the Executive's determination concerning exclusion or deportation of the alien, to which it applied the deferential "some evidence" standard of review, and the Executive's determination of the "jurisdictional fact" of alienage, Tisi, 264 U.S. at 133, which a petitioner was entitled to challenge through a *de novo,* judicial hearing of the evidence. Ng Fung Ho v. White, 259 U.S. 276, 284–85 (1922). As the Court stated:

> Jurisdiction in the executive to order deportation exists only if the person arrested is an alien. The claim of citizenship is thus a denial of an essential jurisdictional fact. The situation bears some resemblance to that which arises where one against whom proceedings are being taken under the military law denies that he is in military service. It is well settled that in such a case a writ of habeas corpus will issue to determine the status.

Id. at 284 (citations omitted). This distinction is entirely consistent with Milligan and Quirin, and it further demonstrates that Padilla is entitled to a *de novo* determination of the "essential jurisdictional fact" whether he is an enemy combatant.

C. *The Executive Cannot Classify a U.S. Citizen Apprehended on U.S. Soil an Enemy Combatant Absent Clear and Convincing Evidence*

"The function of a standard of proof, as that concept is embodied in the Due Process Clause and in the realm of factfinding, is to 'instruct the factfinder concerning the degree of confidence our society thinks he should have in the correctness of factual conclusions for a particular type of adjudication.'" Cruzan v. Dir. Mo. Dept. Health, 497 U.S. 261, 282 (1990) (citations omitted). The degree of confidence in turn depends on the interests at stake on each side of the dispute. See Cruzan, 497 U.S. at 280–87; Addington v. Texas, 441 U.S. 418, 423–33 (1979); Cooper v. Oklahoma, 517 U.S. 348, 362–69 (1996); Heller v. Doe, 509 U.S. 312, 332 (1993).

"In cases involving individual rights, whether criminal or civil, '[t]he standard of proof [at a minimum] reflects the value society places on individual liberty.'" Addington, 441 U.S. at 425 (quoting Tippett v. Md., 436 F.2d 1153, 1166 (4th Cir. 1971)). Indeed, in non-criminal cases, the Supreme Court "has mandated an intermediate standard of proof—'clear and convincing evidence'—when the individual interests at stake in a state proceeding are both 'particularly important' and 'more substantial than mere loss of money.'" Cruzan, 497 U.S. at 282, quoting Santosky v. Kramer, 455 U.S. 745, 756 (1982). The clear and convincing evidence standard, required in many circumstances implicating fundamental individual liberties—such as civil commitment proceedings, deportation proceedings, denaturalization proceedings and proceedings for the termination of parental rights, id.—is the standard most appropriate to test the Executive's contention that Padilla is an enemy combatant.

This proceeding will govern some of Padilla's most fundamental rights. First, Padilla's liberty interest is at stake: "Freedom from imprisonment, from government custody, detention, or other forms of physical restraint—lies at the heart of the liberty that the [Due Process] Clause protects." Zadvydas v. Davis, 533 U.S. 678, 690 (2001). The government seeks the right to detain Padilla, at a minimum, "during wartime." (Gov't Br. at 2.) In a "war" against such an elusive and ephemeral "enemy" as al Qaeda, this effectively means indefinite detention. Indeed, Padilla already has been in military custody, incommunicado, for over a year.

Second, should a court determine that Padilla is indeed an enemy combatant, the government could assert a right to try Padilla by invoking new and as yet untested military tribunal procedures, as it apparently intends to apply to non-citizen enemy combatant detainees. See Military Order of November 13, 2001, 66 Fed. Reg. 57,833 (Nov. 13, 2001). If this occurs, Padilla could ultimately lose his right to trial by jury and many of the other constitutional and statutory rights afforded to a criminal defendant. Cf. Department of Defense, Military Commission Order No. 1 (Mar. 21, 2002), 41 I.L.M. 725 (establishing military commissions to try non-citizen detainees and allowing ex parte presentations to the commission).

Third, much like the stigma of a criminal conviction or even involuntary civil commitment, the Executive's decision to brand Padilla an "enemy combatant"—a traitor to his country—carries a severe stigma. See In re Winship, 397 U.S. 358, 363–64 (1970) (proof beyond a reasonable doubt is required in criminal cases, in part, because of the "certainty" that conviction will stigmatize the defendant); Addington, 441 U.S. at 425–26 (recognizing that the stigma of involuntary commitment "can have a very significant impact on the individual"). A decision of this court affirming the Executive's determination will only lend the weight of judicial authority to that stigmatization.

The government's countervailing interests are also undeniably important, but ultimately insufficient to justify a standard of proof more lenient than clear and convincing evidence. The government argues: "Because the President's determination that Padilla is an enemy combatant represents a core exercise of the Commander-in-Chief authority, that determination is entitled to great deference." (Gov't Br. at 14.) For this proposition it relies principally on the decisions in Hamdi. (Id. at 45–46.) This reliance is entirely misplaced.

The Fourth Circuit determined that Hamdi was captured "in Afghanistan during a time of active military hostilities." Hamdi App III, 316 F.3d at 460. "To compare this battlefield capture to the domestic arrest in Padilla v. Bush is to compare apples and oranges," as the author of the Hamdi III decision bluntly stated. Hamdi v. Rumsfeld, No. 02-7338, WL 21540768, at *3 (4th

Cir. 2003) ("Hamdi App. IV") (Wilkinson, J., concurring in denial of reh'g *en banc*).[14] The Fourth Circuit's opinion is expressly and forcefully limited to the treatment of an enemy combatant who was concededly "captured in a zone of active combat operations abroad." Hamdi App. III, 316 F.3d at 476. The court noted:

> We earlier rejected the summary embrace of a sweeping proposition—namely that, with no meaningful judicial review, any American citizen could be detained indefinitely without charges or counsel on the government's say-so. But Hamdi is not 'any American citizen alleged to be an enemy combatant' by the government; he is an American citizen captured and detained by American allied forces in a foreign theatre of war during active hostilities and determined by the United States military to have been indeed allied with enemy forces.

Id. (internal citations omitted). Padilla, of course, *is* prototypically "any American citizen alleged to be an enemy combatant by the government." He was not captured in a foreign war zone; indeed, he was not "captured" at all, but taken into custody after he was arrested on a material witness warrant. Thus, the Fourth Circuit's observations about "the murkiness and chaos that attend armed conflict," id. at 473, have no relevance here.

Despite the significant differences between the capture of Hamdi and the detention of Padilla, ABCNY recognizes the force of the government's arguments concerning deference to the Executive's powers as Commander-in-Chief. One cannot dispute that imposing *de novo* review under any kind of meaningful standard will require the Court to evaluate facts that implicate serious intelligence, military and foreign policy matters. (See Gov't Br. at 46–47.) But a constitutional government that wages war to protect and preserve a way of life must find a way to accommodate individual liberties so essential to its character. As Quirin and Milligan demonstrate, in cases involving detention on U.S. soil outside a war zone, that accommodation under our Constitution occurs through meaningful participation of the judiciary.

Fortunately, the courts have significant experience discharging their role as Article III adjudicators using procedures that safeguard sensitive factual inquiries implicating military and foreign affairs. For example, the courts have long presided over trials involving espionage offenses. See 18 U.S.C. §§ 792 *et seq.* The Classified Information and Procedures Act, 18 U.S.C. App. 3, in fact sets forth a detailed procedure for cases involving classified information. Although separately constituted by statute, the Foreign Intelligence Surveillance Court, which is routinely asked to determine whether a suspect is an agent of a foreign power, likewise demonstrates that Article III courts can and do handle matters involving sensitive issues of foreign affairs and the collection of intelligence information. See, 50 U.S.C. §§ 1801 *et seq.* Furthermore, if necessary and under the proper conditions and restraints, a court can even consider information *ex parte,* as the government's submission of classified versions of the Mobbs and Jacoby Declarations demonstrate. While the government's interests in intelligence operations and safeguarding sensitive matters of military and foreign affairs are great, there is sufficient precedent to demonstrate that the courts can accommodate them.

"Due process commands that no man shall lose his liberty unless the Government has borne the burden of. . .convincing the factfinder of his guilt." Winship, 397 U.S. at 364 (internal citations omitted). In Winship, the Supreme Court re-affirmed that criminal conviction requires proof beyond a reasonable doubt of every element necessary to constitute the crime. Id. Padilla in one sense has more at stake than a criminal defendant—not just his liberty and the stigma of being branded a traitor, but also, potentially, his right to the very process Winship guarantees. On the other hand, society has a very strong interest in waging a war against a known terrorist enemy. Requiring the government to demonstrate by clear and convincing evidence that Padilla is an enemy combatant strikes an appropriate balance between the significant and competing interests of individual liberty and protection from terrorist threat.

CONCLUSION

For these reasons, ABCNY respectfully submits that if the Court finds that the Executive *may* have had the power to detain Padilla as an unlawful combatant affiliated with al Qaeda, it should remand the matter to the district court to determine whether that power was lawfully exercised as follows:

(1) Padilla is entitled to present facts in support of his petition at a hearing;

(2) Padilla is entitled to consult with counsel in a manner consistent with reasonable national security and intelligence concerns;

(3) At Padilla's hearing, the government will bear the burden of demonstrating by clear and convincing evidence that Padilla is an unlawful combatant working on behalf of al Qaeda.

Dated:	New York, New York July 29, 2003	Respectfully Submitted, WILLKIE FARR & GALLAGHER Benito Romano, Esq. Joseph G. Davis, Esq. Mary Eaton, Esq. Attorneys for the Association of the Bar of the City of New York

NOTES

1. ABCNY takes no position on the constitutionality of the detention order.

2. "Gov't Br." refers to the Brief of Respondent-Appellant Donald Rumsfeld.

3. Of course, even absent the discrete rights that the habeas statutes create, a prisoner has a constitutional right of access to the courts for the purpose of assailing his detention through the writ of habeas corpus. See Bounds v. Smith, 430 U.S. 817, 821–22 (1977); Johnson v. Avery, 393 U.S. 483, 485 (1969). The Executive cannot limit or withhold that right. Ex Parte Hull, 312 U.S. 546, 549 (1941) (holding that "the state may not abridge or impair petitioner's right to apply to a federal court for a writ of habeas corpus"); Johnson, 393 U.S. at 485 (stating that "it is fundamental that access of prisoners to the courts for the purpose of presenting their complaints may not be denied or obstructed"). (See also Part II, infra.)

4. 28 U.S.C. § 2241 authorizes the federal courts to grant writs of habeas corpus to prisoners who, like Padilla, are "in custody under or by color of the authority of the United States," id. at (c)(l), as well as to those who are "in custody in violation of the Constitution or laws or treaties of the United States," id. at (c)(3). Other provisions of the habeas statute, particularly 28 U.S.C. § 2243, establish the procedures to be followed in section 2241 cases.

5. Other provisions of the habeas statute confirm Padilla's right to present facts and the district court's obligation to review the factual predicate for Padilla's detention as an enemy combatant. See e.g., 28 U.S. C. § 2246 (identifying methods for the habeas court to take evidence); 28 U.S.C. § 2247 (stating that documentary evidence "shall" be admissible in habeas cases); 28 U.S.C. § 2248 (directing the habeas court to accept the government's allegations as true unless the court "finds from the evidence that they are not true"). The Executive cannot unilaterally suspend the operation of these statutes and prevent Padilla from presenting facts in support of his petition, just as it cannot suspend the Great Writ itself. See Ex Parte Bollman, 8 U.S. 75, 101 (1807) (holding that Congress alone holds the power to suspend writ and the act that implements it); Ex Parte Merryman, 17 F. Cas. 144, 148–49 (1861) (rejecting executive authority to suspend the writ).

6. Indeed, were the Court to deny Padilla the right to present facts in support of his petition—facts that right now are in his possession alone—it would place itself in the position of ruling on a dispute without the benefit of a fully adversarial proceeding, in violation of the prohibition against advisory opinions. A federal court may not validate an executive action without that "'clear concreteness provided when a question emerges precisely framed and necessary for decision from a clash of adversary argument exploring

every aspect of a multifaceted situation embracing conflicting and demanding interests.'" Flast v. Cohen, 392 U.S. 83, 96–97 (1968) (quoting United States v. Fruehauf, 365 U.S. 146, 157 (1 961)). More generally, a federal court's jurisdiction extends only to cases or controversies, which "implies the existence of present or possible adverse parties, *whose contentions are submitted to the court for adjudication.*" Muskrat v. United States, 219 U.S. 346, 357 (1911) (emphasis supplied). Despite the vigorous and admirable efforts of Padilla's next friend and counsel, it is impossible to know whether the issues presented by the habeas petition they have filed are "precisely framed," because without access to Padilla the Court cannot be assured that the facts relevant to his petition have been aired. The Court cannot and should not exercise its Article III powers to validate the detention of Padilla unless Padilla himself is permitted to submit his contentions to the court.

7. Although the Fourth Circuit appears to have held otherwise, Hamdi App. III, 316 F.3d at 473–76, Hamdi App. III is distinguishable on two significant grounds. The Fourth Circuit viewed the operative facts as undisputed, id. at 473; Padilla's next friend has made no such concession. Moreover, based on the purportedly undisputed facts, the Fourth Circuit concluded that Hamdi was an enemy combatant captured in a "zone of active combat operations." Id. This fact, which the Fourth Circuit viewed as crucial to its decision, see id. at 474, 476–77, likewise makes Hamdi App. III inapplicable to this case. In addition, for the reasons stated above, and those outlined by Judge Motz in Hamdi App. IV, ABCNY respectfully suggests that the decision in Hamdi App. III to adjudicate the petition without hearing directly from the petitioner was error.

8. The government's position also trespasses on Padilla's First Amendment right to petition the court. The First Amendment's Petition Clause guarantees Padilla a right of access to the courts. See U.S. Const. Amend. I (prohibiting infringements on right to "petition the Government for a redress of grievances"); BE & K Const. Co. v. NLRB, 536 U.S. 516, 525 (2002) ("The right of access to the courts is...one aspect of the right of petition" under the First Amendment.) (quotations omitted). "The right to petition government for redress of grievances is 'among the most precious of the liberties safeguarded by the Bill of Rights.'" Franco v. Kelly, 854 F.2d 584, 589 (2d Cir. 1988) (quoting United Mine Workers v. Il. State Bar Ass'n, 389 U.S. 217, 222 (1967)). Hence, the right of access to the court is not satisfied by merely opening the courtroom doors. Rather, as the Supreme Court has held, "meaningful access to the courts is the touchstone." Bounds, 430 U.S. at 823 (internal citations omitted). Incommunicado detention, with no ability to draft a petition or communicate with next friend or counsel can hardly be described as meaningful access.

9. Citations to "JA" refer to the Joint Appendix filed by the parties.

10. The government has no power to detain Padilla as an "enemy" or unlawful combatant unless the laws of war apply to his detention.

11. Cf. Padilla I, 233 F. Supp. 2d at 594 ("Because the Quirin court *found* that the German saboteurs were not only attempting to harm the United States during an armed conflict but doing so as persons associated with an enemy's armed forces, the Court concluded that the saboteurs, unlike Milligan, could be treated as unlawful combatants" (emphasis supplied).

12. The government argued that "jurisdiction is complete under the laws and usages of war." Id. at 121.

13. If the laws of war do not apply, Padilla is at best an alleged criminal, and his detention is patently unlawful. ABCNY notes that the government's position with respect to the laws of war is, at best, inconsistent. On the one hand, the government contends that the "laws" of war apply, but on the other that the entire enemy force with whom we are at war is "unlawful." See id. (noting government's position that neither al Qaeda nor the Taliban are lawful combatants). If so, presumably there would be nothing to stop the Executive from "declaring war" on any form of international criminal organization—or on any international political organization with views hostile to the U.S.—and treating its members as unlawful combatants subject to seizure, indefinite detention and military trial, an outcome that is certainly unconstitutional.

14. Judges of the Fourth Circuit dissenting from the decision not to grant rehearing of the Hamdi App. III ruling disagreed whether that fact had been sufficiently established. See Hamdi App. IV, No. 02-7338, 2003 WL 21540768, at *15–34.

CHAPTER 8

An Act to Amend the Agriculture and Markets Law, in Relation to Unlawful Tampering with Animal Activities

PREFACE BY MARIANN SULLIVAN

Terrorism can harm us in numerous ways, not the least of which is in creating an atmosphere in which legitimate dissent may be squelched in the name of fear. The Committee on Legal Issues Pertaining to Animals was confronted with what appeared to be an example of an attempt to use post-9/11 fears in an inappropriate fashion when a bill was introduced in the New York State legislature that was ostensibly designed to strengthen the hand of law enforcement in fighting "terrorism" motivated by environmental or animal rights philosophies. In fact, the bill went far beyond any legitimate law enforcement concerns and, if enacted, would have, instead, stifled protected speech and characterized as "terrorists" legitimate, mainstream organizations advocating for the protection of animals and the environment. Moreover, while the right to express opinions should be protected regardless of whether they are persuasive or popular, it was clear to the Committee that, in this case, much of the criticism of environmental degradation and cruelty to animals that would have been stifled by this bill is both accurate and extremely alarming.

After the bill came to the Committee's attention, research revealed that it was part of a national post-9/11 movement to enact similar legislation around the country as part of the "war on terrorism." While that movement was led by the National Sportsmen's Alliance, the bills, which were also promoted by the American Legislative Exchange Council, did not deal exclusively, or even primarily, with hunting issues, and appeared to have been influenced by industries vulnerable to criticism on environmental and animal welfare grounds, in particular, agribusiness.[1]

The New York bill, as introduced, was certainly not difficult to criticize, as it was written so broadly and was so blatantly unconstitutional that it would arguably have labeled as a "terrorist" organization the Committee itself. And, as the Committee pointed out, all of the activities that were rendered illegal by the bill that could arguably deserve attention from law enforcement were already illegal under New York's Penal Law. Indeed, in 2005, several animal protection advocates who publicized a videotape they had taken after entering an egg production factory farm in upstate New York, from which they removed several sick and dying hens, were charged with felony burglary. Although two pled guilty to reduced charges, the one who proceeded to trial was acquitted of burglary and petit larceny, but nevertheless received six months of imprisonment for three counts of simple trespass. This appears to be exactly the type of activity toward which the bill is targeted, and this prosecution clearly shows that law enforcement is not without weapons to zealously defend animal use industries from animal advocates.

However, in spite of its blatant unconstitutionality and redundancy, the Committee believed that the bill could not be ignored. Similar, but somewhat toned-down, versions of this bill have been introduced in a variety of state legislatures, and versions have passed in California and Oklahoma. In Missouri and Illinois, only last-minute conference committees prevented the passage of bills prohibiting photography of animal facilities, such as puppy mills and factory farms, even from a legal vantage point, a provision that was also contained in the New York bill. And, the New York bill, even in spite of widespread criticism, was reintroduced in the Assembly in the current session, where it was referred to, and currently remains in, the Agriculture Committee.

These bills are appearing at a time when there is growing public concern regarding animal suffering and environmental degradation, particularly as they relate to conditions on factory farms. These proposed laws, which are clearly unnecessary to combat real terrorism, or even real crimes, have the potential to prevent the legitimate investigation of, dissemination of information about, and debate over the conditions in which animals are kept, by the billions, by an industry that is virtually unregulated on animal welfare grounds. That this should be part of the legacy of 9/11 is anathema, and the Committee strongly felt that it must be actively opposed.

Re: A. 4884 S. 2996	Assemblymember Smith Senators Kuhl, Alesi, Larkin, Maziarz, McGee, Mendez, Rath, Volker, Wright

An Act to amend the agriculture and markets law, in relation to unlawful tampering with animal activities

This Bill is Disapproved

This bill proposes an amendment to Section 378 of the Agriculture and Markets Law, which already sets forth criminal penalties for certain acts in relation to animal research, including stealing animals, appropriating confidential material and releasing animals exposed to infectious agents, and creates a private right of action for its violation. If enacted, this proposed amendment will vastly expand the acts which are made illegal and vastly expand, beyond animal research, the animal related activities that are shielded by the law. Many of the acts that this bill seeks to criminalize are already crimes under New York State law, primarily in the nature of trespass and property damage. This bill would provide for additional, and very substantial, penalties for these crimes when they are "politically motivated," which, according to this bill, renders them terrorist acts. The bill also seeks to criminalize certain acts, if politically motivated, which are not already crimes under New York state law and, further, seeks to criminalize the donation of money to or other support of organizations which commit prohibited acts. Because the bill is both very broad and very vague, it appears that it would criminalize many activities that are protected by the Constitution, including many forms of legitimate protest.

First, this bill would greatly expand the types of "animal activities" that are to receive special treatment, including limitations on protest and criticism, under the law. In addition to three activities which quite clearly involve animals, i.e., hunting, fishing and trapping, it also includes a number of activities which may, or may not, involve animals, including food production, clothing manufacturing, agriculture, recreation and entertainment. It also, oddly, includes activities which do not appear to be significantly related to animal use, including camping and traveling. It is unclear under what circumstances such activities would come within the proposed law. Moreover, the definition contains a catchall provision, i.e., "any other services involving the use of animals" with no indication as to what is meant by "services" or, again, what would constitute a sufficient connection to the "use of animals."

The bill goes on to define an "animal or ecological terrorist organization":

> (j) "Animal or ecological terrorist organization" means any association, organization, entity, coalition, or combination of two or more persons with the primary or incidental purpose of supporting any politically motivated activity through intimidation, coercion, fear, or other means that is intended to obstruct, impede or deter any person from participating in a lawful animal activity, animal facility, research facility, or the lawful activity of mining, foresting, harvesting, gathering or processing natural resources.

Simplified, this section labels as a terrorist organization any two people who, through any means, support politically motivated activity intended to deter someone from participating in any lawful "animal activity" (as described above) or various activities related to natural resources. This definition is broad enough to encompass organizations such as The Sierra Club and the American Society for the Prevention of Cruelty to Animals. Indeed, it might make this Committee a "terrorist organization." Virtually all political and social advocacy is an attempt to "obstruct," "impede" or "deter" some activity or conduct, such as through education, persuasion or legislative change. Moreover, by using the terms "intimidation," "coercion" and "fear" to define the proscribed methods, rather than the proscribed intent, the terms become completely subjective. Legislative action may "coerce" change, people who are the subject of protests are often "intimidated" by the disapproval of their fellow citizens, and people who are informed that there is opposition to their positions may be "fear[ful]" of the ramifications. In this context, these words are so subjective as to be meaningless. But even if those words adequately defined methods of seeking change that should render one a "terrorist," the bill goes on to include the use of any "other means" as well.

The limitation that the activity which is sought to be deterred must be "lawful" does not effectively limit the scope of this definition. Much political advocacy is directed at activities that are lawful, but nevertheless objectionable to the particular advocates, in the hopes of changing the law and/or educating the public or the person involved in the activity.

Moreover, the bill's singling out as "terrorism" of activity that is "politically motivated," does not serve to legitimately focus on terrorist activity. While some terrorists may be politically motivated, that obviously does not make anyone who is politically motivated a terrorist. Indeed, politically motivated activity is at the core of the fundamental freedoms of speech, association and assembly guaranteed by the First Amendment. It is necessary to the successful functioning of a democracy.

It is also troubling that this bill seeks to introduce a definition of terrorism that is not content neutral, but seems to be aimed at setting a lower bar for labeling those in the animal rights or environmental movements as terrorists than is set for those whose political motivation is for a different cause. In this context, it is worth noting that federal criminal law dealing with "terrorism" (see 18 USC 2331 et seq.) as well as those sections of New York's penal law setting forth the crime of "terrorism" (§ 490.00 et seq.) do not attempt to label any entity with a targeted ideology as a "terrorist organization." Instead, these laws define what activities constitute "terrorism" and uniformly identify as a "terrorist" any individual, entity or organization which engages in those activities with the requisite intent, i.e., to intimidate or influence a civilian population or a government. That is the essence of what separates terrorism from other sorts of violent crime.

This bill, on the other hand, seeks to extend the definition of "terrorism" to virtually any politically motivated crime (as well as heretofore non-criminal activities), not where those crimes are targeted at the government or the populace, but where they are targeted at private entities that are the subject of criticism from particular advocacy groups. Of course, crimes that are politically or philosophically motivated are properly considered crimes, and should be prosecuted as such. They are not necessarily terrorism. If terrorist acts were committed in the name of the animal rights or environmental movements, they are already subject to prosecution under existing federal and state laws.

The bill at issue, after defining who is a terrorist, goes on to list the activities which it would prohibit. Though stated much more vaguely than similar sections in the Penal Law, many of the prohibited actions set forth in the bill appear to be targeted at activities that are already prohibited under New York law, including various forms of larceny (Penal Law § 155.00 et seq.), trespass (Penal Law § 140.00 et seq.), burglary (Penal Law § 140.20 et seq.), criminal mischief (Penal Law § 145.00 et seq.), criminal tampering (Penal Law § 145.14 et seq.), reckless endangerment of property (Penal Law § 145.25), and unlawful tampering with animal research (Agriculture and Markets Law § 378). Interestingly, the activities would not fit within the definition of the crime of terrorism (Penal Law § 490 et seq.), which not only requires a specific intent not required here,[2] but is limited to "specified offense" which are much more narrow in scope (*see* Penal Law § 490.05(3)) than the ones set forth herein. By and large, the activities prohibited by this bill also fall far short of the serious nature ("dangerous to human life") of the activities which, if properly motivated, may be deemed to be "domestic terrorism" in the federal law dealing with terrorism.[3] Indeed, this bill focuses primarily on non-violent crimes, and does not even target either murder or kidnapping, which are probably the two crimes most frequently associated with actual terrorism.

While most of the activities prohibited by the bill are already illegal, section (v) specifically defines activity which is not currently a crime, i.e., "entering an animal or research facility to take pictures by photograph, video camera, or other means with the intent to commit criminal activities or defame the facility or its owner." This provision would criminalize even legal entry into a facility if it is for the purpose of taking photographs or making a video recording to "defame" the facility or its owner. In light of the fundamental First Amendment interests involved, defamation has always been a civil matter, not a criminal offense. Moreover, this section goes well beyond the proscriptions of civil law and seeks to criminalize the *intent* to defame. This section appears to create a substantial risk that its effect would be to inhibit investigative reporting and whistle-blowing regarding the cruel treatment of animals.

Furthermore, the activities which would be made crimes under this bill include a catch-all provision, which is so broad, and so vague, that it could clearly include legitimate protest activity, i.e., "interfering with any lawful animal activity or the lawful use of a natural resource or its byproduct." Since legitimate protest is, by definition, designed to "interfere" with the activity it is focused against, the effect of this section would be to criminalize virtually all protest in the area of animal rights and environmental protection. Furthermore, the term "byproduct" of a "natural resource" is undefined and would appear to encompass virtually anything. Moreover, as noted above, the definition of "animal activity" is extraordinarily broad.

In addition to criminalizing (or further criminalizing) these activities, the bill seeks to criminalize the provision of material or financial support to "encourage, plan, prepare, carry out, publicize, promote or aid" any of these activities. This section appears to be targeted at donors and other supporters of animal and environmental protection organizations, though it would also include persons who rent cars or hotel rooms, or provide meals to people who then carry out one of the prohibited activities. First, as noted, many of the activities which are prohibited would normally be assumed to be legal and/or are otherwise clearly protected by the Constitution. Moreover, this section does not require that the donor, or other supporter, intend or even know that the support will be used for these acts. This section would likely have a chilling effect on donors to legitimate organizations performing legitimate activities. Not only would it be difficult for a donor to know whether an activity that an organization is performing fits within the very vague definitions of this bill, but he or she could be held criminally liable even if unaware of the activity. And, the mischief the act would cause if used to prosecute rental car companies, hotels and restaurants, all within the content of the bill, is obvious.

The penalties set forth by this bill are very significant. On the assumption that the bill's reference to "third degree felony" is meant to be a Class C felony, this would mean that a court could sentence a person convicted under this section, if they were a first felony offender, to an indeterminate sentence of up to 5 to 15 years in prison. Since the crime is defined separately and with additional elements from the underlying criminal act, that sentence could likely be made to run consecutively to any sentence imposed for an underlying act.

Moreover, the bill takes the extraordinary step of setting up a website for the keeping and public dissemination of a database containing information about persons who have been convicted of these offenses (including donors). The only thing remotely comparable to this proposal is the requirement that sexual predators and child molesters register to advise people in their neighborhood of their presence (*see* Correction Law § 168-a et seq.). There is no comparable provision for numerous other serious crimes, including murder, rape, arson, kidnapping, robbery, or burglary.

In conclusion, this bill does not appear to be sincerely targeted at fighting terrorism. It is certainly unconstitutional in many respects because of its effect on legitimate protest activities. To the extent it seeks to criminalize activities which may legitimately be classified as crimes, it is unnecessary, as it is redundant of other laws, both state and federal. Moreover, it appears to be an attempt to impose a singular definition of terrorism based on the political beliefs of two groups, i.e., the animal protection movement and the environmental movement. This Committee strongly recommends that the bill be opposed.

NOTES

1. For an extended discussion of these bills, see E.C. Eddy, "Privatizing the Patriot Act: The Criminalization of Environmental and Animal Protectionists as Terrorists," 22 *Pace Environmental Law Review* 261 (2005).

2. . . . intended to

(I) intimidate or coerce a civilian population;

(ii) influence the policy of a unit of government by intimidation or coercion; or

(iii) affect the conduct of a unit of government by murder, assassination or kidnapping. . .

(Penal Law § 490.05(1)(a)).

3. The term "domestic terrorism" means activities that:

(A) involve acts dangerous to human life that are a violation of the criminal laws of the United States or any State;

(B) appear to be intended:

(I) to intimidate or coerce a civilian population;

(ii) to influence the policy of a government by intimidation or coercion; or

(iii) to affect the conduct of a government by mass destruction, assassination or kidnapping; and occur primarily within the territorial jurisdiction of the United States.

(18 USC § 2331)

CHAPTER 9

The Indefinite Detention of "Enemy Combatants": Balancing Due Process and National Security in the Context of the War on Terror

PREFACE BY THOMAS H. MORELAND

Few actions by the Bush Administration pursuant to the war on terror have caused more controversy than its indefinite detention of Jose Padilla. Padilla, a U.S. citizen seized at a Chicago airport in 2002, has remained in military custody pursuant to a determination by President Bush that Padilla was an "enemy combatant" allied with al Qaeda. Although the conduct of which Padilla is suspected would violate the criminal laws, and many other accused terrorists have been prosecuted under those criminal laws, Padilla has been detained without charges. His *habeas* petition challenging his detention puts dramatically at issue the relative powers and responsibilities of the three branches of the U.S. government to balance the interests of national security and civil liberties in the context of the war on terror.

The following Report by the Association's Committee on Federal Courts* contained below analyzes the indefinite detention of enemy combatants as an exercise of the President's war powers, under Article II of the U.S. Constitution, and as a possible violation of core due process rights. In essence, it concludes that the President's war powers, at least absent specific Congressional authorization, do not authorize the indefinite detention of American citizens seized on American soil, and that such detention violates core due process values. This Report was first issued on February 6, 2004, and the revised version that follows was issued on March 18 of the same year.

The Second Circuit, relying principally on the absence of Congressional authorization, invalidated Padilla's detention in its 2003 decision reported at 352 F.3d 695. The U.S. Supreme Court reversed, but on the grounds that the venue of Padilla's *habeas corpus* petition had been improper. 542 U.S. 426 (2004). The petition was then refiled in the District of South Carolina, where Padilla is now detained. District Judge Floyd granted the petition, *Padilla v. Hanft,* 2005 U.S. Dist. Lexis 2921, February 28, 2005. Also finding a lack of Congressional authorization for the detention, the court held that to sustain the detention based on the President's alleged inherent authority as Commander-in-Chief would "offend the rule of law and violate this country's constitutional tradition..." On September 9, 2005, the Fourth Circuit reversed an opinion by Judge Floyd. *Padilla v. Hanft,* 2005 U.S. App. Lexis 19465. The Fourth Circuit did not address the President's inherent powers. Rather it found the detention had been authorized by Congress in its September 18, 2001, Authorization for Use of Military Force Joint Resolution, which authorized the President to use "all necessary and appropriate force" against those responsible for the September 11, 2001, terrorist attacks. The Fourth Circuit found there to be no meaningful distinction between the detention of an armed citizen seized on a foreign battlefield, as in *Hamdi v. Rumsfeld,* 124 S. Ct. 2633 (2004), and the detention of an unarmed citizen seized in the United States and determined by the President, such as was Padilla, to be actively conspiring with al Qaeda.

The U.S. Supreme Court will have an opportunity to address the merits of the Fourth Circuit's decision. While so far only Padilla and one other American citizen have been apprehended in the United States and detained as enemy combatants, the legal principle involved is potentially of far broader application. The indeterminate duration of the war on terror, and the Administration's view that the "battlefield" embraces the entire United States, places at risk in the United States even the most basic of individual rights when opposed by the asserted dictates of national security.

EXECUTIVE SUMMARY

The President, assertedly acting under his "war power" in prosecuting the "war on terror," has claimed the authority to detain indefinitely, and without access to counsel, persons he designates as "enemy combatants," an as yet undefined term that embraces selected suspected terrorists or their accomplices.

Two cases, each addressing a habeas corpus petition brought by an American citizen, have reviewed the constitutionality of detaining "enemy combatants" pursuant to the President's determination:

- *Hamdi v. Rumsfeld*, 316 F.3d 450 (4th Cir. 2003), cert. granted, 124 S. Ct. 981 (Jan. 9, 2004) (No. 03-6696), concerns a citizen seized with Taliban military forces in a zone of armed combat in Afghanistan;
- Padilla ex. rel. Newman v. Bush, 233 F. Supp. 2d 564 (S.D.N.Y. 2002), rev'd sub nom., Padilla ex. rel. Newman v. Rumsfeld, 352 F.3d 695 (2d Cir. 2003), cert. granted, 124 S. Ct. 1353 (Feb. 20, 2004) (No. 03-1027), concerns a citizen seized in Chicago, and suspected of planning a terrorist attack in league with al Qaeda.

Padilla and Hamdi have been held by the Department of Defense, without any access to legal counsel, for well over a year. No criminal charges have been filed against either one. Rather, the government asserts its right to detain them without charges to incapacitate them and to facilitate their interrogation. Specifically, the President claims the authority, in the exercise of his war power as "Commander in Chief" under the Constitution (Art. II, § 2), to detain persons he classifies as "enemy combatants":

- indefinitely, for the duration of the "war on terror";
- without any charges being filed, and thus not triggering any rights attaching to criminal prosecutions;
- incommunicado from the outside world;

- specifically, with no right of access to an attorney;
- with only limited access to the federal courts on *habeas corpus,* and with no right to rebut the government's showing that the detainee is an enemy combatant.

These detentions, effected unilaterally by the executive without congressional authorization and not subject to meaningful judicial review, violate core due process rights under the Constitution, including:

- the right not to be detained except pursuant to a statute authorizing the detention;
- the right not to be detained without the prompt proffer of specific criminal charges;
- the right to test the legality of the detention in the federal courts through the writ of habeas corpus at a meaningful evidentiary hearing;
- the right to consult with and to be represented by counsel concerning the detention, and in connection with a habeas corpus hearing challenging it.

The holding of persons incommunicado in this country, without charges, indefinitely and based solely on the executive's decision, has nothing in common with due process as we know it. Though effected in the perceived interest of national security, these detentions are alien to America's respect for the rule of law. Until now, no court has ever sustained the assertion of such unilateral detention powers by a President, even in times of war.

The President's war power is insufficient to justify such detentions, in derogation of core due process rights. The only Supreme Court precedent said to establish this detention power, Ex parte Quirin, 317 U.S. 1 (1942), did not. Quirin involved only the question of whether saboteurs, members of the German army, could be tried before a military commission for alleged war crimes, as Congress had authorized. In sustaining the prompt trial by commission of the saboteurs, who were represented by counsel, Quirin said nothing supporting the executive's unauthorized, indefinite and incommunicado detentions now at issue.

Apart from the absence of judicial support, recognizing an essentially unlimited and unilateral executive power to detain would have serious negative consequences for our country. The sharp departure from the rule of law inherent in such detentions would threaten many adverse effects beyond the violation of the detainees' rights.

There is a significant risk that persons will be detained erroneously, since they would be permitted no access to counsel or opportunity to rebut their classification as enemy combatants. This risk of error is all the graver because of the obvious potential for ethnic-based actions against men of Middle Eastern extraction, already evidenced in fact in immigration contexts, given the distinct ethnic cast of the terrorists apprehended to date.

Recognition of this unlimited detention power would impose an intolerable pressure on criminal defendants accused of terrorist-related crimes. They could be threatened, if they refuse to plead guilty, with removal from the criminal justice system, and indefinite detention with no access to a lawyer and no opportunity to contest their guilt. This is precisely the fate, to date, of one civilian non-combatant, suspected of providing (but not proven to have provided) logistical support for al Qaeda, who was designated as an enemy combatant and transferred to military jurisdiction shortly before he was to be tried on criminal charges. Al-Marri v. Bush, 274 F. Supp. 2d 1003 (C.D. Ill. 2003).

There is also the danger of further extensions of the war power to curtail other civil liberties. A jurisprudence that holds that the domestic war on terror is indistinguishable from the "total war" circumstances of World War II and the Civil War, and on that basis defers to the President all decisions on the best means to prosecute the war on terror within the United States, leaves the door wide open to an almost unlimited expansion of executive power. Why should the First

Amendment right of free speech, or the Fourth Amendment right to be free of unreasonable searches, be any less subordinate to the President's war power than the core due process right to remain free of unilateral executive detention? Pick your favorite constitutional amendment or right: its survival during the war on terror cannot be assumed if the legitimacy of these indefinite detentions is sustained.

Nor can the assertion of this detention power be comfortably assumed to be only a temporary departure from the rule of law. The war on terror is likely to be a prolonged, if not a permanent feature of our times. Thus, extraordinary departures from due process justified by the existence of this war may prove to be enduring features of the constitutional landscape, not short-term measures easily reversed.

The fact that the administration concedes that *habeas corpus* petitions can be brought on behalf of the detainees provides cold comfort for due process rights, if the basic principle of the detentions is upheld. This is especially so if, as the administration contends, no rebuttal in court is to be permitted to its claim, supported only by "some evidence," that the detainee is an enemy combatant. The Great Writ, under these restrictions, becomes perilously close to an empty gesture.

Finally, to sustain these lawless executive detentions would undermine the position of the United States in promoting the rule of law abroad, and would provide encouragement and cover for repression around the globe. If the United States feels justified in departing from the rule of law in combating terrorism at home, notwithstanding our strong tradition of constitutionalism, regimes in other countries with no such tradition may see such conduct as justifying crackdowns against political dissidents.

We do not question that the President has the power to treat aspects of the war on terror as a "war," a political question traditionally held unreviewable by the courts. Further, the President's war power, coupled with his primacy in the realm of foreign affairs, rightly afford the President a wide discretion in prosecuting the war on terror abroad, a discretion which supports at least the initial detention of Hamdi in Afghanistan in a zone of armed combat.

But no such near total deference is appropriate with respect to the President's actions at home, where due process and the rule of law prevail. The executive's authority to launch military campaigns against al Qaeda and Iraq cannot be conflated with an unlimited power to take actions in this country, in alleged pursuit of the same war on terror, that trammel on core due process rights. The Constitution makes the President the Commander in Chief of the Armed Forces, not Commander in Chief of all persons within the United States.

We do not say that due process is unyielding in the face of dire circumstance. To the contrary, it can accommodate a short-term departure from its usual strictures in an imminent emergency created by terrorism, in which immediate action is essential and can be taken only by the executive. But claims of such a crisis-borne necessity must be scrutinized by the courts, and a heavy presumption weighs against them to the extent they would suspend core due process rights.

No such general claim of necessity can be sustained with respect to the detentions of suspected terrorists in the United States. The criminal laws provide ample means for prosecuting such suspects and imposing heavy sentences upon their conviction, including the death penalty (and using the prospects of such sentences to plea bargain as a means of extracting information). Nor need a criminal prosecution wholly preempt an interrogation for intelligence purposes, if appropriate safeguards are put in place to insure that the fruits of the interrogation are not used against the defendants at the criminal trial.

The absence of Congressional authorization for these detentions further undermines their legitimacy. In other instances of disputed domestic exercises of the President's war power, including Quirin, the courts have looked to whether Congress, the other political branch, had authorized the challenged action. Here Congress has not authorized indefinite detentions. The Joint Resolution of September 2001, authorizing the President to use "all necessary and appropriate force" against al Qaeda, through the "United States Armed Forces," cannot reasonably be read as approving the suspension of basic due process rights in the United States, as distinguished from the use of military force abroad. In the USA Patriot Act passed a month later, which contains numerous expansions of executive power to combat terrorism, Congress notably did not authorize any detentions of citizens, and imposed a seven-day limitation (absent the commencement of removal proceedings) on the detention of aliens suspected of terrorism, a limitation inconsistent with the indefinite detentions now defended. Further, given that neither the Joint Resolution nor the President's war power justifies indefinite detentions, such detentions of citizens also violate 18 U.S.C. § 4001(a), prohibiting detentions of citizens "except pursuant to an act of Congress," as the Second Circuit has now held in Padilla.

There are, to be sure, limits on Congress's own war powers, to the extent legislation would seek to supplant core due process rights. But if Congress did authorize limited and conditional detentions, in specifically defined circumstances, and subject to meaningful judicial review, such a statute would command greater deference than the executive's unilateral assertion of an unlimited detention power.

In addition to its claimed detention power, the administration asserts that alien enemy combatants may be tried at the President's discretion before special military commissions, rather than in Article III courts applying the extensive procedural protections accorded under the Constitution to defendants in criminal prosecutions. Quirin and existing statutory authorization do provide some support for the use of such commissions to prosecute violations of the law of war. Assuming that some enemy combatants could be so charged, nonetheless the use of military commissions should be minimized because of the several advantages offered by criminal prosecutions in the federal courts. Because of the public access to such federal court trials, the procedural safeguards they embrace, and the independence of the federal judiciary, the fairness of such trials and the justness of their verdicts is much more likely to be accepted, in this country and abroad, than would be the case with military trials controlled by the executive. The federal courts have successfully tried numerous terrorism cases. They should be the preferred forum for future terrorism cases.

The war on terror has created many challenges for our country. Not the least is the challenge to preserve the rule of law in acting against enemies that respect no laws. The Constitution is not a "suicide pact," as a Supreme Court justice once famously declared. But neither is it a mere compact of convenience, to be enforced only in halcyon days of civic tranquility. It should take far more than the monstrous brutality of a handful of terrorists to drive us to abandon our core constitutional values. Insistence on the rule of law will not undermine our national security. Abandoning the rule of law will threaten our national identity.

I. INTRODUCTION

Especially since the attacks of September 11, 2001, the United States has viewed itself as engaged in a "war on terror" against the forces of al Qaeda and its adherents, and other terrorist groups, both abroad and at home. The measures taken in response to the threat of terrorism have raised many issues concerning the proper balance between national security and individual liberties. This report addresses, in particular, the role the federal courts should play in striking this balance with respect to the detention and trial of suspected terrorists or their accomplices, designated as "enemy combatants" by the executive branch.

A. Hamdi and Padilla: the President's War Power Trumps Due Process

To date, the constitutionality of detaining "enemy combatants," pursuant to the President's unilateral determination, has been reviewed in two cases, each addressing a habeas corpus petition brought by an American citizen:

- Hamdi v. Rumsfeld, 316 F.3d 450 (4th Cir. 2003) ("Hamdi"), reh'g and reh'g en banc denied, 337 F.3d 335 (4th Cir. 2003), cert. granted, 124 S. Ct. 981 (Jan. 9, 2004) (No. 03-6696);
- Padilla ex. rel. Newman v. Bush, 233 F. Supp. 2d 564 (S.D.N.Y. 2002) ("Padilla"), adhered to on recons. sub nom., Padilla ex. rel. Newman v. Rumsfeld, 243 F. Supp. 2d 42 (S.D.N.Y. 2003), rev'd, 352 F.3d 695 (2d Cir.) ("Padilla Cir."), cert. granted, 124 S. Ct. 1353 (Feb. 20, 2004) (No. 03-1027).

In addition, one alien, a student from Qatar, Ali Saleh Kahlah al-Marri, has been designated as an enemy combatant and transferred to military jurisdiction, shortly before he was scheduled to be tried on criminal charges. See Al-Marri v. Bush, 274 F. Supp. 2d 1003 (C.D. Ill. 2003) ("Al-Marri") (habeas petition dismissed in view of transfer of petitioner to military custody in South Carolina). If the reported facts concerning al-Marri are correct, he is a civilian suspected of providing logistical support for terrorists, specifically helping "other members of al Qaeda 'settle' in the United States."[1]

Padilla and Hamdi, both American citizens, were seized under different circumstances, ultimately declared "enemy combatants," and given over to the custody of the Department of Defense, where they have been held incommunicado, without any access to legal counsel, for well over a year at this point. Padilla at 571–72, 574; see Hamdi at 460.

No criminal charges have been filed against either Hamdi or Padilla.[2] The government disclaims, for now, any interest in pursuing the two "primary objectives of criminal punishment: retribution or deterrence." Padilla at 600, quoting Kansas v. Hendricks, 521 U.S. 346, 361–62 (1997). Rather, the government asserts its right to detain them without charges indefinitely, for the duration of the war on terror, to serve two different purposes: to prevent them from returning to the enemy, and to facilitate their interrogation in the hope of obtaining information to thwart additional terrorist acts. Padilla at 573–74; Hamdi at 465–66.

A brief comparison of Hamdi and Padilla, and of the al-Marri detention, arising as they do out of different factual settings, will help illuminate some of the issues presented by "enemy combatant" detentions.[3]

Hamdi, according to the government's allegations that the Fourth Circuit viewed as indisputable, was "captured in a zone of active combat in a foreign theater of conflict," namely Afghanistan. Hamdi at 459. He allegedly was captured by the Northern Alliance forces, together with other members of a Taliban fighting unit, while in possession of a weapon. The Northern Alliance forces handed Hamdi over to the American armed forces in the fall of 2001. The Department of Defense thereafter has held him in Afghanistan, Guantánamo Bay, Cuba, and ultimately, commencing in April 2002, in Naval Brigs in Virginia (id. at 460, 477) and, commencing July 2003, South Carolina. Brief for the Respondents in Opposition at 4–5, Hamdi v. Rumsfeld (U.S., No. 03-6696) ("Resp'ts Hamdi Brief"). It is not clear when and by whom Hamdi was formally declared to be an "enemy combatant." Compare Hamdi at 461 (Hamdi was so designated "by our Government") with Resp'ts Hamdi Brief at 4 ("the United States military determined that Hamdi is an enemy combatant").

Padilla was arrested in May 2002 by Department of Justice personnel when he arrived at a Chicago airport. The arrest was pursuant to a material witness warrant issued by the Southern District of New York, pursuant to 18 U.S.C. § 3144, to enforce a subpoena to secure Padilla's testimony before a grand jury in the Southern District. Padilla at 568–69. A lawyer appointed to represent Padilla, after consulting with him, filed a petition for a writ of habeas corpus challenging his detention as a material witness. After the motion had been fully submitted, the government suddenly withdrew its grand jury subpoena and transferred Padilla to the custody of the Department of Defense in South Carolina, pursuant to his designation by President Bush, himself, as an "enemy combatant." Id. at 571–74.

To support the classification of the petitioners as enemy combatants, in each case the government presented an affidavit or declaration by Special Advisor to the Undersecretary of Defense for Policy, Michael Mobbs, reciting the circumstances under which each petitioner had been detained and at least some of the alleged facts said to support his designation as an enemy combatant. In Hamdi's case, the evidence was basically his capture, bearing a weapon, as a part of the Taliban fighting forces in Afghanistan. Hamdi at 461, 472. In Padilla's case the facts alleged included his contacts with a senior al Qaeda lieutenant in Afghanistan, allegedly proposing to steal radioactive material so as to build and detonate a "dirty bomb" in the United States, and other contacts with al Qaeda, including training and alleged instructions to journey to the United States to "conduct reconnaissance and/or conduct other attacks on their behalf." Padilla at 572–73.

Both the Hamdi circuit court and the Padilla district court recognized, as the government ultimately conceded, the availability of habeas corpus as a procedural remedy to test the legality of the detentions of these American citizens.[4] But, as a matter of substance, both upheld the constitutionality of the detentions, if the classification of the detainee as an "enemy combatant" were established, as proper exercises of the President's war power as Commander in Chief under Article II, section 2, of the Constitution. Neither court viewed the detainee's U.S. citizenship to limit the President's power to detain them.[5]

The Second Circuit, in its recent decision reversing Padilla, disagreed. It held that, absent explicit congressional authorization, the President's war power did not extend to the detention of American citizens on American soil, removed from any zone of armed combat. Padilla Cir. at 710–18. It also found Padilla's detention to violate 18 U.S.C. § 4001(a), which prohibits the detention of a citizen "except pursuant to an act of Congress." Id. at 718–24.

To sustain the enemy combatant classification, the Padilla district court would have required that the government adduce "some evidence" supporting the classification, while permitting the petitioner to rebut this showing. Padilla at 608. On its interlocutory appeal to the Second Circuit, the government urged that Padilla "has no entitlement to present facts to challenge the basis for his detention," because the "some evidence" standard "turns exclusively on the facts presented by the Executive. . . ." Opening Brief of Respondent-Appellant at 43, 45.

In Hamdi no rebuttal was permitted and Hamdi's counsel was not permitted to consult with him to determine if any rebuttal was feasible: the court found the Mobbs declaration sufficient given that (in its view) the facts supporting Hamdi's classification were beyond dispute. Thus while in its earlier remand decision the Fourth Circuit had refused to sustain the classification "on the government's say so", declining to accept the government's determination as "the first and final word" on the subject, its ultimate resolution based exclusively on the Mobbs declaration—consistent with the government's "no rebuttal" position in the Padilla appeal—seems to have done precisely that in the military battlefield context before it.

Neither Hamdi nor the Padilla district court attempted an all-purpose definition of "enemy combatant," and the administration also seems not to have gone beyond the facts of the individual cases to articulate a generally applicable definition. In Padilla's case, his alleged role in planning a bomb attack bore obvious analogy to the German saboteurs seized as illegal combatants in the World War II case of Ex Parte Quirin, 317 U.S. 1 (1942) ("Quirin"). To the Fourth Circuit, Hamdi's classification as an enemy combatant was self-evident based on his alleged capture while fighting with Taliban forces against the Northern Alliance, America's ally.

Neither Hamdi nor the Padilla district court held that the detainee had a due process right to consult with counsel in connection with the habeas proceeding. In Padilla, however, Judge Mukasey ordered that such consultation be allowed, as a matter of discretion, in part because Padilla had already consulted with his appointed counsel when he had been held as a material witness. The government vigorously resisted this order, resulting in an interlocutory appeal to the Second Circuit, which found Padilla's detention itself to be unconstitutional.

As the Supreme Court is poised to review the Hamdi and Padilla rulings, we offer a review of these decisions, and an analysis of the interests and values at stake.

In different ways, and in different factual contexts, Hamdi and the Padilla district court held that certain basic limits on the power of the executive branch, treated as unquestioned "rights" in most contexts, are of limited or no applicability to accused terrorists. These holdings suggest that a system largely separate from Article III courts and the due process rights they enforce, but rather based on the war power of the President—though still subject to some review via habeas corpus—is appropriate to deal with terrorism. Under this system, "enemy combatants" as determined by the executive branch may be held indefinitely, without charges, perhaps with no access to a lawyer (as in Hamdi), and subject to aggressive interrogation, until the end of the "war on terror." This "enemy combatant" classification can embrace a U.S. citizen seized abroad during a military campaign and accused of fighting with enemy forces (Hamdi), a U.S. citizen accused of planning sabotage in the United States (Padilla), and, given the reported facts concerning al-Marri, a civilian non-combatant perhaps accused of providing logistical support for terrorists in the United States.[6]

The Second Circuit's opinion reversing Padilla does not speak directly to the constitutional rights of detainees to due process. But it does squarely hold that indefinite detentions are not within the President's unilateral war power, to the extent that the person detained is "an American citizen seized on American soil outside a zone of combat." Padilla Cir. at 698. The opinion necessarily does not address the President's powers with respect to non-citizens, such as al-Marri, or with respect to citizens seized abroad or in zones of combat, such as Hamdi.

B. Questions Presented

Since the war on terror has no foreseeable end, it becomes vital to reexamine the role of the federal courts, and the core principles they generally enforce, in the context of terrorism. What is the appropriate role for the courts, the President and Congress with respect to the detention and prosecution of alleged terrorists, given a proper application of the separation of powers doctrine in the light of the war power of the President and the Due Process Clause? Is it likely that denying basic due process rights to alleged terrorists would do lasting damage to those rights traditionally accorded to all persons within the reach of the Constitution? Is it unwise to apply to terrorism the due process limitations on executive power that apply in criminal proceedings? Instead, should the courts find that the President, under his war power, possesses the discretion to fight the war on terror through whatever means he deems appropriate, including here the unlimited detention and interrogation of suspected terrorists? Should the answer to this detention issue depend on whether, for example, the suspect is a citizen, or was arrested, or is detained, in the United States or abroad?

In this report we will:

- restate the basic substantive and procedural "rights" of detainees, outside of the war context;

- examine the precedents construing the war power of the President (and/or Congress), and the extent to which those powers have been held to limit or preempt basic due process rights, including in Padilla and Hamdi;
- analyze the potential damage to civil liberties inherent in upholding the constitutionality of unilateral and indefinite executive detentions of "enemy combatants" in the United States;
- set forth our own analysis of why the President's war power should not be construed to embrace such detentions, at least absent express authorization by Congress; and
- weigh the practical and policy advantages and disadvantages of the federal courts as a trial venue for alleged terrorists, as compared with military commissions, to the extent the use of commissions would be constitutional.

II. THE CORE PRINCIPLES OF INDIVIDUAL LIBERTY AND DUE PROCESS

It is asserted by the administration that, on its determination that an individual is an "enemy combatant", that person may be detained:

- indefinitely, for the duration of the "war against terror";
- without any charges or proceedings being filed, and thus not triggering any rights attaching to criminal prosecutions;
- incommunicado from the outside world;
- specifically, with no right of access to an attorney;
- with only limited access to the federal courts, and no right to rebut the government's showing that the detainee is an "enemy combatant."

Our core constitutional principles of due process and individual liberty prohibit such indefinite and incommunicado detentions in times of peace. After discussing these clear peacetime principles, we will proceed to consider the possible limitation or inapplicability of those principles in the context of the "war on terror."

A. Substantive Rights

1. *No Arbitrary Detentions; The Rule of Law*

The Constitution with its Bill of Rights defines the balance between governmental authority and individual liberty in the United States.

> The United States is entirely a creature of the Constitution. Its power and authority have no other source.

Reid v. Covert, 354 U.S. 1, 5–6 (1957) (Black, J., plurality opinion).

Early on, the Supreme Court sounded the rule of law as central to the Constitution:

> The government of the United States has been emphatically termed a government of laws, and not of men. Marbury v. Madison, 5 U.S. 137, 163 (1803).

Fundamental to our constitutional scheme is the principle that a person can be detained by the government only pursuant to a valid law, and upon a judicial determination that sufficient cause exists to believe it has been violated. The Constitution prohibits detentions based only on the executive's subjective determination.

From at least the Magna Carta of 1215, a major stream in the history of English-speaking peoples has been the increasing protection of individuals from such arbitrary exercises of executive power. The Magna Carta recognized the right to be free from intrusions on personal security "except by the legal judgment of [one's] peers or by the law of the land." The Magna Carta, though initially benefiting only a narrow class of English barons, recognized that even the King was subject to a superior law. The rule of law was gradually extended to protect the rights of commoners. By the time of Edward III, the right to "due process of law" was recognized as protecting personal liberty. See Ingraham v. Wright, 430 U.S. 651, 673 n.41 (1977). Key later developments included the work of Sir Edward Coke in the early 17th century, and the enactment of the English Habeas Corpus Act of 1679 and Bill of Rights of 1689, the latter declaring the supremacy of Parliament and its laws over the power of the crown.

The founding fathers "were opposed to governments that placed in the hands of one man the power to make, interpret and enforce the laws." Duncan v. Kahanamoku, 327 U.S. 304, 322 (1946). The Fourth Circuit, in its Hamdi decision, well articulated the fear of arbitrary governmental power, and specifically unrestrained executive detentions, as a central focus of the Constitution:

> The Constitution is suffused with concern about how the state will yield its awesome power of forcible restraint. And this preoccupation was not accidental. Our forebears recognized that the power to detain could easily become destructive "if exerted without check or control" by an unrestrained executive free to "imprison, dispatch or exile any man that was obnoxious to the government by an instant declaration that such was their will and pleasure." 4 W. Blackstone, Commentaries on the Laws of England 349–50 (Cooley Ed. 1899) (quoted in Duncan v. Louisiana, 391 U.S. 145, 151 (1968)).

Hamdi, 316 F.3d at 464.

The rule of law finds its most explicit constitutional formulation in the Fifth Amendment's guarantee that no person may be "deprived of life, liberty, or property without due process of law...." The "touchstone of due process is protection of the individual against arbitrary action of government." Wolff v. McDonnell, 418 U.S. 539, 558 (1974). The right to due process has both substantive and procedural aspects:

> The Due Process Clause of the Fifth Amendment provides that "No person shall...be deprived of life, liberty, or property, without due process of law...." This Court has held that the Due Process Clause protects individuals against two types of government action. So-called "substantive due process" prevents the government from engaging in conduct that "shocks the conscience," Rochin v. California, 342 U.S. 165, 172 (1952), or interferes with rights "implicit in the concept of ordered liberty," Palko v. Connecticut, 302 U.S. 319, 325–326 (1937). When government action depriving a person of life, liberty, or property survives substantive due process scrutiny, it must still be implemented in a fair manner. Mathews v. Eldridge, 424 U.S. 319, 335 (1976). This requirement has traditionally been referred to as "procedural" due process.

United States v. Salerno, 481 U.S. 739, 746 (1987).

Due process requires an express statutory basis for detentions. Common law crimes, recognized in England, were held incompatible with our Constitution in United States v. Hudson, 11 U.S. 32 (1812). Much more recently, in 1971, Congress acted to rescind the Emergency Detention Act and to prevent any conduct similar to the internment of Americans of Japanese ancestry during World War II. Its remedy was to enact 18 U.S.C. § 4001(a), which provides:

> No citizen shall be imprisoned or otherwise detained by the United States except pursuant to an Act of Congress.

The Fourth Amendment protects not only against unreasonable searches for evidence, but also against arbitrary arrest and detention, in these words:

> The right of the people to be secure in their persons, houses, papers and effects, against unreasonable searches and seizures, shall not be violated, and no Warrants shall issue but upon probable cause,

supported by Oath or affirmation, and particularly describing the place to be searched, and the persons or things to be seized.

The "Fourth Amendment requires a judicial determination of probable cause as a prerequisite to extended restraint of liberty following arrest." Gerstein v. Pugh, 420 U.S. 103, 114 (1975);[7] County of Riverside v. McLaughlin, 500 U.S. 44 (1991) (Fourth Amendment requires prompt judicial determination of probable cause, within 48 hours of arrest, as prerequisite to extended pretrial detention following a warrantless arrest). "Probable cause exists if the facts and circumstances known to the officer warrant a prudent man in believing that the offense has been committed." Henry v. United States, 361 U.S. 98, 102 (1959).

The requirement that probable cause be promptly determined to justify a detention is not limited to the context of criminal prosecutions.[8] It also applies to detentions for investigatory purposes, even where there is no intention of charging the detainee with a crime. Davis v. Mississippi, 394 U.S. 721, 726–27 (1969); see Dunaway v. New York, 442 U.S. 200, 214–16 (1979); cf. United States v. Verdugo-Urquidez, 494 U.S. 259, 264 (1990) (Rehnquist, C.J., plurality opinion) (the Fourth Amendment is violated "at the time of an unreasonable governmental intrusion," and "whether or not the evidence is sought to be used in a criminal trial. . . .").

2. *No Indefinite Detentions (with Rare Exceptions)*

While recognizing exceptions, the Supreme Court has declared that "[i]n our society liberty is the norm, and detention prior to trial or without trial is the carefully limited exception." Salerno, 481 U.S. at 755 (emphasis added). See also id. at 749 (recognizing a "'general rule' of substantive due process that the government may not detain a person prior to a judgment of guilt in a criminal trial"); accord Foucha v. Louisiana, 504 U.S. 71, 83 (1992) ("our present system. . ., with only narrow exceptions and aside from permissible confinements for mental illness, incarcerates only those who are proved beyond reasonable doubt to have violated a criminal law"); Addington v. Texas, 441 U.S. 418, 425 (1979) ("This Court repeatedly has recognized that civil commitment for any purpose constitutes a significant deprivation of liberty that requires due process protection"); see Petition of Brooks, 5 F.2d 238, 239 (D. Mass. 1925) ("There is no power in this court or in any other tribunal in this country to hold indefinitely any sane citizen or alien in imprisonment, except as a punishment for crime").

Though from a dissenting opinion, the following comment on indefinite detentions likewise states the law of the land:

> Fortunately, it still is startling, in this country, to find a person held indefinitely in executive custody without accusation of crime or judicial trial. Executive imprisonment has been considered oppressive and lawless since John, at Runnymede, pledged that no free man should be imprisoned, dispossessed, outlawed or exiled save by the judgment of his peers or by the law of the land.

Shaughnessy v. Mezei, 345 U.S. 206, 218 (1953) (Jackson, J., dissenting from opinion upholding indefinite detention of an excludable alien, held at the border, based on confidential information the Attorney General refused to disclose, even in camera).

The Supreme Court recently declared that "[a] statute permitting indefinite detention of an alien would raise a serious constitutional problem." Zadvydas v. Davis, 533 U.S. 678, 690 (2001) (construing statute to authorize detention of removable aliens only for a "reasonable time," to avoid constitutional question presented by unlimited detention).[9] The Court explained:

> Freedom from imprisonment—from government custody, detention, or other forms of physical restraint—lies at the heart of the liberty [the Due Process] Clause protects. See *Foucha v. Louisiana,* 504 U.S. 71, 80 (1992). And this Court has said that government detention violates that Clause unless the detention is

ordered in a *criminal* proceeding with adequate procedural protections, see *United States v. Salerno,* 481 U.S. 739, 746 (1987), or, in certain special and "narrow" nonpunitive "circumstances," *Foucha, supra,* at 80, where a special justification, such as harm-threatening mental illness, outweighs the "individual's constitutionally protected interest in avoiding physical restraint." *Kansas v. Hendricks,* 521 U.S. 346, 356 (1997).

Id., 533 U.S. at 690.

Kansas v. Hendricks, cited by the Court, upheld the constitutionality of indeterminate civil commitments when a continuing condition of mental illness precluded release, in the interests of the detainee or of public safety. The Kansas statutory scheme passed muster, in important part, because the detainee was guaranteed periodic review by a court to determine whether the condition justifying the detention persisted. Hendricks, 521 U.S. at 364 (annual judicial hearing and finding required to continue commitment).

Dangerousness is the other basis on which the Court has found preventive detention consistent with due process. To pass muster, the detention must serve regulatory rather than punitive purposes: "For under the Due Process Clause, a detainee may not be punished prior to an adjudication of guilt in accordance with due process of law." Bell v. Wolfish, 441 U.S. 520, 535 (1979). Prior to trial, bail can be denied under the Bail Reform Act of 1984, 18 U.S.C. §§ 3141, 3142, after an adversary hearing, on a finding upon "clear and convincing evidence" that no conditions of release "will reasonably assure. . . the safety of any other person and the community."[10] This provision was upheld as a permissible "regulation", and not a punitive measure, in United States v. Salerno, 481 U.S. 739, 746–48 (1987).[11] See United States v. El-Hage, 213 F.3d 74, 80 (2d Cir. 2000), cert. denied, 531 U.S. 881 (2001) (pretrial detention of 30–33 months did not violate due process given, inter alia, gravity of charges against defendant, accused of playing a vital role in al Qaeda, which poses "a substantial threat to national security"). Similarly in Schall v. Martin, 467 U.S. 253 (1984), the Court upheld a statute permitting "a brief pretrial detention" of a juvenile—for a maximum of 17 days (id. at 270)—on a finding that there was a "serious risk" he might commit a crime before the return date. Again, this holding was premised on the conclusion that this statute served the legitimate regulatory and nonpunitive purpose of "protecting both the community and the juvenile himself from the consequences of future criminal conduct." Id. at 264.

In its 2001 Zadvydas opinion, the Supreme Court summarized its preventive detention cases, to the extent based on the dangerousness of the detainees, as follows:

> . . .we have upheld preventive detention based on dangerousness only when limited to specially dangerous individuals and subject to strong procedural protections.

Zadvydas v. Davis, 533 U.S. at 690–91.[12]

There is one 1909 case in which no such "strong procedural protections" were present. The Governor of Colorado detained a union leader for two and one-half months during a "state of insurrection" created by labor strife, until "fears of the insurrection were at an end." Moyer v. Peabody, 212 U.S. 78, 84–85 (1909). After the unionist had been released, he brought suit for damages, claiming the Governor's actions had violated his due process rights. The Court, based on findings that the Governor had acted in good faith, though "without sufficient reason," found no constitutional violation and affirmed dismissal of the damage suit. Justice Holmes' language for the majority was expansive:

> When it comes to a decision by the head of the State upon a matter involving its life, the ordinary rights of individuals must yield to what he deems the necessities of the moment. Public danger warrants the substitution of executive process for judicial process. . . .This was admitted with regard to killing men in the

> actual clash of arms; and we think it obvious, although it was disputed, that the same is true of temporary detention to prevent apprehended harm.

Id. at 85 (citation omitted).[13]

Moyer seems to stand alone in approving an indefinite detention by a local official. See, generally, Note, Riot Control and the Fourth Amendment, 81 Harv. L. Rev. 625, 632–35 (1968). However, it may have some continued relevance to the war on terror.[14]

B. Procedural Rights

1. *Right to a Hearing*

A constitutional right without a remedy for its violation would be antithetical to our system of government under law. The rule of law would mean little

> if the laws furnish no remedy for the violation of a vested legal right.

Marbury v. Madison, 5 U.S. 137, 167 (1803).

The nature of the procedural remedy available to contest a detention is governed by the due process clause. Procedural due process is not a rigid concept. "Due process is flexible and calls for such procedural protections as the particular situation demands." Morrissey v. Brewer, 408 U.S. 471, 481 (1972); see Gilbert v. Homar, 520 U.S. 924, 930 (1997). But while flexible, the courts have evolved certain basic concepts that provide a baseline of individual rights in most circumstances.

The "fundamental right of due process," the Supreme Court has held, "is the opportunity to be heard 'at a meaningful time and in a meaningful manner.'" Mathews v. Eldridge, 424 U.S. 319, 333 (1976), quoting Armstrong v. Manzo, 380 U.S. 545, 552 (1965). See Nat'l Council of Resistance v. Dep't of State, 251 F.3d 192, 208–09 (D.C. Cir. 2001) (designation of terrorist organizations); cf. Yakus v. United States, 321 U.S. 414, 433 (1944) (in context of wartime price control regulations, due process requires that those affected by an administrative order be afforded "a reasonable opportunity to be heard and present evidence").

When the Due Process Clause requires a hearing, "it requires a fair one, one before a tribunal which meets at least currently prevailing standards of impartiality." Wang Yang Sung v. McGrath, 339 U.S. 33, 50 (1950). The particular kind of hearing required will vary in accordance with the relative gravity of the private and public interests at stake in the governmental action challenged. See generally Henry J. Friendly, Some Kind of Hearing, 123 U. of Pa. L. Rev. 1267 (1975).

A person cannot be detained, for more than a short period of time, without being afforded a hearing concerning the legality of his detention. Aside from the immigration context, a detention requires an evidentiary hearing, generally to be conducted by the courts, rather than by an administrative agency, or subject to prompt review by the courts. See Zadvydas v. Davis, 533 U.S. at 692 (noting constitutional problem posed by unreviewable agency determinations affecting fundamental rights). In the criminal context, the initial hearing after an arrest is nonadversarial, conducted by a magistrate to determine probable cause, but the Sixth Amendment's guarantee of a "speedy and public trial" dictates that a full blown evidentiary hearing will soon follow.

2. *Habeas Corpus: The Right of Access to the Federal Courts*

The fundamental procedural remedy to obtain a hearing to test the legality of a detention is the writ of habeas corpus. 28 U.S.C. § 2241. The federal courts have jurisdiction to hear claims that a person is being held "in custody in violation of the Constitution or laws...of the United States." 28 U.S.C. § 2241(c)(3). See Harris v. Nelson, 394 U.S. 286, 290–91 (1969):

> The writ of habeas corpus is the fundamental instrument for safeguarding individual freedom against arbitrary and lawless state action.

If the petition makes specific allegations of fact that, if true, would invalidate the detention, "it is the duty of the court to provide the necessary facilities and procedures for an adequate inquiry" into those facts. Id., 394 U.S. at 300.

The writ, with origins as early as the 14th century in England, was first codified in the English Habeas Corpus Act of 1679, 31 Car. II, c. 2. See generally R.J. Sharpe, The Law of Habeas Corpus (1976). This Act required the jailer, on service of the Writ, to produce the prisoner (except in cases of treason or felony), and to "certify the true causes of his detainer or imprisonment," which led to the release of the prisoner on bail unless the detention was upon a legal process, by a court of jurisdiction, for an offense "for which by the law the prisoner is not bailable...."

The "Great Writ" was guaranteed by the Constitution in Article I, section 9:

> The privilege of the Writ of Habeas Corpus shall not be suspended, unless when in Cases of Rebellion or Invasion, the public Safety may require.[15]

Again the Fourth Circuit's decision in Hamdi well states the role of the writ in our system:

> In war as in peace, habeas corpus provides one of the firmest bulwarks against unconstitutional detentions. As early as 1789, Congress reaffirmed the courts' common law authority to review detention of federal prisoners, giving its explicit blessing to the judiciary's power to 'grant Writs of Habeas Corpus for the purpose of an inquiry into the cause of commitment' for federal detainees. Act of Sept. 24, 1789, ch. 20, § 14, 1 Stat. 81–82. While the scope of habeas review has expanded and contracted over the succeeding centuries, its essential function of assuring that restraint accords with the rule of law, not the whim of authority, remains unchanged.

Hamdi, at 464–65.

More concisely put:

> The historic purpose of the writ has been to relieve detention by executive authorities without judicial trial. Brown v. Allen, 344 U.S. 443, 533 (1953) (Jackson, J., concurring), quoted in Zadvydas v. Davis, 533 U.S. at 699.

See also INS v. St. Cyr, 533 U.S. 289, 301 (2001):

> At its historical core, the writ of habeas corpus has served as a means of reviewing the legality of Executive detention, and it is in that context that its protection has been strongest.

3. *Right to Consult an Attorney (and Usually to Be Represented by One)*

The right to file a writ of habeas corpus provides basic access to the federal courts to test the legality of a detention.[16] But for that right of access and any consequent right to a hearing to be meaningful, legal representation is often a near necessity. The "right to be heard would be, in many cases, of little avail if it did not comprehend the right to be heard by counsel." Powell v. Alabama, 287 U.S. 45, 68–69 (1932).

In criminal prosecutions in federal courts, the Sixth Amendment's guarantee of the accused's right "to have the Assistance of Counsel for his defense" long has been construed to require "the appointment of counsel in all cases where a defendant is unable to procure the services of an attorney...." Betts v. Brady, 316 U.S. 455, 464 (1942).[17]

The constitutional right to legal representation by governmental detainees not charged with a crime is measured by the Due Process Clause.[18] The general test of due process rights outside the criminal and military justice contexts, including whether a right to appointed counsel should be afforded, turns on the three-part balancing test articulated in Mathews v. Eldridge, 424 U.S. 319, 335 (1976). The private interests and the government interests at stake must be weighed, together with the risk of "an erroneous deprivation" of the private interest absent the additional procedural safeguard sought.

While the Mathews v. Eldridge balancing test can require some nice judgments, it seems clear—war power issues aside—that a person faced with a significant period of physical detention has a due process right to counsel to test the legality of the detention. The "fundamental fairness" required by due process requires the appointment of counsel for any indigent litigant who "may lose his physical liberty if he loses the litigation." Lassiter v. Dep't of Social Servs., 452 U.S. 18, 25 (1981) (adopting a case-by-case approach to the right to appointed counsel in parental termination proceedings). It is "the defendant's interest in personal freedom, and not simply the special Sixth and Fourteenth Amendments right to counsel in criminal cases, which triggers the right to appointed counsel...." Id. See In re Gault, 387 U.S. 1, 41 (1967) (since juvenile delinquency proceeding, though civil, may result "in commitment to an institution in which the juvenile's freedom is curtailed," due process mandates appointment of counsel).

Generally, cases concerning a due process right to counsel have focused on the right to appointed counsel, at government expense. But occasionally the right to have retained counsel participate in hearings has been discussed. In the context of welfare benefit termination proceedings, "the recipient must be allowed to retain an attorney if he so desires." Goldberg v. Kelly, 397 U.S. 254, 270 (1970). But the direct participation of even retained counsel may be prohibited in certain proceedings which have only limited consequences, or where an informal, non-adversarial hearing system furthers important governmental interests.[19] Even in these situations where counsel may not attend a hearing, there seems no question that consultation with retained counsel outside the hearing room is permissible. The concept of incommunicado detentions appears to be without precedent, at least outside of the law of war.

4. *Additional Rights in Criminal Prosecutions*

In the context of criminal prosecutions, additional fundamental rights apply. The Fifth Amendment secures the right against double jeopardy and self-incrimination. The Sixth Amendment provides other critical rights:

> In all criminal prosecutions, the accused shall enjoy the right to a speedy and public trial, by an impartial jury...and to be informed of the nature and cause of the accusations; to be confronted with the witnesses against him; to have compulsory process for obtaining witnesses in his favor, and to have the assistance of counsel for his defense."[20]

The Supreme Court articulated this litany of a criminal defendant's rights in Herrera v. Collins, 506 U.S. 390, 398–99 (1993):

> A person when first charged with a crime is entitled to a presumption of innocence, and may insist that his guilt be established beyond a reasonable doubt. In re Winship, 397 U.S. 358 (1970). Other constitutional provisions also have the effect of ensuring against the risk of convicting an innocent person. See, e.g., Coy v. Iowa, 487 U.S. 1012 (1988) (right to confront adverse witnesses); Taylor v. Illinois, 484 U.S. 400 (1988) (right to compulsory process); Strickland v. Washington, 466 U.S. 668 (1984) (right to effective assistance of counsel); Winship, *supra* (prosecution must prove guilt beyond a reasonable doubt); Duncan v. Louisiana, 391 U.S. 145 (right to jury trial); Brady v. Maryland,... [373 U.S. 83 (1963)] (1968) (prosecution must disclose exculpatory evidence); Gideon v. Wainwright, 372 U.S. 335 (1963) (right to assistance of counsel); In re Murchison, 349 U.S. 133, 136 (1944) (right to "fair trial in a fair tribunal").[21]

All of these rights apply only to criminal defendants, and therefore do not apply to detainees against whom no criminal charges have been filed. However, as discussed above, due process precludes more than a brief detention without the proffer of charges. Thus the government is put to a prompt choice: it must either release a detainee, or institute criminal charges and thereby trigger the application of the Fifth and Sixth Amendment rights of a criminal defendant.

C. The Applicability of Core Principles Abroad: To Citizens, but Generally not to Foreign Nationals

To what extent does the application of due process rights turn on whether the detainee is seized in the United States or abroad, or on where the detainee is held subsequent to his initial detention?

Broadly speaking, citizens have the same rights abroad, with respect to actions taken by agents of the United States, as they would with respect to such actions taken within the country. The constitutional rights of citizens—or at minimum those rights deemed "fundamental"—apply anywhere in the world, though always subject to a review of what due process requires under the "particular situation" presented. See United States v. Verdugo-Urquidez, supra, 494 U.S. at 275–78 (Kennedy J., concurring); Reid v. Covert, 354 U.S. 1 (1957) (plurality would so hold with respect to all constitutional rights; concurring opinions would limit to fundamental rights).

In contrast, foreign nationals subject to detention or other action abroad by United States agents generally do not enjoy constitutional protection,[22] including the right to present a habeas corpus petition. The leading case is Johnson v. Eisentrager, 339 U.S. 763 (1950). The petitioners were German nationals convicted of violating the law of war in World War II by furnishing intelligence to Japanese forces in China. They were convicted by a military commission sitting in China with that government's permission, following which petitioners were sent to Germany to serve out their sentences in a military prison. From Germany they filed petitions for writs of habeas corpus, claiming that their right to due process under the Fifth Amendment had been violated. See id. at 765–66.

The district court dismissed the petitions, but the Court of Appeals reversed, holding that any person, including an enemy alien, deprived of his liberty anywhere in the world under the purported authority of the United States is entitled to the writ if he can show his imprisonment to be illegal under any constitutional right. See id. at 767. The Supreme Court reversed the Court of Appeals. The Court wrote:

> We are cited to no instance where a court, in this or any other country where the writ is known, has issued it on behalf of an alien enemy who, at no relevant time and in no stage of his captivity, has been within its territorial jurisdiction. Nothing in the text of the Constitution extends such a right, nor does anything in our statutes.

Id. at 768.

It is, principally, on the precedent of Johnson that the alien suspected terrorists and Taliban fighters held at Guantánamo Bay, Cuba, allegedly outside the sovereign territory of the United States, have been held without any access to U.S. courts via habeas corpus proceedings. Coalition of Clergy v. Bush, 189 F. Supp. 2d 1036 (C.D. Cal.), vacated in part, 310 F.3d 1153 (9th Cir. 2002). But the contrary result was reached in Gherebi v. Bush, No. CV-03-01267 (9th Cir. Dec. 18, 2003), distinguishing the legal status of Guantánamo Bay from that of the prison in Germany involved in Johnson. On November 10, 2003, the Supreme Court granted certiorari in two cases to consider the question of whether "United States courts lack jurisdiction to consider challenges to the legality of the detention of foreign nationals captured abroad in connection with hostilities and incarcerated at the Guantánamo Naval Base, Cuba." Al Odah v. United States, 321 F.3d 1134 (D.C. Cir. 2003), cert. granted, 2003 WL 22070725 (No. 03-343); *Rasul v. Bush*, 215 F. Supp. 2d 55 (D.D.C. 2002), aff'd, 321 F.3d 1134 (D.C. Cir.), cert. granted, 72 U.S.L.W. 3323 (No. 03-334).

D. The Rights of Foreign Nationals in the United States

To what extent do the substantive and procedural due process rights reviewed above apply to foreign nationals detained in the United States? Do they have the same rights as citizens? See generally David Cole, Enemy Aliens, 54 Stan. L. Rev. 953, 978-85 (2002).

Generally, there is no distinction between the procedural due process rights of citizens and those of aliens who are within the jurisdiction of the United States.[23] Procedural due process rights apply to any alien who has entered the country, legally or illegally. Zadvydas v. Davis, 533 U.S. 678, 693–94 (2001); see, e.g., Reno v. Flores, 507 U.S. 292, 306 (1993); Wong Wing v. United States, 163 U.S. 228, 238 (1896); Yick Wo. v. Hopkins, 118 U.S. 356, 369 (1886); Patel v. Zemski, 275 F.3d 299, 307 (3d Cir. 2001).[24]

In contrast to these procedural protections applicable to aliens, their substantive rights to remain in the country are subject to almost unlimited restriction or termination by Congress —"plenary power"—and correspondingly little judicial review:

> Courts have long recognized the power to expel or exclude aliens as a fundamental sovereign attribute exercised by the Government's political departments largely immune from judicial control.

Shaughnessy v. United States ex rel. Mezei, 345 U.S. 206, 210 (1953) (upholding indefinite detention of removable alien held at border, based on national security grounds not disclosed by Attorney General).[25] The Supreme Court has observed that "Congress regularly makes rules [governing aliens] that would be unacceptable if applied to citizens," Matthews v. Diaz, 426 U.S. 67, 80 (1976), a proposition "firmly and repeatedly endorsed," most recently in Demore v. Kim, 538 U.S. 510, 128 S. Ct. 1708 (2003) (case involved "lawful permanent resident"). Further, "when the Government deals with deportable aliens, the Due Process Clause does not require it to employ the least burdensome means to accomplish its goal." Id., 128 S. Ct. at 1720. The rationale for the great discretion accorded Congress with respect to legislation concerning the exclusion or departure of aliens—and the deference accorded to the executive in implementing such legislation—is that "any policy toward aliens is vitally and intricately interwoven with contemporaneous policies in regard to the conduct of foreign relations, the war power and the maintenance of a republican form of government." Id., 128 S. Ct. at 1716 (quoting Mathews, 426 U.S. at 81 n.17, quoting Harisiades v. Shaughnessy, 342 U.S. 580, 588–89 (1952).

Specifically, the Court in *Demore* recognized that "[d]etention during removal proceedings is a constitutionally permissible part" of the deportation process." Id., 128 S. Ct. at 1721–22. The Court sustained the constitutionality of 8 U.S.C. § 1226(c), which requires that deportable aliens convicted of aggravated felonies be detained during "the limited period" of removal proceedings, regardless of whether they constitute a flight risk or threat to the community.[26] The Court contrasted the "limited" and finite period of detention occasioned by removal proceedings—about 47 days on average, plus another four months in the event of an appeal (id., 128 S. Ct. at 1721)—with the "indefinite" and "potentially permanent" detention held constitutionally suspect in Zadvydas of an alien already found to be removable, but not removable as a practical matter. Id., 128 S. Ct. at 1720. In Zadvydas, the Court had found that such continued detention "no longer bear[s] [a] reasonable relation to the purpose for which the individual [was] committed." Id., quoting Zadvydas, 533 U.S. at 690, quoting Jackson v. Indiana, 406 U.S. 715, 738 (1972).

Thus an alien can be deported on any ground sanctioned by Congress, but is entitled to procedural due process with respect to such deportation proceedings. While detention is permissible for the "limited period" during which removal proceedings are pending, this detention must be based on specific charges warranting removal by statute, and on which a hearing will be held resulting in removal if sustained. An indefinite detention without charges would appear no more constitutional for an alien within the country than for a citizen.

E. Hierarchy of Rights

We believe that the above discussion confirms that there is a hierarchy of rights recognized in times of peace, firmly imbedded in our constitutional structure and case law. These rights include, with respect to citizens or aliens detained in the United States or its sovereign territory:

- the right not to be detained except pursuant to a statute authorizing the detention;
- the right (subject to inapplicable exceptions noted above) not to be detained without the prompt proffer of specific criminal charges;
- the right to test the legality of the detention in the federal courts through the writ of habeas corpus and, where the matter has not been previously adjudicated, at a meaningful evidentiary hearing;
- the right to consult with and to be represented by counsel concerning the detention, and in connection with a habeas corpus hearing challenging it.

Our system precludes—again, before considering the implications of the war powers—indefinite detentions without charges, with the detainee held incommunicado without access to a lawyer. Further, the legality of any detention should be testable through the writ of habeas corpus made effective through the assistance of counsel, at least where the detainee is able to retain counsel.

III. POSSIBLE LIMITATIONS AND EXCEPTIONS TO CORE DUE PROCESS RIGHTS, BASED ON THE WAR POWERS

We now review the possible restraints and limitations upon the above core due process values and rights when the President acts in the exercise of his war-making power under Article II of the Constitution. Do the precedents require or suggest that the core rights discussed above, at the heart of our self-identity as a society existing under the rule of law, are inapplicable to persons designated "enemy combatants" by the President, as Commander in Chief prosecuting the war on terror? To what extent can the President so act without congressional authorization? Are these questions for the courts, or rather for the political process?

A. The War Powers

Article I, section 8, of the Constitution grants Congress the power to "provide for the common Defense and general Welfare of the United States...To declare War, grant letters of Marque and Reprisal, and make Rules concerning Captures on Land and Water; To raise and support Armies...and To provide and maintain a Navy." Article II, section 2, declares that "the President shall be Commander in Chief of the Army and Navy of the United States, and of the Militia of the several states, when called into the actual Service of the United States."

The Constitution is held to invest "the President, as Commander in Chief, with the power to wage war which Congress has declared, and to carry into effect all laws passed by Congress for the conduct of war and for the government and regulation of the Armed Forces, and all laws defining and punishing offences against the law of nations, including those which pertain to the conduct of war." Quirin, 317 U.S. at 26. But the scope of the President's powers as Commander in Chief is not clearly defined by Article II, section 2: "These cryptic words have given rise to some of the most persistent controversies in our constitutional history." Youngstown Sheet &. Tube Co. v. Sawyer, 343 U.S. 579, 641 (1952) (Jackson, J., concurring). Few cases—other than Hamdi and Padilla—have considered the authority of the President to detain "enemy combatants" or similar individuals. However, a review of the main stress periods faced by the country reveals some limited case law construing the President's war power and discussing the role of the courts in reviewing exercises of that power.

B. An Historical Perspective

1. *Cases before the Civil War*

Before the Civil War the government used military forces on a number of occasions as a domestic policing force, seizing and holding rebellious or otherwise threatening citizens by a process neither commenced nor supervised by the civilian courts. See Ex parte Milligan, 71 U.S. 2, 50–53 (1866) ("Milligan") (referring to instances of military arrests during Revolutionary War, Shay's Rebellion, and Gen. Andrew Jackson's occupation of New Orleans). The early Supreme Court opinions that discussed the degree of deference owed the President in a national security crisis did not directly address the executive's power to deprive individuals of their liberty. Nonetheless, those decisions concerned related problems occasioned by coercive executive action, and they provided a portion of the analytical framework that has been followed in later cases governing the seizure of individuals suspected of posing a threat to public safety in times of crisis.

The first of these decisions was triggered by President Madison's call-up of the state militias during the War of 1812. Martin v. Mott, 25 U.S. 19 (1827). That step was authorized by a 1795 statute permitting the President to activate the state militias for duty in time of "imminent danger of invasion" or insurrection. Mott had refused to report for militia duty, and as a result was court-martialed, fined and then sentenced to prison by the military authorities when he failed to pay the fine. He sought relief from the civilian courts, in which, among other things, he challenged the validity of the call-up order.

The Supreme Court rejected the notion that the civilian courts may review the President's decision, instead characterizing the President's power as "exclusive" and his decision as "conclusive upon all other persons." Id. at 30. In reaching this conclusion, the Court emphasized not only the wording of the statute, which it read as conferring unlimited discretion on the President to determine whether the danger of invasion existed, but also the impracticality of vesting final authority on that question in the courts. Speed was key:

> The power itself is to be exercised upon sudden emergencies, upon great occasions of state, and under circumstances which may be vital to the existence of the Union. A prompt and unhesitating obedience to orders is indispensable to the complete attainment of the object. The service is a military service, and the command of a military nature; and in such cases, every delay, and every obstacle to an efficient and immediate compliance, necessarily tend to jeopardize the public interests. Id.

According to the Court, any other interpretation of the President's powers would undermine his authority, delegated by Congress, to "regulat[e] the militia and to command[] its services in times of insurrection and invasion." Id. at 30 (quoting The Federalist No. 29).

Apart from the dangers posed by delay inherent in any resort to the courts, the Supreme Court noted other potential inadequacies of the court processes as an instrument of review in such an emergency. Thus, it observed that the grounds for the President's decision "might be of a nature not constituting strict technical proof" and that the disclosure of such information "might reveal important secrets of state, which the public interest, and even safety might imperiously demand to be kept in concealment." Id. at 31.[27]

The inclination of the Supreme Court to defer to the President during a military confrontation, both for constitutional and for practical reasons, was subsequently reiterated in Luther v. Borden, 48 U.S. 1 (1849). The case arose out of the so-called Dorr's Rebellion in Rhode Island. The narrow issue in Luther involved a claim for trespass asserted by a Rhode Island resident in the wake of a state militia's entry into his home during an armed confrontation between two political factions, each claiming to represent the state government. The principal holding of the Court concerned its interpretation of the so-called Guarantee Clause of the Constitution (Art. IV, § 4), which it viewed as leaving to the political branches of the federal government the determination of which faction was the legitimate government of the state. Id. at 41–43.

The Court noted that, under the Guarantee Clause, the Congress is responsible for determining the legitimate government of each state, and has specific responsibility for ensuring the protection of such government against "invasion" and, on request of the state legislature or governor, against "domestic violence". Congress in turn had delegated to the President, by the Act of 1795, the authority to decide whether to call out the militias of the various states to protect a state government against "insurrection" as well as "invasion". Id. at 42–43 (citing Act of Feb. 28, 1795). This constitutional and statutory arrangement required the President to decide which competing faction is the legitimate state government, since that would be a predicate to his determination whether to provide federal protection upon the request of the ostensible state authorities. Id. at 43. Once the President made that decision, practical limitations precluded judicial review:

> After the President has acted and called out the militia, is a Circuit Court of the United States authorized to inquire whether his decision was right? Could the court, while the parties were actually contending in arms for the possession of the government, call witnesses before it and inquire which party represented a majority of the people? If it could, then it would become the duty of the court (provided it came to the conclusion that the President had decided incorrectly) to discharge those who were arrested or detained by the troops in the service of the United States or the government which the President was endeavoring to maintain. If the judicial power extends so far, the guarantee contained in the Constitution of the United States is a guarantee of anarchy, and not of order.

Id. The judicial process was manifestly inadequate to decide these sorts of issues in the midst of conflict:

> When citizens of the same State are in arms against each other, and the constituted authorities unable to execute the laws, the interposition of the United States must be prompt, or it is of little value. The ordinary course of proceedings in courts of justice would be utterly unfit for the crisis.

Id. at 44.

Having concluded that the courts have no role to play in reviewing a President's recognition of a state faction "when the conflict is raging," the Luther Court went on to conclude, as a logical extension, that such judicial power also cannot be constitutionally invoked "when the contest is over." Id. at 43. In short, this type of decision was left to the unreviewable discretion of the political branches of Government.[28] Significantly, the court likened the power of the President to choose among competing state factions to his unquestioned authority to determine which foreign governments to recognize. Id. at 44.

2. *Civil War Cases*

Prior to the Civil War, such matters as the applicability of the Bill of Rights in wartime were "unstudied in law schools, ignored in universities, and unknown in West Point," since such questions had not previously arisen. Harold Hyman, A More Perfect Union: The Impact of the Civil War and Reconstruction on the Constitution 66 (1973) ("Hyman"). Early in the War, President Lincoln declared martial law to be applicable to citizens engaging in disloyal conduct, thus subjecting them to prosecution by courts martial or military commission, and, at the same time, suspending the writ of habeas corpus for such individuals. See Milligan, 71 U.S. at 15–16 (quoting Proclamation dated Sept. 24, 1862).[29] Persons suspected of disloyalty or at least sympathy towards the Confederacy were arrested by federal military and local authorities. These individuals were typically not processed through any civilian court, but rather were either released after subscribing to a loyalty oath, or tried by a military commission, or simply held under some other ad hoc arrangement. See, e.g., Ex parte Vallandigham, 68 U.S. 243, 244–47 (1863). Trials by commission are said to have been extremely rare, in areas where the regular courts were functioning, "since the normal method of dealing with persons suspected of treasonable activity was arrest without warrants, detention without trial, and release without punishment...." Clinton Rossiter, The Supreme Court and the Commander in Chief 28 (1951) ("Rossiter"). Where the military authorities did not trust the civil courts, the practice was "to keep the suspects locked up until the danger had passed." Id. at 36.[30]

While a number of individuals swept up by these measures challenged their detentions in the courts,[31] few challenges resulted in judicial decisions. The Supreme Court, in Ex parte Vallandigham, supra, held itself without jurisdiction to review proceedings before military commissions. See Hyman at 261–62.

One decision of note, though of little practical consequence, was rendered early in the war by Chief Justice Taney, sitting in his capacity as circuit judge. Ex parte Merryman, 17 F. Cas. 144 (1861). The petitioner, a civilian seized by the military in Baltimore,[32] sought release by a habeas petition. Justice Taney ordered the United States Marshal to produce Merryman, but the Marshal proved incapable of doing so because the military authorities in Baltimore would not surrender their prisoner. Id. at 147–48. Taney settled for issuing an opinion in which he held that Merryman's detention violated due process and that the courts had the authority to so rule.

Taney first held that the President himself was not authorized to suspend the writ, a power assigned by the Constitution exclusively to Congress. Id. at 148–50. He then went much further, holding that, regardless of whether the writ was suspended by Congress, the President lacked the authority to arrest a private citizen—that is, "a party not subject to the rules and articles of war"—without judicial process. Id. at 149. The only pertinent authority of the President was to "take care that the laws are faithfully executed", which required him to come to the aid of the judiciary, not to bypass it.[33]

The fact that the country faced a military emergency was, in Justice Taney's view, inconsequential for this point: "I can see no ground whatever for supposing that the president, in any emergency, or in any state of things, can authorize the suspension of the privileges of the writ of habeas corpus, or the arrest of a citizen, except in aid of the judicial power." Id. The federal courts and criminal justice system were functioning, without "the slightest resistance or obstruction," and "there was no reason whatever for the interposition of the military." Therefore the controlling requirements of the Constitution, including due process and the right to a public trial "in a court of justice" still applied, precluding petitioner's seizure and detention by the military. Id. at 152. To Taney, this conclusion flowed from English constitutional law as well as from the Fifth Amendment's guarantee of due process. Id. at 149–50 (citing inter alia "the great habeas corpus act", 31 Car. II).

The full Court gave a broader reading to the President's war power the next year in The Prize Cases, 67 U.S. 635 (1862). An executive order imposing a maritime blockade on a number of Confederate states had led to the seizure of numerous ships and their cargoes. In upholding the President's powers against the claims of cargo and ship owners—including some who disclaimed any sympathy for the Confederate secession—the Supreme Court emphasized traditional principles of international law regarding an executive's powers in wartime, as well as the President's statutory power to use the military to defend against invasion or insurrection. Id. at 668 (citing Acts of Feb. 28, 1795 and March 3, 1807). There had been no formal declaration of war by Congress, but a state of war plainly existed, a war "all the world acknowledges to be the greatest civil war known in the history of the human race...." Id. at 669. The Court emphasized that the determination of what measures were required to counter the insurrection was left to the judicially unreviewable discretion of the President:

> Whether the President in fulfilling his duties, as Commander-in-chief, in suppressing an insurrection has met with such armed hostile resistance, and a civil war of such alarming proportions as will compel him to accord to them the character of belligerents, is a question to be decided by him, and this Court must be governed by the decisions and acts of the political department of the Government to which this power was entrusted. 'He must determine what degree of force the crisis demands.' The proclamation of blockade is itself official and conclusive evidence to the Court that a state of war existed which demanded and authorized a recourse to such a measure under the circumstances peculiar to the case.

Id. at 670 (emphasis in original).[34] Thus, although the Court, echoing Merryman in this respect, defined a civil war in terms of hostilities that prevented the functioning of the "Courts of Justice" (id. at 667–68), it effectively left to the executive the determination of whether such a state of war existed, as well as the degree of force to be used in responding to the insurrection.

3. *After the Civil War: Milligan*

A year after the Civil War, the pendulum swung back toward a narrow reading of the President's war power in Milligan. During the War, Milligan had been arrested by order of the commander of the military district of Indiana, tried before a military commission for crimes relating to his membership in a secret organization sympathetic to the Confederacy, found guilty and sentenced to be hanged.[35] Milligan then proceeded by petition for a writ of habeas corpus in the federal circuit court, challenging the authority of the military to try him given his status as a citizen of a non-belligerent state.

The government, in its brief, boldly asserted that the Bill of Rights was inoperable in wartime:

> [T]hese provisions of the Constitution, like all other conventional and legislative laws and enactments, are silent amidst arms, when the safety of the people becomes the supreme law.

Quoted in Rehnquist at 21.

The Supreme Court, however, upheld Milligan's challenge to his conviction, holding that the military commission had no jurisdiction to try and convict a civilian resident of a non-belligerent state. The constitutional guarantees against trial and punishment except in accordance with the Bill of Rights were unaffected by the War: "The Constitution of the United States is a law for rulers and people, equally in war and in peace, and covers...all classes of men at all times, and under all circumstances." Id. at 120–21. The fact of civil disorder only emphasized the need to preserve these protections:

> [I]f the society is disturbed by civil commotion—if the passions of men are aroused and the restraints of law weakened, if not disregarded—these safeguards need, and should receive, the watchful care of those intrusted with the guardianship of the Constitution and laws.

Id. at 121–22.[36]

The Court summarily rejected the contention that the military commission could try Milligan "under the law and usages of war," holding that such law and usages "can never be applied to citizens in states [such as Indiana] which have upheld the authority of the government, and where the courts are open and their process unobstructed." Id. at 121. Cf. Caldwell v. Parker, 252 U.S. 376, 386–87 (1920) (soldier may be prosecuted in state court, since local courts were open and functioning; military law did not supplant them in wartime). If citizens in non-battlefield states plotted to aid the enemy, they could be arrested and held for trial in the regular courts, which must be deemed adequate to deal with such criminal conduct. Milligan at 126–27. Only in battlefield areas—where the civilian courts were effectively closed—could the military substitute its processes for those of the courts, and only until those courts resumed operation. Id. at 127.

The Milligan holding thus limited the executive's power to proceed by military commission. But the Court in dictum went further, stating that even Congress could not, consistent with the Constitution, authorize the use of military commissions in the fashion that led to Milligan's conviction. Id. at 122. In contrast, four justices in a concurring opinion concluded to the contrary:

> We cannot doubt that, in such a time of public danger, Congress had power, under the Constitution, to provide for the organization of a military commission, and for trial by that commission of persons engaged in this conspiracy.

Id. at 140.[37]

Several Reconstruction cases offered the Supreme Court the opportunity to expand upon its holding in Milligan, but those cases were decided solely on jurisdictional grounds.[38] Some later decisions by state courts and lower federal courts upheld military trials of civilians in the context of violent labor unrest and declarations of martial law by Governors. But the "basis of those decisions was definitely held erroneous in Sterling v. Constantin, 287 U.S. 378 [1932], where the Court said: 'What are the allowable limits of military discretion and whether or not they have been overstepped in a particular case, are judicial questions.' Id. at 401." Duncan v. Kahanamoku, 327 U.S. 304, 321 n.18 (1946). See p. 18, n.13, supra, discussing Sterling.

4. *World War II: Quirin*

World War I did not result in any Supreme Court decision directly focusing on our subject,[39] but the extent of the President's (and Congress's) war powers was revisited in a number of decisions during and after World War II.

In Ex parte Quirin, 317 U.S. 1 (1942) ("Quirin"), the Court upheld the President's use of a military commission to try enemy saboteurs who had been arrested by the FBI after entering the country surreptitiously and in civilian garb for the purpose of carrying out acts of sabotage, operating under German military command. The FBI turned these "illegal belligerents" (id. at 35) or "unlawful combatants" (id. at 31) over to the military for trial before a military commission, pursuant to a Presidential order. The order seemed at odds with the Milligan holding, for clearly the civilian courts were open and functioning. Id. at 23–24. But unlike Milligan, which concerned actions taken by military commanders, the commission reviewed in Quirin had been specifically authorized by the President, and the President, in turn, had been generally authorized by Congress to convene military commissions to try offenses against the law of war. Id. at 26–27.

At the close of the evidentiary presentation before the commission, the saboteurs sought a writ of habeas corpus in federal district court, contending that the commission had no jurisdiction to try them. In opposition the government contended that the petitioners, as illegal combatants, had no right to habeas review by the courts.[40] Alternatively the Government contended that the President had permissibly exercised his powers as Commander in Chief in ordering a military trial for violations of the law of wars. The Court phrased the "question for decision" before it as follows:

> whether the detention of petitioners by respondent for trial by Military Commission, appointed by Order of the President of July 4, 1942, on charges proffered against them purporting to set out their violations of the law of war and of the Articles of War, is in conformity to the laws and the Constitution of the United States. Id. at 18–19.[41]

The answer was affirmative, because violations of the law of war[42] were, by long tradition, triable by a military commission, as authorized by Congress and ordered by the President.

Petitioners had contended that their seizure by civilian authorities within the United States entitled them (or at least the one said to be an American citizen) to a jury trial, under the Fifth and Sixth Amendments. The Court, however, held that pre-existing law at the time of the adoption of these Amendments allowed the use of military commissions for violations of the law of war and that the Amendments did not specifically overrule that legal tradition. "We must conclude that § 2 of Article III and the Fifth and Sixth Amendments cannot be taken to have extended the right to demand a jury to trials by military commission, or to have required that offenses against the law of war not triable by jury at common law be tried only in the civil courts." Id. at 40.[43]

Quirin addressed, albeit briefly, the specific issue of whether a United States citizen could be tried as an unlawful combatant. One of the saboteurs (Haupt) claimed to be a United States citizen, and argued that his citizenship made it improper for him to be tried by a military commission rather than a civil court. The Court rejected this argument:

> Citizenship in the United States of an enemy belligerent does not relieve him from the consequences of a belligerency which is unlawful because in violation of the law of war. Citizens who associate themselves with the military arm of the enemy government, and with its aid, guidance and direction enter this country bent on hostile acts, are enemy belligerents within the meaning of the Hague Convention and the law of war.... It is as an enemy belligerent that petitioner Haupt is charged with entering the United States, and unlawful belligerency is the gravamen of the offense of which he is accused.

Id. at 37–38. See Colepaugh v. Looney, 235 F.2d 429, 432 (10th Cir. 1956) (citing Quirin, and holding a military commission had jurisdiction to try a citizen illegal combatant who had secretly landed in Maine from German submarine).

a. Lawful vs. Unlawful Combatants

The Quirin Court recognized a fundamental distinction under the law of war between lawful and unlawful combatants, a distinction first codified in 1863 in the so-called Lieber Instructions.[44] Lawful combatants are members of an organized army who, if captured in an armed conflict, are entitled to be treated as prisoners of war. Their conduct as combatants is deemed to be lawful and not subject to punishment. Unlawful combatants, in contrast, are not members of a duly organized national military force, do not wear uniforms or other distinctive insignia and do not bear arms openly. As such, if captured, they are not entitled to be treated as prisoners of war and may be tried for violating the law of war:

> By a long course of practical administrative construction by its military authorities, our Government has likewise recognized that those who during time of war pass surreptitiously from enemy territory into our

> own, discarding their uniforms upon entry, for the commission of hostile acts involving destruction of life or property, have the status of unlawful combatants punishable as such by military commission. This precept of the law of war has been so recognized in practice both here and abroad, and has so generally been accepted as valid by authorities on international law that we think it must be regarded as a rule or principle of the law of war recognized by this Government by its enactment of the Fifteenth Article of War.

Quirin, 317 U.S. at 35–36 (footnote omitted). See Spencer J. Crona & Neal A. Richardson, Justice for War Criminals of Invisible Armies: A New Legal and Military Approach to Terrorism, 21 Okla. City U. L. Rev. 349, 360–61 (1996).

The Third Geneva Convention of 1949,[45] in Article 4, defines persons entitled to treatment as prisoner of war[46] as members of the armed forces of a belligerent nation, or of militia and other volunteer corps, including organized resistance movements, provided they are commanded by a person responsible for his subordinates; bear a fixed distinctive sign recognizable at a distance; carry arms openly; and conduct their operation in accordance with the laws and customs of war. By inference, unlawful combatants, a term not used in the Third Geneva Convention, are combatants not satisfying those conditions. Cf. Quirin, 317 U.S. at 35 (by defining lawful combatants entitled to prisoner of war status, the Government "has recognized that there is a class of unlawful belligerents not entitled to that privilege. . . .").

b. Military Commissions: Quirin v. Milligan

It is not easy to harmonize the holdings of Quirin and Milligan with respect to the constitutionality of the use of military commissions in the United States.[47] Milligan certainly suggested that a citizen could never be tried by military commission when the civilian courts were open and functioning. However, Quirin distinguished Milligan on the ground that, unlike the Quirin saboteurs, who were "enemy belligerents" acting pursuant to orders from the German military and intelligence authorities (id. at 45–46), Milligan was not a combatant: he had not been "a part of or associated with the armed forces of the enemy," and, hence, was a "non-belligerent, not subject to the law of war. . . . (id. at 45).[48]

Another distinction is that Quirin relied on congressional authorization for the use of military commissions,[49] while there had been no such authorization in Milligan (though the majority in Milligan opined that such authorization would have been unavailing—see p. 45, above).

Aside from these distinctions, Quirin also appears to reflect a greater deference to the political branches in the midst of a war, in contrast to Milligan's vigorous assertion of judicial authority after the Civil War had ended. Quirin may reflect in part "the reluctance of courts to decide a case against the government on an issue of national security during a war." Rehnquist at 221.

Regardless of the cogency of Quirin or Milligan, it is important to note that neither addresses whether a President has authority to detain enemy combatants indefinitely, without charges. The question did not arise, for in each case the purpose of the detention was to proceed—even with precipitous speed—with a military trial on proffered charges.

5. *World War II: Hirabayashi and Korematsu*

The other major war powers landmarks of World War II reflected extremely broad deference to the President and Congress. In Hirabayashi v. United States, 320 U.S. 81 (1943), and Korematsu v. United States, 323 U.S. 214 (1944), the Court faced challenges to the wartime restrictions imposed by the government on American citizens and residents of Japanese ancestry. The Congress and the President had delegated to the military the authority to exclude from any militarily sensitive area any category of persons deemed a potential threat. The military in turn had declared the entire Pacific Coast to be a sensitive area, and excluded all persons of Japanese ancestry from portions of those areas—choosing to confine those residents in camps—and placed curfews on their out-of-doors activities in other areas. Hirabayashi was convicted of violating militarily-imposed curfew regulations, and Korematsu of refusing to comply with so-called exclusion regulations, which effectively confined Japanese-Americans to detention camps for the duration of military hostilities with Japan.

The Court upheld both convictions and the validity of these national-origin-specific regulations, and did so in terms of broad deference to the war-making powers of Congress and the President. In Hirabayashi, while acknowledging that distinctions based on national origins are "odious", 320 U.S. at 100, the Court nevertheless went on to note that the country was in the midst of a national emergency, and that the political branches had the authority and obligation to take whatever measures they thought necessary to protect against feared invasion or sabotage:

> Since the Constitution commits to the Executive and to the Congress the exercise of the war power in all the vicissitudes and conditions of warfare, it has necessarily given them wide scope for the exercise of judgment and discretion in determining the nature and extent of the threatened injury or danger and in the selection of the means for resisting it. Where, as they did here, the conditions call for the exercise of judgment and for the choice of means by those branches of the Government on which the Constitution has placed the responsibility of warmaking, it is not for any court to sit in review of the wisdom of their action or substitute its judgment for theirs.

320 U.S. at 93 (internal citations omitted). This substantial deferral to the judgment of the executive branch and Congress was based on a broad reading of the war powers, referred to as "the power to wage war successfully." Id. at 92 (quoting Charles Evans Hughes, War Powers Under the Constitution, 42 A.B.A. Rep. 232, 238). The Court held that it need satisfy itself only that the military authorities had "a reasonable basis for the actions taken" (id. at 101), which basis it found by relying on stereotypical characterizations of the Japanese-American community and the unquestioned fact that Japan was waging a war of aggression against the United States. Given "the facts and circumstances with respect to the American citizens of Japanese descent residing on the Pacific Coast",[50] it was rational to suspect a greater loyalty to the enemy among Americans of Japanese ancestry than among others. Id. at 102.

The next year the Court followed further along the same path in upholding in Korematsu the exclusion of all people of Japanese ancestry from large areas of the Pacific Coast and relegating them to detention camps. 323 U.S. at 217–18 (relying on Hirabayashi). Although the Court conceded that exclusion from one's home and community is a far greater deprivation than was inflicted by the Hirabayashi curfew (confinement for ten hours at night in one's home), its foreshortened analysis rested on the same forgiving formula that allowed the executive very broad discretion to protect national security in a crisis:

> As in the Hirabayashi case, we cannot reject as unfounded the judgment of the military authorities and of Congress that there were disloyal members of that population, whose number and strength could not be precisely and quickly ascertained. We cannot say that the war-making branches of the Government did not have ground for believing that in a critical hour such persons could not readily be isolated and separately dealt with, and constituted a menace to the national defense and safety, which demanded that prompt and adequate measures be taken to guard against it.

Id. at 218.[51]

6. *Youngstown (The Steel Seizure Case)*

In Youngstown Sheet & Tube Co. v. Sawyer, 343 U.S. 579 (1952) ("Youngstown"), the Court rejected President Truman's claimed exercise of his war power during the Korean War in seizing steel mills to ensure against disruption of production resulting from labor unrest.

The Court rejected the notion that "broad powers in military commanders engaged in day-to-day fighting in a theater of war" translated into a right of the President "to take possession of private property in order to keep labor disputes from stopping production." Id. at 587 (holding that President could not so act without congressional authorization).

This rhetorical limitation of the war power to battlefield decisions is, in general tenor, in some tension with the Court's sensitivity in Korematsu to the dangers lurking on the home front. Youngstown probably owes something to the less threatening nature of the Korean conflict, and particularly the absence of any suggestion that the enemy, rather than inflexible corporate management, posed a threat within the country.

It also is significant that in Youngstown, unlike in Quirin, Hirabayashi and Korematsu, the President had acted without any congressional authorization, and, in the view of several justices, even contrary to the evident intent of Congress in the Taft-Hartley Act. Id. at 598-604 (Frankfurter, J., concurring). Justice Jackson's concurring opinion argued persuasively that, as a general matter, a President's power is at a maximum when exercised in a manner expressly authorized by Congress, in a "zone of twilight" if taken in the absence of congressional authorization, and at "its lowest ebb" when incompatible with congressional will. Id. at 635–38.

Youngstown has been called "perhaps the Court's most important attempt to fit the needs of executive branch decisionmaking at times of crisis within our constitutional tradition," Neal K. Katyal & Lawrence H. Tribe, Waging War, Deciding Guilt: Trying the Military Tribunals, 111 Yale L.J. 1259, 1273 (2002) ("Katyal & Tribe"), and "a landmark case affirming not only that the President must obey the law but that in general he may act only on the basis of statutory authority." David Currie, The Constitution of the United States 40 (2d ed. 2000). These accolades more properly belong to Justice Jackson's concurring opinion, which has proven widely influential. E.g., Dames & Moore v. Regan, 453 U.S. 654, 668–69 (1981) (adopting the three-tier Jackson analysis of Presidential power). As will be seen, the Second Circuit's opinion reversing *Padilla* relies heavily on that concurrence and its distinction between the war power of the President at home and his war power abroad.

7. *Hamdi and Padilla: Indefinite Detentions under the President's War Power*

The Hamdi and Padilla courts were required to apply the above limited case law on the President's war power to the declared "enemy combatants" before them, both United States citizens. Recall: Hamdi allegedly had been captured in a zone of armed combat in Afghanistan, carrying a gun and in the company of other Taliban fighters, while Padilla was seized in Chicago and ultimately accused of conspiring with al Qaeda operatives abroad to build and detonate a "dirty bomb" in this country. Counsel for each detainee urged that due process barred their indefinite and incommunicado detentions, while the government urged that the President's war power permitted them, based on the government's hearsay representation of the basic facts justifying the detainee's "enemy combatant" status.

As Judge Mukasey noted in Padilla, "it would be a mistake to create the impression that there is a lush and vibrant jurisprudence governing these matters. There isn't." Padilla, 233 F. Supp. 2d at 607. Applying this sparse jurisprudence, and faced with very different factual contexts, Hamdi and the Padilla district court reached somewhat different results, but both sustained the constitutionality of indefinite detentions of "enemy combatants." The Second Circuit, reversing Padilla, held the detention of Padilla unconstitutional.

In Hamdi the petition was denied without an evidentiary hearing, the Fourth Circuit finding that the government's representation of the facts, indisputable in the court's view, was sufficient to justify the enemy combatant classification without the need for further inquiry (or permitting

Hamdi any access to counsel), given the deference due the President's exercise of his war power.

In Padilla Judge Mukasey, while similarly according great deference to the President's war power, withheld ruling on the merits of the petition before him. Instead, he granted Padilla a limited right to consult with his counsel for the purpose of submitting a rebuttal to the Mobbs declaration (Padilla at 599–602), which rested on hearsay reports from "unnamed confidential sources" concerning Padilla's alleged contacts with al Qaeda operatives. Id. at 573. Padilla's "right to present facts" was found "firmly rooted" in the habeas statute, 28 U.S.C. § 2241, and related statutes. Id. at 599. However, the court held that the government ultimately need meet only a low "some evidence" standard to justify Padilla's continued detention. Id. at 608. The Second Circuit did not reach these questions, since it held the President without power to detain Padilla in the first place.

Before turning to our own analysis of the issues posed by enemy combatant detentions, we review the manner in which Hamdi and the two Padilla courts dealt with those issues.

a. Separation of Powers; Deference to Political Branches

The Hamdi circuit court and Padilla district court opinions share much in common. In particular, both decisions place heavy stress on the need for the courts to defer to the political branches in the exercise of their war-making powers, and to avoid any intrusion that would hamper the effective discharge of those powers.

In dismissing Hamdi's petition, the Fourth Circuit stressed the battlefield context of his classification: "an American citizen captured and detained by American allied forces in a foreign theater of war during active hostilities and determined by the United States military to have been indeed allied with enemy forces." Hamdi at 476. The court rejected any "broader categorical holdings on enemy combatant designations" (id. at 465), and disclaimed "placing our imprimatur upon a new day of executive detentions." Id. at 476.[52] It specifically distinguished the Padilla situation, i.e., "the designation as enemy combatant of an American citizen captured on American soil or the role that counsel might play in such a proceeding." Id. at 465.

Hamdi proceeds to analyze at some length what it believes would be unacceptable intrusions in the conduct of military field operations were military commanders required to litigate back in the United States over the factual circumstances of a detainee's capture, detention and interrogation. Id. at 469–71. Because of the deference due to "executive branch decisions premised on military determinations made in the field," and "because Hamdi was indisputably seized in an active combat zone abroad," the Hamdi court did not require any supplementation (or permit any rebuttal) to the Mobbs declaration. Id. at 473. It was persuaded that "a factual inquiry into the circumstances of Hamdi's capture would be inappropriate," and "would entail an unacceptable risk of obstructing war efforts authorized by Congress and undertaken by the executive branch." Id. at 474–75.[53] The Constitution required deference:

> The constitutional allocation of war powers affords the President extraordinarily broad authority as Commander in Chief and compels the courts to assume a deferential posture in reviewing exercises of this authority.

Id. at 474.

The Hamdi court's deference to the executive hence was the product of both institutional deference, which it believed was required by the Constitution's separation of powers, and practical considerations that it found powerfully supported the necessity of such deference in the factual context presented.

In Padilla, which did not involve an overseas military campaign, the practical considerations played much less of a role in the court's analysis. "The prospect of courts second-guessing battlefield decisions...does not loom in this case." Padilla, 243 F. Supp. 2d at 57. In fact, Judge Mukasey noted that federal judges do have the expertise to make and review the sort of factual determinations on which Padilla's classification as an enemy combatant rested. Padilla at 608. However, the court found deference required by the Constitution's separation of powers. It was beyond the appropriate scope of the court's "commission" to consider de novo whether the enemy combatant classification had properly been applied to Padilla:

> The "political branches," when they make judgments on the exercise of war powers under Articles I and II, as both branches have here, need not submit those judgments to review by Article III courts.

Id. at 607.

This observation did not lead the court to deny all review, but rather to craft a highly deferential scope of review. The court's commission, it held, extended "only to deciding two things:"

> (i) whether the controlling political authority—in this case, the President—was, in fact exercising a power vouchsafed to him by the Constitution and the laws; that determination in turn, is to be made only by examining whether there is some evidence to support his conclusion that Padilla was....engaged in a mission against the United States on behalf of an enemy with whom the United States is at war, and (ii) whether that evidence has not been entirely mooted by subsequent events

Id. at 608.[54]

The Second Circuit, on appeal, answered the constitutional question in the negative, holding the President did not have the power, absent express congressional authorization, to detain an American citizen on American soil.

The Hamdi court, while recognizing that the government urged the "some evidence" standard, found it unnecessary to decide that question. It held that, in response to a habeas petition challenging a detention as unlawful, the courts should appropriately "ask that the government provide the legal authority upon which it relies for the detention and the basic facts relied upon to support a legitimate exercise of that authority." Hamdi at 472. It found the requisite legal authority in the "executive's...power to detain under the war powers of Article II," and the basic facts adequately set forth in the Mobbs declaration. Id. at 472–73.

b. Existence of a State of War

None of the three courts viewed itself as entitled to second-guess the government's position that the "war on terror" invoked the President's "war power." All courts treated the question of whether a state of war existed and determinations as to its cessation to be political matters essentially within the authority of the President and/or Congress and not the courts. Padilla at 588–91; Padilla Cir. at 712; Hamdi at 476.

Both Padilla courts placed important reliance for this point on The Prize Cases. Padilla at 589, 595–96; Padilla Cir. at 712. None of the courts placed any significance on the unconventional nature of the war on terror as compared to previous wars, involving massed troops of opposing sovereign states. None found it necessary to probe the question of when the war on terror might come to an end. Hamdi and the Padilla district court expressly found that it plainly had not, given the continued presence of United States troops in Afghanistan. Padilla at 590; Hamdi at 476. Padilla held expressly that the challenge to the alleged indefinite nature of the detention was premature. Padilla at 590–91.[55]

c. Detention of U.S. citizens Arrested on U.S. Soil

The Padilla district court posed as the "central issue" before it this question:

> whether the President has the authority to designate as an unlawful combatant an American citizen, captured on American soil, and to detain him without trial.

Padilla at 593. In reaching an affirmative answer to this question, the Padilla court placed heavy stress on Quirin. Since the Court in Quirin drew no distinction between the alleged American citizen and the other German saboteurs,

> it matters not that Padilla is a United States citizen captured on United States soil.

Id. at 606.

In relying on Quirin, the court adopted as well its limitation of Milligan to "non-belligerent [s]." Quirin, 317 U.S. at 45. The Padilla court held petitioner within the reach of Quirin, not Milligan, since he, "like the Quirin saboteurs, is alleged to be in active association with an enemy with whom the United States is at war." Padilla at 594. See also id. at 608 (relevant showing is whether "Padilla was...engaged in a mission against the United States on behalf of an enemy with whom the United States is at war").

It is on this point that the Second Circuit reversed. Drawing heavily on Justice Jackson's Youngstown concurrence, the Court held that the detention of a citizen was in violation of an express statute, 18 U.S.C. § 4001(a), and hence involved an exercise of Presidential power at its lowest ebb, i.e., Jackson's third category. The President's war power did not support the detention in the United States because the Constitution allocated to Congress, not the President, emergency powers to act in this country, and Congress had not authorized the detention, distinguishing Quirin and The Prize Cases where such authorization had been present. Padilla Cir. at 710–24. Surprisingly, the infringement of individual due process rights inherent in the detention was not a main focus of the opinion.

d. Access to Counsel

As noted, the Padilla district court did not dismiss the writ but rather authorized further proceedings in which Padilla could attempt to rebut the allegations in the Mobbs declaration, and communicate with his counsel for the limited purpose of preparing such a rebuttal. This result proceeded in part from a recognition that normally the purpose of a habeas petition is to allow the presentation of facts (Padilla at 599–602), and the court's view that "Padilla's need to consult with a lawyer to help him do what the statute permits him to do is obvious." Id. at 602. The court, in its opinion on reconsideration, rejected the government's argument that the "some evidence" standard meant that Padilla need be given no opportunity to respond to the government's allegations in support of its enemy combatant classification. Padilla, 243 F. Supp. 2d at 54–56.

The court found it unnecessary to determine whether Padilla had a due process right to counsel. Rather, it authorized counsel as a discretionary matter pursuant to the All Writs Act, 28 U.S.C. § 1651(a), finding that counsel's participation would aid the court in ruling on the merits of the habeas petition, and that its exercise of discretion could be at least informed by the Sixth Amendment right-to-counsel jurisprudence. Padilla at 602–03. The court rejected the government's position that Padilla's contact with counsel would interfere with its ongoing interrogation of Padilla, finding any such interference "would be minimal or nonexistent" since the court was permitting only limited consultations to facilitate the presentation of the facts in the habeas proceeding. Id. at 603. The court also noticed that Padilla, unlike Hamdi, already had consulted with counsel when earlier held as a material witness, and thus there was "no potential prophylactic effect of an order barring access by counsel." Id. at 605.[56]

The Second Circuit had no need to reach the right-to-counsel issue, but Judge Wesley, in dissent, made plain his lack of sympathy for the government's position:

> No one has suspended the Great Writ. See U.S. Const. art. I, § 9, cl. 2. Padilla's right to pursue a remedy through the writ would be meaningless if he had to do so alone. I therefore would extend to him the right to counsel as Chief Judge Mukasey did. [citation omitted]. At the hearing, Padilla, assisted by counsel,

would be able to contest whether he is actually an enemy combatant thereby falling within the President's constitutional and statutory authority.

Padilla Cir. at 732–33.

The Hamdi court, given its conclusion that the Mobbs declaration was not subject to challenge, never expressly addressed the right-to-counsel issue, nor the government's related claim that its ability to interrogate Hamdi would be harmed if, as a result of contacts with counsel, the detainee was placed in an "adversary relationship with the captor." Hamdi at 466 n.4. The court noted that "a capable attorney could challenge the hearsay nature of the Mobbs declaration and each and every paragraph for incompleteness or inconsistency", but found that such "instinctive skepticism, so laudable in the defense of criminal charges," would risk a "constitutionally problematic intrusion into the most basic responsibilities of a coordinate branch." Id. at 473.[57]

e. Congressional Authorization or Prohibition: The Joint Resolution and 18 U.S.C. § 4001(a)

Both Hamdi and the Padilla district court rejected, while the Second Circuit adopted, petitioners' arguments based on 18 U.S.C. § 4001(a), which provides that "No citizen shall be imprisoned or otherwise detained by the United States except pursuant to an Act of Congress". Judge Mukasey found that § 4001(a) did in fact unambiguously require congressional authorization for "enemy combatant" detentions, and the Second Circuit agreed. But while Judge Mukasey found that Congress had provided such authorization in the Joint Resolution adopted by Congress on September 18, 2001, Authorization for Use of Military Force, Pub. Law 107-40 § 2(a), 115 Stat. 224 (2001) (the "Joint Resolution"), the Second Circuit held it had not.

The Joint Resolution, fully titled "To authorize the use of the United States Armed Forces against those responsible for the recent attacks launched against the United States," empowers the President:

to use all necessary and appropriate force against those. . .organizations or persons he determines planned, authorized, committed or aided the terrorist acts that occurred on September 11, 2001. . .in order to prevent any future acts of international terrorism against the United States by such. . .organizations or persons.

Because Padilla was alleged "to have been an unlawful combatant in behalf of al Qaeda," itself deemed responsible for the September 11 attacks, Judge Mukasey held the detention of Padilla authorized by the Joint Resolution and thus in compliance with 18 U.S.C. § 4001(a). Padilla at 596–98.

The Second Circuit, reversing, construed the Joint Resolution only to authorize combat abroad and, possibly, detentions in a battlefield context. It relied on the Supreme Court's opinion in Ex parte Endo for the proposition that the Joint Resolution should be construed to impose no greater restraint on citizens than "clearly and unmistakably indicated" by its language. Padilla Cir. at 723, quoting Endo, 323 U.S. at 300.

The Hamdi court was unwilling to read 18 U.S.C. § 4001(a) as potentially applicable to Hamdi, believing the statute was not intended to override the "well established precedent" authorizing the capture and detention of enemy combatants as an inherent part of warfare. Hamdi at 468. But, in the alternative, the Fourth Circuit also held that the Joint Resolution authorized the detention. Id. at 467.

f. The Geneva Convention

Hamdi and the Padilla district court treated differently the Third Geneva Convention. Padilla held that the detainee's designation as an "enemy combatant," if sustained, meant that he was an "illegal combatant," and thus would not be within the protections of the Geneva Convention as a prisoner of war. Padilla at 592–93, 599. The Hamdi court found the distinction between lawful and unlawful combatants irrelevant to the case before it, since either could be detained under the authority of Quirin. Hamdi at 469. It held, further, that the Geneva Convention afforded no private right of action to any detainee, but rather was enforceable only through diplomatic and reciprocal measures between the warring parties. Id. at 468–69.[58] The Second Circuit had no need to reach this question.

IV. WAR POWERS AND DUE PROCESS: INDEFINITE U.S. DETENTIONS BY UNILATERAL EXECUTIVE ACTION VIOLATE THE CONSTITUTION

We turn now to our own analysis of how the competing considerations of due process and the war power should be applied in the unique and present circumstances of the "war on terror." Our conclusion, in agreement with the Second Circuit's but for somewhat different reasons, is that the Constitution does not permit the President unilaterally, without congressional authorization, to effect indefinite and incommunicado detentions of suspected terrorists seized in the United States.[59] The serious negative consequences of recognizing such an executive power—damaging the rule of law in ways not easily confined to terrorism, opening the door to other abuses of due process, and offering an invitation by example to repressive regimes around the globe—strongly supports not giving the war power such an expansive reading. The limited war power jurisprudence does not justify indefinite detentions in this country of either citizens, as the Second Circuit has now held, or non-citizens, at least until and unless Congress addresses and affirms the President's claim that the national security requires such extraordinary departures from long accepted due process standards.

Much the same could be said with respect to the use of military commissions, based solely on the President's determination of who should be so tried, and in the absence of specific congressional authorization. However, the constitutional question is a closer one. Quirin and the generally worded statute on which it relied do support the use of such commissions to prosecute violations of the law of war. But in any event, after reviewing the military commission orders promulgated for enemy combatant trials, we urge that the use of military commissions be minimized. There are important advantages offered by criminal prosecutions in the federal courts, which have successfully tried many terrorism cases. The most important is that the enhanced fairness of such civilian proceedings will result in a likely greater acceptance in this country and abroad of the justness of their results (see pp. 129–35, below).

A. The Serious Negative Consequences of Recognizing a Unilateral Executive Power to Detain

As we show below, the less than "lush" war power jurisprudence surveyed above does not resolve how to balance the war power and due process in the context of indefinite detentions and the war on terror. Before further discussing this sparse case law, therefore, we look at the possible consequences, legal and practical, of a decision sustaining the constitutionality of such executive detentions. Those serious negative consequences, as we see them, argue strongly against interpreting the war power precedents to sanction the detentions.

1. *The Sharp Departure from the Rule of Law*

Indefinite detentions constitute a sharp departure from core due process principles and the rule of law. The detentions have no finite term, and may continue for as long as the war on terror, which has no foreseeable end. They are effected solely by the executive, without any "probable cause" or other judicial finding. The executive expressly disclaims any intention of bringing charges against the detainees, and thus rules out any assessment by some neutral decision-maker of guilt or innocence. The detainees are isolated, including from any relatives or attorneys, thus precluding any factual challenge by the detainees to the claimed basis for their classification as "enemy combatants". Further, the executive urges that, on any habeas corpus petition brought by a "next friend" of the detainee, no rebuttal should be permitted to its enemy combatant classification.

The holding of persons incommunicado, without access to an attorney, without charges or statutory basis, indefinitely and based solely on the executive's subjective determination, has nothing in common with due process as we know it. The policy has an almost medieval ring to it, harkening back to the days when the sovereign recognized no limitations on its power to detain subjects for whatever reason, uncontrolled by any superior rule of law.

Nor has the term "enemy combatant" even been defined, or limited to persons suspected of planning or carrying out terrorist attacks. Padilla may fit that description as an alleged saboteur. But al-Marri, a civilian in this country legally, seems suspected of providing logistical support for al Queda sleeper cells: presumably criminal activity, if proven, but not "combatant" activity under any likely definition of the term. The scope of the indefinite detentions, in the executive's conception, thus appears to extend to any person believed—on the basis of "some" hearsay—to have provided some form of assistance to al Qaeda, e.g., any form of "material support or resources" to a designated terrorist organization, such as "expert advice or assistance," "currency" or "lodging", 18 U.S.C. § 2339B(g)(4).[60] If the courts sustain the constitutionality of such detentions, the technique may be used against far more people than the three so detained in this country (so far as is known) to date.[61]

Already the use of such a technique by the government appears to have had an impact well beyond the persons detained. It opens the door to the intimidation of non-detainees. Defendants or potential defendants facing charges in criminal proceedings can be threatened, should they not plead or otherwise cooperate, with indefinite detention as enemy combatants terminating their due process rights, as indeed happened to al-Marri on the brink of his criminal trial. Wholly deprived of any protection of the rule of law, or of the interposition of judge and jury, such persons would be subject to an intolerable pressure well beyond the pressure of a criminal prosecution.

We are not sanguine about the practical ability of the courts to cabin the use of such indefinite detentions on a case-by-case basis, if the general technique is accepted as constitutional. While the courts could review evidence concerning whether an alleged terrorist is one in fact, even here the courts' ability to provide meaningful review is dependent on the burden of proof applied to the government. The "some evidence" standard found applicable in Padilla to review of enemy combatant determinations may not provide meaningful review.[62] Surely it will not if, as the government contends, the detainee is not permitted to consult counsel or rebut the government's minimal required showing. Padilla, 243 F. Supp. 2d at 54–56 (rejecting this government contention).

But assuming that the enemy combatant classification is sustained, questions concerning the length and conditions of incommunicado detentions designed to facilitate interrogation may not be subject to effective control by the courts. Our whole tradition is opposed to coerced confessions, including by extended detentions designed to extract information. Once that Rubicon is crossed, the courts are poorly positioned to second-guess executive decisions as to the utility or necessity of extracting information from a particular detainee, or the tactics—including the length and conditions of the detentions—best calculated to perform the extraction.[63] These are largely subjective judgments, based on experience and hunches, informed by whatever has been gleaned from interrogations of other detainees, classified intelligence intercepts and other non-evidentiary information. The courts, on such matters of tactical judgment, would "tend to defer to the executive's assumed greater knowledge and expertise." Katyal & Tribe, 111 Yale L.J. at 1275. Cf. Korematsu v. United States, 323 U.S. 214, 245 (1943) (Jackson, J., dissenting): "In the very nature of things, military decisions are not susceptible of intelligent judicial appraisal."

Nor can the public through the political process, rather than the courts, reasonably be expected to rein in executive excess. That may be a practical possibility in the context of exercises of the President's war power that impact widely on many citizens, such as mobilization, the draft, rationing or higher taxes.[64] But where the exercise of the war power focuses on a discrete minority—the Japanese-Americans in World War II or Arab-Americans and other Muslims in the war on terror—it is unrealistic to expect too much of the political process.[65] The public at large, in the context of the traumatic events of September 11 and continuing acts of lawless terrorism around the world, cannot be expected sua sponte to impose due process constraints on the President's efforts to prevent future terrorist attacks.[66]

Further, the prospects of any political restraint are minimized if the President's war power is found to justify indefinite detentions unless Congress affirmatively passes legislation to prohibit them. Political inertia weighs against such legislation. However, if affirmative congressional authorization is deemed necessary (at a minimum) to sanction such detentions, as we believe and the Second Circuit has held, at least a debate on the wisdom and necessity of such measures is assured.

2. *The Risk of Error*

If such an extraordinarily lawless system could be confined to actual terrorists—lawless in their very essence—at least a certain symmetry would result. But no such limitation can be expected, for the executive branch, of course, like any human institution, is susceptible to error in its detention decisions. The dangers of ethnic profiling are all too apparent in the context of terrorism investigations. In recent times, most international terrorists have been Arabs or other Muslims. Striking the balance between security and individual rights is not an abstract proposition in this context. An estimated 1,200 non-citizens, mostly from the Middle East or South Asia, reportedly were secretly detained after 9/11, of whom only four were subsequently indicted for terrorism-related crimes. Human Rights Watch website (hrw.org/un/chr.59/counter-terrorism-bck4.htm (Dec 17, 2003)).[67] See United States v. Awadallah, 349 F.3d 42, 78 (2d Cir. 2003) (Straub, C.J., concurring) (referring to "the waves of anti-Muslim sentiment that. . .followed September 11"); cf. United States v. Alameh, 341 F.3d 167, 172–74 (2d Cir. 2003) (percentage of Middle Eastern men charged under certain immigration statutes said to increase from 15% before 9/11 to 85% thereafter, though court questioned reliability of these statistics).

We do not believe the country would tolerate today, as did the Court in Korematsu, a wholesale round-up of Arabs or Muslims based on a claim that "there [are]. . .disloyal members of that population," and on a judgment that "such persons could not readily be isolated and separately dealt with. . . ." Korematsu, 323 U.S. at 218. No one has urged any such wholesale detentions.[68] But targeted detentions, limited in number, can be based on "some evidence" that later proves to be faulty. See In re Application of United States for Material Witness Warrant, 214 F. Supp. 2d 356, 358–60 (S.D.N.Y. 2002) (recounting filing of material witness warrant application and criminal charges against Egyptian national following September 11, 2001, based on what proved to be false information provided to government and on an allegedly coerced confession). Indeed, the narrower the scope of court review, the greater the likelihood of such error.

The chance of error inevitably is magnified if detainees, as urged by the government, are held incommunicado, with no opportunity to consult an attorney or to rebut the executive's allegations advanced to justify the detention.

3. *The Long-Term and Expandable Nature of the War on Terror*

The threat to due process posed by indefinite detentions is all the greater because of the likely prolonged nature of the war on terror, which creates a risk that such extraordinary measures adopted in its context may prove to be permanent features of the constitutional land-scape.

In the past, occasional departures in wartime from due process standards have been tolerated in the expectation that, when war ended, the peacetime contours of due process would be resuscitated. Thus, President Lincoln, defending his policy of military arrests of civilians during the Civil War, emphasized the temporary nature of these measures:

> I am unable to appreciate the danger...that the American people will by means of military arrests during the rebellion lose the right to public discussion, the liberty of speech and the press, the law of evidence, trial by jury and *habeas corpus* throughout the indefinite peaceful future which I trust lies before them, anymore than I am able to believe that a man could contract so strong an appetite for emetics during temporary illness as to persist in feeding upon them during the remainder of his healthy life.

Edward S. Corwin, Total War and the Constitution168–69 (1947) ("Corwin").[69]
Others have found Lincoln's optimism as to the temporary nature of war measures misplaced:

> The Court has had little success in preventing the precedents of war from becoming the precedents of peace. We might even go so far as to say that the court has made a positive contribution to the permanent peacetime weakening of the separation of powers, the principle of non-delegation, the Fifth Amendment, and the necessary and proper clauses applicable limits to governmental power. Rossiter at 129.

Justice Jackson, in his Korematsu dissent, feared that the Court's ruling in that case would lie "like a loaded weapon ready for the hand of any authority that can bring forward a plausible claim of an urgent need." 323 U.S. at 246.

But whatever the merits of this debate in the context of "temporary" wars, the war on terror shows few signs of being temporary. There is certainly little expectation that it will be over anytime in the near term. And its scope is expandable, based on the determinations of the President and/or Congress. It is not limited to al Qaeda, as in the Joint Resolution. It has been said by the President to embrace the former Hussein regime in Iraq, Palestinian terror groups and the Abu Sayyaf Group in the Philippines. Numerous other suspected terrorist organizations presumably are within its potential scope: 36 have been designated by the United States. U.S. Dep't of State Press Statement, Oct. 3, 2003.

Accordingly, we must assume a substantial possibility that we will have to live with the war on terror for many years, if not indefinitely. If that is the case, we may not safely await a foreseeable post-crisis period during which the previous contours of due process will be restored. Departures from core due process principles in the context of the war on terror may well be long-lived, not short-term measures easily reversed. This makes all the more important a careful consideration of the relevant constitutional values before due process rights are set aside in obeisance to proclaimed wartime necessity.

4. *The Potential Extension of Anti-Terrorism Measures to Other Criminal Activity*

In theory tactics justified in the war against terror, such as indefinite detentions, might be confined to that context. Terrorism is distinguishable, to some significant degree, from other types of criminal activity. But a bright line between terrorism and other types of criminal activity will not be easy to maintain. If such tactics are deemed constitutionally acceptable with respect to terrorism, and effective in practice, there will be pressure to employ similar tactics with respect to other types of suspected criminal activity.

The Bush administration, arguing for a broadening of the USA PATRIOT Act, has urged that law enforcement agencies be afforded "the same tools to fight terror that they [already] have to fight other crime,"[70] but the dynamic will work in the other direction as well. The two rationales for the detentions of suspected terrorists—to facilitate their interrogation and to incapacitate them (preventive detention)—are not limited to terrorism. Compelling arguments for extracting information from detainees surely could be made in the context of investigations of international drug dealing, serial murders or rapes, or even child abuse. Nor can the rationale of preventive detention logically be limited to terrorism. Undoubtedly, any United States Attorney's office could point to many persons of interest believed to a moral certainty by prosecutors to have committed or to be planning to commit serious crimes, but who have not been arrested because the evidence gathered to date is not deemed sufficient to satisfy "probable cause" or to secure a conviction. If such deficiencies of proof do not preclude the detention of suspected terrorists—if "some evidence" is enough to detain them indefinitely—pressures may build to use preventive detention in other contexts to lock up other persons suspected of other serious criminal activity, based on "some" evidence falling well short of proof of their guilt.[71]

One possible such context is the so-called "war on drugs," which also involves both domestic law enforcement and military efforts abroad, here in aid of governments battling local drug lords, particularly in Colombia and, in the past, in Peru. See, e.g., Thomas Powers, War and its Consequences, N.Y. Review of Books, March 23, 2003, at 19, c. 4 (discussing Dana Priest, The Mission: Waging War and Keeping Peace with America's Military (2003)). In this context, if the war on terrorism leads to a socially accepted notion that constitutional norms are reserved solely for peacetime, we may see a willingness to accept more extreme and potentially extra-constitutional measures in dealing with suspected drug dealers domestically, particularly if they are linked to foreign groups or governments and if the threat they pose to our social fabric is viewed as sufficiently acute.

Granted, it could be argued that the war powers, however expansively construed, could never justify indefinite detentions in pursuit of some rhetorical "war on drugs" or "war on child abuse." But if the focus is on due process, the forecast is more worrisome. If due process is deemed not to preclude indefinite detentions in the context of the domestic war on terror, because of the exigencies and urgencies it presents in the sole judgment of the President, there is reason to fear it might not preclude such detentions in the context of other alleged criminal activity.[72] Our core due process principles should not be subject to this risk.

5. *Further Extensions of the War Power*

If the unilateral war power of the President is sufficient to displace due process with respect to the rights of detainees, might it also be held to trump other constitutional rights, such as free speech under the First Amendment? A separation of powers jurisprudence that places in the executive plenary power to determine the means best suited to prosecute the war on terror offers no comforting reassurance on this score.[73] To vindicate the use of the war power domestically to justify indefinite detentions may open the door to other executive acts heretofore believed beyond the pale, particularly if the courts accept the administration's position that the United States should be viewed as a "battlefield" in the war on terror. N.Y.L.J. Nov. 18, 2003, p. 1, c. 3 (quoting argument of government counsel to Second Circuit in Padilla appeal, Nov. 17, 2003).

6. *The Encouragement of Repressive Regimes Abroad*

Another negative consequence of indefinite detentions is the encouragement or "cover" they could provide for repressive regimes abroad to oppress their non-terrorist dissidents. If the United States feels justified in departing from the rule of law in combating terrorism at home, notwithstanding our strong tradition of constitutionalism, other countries with no such tradition may see such conduct as justifying crackdowns against their citizens for opposition political activity. We will be in a poor position to complain of arbitrary executive detentions by these regimes, bypassing their judicial systems, if we have engaged in much the same conduct ourselves.

This effect, according to Human Rights Watch, is already occurring:

> Over the past two years, numerous governments throughout the world have enacted laws that unduly expand government powers of detention and surveillance. Some governments have pointed to the erosion of civil liberties in the United States after September 11 to deflect criticism of their own rights abuses. www.hrw.org.press (Sept. 30, 2003).[74]

B. The War Powers Jurisprudence Does Not Support Unilateral Executive Detentions in the United States

The negative consequences of sustaining executive detentions, as just reviewed, argue against construing the Constitution to permit such detentions. We now look again at the few relevant war power case precedents. In our view, they provide no definitive answer to the constitutional question, but surely do not require that the detentions be sustained.

1. *The Padilla Analysis: Based on Scant Precedent from "Total War" Contexts*

At base, the Padilla district court's affirmance of the President's indefinite detention power rests on two cases:

- Quirin, for the proposition that in times of war even United States citizens captured in the United States may be detained as illegal combatants;
- The Prize Cases, for the proposition that the question of whether we are at war is a political question within the President's unreviewable discretion.

While relevant, neither case can bear the weight assigned to it, and each case was decided in the very different circumstances of the Civil War (The Prize Cases) and World War II (Quirin).

Quirin is cited in Padilla as virtually the only precedent supporting the constitutionality of the indefinite "enemy combatant" detentions. It is a weak reed for it involved no such detention.[75] In passing dictum the Quirin court did observe that the petitioners in that case (including a citizen), seized in the United States as unlawful combatants, were "subject to capture and detention," like prisoners of war, 317 U.S. at 31. But the issue before the court was not the President's "wartime detention decisions," Hamdi II, 296 F.3d at 282, but rather the President's order that the saboteurs be tried before a military tribunal for war crimes. The constitutionality of that order, supported by congressional authorization as well as a congressional declaration of war, was sustained. Quirin—"just another of the isolated cases. . .that deal with isolated events and have limited application" (Padilla, 243 F. Supp. 2d at 57)—does not speak to the constitutionality of domestic detentions of suspected illegal combatants, held indefinitely with no tribunal passing upon the question of guilt or innocence.

Nor is there other case authority supporting such detentions. The cases do support use of military commissions to prosecute illegal combatants (Quirin), or legal combatants who have committed war crimes. In re Yamashita, 327 U.S. 1 (1946). Clearly the detention of prisoners of war (legal combatants) is permitted for the duration of a war, subject to the observation of the conditions protective of the POWs in the Third Geneva Convention. But no cases are found addressing the detention without charges of alleged illegal combatants seized in this country.[76]

Nor should the power to try illegal combatants before a military commission, sustained on the record before it by Quirin, potentially leading even to the imposition of the death penalty, be viewed as embracing indefinite detentions as a lesser exercise of the war power. A trial before a military commission provides an assessment of guilt or innocence on specific charges, and thereby provides some protection against arbitrary or erroneous executive detentions.

> In a sense, to be sure, detention of an individual without charges is more arbitrary than detention on charges to be tried before a tribunal.

Rehnquist at 50. Certainly many detainees might prefer to be merely held rather than promptly tried by a military commission and, if convicted, punished or even executed. But our concern is not honoring the preference of the detainees, but rather respecting the values of the Constitution.

The Prize Cases likewise provide no compelling precedent in the domestic war on terror. They sustained only Lincoln's power as Commander in Chief to respond with appropriate military force, as he judged it, to the indisputable rebellion of the South. The absence of a declared war between two sovereigns did not mean there was in fact no war. A state of war plainly existing, the President's power to prosecute the war through such military measures as he deemed appropriate—here through a blockade of enemy ports—was undeniable.

But the military decisionmaking discretion of the President sustained in The Prize Cases should not be taken to constitutionalize indefinite detentions, effected far from any military battlefield, simply because the President proclaims that we are in a "war" and deems the detentions helpful in its prosecution. Surely, at minimum, such a fundamental departure from due process should not be seen as an unreviewable wartime measure, based on the military precedent of Abe Lincoln's 1861 blockade.

2. *A Different Analysis for a Different Type of "War"*

Given that the result reached by the Padilla district court is not compelled by the few precedents it cites, and that it has troubling implications for due process rights in the United States, we look again at the war power precedents, and separation of powers principles. We agree with the Second Circuit's decision reversing Padilla: those precedents can and should be read in a way that does not grant the President unilateral power to override core due process principles whenever he declares his actions are part of the war on terror.

a. The Differing Nature of Wars: "Total War" Precedents Should Not Govern the War on Terror at Home

As already noted, there is no specific case support for unilateral executive detentions in the United States. The cases supporting an expansive construction of the President's war power generally, such as The Prize Cases, Korematsu and Quirin, were decided in the very different "total war" circumstances of the Civil War and World War II, which should not control the balance between due process and the war power in the quite different setting of the domestic war on terror. Further, the President's actions sustained in these cases were supported by congressional authorization, while indefinite detentions are not.

The cases involving the President's war power are few in number, and are all but silent in construing the limits or contours of those powers. This post-World War II summary of the case law remains accurate today:

> [T]he Court has refused to speak about the powers of the President as commander in chief in any but the most guarded terms. It has been respectful, complimentary, on occasion properly awed, but it has never embarked on one of those expansive flights of dicta into which it has been so often tempted by other great constitutional questions.
>
> * * *
>
> [I]t has fixed neither the outer boundaries nor the inner divisions of the President's martial authority, and has failed completely to draw the line between his powers and those of Congress....

Rossiter at 4–5.

It has been equally rare for the courts to balance purported exercises of the war powers against the due process rights of individuals affected by such actions. Generally the courts have viewed the invocation of the war powers as a black-and-white proposition: if the war powers are found properly invoked, a due process analysis attempting to limit the means or methods by which such powers are exercised is seldom to be found.

This all-or-nothing approach reached its zenith in the World War II cases reviewed above. In Quirin and Yamashita, with respect to military commissions, and Hirabayashi and Korematsu with respect to the Japanese exclusions, once the action was held within the scope of the war powers there was no further consideration by the majority of whether due process might limit the scope or exercise of the powers.

The contrast between this extreme deference to the President's war powers and the due process jurisprudence prevailing in times of peace led one post-World War II commentator to conclude that there are really "two Constitutions—one for peace, the other for war." Rossiter at 129. In times of war, according to this analysis, the courts recognized the futility of any judicial restraint on the President's freedom of action in prosecuting the war:

> The government of the United States, in a case of military necessity proclaimed by the President, and a fortiori when Congress has registered agreement, can be just as much a dictatorship, after its own fashion, as any other government on earth. The Supreme Court of the United States will not, and cannot be expected to, get in the way of this power (id. at 54).

Rather, the only realistic curb on the use of the war powers was executive self-discipline:

> Most important, the defense of the Constitution rests at bottom exactly where the defense of the nation rests: in the good sense and the good will of the political branches of the national government, which for most martial purposes must mean the President and his military commanders (id. at 131).[77]

Applying the Rossiter analysis to the war on terrorism would lead to the conclusion that it is both inappropriate and futile for the courts to review now, save perhaps in the most cursory fashion, any decision by the President of how to fight terrorism at home or abroad. Any bold judicial pronouncements applying due process to limit overzealous executive action would come only later, following the example of Milligan, after terrorism is licked.[78]

But this declaration of judicial impotence seems overdrawn, at least, in the context of something less than the "total war" circumstances confronting the courts during the Civil War and World War II. Even in the midst of the actual hostilities of the Korean War, the Supreme Court, in Youngstown, rejected President Truman's attempted invocation of his war power to justify his seizure of the steel mills.[79] The court was unanimous that

> the President's action could not be justified as an exercise of his military power as Commander in Chief of the armed forces.

> Indeed, the case should serve as a particularly valuable precedent in precluding an extensive interpretation of the President's autonomous military powers as a basis for executive control of the internal economy when the country is not in a state of declared war and not threatened with imminent invasion.

Kauper, The Steel Seizure Case: Congress, the President and the Supreme Court, 51 Mich. L. Rev. 141, 175 (1952).

Viewed against the general sweep of the thin war powers jurisprudence, the World War II near "total deference" cases are the exception rather than the rule with respect to exercises of the war power in the United States.[80] Nor have the decisions by the Supreme Court in Quirin, Hirabayashi and Korematsu—which exhibited the greatest deference to the executive as crisis manager—well stood the test of time. The Japanese exclusion cases are almost universally condemned. Quirin also has been called into serious question. Another reason not to follow blindly the lead of the World War II precedents is the emergence, in the years since World War II, of a jurisprudence far more vigorous in recognizing and protecting individual rights from excessive governmental action. Katyal & Tribe, 111 Yale L.J. at 1303–04.[81] We trust that today neither the executive nor the courts would countenance the wholesale ethnic-based military orders upheld in Korematsu and Hirabayashi. See generally, E. Muller, 12/7 and 9/11: War, Liberties, and the Lessons of History, 104 W. Va. L. Rev. 1 (2002) (favorably comparing the Bush administration's policies toward Arab Americans after 9/11 with the Roosevelt administration's actions against ethnic Japanese during World War II).

Short of the most pressing emergency circumstances, there should be room to balance civil liberties and national security, i.e., to analyze whether the necessities of national security truly require limiting or abandoning core due process principles. But to achieve such a balance, the courts must go beyond the "yes" or "no" question of whether a state of war exists. The courts recognize the President's power to commit the nation's military forces to combat, though the power to declare war (and finance it) remains with Congress. But this Commander-in-Chief power should not be construed to carry with it the inherent authority to depart from due process at home. Wars and armed conflicts are of too varying kinds, and the war on terror specifically is too multi-faceted, to equate the power to activate the Armed Forces, or even to declare war, with a power to override fundamental individual rights and liberties.

The Padilla district court decision appears to treat the "war on terror" as no different from the Civil War or World War II, in terms of a separation of powers analysis, thus compelling judicial deference to the President's actions as Commander in Chief in pursuit of that war, wherever prosecuted, with the courts without power to "review the level of force selected." Padilla, 533 F. Supp. 2d at 589, quoting Campbell v. Clinton, 203 F.3d 19, 27 (D.C. Cir. 2000) (Silberman, J., concurring).[82] To the contrary, wars or armed conflicts are of different kinds, particularly as they concern the exercise of the President's war power in this country. One size does not fit all. World War II should not be equated, with respect to the scope of the President's war power at home, with our military invasion of Grenada (or Iraq). World War II, a war declared by Congress, was a "total war" fought for national survival, with extensive domestic impacts. It involved a general mobilization of domestic industry for the war effort, a draft, rationing, etc. Grenada, of course, was not even a blip on the domestic screen. The war on terror is no such minor matter, but neither does it, by its nature, involve the military in domestic affairs to the extent required in World War II or, even more so, the Civil War fought on American soil.

As the nature of a war changes, so too should the permissible scope of the President's war power at home and its balance with due process. Youngstown shows that at a minimum. While the power to wage war is "the power to wage war successfully," what may be necessary for success in the context of one war may be gratuitous in another—or at least not so necessary as to sacrifice our core due process principles.

The relevant question, then, is not whether the war on terror is truly a "war," but rather what kind of war it is. Does it exhibit the conditions that, in past conflicts, have justified expansive interpretations of the war power? The war on terror, in fact, has many different aspects involving widely differing circumstances, ranging from the military campaign in Afghanistan to domestic law enforcement efforts to root out "sleeper cells." To use the Afghanistan campaign to justify limits on due process at home—on the ground that the "war on terror" embraces both venues—is dangerous and unnecessary business in the context of due process. The words of Justice Jackson, concurring in *Youngstown*, are salient here:

> . . . [N]o doctrine that the Court could promulgate would seem to me more sinister and alarming than that a President whose conduct of foreign affairs is so largely uncontrolled, and often even is unknown, can vastly enlarge his master over the internal affairs of the country by his own commitment of the Nation's armed forces to some foreign venture.

343 U.S. at 642.[83]

Any analysis of the balance between the war power and due process should distinguish between the two principal theaters of the war on terror, domestic and foreign. The rule of law speaks very differently to these two venues, as do the justifications typically advanced in support of an expansive reading of presidential power in wartime.

b. The War on Terror Abroad: Broad Presidential Discretion, and Maximum Judicial Deference

The courts are most deferential to exercises of the war power when the President is acting in a military context, as Commander in Chief, or as the architect of foreign policy, and especially "in time of war and of grave public danger." See, e.g., Quirin, 317 U.S. at 25 (detention and trial of saboteurs ordered by President in the exercise of his powers as Commander in Chief should not "be set aside by the courts without the clear conviction that they are in conflict with the Constitution or the laws of Congress constitutionally enacted"). Such judicial deference, strongest when Congress has specifically authorized the challenged action, appears to follow from the courts' acceptance of two related notions. First, that military and foreign affairs are seen as areas in which the President is constitutionally vested with unique authority and possesses presumed expertise. See, e.g., Chicago & Southern Air Lines v. Waterman Steamship Co., 333 U.S. 103, 111 (1948); United States v. Curtiss-Wright Export Corp., 299 U.S. 304, 319 (1936). Second, the courts view themselves as particularly ill-equipped to make decisions in these areas, because they require policy judgments not within the judges' special knowledge and because decisions often must be made rapidly and in a manner that court processes are not designed to accommodate. In addition, judicial deference is also heightened by the fact that the President and Congress are the "political" branches, and thus charged with making life-and-death decisions in times of crisis. As the one unelected branch, the judiciary is properly reluctant at such times to take positions that either potentially threaten, or may be seen as threatening, national survival.

The Fourth Circuit in Hamdi articulated the reasons for this deference in the context of overseas conflicts in these words:

> Through their departments and committees, the executive and legislative branches are organized to supervise the conduct of overseas conflict in a way that the judiciary simply is not. The Constitution's allocation of the warmaking powers reflects not only the expertise and experience lodged within the executive, but also the more fundamental truth that those branches most accountable to the people should be the ones to undertake the ultimate protection and to ask the ultimate sacrifice from them.

Hamdi III, 316 F.3d at 463. The very notion of a court attempting to adjudicate facts that may be concealed by the fog of foreign wars suggests caution. Hence we see the courts reluctant to become involved in cases that may call upon them to decide factual and policy-laden questions that are either not susceptible of direct proof by competent evidence, or that may require, for proper illumination, substantial disruption of military or other national security activities by the executive branch.

These justifications for extreme judicial deference speak most strongly to the overseas and military aspects of the war on terror. The military campaigns in Afghanistan and Iraq squarely implicate the President's powers as Commander in Chief. Their international aspects speak to the President's primacy in foreign affairs. The need for speedy executive action in response to terrorist-inspired crises abroad is self-evident. The need broadly to gather information (often not of evidentiary quality) from a wide variety of sources, including foreign intelligence services, is one that only the executive can meet.

For these reasons, an expansive view of the President's powers to pursue the war on terror abroad is justified. Further, the exercise of such powers abroad rarely will implicate due process concerns in view of the traditionally limited role of due process outside the country. The Hamdi decision, in these respects, was an easier one than Padilla.[84]

c. The War on Terror at Home: Due Process Still Applies

But when the focus is shifted to the detention of alleged enemy combatants seized in this country, such as in Padilla and now al-Marri, the case for deference to the President's unilateral war power becomes problematic. In this context, the President's foreign affairs primacy is of lesser moment. Nor is the President's role as a military commander dominant, for the domestic war on terror seems closer to a law enforcement effort than to a military campaign.[85] Most suspected terrorists detained in this country in fact have been prosecuted through the criminal justice system.[86] Nor does the war on terror at home, as a general matter, involve an emergency requiring action so hasty as to preclude the use of judicial processes, though particular crises may occur that do so temporarily (as in the immediate aftermath of 9/11). Speed surely is not the essence of the indefinite detentions, which are expressly intended to be long-term.

There is a vital line to be drawn between the exercise of the President's war power at home versus abroad. In the words of an FBI agent engaged in anti-terrorism investigations:

> Inside the borders of the United States, there is the rule of law. We had U.S. citizens. I was not just going to go up and scoop them off the street. N.Y. Times, The First Home-Front Battle in the War on Terror, Oct. 16, 2003, E8, c.3, 8 (quoting special agent Peter Ahearn on why he had not acted to seize the "Lackawanna Six" in the absence of sufficient evidence for an arrest).

A protest might be raised to the distinction of the war on terror abroad from the war on terror at home on the ground that it is all one war waged by the same enemy: an international conspiracy that respects no national boundaries. But while the war may be one, due process operates (generally) only at home, not abroad. The constitutional calculus is different, and it must be if the war on terror is not to swallow domestic liberties whole.

The contrary view of an undifferentiated global war on terror, with America viewed as part of the "battlefield," would hold all civil liberties hostage to the Commander in Chief's unilateral military judgment as to the "level of force" required to combat al Qaeda or other terrorists. With the President possessed of unreviewable powers to determine (i) when we are "at war," (ii) the dimensions of the "battlefield," and (iii) the "level of force" to be used, the elements of a "constitutional dictatorship," in Rossiter's phrase,[87] would be in place. The courts must abandon their role as protectors of core due process rights if they take Quirin and The Prize Cases to justify such an extreme result.

The Second Circuit did not. In reversing Padilla it drew a clear distinction between exercises of the war power abroad and at home. Again turning to Justice Jackson's concurrence in Youngstown, it cited his articulation (343 U.S. at 644) of the "Constitution's policy that Congress, not the Executive, should control utilization of the war power as an instrument of domestic policy." Padilla Cir. 713. The separation of powers as enforced by the courts, in sum, requires congressional authorization for Presidential action at home, as distinguished from his action abroad, which the courts generally will not scrutinize. Cf. United States v. Verdugo-Urquidez, 494 U.S. 259, 275 (1990) (any restrictions on actions by American armed forces abroad "must be imposed by the political branches through diplomatic understanding, treaty, or legislation," and not by the courts).

3. *The Claimed Necessity for Indefinite Detentions*

The exigencies of the war on terror at home surely warrant some deference by the courts to the executive's anti-terror initiatives, and the "flexible" nature of due process permits it. Such measures as heightened screening of luggage at airports and the use of police checkpoints during terrorism alerts are two examples of reasonable restrictions of liberty that should cause little pause. But the question of necessity cannot be left entirely in the hands of the executive branch, given its institutional need to place primary emphasis on national security. Political realities almost compel the President, by virtue of his role, to tilt the balance between national security and the due process rights of suspected terrorists strongly in favor of national security. He may be held responsible by the voters if he fails to prevent another terrorist attack, but likely not for any violation of due process in the course of seeking to prevent such an attack.

Chief Justice Rehnquist, writing in his private capacity as historian, sees the need for "more careful" judicial review of exercises of the war powers based on claims of necessity:

> It is all too easy to slide from a case of genuine military necessity, where the power sought to be exercised is at least debatable, to one where the threat is not critical and the power either dubious or non-existent.
>
> * * *
>
> It is neither reasonable nor is it remotely likely that civil liberty will occupy as favored a position in wartime as it does in peace-time. But it is both desirable and likely that more careful attention will paid by the courts to the basis for the government's claims of necessity as a basis for curtailing civil liberty. The laws will thus not be silent in time of war, but they will speak with a somewhat different voice.

Rehnquist at 224–25.

The courts, to be sure, are not ideally positioned to judge the military necessity of particular exercises of a President's claimed war power. But they are familiar with and responsible for enforcing due process principles. When a President's actions so sharply depart from core due process principles as do indefinite detentions, a heavy burden is fairly placed on the executive to justify the necessity of such unilaterally adopted measures.

With these observations in mind, we turn to the two bases on which the executive has claimed a necessity to employ indefinite detentions: to incapacitate suspected terrorists, and to interrogate them.

a. *Incapacitation: Achieved Well by the Criminal Justice System*

The first rationale is simply incapacitation: detaining a suspected terrorist prevents him from committing further acts of terrorism.[88] But so, too, does a successful criminal prosecution followed by a sentence commensurate with the crime. Accordingly, indefinite detentions could be justified on this rationale only if we lack confidence in the ability of the Justice Department, juries and judges to prosecute, convict and sentence terrorists. No such lack of confidence is warranted in light of the record of Article III courts in handling terrorist cases to date.

Are there an appreciable number of cases in which there exists "some evidence" that a suspect is a terrorist, but not enough to convict him of terrorism "beyond a reasonable doubt"? We have not heard of such an argument being seriously advanced. If there is any basis for it, it should be presented to Congress for it to consider whether legislation permitting indefinite detentions under some circumstances is justified.

b. Intelligence Gathering: Prosecutions Need Not Short Circuit the Process

The more serious alleged need for indefinite, incommunicado detentions is to facilitate intelligence-gathering interrogation designed to extract information helpful in preventing future terrorist attacks. It is with respect to this alleged need that the question of how to balance due process and security is most acutely posed, in the context of executive detentions.

It seems apparent, if press reports can be believed, that interrogations of al Qaeda leaders and some lower level operatives have yielded some valuable information concerning ongoing terrorist plots. The professed purpose of these enemy combatant detentions is indeed to extract information, rather than to impose a penalty for past conduct. To require prompt trials of the detainees on charges, the government urges, will defeat this purpose: a criminal proceeding, with its requirement that the defendant have access to counsel and to information in the possession of the government that is pertinent to his defense, may interfere with the continuity of debriefing of terrorist suspects, including both the defendant and others.

The premise for this point is summarized in a declaration submitted by the government on its re-argument motion in Padilla. In that declaration, an official from the Defense Intelligence Agency ("DIA") summarized the technique of debriefing favored by the DIA in this context. As quoted by Chief Judge Mukasey, the government represented:

> DIA's approach to interrogation is largely dependent upon creating an atmosphere of dependency and trust between the subject and the interrogator. Developing the kind of relationship of trust and dependency necessary for effective interrogations is a process that can take a significant amount of time. There are numerous examples of situations where interrogators have been unable to obtain valuable intelligence from a subject until months, or even years, after the interrogation process began.
>
> Anything that threatens the perceived dependency and trust between the subject and interrogator directly threatens the value of interrogation as an intelligence-gathering tool. Even seemingly minor interruptions can have profound psychological impacts on the delicate subject-interrogator relationship. Any insertion of counsel into the subject-interrogator relationship, for example—even if only for a limited duration or for a specific purpose—can undo months of work and may permanently shut down the interrogation process. Therefore, it is critical to minimize external influences on the interrogation process.

Padilla, 243 F. Supp. 2d at 49.

The interference posited by the government could come in two ways. First, once criminal charges are filed the interrogation process could come to an immediate halt since the defendant must be warned of his rights to silence and to counsel.[89] Second, the defendant might seek and obtain court authorization to contact other detainees who may be undergoing such interrogation, and such contacts could imperil the gathering of information even from individuals who are being held abroad, outside of the criminal justice system.

Although these concerns are not fanciful, there are at least some potential avenues for dealing with them. First, in many instances, the government might most effectively obtain information from a detainee by pursuing criminal charges, having counsel assigned and then allowing the attorney to seek to persuade his client to cooperate in exchange for leniency. See Padilla, 243 F. Supp. 2d at 51–53 (suggesting the same scenario). In fact, the Department of Justice touts its success at obtaining information from accused terrorists in precisely this manner:

- **[W]e are gathering information by leveraging criminal charges and long prison sentences.** When individuals realize that they face a long prison term, they often try to cut their prison time by pleading guilty and cooperating with the government. Since September 11, we have obtained criminal plea agreements from more than 15 individuals, who must, and will continue to, cooperate with the government in its terrorist investigations.
- These individuals have provided critical intelligence about al Qaeda and other terrorist groups, safehouses, training camps, recruitment, and tactics in the U.S., and the operations of those terrorists who mean to do American citizens harm.
- One individual has given us intelligence on weapons stored here in the United States.
- Another cooperator has identified locations in the U.S. being scouted or cased for potential attacks by al Qaeda.

(Dept. of Justice Website, Jan. 30, 2004: www.lifeandliberty.gov/subs/a_terr.htm) (emphasis in original).

Second, since there is little doubt that after arrest accused terrorists will be subject to pre-trial preventive detention, while they are so detained the government could possibly subject them to an intelligence-gathering process, and yet protect its ability to prosecute, by having the interrogation conducted by someone who is involved solely in intelligence-gathering and will be walled off from any participants in any subsequent criminal proceeding. See, e.g., Padilla, 243 F. Supp. 2d at 51 (citing cases).[90] The privilege against self-incrimination is an evidentiary one: a "fundamental trial right," the violation of which "occurs only at trial." United States v. Verdugo-Urquidoz, 494 U.S. at 264. It is not offended by questioning if the fruits are not used at trial. Therefore, so long as the interrogation is isolated from the criminal proceeding, with no information elicited from the suspect introduced at trial against the suspect or made available to the prosecuting attorneys, due process and the right to assistance of counsel may be flexible enough to permit some interrogation of suspected terrorists. The precise extent to which such interrogations might be permitted is not a question we need answer for the purpose of this discussion, except to note that such interrogation is not necessarily precluded if due process, as we urge, is construed to prevent indefinite and incommunicado detentions in service of the domestic war on terror.

The danger of interference with other ongoing interrogations is not entirely speculative, as illustrated by the case of Zacarias Moussaoui, the accused "twentieth hijacker". Moussaoui has successfully sought from the trial court some form of access to Ramzi Bin Al-Shibh, an allegedly high-level al Qaeda operative recently seized in Pakistan and now being held and interrogated overseas. The government's refusal to permit such access has resulted in the dismissal of portions of the indictment and the preclusion of the death penalty, a ruling now on appeal. United States v. Moussaoui, 282 F. Supp. 2d 480 (E.D. Va. 2003), appeal pending, No. 03-4792 (4th Cir.).

We do not know the eventual fate of the Moussaoui prosecution, but it appears to present quite a unique circumstance: a charge of conspiracy to commit a specific act (the 9/11 attacks), supported by (it would appear) scant evidence, and with the defendant able credibly to identify another suspect in a position to refute the charge. There are likely to be very few similar cases, in part because the argument for the necessity of access to another detainee will not appeal to most courts. Moreover, even if some access is deemed necessary, the less intrusive approach may involve either providing defense counsel with some of the fruits of the other suspect's interrogation or, still more likely, having the trial judge review those fruits and, if they are helpful to the defendant, grant relief comparable to what is authorized by the Classified Information

Procedures Act, 18 U.S.C. App. 3, § 1 et seq., as a substitute for production of classified information.

While we recognize that the above measures fall short of the unlimited opportunity for interrogation desired by the executive, they accommodate the proclaimed need to some degree. If due process is to be bent further, perhaps to the breaking point, we submit that statutory authority is required at a minimum based on a showing of compelling necessity found persuasive by Congress.

4. *Emergencies*

While we conclude that indefinite detentions in this country should not be held within the executive's war power, absolutism is not necessary or prudent in this context. Due process is not unyielding in the face of dire emergency. It can accommodate transient, short-term departures from its normal strictures in truly emergency situations, requiring immediate action to protect the nation's security that only the executive is capable of initiating. Temporary detentions by the executive in such emergency circumstances might pass due process muster in "the particular situation" presented. Morrissey v. Brewer, 408 U.S. at 481.

The Second Circuit appears to disagree, holding that "the Constitution lodges these [emergency] powers with Congress, not the President," again relying on the Jackson concurrence in Youngstown. Padilla Cir. at 714–15.[91] We do not agree with this total negation of a President's ability to act swiftly in a dire emergency at home under his war power given the possibility—not so remote in light of 9/11—of an unpredictable circumstance in which awaiting congressional action would be folly and reliance on criminal procedures futile.

But to say that the domestic war on terror presents such circumstances of emergency necessity in general—throughout its indeterminate duration and wherever prosecuted—would be not only contrary to fact but deeply threatening to our core due process values. The courts cannot abdicate meaningful review of Presidential claims of emergency circumstances and remain true to their role as protectors of constitutional liberties.

C. The Necessity of Congressional Authorization

1. *A Clear If Not Loud Message: Congress Counts*

The question of the extent to which due process should yield to the demands of the war on terror is not an easy one. But when the President's actions at home so clearly conflict with core due process principles, we do not believe that the President's war-making power alone should be held sufficient to sustain those actions under the Constitution. Rather, we believe that congressional authorization is essential for any indefinite domestic detentions conceivably to pass constitutional muster, given that they depart so sharply from core due process principles. Striking the balance between national security and due process rights cannot and should not depend on the courts' naked review of unilateral executive actions, not supported by the other political branch.

One fairly consistent theme that runs through the relatively sparse relevant case law is that the courts are more willing to approve the President's actions in the United States pursuant to his war powers when there has been specific congressional authorization for those actions. See, e.g., Martin v. Mott, 25 U.S. 19 (1827) (President's activation of state militias authorized by 1795 statute); Luther v. Borden, 48 U.S. 1, 42–43 (1849) (citing same statute); Quirin, 317 U.S. 1 (1942) (use of military commissions to try unlawful combatants seized in U.S.); Hirabayashi v. United States, 320 U.S. 81 (1944), and Korematsu v. United States, 323 U.S. 214

(1944) (congressional authorization found for the curfew and relocation orders imposed by the executive branch on Japanese resident aliens and citizens).[92]

In contrast, several important cases have struck down executive action in the United States as beyond the President's war power, in the absence of specific congressional authorization. See Milligan, 71 U.S. 2 (no congressional authorization for use of military commissions in areas in which civil courts were functioning; four concurring justices in Milligan would have affirmed the challenged military commissions had they been authorized by Congress); Youngstown, 343 U.S. 579 (no congressional authorization for seizure of steel mills). The absence of congressional authorization, in fact, is the principal basis of the Second Circuit's invalidation of citizen detentions in its Padilla decision.[93]

It is true that the presence or absence of congressional authorization has not been the central focus of the above-cited Supreme Court decisions. The clearest expression of the importance of congressional action is probably Justice Jackson's concurring opinion in Youngstown, heavily relied upon the Second Circuit's Padilla opinion, in which he urged that the presumption in favor of the constitutionality of presidential action is strongest when the action is supported by specific congressional authorization. There is compelling wisdom in this observation. It is consistent with a sensitive application of the separation of powers doctrine for the courts to show greater deference to action authorized by both of the political branches of government, rather than to action taken by the executive alone.

The sharp departure from due process inherent in indefinite detentions should require, at minimum, affirmative congressional authorization after consideration of the difficult relevant policy considerations. There is, we recognize, a rational basis for some special treatment of terrorist activities under the law, for terrorism, to some degree, can be distinguished from other types of criminal activity. International terrorism represents an organized and violent conspiracy directed against the United States, as distinguished from other criminal activity, which is typically more private and limited in its objectives. As September 11 demonstrated, terrorism can cause a uniquely grave impact on the national sense of well-being as well as terrible loss of life. The demonstrated willingness of religious fanatics to engage in suicidal attacks places their actions beyond the normal variety of criminal conduct, and beyond the likely deterrent capacity of any threat of punishment by our criminal justice system.

In criminal prosecutions, the requirement that the government prove guilt beyond a reasonable doubt is "designed to exclude as nearly as possible the likelihood of an erroneous judgment," and thereby "our society imposes almost the entire risk of error upon itself." Addington v. Texas, 441 U.S. 418, 424–25 (1979). With respect to terrorism, when the consequence of error may be not just the acquittal of a defendant but the perpetration of further terrorist acts, the graver risk of error may argue against reading the Constitution to impose the "entire risk of error" on society. Cf. Kennedy v. Mendoza-Martinez, 372 U.S. 141, 160 (1963) (the Constitution "is not a suicide pact"; case involved compulsory military service).

Congress is in a position to weigh the interests of due process and national security in this context. It "can see the problem whole," not limited to the President's necessary emphasis on national security or by the courts' necessary focus on individual cases. Katyal & Tribe, 111 Yale L.J. at 1275. Specifically, it can explore through hearings and debate the extent to which indefinite detentions are necessary to facilitate the interrogations of terrorists, and the degree to which such interrogations are essential in preventing future terrorist attacks. It can consider ways in which such interrogations can be facilitated without wholesale departure from the rule of law and due process.[94]

There are, it is important to note, constitutional limitations on what Congress itself can authorize in the war on terror. See Humanitarian Law Project v. Ashcroft, No. CV 03-6107

(C.D. Cal. Jan. 22, 2004) (invalidating section of USA Patriot Act as unconditionally vague); cf., e.g., Reid v. Covert, 354 U.S. 1 (1957) (ruling unconstitutional, as violative of Article III and the Fifth and Sixth Amendments, the congressionally-authorized use of courts marshal to try dependents of military personnel abroad on capital charges). To the extent legislation abrogates core due process principles in authorizing enemy combatant detentions, its constitutionality cannot be assumed.[95] But no question: the judgment of both political branches as to the necessity of enemy combatant detentions, and their appropriate extent and limitations, would carry a stronger presumption of constitutionality than does unilateral executive action.

If legislation in this area is deemed desirable, it could and should address the circumstances (if any) warranting detentions without charges, and the appropriate role of the courts in reviewing such detentions.[96] Among the many relevant questions:

- What type of activity is sufficient to warrant detention (as distinguished from a trial on criminal charges), e.g., should only direct involvement in a violent terrorist plot be sufficient or should providing logistical support for a terrorist organization also be sufficient, as the administration seems to believe?
- What standard of proof concerning the detainee's activities must the government meet in court to justify the detention (e.g., "some evidence," probable cause, clear and convincing evidence)?
- What type of hearing should the courts conduct to test the government's justification (a full adversary proceeding or something less rigorous)?
- Is the detainee to be afforded the right to counsel by statute, as is the case in proceedings under the Alien Terrorist Removal Act, 8 U.S.C. § 1534(c)(1)?
- For what purposes can the detention be continued (e.g., preventive detention, ongoing interrogation), and what standard of proof applies to such a showing by the government?
- For how long can the detention be continued before additional justification must be presented by the government in court?
- Are the rules for detention to be different for citizens and non-citizens?[97]

There is a risk that the Second Circuit's opinion in Padilla, relying as it does on a statute prohibiting the detention (only) of citizens, and deciding as it must only the case before it, involving a citizen, might encourage arbitrary distinctions between citizens and non-citizens. Any such bright line distinctions are to be avoided. They would violate the equal protection and due process rights of aliens, and encourage additional discrimination against Arabs and Muslims.

Nor would such distinctions make sense. Padilla and Hamdi, both citizens, probably have less attachment to this country than millions of Arab-Americans who have lived here for many years. Any detentions, if at all justified outside the criminal justice system, should be based on individualized considerations, and not ethnic stereotyping or arbitrary citizen vs. non-citizen categories.

2. *Congress Has Not Authorized Indefinite Detentions*

a. The Joint Resolution Does Not

We agree with the Second Circuit that the Joint Resolution of September 18, 2001, does not constitute authorization for indefinite enemy combatant detentions in the United States. The Joint Resolution broadly authorizes the President to use "all necessary and appropriate force" against terrorist organizations (and their members) responsible for the September 11 attacks. By its title it speaks expressly of "Military Force" and "the use of the United States Armed Forces," and its text specifies that it constitutes authorization, under sections 5(b) and 8(a)(1) of the War Powers Resolution, 50 U.S.C. § 1544(b), 1547(a)(1), for the use of the United States

Armed Forces. This generally worded enactment, speaking most directly (and perhaps exclusively) to military action abroad, should not be sufficient to suspend or abridge basic due process rights of individuals detained in the United States.[98] Specific congressional legislation addressing the enemy combatant context, and invoking Congress' own war powers, properly would elicit greater judicial deference, though not an abdication of the courts' role to pass on the constitutionality of legislation.

b. The USA PATRIOT Act Does Not, and by Implication Restricts Detentions

Legislation more specific than the Joint Resolution is found in the USA PATRIOT Act, Pub. L. No. 107-56, 115 Stat. 272 (2001), but it does not support detentions of an extended or indefinite nature, and its detention provisions do not apply at all to U.S. citizens. The statute authorizes only the detention for up to seven days of an alien "the Attorney General has reasonable grounds to believe" is engaged in activity that "endangers the national security," following which the Attorney General must either commence removal proceedings or release the detainee. Title IV, §§ 411-12, codified at 8 U.S.C. § 1226a(a)(3) and (5) (2001).

Further, "[i]f an alien is finally determined not to be removable", then the detention "shall terminate." 8 U.S.C. § 1226a(a)(2). If the alien is found to be removable, but cannot be removed, then but only then is the Attorney General authorized to detain such an individual for successive six-month periods until the alien either is removed or is no longer a threat to "the national security of the United States or the safety of the community or any person." Id. § 1226a(a)(6).

Thus the PATRIOT Act authorizes continuing detentions of aliens only if a) they are adjudged to be removable, pursuant to proceedings which must be commenced within 7 days of detention; b) they cannot be removed; c) and they pose a threat to national security.[99] The designation of an individual as an "enemy combatant" is not a substitute for a final order of removal. Therefore, it cannot be said that Congress authorized such indefinite detentions in the PATRIOT Act.

c. 18 U.S.C. § 4001(a) Prohibits Detentions Not within the War Power

The Second Circuit held that the detention of citizens as enemy combatants is prohibited (since not authorized by the Joint Resolution) by 18 U.S.C. § 4001(a), which provides:

> No citizen shall be imprisoned or otherwise detained by the United States except pursuant to an Act of Congress.

This statute was passed in 1971 to preclude any detentions analogous to the widely condemned removals of Japanese citizens in World War II upheld in the Korematsu case. In our view, this generally worded statute, enacted in a context far removed from terrorism, should not be construed to abrogate any long-standing war power of the President.[100] But, as argued above, such power does not include indefinite detentions in the United States, and to that extent the statute does have force.

V. MILITARY COMMISSIONS: THEIR USE IN THE WAR ON TERROR SHOULD BE MINIMIZED

If we are correct in arguing that accused terrorists seized in the United States and citizens seized abroad must be tried (or released),[101] the question of the trial tribunal becomes ripe.

The President's Military Order issued on November 13, 2001 (the "PMO"),[102] authorized the trial by military commission of non-citizens—whether seized at home or abroad—accused of being members of al Qaeda or committing or aiding terrorist acts. In July 2003 six detained "enemy combatants" were designated as subject to the PMO, but no commissions have yet been scheduled.

As a matter of constitutional law, we believe the President's war power alone would be insufficient to override the Sixth Amendment right of suspects seized in this country to a "speedy and public trial before an impartial jury." But, unlike with respect to indefinite detentions, there is express congressional authorization for the use of military commissions to try offenses violating the law of war: the same statute on which the Quirin court relied.

Quirin, although it has been questioned,[103] stands as precedent authorizing the use of military commissions to try violations of the law of war, even by a United States citizen seized in the United States. It is true that the statute on which Quirin relied, Article 15 of the Articles of War, was general. It merely confirmed, without defining, the pre-existing jurisdiction of military commissions to try "offenders or offenses that by statute or by the law of war may be tried by military commissions...." It was arguably inadequate to support the result reached in Quirin, for there was little precedent for the use of military commissions outside occupied territories or theaters of active combat, or in any area where the civilian courts were functioning. However, Congress reenacted Article 15 in 1950 as part of the Uniform Code of Military Justice. 10 U.S. C. § 821.[104] That congressional action, with knowledge of the Quirin precedent, can fairly be read as endorsing Quirin's view that Congress has authorized the use of military commissions in the United States to prosecute violations of the law of war.[105]

Thus, given Quirin, we do not say "never" with respect to the use of military commissions to prosecute alleged violators of the law of war seized in the United States. We note, however, that whether acts of terrorism by non-state actors violate the law of war is far from clear. Neither customary international law nor any treaties to which the United States is a party recognize a state of war or "armed conflict," thereby implicating the law of war, in the absence of any organized armed forces. An international terrorist conspiracy, though subject to criminal prosecution, is not easily viewed as governed by the law of war. See generally, Congressional Research Service, Terrorism and the Law of War: Trying Terrorists as War Criminals Before Military Commissions, CRS 10–17 (Dec. 11, 2001); Nat'l Inst. of Military Justice, Annotated Guide, Procedures for Trials by Military Commission of Certain Non-United States Citizens in the War Against Terrorism 9–10 (2002) ("NIMJ Guide"). For a thorough discussion of this and related issues concerning the use of military commissions in the war on terror, see Association of the Bar of the City of New York, Inter Arma Silent Leges: In Times of Armed Conflict, Should the Laws be Silent? A Report on The President's Military Order of November 13, 2001 Regarding "Detention, Treatment, and Trial of Certain Non-Citizens in the War Against Terrorism" ("City Bar Report").

But assuming that, to some extent, the use of military commissions to try suspected terrorists would be constitutional, we urge that they be sparingly used, given the competence and advantages of the federal court forum.

As a practical matter, the federal courts have proven their ability effectively to try terrorists, aided by the enactment in 1980 of the Classified Information Procedures Act, 18 U.S.C. App. 3, § 1 et seq. ("CIPA"), which protects national security information in the context of such trials.

As a policy matter, trials in Article III courts serve the national interest by providing a public determination of guilt or innocence by an impartial jury overseen by an independent judge. The far greater likely acceptance of the fairness of such trials more than compensates for any marginal increase in the protection of classified information, or any higher likelihood of convictions, that may be available in military commissions controlled by the executive branch.

A. Military Justice System (Courts Martial)

Since September 11th, both courts-martial and military commissions have been proposed as venues for trying terrorists. These proposals often conflate two very different mechanisms. Each system has a unique function, constitutional foundation and relationship with what this report has labeled "core values". See NIMJ Guide 78–80. While in general the federal judiciary has had minimal contact with and oversight of these forms of military justice, civilian and military judicial structures have interacted in important ways.

1. *Constitutional and Statutory Basis*

The United States Constitution empowered the Congress to create a military justice system, including a courts-martial system. This congressional power springs from Article I, section 8, clause 1 (to "provide for the common defense") and clause 11 ("To make Rules for the Government and Regulation of the land and naval Forces."). Statutory authority for courts-martial derives from the Articles of War, initially adopted by the Second Continental Congress in 1775 (NIMJ Guide 78), its numerous amendments,[106] and the Uniform Code of Military Justice ("UCMJ"), enacted by Congress in 1950, which in part codifies the Articles of War. 10 U.S.C. §§ 801–950.

The UCMJ amended the Articles of War to create the system of military courts-martial in existence today.[107] It authorizes the President (and the Secretary of Defense) to convene courts-martial (Article 22(a)(1)(2)) and to compel, insofar as the President considers "practicable," the enforcement of civilian standards of criminal procedure.[108] The Supreme Court has upheld the constitutionality of this delegation of power.[109]

Both the Articles of War and the UCMJ reflect the initial conception of the military justice system as primarily a system for disciplining soldiers, and only secondarily a venue for trying non-military personnel.[110] But the UCMJ contains provisions that give courts-martials jurisdiction over non-servicemen in narrow circumstances.[111] Most notably, the UCMJ provides that courts-martial have jurisdiction, concurrent with military tribunals and commissions (Article 21), "to try any person who by the law of war is subject to trial by a military tribunal and may adjudge any punishment permitted by the law of war" (Article 18), and also jurisdiction over prisoners of war (Article 2(a)(9)). In practice, however, these functions have generally been fulfilled by special military commissions.

2. *Protection of Core Values and Judicial Oversight*

The Due Process Clause is applicable to legislation dealing with military affairs, though the courts afford great deference to Congress given its "plenary control" over the military under the Constitution (Art. I, § 8). Weiss v. United States, 510 U.S. 163, 176–77 (1994), quoting Chappell v. Wallace, 462 U.S. 296, 301 (1983).

The UCMJ contains many provisions recognizing rights also enforced in civilian courts:

> By enacting the Uniform Code of Military Justice in 1950, and through subsequent statutory changes, Congress has gradually changed the system of military justice so that it has come to more closely resemble the civilian system. Weiss, 510 U.S. at 174.

Thus the UCMJ includes a prohibition on compulsory self-incrimination (Article 31), and a right to be represented by civilian counsel or military counsel of one's own selection (Article 38), and imposes a burden of proof on the United States to establish guilt beyond a reasonable doubt (Article 51). The UCMJ also establishes an appeals court of five civilian judges, the United States Court of Appeals for the Armed Forces, which is located within, but independent of, the Department of Defense (Articles 59–76).[112]

The most widely criticized weakness of the courts-martial system has been its lack of independence from the military command structure. Courts-martial judges have significantly less independence than civilian judges since their selection, as well as many pre-trial procedural decisions, are made by commanding officers, who often also have initiated the prosecutions.[113]

In general, the military justice system has not been the subject of significant judicial oversight. Most procedural issues and appeals have been dealt with by the Court of Appeals for the Armed Forces. However, the federal courts have intervened to adjudicate the overlapping or conflicting jurisdictions of the courts-martial and civilian courts in the context of habeas petitions.[114] A series of post-World War II cases ruled that courts-martial jurisdiction could not be extended to non-military personnel, including discharged soldiers,[115] civilian employees of the military overseas (for capital offenses),[116] and civilian dependents of overseas military personnel.[117] With respect to members of the Armed Forces, in 1987 the Supreme Court overruled its 1969 decision that had limited the jurisdiction of courts-martial to crimes committed by military personnel that had a relationship to their military service (a "service connection").[118]

The federal courts have heard habeas petitions from courts-martial rulings and on occasion intervened in the procedural area of courts-martials. For instance, in Loving v. United States, 517 U.S. 748 (1996), the Supreme Court held that Supreme Court jurisprudence on the death penalty applied to the military court system. At the same time, the Court endorsed the power of the President to circumscribe courts-martial procedural rules (a power delegated to him under the UCMJ).

In summary, while the traditional role of the military justice system has been to discipline soldiers and other individuals working for or under the control of the military, it could nonetheless be used as a tool for prosecuting terrorists for offenses violating the "law of war", under the jurisdiction accorded by Article 18. While the courts-martial's lack of independence presents a risk of manipulation by military commanders, the UCMJ and the Manual for Courts-Martial offer significant protection to core values.

B. Special Military Commissions

1. *Constitutional and Statutory Basis*

Military commissions, as Quirin observed, have a long history of use both in this country and elsewhere in the world. See Quirin, 317 U.S. at 35–36. They have been the historic and traditional venue for the trial of war crimes. See Wedgwood, 96 Am. J. Int'l L. at 332.[119]

The historical precedent for the use in the United States of special military tribunals (hereinafter "military commissions"), extends back to the Revolutionary War trial of Major John Andre.[120] While the Constitution makes no mention of military commissions, Presidential authority to establish them is traceable to the Commander in Chief war power clause of Article II, section 2. During the occupation of parts of Mexico during the Mexican American War, military commissions were set up to try civilian offenses committed in the occupied territory, and "councils of war" were set up to try violations of the law of war.[121] During the Civil War, the use of military commissions flourished, with over 4000 trials covering both violation of the laws of war and ordinary crimes.[122] President Lincoln declared a state of martial law throughout the country in 1862, and set up tribunals to try both military personnel and civilians.

During World War II, as most notably upheld in Quirin, military commissions were once again put into place to try spies and enemy combatants both on American soil and abroad, in

Germany, Japan and other countries occupied by the Allies. The year after World War II ended, the Court again upheld the use of a military commission in In re Yamashita, 327 U.S. 1 (1946). Japanese General Tomoyuki Yamashita, though captured as a lawful combatant, was accused of committing war crimes: failure to take steps to prevent the commission of atrocities by Japanese troops under his command during the U.S. Army's retaking of the Philippines. 327 U.S. at 16. The Court affirmed the authority of military commissions to try offenses against the law of war, even after active hostilities had ceased.[123] It further held, based on congressional grants of power in the Articles of War and the Espionage Act of 1917, that proceedings before military tribunals were free from review by the Supreme Court, save only inquiry as to whether the trial was within the authority of the military power.

In Madsen v. Kinsella, 343 U.S. 341 (1952), the Supreme Court surveyed the history of military commissions as follows:

> Since our nation's earliest days, such commissions have been constitutionally recognized agencies for meeting many governmental responsibilities related to war. They have been called our common law war courts. They have taken many forms and borne many names. Neither their procedure nor their jurisdiction has been prescribed by statute. It has been adopted in each instance to the need that called it forth. . . .

Id. at 348 (footnotes and citation omitted).

In Madsen, the wife of an American officer stationed in occupied Germany was tried by the United States Court of the Allied High Commission for Germany for murdering her husband and was convicted. The Supreme Court upheld the High Commission Court's authority, stating that the establishment of a military tribunal in an occupied country after the cessation of hostilities was within the President's authority, absent any attempt to limit that authority by Congress:

> In absence of attempts by Congress to limit the President's power, it appears that, as Commander-in-Chief of the Army and Navy of the United States, he may, in time of war, establish and prescribe the jurisdiction and procedure of military commissions and of tribunals in the nature of such commissions, in territory occupied by Armed Forces of the United States. His authority to do so sometimes survives cessation of hostilities. The President has the urgent and infinite responsibility not only of combating the enemy but of governing any territory occupied by the United States by force of arms. The policy of Congress to refrain from legislating in this uncharted area does not imply its lack of power to legislate.

Id. at 348–49 (emphasis added).

The UCMJ, the Constitution, and federal jurisprudence limit the subject matter jurisdiction of military tribunals to violations of the law of war, with the narrow exception, as affirmed by *Madsen*, of the temporary use of tribunals to try civilian offenses during military occupation by United States forces abroad. See American Bar Association Task Force on Terrorism and the Law, Report and Recommendations on Military Commissions, Army Law 8, 12–13 (March 2002); City Bar Report at 10–14.[124] If, then, the President seeks to prosecute suspected terrorists before military commissions, one necessary role for the federal courts will be to review whether the actions charged constitute violations of the law of war, a question not free from doubt in the context of stateless terrorism.

2. *The Enemy Combatant Commission Orders*

Language in the Manual for Courts-Martial suggests that, barring other regulations set forth by the President or Congress, the UCMJ governs military commissions.[125] However, the Bush administration chose to promulgate specific procedures to govern the trial of any suspected terrorists, initially in the PMO issued November 13, 2001, and, later, in Military Commission Order No. 1 issued on March 21, 2002, by the Department of Defense (the "DOD Order"). See generally NIMJ Guide (comprehensive analysis of the DOD Order).

The PMO presented an array of potential due process issues.[126] This is foreshadowed in Section 1(f) of the PMO, stating "it is not practicable to apply in military commissions under this order the principles of law and the rules of evidence generally recognized in the trial of criminal cases in the United States district courts." The PMO provided for preventive arrest,[127] seemingly indefinite detention,[128] suspension of the exclusionary rule,[129] and exclusive jurisdiction, the latter provision perhaps intended to prohibit habeas corpus relief.[130] Under the PMO, a detainee could be convicted, and even sentenced to death, on secret evidence (§ 4(c)(4)), and on a vote of only two-thirds of the members of the commission (§ 4(c)(6) and (7); conviction could be premised on evidence well short of proof beyond a reasonable doubt; the decision was to be rendered, not by a jury of the detainee's peers, but by military officers subject to executive command; and the trials could be closed to the public (§ 4(c)(4)). In the opinion of this Association, the framework set forth in the PMO was inconsistent with the procedural protections of the UCMJ, thereby violating the requirement of UCMJ Article 36 that procedural changes made by the President "not be contrary or inconsistent with this chapter [the UCMJ]." City Bar Report at 18.

The March 2002 DOD Order responded to numerous complaints about the lack of protection of core values in the PMO. For instance, the DOD Order articulates a presumption of innocence, a right to counsel, a right to cross-examine witnesses, and a right not to testify during trial with no adverse inference to be drawn. § 5 ("Procedures Accorded the Accused"). It also establishes a procedure for limited appeals to a review panel appointed by the "Appointing Authority" (§ 6H(4) and (5)), defined as "the Secretary of Defense or a designee." § 2.

However, the DOD Order does little to answer concerns that the commission structure lacks independence, fails to provide some very basic protections for 'core values', and falls substantially short of the procedural safeguards embodied in the UCMJ. For instance, the Order gives the President, the Secretary of Defense or their designee control over the appointment of tribunal members (§ 4A) and members of the review panel (§ 6H(4)), and the authority to review the rulings of the review panel (§ 6H(5) and (6)). The DOD Order's guarantee of a right to civilian counsel is conditioned on such counsel being approved by the government, and their employment at no government expense. (§ 4(C)(3)). The DOD Order allows for public hearings (§ 5O), but also empowers the Appointing Authority to close those hearings for security reasons and to exclude the accused and civilian defense counsel from closed hearings in certain circumstances. § 6B(3). It further authorizes the government to withhold information "concerning... national security interests" (§ 6D(5)), or "state secrets." § 9.[131] It does not supersede (see § 7B) the terms of the PMO providing for preventive arrest, indefinite detention, suspension of the exclusionary rule and exclusive jurisdiction § 6(b).

Thus from the standpoint of due process values, the DOD Order, while a significant improvement from the PMO, still stops considerably short of the procedural protections available in Article III courts, or even those available in courts-martial under the UCMJ. See NIMJ Guide 80–83.

VI. THE ADVANTAGES AND DISADVANTAGES OF THE FEDERAL COURT FORUM

Our review of legal and historical precedent suggests that the government, consistent with the Constitution, may have the authority to try suspected terrorists for violations of the law of war, in the United States or elsewhere, before military commissions. We turn to the question of whether such an approach, to the extent constitutional, is desirable public policy, and, if so, in what circumstances.[132]

The principal articulated argument for avoiding the civilian courts is that both procedural and substantive legal requirements applicable in these courts pose significant practical problems for the war on terrorism. In substance, the proponents of alternative remedies suggest that the civilian courts are not equipped to handle cases of this sort without endangering either national security or the participants in the proceeding. See, e.g., Ruth Wedgwood, After September 11, 36 New Eng. L. Rev. 725, 728 (2002); Wedgwood, 96 Am. J. Int'l L. at 330–32 (2002). This argument rests on explicit or implicit assumptions about how the civilian legal system works and what its limitations may be in dealing with the prosecution of terrorists. To test these assumptions, we look to the courts' experience in dealing with similar types of cases, and also assess the procedures available to the courts under current law to protect national security and other vital interests in the context of terrorism prosecutions.

A. The Feasibility of Criminal Prosecutions of Terrorists in Article III Courts

As an initial matter, we note that the criminal justice system today clearly has the statutory authority to deal with acts of terrorism. This has not always been the case. During the Civil War, one reason for the frequent resort to military commissions was that few if any criminal statutes reached the actions of Confederate sympathizers and activists. See, e.g., Hyman at 65–75. Prosecutors lacked any legal basis for charging many such suspects with serious and provable criminal violations. Absent clear proof of violent activity, the only available legal theory was treason, and that charge carries with it a very difficult, constitutionally mandated burden of proof.[133] See Hyman at 94–95. See generally United States v. Rahman, 189 F.3d 88, 111–12 (2d Cir. 1999).

In contrast, the current federal criminal code is well stocked with provisions criminalizing a significant array of activities that are said to bear the hallmark of terrorist intent. As recent prosecutions illustrate, the potential legal charges are many and varied.

For example, the defendants in the Rahman prosecution faced charges of seditious conspiracy, 18 U.S.C. § 2384; illegal use of explosives to destroy property, 18 U.S.C. § 844(i); conspiracy to kill foreign officials, 18 U.S.C. §§ 1416–17; and the use of violence or other criminal acts to assist a racketeering organization, 18 U.S.C. § 1959. See Rahman, 189 F.3d at 126. In the embassy bombing case, the defendants were charged, inter alia, with possession of firearms in a federal facility, 18 U.S.C. § 930; dealing in, possessing or distributing explosives without a license, 18 U.S.C. § 842; murder within the territorial jurisdiction of the United States, 18 U.S.C. § 1111; destruction of national-defense materials, premises or utilities, 18 U.S.C. § 2155(b); the killing of a United States official or employee in the course of his official functions, 18 U.S.C. § 1114; maiming within the territorial jurisdiction of the United States, 18 U.S.C. § 114; malicious destruction of government property, 18 U.S.C. § 844(f)(1); and use of explosives against United States nationals, 18 U.S.C. §§ 844(n) & 2332(b). See, e.g., United States v. Bin Laden, 92 F. Supp. 2d 189, 192, 198, 201–04 (S.D.N.Y. 2000); United States v. Bin Laden, 160 F. Supp. 2d 670, 672 n.1 (S.D.N.Y. 2001). Other recent prosecutions have featured charges of fraud in connection with the possession or use of identification documents, visas and passports, 18 U.S.C. §§ 1546(a), 1028(a)(6), see United States v. Koubriti, 199 F. Supp. 2d 656, 658 (E.D. Mich. 2002), and providing material support and resources to a registered terrorist organization, 18 U.S.C. § 2339B. See United States v. Sattar, No. 02 CR 395, 2002 WL 1836755 *1 (S.D.N.Y. Aug. 12, 2002).[134]

The federal courts have had significant experience trying terrorists, with a high rate of convictions.[135] Since criminal prosecutions in Article III federal courts are a readily available option for proceeding against accused terrorists, we turn to the question of whether such prosecutions are preferable to the use of military commissions. We start with the evident benefits of such an approach, and then address the principal articulated drawbacks.

B. The Benefits of Using Article III Courts to Deal with Terrorism Offenses

The considerations militating in favor of using the federal courts to deal with criminal conduct that involves terrorist aims or methods are easy to cite and compelling in their simplicity.

1. *Justice*

As we have noted earlier in this report, our Constitution—as interpreted by the Supreme Court—embodies a set of requirements that evolve from the twin concepts that the government may not seize an individual and hold him against his will absent evidence of criminal conduct or some other constitutionally cognizable basis for detention (the substantive due-process principle) and that any such detainee is entitled to certain procedural protections to ensure that his loss of liberty is justified by governing legal rules (the procedural due-process principle). In substance, any person seized by the government is presumed to be entitled to be restored to freedom, and the government must persuade a neutral decision-maker that the detainee is permissibly deprived of his liberty for whatever length of time and under whatever circumstances may be involved.

The rules that ordinarily apply to enforce this principle in the context of criminal prosecutions include a host of requirements to ensure both a tolerable level of reliability to the process and respect for the dignity and presumptive autonomy of the individual. Each of the procedural protections offered by the Constitution adds a quantum of assurance of both fairness to the detainee and reliability in the result of the process. Collectively, they reflect our society's understanding of what is required to ensure that individuals are not held by the government without basis and that the factual and legal validity of the asserted bases for detention are reliably judged. They are recognized by our society as necessary to protect a detainee's liberty interest when he is faced with the prospect of prolonged detention because of alleged misconduct.

It seems self-evident that the same protections should presumptively extend to those individuals whom the government has seized and proposes to detain for an extended, and perhaps indefinite, period of time because they are suspected of having engaged in conduct intended to further terrorist aims, thus violating applicable criminal laws. Such a presumption serves the precise goals of honoring the substantive and procedural due-process principles to which we have adverted.

Many of the protections afforded in the civilian criminal process are denied in the context of military commissions, even under the DOD Order, as discussed above. To the extent such protections are denied, so too is justice as our society traditionally defines it under the Constitution.[136]

In short, the demand for a just result is a persuasive reason for resorting to the Article III forum in which the full panoply of rights are available to a detainee, unless there are compelling reasons for depriving him of some of those protections. These considerations justify a presumption in favor of resorting to the civilian courts.

2. *Appearance of Fairness*

As we have suggested, the protections for the detainee that are recognized by the Supreme Court in the context of criminal proceedings form the basis of a regime acknowledged by our society as necessary to ensure fair procedure and a reliable result in determining criminal liability. In view of this societal consensus, these protections provide not merely the substance of fairness to the detainee—both a fair process and, hopefully, a just result—but also the appearance of fairness. In short, they lend legitimacy both to the process and to its outcome.

The significance of this consideration extends beyond the boundaries of our society. Just as the use of indefinite detentions may encourage repression abroad, so too may any prominent resort to military commissions. Our leaders have not been shy in trumpeting the civic virtues of our constitutional system to other nations, including those with little, if any, tradition of respect for individual autonomy and limitation on government authority. Necessarily, the manner in which our government actually conducts itself in dealing with perceived misconduct both by citizens and by foreigners—including acts that may be considered threats to our civil peace and security—offers the world a strong indicator as to whether our system of self-governance actually adheres to the high standards that we profess to honor.

3. *Maintaining the Health of the Bill of Rights Generally*

For many of the reasons cited above with respect to indefinite detentions, the unnecessary bypassing of the criminal justice system in dealing with accused terrorists would create the risk of weakening our observance of core due process principles in other areas protected by the Bill of Rights. By the same token, if we can adhere to pre-existing rigorous norms of procedural fairness even in a time of fear and potentially serious threats to our national security, we reinforce the strength of those shared values in all contexts. In short, we diminish the temptation to cut corners in connection with both procedural and substantive requirements of regularity and fairness in all circumstances. If—despite the severity of the threat—we avoid ad hoc solutions designed to achieve an easy result in terms of the government's ability to ensure security, we will inevitably reinforce adherence to those norms in the face of other, and hopefully less extreme, circumstances.

4. *Public Participation in the Process*

In summarizing the various protections offered by the civilian criminal justice system, we have mentioned, among others, the right to a trial by a jury of the defendant's peers and the right to a public trial. These guarantees are deemed to offer some affirmative assurance as to the fairness of the process to the detainee, but they also serve another function, which benefits society as a whole.

The openness of the process gives the public itself the assurance that this aspect of governance is carried out in a manner consistent not only with constitutional norms, but with society's expectations. As the Supreme Court has recently noted, "[t]ransparency is essential to maintaining public respect for the criminal justice system, ensuring its integrity, and protecting the rights of the accused." Smith v. Doe, 528 U.S. 84, 99 (2003). Thus, the guarantee of a public trial is not merely a benefit to the defendant, but also a benefit to the public at large. Indeed, the courts have recognized that the principle of public access to the proceedings of the courts has a basis in the First Amendment.

Apart from the benefits of such access for purposes of public observation and monitoring, the direct participation of the community in the process, as jurors or potential jurors, offers further assurance that the government, when exercising its most coercive function, operates only with the consent and at the behest of the public. In effect, the executive branch is held to account for its actions in a very direct and public fashion. Moreover, when a verdict is rendered by a jury of citizens chosen from the community, it most consistently reflects the voice and judgment of that community, not only on the alleged actions of the defendant, but also on the conduct of the government.

Resort to the civilian courts ensures such participation to a far greater degree than other proposed means of handling detainees. The guarantee of a public trial in the civilian courts is not absolute, but the court is required to minimize any closure to the narrowest possible scope consistent with any compelling need for closed proceedings. See, e.g., Waller v. Georgia, 467 U.S. 39, 48 (1984); Ayala v. Speckard, 131 F.3d 62, 68-69 (2d Cir. 1997) (en banc), cert. denied, 524 U.S. 958 (1998). Moreover, the right to a jury trial on criminal charges filed in federal court remains inviolate, and thus ensures direct public participation in the process.

In a period when the government may seek, presumably for legitimate reasons, to exert its coercive authority to the greatest extent that may be consistent with constitutional limitations, the participation of the public, both as observer and as fact-finder, will serve to legitimize defensible applications of government powers. In this respect, it bears emphasis that the trust presumably desired by the executive branch must be earned, and that a failure to shine a light on government processes is conducive to abuse. See generally NLRB v. Robbins Tire & Rubber Co., 437 U.S. 214, 242 (1978) (describing policy underlying Freedom of Information Act). See also Jane Mayer, Annals of Justice: Lost in the Jihad, The New Yorker, 50, 57–59 (March 10, 2003) (recounting circumstances in which John Walker Lindh was allowed to plead to lesser charges); Al-Najjar v. Reno, 97 F. Supp. 2d 1329, 1352–61 (S.D. Fla. 2000) (rejecting INS detention order against suspected terrorist sympathizer, which was based on ex parte and hearsay evidence), vac. as moot, 273 F.3d 1330 (11th Cir. 2001).

Viewed in this context, a decision to use the civilian courts brings with it the evident advantage that public participation is assured. In contrast, military commissions lack equivalent protections, and are in fact designed to exclude them. For the reasons noted, such a choice would bring with it a serious cost in terms of both the regularity of the process and public acceptance of its legitimacy.

C. Possible Drawbacks to the Use of Article III Courts

Having taken account of the advantages to be derived by a consistent adherence to the processes of the civilian courts in dealing with terrorism detainees, we address those points principally made in favor of military commissions, and offer, if not a rebuttal, at least a context in which to assess them.

The principal difficulties cited by critics of the use of the civilian judicial process include i) the danger of detainees obtaining access to classified or otherwise sensitive information, ii) possible leakage of such information to the public through its compelled disclosure at a public trial or through intentional or inadvertent revelation by defense counsel, iii) the stringency of the standards for admission of relevant evidence, iv) the threat of physical harm to the civilian participants in the trial (including, presumably, jurors, judges and prosecutors), v) juror intimidation by fear of terrorist retaliation, and vi) the administrative and fiscal burden of these types of cases on the judicial system. We address each of these issues in turn.

1. *Detainees' Demand for Access to Sensitive Information and the Conduct of the Trial*

The defendant in a criminal proceeding is constitutionally entitled to see potentially exculpatory information, Brady v. Maryland, 373 U.S. 83, 84-87 (1963), and is also permitted, as a matter of discovery, to see a variety of other information pertinent to the prosecutor's case, including statements by witnesses. See 18 U.S.C § 3500; Fed. R. Crim. P. 16. In the trial of an accused terrorist, even good-faith requests by defense counsel for such information might pose the hazard that a defendant will obtain access to sensitive information that, if revealed to others in a position to act on it, could cause serious harm to national security. Moreover, there may be circumstances in which a defendant exercises his right to discovery for purposes antithetical to its governing purpose, which is the assurance of a fair trial. Thus, the defendant may seek sensitive and arguably relevant data precisely because it may be helpful to those of his conspirators who are still at liberty. In other circumstances, he may seek the most sensitive information arguably available in order to place the government on the horns of a dilemma, in which it must choose between (1) risking the dangerous disclosure of secret information (either to the defendant or at trial or both) as the price of prosecution and (2) foregoing prosecution.

Obviously these dangers would be entirely avoided by subjecting the detainee to a court process in which he is not entitled to disclosure of information by the prosecutor, in which evidence deemed necessary for proof of guilt can be disclosed ex parte by the government to a reliable set of military judges, and to which the public, including the press, has no access.

The concern with disclosure of sensitive information to a defendant accused of threatening national security is not a new phenomenon. Indeed, from the earliest espionage cases, it appears that the government has been compelled to address the question of how to obtain convictions consistent with legal requirements while protecting national security.[137] Ultimately in 1980 Congress addressed concerns about the potential for abuse of classified information by defendants in criminal prosecutions by enacting the CIPA. See generally Timothy J. Shea, CIPA Under Siege: The Use and Abuse of Classified Information in Criminal Trials, 27 Am. Crim. L. Rev. 657 (1990). The CIPA is designed to ensure a fair trial while at the same time minimizing the risk that a defendant can disclose classified information, whether as part of an effort to present a defense at trial or as a tactic to preclude his prosecution (euphemistically referred to as "greymail"), or even as part of an effort to assist enemies of the country. See, e.g. United States v. Pappas, 94 F.3d 795, 799 (2d Cir. 1996) (quoting United States v. Wilson, 571 F. Supp. 1422, 1426 (S.D.N.Y. 1983)). The pertinent provisions impose a series of procedural requirements on a defendant who proposes to use classified information in his defense and authorize several forms of remediation by the court to harmonize the conflicting legitimate interests of the defendant and the government.[138]

The statute addresses three circumstances in which the question of disclosure of classified information may arise. First, the defendant may seek production of such information from the government and may propose to use it at trial. Second, the defendant may already be in possession of classified data, and may wish to use it at trial. Third, the government may find it necessary to use such information as evidence.

To deal with any of these circumstances, the government may demand a pre-trial conference to consider matters related to the use of classified information in the case. These issues include discovery, the defendant's obligation to provide notice of his intent to use such information at trial, and the conducting of hearings to determine whether and in what circumstances classified information must be produced to the defendant or may be used at trial. See Shea, 27 Am. Crim. L. Rev. at 662–64.

With respect to discovery, the CIPA entitles the government, on an ex parte submission, to seek an order excusing it from disclosing classified information to the defense. See, e.g., United States v. Rezaq, 156 F.R.D. 514, 525–26, vac. in part, 899 F. Supp. 697 (D.D.C. 1995). The statute gives the court three options in ruling on the government's request: first, to conclude that the classified information is not sufficiently relevant to require its disclosure (e.g., United States v. Fowler, 932 F.2d 306, 310 (4th Cir. 1991)); second, even if some disclosure is deemed necessary, to authorize the government to substitute for the classified information either a summary of it or "a statement admitting relevant facts that the classified information would tend to prove" (CIPA § 4; see, e.g., United States v. Rezaq, 134 F.3d 1121, 1142 (D.C. Cir.)); or third, to conclude that the latter substitutes are not adequate to protect the defendant's interests (see, e.g., United States v. Fernandez, 913 F.2d 148, 150 (4th Cir. 1990)), in which event the court has broad discretion to enter a protective order conditioning the discovery required on compliance with terms that ensure against improper use of the sensitive information. CIPA § 3.[139]

The CIPA further provides that if the defendant wishes to use classified information at trial or intends to cause it to be disclosed (presumably by questioning government witnesses), he must notify the prosecutor and the court at least thirty days before trial and identify the information in question. CIPA, § 5(a). See, e.g., United States v. Wilson, 750 F.2d 7, 8 (2d Cir. 1984), cert. denied, 479 U.S. 839 (1985). In response, the government may request an in camera hearing on "the use, relevance, or admissibility of classified information" (§ 6(a)), and, in support of a motion to limit or exclude classified information at trial, may submit an affidavit by the Attorney General, to be reviewed in camera and ex parte if the government requests,[140] "certifying that disclosure of classified information would cause identifiable damage to the national security of the United States and explaining the basis for the classification of such information." § 6(c).

In deciding whether to permit the use of classified information at trial, the courts have generally held that CIPA does not change the law on privilege or admissibility, but requires the trial judge to apply a balancing test, weighing the relevance and probative weight of the information, the public interest in its non-disclosure,[141] and the adequacy of a summary or statement in lieu of its use. See, e.g., United States v. Smith, 780 F.2d 1102, 1107 (4th Cir. 1985); United States v. Yunis, 924 F.2d 1086, 1095 (D.C. Cir. 1991) (citing United States v. Sarkissian, 841 F.2d 959, 965 (9th Cir. 1988). See also United States v. Rahman, 870 F. Supp. 47, 50–51 (S.D.N. Y. 1994). But see United States v. Baptista-Rodriguez, 17 F.3d 1354, 1164 (11th Cir. 1994).

If the court authorizes the disclosure at trial, the government may request that instead the court permit a summary or statement admitting relevant facts to be substituted, and the court must grant the motion if the summary or statement will provide the defendant "with substantially the same ability to make his defense as would disclosure of the specific classified information." § 6(c)(1);[142] see, e.g., Rezaq, 134 F.3d at 142–43. If the court denies the government's substitution motion, the Attorney General can still block the disclosure by filing an affidavit objecting to it. CIPA, § 6(e)(1). The resulting limitation on the defense, however, requires that the court dismiss the indictment,[143] unless it concludes "that the interests of justice would not be served by dismissal" (id.), in which event the court has broad discretion in designing an appropriate remedy.[144]

The statute also deals with trial procedure. See, e.g., United States v. O'Hara, 301 F.3d 563, 567 (7th Cir.). It authorizes the court to minimize the use of classified materials at trial by admitting only selected parts of a document or by requiring the deletion of classified portions "unless the whole ought in fairness to be considered." CIPA, § 8(b). The government may object to any question or line of inquiry by the defense on the ground it will lead to the unauthorized disclosure of classified information, in response to which objection the court must ensure against such unauthorized disclosure, such as by requiring an explanation by the defense as to the nature of the information it seeks to elicit. § 8(c).

The CIPA also requires the Chief Justice, in consultation with specified executive branch agencies, to issue procedural rules to protect against the unauthorized disclosure of classified information through the courts. § 9(a). Those rules, issued in 1981 by then-Chief Justice Burger, require, inter alia, the appointment of a court security officer to supervise security measures, the identification of secure quarters within the courthouse in which proceedings concerning classified information are to take place, and security investigations and clearances for any court personnel who may have access to such information. Security Procedures Published By the Chief Justice of the United States for the Protection of Classified Information, ¶¶ 3–4 ("Security Procedures"), reprinted following 18 U.S.C.A. App. 3, § 9 (West 2000).[145]

The requirements imposed by CIPA and the rules of the Chief Justice have been repeatedly upheld as constitutional. See, e.g., Wilson, 750 F.2d at 9 (upholding requirement that defendant notify government of his intention to use classified information); United States v. Lee, 90 F. Supp. 2d 1324, 1326–28 (D.N.M. 2000); United States v. Poindexter, 725 F. Supp. 13, 31-35 (D.D.C. 1989) (same); United States v. Collins, 603 F. Supp. 301, 303–06 (S.D. Fla. 1985) (upholding provisions authorizing court to substitute admission or summary for original document); United States v. Wilson, 571 F. Supp. 1422, 1426–27 (S.D.N.Y. 1983) (definitions not void for vagueness); United States v. Joliff, 548 F. Supp. 229, 231–32 (D. Md. 1981) (upholding discovery limitations); United States v. Smith, 899 F.2d 564, 569-70 (6th Cir.), cert. denied, 498 U.S. 848, reh. denied, 498 U.S. 848 (1990) (upholding rules of Chief Justice). The provisions of CIPA have been consistently applied by the federal courts in a variety of prosecutions, including cases involving charges of terrorism. E.g., Rezaq, 134 F.3d at 1142–43 (upholding substitution order in aircraft piracy case); Bin Laden, 58 F. Supp. 2d at 115–17, 121–23 (requiring security clearances for defense counsel and imposing stringent rules for handling classified materials in terrorism case); Rahman, 870 F. Supp. at 52 (authorizing summary of pertinent part of classified document in terrorism prosecution). See also United States v. Bin Laden, 2001 WL 66393, * 2–4 (S.D.N.Y. Jan. 25, 2001).

Based on this body of experience, we are aware of no indication that the statute, reasonably interpreted by federal judges, is inadequate to the task of protecting national security interests while affording defendants a fair trial. Indeed, the recent experience of the Southern District of New York in hosting a series of trials involving al Qaeda defendants suggests that available procedures can minimize the dangers of either public disclosure or defendant misuse of classified information.

We particularly note that periodic review of classified information was required in the recent prosecution of defendants in the embassy bombing case in the Southern District of New York. The district court ordered that all defense counsel be subjected to security checks; directed that to the extent that the defense required access to classified information, the documents were to be shown only to counsel and not to the defendants; conducted in camera reviews and ex parte hearings, as necessary; and determined on an item-by-item basis whether disclosure of classified data was required. E.g., Bin Laden, 58 F. Supp. 2d at 115–17, 121–23; Bin Laden, 2001 WL 66393, *4–7. Further, a number of testifying witnesses possessed highly sensitive information (including not only law-enforcement agents, but also one or more formerly highly placed members of al Qaeda who were cooperating with the government), and the district court supervised the questioning to avoid disclosing any such information not clearly necessary for the defense. We have no reason to believe at this point that this manner of proceeding was inadequate either to safeguard sensitive information or to ensure a fair trial for all of the defendants.

In reaching these conclusions, we recognize that the CIPA does not remove all risks in the prosecution of terrorists. The statute itself creates the possibility that an indictment charging an alleged terrorist suspect with heinous crimes could be dismissed if the court ordered disclosure of sensitive information and the government declined. The Moussouai case demonstrates, in analogous circumstances, the potential of such an outcome.[146]

Nonetheless, the CIPA gives the courts broad discretion to find other alternatives that, in most if not all circumstances, should give adequate assurance to the government that its interest in protecting the public will not be significantly threatened by the need to disclose classified information as a condition for prosecuting the detainee. We are confident that, given the importance of permitting such prosecutions to go forward, the courts will continue to make every effort to design procedures that would provide reasonable assurance that the legitimate concerns of the government are met.

Finally, we view the CIPA and other governing law as likely to be adequate to deal with the concern that if classified information must be used at trial, it will filter out to terrorist groups or others who could make use of it to harm this country. The potential sources of such disclosure presumably are members of the public and the press who attend the trial, and the jurors.[147] But the long-recognized authority of the court to protect sensitive information even at trial suggests that this concern does not pose an irremediable problem.

As noted, the Supreme Court has explicitly recognized that an otherwise public trial may be closed for as long as necessary to avoid disclosure of information that could cause public injury. This principle has most commonly been applied to protect the identity of undercover agents in narcotics prosecutions. Brown v. Artuz, 283 F.3d 492, 498–500 (2d Cir. 2002); Bowden v. Keane, 237 F.3d 125, 127 (2d Cir. 2001). Nonetheless, it plainly would extend to portions of a terrorism or other criminal trial in which sensitive information must be disclosed or national security concerns are present. E.g., Abu-Jamal v. Horn, 2001 WL 1609690, *87–90 (E.D. Pa. Dec. 18, 2001); United States v. Poindexter, 732 F. Supp. 165, 167–69 (D.D.C. 1990); see generally Noble, The Independent Counsel Versus the Attorney General in a Classified Information Procedures Act—Independent Counsel Statute Case, 33 B.C.L. Rev. 539, 585–90 (1992).

Similarly, although the jurors could be exposed to such information if it was received in evidence, there are precautions available to minimize the risk that they will disclose what they have seen. First, as noted, the CIPA allows the court to mask classified data through the substitution of summaries or findings, so that actual disclosure of highly sensitive information to the jury is unlikely. Second, the voir dire process is likely to weed out individuals who might pose a possible risk of disclosing very sensitive information. Third, although the rules promulgated by the Chief Justice specify that security clearances for jurors are not required, neither the statute nor the rules preclude a thorough background check of potential jurors, up to and including an inquiry at the level of a security investigation. Between these forms of assurance and the court's authority to instruct the jurors that they are not to make any such disclosure, on pain of potential criminal prosecution, again we view the cited danger as in the realm of fairly remote speculation.[148]

2. *Stringency of Evidentiary Rules*

Another criticism of the use of civilian courts is the suggestion that the rules of evidence applicable in federal court are too stringent to permit proper proof of guilt when dealing with an organization as shadowy and difficult to track as al Qaeda. In general terms, the stated concern is that information that may be quite compelling may be found inadmissible in a civilian court because of the restrictions on hearsay, authentication requirements (for example, how to establish chain of custody for objects found on a foreign battlefield) and the possible effect of the exclusionary rule for illegal searches. Since a military commission may be empowered to consider such evidence, albeit with the discretion to discount its weight if there are serious questions about its reliability, proponents of that approach suggest that the commission will be a better tool for dealing with the threat of organizations that are based overseas and have far-flung and very secretive means of operating. See, e.g., Wedgwood, 96 Am. J. Int'l L. at 330–31.

We do not doubt that lowering these evidentiary barriers would make successful prosecution of suspects somewhat easier. To the extent that some of the cited rules are designed to ensure reliability, however, we question whether sacrificing that goal is necessarily desirable.

In any event, we believe that the concern that the Federal Rules of Evidence will prevent successful prosecutions in cases in which the government has persuasive evidence of guilt is overstated. For example, the rules governing authentication give the trial court significant discretion, and if the evidence in question is probably what it purports to be, then the court is likely to treat chain-of-custody issues with some flexibility. See, e.g., United States v. Tropeano, 252 F.3d 653, 660 (2d Cir. 2001); United States v. Bin Laden, 2001 WL 276714, *1–2 (S.D.N.Y. March 20, 2001).

As for the hearsay rule, apart from the numerous specific exceptions found in Fed. R. Evid. 803 and 804, the catch-all provisions of Rule 807 allow for admission of a statement that would otherwise be barred if the statement "is offered as evidence of a material fact" and "is more probative on the point for which it is offered than any other evidence which the proponent can procure through reasonable efforts" and, finally, if "the general purposes of these rules and the interests of justice will best be served by admission of the statement into evidence." This provision also gives the court ample latitude, and if the statement in question is deemed to bear indicia of reliability and it is relevant to a material issue, it will presumably be admitted.[149]

With regard to the possibility of Fourth or Fifth Amendment suppression due to irregularities in evidence-gathering overseas, the courts have recognized that information-gathering in foreign countries may not permit all of the formalities that pertain to police searches or investigations here. For example, in the embassy bombing case, the defendants sought to suppress statements that they had made to law enforcement agents in Kenya because they were not supplied with lawyers at the time and were informed that none were available there but that they could receive help if they confessed. The court denied suppression. In doing so, it held that the American agents had undertaken reasonable measures in view of all of the circumstances when questioning the defendants, and that in general terms a defendant being interrogated in Kenya by Kenyan law enforcement agents is not entitled to the same protections as would apply if he were in the United States or being questioned overseas under the supervision of American agents. United States v. Bin Laden, 132 F. Supp. 2d 168, 185–89 (S.D.N.Y. 2001). Similarly, when defendants sought to suppress the fruits of electronic surveillance and searches of a residence undertaken overseas, the court held that foreign intelligence surveillance is not governed by a warrant requirement, and it denied the motion, holding that both the electronic surveillance and the residential searches had been reasonable. United States v. Bin Laden, 126 F. Supp. 2d 264, 277 (S.D.N.Y. 2001); United States v. Bin Laden, 160 F. Supp. 2d 670, 678–79 (S.D.N. Y. 2001).

In short, although the federal rules of evidence may make proof somewhat more difficult in some circumstances, they are unlikely to pose a serious obstacle to the successful prosecution of a strong case. This is evident from the convictions secured in the various World Trade Center and related prosecutions, e.g., United States v. Salameh, 152 F.3d 88 (2d Cir. 1998); United States v. Youssef, 327 F.3d 56 (2d Cir. 2003); United States v. Rahman, 189 F.3d 88 (2d Cir. 1999); the embassy bombing case, see, e.g., United States v. Bin Laden, 2001 WL 1160604 (S.D.N.Y. Oct. 2, 2001); United States v. Bin Laden, 156 F. Supp. 2d 359, 361 (S.D.N.Y. 2001); and other terrorism cases in which defendants have ultimately pled to serious charges despite possible difficulties of proof. See, e.g., United States v. Lindh, 227 F. Supp. 2d 565 (E.D. Va. 2002); Another Man in Buffalo Case Pleads Guilty to Qaeda Link, N.Y. Times, March 25, 2003, at D7, c. 5.

3. *Possible Harm to Trial Participants*

Another concern voiced by proponents of alternatives other than civilian court trials is the danger of retaliation against the participants in such a trial. E.g., Wedgwood, 96 Am. J. Int'l L. at 331. The implied assumption is that military prosecutors and judges are more used to taking physical risks and can more readily be protected.

We understand that the judges who have presided at terrorism trials have been offered continued security protection after the completion of the trials, and that some have accepted.

Theoretically the same danger might be found in cases involving other types of charges of organized mayhem, including gang cases, organized-crime cases and drug prosecutions. Indeed, the few incidents of actual violence directed at federal judges have taken place in a variety of settings. These include the murder of a judge in the Southern District of New York following an unfavorable decision in a civil case brought by the daughter of the assailant; the bombing death of a federal appellate judge in Georgia; and the shooting of a judge in Texas at the behest of a convicted drug dealer. See Zagel & Winkler, The Independence of Judges, 46 Mercer L. Rev. 775, 830–31 (1995).

As for risks to jurors or prosecutors, this concern seems quite speculative. The use of anonymous juries seems adequate to shield jurors. We know of no evidence that prosecutors are significantly more at risk in handling terrorism cases than in pursuing drug, gang or organized crime cases. In fact, the general animus of terrorist groups toward American society generally may make it less likely, than with other criminal suspects, that their confederates would seek vengeance against specific federal actors.

In sum, the danger posed by participation in a terrorist trial is not a compelling argument for denying this class of detainees the same procedural protections as have been afforded to all criminal defendants under the Constitution.

4. *Juror Intimidation*

A related potential area of concern is based on the perception that trial participants may face threats of retaliation from terrorist groups. Regardless of whether that is a realistic possibility, it might be argued that the perception of such a threat exposes jurors—who have no training or perspective to deal with the fear—to subtle pressures to alter their analysis of the evidence.

It is certainly conceivable that some potential jurors may be fearful of serving and, if left on the jury, might tailor their verdict to some degree to accommodate that fear. This is a concern in other types of case as well, however, particularly in prosecutions of organized-crime figures and possibly some other cases involving violence-prone defendants who belonged to criminal organizations. See, e.g., United States v. Ruggiero, 928 F.2d 1289, 1300–02 (2d Cir. 1991). In those cases, the problem is dealt with in two ways: first, by careful and searching voir dire, with ample opportunity for both sides to exercise peremptory challenges and with heightened sensitivity by the court to challenges for cause, and, second, by the availability of anonymity for jurors.

We recognize that this may not be a perfect solution. A recent article that was based on interviews with a number of jurors who had participated in the embassy-bombing trial suggested that at least one may have been partly influenced by a personal concern for safety in assessing the death-penalty question, although apparently not the issue of guilt. See Weiser, A Jury Torn and Fearful in 2001 Terrorism Trial, N.Y. Times, Jan. 5, 2003 at 1 (reprinted at http://www.why-war.com/news/2003/01/05/ajuryfor.html). Nonetheless, perfection is obviously not a tenable standard on which to base the decision as to how we are to treat detainees in the current circumstances, since none of the other proposed solutions even approach that lofty criterion.

In truth, we are left with a variety of quite imperfect approaches, but the highly subjective concern with the mental processes of jurors seems a very weak reed on which to rest a serious deviation from accepted standards of procedural fairness.

5. *Administrative and Fiscal Burdens*

A further concern that has been voiced at the use of the civilian courts is related to the security issues. Simply stated, the argument, as we understand it, is that the procedures for ensuring that the national security is adequately protected and that the participants are secure will prove too cumbersome and delay resolution of the charges. See, e.g., Byard Q. Clemmons, The Case for Military Tribunals, 49 The Federal Lawyer 27, 31 & nn.51–52 (2002). This concern is that the financial and administrative headaches of managing a Rube Goldberg set of procedures will put an excessive strain on the courts.

We view this concern as entirely unpersuasive. First, compared to the wealth of other legal proceedings handled by the federal courts—some of them of great length and complexity—terrorism trials are a minor drain on the courts' resources. Second, the considerations going to the fairness of our treatment of detainees and the legitimacy for which our society should properly strive in its handling of proceedings involving charges of serious crimes plainly outweigh dollar-and-cents calculations. If the war on terrorism is of sufficient moment, our country is capable of paying for it. Third, the speed with which verdicts are rendered is not a determinant of the fairness of the result nor should it dictate the availability of fundamental due process protections to a defendant.

D. On Balance: Maximize Use of the Federal Court Forum

The case for using the federal courts as the preferred forum for the trial of terrorism cases is in our view compelling. Conceivably there may be exceptional circumstances from time to time that would warrant proceeding before a military commission. But as a general matter, the powerful benefits derived from the transparency and perceived fairness of federal court trials will strongly militate in favor of that venue.

We note that with the recent capture of Saddam Hussein, the Administration has been careful to emphasize the importance of a transparent and open trial proceeding that will give the world confidence that justice has been served at the end of the process. These same considerations are what impels us to recommend the use of the federal courts to try domestic terrorism cases.

VII. CONCLUSION

While to date only three enemy combatants are known to have been detained in the United States, the importance of the issues discussed in this report extend well beyond those three individuals. It must be expected that there will be further terrorist attacks against the United States, and also further suspected terrorists apprehended before they have been able to put their plans into effect. The precedents set with respect to the three existing cases will influence the treatment of such later cases, and more generally the degree to which our country preserves its due process values while it maintains its homeland security.

The issues are not easy ones, and the dearth of case law and practical experience truly on point is striking. But the fundamental due process principles that form the rule of our law under the Constitution are not obscure. In our view, those basic principles cannot be set aside and avoided, in the context of terrorism, without doing likely permanent damage to the constitutional values we honor in all other circumstances.

The Constitution is not a "suicide pact", as a Supreme Court Justice once famously declared. But neither is it a mere compact of convenience, to be enforced only in times of civic tranquility. It should take far more than the monstrous brutality of a handful of terrorists to drive us to abandon our core constitutional values. We can effectively combat terrorism in the United States without jettisoning the core due process principles that form the essence of the rule of law underlying our system of government.

Insistence on the rule of law will not undermine our national security. Abandoning the rule of law will threaten our national identity.

February 6, 2004
(revised March 18, 2004)

NOTES

* **Committee on Federal Courts:** Thomas H. Moreland (chair; subcommittee member), Jill S. Abrams, Stuart M. Altman, David JB Arroyo, Carmine D. Boccuzzi, Francisco E. Celedonio (subcommittee member), Lewis Richard Clayton (abstained from consideration of this report), Eric O. Corngold (abstained from consideration of this report), James L. Cott (abstained from consideration of this report), Michael H. Dolinger (subcommittee member), Thomas A. Dubbs, Martin D. Edel, William C. Fredericks, Barry S. Gold, Thomas H. Golden, Rita W. Gordon, Marc L. Greenwald, Caitlin J. Halligan, Lynne Troy Henderson (subcommittee member), Fran M. Jacobs, Lowell Johnston, Bruce Robinson Kelly, Lynn Mary Kelly, Richard Mancino (subcommittee member), Michael B. Mushlin, Lynn K. Neuner, Katherine Huth Parker, Douglas J. Pepe, Amy Rothstein, Gail P. Rubin, Peter Salerno, Wendy H. Schwartz, Alexandra Shapiro (abstained from consideration of this report), James A. Shifren (subcommittee member), Ellen B. Unger, Alan Vinegrad, Hilary M. Williams, and Victor Worms.

1. The New York Times reported as follows concerning al-Marri:

> Mr. Marri 37, came to the United States a day before the 9/11 attacks on a student visa. He was held in December 2001 as a material witness in the Sept. 11 investigation and later charged with lying to the F.B.I. in an interview and credit card fraud.
>
> Officials said the recent information from Qaeda operatives in American custody, including Khalid Shaikh Mohammed, pointed to Mr. Marri as a "sleeper" operative assigned to help other members of al Qaeda "settle" in the United States. Mr. Marri visited a Qaeda training camp in Afghanistan and met with Osama bin Laden, officials said. Eric Lichtblau, Wide Impact From Combatant Decision Is Seen, N.Y. Times, June 25, 2003, at A14.

In the same article, the purpose of the detention was described as follows:

> Administration officials said the decision to imprison. . .al-Marri in a brig in South Carolina. . .was intended in part to try to cull more information from him about possible links to al Qaeda. That avenue would probably have been foreclosed if Mr. Marri's case had gone to trial the next month.
>
> "This way," an administration official said, "we'll obviously be able to continue to interrogate him. We may be able to obtain valuable intelligence from him." (Id.).

It appears al-Marri was arrested as a material witness by FBI agents in Peoria, Illinois, at the direction of the U.S. Attorney's Office for the Southern District of New York, and transferred to New York. He was formally arrested on a complaint charging him with credit card fraud in January 2002. In February an indictment was returned with additional charges, none expressly tied to terrorism. Ultimately he was scheduled to be tried on these charges in Peoria on July 21, 2003. On June 23 President Bush designated him an enemy combatant. The indictment thereupon was dismissed and he was "immediately transferred into military custody and transported to the Naval Consolidated Brig in Charleston, South Carolina, where he continues to be held." Al-Marri, 274 F. Supp. 2d at 1004–05. In the cited order, al-Marri's subsequent habeas corpus petition was dismissed by the Central District of Illinois for improper venue, given al-Marri's transfer to South Carolina and the general rule that "habeas cases should be brought in the district of confinement." Id. at 1009–10.

2. Padilla's alleged conduct as a saboteur undoubtedly violated numerous criminal statutes directed against terrorist acts and conspiracies. Hamdi's criminal liability as a Taliban foot soldier is less clear.

3. For a more complete analysis of the Padilla and Hamdi decisions see [discussion below].

4. The government initially contested Hamdi's right to bring the writ. It argued, in the Fourth Circuit's words, that the federal courts "may not review at all its designation of an American citizen as an enemy

combatant" because "[the government's] determinations on this score are the first and final word." Hamdi v. Bush 296 F.3d 278, 283 (4th Cir. 2002). The Fourth Circuit refused to dismiss the habeas petition on this ground and remanded it to the District Court, declining to embrace by such a dismissal "a sweeping proposition, namely that, with no judicial review, any American citizen alleged to be an enemy combatant could be detained indefinitely without charges or counsel on the government's say so" (id.). After the Fourth Circuit's remand, apparently the government revised its position and did not dispute Padilla's or Hamdi's right to bring a habeas petition.

5. Both Padilla and Hamdi are American citizens. Padilla grew up in Chicago and New York, and then moved to Egypt after serving a prison sentence (Padilla at 572). Hamdi was born in this country, but moved to Saudi Arabia as a young child. (Hamdi at 460).

6. Alternatively, such suspected "enemy combatants," or at least the foreign nationals among them, may be tried at the President's discretion before special military commissions, rather than in Article III courts, which apply the extensive procedural protections accorded under the Constitution to defendants in criminal prosecutions.

So far no trials before military commissions have been ordered, though detailed rules to govern such trials have been promulgated. Those rules do not provide for such military trials of citizens.

7. The procedure used to determine probable cause, though it need not be adversarial in nature, "must provide a fair and reliable determination of probable cause as a condition for any significant pretrial restraint of liberty, and this determination must be made by a judicial officer either before or promptly after arrest". Id., 420 U.S. at 125.

8. Though concerned with a criminal prosecution, the Gerstein court pointed out "consequences of prolonged detention" that are not limited to the criminal context: confinement "may imperil the suspect's job, interrupt his source of income, and impair his family relationships." Id., 420 U.S. at 114.

9. The Court distinguished Shaughnessy v. Mezei as involving the indefinite detention of an alien held at the border, and therefore not subject to the due process protection afforded to aliens within the United States. 533 U.S. at 692–93. See p. 29 n.23. The Supreme Court recently has granted certiorari in a case challenging the indefinite detention of an illegal immigrant from Cuba who cannot be removed to Cuba. Benitez v. Wallis, 337 F.3d 1289 (11th Cir. 2003), cert. granted, 72 U.S.L.W. 3460 (U.S. Jan. 16, 2004) (No. 03-7434).

10. The "clear and convincing evidence" standard is required by 18 U.S.C. § 3142(e). However, cutting the other way, under § 3142(f) there is a "presumption," subject "to rebuttal," that the conditions justifying detention exist if the judicial officer finds "probable cause to believe" that the detainee has committed certain serious enumerated crimes: crimes of violence, serious drug offences, repeat offenses, and crimes for which the sentence can be life imprisonment or the death penalty. See United States v. Millan, 4 F.3d 1038, 1047 (2d Cir. 1993) (citing presumption, inter alia, in sustaining pre-trial detentions that to date of decision had exceeded two years).

11. The test distinguishing permissible regulatory from impermissible punitive confinement looks at the apparent statutory purpose, and also asks whether that alleged non-punitive purpose is rationally assignable to the detention, and whether the detention is excessive in relation to such purpose. *Salerno*, 481 U.S. at 746–47; Schall v. Martin, 467 U.S. 253, 269 (1984).

12. To anticipate the later portions of this report, we note the Court observed that terrorism might justify a different result:

> Neither do we consider terrorism or other special circumstances where special arguments might be made for forms of preventive detention and for heightened deference to the judgments of the political branches with respect to matters of national security.

Id. at 696.

13. In Sterling v. Constantin, 387 U.S. 378 (1932), the Court cited Moyer for the proposition that the executive (the President or a Governor) has discretion "to determine whether [there existed] an exigency requiring military aid" to suppress insurrection and disorder, and possesses "a permitted range of honest judgment as to the measures to be taken in meeting force with force. . . ." Id. at 399–400.

But the Sterling Court upheld a lower court injunction against action by the Governor of Texas to enforce through the national guard a state order limiting the production of oil, a restriction the federal court had ruled arbitrary and a violation of due process. The Governor had justified this action as required by "military necessity" due to an alleged state of insurrection in the East Texas area affected by the order. The Court, based on the factual record compiled below, in essence held this justification a pretext advanced in bad faith—there was no actual or threatened insurrection—and therefore beyond the "permitted range of honest judgment" accorded to the Governor in responding to disorder. Id. at 399–404.

14. In its 1987 Salerno decision, the Supreme Court cited Moyer for this rather sweeping dictum:

> . . . in times of war or insurrection, when society's interest is at its peak, the Government may detain individuals whom the Government believes to be dangerous.

Salerno, 481 U.S. at 748.

15. Some do not believe that the Constitution's prohibition of the suspension of the writ is equivalent to a constitutional mandate that the writ be recognized in the first place. The question has been academic, since Congress as one of its first acts gave statutory recognition to the writ in the Judiciary Act of 1789. William H. Rehnquist, All the Laws But One: Civil Liberties in Wartime 37 (1988) ("Rehnquist").

16. As noted above, there seems to be no dispute that alleged enemy combatants detained in the United States have the procedural right to challenge their detention by means of a habeas corpus petition. The areas of procedural controversy concern the nature of the hearing to be afforded such petitioners: whether detainees have a right to counsel in connection with the hearing and a right to rebut at the hearing the government's showing that they are enemy combatants, and what showing is required by the government to justify the detention.

17. Gideon v. Wainwright, 372 U.S. 335 (1963), applied the same per se requirement to the states, through the Due Process Clause of the Fourteenth Amendment, rejecting the case-by-case approach of Betts v. Brady. See also Argersinger v. Hamlin, 407 U.S. 25 (1972).

After a conviction at a trial at which that right to counsel (and other procedural protections) has been respected, the prisoner does not have a right to appointed counsel when pressing a habeas or other collateral attack on the conviction. Coleman v. Thompson, 501 U.S. 722, 752–57 (1991); Pennsylvania v. Finley, 481 U.S. 551, 555–58 (1987); Murray v. Giarratano, 492 U.S. 1 (1989) (Finley rule applies to death penalty case). But no court appears to have denied petitioner the right, in connection with such collateral attacks, to appear through retained or pro bono counsel. Further, the government has some duty to facilitate a petitioner's pro se efforts to pursue a habeas petition. Bounds v. Smith, 430 U.S. 817, 828 (1977) (right of access to courts requires prison authorities to provide facilities to enable prisoners to prepare meaningful legal papers).

18. Statutes have extended a right to counsel in some circumstances where due process might or might not so require. Somewhat ironically, in light of the executive's refusal to afford "enemy combatant" suspected terrorists access to counsel, accused terrorists are guaranteed by statute the right to appointed counsel in proceedings under the Alien Terrorist Removal Act. 8 U.S.C. § 1534(c)(1).

19. For example, in school suspension hearings, in which the maximum suspension was 10 days, the Court did not construe due process to require that the student be afforded "the opportunity to secure counsel. . . ." Goss v. Lopez, 419 U.S. 565, 583 (1973); see also Wolff v. McDonnel, 418 U.S. 539, 570 (1974) (no right to retained or appointed counsel in prison disciplinary proceedings); see Walters v. Nat'l Ass'n of Radiation Survivors, 473 U.S. 305 (1985) (statute prohibiting more than de minimis attorneys' fees in veterans benefit hearings upheld); Middendorf v. Henry, 425 U.S. 25 (1976) (a soldier faced with a summary court martial has no right to be represented by retained counsel; defendant could obtain counsel by demanding special court martial, thereby risking greater penalties if convicted).

The Court has twice declined to address whether a parolee, in a revocation hearing, "is entitled to the assistance of retained counsel," or to appointed counsel if indigent. Morrissey v. Brewer, 408 U.S. 471, 489 (1972); Gagnon v. Scarpelli, 411 U.S. 778, 783 n.6, 783–91 (1973) (adopting a case-by-case approach with respect to a right to appointed counsel, in probation revocation hearings, while not deciding whether parolee "has a right to be represented at a revocation hearing by retained counsel" under circumstances in which indigent parolee would not be entitled to appointed counsel).

20. The public, including the media, has a First Amendment right of access to criminal trials independent of the accused's Sixth Amendment right to a "public trial." Richmond Newspapers, Inc. v. Virginia, 448 U.S. 555 (1980). That public right of access has been extended to pretrial criminal proceedings,

Press-Enterprise Co. v. Superior Court, 478 U.S. 1 (1986), and, by circuit court authority, to civil trials, e.g., Westmoreland v. CBS, 752 F.2d 16, 23 (2d Cir. 1984), and, with the courts divided, to some administrative proceedings. Compare Detroit Free Press v. Ashcroft, 303 F.3d 681 (6th Cir. 2002) (recognizing right of access, subject to case-by-case determination, to deportation hearings), with North Jersey Media Group, Inc. v. Ashcroft, 308 F.3d 198 (3d Cir. 2002) (finding no such right of access), cert. denied, 123 S. Ct. 2215 (2003).

21. The requirement that the state prove guilt in a criminal case "beyond a reasonable doubt," expressly held a requirement of due process by In re Winship, 397 U.S. 358, 364 (1970), has been said to be "bottomed on a fundamental value determination of our society that it is far worse to convict an innocent man than to let a guilty man go free." (Id. at 372) (Harlan, J., concurring).

More expansively, the procedural protections of criminal law are sometimes said to reflect the sentiment that it is "better that 10 guilty persons escape than that one innocent suffer." However, the quoted sentiment is from Blackstone. 4 W. Blackstone Commentaries § 358.

22. See United States v. Verdugo-Urquidez, supra, 494 U.S. at 274–75 (search of Mexican national's home in Mexico by United States agents was not subject to Fourth Amendment's prohibition of unreasonable searches).

23. In stark contrast, procedural due process rights do not apply to aliens who have been excluded and held at the border (and therefore not deemed to have entered the country):

> ...an alien seeking initial admission to the United States requests a privilege and has no constitutional rights regarding his application, for the power to admit or exclude aliens is a sovereign prerogative. Landon v. Plasencia, 459 U.S. 21, 32 (1981).

"Whatever the procedure authorized by Congress is, it is due process as far as an alien denied entry is concerned." United States ex rel. Knauff v. Shaughnessy, 338 U.S. 537, 544 (1950). Even such a detained and excluded alien, however, has the right to file a habeas proceeding to challenge his detention. Ekiu v. United States, 142 U.S. 651, 660 (1892).

24. Most constitutional rights have been held applicable to resident aliens, whether legal or illegal:

> [P]ersons who are not citizens receive the protection of all of the civil liberties guaranties of the constitution, and its amendments, except for the privileges and immunity clauses." R. Rotunda and J. Nowak, Treatise on Constitutional Law 528 (3d Ed. 1999).

See United States v. Verdugo-Urquidez, 494 U.S. 259, 271 (1990) (listing cases extending rights to aliens); Harisiades v. Shaughnessy, 342 U.S. 580, 586–87 n.10 (1952) (listing the respects in which the alien is not "conceded legal parity with the citizen", such as the right to vote and hold public office).

To be distinguished are "enemy aliens"—citizens of a country with whom the United States is engaged in a declared war—whom the President may detain or deport pursuant to the Enemy Alien Act, 50 U.S.C. §§ 21–24. Ludecke v. Watkins, 335 U.S. 160 (1948).

25. For a critical view of this "plenary power" doctrine, see Louis Henkin, The Constitution and United States Sovereignty: A Century of Chinese Exclusion and its Progeny, 100 Harv. L. Rev. 853 (1987).

26. Justice Kennedy, providing the fifth vote in a 5 to 4 decision, in a concurring opinion stated that due process required, as a condition to continued detention, that the alien be afforded a hearing at which the government would need to meet a "minimal, threshold burden" of showing there was "at least some merit" to its claim that the alien was within the class subject to mandatory detention, and that, consistent with Zadvydas, the alien "could be entitled to an individualized determination as to his risk of flight and dangerousness if the continued detention became unreasonable and unjustified." (Demore, 128 S. Ct. at 1722).

27. The concern about the release of state secrets is relevant to the current debate over whether terrorist suspects should be tried in Article III courts or by military commissions.

28. It bears noting, however, that the Court then acknowledged, albeit in dictum, some legal limits to the military authorities' power to intrude on the property and liberty of civilians, even during a period of civil unrest or insurrection. The Court said the state militia members "were justified in breaking and entering the plaintiff's house" if they acted upon "reasonable grounds." Id. at 45–46. The Court went on to specify that "[n]o more force...can be used than is necessary to accomplish the object," and that if "the

power is exercised for the purposes of oppression, or any injury willfully done to person or property, the party by whom or by whose order it is committed would undoubtedly be answerable," id. at 46, though the Court did not specify in what forum or at whose behest. See also Mitchell v. Harmony, 54 U.S. 115, 134–35 (1851) (claim in trespass sustained against lieutenant-colonel in army for seizure of private goods to facilitate lawful U.S. military expedition in Mexico; such seizures lawful only if officer has "reasonable ground for believing" they are required by an "immediate and impending" danger).

29. There was substantial political opposition to President Lincoln's wartime measures: "evidence from secession notwithstanding...educated Americans were convinced that Americans lived always under a rule of law." Hyman at 67. By the end of the war, it is said that the public seemed supportive of Lincoln's position that wartime necessity did not permit strict observance of peacetime legal restrictions on executive action. Id. at 131–40.

30. In 1863 Congress regularized Lincoln's procedures to a degree by formal legislation. It authorized the President to suspend the writ whenever during "the present rebellion" he judged that the public safety so required, while requiring that "political prisoners," as listed by the Secretaries of State and War within 20 days of their detention, be released unless indicted by a succeeding grand jury. Milligan, 71 U.S. at 114–15; see generally Hyman at 249–56. Excluded in practice from these lists of political prisoners were civilians facing courts-martial or military commission trials for military offenses, including guerrillas, saboteurs and spies, the closest analogues to today's terrorists. Hyman at 253–54.

31. It quickly became customary, and later official policy, to allow "prisoners who could afford the luxury to enjoy access to lawyers". Hyman at 82.

32. Merryman was accused of trying to block the passage of Union troops by railway from the north to the beleaguered Washington, D.C.

33. Chief Justice Taney's narrow view of the President's wartime powers may be viewed as in some tension with the general tenor of the Supreme Court's analysis in Luther, which Taney also authored. His hostility to the increase in federal power in service of the Union cause, and his enduring sympathy for states rights, is well documented. Hyman at 256–60.

34. The Court indicated that legislative recognition of a state of war was not required, but observed that if such congressional assent were needed, it could be found in many pieces of legislation enacted since the start of the war to assist in its prosecution. Id. at 670.

35. Lambdin P. Milligan, a well-known lawyer sympathetic to the Confederate cause, was convicted and sentenced to death for planning and organizing an attack upon the Democratic convention which was to be held in Chicago in 1864. Rehnquist at 21–23; Alex Abella & Scott Gordon, Shadow Enemies 140 (2002) ("Shadow Enemies").

36. The Court's clarion words echoed those of Milligan's brief, authored by future President James Garfield. Of a decision favorable to Milligan, he wrote:

> It will establish forever this truth, of inestimable value to us and to mankind, that a republic can wield a vast engine of war without breaking down the safeguards of liberty; can suppress insurrection, and put down rebellion, however formidable, without destroying the bulwarks of law; can by the might of its armed millions, preserve and defend both nationality and liberty. Quoted in Rehnquist at 23.

37. The majority's dictum against congressional power was highly controversial, regarded "as a gratuitous salvo against the plans of the Radicals for congressional reconstruction...." Rossiter at 30–31.

38. See Ex parte McCardle, 74 U.S. 506 (1868) (challenge by civilian facing military commission in Mississippi; Court holds it lacks appellate jurisdiction under Judiciary Act of 1867 in view of 1868 repeal of jurisdiction); Ex parte Yerger, 75 U.S. 85 (1868) (challenge by civilian held for military tribunal; Court finds continuing appellate jurisdiction under 1789 Judiciary Act).

To the extent that these jurisdictional decisions have relevance to our inquiry, they emphasize the strong reluctance of the Supreme Court to treat even a congressional enactment as effectively depriving the court of habeas appellate jurisdiction. See e.g., Yerger, 75 U.S. at 94–98, 100–02; Sandoval v. Reno, 166 F.3d 225, 231–32 (3d Cir. 1999) (discussing McCardle and Yerger). See also Felker v. Turpin, 518 U.S. 651, 660 (1996).

39. Decisions after the termination of hostilities in World War I did uphold the power of the political branches to decide when the consequences of the war, and therefore the need for wartime emergency statutes, had expired. See, e.g., Hamilton v. Kentucky Distilleries & Warehouse Co., 251 U.S. 146 (1919). See generally Note, Judicial Determination of the End of the War, 47 Colum. L. Rev. 255 (1947).

40. The Government's position was clearly stated in its brief:

> "The fact is that ordinary constitutional doctrines do not impede the Federal Government in its dealings with enemies." [citations omitted]
>
> The President's power over enemies who enter this country in time of war, as armed invaders intending to commit hostile acts, must be absolute. 317 U.S. at 12.

41. The district court had denied leave to file a petition, and the case was then heard within a few days by the Supreme Court. The Court announced its decision on the day after oral argument had been completed, summarily ruling against the petitioners on the merits. Id. at 11. At the same time it promised a written decision, which it issued several months later, after sentence had been pronounced by the Commission and a number of the detainees had been executed.

42. The law of war is a centuries' old branch of international law that "prescribes the rights and obligations of belligerents," and which "define[s] the status and relations not only of enemies—whether or not in arms—but also of persons under military government or martial law and persons simply resident or being upon the theatre of war, and which authorizes their trial and punishment when offenders." William Winthrop, Military Law and Precedents 773 (2d ed. 1920). "Such laws and customs would especially be taken into consideration by military commissions in passing upon offences in violation of the laws of war." Id. at 42.

43. The Court read the Constitution in this light even though the Amendments do contain a specific exception for "cases arising in the land and naval forces," and do not otherwise restrict the scope of the grand jury and civil jury guarantees for any other persons. Id. at 41–44. The Court held: "We cannot say that Congress in passing the Fifth and Sixth Amendments intended to extend trial by jury to the cases of alien or citizen offenders against the law of war otherwise triable by military commission, while withholding it from members of our own armed forces. . . ." Id. at 44.

44. See Instructions for the Government of Armies of the United States in the Field, promulgated as General Orders No. 100 by President Lincoln, April 24, 1863, reprinted in The Laws of Armed Conflicts 3 (D. Schindler & J. Toman, eds., 1988). The Lieber Instructions were prepared by Francis Lieber, then a professor of Columbia College. They became a strong influence on later codifications of the law of war by other states and international tribunals.

45. Convention (III) Relative to the Treatment of Prisoners of War, signed at Geneva, August 12, 1949 (consented to by the United States Senate on July 6, 1955, with reservations). 6 U.S.T 3316, 75 U.N.T.S. 136 ("Third Geneva Convention").

46. Prisoners of war are entitled to various rights and privileges as set forth in the Third Geneva Convention. As lawful combatants they are not subject to prosecution and "shall be released and repatriated without delay after the cessation of active hostilities." Art. 18. See Ruth Wedgwood, al Qaeda, Terrorism and Military Commissions, 96 Am. J. Int'l L. 328, 333 (April 2002) (hereafter cited as "Wedgwood").

47. The Supreme Court's decision in Duncan v. Kahanamoku suggests that Milligan remained good law after Quirin, to the extent that Milligan prohibits the trial of civilians by military commission for actions not constituting violations of the law of war. The majority opinion cited Milligan with approval (id. at 322, 324), and Justice Murphy, concurring, expressly reaffirmed Milligan's "open court" rule (id. at 328–35).

48. But see Mudd v. Caldera, 134 F. Supp. 2d, 138, 145–47 (D.D.C. 2001), appeal denied, 309 F.3d 819 (D.C. Cir. 2002) (military commission had jurisdiction to try Dr. Samuel Mudd for aiding and abetting assassination of Lincoln, a military offense violating the law of war; Quirin does not limit the jurisdiction of military commissions to persons acting under direction of enemy armed forces).

49. Quirin found it did not need "to determine to what extent the President as Commander in Chief has constitutional power to create military commissions without the support of Congressional legislation," for "here Congress has authorized trial of offenses against the law of war before such commissions." 317 U.S. at 29.

50. The Court referred to the asserted facts, inter alia, that (i) "social, economic and political conditions which have prevailed since the close of the last century, when the Japanese began to come to this country in substantial numbers, have intensified their solidarity and have in large measure prevented assimilation as an integral part of the white population," (ii) many children of Japanese parentage were sent to after-school Japanese language training, sometimes at schools "generally believed to be sources of Japanese nationalistic propaganda, cultivating allegiance to Japan," and (iii) Japan recognized dual citizenship. Id. at 96–97.

51. Korematsu, widely condemned in retrospect, was not without vigorous dissents. Justice Murphy, for one, opined that the exclusion order "'goes over the very brink of constitutional power' and falls into the ugly abyss of racism." Id. at 233.

It also bears noting that, on the same day it upheld the exclusion order in Korematsu on constitutional grounds, the Court, in Ex parte Endo, 323 U.S. 283 (1944), construed the regulations governing the relocation centers to require the release of "citizens who are concededly loyal." Id. at 297.

52. The Fourth Circuit's opinion, in fact, is notable for its several rhetorical flourishes recognizing the importance of civil liberties and the writ of habeas corpus, even in times of war. It was emphatic that "the detention of United States citizens must be subject to judicial review" by means of the writ of habeas corpus, consistent with the writ's "essential function of assuring that restraint accords with the rule of law, not the whim of authority. . . ." Id. at 464–65. See also:

> The duty of the judicial branch to protect our individual freedoms does not simply cease whenever our military forces are committed by the political branches to armed conflict. Id. at 464.

53. The court vigorously criticized the district court's orders in connection with that court's plan to conduct an evidentiary hearing on the legality of the detention, i.e., that Hamdi have unmonitored access to his court-appointed lawyer and that the government disclose detailed information concerning Hamdi's seizure and interrogation. The Fourth Circuit found those orders, which it had earlier stayed, unacceptably to intrude into the President's authority and to show insufficient deference to the war-making powers of the two political branches. Id. at 462, 469–71.

54. In United States v. Lindh, 212 F. Supp. 2d 541 (E.D. Va. 2002), the District Court was similarly deferential to the President's finding that an American citizen fighting with the Taliban and captured in Afghanistan was an 'unlawful combatant' and so not subject to immunity from prosecution as a prisoner of war under the Geneva Convention. The court found that "conclusive deference, which amounts to judicial abstention, is plainly inappropriate." Id. at 556–57. The court proceeded to examine the President's finding in light of Geneva Convention Article 4, which sets forth the criteria for determining unlawful combatant status, and held that the Taliban forces were unlawful as lacking a command structure, distinctive uniforms and compliance with the law of war. Id. at 557–58.

55. Padilla did refer to Padilla's potential ability to demonstrate, at some point in the future, that the evidence used to support his enemy combatant classification had been "entirely mooted by subsequent events." Id. at 608. This may envision a possible showing that operations against al Qaeda had ended, or that "the operational capacity of al Qaeda [had been]. . .effectively destroyed" (id. at 590), or that Padilla's usefulness as a source of intelligence had been exhausted, at which point continuing the detention might no longer bear "a reasonable relation to the purpose for which the individual [was] committed." Zadvydas, 533 U.S. at 690.

Judge Wesley's dissenting opinion in the Second Circuit strikes a somewhat similar note with respect to the purpose of the detention:

> Certainly, a court could inquire whether Padilla continues to possess information that was helpful to the President in prosecuting the war against al Qaeda. Presumably, if he does not, the President would be required to charge Padilla criminally or delineate the appropriate process by which Padilla would remain under the President's control. See, e.g., Zadvydas v. Davis, 533 U.S. 678 (2001).

Padilla Cir. at 733.

56. As to the government's argument that Padilla might use his lawyer to pass messages to terrorists—echoing charges in an unrelated pending case—the court found, after reviewing the sealed Mobbs declaration, that such conjecture amounted to only "gossamer speculation." Id. at 604. It noted that the military

would be able to monitor the attorney-client communications, so long as the monitors were insulated from any further involvement with court proceedings. Id. The court cited in this regard the procedures for monitoring attorney-client communications recently promulgated at 28 C.F.R. § 501.3(a).

57. Since these decisions, in December 2003 the government announced it would permit Hamdi to consult with his attorneys. The Department of Defense announced on December2, 2003, that Hamdi "will be allowed access to a lawyer" because it had "completed its intelligence collection with Hamdi." Its press release billed this decision as a matter of discretion," and "not required by domestic or international law ...." The government, in its unsuccessful brief in opposition to Hamdi's petition for a writ of certiorari, described the new position in these words:

> As a matter of discretion and military policy, the Department of Defense (DOD) has adopted a policy of permitting access to counsel by an enemy combatant who is a United States citizen and who is detained by the military in the United States, when DOD has determined that such access will not compromise the national security of the United States, and when DOD has determined either that it has completed intelligence collection from the enemy combatant or that granting access to counsel would not interfere with such intelligence gathering. In accordance with DOD's policy and the military's ongoing evaluation of Hamdi's detention, DOD has determined that Hamdi may be permitted access to counsel subject to appropriate security restrictions. See http://www.dod.gov/releases/2003/ nr20031202-0717.html.

Resp't Hamdi Brief at 25–26 n.11.

58. As a practical matter the Hamdi court's holding would mean that the Geneva Convention is unenforceable in the war on terror, since neither the defeated and dissolved Taliban nor the terrorist organization al Qaeda is capable of diplomacy.

The Lindh court held, consistent with Padilla, that the Geneva Convention was enforceable by the defendant before it, but that he was an unlawful combatant and thus not entitled to immunity from prosecution under the Convention. Lindh, 212 F. Supp. 2d at 553.

59. Some urge that the principles of international law should be applied by American courts in reviewing or limiting the purported exercise of the war power by the President. See Jordan J. Paust, Judicial Power to Determine the Status and Rights of Persons Detained Without Trial, 44 Harv. Inter. L.J. G4 (2003). But the invocation of "customary international law" as part of American law is problematic, for there often is no clear consensus on its content. See generally Flores v. Southern Peru Cooper Corp., 343 F.3d 140 (2d Cir. 2003) (construing the Alien Tort Claims Act's embrace of torts "committed in violation of the law of nations," 28 U.S.C. § 1350). No principles of customary international law—"those rules that States universally abide, or to which they accede, out of a sense of legal obligation and mutual concern" (id. at 158)—appear to either clearly permit or prohibit the detention of illegal combatants in the context of the war on terror. Like the law of war, customary international law speaks with an especially uncertain voice in the context of stateless terrorism. See Paust, supra, at G11 n.30.

60. The Central District of California recently enjoined the enforcement of the "expert advice and assistance" clause of the cited section of the USA PATRIOT ACT, finding it to be unconstitutionally vague. Humanitarian Law Project v. Ashcroft, No. CV 03-6107 (C.D. Cal. Jan. 22, 2004). For an analogous holding by the Southern District of New York.

61. It may well be that the "enemy combatant" detentions have been infrequently employed in the United States to date because the executive has been able to detain other suspects in other ways. Numerous aliens have been detained on immigration charges and a lesser number have been detained as "material witnesses," Padilla's initial status, under 18 U.S.C. § 3144. Further, a large group of alleged "enemy combatants" seized abroad is being held at the Guantanamo Bay Naval Base in Cuba, detentions which present distinct issues not addressed in this report.

62. The usual predicate for the "some evidence" standard is a review of administrative fact-finding. In that context, "some" evidence can be "meager" evidence. See Superintendent v. Hill, 472 U.S. 445, 457 (1985) (review of prison disciplinary decision). The "some evidence" standard "is not intended as a substantive check on the accuracy of administrative fact-finding." Butler v. Oak Creek-Franklin School District, 172 F. Supp. 2d 1102, 1118 (E.D. Wis. 2001) (school disciplinary hearing).

63. Truly extreme instances of abuse might be held to violate substantive due process, but the vagueness of that standard makes it a poor vehicle for controlling exercises of the war power.

64. Compare this observation by Justice Stewart, concurring in the "Pentagon Papers" case, commenting on the Executive's "enormous powers in the two related areas of national defense and international relations":

> In the absence of the governmental checks and balances present in other areas of our national life, the only effective restraint upon executive policy and power in the areas of national defense and international affairs may lie in an enlightened citizenry—in an informed and critical public opinion which alone can here protect the values of democratic government.

New York Times Co. v. United States, 403 U.S. 713, 728 (1971).

65. Cf. Graham v. Richardson, 403 U.S. 365, 372 (1971):

> Aliens as a class are a prime example of a "discrete and insular" minority. . . for whom. . . heightened judicial solicitude is appropriate. (citations omitted).

66. In a poll conducted for National Public Radio in November 2001, the respondents were equally divided—48% to 48%, with 4% "don't know"—on whether the government should have the authority to "detain terrorist suspects indefinitely without charging them." NPR/Kaiser/Kennedy School Survey on Civil Liberties, available at www.npr.org/programs/specials/poll/civilliberties/civillibertiesstaticresults_4.html.

67. The government's secret detentions of these unidentified aliens, most held on immigration charges, have (so far) been upheld by the courts. Center for National Security Studies v. United States Department of Justice, 331 F.3d 918 (D.C. Cir. 2003), cert. denied, No. 03-472 (Jan. 12, 2004). Compare, in the non-immigration context, the comment that "secret arrests" represent a "concept odious to a democratic society." Morrow v. District of Columbia, 417 F.2d 728, 741–42 (D.C. Cir. 1969).

68. However, nationality-based immigration policies have been implemented. See David Stout, Ridge Moves to Tighten Security Ahead of an Iraq War, N.Y. Times, WYSIWYG//12/ http://www.nytimes.com/2003/03/18/politics/18CND-Home.htm (noting new order by Homeland Security Department to detain all persons seeking political asylum if they arrived from any of 34 countries).

69. Similarly, President Roosevelt in World War II, in announcing to Congress that he would impose stringent ceilings on food prices if Congress failed to act, proclaimed:

> When the war is won, the powers under which I act automatically revert to the people—to whom they belong.

Quoted in Edward S. Corwin, The War and the Constitution: President and Congress, 37 American Political Science Review 18, 19 (1943).

70. Remarks of President Bush, Sept. 10, 2003, at FBI Academy, Quantico, Virginia (White House website).

71. Salerno opens the door to preventive detentions in the context of pre-trial detentions, but still subject to both a prior probable-cause finding and the speedy trial guarantee of the Sixth Amendment.

72. Concerns of this nature informed Justice Jackson's dissent in Korematsu. Citing Cardozo's reference to "the tendency of a principle to expand itself to the limits of its logic" (Nature of the Judicial Process 51), Jackson argued that the Court should not lend its imprimatur to a military decision, reasonable as such but unconstitutional in principle, since the Court's ruling would have a "generative power of its own," beyond that of the military order. Korematsu, 323 U.S. at 246.

73. Compare Center for National Security Studies v. United States Dep't of Justice, 331 F.3d at 932 (D.D.C. 4003) (reversing decision under FOIA requiring disclosure concerning post 9/11 detainees: "the courts must defer to the executive on decisions of national security"), with United States v. Moussaoui, 336 F.3d 279, 282 (4th Cir. 2003) (Wilkins, C.J., concurring in denial of rehearing en banc) ("Siding with the Government in all cases where national security concerns are asserted would entail surrender of the independence of the judicial branch and abandon our sworn commitment to the rule of law").

74. Examples from the Human Rights Watch website of such statements include:

> On December 16, 2001, [Egyptian] President Mubarak asserted that new U.S. policies "prove that we were right from beginning in using all means, including military tribunals. . . . There is no doubt that the events of September 11 created a new concept of democracy that differs from the concept that Western states defended before these events, especially in regard to the freedom of the individual," Mubarak said.
>
> In comments to a Washington Post columnist in November 2002, Eritrea's Ambassador to the United States justified his government's arrest of journalists by claiming that detention without charge was consistent with the practices of democratic countries. He cited the roundup of material witnesses and aliens suspected of terrorist activities in the United States as proof.

www.hrw.org/campaigns/september11/opporrtunismwatch.htm (Dec. 17, 2003).

75. In addition, as Judge Mukasey observed, neither Quirin nor any other case addresses the appropriate standard of review with respect to the classification of a particular person as an illegal combatant. Padilla necessarily covered new ground in holding that such classifications are subject to judicial review only on a deferential "some evidence" standard.

76. The absence of case law does not end the inquiry, for "practical construction"—action on the ground—may constitute relevant precedent. See Quirin, 317 U.S. at 35–36 (relying on the practice of military authorities recognizing illegal combatants); see also Hyman at 558–59 (bemoaning distorted "case-centered" historical analysis). Justice Frankfurter, in his Youngstown concurrence, would recognize an "executive construction of the Constitution," (Youngstown, 343 U.S. at 613), citing United States v. Midwest Oil Co., 236 U.S. 459 (1915), but only on a showing of "a systematic, unbroken, executive practice, long pursued to the knowledge of the Congress and never before questioned. . . ." (Youngstown, 343 U.S. at 610–11).

The only apparent candidate for such an "executive construction" with respect to detentions appears to be Lincoln's policy during the Civil War, when military detentions of alleged Confederate sympathizers are said to have been frequent.

However, the dramatically different circumstances of the Civil War, an armed rebellion on American soil, minimize the relevance of any such precedents to the domestic war on terror. Further, Lincoln's unique actions hardly meet the Frankfurter test of a "systemic unbroken" practice "long pursued," and in fact were sharply questioned at the time and invalidated in the only two court decisions on point, Merryman and Milligan.

77. Edward S. Corwin, writing in 1947, came out at about the same place:

> The restrictive clauses of the Constitution are not, as to the *citizen at least,* automatically suspended, but the scope of the rights to which they extend is capable of being reduced in face of the urgencies of war, sometimes even to the vanishing point, depending on the demands of the war. Theoretically these will be determined by the President and then Congress, subject to judicial review; actually the Court will not intrude its veto while war is flagrant.

Corwin at 131.

78. Milligan, decided the year after the Civil War ended, emphasized, with surprising candor, that the Court was able to address the question before it dispassionately precisely because the war had concluded:

> During the late wicked Rebellion, the temper of the times did not allow that calmness in deliberation and discussion so necessary to a correct conclusion of a purely judicial question. *Then,* considerations of safety were mingled with the exercise of power; and feelings and interests prevailed which are happily terminated. *Now* that the public safety is assured, this question, as well as all others, can be discussed and decided without passion or the admixture of any element not required to form a legal judgment. 71 U.S. at 109 (italics in original).

As Rossiter observes:

> It is one thing for a court to lecture a President when the emergency has passed, quite another to stand up in the middle of the battle and inform him that he is behaving unconstitutionally.

Rossiter at 38.

The hazard in the latter course is illustrated by Justice Taney's 1861 decision in Merryman, in the early days of the Civil War, ruling Lincoln's suspension of habeas corpus unconstitutional: the President simply ignored the ruling in his conduct of the war. Hyman at 89.

79. The Court offered no explanation for its conclusion that the President's war power, absent congressional authorization, did not embrace the seizure of domestic industries. The conclusion seemed obvious to the Court, but for reasons it chose not to articulate.

This assertion of judicial power in Youngstown must have surprised Rossiter, who only the year before had written as follows concerning a President's power to seize industries to aid the war effort:

> Nor can there be any doubt that under the conditions of modern war the President has a broad constitutional power to seize and operate industrial facilities in which production has been halted, a power which, like his other powers of martial law, is virtually impossible to define or control.

Rossiter at 63.

80. At the other extreme, the insistence of Milligan that war and peace make no difference in constitutional terms also finds little echo in the caselaw (or common sense). Milligan's words are clarion: the Constitution "is a law for rulers and people, equally in war and in peace, and covers. . .all classes of men at all times, and under all circumstances." Milligan, 71 U.S. at 120–121. But no case has adopted Milligan's view that it is constitutionally impossible even for Congress and even in emergency circumstances to adopt wartime measures that limit individual rights in a way not limited in peacetime. Due process is not so rigid:

> Early constitutional absolutism is replaced by constitutional relativity; it all depends—a result that has been definitely aided in the case of substantive rights by the modern conception of due process of law as 'reasonable law'—that is to say, what the Supreme Court finds to be reasonable in the circumstances.

Corwin at 80.

81. Louis Henkin, writing in 1972, pointed out the transformation in the role of the Constitution, as applied by the Supreme Court, with respect to individual rights. While "there was hardly a case during more than a hundred years [after adoption of the Constitution] in which the courts invalidated federal action on the ground that it violated an individual's constitutional rights"—Dred Scott (recognizing the property rights of the slave owner) being the only such pre-Civil War case—more recently for the courts "the Constitution has become primarily a bulwark for the individual against government excess." Louis Henkin, Foreign Affairs and the Constitution 251–52 (1972).

82. In Campbell, a group of Congressmen challenged President Clinton's authority to direct American armed forces to participate in the NATO military campaign in Yugoslavia, in the absence of a congressional declaration of war or authorization under the War Powers Resolution (50 U.S.C. § 1541 et seq.). The court held the plaintiffs lacked standing and Judge Silberman, concurring, also added that "what constitutes a war" was a non-justifiable political question.

83. Admittedly, the Korean War, which Justice Jackson addressed, did not involve attacks on American soil. Nor is the labor-management context of Youngstown closely analogous to Padilla, involving seizure of a suspected terrorist as he entered this country. But, on the other side, Truman's action in Youngstown affected only property rights, while the indefinite detentions violate core due process values.

84. As Hamdi illustrates, a citizen has the right to pursue habeas relief in the domestic courts even when detained abroad. But given the scope of the President's war power abroad, a citizen seized abroad as an illegal combatant in a military setting may well be denied substantive relief, as Hamdi also illustrates, at least in the short term when such relief might interfere with an ongoing military campaign.

By this we do not mean to minimize the issues in Hamdi, which also implicates due process concerns. The justification for the incommunicado, long-term interrogation and detention of a foot soldier in the Taliban armed forces, if that is all Hamdi was, seems hard to square with the Third Geneva Convention, or to justify on the basis of any apparent need. As to what Hamdi was, the facts concerning his combatant status may not be as indisputable as the court concluded. See Hamdi v. Rumsfeld, 337 F.3d 335, 357–64 (4th Cir. 2003) (Luttig, J. dissenting from denial of rehearing en banc, arguing that circumstances of Hamdi's seizure were neither conceded in fact nor "susceptible to concession in law, because Hamdi has not been permitted to speak for himself or even through counsel" (id. at 357)).

85. Congress, in the Posse Comitatas Act, 18 U.S.C. § 1385, passed in 1878 in reaction to the use of the armed forces to support reconstruction in the south, precluded the use of the armed forces "to execute the laws," except "in cases and under circumstances expressly authorized by the Constitution or act of Congress. . . ."

In passing the Homeland Security Act in 2002, Congress reaffirmed "the continued importance" of the Posse Comitatas Act, 6 U.S.C. § 466(b). However, it also affirmed that the Act did not bar the President's use of the armed forces when required "to respond promptly in time of war, insurrection or other serious emergency" (6 U.S.C. § 466(a)(4)).

86. According to the Department of Justice's website, as of January 30, 2004, 284 suspected terrorists have been charged in United States courts, with 149 convicted. (www.lifeandliberty.gov/ subs/a_terr.htm).

87. See generally Clinton Rossiter, Constitutional Dictatorship (1948) (arguing that such is necessary in times of great national peril, such as total war).

88. Having exhausted its interrogation of Hamdi, the Department of Defense explains his continued detention as "not criminal in nature but. . .permitted under the law of war to prevent an enemy combatant from continuing to fight against the United States" (Press Release, Dec. 2, 2003).

89. Here is one forceful expression of this concern:

> The prime source of intelligence [concerning anticipated terrorist attacks] will be captured combatants; and lawyers, alas, will inevitably turn off that flow of time critical information.
>
> * * *
>
> Any lawyer worth his salt will deliver standard form advice to a client: Keep your mouth shut. Don't talk. Not in court and not in military interviews.

Ruth Wedgwood, Lawyers at War, Wall St. J., Feb. 18, 2003.

90. The case also might be held in a state of suspense—with appropriate Speedy Trial Act findings—while intelligence officials pursue their inquiries.

91. Justice Jackson cautions about permitting the President "of his own volition," to "invest himself with undefined emergency powers." "[E]mergency powers are consistent with free government only when their control is lodged elsewhere than the Executive who exercises them." Youngstown, 343 U.S. at 651.

92. Hirabayashi is said to be:

> perhaps the most clear-cut case on record of the Court's tendency to insist that unusual military actions be grounded, whenever possible, on the combined powers of President and Congress, which when merged are called simply the war powers of the United States.

Rossiter at 47.

93. The Second Circuit's opinion relies principally on the Constitution's allocation of certain specific powers to Congress, not the President: Article I, § 8, cl. 10 (power to define offenses against the laws of nations), Article I, § 9, cl. 2 (suspension of habeas corpus), and the Third Amendment (quartering of soldiers in houses in time of war without owner's consent, permitted only as "prescribed by law"). Padilla Cir. at 714–15.

In our view this analysis is somewhat conclusory. Enemy combatant detentions inescapably require the courts to balance the interests of national security with due process rights. The Constitution's allocation of specific powers to Congress may help inform this balancing task, but it does not avoid it. The balancing required should place heavy weight on the due process values at stake. The Second Circuit's opinion does not expressly recognize those constitutional values as having independent force, entitled to protection by the courts (at least presumptively) even in times of war. It makes only passing reference to the "individual liberty rights" implicated by the detentions, in distinguishing the property interests at stake in The Prize Cases (Padilla Cir. at 717–18), and pays an unexplained tribute to the "guarantees of the Fourth and Fifth Amendments to the Constitution." Id. at 724.

We also would not be as absolutist as the Second Circuit's separation of powers analysis. We believe that the President has some war power to act domestically in emergency circumstances. On the other hand, congressional action authorizing indefinite detentions would not obviate the need for the courts to address due process concerns, as the Second Circuit's opinion may assume.

94. Compare the op ed comment by Prof. Viet Dinh, a former assistant attorney general: "After two years of unofficial criticism. . . it is time for Congress to contribute its voice—either to affirm the president's authority or suggest refinements to administration policy." Justice for All, Wall St. J., Dec. 15, 2003, at A14.

95. In this context we are troubled by this Second Circuit's dictum in its Padilla decision, quoting the discredited Hirabayashi:

> To be sure, when Congress and the President act together in the conduct of war, "it is not for any court to sit in review of the wisdom of their action and substitute its judgment for theirs." Hirabayashi v. United States, 320 U.S. 81, 93 (1943).

Padilla Cir. at 713.

Again, we say it depends on what kind of "war" and just what measures are taken in its pursuit. Surely the Second Circuit would not hesitate to "sit in review," during the "war" on terror, of a congressionally authorized curfew directed solely at all Arabs and Muslims, similar to the Japanese curfew upheld in Hirabayashi itself.

96. Other suggested approaches may include the creation of specialized so-called "terrorism courts" that would be empowered to try individuals charged with specified terrorism-related offenses while offering core due-process protections. See, e.g., Powers, Due Process for Terrorists? The Case for a Federal Terrorism Court, The Weekly Standard, Jan. 12, 2004. We take no position on any such proposals, but strongly urge that any dilution of long-accepted due process procedures be rejected without, at a minimum, a clear and considered congressional imprimatur.

97. Compare the reported recent remarks by Judge Michael Chertoff, former head of the Justice Department's Criminal Division, suggesting that "we need to debate a long-term sustainable architecture for the process of determining when, why and for how long someone may be detained as an enemy combatant, and what judicial review should be available." R. Schmitt, Patriot Act Author Has Concerns, L.A. Times, Nov. 3, 2003 (www.informationclearinghouse.info/articles5325.htm).

98. The Joint Resolution would appear to authorize at least Hamdi's initial detention in Afghanistan, which was closely related to the engagement of the Armed Forces pursuant to the Joint Resolution against the Taliban, because of its sheltering of al Qaeda.

99. Such a continuing detention, of course, would require confronting the due process question posed by indefinite detentions, a question the Zadvydas Court avoided by narrowly construing the statute before it.

100. The Second Circuit views 18 U.S.C. § 4001(a) as casting in doubt the continuing "usefulness" of Quirin (Padilla Cir. at 716), and it did unearth a few references in the congressional debates on 18 U.S.C. 4001(a) that focused specifically on the possible impact of the proposed statute in precluding executive detentions of suspected spies and saboteurs in wartime (id. at 719–20).

Since we do not view Quirin as a detention case, we do not view the statute as relevant to Quirin. If, as Quirin held, trial by military commission has been authorized by Congress, it follows that a detention in service of such a trial has congressional sanction.

101. A caveat is in order with respect to the seizure of citizens abroad in a theater of armed military conflict, the facts presented in Hamdi.

102. Military Order Regarding Detention, Treatment, and Trial of Certain Non-Citizens in the War Against Terrorism, 66 Fed. Reg. 57833 (November 13, 2001).

103. Quirin's analysis, predicated on no directly supportive legal authority, has come into considerable question since its issuance, including by some of the participating justices. See, e.g., David J. Danelski, The Saboteurs' Case, 21 J. Sup. Ct. Hist. 61, 72–80 (1996); Michael R. Belknap, The Supreme Court Goes to War: The Meaning and Implications of the Nazi Saboteur Case, 89 Mili. L. Rev. 59, 81–90 (1980); Katyal & Tribe, 111 Yale L.J. at 1282–83, 1290–91.

104. Article of War 15, as now codified as Article 21 at 10 U.S.C. § 821, states:

> The provisions of this chapter conferring jurisdiction upon courts-martial do not deprive military commissions, provost courts, or other military tribunals of concurrent jurisdiction with respect to offenders or offenses that by the law of war may be tried by military commissions, provost courts, or other military tribunals.

105. For a tightly reasoned contrary view, see Katyal & Tribe, 111 Yale L.J. at 1286–90.
106. E.g., Articles of War, 15 H.R. Doc. No. 81-491 (1949); S. Rep. No. 81-486 (1949). See generally Loving v. United States, 517 U.S. 748, 752–53 (1996).
107. These reforms were made in response to allegations that courts-martial held during World War II (up to 2 million) were arbitrary and lacked independence. Cox Commission, Report of the Commission on the 50th Anniversary of the Uniform Code of Military Justice 2 (May 2001) ("Cox Commission").
108. Article 36(a), UCMJ, provides that procedures, including "modes of proof," for courts-martial, as well as military commissions

> may be prescribed by the President by regulations which shall, so far as he considers practicable, apply the principles of law and the rules of evidence generally recognized in the trial of criminal cases in the United States district courts.

Courts-martial procedure is governed by the detailed and comprehensive Manual for Courts-Martial (2002 ed.)
109. Loving v. United States, 517 U.S. 748, 770 (1996) (the Supreme Court interpreted Article 36 as "indicative of congressional intent to delegate [the authority to proscribe aggravating circumstances in capital cases] to the President...").
110. The courts-martial system has jurisdiction over, *inter alia,* active duty members of the armed forces or those working with the armed forces, persons accompanying an armed force in the field during times of war, certain retired servicemen, certain areas under the control of the armed forces "subject to any treaty or agreement", volunteers and those under reserve duty. UCMJ Art. 2.
111. Courts-martials under the Articles of War also applied "in time of war" to "all persons not citizens of, or owing allegiance to, the United States of America, who shall be found lurking as spies in or about the fortifications or encampments of the armies of the United States...." Articles of War, Spies, Sec. 2. 2 Stat. 359–72 (1806).
112. Formerly the United States Military Court of Appeals. See http://www.armfor.uscourts.gov.
113. See generally Cox Commission. An informative website on this topic is Citizens Against Military Injustice, http://www.militaryinjustice.org.
114. Petitions for certiorari are also possible from the Court of Appeals for the Armed Forces to the Supreme Court. UCMJ Article 67 (a), and 28 U.S.C. § 1259.
115. United States ex rel. Toth v. Quarles. 350 U.S. 11 (1955).
116. McElroy v. United States ex rel. Guagliardo, 361 U.S. 281 (1960).
117. Reid v. Covert, 354 U.S. 1 (1957); Kinsella v. United States ex rel. Singleton, 361 U.S. 234 (1960) (wife of soldier charged with his murder).
118. In O'Callahan v. Parker, 396 U.S. 258 (1969), the Court had ruled that the rape of a civilian woman in an off-base hotel room by an active duty soldier was outside of the jurisdiction of a court-martial. The Court's opinion rejected, largely on due process grounds, the courts-martial system as an appropriate venue for trying either civilians or military personnel charged with non-military related criminal acts. In 1987 the Court overruled O'Callahan, and a subsequent case, Relford v. Commandant, 401 U.S. 355 (1971), and reinstated the former rule which based jurisdiction solely upon the military or civilian status of the accused. Solario v. United States, 483 U.S. 435, 447 (1987).
119. See also Shadow Enemies at 136–141 (discussing the use of military commissions in the Revolutionary War, the Mexican-American War, the Civil War and other conflicts); Maj. Michael O. Lacey, Military Commissions: A Historical Survey, Army Law. 41, 41–47 (March 2002) ("Lacey"); NIMJ Guide 4–5.
120. Maj. Timothy C. MacDonnell, Military Commissions and Courts-Martial: A Brief Discussion of the Constitutional and Jurisdictional Distinctions Between the Two Courts, Army Law 19 (March 2002) ("MacDonnell").

121. Quirin at 13 n.10; MacDonnell at 28.

122. Quirin at 13 n.10. Military commissions were used during the Civil War to try Confederate soldiers who had shed their uniforms in attempts to take over civilian ships or commit acts of sabotage, as well as to try spies. Id., 317 U.S. at 31–32, n.9, n.10.

123. Like Quirin, Yamashita upheld the right of habeas corpus to test the authority of the military commission to proceed. "[Congress] has not withdrawn, and the Executive branch of the government could not, unless there was a suspension of the writ, withdraw from the courts the duty and power to make such inquiry into the authority of the Commission as may be made by habeas corpus." 327 U.S. at 9.

124. Duncan v. Kahanamoku, 327 U.S. 304 (1946), reaffirmed this limiting principle in construing the legislation that authorized the declaration of "martial law" in Hawaii during World War II. The Court emphatically rejected the argument that Congress had authorized the military to arrest civilians in Hawaii and try them before military commissions, not for violations of the law of war but rather for civilian offenses. The Court's conclusion that the statutory use of the term "martial law" did not permit the military to supplant otherwise available civilian courts in trying civilian offenses was said to rest on the bedrock of constitutional case law and practice since the Revolutionary War. See id. at 319–24 (citing inter alia, Milligan and emphasizing that "[c]ourts and their procedural safeguards are indispensable to our system of government." Id. at 322).

125. Manual for Courts-Martial, Preamble paragraph 2(b) (2); see generally NIMJ Guide 77–80.

126. City Bar Report at 18.

127. Section 2(c) provides that "any individual subject to this order...shall...forthwith be placed under the control of the Secretary of Defense."

128. Section 3 provides that "[a]ny individual subject to this order shall be—(a) detained at an appropriate location designated by the Secretary of Defense outside or within the United States."

129. Section 4(c)(3): permits the "admission of such evidence as would...have probative value to a reasonable person."

130. Section 7(b) provides, with respect to "any individual subject to this order," that

> (1) military tribunals shall have exclusive jurisdiction with respect to offenses by the individual; and (2) the individual shall not be privileged to seek any remedy or maintain any proceeding, directly or indirectly, or to have any such remedy or proceeding sought on the individual's behalf, in (i) any court of the United States, or any State thereof, (ii) any court of any foreign nation, or (iii) any international tribunal.

The Supreme Court has in the past heard habeas petitions and reviewed the jurisdiction and authority of a military commission despite similarly limiting language. See p. 45 n.38 above; Quirin, 317 U.S. at 23–25.

131. The term "state secrets" is not well-defined in the law, even in the privilege context. See NIMJ Guide 87.

132. Another alternative alluded to by commentators is the possibility of referring at least some terrorism detainees to an international tribunal. See, e.g., Harold Hongju Koh, "The Case Against Military Commissions", 96 Am. J. Int'l L. 337, 339 n.30 (2002). Since our government has forcefully opposed the creation of a permanent international criminal court and has offered no indication that it sees a special multi-national court to be an appropriate means of dealing with suspects detained by the United States, we focus on American-controlled methods of handling such detainees.

133. Article III, section 3, of the Constitution provides:

> Treason against the United States, shall consist only in levying War against them, or in adhering to their Enemies, giving them Aid and Comfort. No Person shall be convicted of Treason unless on the Testimony of two Witnesses to the same overt Act, or on Confession in open Court.

134. The court in Sattar later held that 18 U.S.C. § 2339B was unconstitutionally vague as applied to the specific allegations of the indictment that defendants had "provided" telecommunications equipment (through use of a telephone) and personnel (by their own conduct) to a terrorist organization. See , 272 F. Supp. 2d 348, 356–61 (S.D.N.Y. 2003). The government has since filed a superseding indictment

charging the defendants with an alternative violation involving the provision of assistance to a terrorist organization.

135. In the 1990s the federal courts heard numerous high profile cases involving international terrorists, including the trial of members of the Provisional IRA, the Abu Nidal Organization, the Nestor Paz Zamora Commission (CPNZ), the Japanese Red Army, and Cuban National Movement, and the prosecutions arising out of the 1993 attack on the World Trade Center and the 1998 bombing of the American embassies in Kenya and Tanzania. For a detailed discussion and statistical analysis of the prosecution of international and domestic terrorists in federal courts during the 1980s and 1990s, see Brent L. Smith et al., The Prosecution and Punishment of International Terrorists in Federal Courts: 1980–1998, Criminology & Public Policy 311–38 (July 2002) (accounting for 427 defendants charged with terrorists crimes from 1980 to 1998) of those tried from 1988 to 1998, the conviction rate exceeded 80%).

Since September 11, 2001, 284 suspected terrorists have been charged in the federal courts and 149 convicted to date.

136. This observation applies to both citizens and non-citizens. Indeed, due process concerns presumptively give even aliens illegally in the country access to the courts to review removal orders. See, e.g., Wang v. Ashcroft, 320 F.3d 130 (2d Cir. 2003) (applying INS v. St. Cyr, 533 U.S. 289); see also Plyler v. Doe, 457 U.S. 202, 210 (1982).

137. In 1949, at a time of much public concern about the threat posed by the Soviet Union, Attorney General J. Howard McGrath, in his annual report to the United States Judicial Conference, addressed this very question of "protecting against the disclosure of information during espionage trials or other trials involving the national security, which in the interest of national security should be kept secret." Report of the Proceedings of the Annual Meeting of the Judicial Conference of the United States, Report of the Attorney General at 34 (Sept. 22, 1949). The Attorney General indicated that, as a general matter, a series of decisions by the Second Circuit had adequately addressed the issue in upholding the practice of trial courts in declining to admit confidential government documents at trial unless the defendant demonstrated that they were "directly material to his defense." United States v. Andolschek, 142 F.2d 503, 506-07 (2d Cir. 1944); United States v. Cohen, 145 F.2d 82, 92 (2d Cir. 1944); United States v. Krulewich, 145 F.2d 76, 78–79 (2d Cir. 1944); United States v. Ebeling, 146 F.2d 254, 256–57 (2d Cir. 1945).

As Mr. McGrath explained these decisions, the court is to exclude and "seal" any confidential document not "directly material" to the defense, and he suggested that even the sensitive evidence admitted at trial would be shown only to the attorneys, the jurors and the judge (and apparently not to the defendant), an arrangement that he appeared to view as satisfactory. As for appeals, he suggested that any such documents would be filed under seal with the appellate court.

Mr. McGrath did note a practical problem involving cases in which the information needed for trial of the charges was so sensitive "that it cannot be disclosed even to the court, the attorneys or the jury." Id. at 35. He advised that because of this problem, "[i]n many cases of this type the Department [of Justice] has been compelled to refrain from prosecuting, and known violators of the law remain at large." Id.

138. The statute also requires the Attorney General to issue guidelines specifying what factors the Department of Justice is to consider in determining whether to pursue a prosecution in which classified information may be disclosed. CIPA, 18 U.S.C. App. 3, §12.

139. Under this provision, the courts have imposed a variety of conditions, including prohibiting public revelation of the information, requiring that the disclosure of sensitive information be limited to defense counsel only and not to the defendant, and compelling the defense attorney to undergo a formal security clearance by the government as a condition for receiving such information. See, e.g., United States v. Pappas, 94 F.3d at 795, 799-800 (2d Cir. 1996); United States v. Moussaoui, No. 01-455-A, 2002 WL 1987964, *1 (E.D. Va. Aug. 29, 2002); United States v. Bin Laden, No. S (7) 98 CR. 1023, 2001 WL 66393, *2 (S.D.N.Y. Jan. 25, 2001); United States v. Bin Laden, 58 F. Supp. 2d 113, 116–17 (S.D.N.Y. 2000).

140. See, e.g., United States v. Klimavicius-Viloria, 144 F.3d 1249, 1261 (9th Cir. 1998).

141. That public interest is embodied in a number of recognized privileges, including the state secret, informant and various law-enforcement privileges, and in applying the CIPA the courts have plainly been sensitive to the policy considerations undergirding them. See generally Shea, 27 Am. Crim. L. Rev. at 693–96 (citing cases).

142. If the court rules against the government on the disclosure question, the prosecutor may obtain interlocutory appellate review. § 7(a). But cf. United States v. Moussaoui, 336 F.3d 279 (4th Cir. 2003) (Wilkens, C.J., concurring in denial of en banc review) (appellate jurisdiction attaches only after district court imposes sanctions on government). The procedures on appeal are expedited, and appropriate security measures must be taken to avoid disclosure of the classified information while the issue is under appeal. §§ 7(a), 9(b).

143. See, e.g., Fernandez, 913 F.2d at 151, 162-65 (affirming dismissal of indictment).

144. The statute mentions, as some alternatives, the dismissal of specific counts of the indictment, entering findings against the government on issues pertaining to which the classified information is relevant, and either striking or precluding pertinent portions of the testimony of specific witnesses. § 6(e)(2). See, e.g., United States v. Moussaoui, 282 F. Supp. 2d 480, 482–87 (E.D. Va. 2003).

145. The rules also authorize the government to investigate the background, or "trustworthiness", of any individuals "associated with the defense", and to provide such information to the court to consider in framing a protective order under section 3 of CIPA. Id. at § 5. The rules also refer to the jurors, stating that security checks of them are not require[d], but advising that the trial judge should honor any government request for a post-trial instruction cautioning the jurors not to reveal the contents of any classified documents shown to them during the trial. § 6. The rules go on to require specific procedures for the storage and transmittal of such documents within the court, establishment of operating routines in handling sensitive materials, coordination with Justice Department security personnel, and procedures for disposal of the materials after the completion of court proceedings. §§ 7, 8, 9, 11 & 13.

146. Strictly speaking, the Moussouai issue does not concern the required disclosure of classified information, but rather the asserted interest of the government in unhampered access to terrorist sources of intelligence.

147. The portrayal of defense counsel as a potential threat to national security presents a minimal risk, at best. As Chief Judge Mukasey observed, in rejecting the government's objection to provision of counsel to an alleged al Qaeda supporter and activist, when counsel are known to the court as reliable officers of the court and there is no reason to suspect that they would violate stringent and specific requirements concerning the non-disclosure of sensitive information, the risks to national security are minimal or non-existent, and a detainee's access to counsel should therefore be accommodated. Padilla, 233 F. Supp. 2d at 599–605.

We recognize that a member of the bar who represented one defendant in United States v. Rahman, 189 F.3d 88 (2d Cir. 1999), stands charged with having assisted her now-convicted client in communicating to his followers a statement encouraging the commission of terrorist acts overseas. See United States v. Sattar, 2002 WL 1836755, *1 (S.D.N.Y. Aug. 12, 2002). Whatever the merits of this charge, it does not suggest that this attorney had access to classified information during the trial, or that she improperly disclosed any such information during or after the trial, or, of course, that any actual wrongdoing by this attorney exemplifies the behavior of the criminal defense bar.

148. It is also worth observing that the danger of some outsider pressuring a former juror to disclose the substance of secret evidence is remote in view of the ability of the court to require an anonymous jury. See, e.g., United States v. Aulicino, 44 F.3d 1102, 1116–17 (2d Cir. 1995); United States v. Thai, 29 F.3d 785, 800–01 (2d Cir. 1994).

149. Prof. Wedgwood's hypothetical example of reliable evidence that would be inadmissible in a civilian court is a statement by Bin Laden's mother to someone else that her son had called her just before September 11, 2001, and warned her that "a major event was imminent". Wedgwood, 96 Am. J. Int'l L. at 331. It is not self-evident that, if confronted with the question, a court would bar the mother's interlocutor from testifying to the statement under the provisions of Rule 807.

CHAPTER 10

Recommendations Related to the Trial of Saddam Hussein

PREFACE BY MARK R. SHULMAN

Following brief but vigorous military operations, the Ba'athist government led by Saddam Hussein fell to the U.S.–led coalition on April 9, 2003. Mr. Hussein, his family, and many other leaders of his regime fled Baghdad. Within a few weeks President George W. Bush announced the end of major combat operations. At the same time, President Bush acknowledged that much work remained to be done in Iraq. Capturing key Ba'athist leaders was a top priority. In addition, the coalition had soon to acknowledge that it faced a guerrilla war. Searching for fugitives while attempting both to quell the insurgency and rebuild Iraq's infrastructure proved to be a considerable challenge. Nonetheless, acting on a tip secured with the assistance of a large bounty, U.S. troops managed to locate and eventually kill Mr. Hussein's widely feared sons in a July 22, 2003, raid.

Over the half year that followed, the search for Mr. Hussein himself focused increasingly on the vicinity of Tikrit, where he had been born and raised. Tikrit was Mr. Hussein's original power base and remained a center for the resistance. Eventually, the United States offered a bounty of $25 million that appears to have enticed one of Mr. Hussein's entourage to furnish the information necessary to capture him. This dramatic chapter closed with a whimper on December 13, 2003—nearly eight months after the fall of Mr. Hussein's regime. U.S. troops located Mr. Hussein in an underground hideout and took him prisoner without a fight. Talk turned immediately to his trial, in part perhaps to forestall summary execution of a man apparently responsible for significant crimes against humanity.

As did much of the world, the Association's Council on International Affairs took considerable interest in the prospect of Mr. Hussein's trial. A Task Force of the Council looked into such diverse issues as Iraqi criminal law, the state of the Iraqi judicial system, and the various proposals for venue, in addition, of course, to the principal allegations that Mr. Hussein was likely to face.

The following Report reflects the Council's best judgment about how to move forward as of the Spring of 2004. At that point, the Constitutional status of the government of Iraq seemed ambiguous. Also, duties owed by the United States, as an occupying power, were in flux, as Iraq's own government gained competencies. The growing insurgency appeared to be leading to a split between the minority Sunni population that had enjoyed disproportionate benefits under the Ba'athist regime and the majority Shi'ite and Kurdish people who had suffered mightily under Mr. Hussein's rule. Moreover, the ethnic divide had significant implications beyond Iraq's borders, as nearby Shi'ite Iran and Kuwait had considerable claims against the Ba'athists. Failure to provide them with justice only threatened to spread the conflict.

Many of the issues raised in this Report remain unresolved today. Shortly after this Report was issued, the Iraqi Governing Council did establish the Tribunal and the United States remanded Mr. Hussein to its jurisdiction. The Iraqi High Tribunal was composed of Iraqis only. Its first chief judge was quickly removed, probably because he was related to someone closely tied to the intelligence used to support the move to war in the first place. Mr. Hussein's trial was postponed several times. During the Summer of 2004, the investigative tribunal filed a criminal case against Mr. Hussein and three other former senior officials, for a specific atrocity, the 1982 massacre of Shi'ites in Dujail. After numerous delays, the trial of Mr. Hussein and seven co-defendants began inauspiciously in October 2005; within days of its opening, a defense lawyer had been assassinated. A similar attack killed another defense lawyer and seriously injured a third in November. Meanwhile Mr. Hussein launched his own attacks on the Iraqi High Tribunal's legitimacy and its jurisdiction over him. During succeeding months, the trial was punctuated by grisly allegations and occasional admissions, by political grandstanding, and by a variety of irregularities that continued to call into question the Tribunal's ability to provide a fair trial.

In November 2006, Mr. Hussein was found guilty and sentenced to death. After his appeal failed, he was hanged in December 2006. His speedy execution halted his trial on charges of committing genocide against Iraqi Kurds during the 1988 Anfal Campaign. Respected analysts at Human Rights Watch have concluded that the first trial of Mr. Hussein was deeply flawed and that the special purpose Tribunal was incapable of holding a fair trial for several reasons:

> These include: 1) An almost complete lack of familiarity with international criminal law on the part of all Iraqi lawyers and judges involved in the trial; 2) Chaotic and inadequate administration which has given rise to major problems in performing basic administrative tasks necessary for a trial of this magnitude to run fairly; and 3) Such extensive use of anonymous witnesses that the defendants did not get right to contest the evidence against them.
>
> These shortcomings have been compounded by the sharp deterioration of the security environment in Iraq which has resulted in the murder of three defense lawyers, the reluctance of numerous witnesses to come forward, and serious limitations on the defense's capacity to investigate and test evidence gathered by the prosecution.[1]

The concerns of Human Rights Watch echo those expressed in the Report that follows and bode ominously for the Anfal Trial, for the rule of law in Iraq, and for the Iraqi nation more generally. The stakes remain high, since the success of the war in Iraq and of the Iraqi state will inevitably be judged in large part by history's verdict of the justice meted out to Saddam Hussein.

INTRODUCTION

In light of the enormity of the crimes with which Saddam Hussein is likely to be charged, the unique circumstances leading up to his disposition and capture and the fact that his trial presents a timely and significant occasion to promote the rule of law and end the cycle of lawlessness abhorrent to the Association and tragic for the people of Iraq and civilized societies, the Association offers the following observations and recommendations concerning the substance and procedures to be used in the anticipated trial of Mr. Hussein.

The Association believes that clearly articulated and universally accepted legal principles continue to provide instruction even where the particular circumstances found in post-Saddam Hussein Iraq may challenge the successful application of traditional legal solutions.

First, the Association recognizes that the current Iraqi judicial system, after years of neglect and misuse by the Ba'athist regime, is ill equipped to conduct or even support a complex trial involving allegations of such crimes as aggression, crimes against humanity, war crimes and genocide without the participation, in some way, of international experts.

Second, the Association recognizes that with respect to the death penalty the people of Iraq retain the right and burden of determining such a fundamental element in the relationship between a state and its citizens. However, consistent with most relevant human rights international treaties and its own longstanding position, the Association urges that the death penalty not be available for use in this case.

Third, while the Association strongly supports the use and improvement of the multilateral instrumentalities of international law, including the International Criminal Court, it recognizes that the principles of complementarity, sovereignty and dignity accord to the Iraqi people the right to try, in a duly constituted court of law, their former leaders, since the people of Iraq were the primary victims of the crimes alleged. However, serious crimes against non-Iraqi citizens, such as Iranians and Kuwaitis, may require that there be an international component in any trial that is conducted.

The Ba'athist regime led by Mr. Hussein stands accused of some of the most grievous crimes mankind has experienced. Its principal victims were the Iraqi people, mainly ethnic and religious groups disfavored by his regime. Under the totalitarian rule of Mr. Hussein, Iraq also conducted vicious wars against its neighbors and their allies. Trial and punishment by an Iraqi government without international participation might not provide sufficient accountability. To promote the process of creating an accurate historical record and to ensure that justice is done for victims as well as for the accused, the Iraqi people must ensure that any trial meets internationally recognized standards of professionalism, independence, openness and thoroughness.

Compilation of the vast amount of evidence necessary to form the basis for a comprehensive indictment and successful prosecution would launch the healing process in Iraq. This process would likely be enhanced by the experience of trials for the senior leaders of the Ba'athist regime that meet the internationally recognized standards and also by some form of national truth and reconciliation process that enables Iraqi society to come to terms with crimes perpetrated by other agents of the regime.

RECOMMENDATIONS

In addition to bringing Mr. Hussein and his principal accomplices to justice before a duly constituted and competent court of law, an indictment and trial under appropriate international standards would further the following objectives: (*i*) developing the rule of law in Iraq; (*ii*) strengthening the perception of the United States and its coalition partners as helping to spread democratic values; and (*iii*) confirming the United States' commitment to international cooperation and standards. Of the possible venues, a modified form of the recently chartered Iraqi Special Tribunal for Crimes Against Humanity may best be able to fulfill these objectives. Should the charter of the Special Tribunal not be modified to meet these objectives, an international or hybrid national-international court or an international tribunal could be established by the Iraqi government to try Mr. Hussein.

Before turning Mr. Hussein and his principal accomplices over to any tribunal for trial on charges of both domestic and international human rights violations, the United States and its coalition partners should be assured that the trial will be conducted in accordance with established legal standards codified in the Geneva Conventions, the International Covenant for Civil and Political Rights and the Universal Declaration of Human Rights. Political expediency should not permit such standards to be ignored or glossed over. To best ensure legal sufficiency and political legitimacy, remand should be premised on the following conditions:

- Strengthening the Special Tribunal to provide for both Iraqi and non-Iraqi judges, prosecutors, defense counsel and investigative and administrative staffs, with qualifications/experience in handling cases involving complex human rights violations to ensure the competence of the tribunal as required under Article 14 of the International Covenant on Civil and Political Rights. At least one non-Iraqi jurist would serve on each Trial Chamber and at least two on the Appeals Chamber. These non-Iraqis would serve in addition to advisors to the Special Tribunal courts and the Prosecutions Department. A training program for Iraqi judges could be instituted if necessary.
- Selection of judges, prosecutors, counsel and support staff would be made jointly by the Iraqi Governing Council (or its successor) and the United Nations Security Council (or some other international or regional authority). Some preference could be given to the empanelling of secular jurists from countries near Iraq.
- Amending or reenacting the provisions of the Statute of the Iraqi Special Tribunal by the new Iraqi government that assumes power after June 2004 to accommodate these provisions and those that follow:

1. The charges to be considered would be those involving international crimes, and, where appropriate, domestic offenses involving serious crimes.
2. The Special Tribunal would adopt rules of evidence and procedure of what are generally regarded by the international community as the highest standards such as those developed for the International Criminal Court, and would require for conviction evidence of guilt beyond a reasonable doubt. The evidence should be compelling, substantial and well documented.
3. The maximum penalty would be life imprisonment. A finite right of appeal would be included in the trial procedures, as would be customary under international law.
4. The trial would take place in Baghdad, be conducted in the Arabic language (with simultaneous interpretation) and be open to the public and the media. Evidence accepted by the judges would be available in its original language to the public and the media, except where necessary to protect the innocent.
5. Robust security must be provided for all participants in the proceedings. Appropriate provisions would also be made to protect witnesses, including, where appropriate, the identity of a witness.

NOTES

1. See http://hrw.org/english/docs/2006/08/14/iraq13982.htm.

CHAPTER 11

Human Rights Standards Applicable to the United States' Interrogation of Detainees

PREFACE BY MARTIN S. FLAHERTY

On April 28, 2004, CBS first broadcast the now infamous photographs of prisoner abuse, mistreatment, and torture at Abu Ghraib prison. That same week, the Association released its Report, which had been long in the making, on international human rights and humanitarian standards applicable to U.S. interrogation of detainees. The timing of these two developments was entirely accidental but sadly appropriate. The Abu Ghraib photographs touched off a firestorm of moral outrage both inside the United States and around the world. Though its authors had no firm evidence of the Abu Ghraib abuses beforehand, the Association's Report set forth bases for outrage on legal grounds. More generally, the Report almost overnight became among the most widely consulted guides as to how U.S. forces should conduct themselves not just in Iraq, but Afghanistan, Guantanamo Bay, and indeed wherever U.S. forces held individuals in custody in the name of the "global war on terror."

As the Report itself makes clear, the Association first undertook the project in response to widely reported allegations that individuals detained by the United States were being subjected to mistreatment in connection with the conflict in Afghanistan. Yet, as the Report also states, most of the standards it discusses "apply broadly and with equal force to the treatment of detainees captured in other situations." Unfortunately, the broader applicability of the Report proved to be grimly prophetic. In the wake of the Abu Ghraib scandal, the Association nonetheless saw a need to address issues arising out of detention in Iraq, as well as additional issues that had come to light out of Afghanistan. These concerns led to the release of a Supplement to the main Report a month later, in May 2004, to analyze these additional legal settings.

The Report represents what became a fruitful collaboration between the Committee on International Human Rights,* initially led by Scott Horton and succeeded by Martin Flaherty, and the Committee on Military Affairs and Justice, chaired by Miles P. Fischer. Although military lawyers and human rights advocates might not initially have appeared as natural allies, a close collaboration developed over the year-long process of generating the two documents. Not only did the two groups supplement one another's knowledge with regard to human rights law on one hand and humanitarian law on the other, they also discovered the ways in which the two bodies of law complemented one another and reinforced a mutual commitment to uphold the United States' position as a traditional champion of the rule of law internationally. Importantly, much the same partnership emerged in the nation at large. Human rights lawyers and nongovernmental organizations (NGOs) took the lead in criticizing the Bush Administration's actions with regard to human rights law. But so too did military lawyers, especially from within the Judge Advocate General's Corps, who in various formal and informal ways expressed dismay at the Administration's apparent unconcern for abiding by laws of war that the United States had in large part fashioned.

The Report describes "the legal principles which should guide our military and intelligence personnel in their conduct." First and foremost of these is the Convention Against Torture and Other Cruel, Inhuman or Degrading Treatment (CAT) to which the United States is a party. More contentious are the Geneva Conventions, since there remain legitimate questions as to whether members of the Taliban or, more controversially, al Qaeda, qualify for prisoner of war (POW) status and the extensive protections it entails. The Report nonetheless concludes that in cases of doubt POW status should be accorded liberally, and that in any instance, Common Article 3 provides important protections for those detainees who do not qualify for POW status. In addition, the Report also considers safeguards afforded by other international standards, including the International Covenant on Civil and Political Rights, the Universal Declaration of Human Rights, and the Inter-American Convention on Human Rights; customary international law; and *jus cogens*. As a final matter, the Report consults the comparative experience of the United Kingdom and Israel in combating terrorist violence while nonetheless observing strictures against torture and other cruel, inhuman, and degrading treatment.

In light of Abu Ghraib, the Supplement provides additional analysis focusing on the legal standards applicable to detainees in Iraq. Here the Association analyzes the Geneva Conventions with regard to several important questions, among them the broad coverage for "protected persons" during occupations, its conclusion that U.S. detainees do not fall into the few narrow exceptions to protected-person status, and the standards that apply once the formal U.S. occupation in Iraq ends. The Supplement also underlines the Association's position that Common Article 3 provides baseline human rights protections and is not subject to exceptions for persons affiliated with non-state organizations such as al Qaeda that have not signed the Geneva Conventions. In this regard, both the Report and the Supplement flatly contradict positions taken in internal Bush Administration memoranda written by Professor John Yoo, as well as the position later adopted by the D.C. Circuit in *Hamdan*.

The Report concludes with a series of recommendations, which the Supplement reiterates and amplifies. These include calls upon the U.S. government (1) to train and educate all relevant officials in the international legal standards that apply to detention and interrogation, (2) to conduct prompt investigations of possible violations, (3) to expand the scope of 18 U.S.C. sec. 2340 to expressly prohibit torture in extraterritorial detention centers under U.S. jurisdiction, (4) to fully apply and utilize the Uniform Code of Military Justice, (5) to conduct independent investigations with regard to the human rights compliance of countries to which the U.S. might "render" detainees, (6) to grant POW status to detainees whose status is in doubt as a matter of policy, and (7) to restore the role of the Judge Advocate Officers in providing legal advice in connection with detention and interrogation.

The legal conclusions set forth become even more important in light of official responses to both the Association and others regarding U.S. policy. Both the inquiries and the responses are set forth in the appendices. Among these exchanges, William J. Haynes responded to Ken Roth of Human Rights Watch asserting that "the United States condemns and prohibits torture," and that "U.S. personnel are required to follow this policy and applicable laws prohibiting torture." Haynes responded even more fully to an inquiry made by Senator Patrick Leahy that U.S. policy consists of undertaking interrogations in a manner consistent with the Convention Against Torture and other Cruel, Inhuman and Degrading Treatment as ratified by the United States, as well as the Federal Torture Statute, 18 U.S.C. sec. 2340–2340A. Haynes further stated that it was U.S. policy not simply to refrain from torture, but to refrain from cruel, inhuman, and degrading treatment not amounting to torture.

The Report and the Supplement made a significant impact when they were released. Among other things, they served as a basis for press reports on detainee mistreatment in such publications as the *Washington Post, The New Yorker,* and the *New York Times.* They have repeatedly served as a resource for Congress, including the questioning of Alberto Gonzales during the hearing held on his appointment as Attorney General. They were also among the few non-government documents reprinted in the book, *The Torture Papers: The Road to Abu Ghraib,* edited by Karen J. Greenberg and Joshua L. Dratel and published by Cambridge University Press. In these and other ways, the work of the two Committees has sought to live up to the Association's highest ideals of providing dispassionate legal analysis on great public questions. The countervailing regret is that this analysis calls into question the actions and policies of our own government in upholding humanitarian law, international human rights law, Federal law, and the rule of law itself.

In *Hamdan v Rumsfeld,*[1] the Supreme Court confirmed and expanded its commitment to the rule of law against the Administration's ongoing claims of unchecked executive authority. Reversing a D.C. Circuit panel that included now Chief Justice John Roberts, the Court held that special military commissions constituted to try Guantanamo detainees violated the Uniform Code of Military Justice (UCMJ) in two respects. The military commissions failed first because their procedures substantially differed from those guaranteed in courts martial, with no government showing justifying the divergence. In addition, the commissions violated Common Article 3 of the 1949 Geneva Conventions, as incorporated by the UCMJ, insofar as they were not regularly constituted courts. The Association may take some credit for this second rationale because its amicus briefs, both before the D.C. Circuit and Supreme Court, first raised the relevance of Common Article 3's requirements.

HUMAN RIGHTS STANDARDS APPLICABLE TO THE UNITED STATES' INTERROGATION OF DETAINEES

EXECUTIVE SUMMARY/INTRODUCTION

This Report is a joint effort of the Association of the Bar of the City of New York's Committees on International Human Rights and Military Affairs and Justice, undertaken to consider allegations—reported in the press and by human rights and humanitarian organizations conducting their own investigations—that individuals detained by the United States at its military and intelligence facilities in connection with the initial War in Afghanistan and the subsequent ongoing conflict in Afghanistan, are being subjected to interrogation techniques that constitute torture or cruel, inhuman or degrading treatment.[2] We note at the outset, however, that although this project was initially motivated by allegations regarding the treatment of detainees from the War in Afghanistan, the international law and human rights standards discussed herein—with the exception of Geneva Convention protections applicable only to situations of international armed conflict—apply broadly and with equal force to the treatment of detainees captured in other situations, including detainees picked up in other countries in connection with the broader "War on Terror."[3] In this Report, we will examine the international legal standards governing United States military and civil authorities in interrogating detainees and propose ways of assuring that those standards are enforced.

The Alleged Interrogation Practices

These allegations first surfaced in December 2002, when the U.S. military announced that it had begun a criminal investigation into the death of a 22 year-old Afghan farmer and part-time taxi driver who had died of "blunt force injuries to lower extremities complicating coronary artery disease" while in U.S. custody at Bagram Air Force Base in Afghanistan.[4] Since then, details about interrogation techniques allegedly employed at U.S. detention facilities—most of which are off-limits to outsiders and some of which are in undisclosed locations—have come from government officials speaking on the condition that they would not be identified and from the few prisoners who have been released. Some examples of "stress and duress" interrogation "techniques" reportedly being practiced by U.S. Department of Defense ("DOD") and Central Intelligence Agency ("CIA") personnel at U.S. detention facilities include: forcing detainees to stand or kneel for hours in black hoods or spray-painted goggles, 24-hour bombardment with lights, "false-flag" operations meant to deceive a captive about his whereabouts, withholding painkillers from wounded detainees, confining detainees in tiny rooms, binding in painful positions, subjecting detainees to loud noises, and sleep deprivation.[5] In addition, the U.S. is reportedly "rendering" suspects to the custody of foreign intelligence services in countries where the practice of torture and cruel, inhuman or degrading treatment during interrogation is well-documented.[6]

The Administration's Responses

The Association and others have written to U.S. government officials to ask whether there is any factual basis for these allegations and whether steps are being taken to ensure that detainees are interrogated in accordance with U.S. law and international standards prohibiting torture and "cruel, inhuman or degrading" treatment falling short of torture ("CID").[7]

In response to inquiries from Human Rights Watch, U.S. Department of Defense General Counsel William J. Haynes has stated that: "United States policy condemns and prohibits torture" and that, when "questioning enemy combatants, U.S. personnel are required to follow this policy and applicable laws prohibiting torture."[8] CIA General Counsel Scott W. Muller, citing to the need to protect intelligence sources and methods, has responded to our inquiries by stating only that "in its various activities around the world the CIA remains subject to the requirements of U.S. law" and that allegations of unlawful behavior are reported by the CIA to the Department of Justice and are subject to investigation.[9]

In response to an inquiry made by U.S. Senator Patrick J. Leahy regarding U.S. policy, Haynes stated that U.S. policy entails "conducting interrogations in a manner that is consistent with the Convention Against Torture and Other Cruel, Inhuman, or Degrading Treatment or Punishment ("CAT"), as ratified by the U.S. in 1994, and with the Federal anti-torture statute, 18 U.S.C. §§ 2340–2340A, which Congress enacted to fulfill U.S. obligations under the CAT."[10] Haynes also stated that U.S. policy is "to treat all detainees and conduct all interrogations, wherever they may occur, in a manner consistent with" the U.S. obligation, pursuant to Article 16 of CAT, namely, "to prevent other acts of cruel, inhuman, or degrading treatment or punishment which do not amount to torture" insofar as such treatment is "prohibited by the Fifth, Eighth, and/or Fourteenth Amendments."[11] Haynes assured Senator Leahy "that credible allegations of illegal conduct by U.S. personnel will be investigated and, as appropriate, reported to proper authorities."[12] Furthermore, Haynes stated that the U.S. does not "expel, return ('*refouler*') or extradite individuals to other countries where the U.S. believes it is 'more likely than not' that they will be tortured," that "United States policy is to obtain specific assurances from the receiving country that it will not torture the individual being transferred to that country," and that "the United States would take steps to investigate credible allegations of torture and take appropriate action if there were reason to believe that those assurances were not being honored."[13]

Both Haynes and Muller have declined, however, to give details concerning the specific interrogation methods used by U.S. personnel at U.S. military and CIA detention facilities.

Legal Standards Prohibiting Torture and Cruel, Inhuman or Degrading Treatment

Although we are not in a position to investigate the factual basis for the allegations of torture and cruel, inhuman or degrading interrogation practices at U.S. detention facilities that have been made, we can describe the legal principles which should guide our military and intelligence personnel in their conduct. Accordingly, in this Report we examine the international and U.S. law standards against which the interrogation practices used on detainees should be assessed. We also address the question of whether there are any circumstances posed by the post-September 11 world in which abrogation of our country's obligations to prevent and punish torture and cruel, inhuman or degrading treatment should be permitted in the interrogation of terrorist suspects.

The Convention Against Torture

First and foremost, the U.S. obligation to prohibit and prevent the torture and cruel, inhuman or degrading treatment of detainees in its custody is set forth in the Convention Against Torture And Other Cruel, Inhuman, or Degrading Treatment ("CAT"), to which the U.S. is a party.[14] When the U.S. ratified CAT in 1994, it did so subject to a reservation providing that the U.S. would prevent "cruel, inhuman or degrading treatment" insofar as such treatment is prohibited under the Fifth, Eighth, and/or Fourteenth Amendments.[15] Thus, the U.S. is obligated to prevent not only torture, but also conduct considered cruel, inhuman or degrading under international law if such conduct is also prohibited by the Fifth, Eighth and Fourteenth Amendments. In interpreting U.S. obligations, we look to the U.N. Committee Against Torture's interpretations of CAT as well as U.S. case law decided in the immigration and asylum law context, under the Alien Tort Claims and Torture Victim Protection Acts and concerning the treatment of detainees and prisoners under the Fifth, Eighth and/or Fourteenth Amendments. We also examine the procedural mechanisms available under U.S. law to punish violations of CAT—including prosecution under federal criminal law (18 U.S.C. §§ 2340—2340A) and the Uniform Code of Military Justice ("UCMJ").

Other International Legal Standards which Bind the United States

While there is a dearth of U.S. case law applying CAT's prohibition against torture and cruel, inhuman or degrading treatment in the interrogation context, there is a wealth of international law sources which offer guidance in interpreting CAT. Some of these international legal standards are, without question, binding on the U.S., such as: the International Covenant on Civil and Political Rights (the "ICCPR"),[16] the law of *jus cogens* and customary international law. Another international legal instrument which has been ratified by the U.S. and is relevant to the interrogation practices being examined by this Report is the Inter-American Declaration on the Rights and Duties of Man.[17] Other sources, such as the European Convention for the Protection of Human Rights and Fundamental Freedoms,[18] also provide guidance.

The applicability of the Geneva Conventions to the detainees from the War in Afghanistan, however, presents a more contentious issue. The Administration's official position is that the Geneva Conventions do not apply to Al Qaeda detainees, and that neither the Taliban nor Al Qaeda detainees are entitled to prisoner of war ("POW") status thereunder. Nevertheless, the Administration has stated that it is treating such individuals "humanely and, to the extent appropriate and consistent with military necessity, in a manner consistent with the principles of the Third Geneva Convention of 1949," and that the detainees "will not be subjected to physical or mental abuse or cruel treatment."[19] The Administration has never explained how it determines what interrogation techniques are "appropriate" or "consistent with military necessity," or how it squares that determination with U.S. obligations under human rights and customary international law. For POW and civilian detainees who meet the relevant criteria of Geneva Convention (III) Relative to the Treatment of Prisoners of War ("Geneva III") and Geneva Convention (IV) Relative to the Protection of Civilian Persons in Time of War ("Geneva IV"), respectively, all coercion is prohibited.[20] Moreover, any detainee whose POW status is in doubt is entitled to a hearing and determination by a competent tribunal and, pending such determination, any such detainee must be treated as a POW. Concern for the safety of U.S. forces weighs in favor of extending POW status liberally. At a minimum, all detainees—regardless of POW or civilian status—are entitled to humane treatment and prompt hearings under human rights and customary international law, including the protections of Article 3 common to all four Geneva Conventions ("Common Article 3") and Article 75 of the Protocol Additional to the Geneva Conventions of 12 August 1949 and Related to the Protection of Victims of International Armed Conflicts ("Additional Protocol I").[21] We urge the U.S. to promptly establish proper screening procedures for all detainees, whether or not they served with forces that met the specific criteria of Geneva III.

Legal Standards which the United States Should Look to for Guidance

Other relevant sources of law, such as the seminal 1999 Israeli Supreme Court decision on interrogation methods employed by the Israeli General Security Service, *Judgment Concerning The Legality Of The General Security Service's Interrogation Methods,*[22] and decisions of the European Court of Human Rights, although not legally binding on the U.S., also offer useful guidance in our interpretation of CAT. These foreign decisions indicate that the "War on Terror" is not unprecedented. As the Israeli and Northern Ireland experiences demonstrate, the U.S. is not the only country to have faced terrorism within its borders, despite the unique tragedy of September 11 and the potential threat of weapons of mass destruction that could expand the loss of life by orders of magnitude. We can and should learn from the experience of other countries whose courts have grappled with the need to permit effective interrogation while at the same time upholding the standards of human rights and the rule of law.

Standards in the Time of Terror

There is an inherent tension between the need to obtain potentially life-saving information through interrogation of terrorist suspects and the legal requirement of upholding the standards set forth in CAT. We grappled with the question of whether there are any circumstances under which torture or cruel, inhuman or degrading treatment would be permissible in a post-September 11 world. While we acknowledge the real danger posed to the United States by Al Qaeda and other terrorist organizations, we concluded that there are no such exceptions to CAT's absolute prohibition of torture.

Condoning torture under any circumstances erodes one of the most basic principles of international law and human rights and contradicts our values as a democratic state. Permitting the abuse of detainees in U.S. custody, perhaps under so-called "torture warrants," not only harms the detainees themselves; it compromises the moral framework of our interrogators and damages our society as a whole. If U.S. personnel are allowed to engage in brutal interrogation methods which denigrate the dignity and humanity of detainees, we sanction conduct which we as a nation (along with the international community) has clearly determined is wrong and immoral. Accordingly, we unanimously condemn the torture of detainees under any circumstances. We note that U.S. constitutional jurisprudence on "cruel, inhuman or degrading" treatment, which has been made relevant to CAT by the U.S. reservation, is an extremely important source of guidance on this subject. On the other hand, much of this jurisprudence evolved in the context of domestic criminal justice administration, and how these precedents would be applied in a case arising out of the interrogation and detention covered by this Report is, in the absence of more definitive authority, a matter of some speculation.

Recommendations

We applaud the statements in William Haynes' June 25, 2003 letter to Senator Leahy affirming the policy of the U.S. regarding its commitment to CAT. To make that policy meaningful, we make the following recommendations:

1. Training and Education. All law enforcement personnel, civilian or military, medical personnel, public officials and other persons who may be involved in the custody, interrogation or treatment of anyone under any form of detention or imprisonment should be informed and educated regarding the prohibition against torture and cruel, inhuman or degrading treatment, as applied in practice. This requires, as provided in Article 11 of CAT, that the U.S. keep under systematic review interrogation rules, instructions, methods and practices as well as arrangements for the custody and treatment of such detainees.[23] Above all, commanders should not condone non-compliance nor permit an environment in which troops are encouraged to provide lip service to compliance but yet think that non-compliance is acceptable.

Given that CIA personnel are not generally subject to the UCMJ, possibly not even when accompanying the armed forces in the field, special procedures should be available to provide reasonable assurance that compliance with CAT is being taught and maintained by intelligence agencies. That assurance might best be provided by the applicable committees of the Congress exercising oversight responsibility in conjunction with the inspectors general of the applicable agencies.

2. Prompt Investigation of Violations. As required by Article 12 of CAT, the U.S. must ensure that allegations of abusive conduct are taken seriously and are fully and impartially investigated.[24] Thus, any individual who alleges that he or she has been subjected to torture must be provided with a meaningful opportunity to complain to, and to have his/her case promptly and impartially examined by, competent authorities. Steps must be taken to ensure that the complainant and witnesses are protected against all ill-treatment and intimidation.

3. Expand the Scope and Reach of Section 2340. Consistent with its obligation under Article 4 of CAT to ensure that all acts of torture are offenses under its criminal law[25]—and since 18 U.S.C. § 2340 does not, by its terms, apply to acts constituting torture committed in extraterritorial detention centers under U.S. jurisdiction—the U.S. must expand the geographic reach of Section 2340 so that the prescriptions of CAT are applicable at all U.S. detention centers.

4. Fully Utilize the UCMJ. The U.S. must more fully utilize the procedures and protections available under the UCMJ to prosecute all violations of CAT by the armed forces or others subject to the UCMJ.

5. Independent Investigation of Human Rights Compliance in Other Countries. As provided by Article 3 of CAT, the U.S. must not "render" detainees to other countries where there are substantial grounds for belief that the detainees would be in danger of being subjected to torture.[26] In determining whether there are "substantial grounds for belief" that a detainee would be in danger of torture if rendered to another country, U.S. authorities must take into account all the relevant considerations concerning that country, including independently investigating whether there exists a consistent pattern of gross, flagrant or mass violations of human rights in the country.[27]

6. Grant POW Status to Detainees Whose Status is in Doubt and Possibly as a Matter of Policy. The U.S. should adhere to Geneva III's requirement that any detainee whose POW status is in "doubt" is entitled to POW status—and, therefore, cannot be subjected to coercive treatment—until a "competent tribunal," which must be convened promptly, determines otherwise.[28] We urge the U.S. to consider the policy grounds for extending POW treatment to regular force combatants, whether or not legally required to do so, as it has done in prior conflicts.

7. Prompt Screening and Hearings for All Detainees. In keeping with the spirit of the Geneva Conventions and human rights law, we urge the U.S. to provide proper screening procedures and hearings to all detainees.[29]

We now turn to a more detailed discussion of the international standards applicable to interrogation procedures.

I. THE CONVENTION AGAINST TORTURE

The U.N. Convention Against Torture and Other Cruel, Inhuman or Degrading Treatment or Punishment ("CAT") is the primary source of international law relevant to the treatment of detainees.[30] CAT has been ratified by the U.S., and its prohibitions against torture and cruel, inhuman or degrading treatment or punishment have been implemented in our domestic law.

Specifically, U.S. law implements CAT's prohibition against torture in the immigration and asylum contexts, under the Alien Tort Claims and Torture Victim Protection Acts, by criminal statute and under the UCMJ. Under CAT, the U.S. is also obligated to prevent "cruel, inhuman or degrading treatment or punishment" as defined in international law; however, by express reservation, the U.S. interprets this obligation in keeping with standards of treatment required by the Fifth, Eighth and Fourteenth Amendments. Accordingly, under CAT, American military and intelligence personnel involved in the interrogation of detainees may not torture those detainees, nor may they subject them to cruel, inhuman or degrading treatment that is, or would be, forbidden under the Fifth, Eighth and/or Fourteenth Amendments.

A. CAT's Definitions of—and Prohibitions against—Torture and Cruel, Inhuman or Degrading Treatment

CAT defines and prohibits torture, as defined, and cruel, inhuman or degrading treatment or punishment in general terms. In addition, it also sets out steps ratifying countries must take to prevent, investigate, and criminalize acts of torture;[31] prohibits the extradition or other rendering (also known as "*refoulement*") of a person to a country that would likely subject such person to torture;[32] creates a Committee to oversee the implementation of CAT by ratifying countries; and sets forth procedures for inquiries, individual communications, and inter-State complaints.

CAT's preamble acknowledges that torture and other cruel, inhuman or degrading treatment or punishment are already prohibited under Article 5 of the Universal Declaration of Human Rights and Article 7 of the ICCPR. Thus, rather than simply mirroring the prohibitions from these instruments, Article 1 of CAT provides additional guidance to states parties in preventing and punishing torture by setting forth an explicit definition of torture:

> ...torture means any act by which severe pain or suffering, whether physical or mental, is intentionally inflicted on a person for such purposes as obtaining from him or a third person information or a confession, punishing him for an act he or a third person has committed or is suspected of having committed, or intimidating or coercing him or a third person, or for any reason based on discrimination of any kind, when such pain or suffering is inflicted by or at the instigation of or with the consent or acquiescence of a public official or other person acting in an official capacity. It does not include pain or suffering arising only from, inherent in or incidental to lawful sanctions.

This definition makes it clear that the result of torture need not be physical pain or suffering, but can also be mental. In addition, torture is defined to include such conduct undertaken for the purpose of obtaining information. Finally, the prohibition is not directed at private citizens, acting independently of government; it applies rather to acts committed by government officials and agents, or persons acting with official consent or acquiescence.

CAT's prohibition of torture is absolute. An order from a superior officer or a public authority may not be invoked as a justification of torture. Specifically, Article 2(2) provides: "No exceptional circumstances whatsoever, whether a state of war or a threat or war, internal political instability or any other public emergency, may be invoked as a justification of torture."

Although CAT does not provide a definition of CID punishment or treatment, Article 16 requires ratifying countries to prevent "other acts of cruel, inhuman or degrading treatment or punishment which do not amount to torture...." This language suggests that cruel, inhuman or degrading treatment is on a continuum with torture.

CAT requires each signatory state to prevent the commission of the prohibited acts within any territory under the state's jurisdiction. Specifically, each ratifying country must ensure that any official who may be involved in the interrogation of anyone under any form of detention or imprisonment is informed of and educated about the prohibitions against torture and cruel, inhuman or degrading treatment. CAT also requires each ratifying country to ensure that allegations of torture and CID treatment are fully and impartially investigated. *See* CAT Articles 12 and 16(1).

B. CAT's Prohibition against Torture and CID Treatment as Interpreted by the U.N. Committee Against Torture

The U.N. Committee Against Torture, created by CAT, is charged with monitoring implementation of the treaty by ratifying countries through the determination of individual complaints, considering country reports submitted under CAT, and resolving inter-State disputes. Given the importance of international standards in interpreting U.S. domestic law[33] as well as the recent *Lawrence v. Texas* decision, in which the U.S. Supreme Court expressly looked to foreign and international law for guidance,[34] U.N. Committee decisions are relevant to the assessment of whether the actions of U.S. personnel involved in the interrogation of detainees constitute torture or cruel, inhuman or degrading treatment.

The U.N. Committee has concluded that the following acts[35] constitute torture under CAT:

- daily beatings and detaining someone in a small, uncomfortable space for two weeks;[36]
- forcing someone to sleep on the floor of a cell while handcuffed following interrogation;[37]
- in severe cases, sleep deprivation;[38] and
- the threat of torture.[39]

Furthermore, the U.N. Committee has recommended that the use of a blindfold during questioning be expressly prohibited.[40] More generally, the U.N. Committee has expressed concern that States have defined torture too narrowly, covering only "systematic blows or other violent acts."[41] The U.N. Committee has also expressed concern whether the penal law of one State was too narrow in defining torture because it failed to prohibit "certain aspects of torture, such as psychological pressure, threats and intimidation."[42]

The U.N. Committee has found that the following acts amount to cruel, inhuman or degrading treatment or punishment under CAT:

- depriving someone of food and/or water;[43]
- in some cases, binding someone in a restraint chair;[44]
- the use by prison authorities of instruments of physical restraint that may cause unnecessary pain and humiliation;[45] and
- long periods of detention (two weeks or more) in detention cells that are sub-standard (this conduct may amount to torture if the period of detention is extremely long).[46]

The U.N. Committee has found that the following acts may amount to torture when used in combination with other forms of CID:

- being restrained in very painful conditions;
- being hooded;
- the sounding of loud music for prolonged periods;
- sleep deprivation for prolonged periods;
- violent shaking; and
- using cold air to chill.[47]

In sum, the U.N. Committee Against Torture has indicated that the classification of treatment as CID or torture is often a matter of severity, intensity, and the totality of the circumstances. Combining several forms of cruel, inhuman or degrading treatment will frequently amount to torture, and ratifying countries are required under CAT to refrain from all such practices, whether they reach the level of severity to be considered torture or not. Thus, according to

U.N. Committee jurisprudence, alleged interrogation practices such as forcing detainees to stand or kneel for hours in black hoods or spray-painted goggles, 24-hour bombardment with lights, binding detainees in painful positions, withholding painkillers from wounded detainees, and subjecting detainees to loud noises and sleep deprivation, at a minimum, constitute cruel, inhuman or degrading treatment and may, depending on the circumstances, rise to the level of torture. U.N. Committee decisions critical of blindfolding, psychological pressure and threats and intimidation strongly suggest that "false-flag" operations meant to deceive detainees about their whereabouts and "stress and duress" interrogation techniques are also prohibited.

C. U.S. Law Implementing CAT's Prohibitions against Torture and Cruel, Inhuman or Degrading Treatment or Punishment

The Senate adopted a resolution of advice and consent to U.S. ratification of CAT, subject to the declaration that it be deemed non-self-executing, on October 27, 1990.[48] The U.S. ratified CAT in October 1994, and CAT entered into force with respect to the United States on 20 November 1994.[49] The implementation in U.S. immigration, extradition, criminal and civil tort law of CAT's prohibition against torture, as well as the express application of U.S. constitutional standards to CAT's prohibition against CID treatment, indicates that many of the interrogation practices allegedly being used by the U.S. against detainees may be prohibited under international <u>and</u> U.S. law.

1. *U.S. Understandings and Reservations in Ratifying CAT*

The United States conditioned its ratification of CAT upon certain understandings related to CAT's definition of torture in Article 1. In one such understanding, the U.S. specified that mental pain or suffering within the meaning of "torture" refers to prolonged mental harm caused by or resulting from: (1) the intentional infliction or threatened infliction of severe physical pain or suffering; (2) the administration or application, or threatened administration or application, of mind-altering substances or other procedures calculated to disrupt profoundly the senses or the personality; (3) the threat of imminent death; or (4) the threat that another person will imminently be subjected to death, severe physical pain or suffering, or the administration or application of mind-altering substances or other procedures calculated to disrupt profoundly the senses or the personality.[50] Another U.S. understanding pertains to defects in criminal procedure: noncompliance with applicable legal procedural standards (such as Miranda warnings) does not per se constitute "torture."[51]

When ratifying CAT, the United States also took the following reservation: "the United States considers itself bound by the obligation under Article 16 to prevent 'cruel, inhuman or degrading treatment or punishment,' only insofar as the term 'cruel, inhuman or degrading treatment or punishment' means the cruel, unusual and inhumane treatment or punishment prohibited by the Fifth, Eighth, and Fourteenth Amendments to the Constitution of the United States."[52]

2. *The Implementation of CAT's Prohibition against Torture in U.S. Legislation, Regulation and Case Law*

CAT's prohibition of official acts amounting to torture has been implemented in the United States through legislation, regulations and case law pertaining to, *inter alia,* (1) immigration, (2) claims of torture in removal and extradition proceedings, (3) criminal sanctions for torture, and (4) tort claims alleging torture. Through the application of these implementing laws and regulations, U.S. courts have interpreted CAT's substantive provisions in a variety of contexts.[53]

(a) U.S. Immigration Law and Torture

As previously noted, all countries that ratify CAT are obligated to ensure that detainees are not deported or extradited to countries where they are likely to be tortured. In 1998, the United States enacted the Foreign Affairs Reform and Restructuring Act of 1998, § 2242, Pub. L. No. 105-277, Div. G, 112 Stat. 2681, 2681-822 (Oct. 21, 1998) (the "FARR Act"), implementing this obligation. In 1999, the Immigration and Naturalization Service ("INS") promulgated regulations effectuating the FARR Act in the immigration and asylum context, providing aliens in exclusion, deportation or removal proceedings with grounds to seek withholding of removal based on CAT. *See* 8 C.F.R. § 208.18 (2004), *et seq*. These regulations incorporate CAT's definition of torture verbatim, with the following qualification: "Torture is an extreme form of cruel and inhuman treatment and does not include lesser forms of cruel, inhuman or degrading treatment or punishment that do not amount to torture." *See* 8 C.F.R. § 208.18(a)(2) (2004). These regulations further define mental pain or suffering consistently with the U.S. understandings to CAT, and exclude from the definition of torture acts which result in "unanticipated or unintended severity of pain and suffering." *See* 8 C.F.R. § 208.18(a)(5) (2004).

A number of federal court cases and Board of Immigration Appeals ("BIA") decisions address torture claims in the immigration context. The BIA has held that the following abuses of detainees and prisoners, for example, amount to torture: "'suspension for long periods in contorted positions, burning with cigarettes, sleep deprivation, and...severe and repeated beatings with cables or other instruments on the back and on the soles of the feet,'...beatings about the ears, resulting in partial or complete deafness, and punching in the eyes, leading to partial or complete blindness." *Matter of G-A-*, 23 I & N Dec. 366, 370 (BIA 2002) (internal citations omitted).[54] Furthermore, persons seeking asylum or withholding of removal have successfully challenged deportation under Sections 208 and 241(b)(3) of the Immigration & Nationality Act ("INA") when they have a well-founded fear of future persecution. Although "persecution" is not defined in the INA, it is understood to encompass treatment falling short of torture.

(b) U.S. Extradition of Fugitives Who Face Threat of Torture

In the extradition context, torture claims are governed by regulations enacted by the Department of State under the FARR Act. Under these regulations, individuals sought for extradition may present a claim that they are likely to be tortured if surrendered to the requesting state. These claims are considered by the U.S. Secretary of State, who is responsible for implementing CAT's obligation not to extradite an individual to a State where he or she is in danger of being subject to torture. Specifically, section 95 of 22 C.F.R. (2004) provides, in relevant part, that the Secretary of State must consider whether a person facing extradition from the U.S. "is more likely than not" to be tortured in the State requesting extradition, and that appropriate policy and legal offices must review and analyze the information relevant to the torture allegation. The extradition regulations, and the decisions interpreting them,[55] demonstrate that U.S. administrative bodies and courts view CAT's prohibition against extradition to torture as binding on the U.S. even when the extraditable individual is accused of wrongdoing.

(c) U.S. Implementation of CAT's Criminal Law Requirements

18 U.S.C. §§ 2340 and 2340A were enacted to fulfill CAT's requirement that each ratifying country criminalize all acts of torture, including attempts to commit torture and complicity in torture.[56] Section 2340 defines torture as:

> an act committed by a person acting under the color of law specifically intended to inflict severe physical or mental pain or suffering (other than pain or suffering incidental to lawful sanctions) upon another person within his custody or physical control...

"Severe mental pain or suffering" is also defined, using the same wording as the U.S. understandings concerning Article 1 of CAT set forth in Section I(C)(1) above. *See* 18 U.S.C. § 2340. As discussed further below, however, this statute applies only to U.S. nationals (or others present in the U.S.) who have committed or attempted or conspired to commit acts of torture "outside of the United States."[57]

(d) U.S. Case Law Interpretations of Torture in Tort Claims

Two U.S. statutes provide for civil suits against those who commit acts of torture abroad. The Alien Tort Claims Act of 1789 ("ATCA"), 28 U.S.C. § 1350, states that "[t]he district courts shall have original jurisdiction of any civil action by an alien for a tort only, committed in violation of the law of nations or a treaty of the United States." The Torture Victim Protection Act of 1991 ("TVPA"), 28 U.S.C. § 1350, provides that:

> [a]n individual who, under actual or apparent authority, or color of law, of any foreign nation—(1) subjects an individual to torture shall, in a civil action, be liable for damages to that individual; or (2) subjects an individual to extrajudicial killing shall, in a civil action, be liable for damages to the individual's legal representative, or to any person who may be a claimant in an action for wrongful death.[58]

The TVPA extends a civil remedy to U.S. citizen torture victims, while the ATCA provides a remedy for aliens only.

U.S. courts applying the ATCA and TVPA have found that the following acts constitute torture: subjecting detainees to interrogation sessions lasting 14 hours (*Xuncax v. Gramajo,* 886 F. Supp. 162, 170 (D. Mass 1995)); beating with hands (*Tachiona v. Mugabe,* 234 F. Supp. 2d 401, 420–423 (S.D.N.Y. 2002); *Cabiri v. Assasie-Gyimah,* 921 F. Supp. 1189, 1191, 1196 (S.D.N.Y. 1996); *Abebe-Jira v. Negewo,* 72 F.3d 844, 845 (11th Cir. 1996)); threatening with death (*Abebe-Jira v. Negewo,* 72 F.3d 844, 845 (11th Cir. 1996)); and using techniques to exacerbate pain or injury (*Abebe-Jira v. Negewo,* 72 F.3d 844, 845-6 (11th Cir. 1996)).

(e) Conclusion: CAT's Prohibition against Torture as Implemented in U.S. Legislation and Regulation

U.S. domestic laws prohibiting, or providing a cause of action to victims of, torture are consistent with the standards of CAT. However, these U.S. statutes and regulations are limited to specific contexts—such as, refugee claims, extradition of foreign fugitives, criminalizing acts of torture committed outside the U.S. by U.S. officials, and providing compensation to victims of torture committed by aliens. Accordingly, the U.S. has yet to fulfill its obligation, under CAT, to enact laws which adequately prevent U.S. officials and individuals acting with their consent from subjecting any detainee to torture and which punish such conduct wherever it occurs.

3. *CAT's Prohibition against "Cruel, Inhuman or Degrading Treatment," as Interpreted by United States Law*

As previously noted, the U.S.'s reservation to Article 16 of CAT provides that the United States considers itself bound by Article 16 only insofar as CID treatment is understood to mean "the cruel, unusual and inhumane treatment or punishment prohibited by the Fifth, Eighth and Fourteenth Amendments."

The Senate Foreign Relations Committee report states that this reservation is the outgrowth of concern that "degrading treatment or punishment…has been interpreted as potentially including treatment that would probably not be prohibited by the U.S. Constitution" and cites, as an example of what the United States would not find "degrading" under the U.S. Constitution, a holding by the European Commission of Human Rights that the refusal of authorities to give formal recognition to an individual's change of sex might constitute degrading treatment.[59] This explanation suggests that the reservation was intended to prevent the importation of foreign social values or mores into U.S. law, rather than any view that international norms of CID treatment are out of step with U.S. law.

In assessing interrogation conduct under Article 16 of CAT, the U.S. should look to international standards defining cruel, inhuman or degrading treatment. If such conduct is prohibited under international law, the U.S. is bound to prevent such conduct unless it would not be prohibited under the Fifth, Eighth and Fourteenth Amendments. The Committees take note that much of the case law under the three Amendments arises in the context of domestic criminal justice proceedings. How this jurisprudence would be applied in a case relating to the detention and interrogation of foreign combatants is not completely clear. For instance, on the one hand some of the special protections provided in the American criminal justice system with respect to interrogations would be of doubtful applicability, particularly considering an asserted state interest in national security. On the other, the absence of a legitimate state interest in punishment might mandate a higher standard of treatment of detainees generally.

(a) Fifth and Fourteenth Amendment Standards

The Constitution's guarantee of due process forbids compulsion to testify, at least for domestic law enforcement purposes, by fear of hurt, torture or exhaustion. *See Adamson v. California,* 332 U.S. 46 (1947) (armed Texas Rangers on several successive nights took defendant from county jail into the woods, whipped him, asked him each time about a confession, interrogated him from approximately 11 p.m. to 3 a.m. and warned him not to speak to anyone about the nightly trips); *Brown v. Mississippi,* 297 U.S. 278 (1936) (confessions obtained by mock executions and whippings); *Ashcraft v. Tennessee,* 322 U.S. 143, 154 (1944) (defendant was taken into custody by police officers and for 36 hours thereafter was held incommunicado, without sleep or rest, and interrogated without respite by relays of officers, experienced investigators, and highly trained lawyers); *see also Ashcraft v. Tennessee,* 327 U.S. 274 (1946). However, the presence of unlawful police coercion motivated by "immediate necessity to find the victim and save his life" to extract a confession has been found by one appeals court to be insufficient to exclude a subsequent confession.[60]

Due process also prohibits actions taken under color of law that are "so brutal and offensive to human dignity" that they "shock the conscience."[61] The Supreme Court has given content to the phrase "shocks the conscience" by reference to the spectrum of fault standards in tort law. Intentional infliction of injury unjustifiable by any government interest is the sort of official action which could rise to the conscience-shocking level.[62] All applicable sources of law are consistent in prohibiting such extreme conduct.

(b) Eighth Amendment Standards

The Eighth Amendment prohibits "cruel and unusual punishments."[63] In the context of law enforcement, U.S. courts have long held that the norms articulated under the Cruel and Unusual Punishment Clause establish a minimum level of protection, applicable even to pretrial detainees.[64]

While the Supreme Court initially interpreted the Eighth Amendment as prohibiting only barbaric or torturous punishments, this interpretation was early broadened in two respects: (i) to prevent disproportionate punishments (*Weems v. United States,* 217 U.S. 349 (1910)) and (ii) to address non-physical forms of cruel and unusual punishment (*e.g., Trop v. Dulles,* 356 U.S. 86 (1958) (in case involving denationalization as a punishment for desertion from the United States Army, the Court noted that "evolving standards of decency that mark the progress of a maturing society" should inform interpretation of the Eighth Amendment)). In 1947, the Supreme Court recognized that wanton or unnecessary infliction of pain also constitutes cruel and unusual punishment. *Louisiana ex rel. Francis v. Resweber,* 329 U.S. 459, 463 (1947).

In cases brought by prisoners under the Eighth Amendment alleging that excessive force was used against them by government officials, courts consider both the objective component (whether the wrongdoing was "harmful enough" to implicate the Eighth Amendment) and the subjective component (whether the officials acted with a sufficiently culpable state of mind) of the challenged conduct. *Hudson v. McMillian,* 503 U.S. 1, 8 (1992). In order to establish that the objective component of an Eighth Amendment violation is satisfied, a prisoner need not prove he has sustained significant injury. However, the extent of injury suffered is one factor that may suggest "whether the use of force could plausibly have been thought necessary" in a particular situation, "or instead evinced such wantonness with respect to the unjustified infliction of harm as is tantamount to a knowing willingness that it occur."[65] The subjective component involves, in the context of force used by prison officials, "whether force was applied in a good-faith effort to maintain or restore discipline, or maliciously and sadistically for the very purpose of causing harm."[66]

D. Enforcement of CAT under U.S. Law

1. 18 U.S.C. §§ 2340–2340B

As stated above, the United States' attempt to comply with its obligation under CAT to criminalize torture is codified in 18 U.S.C. § 2340A. Section 2340A criminalizes conduct by a U.S. national or a foreign national present in the U.S. who, acting under color of law, commits or attempts to commit torture outside the United States. The statute is exclusively criminal and may not be construed as creating any right enforceable in a civil proceeding. *See* 18 U.S.C. § 2340B. Section 2340A generally applies to acts committed by U.S. nationals overseas (everywhere *except* "all areas under the jurisdiction of the United States, including any of the places described in sections 5 and 7 of this title and Section 46501(2) of Title 49.") When the Section was enacted the reach of the cross-referenced provisions, notably 18 U.S.C. § 7, was uncertain.[67] However, Section 7 was broadened in the USA PATRIOT Act to clarify jurisdiction over crimes committed against U.S. citizens on U.S. property abroad by extending U.S. criminal jurisdiction over certain crimes committed at its foreign diplomatic, military and other facilities, and by cross-reference excluded those places from the reach of Section 2340A. The resulting drastic limitation of jurisdiction under 18 U.S.C. § 2340A appears unintended. We recommend that Congress amend Section 2340A to assure that it applies to U.S. government premises abroad without prejudice to the expansion of U.S. criminal jurisdiction under other statutes.

The U.S. did not enact a specific criminal statute outlawing torture within the United States, out of deference to federal-state relations and because it determined that existing federal and state criminal law was sufficient to cover any domestic act that would qualify as torture under CAT.[68] It is submitted that the inapplicability of state law to U.S. facilities abroad and the lack of other federal criminal law comparable to Section 2340A leaves a serious vacuum in carrying out the obligations of the U.S. under CAT.

Unfortunately the U.S. has never enforced 18 U.S.C. § 2340A, and has thereby fallen far short of its obligations under international law and its professed ideals. The United States has failed to utilize 18 U.S.C. § 2340A to prosecute either U.S. agents suspected of committing torture outside the jurisdiction of the U.S. or foreign torturers living within the United States. Indeed, Amnesty International reported in 2002 that in the eight years following the enactment of 18 U.S.C. § 2340 and § 2340A, not a single case had been brought under that section.[69]

2. *Uniform Code of Military Justice*

The UCMJ may be used to prosecute in courts-martial certain acts of ill-treatment carried out, whether within the United States or overseas, by American military personnel and possibly certain civilians accompanying such personnel. This federal statute is essentially a complete set of criminal laws that includes both crimes that are normally part of a criminal code as well as uniquely military and wartime offenses.

As a jurisdictional matter, the UCMJ applies worldwide (10 U.S.C. § 805), and persons subject to the UCMJ include any U.S. service member (10 U.S.C. § 802) as well as certain civilians "[i]n time of war...serving with or accompanying an armed force in the field" (10 U.S.C. § 802(a)(10)) and POWs (10 U.S.C. § 802(a)(9)).[70] Because courts-martial have jurisdiction to try "any person who by the law of war is subject to trial by a military tribunal" for any offense against the laws of war (10 U.S.C. § 818), the UCMJ would seem to apply also to "unlawful combatants" deemed by the Administration not to qualify for POW status under Geneva III.

The broad statutory application of the UCMJ to civilians associated in various ways with the armed forces has been judicially limited in deference to the requirements of Article III, Section II, of the Constitution and the Fifth and Sixth Amendments protecting the right to trial by jury. As so limited, the UCMJ does not apply to civilians who have no military status in peacetime, even if they are accompanying United States forces overseas as employees or dependents. Although courts' interpretations of the terms "serving", "accompanying" and "in the field" suggest a broad application, the "time of war" requirement is construed narrowly when applied to civilians.[71] As recently as 1998, the Court of Appeals for the Armed Forces[72] analyzed the propriety of the application of the UCMJ to civilians and stated:

> As a matter of constitutional law, the Supreme Court has held that Congress may not extend court-martial jurisdiction to cover civilians who have no military status in peacetime, even if they are accompanying United States forces overseas as employees or dependents.

Willenbring v. Neurauter, 48 M.J. 152, 157, 1998 CAAF LEXIS 43 (C.A.A.F. 1998). The line of cases in this area generally focuses on the application of the UCMJ to civilian contractors and civilian dependents of service members. *See, e.g., Robb v. United States,* 456 F.2d 768 (Ct. Cl. 1972) (civilian engineer employed by U.S. Navy in Vietnam was not subject to UCMJ); *Reid v. Covert,* 354 U.S. 1 (1957) (no jurisdiction over civilian dependents of service members stationed overseas in peacetime for capital offenses). No cases directly address whether CIA operatives conducting para-military operations with the regular armed forces or interrogations within a military base are considered civilians for purposes of UCMJ application. In *Reid v. Covert,* the Supreme Court stated, "[e]ven if it were possible, we need not attempt here to precisely define the boundary between 'civilians' and members of the 'land and naval Forces.' We recognize that there might be circumstances where a person could be 'in' the armed services ...even though he had not formally been inducted into the military or did not wear a uniform." *See* 354 U.S. at 22.[73] In any event, where a CIA operative is a detached service member who has not been formally discharged from military service (as is often the case in practice), the UCMJ would generally apply to such person in time of war or peace.

The UCMJ provides the strongest substantive basis for potential prosecution of torture or CID treatment in federal criminal law, specifically outlawing cruel or unusual punishment, torture under 18 U.S.C. § 2340 and a variety of related offenses. Article 55 of the UCMJ provides that:

> Punishment by flogging, or by branding, marking, or tattooing on the body, or any other cruel or unusual punishment, may not be adjudged by any court-martial or inflicted upon any person subject to this chapter. The use of irons, single or double, except for the purpose of safe custody, is prohibited.

10 U.S.C. § 855.[74] Article 55 is unique in its specific definition of "cruel *or* unusual punishment" as an offense.[75] While most military courts have followed the Supreme Court's analytical framework of protections under the Eighth Amendment as they pertain to cruel and unusual punishment,[76] several military courts have found that Article 55 provides greater protections than those given under the Eighth Amendment.[77] It is notable that Article 55 applies at least the equivalent of the protection afforded by the Eighth Amendment even if the victim is not otherwise entitled to constitutional rights (*e.g.,* a non-citizen apprehended and detained outside the U.S. and arguably not entitled to such rights).[78]

Moreover, the UCMJ effectively provides a basis for the prosecution of military personnel in courts-martial for the offense of torture in violation of 18 U.S.C. § 2340. Article 134 of the UCMJ (10 U.S.C. § 934) provides:

> Though not specifically mentioned in this chapter, all disorders and neglects to the prejudice of good order and discipline in the armed forces, all conduct of a nature to bring discredit upon the armed forces, and crimes and offenses not capital, of which persons subject to this chapter may be guilty, shall be taken cognizance of by a general, special, or summary court-martial, according to the nature and degree of the offense, and shall be punished at the discretion of that court.

Article 134 makes punishable acts in three categories of offenses not specifically covered in any other article of the UCMJ: Clause 1 offenses involving disorders and neglect to the prejudice of good order and discipline; Clause 2 offenses involving conduct of a nature to bring discredit upon the armed forces; and Clause 3 offenses entailing non-capital crimes or offenses that violate Federal law.

In order to successfully charge an individual under Clauses 1 and 2 of this Article, the government must show: (i) that the accused did or failed to do certain acts; and (ii) that, under the circumstances, the accused's conduct was to the prejudice of good order and discipline in the armed forces or was of a nature to bring discredit upon the armed forces.[79] Under Clause 1, the acts must be directly prejudicial to good order and discipline, rather than remotely so. Under Clause 2, discredit is interpreted to mean "injure the reputation of," and encompasses conduct that brings the service "into disrepute or which tends to lower it in public esteem."[80] With respect to Clause 3 offenses, as a general rule, any offense created by Federal statute may be prosecuted as an Article 134 offense. *United States v. Perkins,* 47 C.M.R. 259 (Ct. of Mil. Rev. 1973).[81]

Thus, a service member whose conduct is alleged to violate 18 U.S.C. § 2340, the federal enactment of CAT, could be prosecuted under Article 134 of the UCMJ, as a Clause 3 violation. Moreover, multiple counts alleging Article 134 violations also could be brought in such a situation, as such conduct could be construed as prejudicial to good order and discipline and/or of a nature to bring discredit upon the armed forces. *Perkins,* 47 C.M.R. at 263–264.

Finally, criminal charges for torture or CID conduct could be brought under a variety of other provisions[82] including "cruelty."[83] The last of these offenses is generally intended to be applied to mistreatment of U.S. service members by their superiors, but by its terms it is not so limited and has been applied to intentional mistreatment of detainees.[84] And in instances where specific orders are in place regarding the treatment of detainees, as is recommended in this Report, failure to obey such orders is punishable under 10 U.S.C. § 892. A number of service members in Iraq are or have been investigated or tried for assaulting detainees, under the assault provision of the UCMJ (Article 128), and in at least one case the alleged assault occurred in the context of an interrogation.[85]

The UCMJ is thus the substantively most extensive body of federal criminal law relating to the interrogation of detainees by U.S. military personnel and, in time of war, its reach could possibly extend to civilians such as CIA agents accompanying such personnel. It prohibits such persons from subjecting detainees to torture and "cruel or unusual punishment" within or without the United States and regardless of the applicability of constitutional rights.

E. Summary

CAT's prohibition against torture is absolute. By ratifying CAT, the United States has accepted that the prohibition of torture is non-derogable. Moreover, by implementing prohibitions against torture in immigration, extradition, criminal and civil tort law contexts, the U.S. has given CAT's prohibition against torture the force of U.S. law. Furthermore, by stipulating that CAT's prohibition on CID treatment or punishment means the cruel and unusual treatment or punishment prohibited by the U.S. Constitution, the U.S. has made relevant the case law providing that detainees cannot be subjected to interrogation techniques: that force them to answer law enforcement questions by "fear of hurt, torture or exhaustion," *Adamson v. California, supra;* that are "brutal and offensive to human dignity," *Rochin v. California, supra;* that fall below the "evolving standards of decency that mark the progress of a maturing society," *Trop v. Dulles, supra;* or which deliberately inflict force or pain (in the context of restoring prison order or safety), *Hudson v. McMillian, supra.* However, U.S. enforcement of CAT in our domestic criminal law—particularly with respect to acts of torture or CID treatment by U.S. civilians or by U.S. officials in extra-territorial areas under U.S. jurisdiction—has been incomplete. We urge the U.S. to fill in the gaps in preventing and punishing torture and CID treatment left by 18 U.S.C. § 2340A and to fully utilize the UCMJ to fulfill its obligations under CAT.

II. THE GENEVA CONVENTIONS

The four Geneva Conventions of 1949 are the core of the international law of armed conflict applicable to the treatment of detainees, albeit not the complete body of applicable law. The applicability of the Geneva Conventions to persons captured by the United States in connection with the War In Afghanistan and the ongoing conflict in Afghanistan, however, is highly controversial. The most hotly contested issue is whether those Al Qaeda and Taliban detainees who were captured before the creation of the Karzai government are entitled to POW status under Geneva Convention III Relative to the Treatment of Prisoners of War ("Geneva III"). This issue is of particular significance because Geneva III flatly prohibits "any form of coercion" of POWs in interrogation—the most protective standard of treatment found in international law. Likewise, Geneva Convention IV Relative to the Protection of Civilian Persons in Time of War ("Geneva IV") protects "civilian" detainees who qualify as "protected persons" from "coercion."[86] We also should note that the issues regarding Geneva III and Geneva IV are affected by whether the person was detained either before or after the Karzai government was established. Before the Karzai government, the U.S. was engaged in an international armed conflict with Afghanistan, which was governed by the Taliban (albeit the U.S. did not recognize that government). After the establishment of the Karzai government, the conflict in Afghanistan became an internal one—as the U.S. and other international organizations were present in Afghanistan with the consent of the Karzai government to assist in maintaining order. Geneva III and Geneva IV apply only in situations of international armed conflict and, therefore, ceased to apply once the Afghan conflict became an internal one. *See* Geneva IV, Art. 6.

In this section, we will examine the Administration's position that Al Qaeda and Taliban detainees are not POWs under Geneva III and some critiques of the Administration's position. We submit that, regardless of whether a detainee enjoys status as a POW or civilian protected person under the Geneva Conventions, the Conventions nevertheless are relevant to the interrogation of detainees in the following respects:

First, the requirements of humane treatment embodied in Common Article 3 of the Geneva Conventions and Article 75 of Additional Protocol I protect all detainees captured in situations of international or internal armed conflict, regardless of "legal" status.[87] Of course, all detainees—including those captured outside of Afghan territory or in connection with the "War on Terror"—are entitled to the protection provided by human rights law, including CAT, the ICCPR and customary international law.

Second, notwithstanding its position on the POW status of Taliban and Al Qaeda detainees, the Administration has undertaken that it will treat all detainees in a manner consistent with the principles of Geneva III. Accordingly, the interrogation techniques reportedly being used on detainees at Bagram and other U.S. detention facilities should be considered in light of the text and spirit of the Geneva Conventions.

Third, if there is doubt as to whether a detainee meets Geneva III criteria for POW status, that detainee is entitled to interim POW status until a "competent tribunal" determines his or her legal status. Because the U.S. government has not convened "competent tribunals" to determine the status of any detainees, all detainees for whom POW status is in doubt are entitled to interim POW status.[88]

Finally, even accepting the interpretation that the Third and Fourth Geneva Conventions contain gaps leaving certain detainees captured in the War in Afghanistan (*i.e.,* citizens of co-belligerents and neutrals) without POW or "protected person" civilian status, the Geneva Conventions are supplemented by human rights law and customary international legal norms which have the force of law in the United States. For example, even where a detainee may not be entitled to a hearing under Geneva III, he is entitled to a hearing to determine the justification for his detention under Article 9 of the ICCPR. Many detainees may not be combatants at all and may be simply innocent bystanders mistakenly detained or wrongfully turned over to the U.S. military by the Northern Alliance.[89] They deserve prompt hearings in which they are given an opportunity to establish their non-combatant status.

A. Application of the Geneva Conventions to the Afghan Conflict Generally

Both the U.S. and Afghanistan are parties to the Geneva Conventions. Article 2 common to all four Conventions provides that the Conventions "apply to all cases of declared war or of any other armed conflict" between two or more parties to the Conventions so long as a state of war is recognized by a party to the conflict. The Conventions also apply to all cases of partial or total occupation of the territory of a signatory, even if the occupation meets with no armed resistance. *See* Geneva Conventions, Art. 2. Signatories to the Conventions are bound by its terms regardless of whether an additional party to the conflict is a signatory. *Id.* The Administration's position is that the Geneva Conventions apply to the War in Afghanistan.[90]

B. Geneva III

1. *Relevant Legal Standards*

Under Geneva III, combatants are entitled to POW status if they are members of the armed forces (other than medical personnel and chaplains). The specific requirements for combatant/POW status are set forth in Article 4 of Geneva III[91] and Articles 43 and 44 of Additional Protocol I.[92]

If there is any doubt as to whether captured persons meet Article 4's criteria for POW status, such persons are entitled to interim POW status until a "competent tribunal" determines their legal status.[93]

Geneva III mandates that POWs be treated humanely at all times. This includes freedom from physical and mental torture, acts of violence, intimidation and insult, and exposure to public humiliation.[94] Pursuant to Article 14, POWs also "are entitled in all circumstances to respect for their persons and their honour.... [and] shall retain the full civil capacity which they enjoyed at the time of their capture."

With respect to interrogation, in particular, Article 17 of Geneva III provides: "No physical or mental torture, nor any other form of coercion, may be inflicted on prisoners of war to secure from them information of any kind whatever. Prisoners of war who refuse to answer may not be threatened, insulted, or exposed to any unpleasant or disadvantageous treatment of any letter="default"/>kind." Under Article 17, POWs are only obligated to provide their name, rank, date of birth, and army, personal or serial identification number or equivalent information. Geneva III does not, however, prohibit non-coercive interrogation of POWs. POWs may be interrogated, but they are not obliged to respond to such interrogation, nor may they be threatened, coerced into responding or punished for failing to respond. The Geneva Conventions also do not "preclude classic plea bargaining"—*i.e.,* the offer of leniency or other incentives in return for cooperation.[95]

Thus, to the extent detainees from the War in Afghanistan are considered POWs or to the extent their POW status is in "doubt" pending the determination of status by a competent tribunal, interrogation tactics which rise to the level of "coercion" are prohibited by Geneva III.

2. *The United States' Position*

In sharp contrast with past conflicts (such as Vietnam and Korea) in which it was U.S. policy to presume that military prisoners were entitled to POW status regardless of the possible non-qualification of their forces under Geneva III, from the very outset of the War in Afghanistan, United States officials labeled captured Al Qaeda and Taliban prisoners "unlawful combatants," and stated that the Geneva Conventions were, therefore, entirely inapplicable to their treatment.[96] The United States reasoned that Al Qaeda was not entitled to the protections of the Geneva Conventions because: (1) Geneva III could not apply to members of a nonstate organization, such as Al Qaeda, (2) the conflict was not an internal conflict such that Al Qaeda members could benefit from the protection of Common Article 3, and (3) in any event, Al Qaeda members failed to meet the requirements set forth in Article 4(A)(2) of Geneva III.[97] The United States argued further that, since Afghanistan was not a functioning state during the conflict and the Taliban was not recognized as a legitimate government, Geneva III could not apply to the Taliban.[98]

After vigorous criticism was leveled against these arguments, Secretary of State Colin Powell requested that the Administration reconsider its position.[99] On February 7, 2002, in response to Powell's comments, the Administration partially reversed its initial position. Although the Administration continues to argue that the Geneva Conventions are inapplicable to Al Qaeda captives, President Bush announced that Geneva III was applicable to the Taliban because both the U.S. and Afghanistan were signatories to the Convention and the parties had been involved in an armed conflict. However, President Bush further argued that because the Taliban had violated the laws of war and associated closely with Al Qaeda, "[u]nder the terms of the Geneva Convention...the Taliban detainees do not qualify as POWs."[100] The decision in *United States v. Lindh,* 212 F. Supp. 2d 541 (E.D. Va. 2002), which specifically addresses the issue of whether the Taliban are entitled to POW status under Geneva III, sheds further light on the U.S. position.[101]

3. *Critiques of the United States' Position*

International humanitarian and human rights organizations and legal bodies, including the International Committee of the Red Cross ("ICRC"),[102] the Inter-American Court of Human

Rights,[103] Amnesty International,[104] the International Commission of Jurists,[105] the Secretary General of the United Nations,[106] the United Nations High Commissioner for Human Rights,[107] as well as certain U.S. and foreign international law scholars[108] have criticized the U.S. position on several grounds.

(a) Article 5 Presumes POW Status Until the Determination of Status by a Competent Tribunal

Critics of the Administration position argue that non-civilian detainees from the War in Afghanistan either clearly qualify as POWs or their POW status is in "doubt." Geneva III mandates that a detainee whose status is in "doubt" must be treated as a POW until his status is decided otherwise by a competent tribunal under Article 5. Indeed, Article 5's presumption that captured combatants are entitled to POW status until their status is determined by a competent tribunal is one that has been consistently honored by the U.S. since World War II.[109] Moreover, like Article 5, customary international law also includes the principle that a competent tribunal must resolve any doubt about the status of a captured combatant.[110] We agree with critics of the Administration position that all combatants whose claim to POW status is "in doubt" must be treated as POWs until such doubt has been resolved by a "competent tribunal." Accordingly, since no tribunals have been convened for detainees from the War in Afghanistan, all such detainees must be considered POWs under Geneva III.

(b) The Taliban Detainees Were "Regular Armed Forces" and, Therefore, Are Encompassed by Article 4(A) of Geneva III

Critics of the Administration's position that Taliban fighters are not entitled to POW status because they do not satisfy the requirements of Article 4(a)(2) of Geneva III[111] assert that Taliban captured in the War in Afghanistan are entitled to POW status either under: Article 4(a)(1) because they are "[m]embers of the armed forces" of Afghanistan; or Article 4(a)(3) as they are "[m]embers of regular armed forces who profess allegiance to a government of an authority not recognized by the Detaining Power."[112]

(c) Policy Arguments Favoring Broad Grant of POW Status to Non-Civilian Detainees from the War in Afghanistan

Several policy arguments favor granting POW status liberally even assuming that Geneva III does not apply to Taliban or Al Qaeda detainees captured in the War in Afghanistan.

First, depriving Taliban and Al Qaeda of POW status because they do not obey the laws of war sets a dangerous precedent, inviting other state parties to claim that another party is not obeying the rules of war and that they are, therefore, free from the obligations of Geneva III. International humanitarian law applies regardless of whether or not the other party to the conflict respects such laws.[113] Reciprocity arrangements are generally rejected in international humanitarian law as they can so easily be abused at the expense of civilians or persons rendered "hors de combat."[114]

Second, it is in the U.S.'s self-interest to ensure that the Geneva Conventions—a regime of vital importance to the safety of our own armed forces—are interpreted as broadly as possible. Otherwise, an opposing state party could use the argument that the U.S. has violated the laws of war to deny captured U.S. soldiers POW status. In fact, North Korea and Vietnam have already used this argument as a basis to deny captured U.S. prisoners POW protections under the Geneva Conventions.[115] Indeed, it was reportedly these very examples that prompted Colin Powell, out of concern for the safety of U.S. forces, to request that President Bush reconsider the Administration's initial position.[116]

We accordingly urge liberal extension of POW treatment where that would encourage reciprocal treatment of U.S. service personnel and advance more generally foreign policy and national security interests. We further believe that, even to the extent that POW status is denied to detainees, such detainees must be afforded the protections of international criminal law, as well as international human rights and humanitarian law.

C. Geneva IV

Geneva IV applies in international armed conflicts to the same extent as Geneva III. It covers "protected persons" defined as "those who, at a given moment and in any manner whatsoever, find themselves, in case of a conflict or occupation, in the hands of a Party to the conflict or Occupying Power of which they are not nationals." *See* Geneva IV, Article 4.[117]

The fact that a person may have unlawfully participated in a conflict is not relevant to Geneva IV protections, apart from a significant national security exemption. The term "protected persons" includes persons detained as spies or saboteurs as well as other persons suspected of engaging in activities hostile to the security of the detaining power. Specifically, Article 5 provides:

> Where in the territory of a Party to the conflict, the *latter* is satisfied that an individual protected person is definitely suspected of or engaged in activities hostile to the security of the State, such individual person shall not be entitled to claim such rights and privileges under the present Convention as would, if exercised in the favour of such individual person, be prejudicial to the security of such State
>
> ....
>
> In each case, such persons shall nevertheless be treated with humanity and, in case of trial, shall not be deprived of the rights of fair and regular trial prescribed by the present Convention. They shall also be granted the full rights and privileges of a protected person under the present Convention at the earliest date consistent with the security of the State or Occupying Power, as the case may be.

As drafted, (*i.e.,* the use of the words "the latter"), it would appear that the national security derogation is available only to the State on whose territory the conflict is occurring (*i.e.,* in the War in Afghanistan, only to the Northern Alliance), and there is no authority whether or not an allied State, such as the United States, can benefit from such exemption.

In an exception of great importance in Afghanistan, given the number of third country participants in the conflict, "protected persons" does not include "[n]ationals of a State which is not bound by the Convention," "[n]ationals of a neutral State who find themselves in the territory of a belligerent State" and "nationals of a co-belligerent State...while the State of which they are nationals has normal diplomatic representation in the State in whose hands they are." *See* Geneva IV, Article 4. For example, a Pakistani picked up on the battlefield in Afghanistan would fall within the exceptions to "protected person" status under Geneva IV.

However, in no event would such provision permit the State to commit "grave breaches" as defined in Article 147, which includes torture or inhuman treatment and willfully causing great suffering or serious injury to body or health, upon a "protected person". *See* Geneva IV, Art. 146. Furthermore, to the extent that any physical or moral coercion (otherwise prohibited by Article 31 of Geneva IV) might fall below the level of "grave breach" and thus be derogable, the ICRC commentary to the national security derogations contained in Article 5 of Geneva IV, involving persons engaged in activities hostile to the security of the state notes that:

> widespread application of the Article may eventually lead to the existence of a category of civilian internees who do not receive the normal treatment laid down by the Convention but are detained under conditions which are almost impossible to check. It must be emphasized most strongly, therefore, that Article 5 can only be applied in individual cases of an exceptional nature, when the existence of specific charges makes it almost certain that penal proceedings will follow. This article should never be applied as a result of mere suspicion.

Like POWs under Geneva III, "protected persons" under Geneva IV cannot be subjected to coercive interrogation tactics. Specifically, Article 31 of Geneva IV provides that "[n]o physical or moral coercion shall be exercised against protected persons, in particular to obtain information from them or from third parties." Article 32 further provides that "any measure of such a character as to the cause the physical suffering or extermination of protected persons" is prohibited and that "[t]his prohibition applies not only to murder, torture, corporal punishments, mutilation and medical or scientific experiments not necessitated by the medical treatment of a protected person, but also to any other measures of brutality, whether applied by civilian or military agents."

By its terms, Geneva IV ceases to apply "on the general close of military operations" in the case of an international conflict. *See* Geneva IV, Art. 6. Whether military operations have reached a "general close" after the establishment of the Karzai government in June 2002 and whether the change in character of the conflict from an international one to a multi-national conflict within a single State against non-State opponents terminated application of Geneva IV are issues open to controversy.[118] Thus, the ability of some civilians captured in Afghanistan to claim "protected person" status under Geneva IV today is subject to additional debate. However, regardless of the characterization of the current conflict, torture and inhumane treatment of civilian detainees from the War in Afghanistan or the ongoing conflict in Afghanistan, whether or not they qualify as "protected persons" under Geneva IV, is not permitted. All such persons are still entitled to the protections of international human rights law and to humane treatment under Common Article 3 and Article 75 of Additional Protocol I.

D. Summary

None of the detainees from the War in Afghanistan or the ongoing conflict in Afghanistan fall outside of international humanitarian law. An individual detained during the armed conflict in Afghanistan—whether considered an international or internal armed conflict—is either protected by Geneva III as a POW, by Geneva IV as a civilian "protected person," or, at the very minimum, by Common Article 3 and Article 75 of Additional Protocol I. Of course, all detainees—regardless of where or when they were captured—are entitled to the protection of human rights law (including CAT and the ICCPR) and customary international law.

Detainees protected as POWs or civilians under Geneva III or Geneva IV cannot be subjected to coercion of any kind. In addition, those detainees whose POW status is in doubt are entitled to interim POW status until a competent tribunal determines otherwise. At least some Afghan detainees are entitled to such tribunals, and the U.S. is long overdue in providing any process whatsoever to detainees, many of whom may simply be innocent non-combatants, wrongfully detained. We, therefore, urge the U.S. to establish proper screening procedures for all detainees.

III. OTHER INTERNATIONAL LEGAL STANDARDS

The legal standards set forth in the International Covenant on Civil and Political Rights, the American Declaration of the Rights and Duties of Man, and customary international law also apply to the treatment of detainees held by the United States.

A. The International Covenant on Civil and Political Rights[119]

1. *Relevant Legal Standards*

Like CAT, the ICCPR expressly prohibits both torture and CID. Specifically, Article 7 of the ICCPR provides: "No one shall be subjected to torture or to cruel, inhuman or degrading treatment or punishment."[120] However, the ICCPR goes further than CAT in its non-derogability provision, expressly stating that neither torture *nor* CID treatment can be justified by exceptional circumstances such as war, internal political stability or other public emergencies. (*See* ICCPR, Art. 4). Article 10 also provides that: "All persons deprived of their liberty shall be treated with humanity and with respect for the inherent dignity of the human person."

The Human Rights Committee, established under Article 28, adjudicates complaints filed by individuals or states parties alleging violations of the ICCPR. The Committee has found the following conduct to violate Article 7's prohibition against cruel, inhuman or degrading treatment or punishment: threatening a victim with torture, prolonged solitary confinement and incommunicado detention, and repeated beatings.[121] Moreover, the Human Rights Committee has specifically criticized interrogation procedures such as handcuffing, hooding, shaking and sleep deprivation as violations of Article 7 in any circumstances.[122]

Although the ICCPR does not expressly prohibit states parties from "rendering" individuals to countries where they are likely to be mistreated, the Human Rights Committee has explained that, under Article 7, states parties "must not expose individuals to the danger of torture or cruel, inhuman or degrading treatment or punishment upon return to another country by way of their extradition, expulsion or refoulement."[123] Accordingly, the Human Rights Committee has stated that "[i]f a State party extradites a person within its jurisdiction in circumstances such that as a result there is a real risk that his or her rights under the Covenant will be violated in another jurisdiction, the State party itself may be in violation of the Covenant."[124]

2. *Enforcement*

(a) U.S. Courts

In ratifying the ICCPR, the U.S. Senate declared that Articles 1 through 27 are not self-executing. Thus, while the Supreme Court has not squarely decided the issue, the majority of federal appeals courts have held that the ICCPR provides no privately enforceable rights and is not binding on federal courts.[125] The Second and Ninth circuit courts, however, have cited the ICCPR as evidence that customary international law prohibits arbitrary arrest, prolonged detention and torture.[126]

(b) The Human Rights Committee

The Human Rights Committee is empowered to: (i) receive state party reports and comment on those reports (*see* ICCPR, Art. 40(4)); (ii) rule on complaints filed by a state party that another state party is not fulfilling its obligations under the ICCPR (*see* ICCPR, Art. 41);[127] and (iii) rule on complaints filed by individuals "who claim that any of their rights enumerated in the Covenant have been violated and who have exhausted all available domestic remedies."[128]

B. Organization of American States' Instruments

1. *Relevant Legal Standards*

The U.S. is a member of the Organization of American States (the "OAS"). Article XXV of The American Declaration of the Rights and Duties of Man (the "American Declaration"), which was adopted by the Ninth International Conference of the OAS in 1948, provides:

> Every individual who has been deprived of his liberty has the right to have the legality of his detention ascertained without delay by a court, and the right to be tried without undue delay or, otherwise, to be released. He also has the right to humane treatment during the time he is in custody.

On June 1, 1997, the U.S. signed, but has not yet ratified, the American Convention On Human Rights (1969) (the "American Convention").[129] Article 5 of the American Convention, which sets forth Rights to Humane Treatment, provides:

1. Every person has the right to have his physical, mental, and moral integrity respected.
2. No one shall be subjected to torture or to cruel, inhuman or degrading punishment or treatment. All persons deprived of their liberty shall be treated with respect for the inherent dignity of the human person.

Moreover, pursuant to Article 27(2) of the American Convention, the Rights to Humane Treatment may not be suspended "[i]n time of war, public danger, or other emergency that threatens the independence or security of a State Party."

With respect to the treatment of detainees, the Inter-American Commission on Human Rights (the "Inter-American Commission")—which represents all member countries of the OAS and was established under Chapter VII of the American Convention—has determined that, "when the State holds a person in detention and under its exclusive control, it becomes the guarantor of that person's safety and rights."[130] In this regard, the Commission has found the following practices to be violations of Article 5 of the American Convention: threats to summon family members and pressure them to "talk"; threats to kill detainees; blindfolding detainees and forcing them to run around; "prolonged isolation and deprivation of communication"; solitary confinement; confining detainees in small cells with other prisoners; keeping detainees in cells that are damp and/or without adequate ventilation; keeping detainees in cells without beds; forcing detainees to sleep on the floor or on newspaper; depriving detainees of necessary hygiene facilities; beatings with rifles; and kicks in various parts of the body, especially in the stomach.[131]

The Inter-American Court of Human Rights (the "Inter-American Court")—established pursuant to Chapter VIII of the American Convention—has held that, "in order to establish if torture has been inflicted and its scope, all the circumstances of the case should be taken into consideration, such as the nature and context of the respective aggressions, how they were inflicted, during what period of time, the physical and mental effects and, in some case, the sex, age and state of health of the victims."[132] "The violation of the right to physical and psychological integrity of persons is a category of violation that has several gradations and embraces treatment ranging from torture to other types of humiliation or cruel, inhuman or degrading treatment with varying degrees of physical and psychological effects caused by endogenous and exogenous factors which must be proven in each specific situation."[133]

The Inter-American Court has found the following practices to violate Article 5 of the American Convention and/or Article 2 of the Inter-American Convention To Prevent and Punish Torture:[134] forcing detainees to stand blindfolded with their hands cuffed behind their backs; forcing detainees to listen to the cries of others being beaten; threatening detainees with physical torture; restriction of visiting rights; incommunicado detention; incarceration in solitary confinement and/or in a small cell with no ventilation or natural light; prohibiting detainees from engaging in physical exercise or intellectual efforts; deprivation of necessary hygiene facilities; deficient medical treatment; and throwing detainees to the ground.[135] "[A]ccording to international standards for protection, torture can be inflicted not only via physical violence, but also through acts that produce severe physical, psychological or moral suffering in the victim."[136] The Inter-American Court also has held that: "Prolonged isolation and being held incommunicado constitute, in themselves, forms of cruel and inhuman treatment, harmful to the mental and moral integrity of the person and to the right of all detainees of respect for the inherent dignity of the human being."[137]

Moreover, the Inter-American Court has warned that the fact that a State is confronted with terrorism does not, in itself, warrant the use of force:

Any use of force that is not strictly necessary, given the behavior of the person detained, constitutes an affront to human dignity...in violation of Article 5 of the American Convention. The need to conduct investigations and the undeniable difficulties inherent to combating terrorism are not grounds for placing restrictions on the protection of the physical integrity of the person.[138]

In a case brought before the Inter-American Commission by detainees alleging violations of the United States' obligations under the American Declaration by U.S. armed forces in Grenada in 1983, *Coard, et al. v. United States,* the Inter-American Commission expressly extended the protections of human rights and humanitarian norms to extraterritorial conduct by U.S. military forces and criticized the U.S. for delay in providing procedure to detainees.[139] Acknowledging the need to balance between public security and individual rights, the Inter-American Commission in *Coard* held that: "What is required when an armed force detains civilians is the establishment of a procedure to ensure that the legality of the detention can be reviewed without delay and is subject to supervisory control....[C]ontrol over a detention [cannot] rest[] exclusively with the agents charged with carrying it out." *Coard,* at paras. 58–59.

2. *Enforcement*

The Inter-American Commission has competence with respect to matters relating to the fulfillment of the commitments made by the States Parties to the American Convention.[140] "The main function of the Commission" is "to promote respect for and defense of human rights."[141] Any person may lodge a petition with the Commission complaining of violation of the American Convention by a State Party, so long as effective domestic remedies available to the petitioner have been exhausted.[142]

On March 12, 2002, in response to a petition challenging detentions at Guantánamo Bay coordinated by the Center for Constitutional Rights,[143] the Inter-American Commission adopted precautionary measures addressed to the United States concerning the Guantánamo detainees.[144] Specifically, the Commission asked the U.S. "to take the urgent measures necessary to have the legal status of the detainees at Guantánamo Bay determined by a competent tribunal."[145] In so doing, the Inter-American Commission explained:

[W]here persons find themselves within the authority and control of a state and where a circumstance of armed conflict may be involved, their fundamental rights may be determined in part by reference to international humanitarian law as well as international human rights law. Where it may be considered that the protections of international humanitarian law do not apply, however, such persons remain the beneficiaries at least of the non-derogable protections under international human rights law. In short, no person under the authority and control of a state, regardless of his or her circumstances, is devoid of legal protection for his or her fundamental and non-derogable human rights.[146]

With regard to the Guantánamo Bay detainees in particular, the Inter-American Commission observed that: "[T]he information available suggests that the detainees remain entirely at the unfettered discretion of the United States government. Absent clarification of the legal status of the detainees, the Commission considers that the rights and protections to which they may be entitled under international or domestic law cannot be said to be the subject of effective legal protection by the State."[147] The Inter-American Commission further noted that, regardless of the legal status of the Guantánamo Bay detainees, their legal protections "may in no case fall below the minimal standards of non-derogable rights."[148] Thereafter, the Commission issued a renewed request to the U.S. government for precautionary measures, stating that new factual allegations regarding torture or other ill-treatment of detainees "raise questions concerning the extent to which the United States' policies and practices in detaining and interrogating persons in connection with its anti-terrorist initiatives clearly and absolutely prohibit treatment that may amount to torture or may otherwise be cruel, inhuman or degrading as defined under international norms."[149]

C. Customary International Law and *Jus Cogens*

1. *Relevant Legal Standards*

Customary international law has long prohibited the state practice of torture, without reservation, in peace or in wartime.[150] On December 9, 1975, the United Nations General Assembly adopted by consensus the Declaration on the Protection of All Persons from Being Subjected to Torture and Other Cruel, Inhuman or Degrading Punishment.[151] The Torture Resolution together with CAT and the ICCPR—ratified by 133 and 151 States, respectively—embody the customary international law obligation to refrain from behavior which constitutes torture.[152] In addition, in 1985 the United Nations Special Rapporteur on Torture, Pieter Koojimans, noted the widespread existing domestic legislation in many countries, including the United States, expressly or by implication prohibiting torture as well as cruel, inhuman and degrading punishment.[153]

The prohibition of torture is, moreover, one of the few norms which has attained peremptory norm or *jus cogens* status, and is recognized as such by United States courts.[154] *Jus cogens* is defined as a peremptory norm "accepted and recognized by the international community of states as a whole as a norm from which no derogation is permitted and which can be modified only by a subsequent norm of general international law having the same character."[155] While many international agreements expressly prohibit *both* torture and cruel, inhuman and degrading treatment,[156] it remains an open question as to whether *jus cogens* status extends to the prohibition against cruel, inhuman or degrading treatment. What is clear, however, is that cruel, inhuman and degrading treatment or punishment is prohibited by customary international law.

U.S. ratification of the ICCPR and CAT are clear pronouncements that we condemn the practice of torture and CID treatment and that we consider ourselves legally bound to prohibit such conduct. Indeed, in 1999, the United States issued a report to the U.N. Committee Against Torture categorically affirming that:

> Every act constituting torture under the Convention constitutes a criminal offense under the law of the United States. No official of the Government, federal, state or local, civilian or military, is authorized to commit or to instruct anyone else to commit torture. Nor may any official condone or tolerate torture in any form. No exceptional circumstances may be invoked as justification for torture. United States law contains no provision permitting otherwise prohibited acts of torture or other cruel, inhuman or degrading treatment or punishment to be employed on grounds of exigent circumstance (for example, during a "state of public emergency") or on orders from a superior officer or public authority, and the protective mechanisms of an independent judiciary are not subject to suspension.[157]

Furthermore, the United States has enacted the Torture Victim Protection Act,[158] has imposed civil liability for acts of torture regardless of where such acts take place,[159] and has enacted the Torture Victims Relief Act, providing for monetary assistance for torture victims.[160] As previously discussed, not only does the U.S. Constitution prohibit cruel and unusual punishment or treatment by state officials (including under the military justice system), but almost all of the U.S. State constitutions have similar prohibitions.[161] Finally, a number of federal judicial proceedings have recognized that the right to be free from torture as well as cruel, inhuman or degrading treatment or punishment is a norm of customary international law.[162]

In the State Department Country Reports On Human Rights Practices, for example, the United States has expressly characterized the following types of conduct—some of which are allegedly occurring at U.S. detention centers—as "torture" or "other abuse": tying detainees in painful positions; forcing detainees to stand for long periods of time; incommunicado detention; depriving detainees of sleep; dousing naked detainees with cold water; denial of access to medical attention; interrogation techniques designed to intimidate or disorient; subjecting a detainee to loud music; forcing a detainee to squat or to assume "stressful, uncomfortable or painful" positions for "prolonged periods of time"; long periods of imprisonment in darkened rooms; verbal threats; and instilling detainees with the false belief that they are to be killed.[163] The following types of conduct have been defined as cruel, inhuman or degrading treatment: stripping; confinement in severely overcrowded cells; beating; imprisonment in small containers; and threats against family members of detainees.[164]

2. *Enforcement*

As the Second Circuit stated in *Filartiga v. Peña-Irala,* 630 F.2d 876 (1980), the United States is bound by customary international law. Thus, in cases where jurisdictional hurdles have been met, the bans on torture, arbitrary detention, and at least some aspects of cruel, inhuman and degrading treatment have been enforced by U.S. courts as violations of customary international law.[165]

IV. SHOULD EXCEPTIONS BE MADE FOR THE "WAR ON TERROR"?: THE EXPERIENCE OF OTHER JURISDICTIONS

Notwithstanding the clear legal prohibitions against the use of torture and cruel, inhuman or degrading treatment in U.S. and international law, we considered whether, in a post-September 11 world, the threat posed by terrorists to the United States could ever justify the use of prohibited interrogation practices. We sought to answer the question of whether there are any circumstances in which torture and CID treatment in the interrogation of detainees should be permitted.

For additional guidance in answering these questions, we looked to the experiences of Northern Ireland and Israel, other places where the struggle between fighting terrorism and upholding the rule of law has been waged. Both the European Court of Human Rights and the Israeli Supreme Court have confronted the contradictory demands of national security and human rights against the backdrop of terrorism. The legal debate that infuses these courts' seminal decisions on the use of torture and CID treatment in the interrogation of terrorist suspects offers guidance to the United States in interpreting CAT. These courts have ruled that there are no exceptions to the prohibition against torture and CID treatment. Their rulings express the conviction that the torture and CID treatment of detainees—even when those detainees are suspected terrorists—cannot be justified.

A. Legal Challenges to Interrogation Practices in Northern Ireland and Israel

1. The Republic of Ireland v. The United Kingdom

The European Convention for the Protection of Human Rights and Fundamental Freedoms (the "European Convention") came into force in 1953.[166] Article 3 of the European Convention provides: "No one shall be subject to torture or to inhuman or degrading treatment or punishment." The judicial body primarily charged with interpreting and enforcing the European Convention is the European Court of Human Rights (the "ECHR"). The ECHR has, in several decisions, applied the European Convention's prohibition against torture and inhuman or degrading treatment to cases involving interrogation of suspected terrorists who pose a threat to national security.

The most important of these decisions is *The Republic of Ireland.*[167] The Republic of Ireland case was decided in a legal and political environment conditioned by several years of terrorism in Northern Ireland perpetrated by members of the Irish Republican Army (IRA) and Loyalist groups. By March 1975, over 1,100 people had been killed, over 11,500 injured and £140 million worth of property destroyed.[168] To combat a campaign of violence being carried out by the IRA, in 1971, the Northern Ireland Government introduced regulations providing authorities with extrajudicial powers, including arrest for interrogation purposes and internment.[169]

The Republic of Ireland Decision is a landmark legal discussion of whether specific interrogation practices committed by British security forces against IRA detainees constituted torture or inhuman or degrading treatment. The impetus for the ECHR's decision was the Republic of Ireland's application before the European Commission of Human Rights alleging, among other things, that various interrogation practices—including specific practices referred to as the "five techniques"—amounted to torture and inhuman or degrading treatment, in contravention of Article 3 of the European Convention.[170] The "five techniques"—described by the ECHR as methods of "disorientation" or "sensory deprivation"—include a number of practices allegedly being used today by U.S. interrogators:

- Wall-standing: Forcing a detainee to remain spread-eagled against a wall with his fingers placed high above his head against the wall, his legs spread apart and his feet positioned such that he must stand on his toes with the weight of his body resting on his fingers;
- Hooding: Keeping a dark bag over a detainee's head at all times, except during interrogation;
- Subjection to noise: Holding a detainee in a room where there is a continuous loud and hissing noise;
- Deprivation of sleep; and
- Deprivation of food and drink.[171]

The European Commission of Human Rights unanimously found that the "five techniques" constituted torture, and that other challenged interrogation practices amounted to inhuman and degrading treatment.[172] Although the British Government subsequently discontinued the "five techniques" and did not contest the underlying allegations of the case or the Commission's findings in connection therewith, the Republic of Ireland nevertheless referred the case to the ECHR.[173] The ECHR took the opportunity to rule upon the legality of the "five techniques," citing to the European Court's responsibility "to elucidate, safeguard and develop the rules instituted by the Convention."[174]

In *The Republic of Ireland* decision, the ECHR explained that ill-treatment "had to attain a minimum level of severity to fall within Article 3, the assessment of which was necessarily relative, depending on all the circumstances, including the duration of the treatment, its physical or mental effects and, sometimes, the sex, age or state of health of the victim."[175] The ECHR pointed out that, while the term "torture" attached "a special stigma to deliberate inhuman treatment causing very serious and cruel suffering," the distinction between torture and inhuman or degrading treatment "derived principally from a difference in the intensity of the suffering inflicted."[176] The ECHR held that since the "five techniques" "were applied in combination, with premeditation and for hours at a time, causing at least intense physical and mental suffering and acute psychiatric disturbances, they amount to inhuman treatment."[177] The ECHR further held that since the "five techniques" aroused "in the victims feelings of fear, anguish and inferiority capable of humiliating and debasing them and possibly breaking their physical or moral resistance, they were also degrading."[178] The ECHR concluded that the "five techniques" violated

Article 3's prohibition against inhuman or degrading treatment, but that they did not amount to torture.[179]

2. Israeli Supreme Court Judgment Concerning The Legality of the General Security Service's Interrogation Methods

As the Israeli Supreme Court notes at the outset of its *Judgment Concerning The Legality Of The General Security Service's Interrogation Methods,*[180] the State of Israel "has been engaged in an unceasing struggle for both its very existence and security, from the day of its founding":

> Terrorist organizations have established as their goal Israel's annihilation. Terrorist acts and the general disruption of order are their means of choice. In employing such methods, these groups do not distinguish between civilian and military targets. They carry out terrorist attacks in which scores are murdered in public areas, public transportation, city squares and centers, theaters and coffee shops. They do not distinguish between men, women and children. They act of cruelty and without mercy.[181]

In 1987, the Landau Commission of Inquiry into the Methods of Investigation of the GSS Regarding Hostile Terrorist Acts (the "Landau Commission") was established to investigate the interrogation practices of the main body responsible for fighting terrorism in Israel, the General Security Service (the "GSS"), and to reach legal conclusions concerning them. The resulting Landau Report,[182] concluded: "The effective interrogation of terrorist suspects is impossible without the use of means of pressure, in order to overcome an obdurate will not to disclose information and to overcome the fear of the person under interrogation that harm will befall him from his own organization, if he does not reveal information."[183] The Landau Report explained that: "The means of pressure should principally take the form of non-violent psychological pressure through a vigorous and extensive interrogation, with the use of stratagems, including acts of deception. However, when these do not attain their purpose, the exertion of a moderate measure of physical pressure cannot be avoided."[184] The Landau Commission recommended, however, that GSS interrogators should be guided by clear rules "to prevent the use of inordinate physical pressure arbitrarily administered," and formulated a code of guidelines (set forth in a secret part of the Landau Report) which defined, "on the basis of past experience, and with as much precision as possible, the boundaries of what is permitted to the interrogator and mainly what is prohibited to him."[185] The Landau Commission asserted that the latitude it afforded GSS interrogators to use "a moderate measure of physical pressure" did not conflict with the standards set forth in international human rights conventions—such as the UDHR, the ICCPR and the European Convention—which prohibited torture and cruel, inhuman or degrading treatment or punishment.[186]

In 1999, in the *GSS Interrogation Methods Decision,* the Israeli Supreme Court took up the legality of certain interrogation practices employed by the GSS. The Israeli Supreme Court acknowledged that the Landau Commission had approved the use of "a moderate degree of physical pressure," and that the Landau Commission's recommendations had been accepted by the Israeli Government.[187] The interrogation methods considered by the Israeli Supreme Court in the *GSS Interrogation Methods Decision* were:

- Shaking: Forcefully shaking a detainee's upper torso back and forth, repeatedly, and in a manner which causes the neck and head to dangle and vacillate rapidly.
- The "shabach" position: Forcing a detainee who has his hands tied behind his back to sit on a small and low chair whose seat is tilted forward and towards the ground, where one hand is placed inside the gap between the chair's seat and back support, the detainee's head is covered by an opaque sack falling down to his shoulders, and powerfully loud music is played in the room.
- The "frog crouch": Forcing a detainee to crouch on the tips of his/her toes for five minute intervals.

- Excessive tightening of handcuffs: Using particularly small cuffs, ill-fitted in relation to the suspect's arm or leg size.
- Sleep deprivation: A detainee is deprived of sleep as a result of being tied in the "shabach" position, being subjected to powerfully loud music or intense non-stop interrogations.[188]

In examining the legality of these GSS interrogation methods, the Israeli Supreme Court acknowledged that, taken individually, some of the components of the "shabach" position have "legitimate" goals: for example, hooding prevents communication between suspects, the playing of powerfully loud music prevents the passing of information between suspects, the tying of the suspect's hands to a chair protects investigators, and the deprivation of sleep can be necessitated by an interrogation.[189] According to the Israeli Supreme Court, however, there is a necessary balancing process between a government's duty to ensure that human rights are protected and its duty to fight terrorism. The results of that balance, the Israeli Supreme Court stated, are the rules for a "reasonable interrogation"—defined as an interrogation which is: (1) "necessarily one free of torture, free of cruel, inhuman treatment of the subject and free of any degrading handling whatsoever"; and (2) "likely to cause discomfort."[190] "In the end result," the Court noted, "the legality of an investigation is deduced from the propriety of its purpose and from its methods."[191]

Turning to the specific interrogation methods before it, the Court concluded that shaking, the "frog crouch," the "shabach" position, cuffing causing pain, hooding, the consecutive playing of powerfully loud music and the intentional deprivation of sleep for a prolonged period of time are all prohibited interrogation methods.[192] "All these methods do not fall within the sphere of a 'fair' interrogation. They are not reasonable. They impinge upon the suspect's dignity, his bodily integrity and his basic rights in an excessive manner (or beyond what is necessary). They are not to be deemed as included within the general power to conduct interrogations."[193] The Israeli Supreme Court explained that restrictions applicable to police investigations are equally applicable to GSS investigations, and that there are no grounds to permit GSS interrogators to engage in conduct which would be prohibited in a regular police interrogation.[194]

In so ruling, the Israeli Supreme Court considered the "ticking time bomb" scenario often confronted by GSS interrogators:

> A given suspect is arrested by the GSS. He holds information respecting the location of a bomb that was set and will imminently explode. There is no way to defuse the bomb without this information. If the information is obtained, however, the bomb may be defused. If the bomb is not defused, scores will be killed and maimed. Is a GSS investigator authorized to employ physical means in order to elicit information regarding the location of the bomb in such instances?[195]

The Israeli Supreme Court stated that it was prepared to presume that if a GSS investigator—who applied physical interrogation methods for the purpose of saving human life—is criminally indicted, the "necessity" defense recognized under Israeli Penal Law would be open to him in the appropriate circumstances.[196] The Israeli Supreme Court also acknowledged that the legislature could enact laws permitting the interrogation methods that its decision struck down.[197] However, the Israeli Supreme Court refused to imply from the existence of the "necessity" defense, as the State argued for it to do, "an advance legal authorization endowing the investigator with the capacity to use physical interrogation methods."[198]

B. The Legal and Moral Implications of the "Ticking Bomb" Scenario

As the *Republic of Ireland* and *GSS Interrogation Methods Decision* demonstrate, in the face of a terrorist threat there is an inherent tension between obtaining potentially life-saving intelligence information through abusive interrogation of detainees and upholding human rights:

In crystallizing the interrogation rules, two values or interests clash. On the one hand, lies the desire to uncover the truth, thereby fulfilling the public interest in exposing crime and preventing it. On the other hand, is the wish to protect the dignity and liberty of the individual being interrogated.[199]

International and human rights law is clear: torture and cruel, inhuman or degrading treatment of detainees is prohibited. Those who would, nevertheless, support the use of moderate physical force, sensory deprivation or disorientation techniques in the interrogation of terrorist suspects argue that resort to such methods is, at times, the only way to prevent the death of innocent persons and is, therefore, justified in such cases as the "lesser of two evils." Proponents of this view would argue that the legitimacy of an act can be measured by whether its utility exceeds its harm. On this point, the Landau Commission took the following position:

To put it bluntly, the alternative is: are we to accept the offense of assault entailed in slapping a suspect's face, or threatening him, in order to induce him to talk and reveal a cache of explosive materials meant for use in carrying out an act of mass terror against a civilian population, and thereby prevent the greater evil which is about to occur? The answer is self-evident.

Everything depends on weighing the two evils against each other.[200]

In the case of detainees being held by the U.S. in connection with the "War on Terror," however, the "ticking bomb" scenario is further complicated. Any utilitarian justification for subjecting these detainees to interrogation practices prohibited by CAT must necessarily be premised on the certainty (or, at least, the substantiated suspicion) that these individuals do, in fact, possess vital intelligence information. But, here, there is no such certainty. Instead, hundreds of detainees at Guantánamo Bay, Bagram Air Force Base and other U.S. detention facilities have been detained for months without any type of hearing or legal challenge permitted to their detention.

Our answer to the question of whether torture of detainees should ever be permitted in a post-September 11 world is that there are no such circumstances. We condemn the use of torture in interrogation of detainees, without exception. By its terms, CAT permits no derogation of the prohibition against torture—stating that "[n]o exceptional circumstances whatsoever, whether a state of war or a threat of war, internal political stability or any other public emergency, may be invoked as a justification of torture."[201] As the Israeli Supreme Court has explained, "A democratic, freedom-loving society does not accept that investigators use any means for the purpose of uncovering the truth. 'The interrogations practices of the police in a given regime are indicative of a regime's very character.' "[202]

We recognize that some legal scholars and ethicists may well argue that circumstances exist (as in the "ticking bomb" scenario) in which torture and CID treatment in the interrogation of detainees should be permitted. However, we stress that torture of detainees—which is prohibited under international and U.S. law—is never permissible, and should be fully investigated and prosecuted in all cases.

* * *

In summary, the Association makes the following recommendations:

First, we urge the United States to amend 18 U.S.C. § 2340 to encompass the actions of military and intelligence personnel at U.S. facilities overseas, to fully utilize the UCMJ to protect all detainees from abuse and to independently investigate human rights compliance in countries to which we are "rendering" detainees.

Second, U.S. military and intelligence personnel involved in interrogation of terrorist suspects should be educated regarding the prohibition against torture and CID, and should receive training to comply with those rules.

Third, the U.S. should adhere to its commitments under the Geneva Conventions, extend POW treatment to regular force combatants as a matter of policy, and promptly establish proper screening procedures and hearings for all detainees.

Finally, the Association notes that particularly in these times of terrorism and violence, it is important to protect the rule of law and the standards of decency to which our nation and the community of nations are committed. As the Israeli Supreme Court has stated:

> This is the destiny of democracy, as not all means are acceptable to it, and not all practices employed by its enemies are open before it. Although a democracy must often fight with one hand tied behind its back, it nonetheless has the upper hand.[203]

NOTES

* **The Committee on International Human Rights:** Martin S. Flaherty (chair; member of the subcommittee who prepared the Report), Scott Horton (immediate past chair; member of the subcommittee who prepared the Report), Jeanmarie Fenrich (secretary), Charles Adler, Patricia C. Armstrong, Hon. Deborah A. Batts, Nicole Barrett, Aarthi Belani (student member; member of the subcommittee who prepared the Report), Seymour H. Chalif, Amy Christina Cococcia, Catherine Daly, Eric O. Darko, Jane M. Desnoyers, Mark K. Dietrich, Fiona M. Doherty, Barbara Fortson (former member; member of the subcommittee who prepared the Report), Aya Fujimura-Fanselow (student member), Douglas C. Gray, William M. Heinzen, Alice H. Henkin, Sharon K. Hom, Miranda Johnson (student member), Anil Kalhan, Mamta Kaushal, Christopher Kean, Elise B. Keppler, Katharine Lauer (member of the subcommittee who prepared the Report), Sara Lesch, Yvonne C. Lodico, Marko C. Maglich, Elisabeth Adams Mason, Nina Massen, Sam Scott Miller, Elena Dana Neacsu, Dyanna C. Pepitone, Marny Requa (student member), Sidney S. Rosdeitcher (chair of the subcommittee responsible for preparing the Report), Margaret L. Satterthwaite (member of the subcommittee who prepared the Report), Joseph H. Saunders, Christopher A. Smith (student member), and Katherine B. Wilmore.

The Committee on Military Affairs and Justice: Miles P. Fischer (chair; member of the subcommittee who prepared the Report), Michael Mernin (secretary), Donna Ahlstrand (former member; member of the subcommittee who prepared the Report), Steven Barrett, Myles Bartley, Philip Blum, Kenneth Carroll, Brian Cogan, Joshua Eisenberg, Matthew Hawkins, Peter Jaensch, Peter Kornman, Peter Langrind, Gerald Lee, Patricia Murphy, Rose Murphy, Harold Nathan, Timothy Pastore, Stanley Paylago (member of the subcommittee who prepared the Report), Visuvanathan Rudrakumaran, and Lawrence Sloan.

The views expressed herein are solely those of the Association and the participating Committees.

The Committee on International Human Rights and Military Affairs and Justice would like to thank the following persons for their assistance in the preparation of the Report: John Cerone (Executive Director, War Crimes Research Office, Washington College of Law, American University); Ken Hurwitz (Human Rights First); Professor Marco Sassòli (University of Geneva, professor of international law); Brigitte Oederlin and Gabor Rona (International Committee of the Red Cross); Paul, Weiss, Rifkind, Wharton & Garrison LLP ("Paul Weiss") associates Katarina Lawergren and Marc Miller and former Paul Weiss associate Matias Milet; and New York University School of Law students Ari Bassin, Amber A. Baylor, Angelina Fisher, Tzung-lin Fu, David R. Hoffman, Jane Stratton and Stephanie S. Welch; and New York Law School student Holly Higgins. This Report could not have been completed without the indefatigable efforts of Paul Weiss associate Liza Velazquez in helping edit the many drafts of the Report and consolidating the many views and comments of the Committees and Subcommittee into a coherent whole.

1. 548 U.S. __ (2006).

2. For purposes of this Report, the term "War in Afghanistan" refers to the period of international armed conflict in Afghanistan—from October 2001 to June 2002, when the Taliban was the governing force in Afghanistan, and the phrase "ongoing conflict in Afghanistan" refers to the period after June 18,

2002 when Hamid Karzai was elected as Afghanistan's transitional head of state, and the U.S. and other international parties were operating in Afghanistan at the invitation of this new Afghanistan government. This distinction becomes important in discussing the protections afforded to detainees by the Geneva Conventions. *See* Section II of this Report.

3. An assessment of the parameters and legal implications of the "War on Terror," a term coined by the Administration, is beyond the scope of this Report.

4. Carlotta Gall, *U.S. Military Investigating Death of Afghan In Custody,* N.Y. TIMES, Mar. 4, 2003, at A14. According to the *New York Times,* another Afghan man died of a pulmonary embolism or a blood clot in the lung while in U.S. custody at Bagram on December 3, 2002. Both men died within days of arriving at Bagram. Human Rights Watch has criticized the U.S. government for failing, one year after the first two deaths at Bagram—which were classified as homicides, to release the results of its investigation. *See* Press Releases & Documents, Voice of America, Rights Group Criticizes U.S. Military for Treatment of Afghan Detainees (Dec. 1, 2003) (printed at 2003 WL 66801402).

5. *See, e.g.,* Dana Priest & Barton Gellman, *U.S. Decries Abuse but Defends Interrogations; "Stress and Duress" Tactics used on Terrorism Suspects Held in Secret Overseas Facilities,* WASH. POST, Dec. 26, 2002, at A01; Eric Lichtblau & Adam Liptak, *Questioning to Be Legal, Humane and Aggressive, The White House Says Now,* N.Y. TIMES, Mar. 4, 2003, at A13; Jess Bravin & Gary Fields, *How do U.S. Interrogators Make A Captured Terrorist Talk,* WALL ST. J., Mar 4, 2003, at B1; Tania Branigan, *Ex-Prisoners Allege Rights Abuses By U.S. Military,* WASH. POST, Aug. 19, 2003, at A02. While standards and conditions of confinement—addressed by many of the international legal instruments examined in this Report—would be included in any exhaustive inquiry into the treatment of detainees at U.S. detention centers, in this Report we are focusing more narrowly on the legality of interrogation methods.

6. Captives have reportedly been "rendered" by the U.S. to Jordan, Egypt, Morocco, Saudi Arabia and Syria, in secret and without resort to legal process. *See, e.g.,* Peter Finn, *Al Qaeda Recruiter Reportedly Tortured; Ex-Inmate in Syria Cites Others' Accounts,* WASH. POST, Jan. 31, 2003, at A14; Dana Priest and Barton Gellman, *U.S. Decries Abuse but Defends Interrogations; "Stress and Duress" Tactics used on Terrorism Suspects Held in Secret Overseas Facilities,* WASH. POST, Dec. 26, 2002, at A01; Rajiv Chandrasekaran & Peter Finn, *U.S. Behind Secret Transfer of Terror Suspects,* WASH. POST, Mar. 11, 2002, at A01.

7. *See, e.g.,* Letter from Kenneth Roth, Executive Director, Human Rights Watch to President George W. Bush (Dec. 26, 2002) (*available at* http://www.hrw.org/press/2002/12/us1227.htm); Letter from Human Rights Groups to President George W. Bush (Jan. 31, 2003); Letter from Ernest Duff, The National Consortium of Torture Treatment Programs to President George W. Bush (Feb. 5, 2003); Letter from Sen. Patrick Leahy to Condoleezza Rice (June 2, 2002); Letter from ABCNY Committees on Military Affairs and Justice and International Human Rights to Scott W. Muller, General Counsel, CIA (June 4, 2003); Letter from Sen. Patrick J. Leahy to William J. Haynes, II, General Counsel, DOD (Sept. 9, 2003).

8. *See* Letter from William J. Haynes II, General Counsel, DOD, to Kenneth Roth, Executive Director, Human Rights Watch (Apr. 2, 2003). The Administration's use of the terms "enemy combatants" and "unlawful combatants" to detain persons indefinitely without administrative or judicial proceedings is novel.

9. *See* Letter from Scott W. Muller, General Counsel, CIA to Miles P. Fischer and Scott Horton, chair of the Committee on Military Affairs and Justice and then-chair of the Committee on International Human Rights, respectively (June 23, 2003). A CIA senior official has informally indicated that the agency complies with applicable law in reliance on the advice of its legal staff. However, we have been unable to confirm what legal advice has been given by CIA counsel or what means have been used to assure compliance with that advice.

10. *See* Letter from William J. Haynes II, General Counsel, DOD, to Sen. Patrick J. Leahy (June 25, 2003). At the November 20–21, 2003, Annual Review of the Field of National Security Law conference of the American Bar Association's Standing Committee on National Security Law, Muller stated publicly in response to a question by a member of the Committee on Military Affairs and Justice that Haynes' June 25, 2003 letter to Sen. Leahy articulates the policy position of "the entire U.S. government."

11. *Id.*

12. *Id.*

13. *Id.*

14. Convention Against Torture and Other Cruel, Inhuman or Degrading Treatment or Punishment, *opened for signature* Feb. 4, 1985, G.A. Res. 46, U.N. GAOR 39th Sess., Supp. No. 51, at 197, U.N. Doc. A/RES/39/708 (1984), *reprinted in* 23 I.L.M. 1027 (1984) ("CAT").

15. 136 Cong. Rec. S17486-01, 1990 WL 168442.

16. G.A. Res. 2200A (XXI), U.N. GAOR, 21st Sess., Supp. No. 16, at 52, U.N. Doc. A/6316.

17. O.A.S. RES. XXX, OEA/Ser. L.V./II. 82 Doc. Rev. 1, at 17.

18. 213 U.N.T.S. 221.

19. *See White House Fact Sheet: Status of Detainees at Guantánamo* (Feb. 7, 2002) (*available at* http://www.whitehouse.gov/news/releases/2002/02/print/20020207-13.html).

20. Geneva Convention (III) Relative to the Treatment of Prisoners of War, 6 U.S.T. 3316, 1949 U.S.T. LEXIS 483 ("Geneva III"); Geneva Convention (IV) Relative to the Protection of Civilian Persons in Time of War, 6 U.S.T. 3516, 1949 U.S.T. LEXIS 434 ("Geneva IV").

21. Additional Protocol I, *reprinted in*16 I.L.M. 1391. While neither the United States nor Afghanistan is a signatory to Additional Protocol I, it is generally acknowledged that certain provisions are binding as a matter of customary international law. And although the terms of Common Article 3 specifically limit its scope to internal conflicts, it is considered by customary international law to have broader scope.

22. 38 I.L.M. 1471 (Sept. 6, 1999).

23. CAT, Art. 11.

24. *Id.,* Art. 12.

25. *Id.,* Art. 4.

26. *Id.,* Art. 3.

27. For example, a lawsuit was recently filed by the Center for Constitutional Rights on behalf of Maher Arar, a Syrian-born Canadian citizen alleging that U.S. authorities deported him to Jordan in September 2002, where he was driven across the border and handed over to Syrian authorities. The Arar Complaint alleges that, although the U.S. Department of State's 2003 Country Reports designated Syria as a government that practices systemic torture, U.S. officials allegedly relied on assurances from the Syrian government that Arar would not be tortured. Arar has alleged that he was tortured repeatedly in a Syrian prison for 10 months, often with cables and electrical cords. *See* Complaint in *Maher Arar v. John Ashcroft, et al.* (*available at* http://www.ccr-ny.org/v2/legal/September_11th/docs/ArarComplaint.pdf).

28. Geneva III, Art. 5.

29. We note that the Department of Defense has recently circulated for comment administrative review procedures for enemy combatants at Guantánamo Bay Naval Base. *See* http://www.defenselink.mil/news/Mar2004/d20040303ar.pdf. While welcoming such a review process, we do not consider it to meet the requirement for status determination under the Geneva Conventions.

30. *Supra* note 13.

31. *Id.* Article 4.1 states: "Each State Party shall ensure that all acts of torture are offences under its criminal law. The same shall apply to an attempt to commit torture and to an act by any person which constitutes complicity or participation in torture."

32. *Id.* Article 3.1 states: "No State Party shall expel, return ('*refouler*') or extradite a person to another State where there are substantial grounds for believing that he would be in danger of being subjected to torture."

33. *See Murray v. The Charming Betsy,* 6 U.S. (2 Cranch) 64, 118 (1804) (a statute "ought never to be construed to violate the law of nations, if any other possible construction remains"). *See also United States v. P.L.O.,* 695 F. Supp. 1456, 1468 (S.D.N.Y. 1988) (noting "the lengths to which our courts have sometimes gone in construing domestic statutes so as to avoid conflict with international agreements...").

34. *Lawrence v. Texas,* 539 U.S. 558 (2003).

35. This list is by no means comprehensive. Practices were selected for inclusion here because of their similarity to the practices allegedly used by U.S. agents with respect to detainees held in connection with the War in Afghanistan and the ongoing conflict in Afghanistan. The findings and concluding observations of the Committee Against Torture are available at http://www.unhchr.ch/tbs/doc.nsf.

36. *Case of A. (name withheld) v. The Netherlands,* Committee Against Torture, Comm. No. 91/1997 (1998), U.N. Doc. No. CAT/C/21/D/91/1997.

37. *See* Inquiry under Article 20: Committee Against Torture, Findings concerning Peru (2001), U.N. Doc. No. A/56/44, at para. 35.

38. Concluding Observations concerning Republic of Korea (1996), U.N. Doc. No. A/52/44, at para. 56.

39. Concluding Observations concerning New Zealand (1993), U.N. Doc. No. A/48/44, at para. 148.

40. *See* Inquiry Under Article 20: Committee Against Torture, Findings concerning Turkey (1993), U.N. Doc. No. A/48/44/Add.1, at para. 48.

41. Concluding Observations concerning Azerbaijan (2003), U.N. Doc. No. CAT/C/CR/30/1, at para. 5(b).

42. Concluding Observations concerning Germany (1993), U.N. Doc. No. A/48/44, at para. 167.

43. *Id.; see also* Concluding Observations concerning New Zealand (1998), U.N. Doc. No. A/53/44, at para. 175.

44. Concluding Observations concerning the United States (2000), U.N. Doc. No. A/55/44, at para. 179(e).

45. Concluding Observations concerning Australia (2000), U.N. Doc. No. A/56/44, at para. 52(b).

46. *Supra* note 36.

47. These techniques were found by the Committee to constitute "breaches of article 16 and also constitute torture as defined in article 1 of the Convention. This conclusion is particularly evident where such methods of interrogation are used in combination, which appears to be the standard case." Concluding Observations concerning Israel (1997), U.N. Doc. No. A/52/44, at para. 257.

48. *See* 136 Cong. Rec. 36,198 (daily ed. Oct. 27, 1990). The instrument of ratification included the declaration that "the provisions of Articles 1 through 16 of [CAT] are not self-executing." *See* United Nations Treaty Collection: Declarations and Reservations, (*available at* http://www.unhchr.ch/html/menu3/b/treaty12_asp.htm).

In the case of a self-executing treaty, "no domestic legislation is required to give [it] the force of law in the United States." *Trans World Airlines, Inc. v. Franklin Mint Corp.,* 466 U.S. 243, 252 (1984). By contrast, a non-self-executing treaty is one that "must be implemented by legislation before it gives rise to a private cause of action." *Mannington Mills, Inc. v. Congoleum Corp.,* 595 F.2d 1287, 1298 (3d Cir. 1979).

49. *See* Ratification Status for CAT, United States of America (*available at* www.unhchr.ch). The U.S. has not opted out of the inquiry procedure under Article 20. It has entered a declaration accepting the inter-state complaint procedure set up by Article 21. The U.S. has not, however, accepted the competence of the Committee under Article 22 to receive and consider complaints on behalf of individuals subject to its jurisdiction who claim to be victims of a violation of CAT.

50. *See*136 Cong. Rec. S17486-01 (daily ed. Oct. 27, 1990).

51. *See* 136 Cong. Rec. 36192, 36198 (daily ed. Oct. 27, 1990).

52. Under international law, reservations are invalid if they violate the "object and purpose" of the treaty. *See* Vienna Convention on the Law of Treaties, *opened for signature* May 23, 1969, 1155 U.N.T.S. 331, at Art. 19(c). This Report assumes that the U.S. reservation with respect to Article 16 of CAT is valid.

53. Because the focus of this Report is on what laws apply to agents of the United States government in detention centers located outside of United States territory, this discussion does not examine state or federal penal or civil rights statutes that would also apply to interrogation occurring on American soil.

54. This had also been the position of the Ninth Circuit. *See Al-Saher v. INS,* 268 F.3d 1143 (9th Cir. 2001) (holding that severe beatings and cigarette burns sustained over periods of days, weeks and months constitutes torture). More recently, however, the Ninth Circuit has held that neither serious persecution (*e.g.*, threats, unjust charges, fines, illegal searches and seizures) nor verbal abuse alone amount to torture. *See Gui v. INS,* 280 F.3d 1217 (9th Cir. 2002); *Quant v. Ashcroft,* 2003 U.S. App. LEXIS 6616 (9th Cir. 2003).

55. *See, e.g., Cornejo-Barreto v. Seifert,* 218 F.3d 1004, 1016-17 (9th Cir. 2000) (individuals certified as extraditable by the Secretary of State who fear torture may petition for judicial review of the Secretary's decision using CAT standards protecting against *non-refoulement*); *Mu-Xing Wang v. Ashcroft,* 320 F.3d 130 (2d Cir. 2003) (following *Cornejo-Barreto*'s holding that habeas review is available for CAT claims, but in the context of removal); *Ogbudimkpa v. Ashcroft,* 342 F.3d 207 (3d Cir. 2003) (same).

56. The Senate Committee on the Judiciary acknowledged the relationship of 18 U.S.C. § 2340 to CAT and the Torture Victim Protection Act in a 2002 report. *See* S. Rep. No. 107-44 (2002), at 10–11.

57. A restrictive interpretation of the scope of the statute is found in the U.S. Dept. of Justice, Criminal Resource Manual 20 (Oct. 1997), which provides: "Section 2340A of Title 18, United States Code, prohibits torture committed by public officials under color of law against persons within the public official's custody or control. . . . The statute applies only to acts of torture committed outside the United States. There is Federal extraterritorial jurisdiction over such acts whenever the perpetrator is a national of the United States or the alleged offender is found within the United States, irrespective of the nationality of the victim or the alleged offender."

58. *See* S. Rep. No. 102-249 (1991) (stating that the TVPA would "carry out the intent of the Convention Against Torture and Other Cruel, Inhuman or Degrading Treatment or Punishment, which was ratified by the U.S. Senate on October 27, 1990").

59. *See* Report of the Committee on Foreign Relations, Convention Against Torture and Other Cruel, Inhuman, or Degrading Treatment or Punishment, S. Exec. Rep. No. 30, 101st Cong., 2d Sess. 25 (1990) (statement of Mr. Pell) (citing *Case of X. v. Federal Republic of Germany* (No. 6694/74)).

60. *Leon v. Wainwright,* 734 F.2d 770 n.5 (11th Cir. 1984) (kidnapping conviction confirmed based on a confession obtained following a prior coerced confession).

61. *Rochin v. California,* 342 U.S. 165, 172 (1952).

62. *County of Sacramento v. Lewis,* 523 U.S. 833, 848-49 (1998).

63. The UCMJ, discussed below, provides that no "cruel or unusual punishment" may be adjudged by any court-martial or inflicted upon any person subject to the UCMJ (10 U.S.C.S. § 855). In general, military courts have applied the Supreme Court's interpretation of the Eighth Amendment to claims raised under this provision. *See, e.g., United States v. Avila,* 53 M.J. 99, 2000 CAAF LEXIS 569 (C.A.A.F. 2000). Thus, under the UCMJ, POWs and persons who under the law of war are subject to trial for military offences by a military tribunal are not to be punished in a cruel or unusual manner, within the meaning of the Eighth Amendment.

64. *City of Revere v. Massachusetts Gen. Hosp.,* 463 U.S. 239, 244 (1983). *See also County of Sacramento v. Lewis,* 523 U.S. 833, 849–50 (1998) (citation omitted) ("We held in *City of Revere v. Massachusetts Gen. Hospital* that 'the due process rights of a [pretrial detainee] are at least as great as the Eighth Amendment protections available to a convicted prisoner'").

65. *Hudson v. McMillian,* 503 U.S. 1, 7 (1992) (quoting *Whitley v. Albers,* 475 U.S. 312, 321 (1986)).

66. *Whitley v. Albers,* 475 U.S. 312, 320-21 (1986) (quoting *Johnson v. Glick,* 481 F.2d 1028, 1033 (2d Cir. 1973)).

67. *Compare U.S. v. Gatlin,* 216 F.3d 207 (2d Cir 2000) *with U.S. v. Corey,* 232 F.3d 1166 (9th Cir 2000). However, the question was substantially mooted for most purposes by the passage of the Military Extraterritorial Jurisdiction Act of 2000, Pub. L. 106-503, 112 Stat. 2488, which subjects persons accompanying the armed forces abroad to U.S. civilian criminal jurisdiction, even if outside the "special maritime and territorial jurisdiction."

68. *See* U.S. Dept. of State, Initial Report of the United States of America to the U.N. Committee against Torture, U.N. Doc. CAT/C/28/Add.5 (1999), at para. 178.

69. *Amnesty International Report Charges U.S. is "Safe Haven" for Torturers Fleeing Justice; Eight Years On, U.S. Has Failed to Prosecute Single Individual for Torture,* Amnesty International Press Release (2002) (*available at* http://www.amnestyusa.org/news/2002/usa04102002.html). *See also* William J. Aceves United States of America: A Safe Haven For Torturers (Amnesty International USA Publications 2002), at 50.

70. The UCMJ does not define the term POW. Thus it is uncertain whether POW in the UCMJ has the same meaning as in Geneva III.

71. *United States v. Averette,* 19 U.S.C.M.A. 363, 365–66, 41 C.M.R. 363, 365–66 (1970) (the phrase "in time of war" is limited to "a war formally declared by Congress"; even though the Vietnam conflict "qualified as a war as that word is generally used and understood[,]...such a recognition should not serve as a shortcut for a formal declaration of war, at least in the sensitive area of subjecting civilians to military jurisdiction"). *Cf. United States v. Anderson,* 17 U.S.C.M.A. 588, 589, 38 C.M.R. 386, 387 (1968) (United States' involvement in Vietnam conflict "constitutes a 'time of war'...within the meaning of" Article 43

(a) of the UCMJ, which provides that there is no statute of limitations over certain offenses committed "in time of war").

72. The Court of Appeals for the Armed Forces (formerly the Court of Military Appeals) is a civilian Article I court hearing appeals from the intermediate appellate courts for each of the Army, Navy (and Marines) and Air Force, subject to possible appeal to the United States Supreme Court.

73. As previously noted, the Military Extraterritorial Jurisdiction Act of 2000, *see supra* note 67, eliminated any gap in jurisdiction resulting from *Reid v. Covert* by conferring jurisdiction on federal courts over civilians accompanying the armed forces abroad.

74. The protections of Article 55 apply to "any person subject to" the UCMJ. And as stated previously, the UCMJ would seem to apply to unlawful combatants under 10 U.S.C. § 818.

75. The Articles of War preceding the UCMJ prohibited "cruel and unusual punishment," but the phrase was changed to "cruel *or* unusual punishment" in Article 55 (emphasis added). *See* Articles of War 41, Manual for Courts-Martial, U.S. Army, 1929 at 212, and 1949 at 284. The legislative history of Article 55 provides no rationale why the word "and" was changed to "or." *United States v. White,* 54 M.J. 469, 2001 CAAF LEXIS 497 (C.A.A.F. 2001).

76. *See United States v. Kinsch,* 54 M.J. 641, 2000 CCA LEXIS 237 (A.C.C.A. 2000). *See also* Section I(C)(3)(b) of this Report for a fuller discussion of the Eighth Amendment prohibition of cruel and unusual treatment and punishment.

77. *See United States v. Wappler,* 2 C.M.A. 393, 9 C.M.R. 23, 1953 CMA LEXIS 897 (C.M.A. 1953); *White,* 54 M.J. at 473; *United States v. Avila,* 53 M.J. 99, 2000 CAAF LEXIS 569 (C.A.A.F. 2000).

78. Compare the federal criminal civil rights statutes, 18 U.S.C. §§ 241 and 242, and the civil statute 42 U.S.C. § 1983, all of which apply only where the victim is entitled to constitutional rights.

79. Manual for Courts-Martial, United States (1995 edition) (the "Manual"), Paragraph 60.b (1–2). The Manual is issued by the President as a regulation under the authority granted by Congress under Article 3 of the UCMJ.

80. Manual, Paragraph 60.c (3).

81. According to the Manual, however, the doctrine of preemption "prohibits application of Article 134 to conduct covered by Articles 80 through 132. For example, larceny is covered in Article 121, and if an element of that offense is lacking—for example, intent—there can be no larceny or larceny type offense, either under Article 121 or, because of preemption, under Article 134." Manual, Paragraph 60.c (5)(a). In effect, Article 134 may not be employed to salvage a charge where the charge could not be sustained under the substantive offense provisions of the UCMJ or Federal statute. Accordingly, conduct which violated Article 55 discussed above or any other substantive provision of the UCMJ could not be charged under Article 134. These remain alternative, not cumulative provisions.

82. For example, murder (10 U.S.C. § 918), manslaughter (10 U.S.C. § 919), dereliction of duty (10 U.S.C. § 892).

For purposes of this Report, we assume that U.S. military interrogations of detainees are conducted for intelligence gathering purposes and not with an investigatory intent to elicit incriminating responses in anticipation of criminal prosecution. However, should the focus of the interrogation shift from an intelligence to a law enforcement nature, Miranda warnings under Article 31 of the UCMJ (10 U.S.C. § 831) would be required. The failure to give such warnings is a criminal offense under Article 98 of the UCMJ (10 U.S.C. § 898).

83. *See* Article 93 of the UCMJ (10 U.S.C. § 893). Two Marines face charges for assault, cruelty and dereliction of duty involving the treatment and death of an Iraqi prisoner. *See* Associated Press Newswires, *Two Marines Face Trial After Iraqi Dies,* Apr. 14, 2004; Tony Perry, *Iraqi Prisoner Died After Marine Grabbed His Throat, Officials Say,* L.A. TIMES, Oct. 22, 2003, at B06. It is not believed that the incident involved interrogation, but it is notable that such alleged offenses involved Marine infantry reservists who had not been trained in the treatment of prisoners (apart from one with relevant peacetime background) and are reported to have been given only a brief orientation before being assigned to this duty. As advocated elsewhere in this Report, proper training of U.S. military and intelligence personnel is essential to achieve compliance with the U.S.'s obligations under CAT.

84. Article 93 prohibits a person subject to the jurisdiction of the UCMJ from committing acts of "cruelty toward, or oppression or maltreatment of, any person subject to his orders." The phrase "any person

subject to his orders" in Article 93 is defined as: "not only those persons under the direct or immediate command of the accused but extends to all persons, subject to the...[UCMJ] or not, who by reason of some duty are required to obey the lawful orders of the accused, regardless whether the accused is in the direct chain of command over the person." Manual for Courts-Martial, United States, (1995 edition), Part IV, P 17c(1).

85. An officer in Iraq was charged under Article 28 (10 U.S.C. § 928) for firing his pistol near an Iraqi detainee's head in the course of an interrogation in order to elicit details about a planned ambush or assassination. Thomas E. Ricks, *Army Accuses Officer In Iraq Of Firing Pistol Near Prisoner,* WASH. POST, Oct. 30, 2003, at A14. The officer faced a possible court-martial and up to eight years imprisonment. Following a UCMJ Article 32 hearing (which is akin to a grand jury or preliminary hearing), the division's commanding general ordered that the officer be fined and allowed to retire. *See U.S. Officer Fined for Harsh Interrogation Tactics* (Dec. 13, 2003) (*available at* http://www.cnn.com/2003/US/12/12/sprj.nirq .west.ruling).

86. *See* Section II(C) for a discussion of who qualifies as a "protected person" under Geneva IV.

87. "Common Article 3" provides that detainees "shall in all circumstances be treated humanely" and prohibits the following acts "at any time and in any place whatsoever": "violence to life and person, in particular murder of all kinds, mutilation, cruel treatment and torture;" and "outrages upon personal dignity, in particular humiliating or degrading treatment." Common Article 3 also provides that the "wounded and sick shall be collected and cared for."

Although neither the United States nor Afghanistan is a party to Additional Protocol I, it is generally acknowledged that relevant sections of Protocol I constitute either binding customary international law or good practice, in particular the minimum safeguards guaranteed by Article 75(2). *See* Michael J. Matheson, *Remarks on the United States Position on the Relation of Customary International Law to the 1977 Protocols Additional to the 1949 Geneva Conventions, reprinted in The Sixth Annual American Red Cross-Washington College of Law Conference on International Humanitarian Law: A Workshop on Customary International Law and the 1977 Protocols Additional to the 1949 Geneva Conventions,* 2 AM. U. J. INT'L L. & POL'Y 415, 425–6 (1987).

Article 75 provides that "persons who are in the power of a Party to the conflict and who do not benefit from more favourable treatment under the Conventions" "shall be treated humanely in all circumstances" and that each state Party "shall respect the person, honour, convictions and religious practices of all such persons." Paragraph 2 of Article 75 prohibits, "at any time and in any place whatsoever, whether committed by civilian or military agents": "violence to the life, health, or physical or mental well-being of persons, in particular...torture of all kinds, whether physical or mental," "corporal punishment," and "mutilation"; "outrages upon personal dignity, in particular humiliating and degrading treatment ...and any form of indecent assault"; and "threats to commit any of the foregoing acts."

The U.S. rejection of Additional Protocol I was explained in a presidential note to the Senate in the following terms: "Protocol I.... would grant combatant status to irregular forces even if they do not satisfy the traditional requirements to distinguish themselves from the civilian population and otherwise comply with the laws of war. This would endanger civilians among whom terrorists and other irregulars attempt to conceal themselves. These problems are so fundamental in character that they cannot be remedied through reservations...." *See* 1977 U.S.T. LEXIS 465.

88. *See* Geneva III, Art. 5; *see also* U.S. Dept. of Army, Field Manual 27-10, "Law of Land Warfare", Art. 71 (1956); U.S. Dept. of Army, Regulation 190-8 Military Police, "Enemy Prisoners of War, Retained Personnel, Civilian Internees and Other Detainees," § 1-5 (a)(2) (1997).

89. *See, e.g.,* Dep't of Defense, Secretary Rumsfeld Media Availability en route to Camp X-Ray (Jan. 27, 2002) (*available at*http://www.defenselink.mil/news/Jan2002/t01282002_t0127sd2.html) ("Sometimes when you capture a big, large group there will be someone who just happened to be in there that didn't belong in there.") (remarks of Respondent, Secretary of Defense Donald H. Rumsfeld); Carlotta Gall, *Freed Afghan, 15, Recalls a Year at Guantánamo,* N.Y. TIMES, Feb. 11, 2004, at A03 (quoting released teenager claiming to have been captured by non-U.S. forces and handed over to the Americans while looking for a job); Jan McGirk, *Pakistani Writes of His U.S. Ordeal,* BOSTON GLOBE, Nov. 17, 2002, at A30 ("Pakistan intelligence sources said Northern Alliance commanders could receive $5000 for each Taliban

prisoner and $20,000 for a[n] [al] Qaeda fighter. As a result, bounty hunters rounded up any men who came near the battlegrounds and forced them to confess.").

90. *See, e.g.,* Sean D. Murphy, *Contemporary Practice of the United States Relating to International Law,* 96 Am. J. Int'l L. 461, 476–77 (2002).

91. Article 4-A of Geneva III provides, in part:

> Prisoners of war, in the sense of the present Convention, are persons belonging to one of the following categories, who have fallen into the power of the enemy:
>
> Members of the armed forces of a Party to the conflict as well as members of militias or volunteer corps forming part of such armed forces.
>
> Members of other militias and members of other volunteer corps, including those of organized resistance movements, belonging to a Party to the conflict and operating in or outside their own territory, even if this territory is occupied, provided that such militias or volunteer corps, including such organized resistance movements, fulfill the following conditions:
>
> (a) of being commanded by a person responsible for his subordinates;
> (b) that of having a fixed distinctive sign recognizable at a distance;
> (c) that of carrying arms openly;
> (d) that of conducting their operations in accordance with the laws and customs of war.
>
> Members of regular armed forces who profess allegiance to a government or an authority not recognized by the Detaining Power. . . .

92. Article 43 of Additional Protocol I provides: "The armed forces of a Party to a conflict consist of all organized armed forces, groups and units which are under a command responsible to that Party for the conduct or its subordinates, even if that Party is represented by a government or an authority not recognized by an adverse Party. Such armed forces shall be subject to an internal disciplinary system which, inter alia, shall enforce compliance with the rules of international law applicable in armed conflict."

93. *See* Geneva III, Art. 5; *see also,* U.S. Dept. of Army, Field Manual 27-10, "Law of Land Warfare", Art. 71 (1956); U.S. Dept. of Army, Regulation 190-8 Military Police, "Enemy Prisoners of War, Retained Personnel, Civilian Internees and Other Detainees," § 1-5 (a)(2) (1997). Under U.S. military regulations, a "competent tribunal" pursuant to Article 5 of Geneva III consists of three commissioned officers. The regulations also require that persons whose status is to be determined be advised of their rights; be permitted to attend all open sessions, call witnesses and question witnesses called by the tribunal; be permitted (but not compelled) to testify or otherwise address the tribunal; and be provided with an interpreter. The regulations provide for the tribunal's determination of a detainee's status in closed session by a majority vote and require a preponderance of the evidence to support the tribunal's finding. *See* Erin Chlopak, *Dealing with the Detainees at Guantánamo Bay: Humanitarian and Human Rights Obligations Under the Geneva Conventions,* Hum Rts. Br. (Spring 2002), at 6, 8.

It should be noted that the "competent tribunal" outlined in ARMY REG. 190-8, § 1-6 is a quick, administrative process that is highly dependent upon the availability of witnesses during ongoing combat and support operations. Unsworn statements may be presented as evidence, and a record of the proceedings is developed. Although the tribunal may or may not include military lawyers such as members of the Staff Judge Advocate General ("JAG"), JAG lawyers will subsequently review the record. The record may also be the basis for any further proceedings for war crimes or for any other penalty.

Fundamentally, the tribunal determines only status and does not adjudicate liability. Tribunals are required under Geneva III only when status of the detainee is in doubt. When, for example, ten thousand uniformed members of a regular enemy infantry division surrender as a body, there is no need for a tribunal. When, however, non-uniformed, but possibly military, personnel mix with refugees, that is a classic situation for such tribunals.

94. Specifically, Article 13 of Geneva III provides:

> Prisoners of war must at all times be humanely treated. Any unlawful act or omission by the Detaining Power causing death or seriously endangering the health of a prisoner of war in its custody is prohibited, and will be regarded as a serious breach of the present Convention. In particular, no prisoner of war may be subjected to physical mutilation or to medical or scientific experiments of any

kind which are not justified by the medical, dental or hospital treatment of the prisoner concerned and carried out in his interest.

Likewise, prisoners of war must at all times be protected, particularly against acts of violence or intimidation and against insults and public curiosity.

95. Manooher Mofidi and Amy E. Eckert, *"Unlawful Combatants" or "Prisoners of War": The Law and Politics of Labels,* 36 Cornell Int'l L.J. 59, 89 (2003).

96. Murphy, *supra* note 90, at 476–77.

97. *Id.*

98. *Id.*

99. Powell asked that the Administration recognize that the Geneva Conventions apply to the conflict between the U.S. and Taliban regime and that the Administration convene a "competent tribunal" to determine the status of the prisoners pursuant to Article 5 of Geneva III. *See* Katharine Q. Seelye, *A Nation Challenged: The Prisoners; Powell Asks Bush to Review Stand on War Captives,* N.Y. Times, Jan. 27, 2002, at A01; William Safire, Editorial, *Colin Powell Dissents,* N.Y. Times, Jan. 28, 2002, at A15.

100. *See supra* note 19.

U.S. Secretary of Defense Donald Rumsfeld, responding to a request for clarification, referred to Article 4(a)(2) of Geneva III to explain why the Taliban could not qualify for POW status: "The Taliban [like Al Qaeda] also did not wear uniforms, they did not have insignia, they did not carry their weapons openly, and they were tied tightly at the waist to Al Qaeda. They behaved like them, they worked with them, they functioned with them, they cooperated with respect to communications, they cooperated with respect to supplies and ammunition." Secretary of Defense Donald H. Rumsfeld, Remarks on Ferry from Air Terminal to Main Base, Guantánamo Bay, Cuba (Jan. 27, 2002) (transcript *available at* http://www.defenselink.mil/transcripts/2002/t01282002_t0127sd2.html).

101. Applying the four-part test from Article 4(a)(2) of Geneva III to the determination, the *Lindh* court found that the Taliban had an insufficient internal system of military command or discipline, that the "Taliban typically wore no distinctive sign that could be recognized by opposing combatants," and that the "Taliban regularly targeted civilian populations in clear contravention of the laws and customs of war." *Lindh,* 212 F. Supp. 2d at 558. Implicitly the *Lindh* Court held that the four conditions listed in Geneva III, Article 4(a)(2) also apply to "regular armed forces." *Id.* at 557. In concluding that the Taliban were not regular armed forces, the *Lindh* court stated "[i]t would indeed be absurd for members of a so-called 'regular armed force' to enjoy lawful combatant immunity even though the force had no established command structure and its members wore no recognizable symbol or insignia, concealed their weapons, and did not abide by the customary laws of war. Simply put, the label 'regular armed force' cannot be used to mask unlawful combatant status." *Id.,* at n.35.

See also Int'l Comm. of the Red Cross, *Commentaries to Article 4(a)(1) Convention (III) relative to the Treatment of Prisoners of War, Geneva, 12 August 1949,* ICRC Database on Int'l Humanitarian Law (*available at* http://www.icrc.org./ihl.nsf/b466ed681ddfcfd241256739003e6368/3ca76fa4dae5b32ec12563ed00425040?Open Document) ("It is the duty of each State to take steps so that members of its armed forces can be immediately recognized as such and to see to it that they are easily distinguishable from members of the enemy armed forces or from civilians."). *See also, generally,* Ingrid Detter, THE LAW OF WAR (Cambridge Univ. Press, 2nd ed., 2000), at 136; Christopher Greenwood, *International Law and the War Against Terrorism,* 78 International Affairs 301, 316 (2002); Ruth Wedgwood, *Al Qaeda, Terrorism, and Military Commissions,* 96 Am. J. Int'l L. 328, 335 (2002).

102. ICRC, *Geneva Convention on Prisoners of War* (Feb. 9, 2002) (*available at* http://www.icrc.org/Web/Eng/siteeng().nsf/iwpList454/26D99836025EA80Dc1256B6600610C90) ("International Humanitarian Law foresees that the members of armed forces as well as militias associated to them which are captured by the adversary in an international armed conflict are protected by the Third Geneva Convention. There are divergent views between the United States and the ICRC on the procedures which apply on how to determine that the persons detained are not entitled to prisoner of war status.")

103. IACHR, Decision on Request for Precautionary Measures (Detainees at Guantánamo Bay, Cuba), 41 I.L.M. 532, 533 (2002) ("It is. . .well-known that doubt exists as to the legal status of the detainees.")

104. Amnesty International, *Memorandum to the U.S. Government on the rights of people in U.S. custody in Afghanistan and Guantánamo Bay* (*available at* http://web.amnesty.org/aidoc/aidoc_pdf.nsf/Index/AMR510532002ENGLISH/$File/AMR510532.pdf) (The United States' "selective approach to the Geneva Conventions threatens to undermine the effectiveness of international humanitarian law protections for any U.S. or other combatants captured in the future.")

105. ICJ, *Rule of Law Must be Respected in Relation to Detainees in Guantánamo Bay* (Jan. 17, 2002) (*available at* http://www.icj.org./ews.php?id_article=2612&lang=eng) ("The United States has refused [POW] status to Taliban fighters even though, as members of the armed forces, they are entitled to it.")

106. Kofi Annan, Press Encounter outside No. 10 Downing Street, London, (Feb. 25, 2002) (unofficial transcript *available at* http://www.un.org/aps/sg/offthecuff.asp?nid=103) ("The Red Cross has indicated that anyone who was arrested in the battlefield, or picked up in the battlefield, is a prisoner of war and they do not make a difference between the Al Qaeda and the Taliban. And under the convention, where there is a disagreement, normally you have an independent tribunal to resolve this.").

107. Mary Robinson, Statement of the High Commissioner for Human Rights on Detention of Taliban and Al Qaeda Prisoners at U.S. Base in Guantánamo Bay, Cuba (Jan. 16, 2002) (*available at* http://www.unhchr.ch/hurricane/hurricane.nsf/0/C537C6D4657C7928C1256B43003E7D0B?opendocument) ("All persons detained in this context are entitled to the protection of international human rights law and humanitarian law, in particular the relevant provisions of the International Covenant on Civil and Political Rights (ICCPR) and the Geneva Conventions of 1949.")

108. *See, generally,* George H. Aldrich, *The Taliban, Al Qaeda, and the Determination of Illegal Combatants,* 96 Am. J. Int'l L. 891 (2002); Harold Hongju Koh, *Agora: Military Commissions—The Case Against Military Commissions,* 96 Am. J. Int'l L. 337 (2002); Neil McDonald & Scott Sullivan, *Rational Interpretation in Irrational Times: The Third Geneva Convention and the War on Terror,* 44 Harv. Int'l L.J. 301 (2003); Manooher Mofidi and Amy E. Eckert, *"Unlawful Combatants" or "Prisoners of War": The Law and Politics of Labels,* 36 Cornell Int'l L.J. 59 (2003); Michael Ratner, *Moving Away from the Rule of Law: Military Tribunals, Executive Detentions and Torture*, 24 Cardozo L. Rev. 1513 (2003).

109. *See* Jennifer Elsea, Treatment of "Battlefield Detainees" in the War on Terrorism, Cong. Research Serv., RL31367, at 30 (2002) (*available at* http://fpc.state.gov/documents/organization/9655.pdf) (stating that the United States "has in the past interpreted [Article 5] as requiring an individualized assessment of status before privileges can be denied"). *See also* The Judge Advocate General's School, Operational Law Handbook 22 (William O'Brien ed., 2003) (instructing judge advocates to "advise commanders that, regardless of the nature of the conflict, all enemy personnel should initially be accorded the protections of [Geneva III], at least until their status may be determined").

110. Michael J. Matheson, while serving as Deputy Legal Advisor of the U.S. State Department, stated:

> We [the United States] do support the principle that, should any doubt arise as to whether a person is entitled to combatant status, he be so treated until his status has been determined by a competent tribunal, as well as the principle that if a person who has fallen into the power of an adversary is not held as a prisoner of war and is to be tried for an offense arising out of the hostilities, he should have the right to assert his entitlement before a judicial tribunal and to have that question adjudicated.

Matheson, *supra* note 86.

111. Some have argued that the Taliban did comply with the requirements for Article 4(a)(2). *See, e.g.,* Robert Goldman and Brian Tittemore, Unprivileged Combatants and the Hostilities in Afghanistan: Their Status and Rights under International Humanitarian Rights Law (The Am. Soc. of Int'l Law Task Force on Terrorism, Task Force Paper) (*available at* http://asil.org/taskforce/goldman.pdf.)

112. Not only did the Taliban profess such an allegiance, but they were the strongest military partner in the Alliance, effectively controlling Afghanistan. *See* "Taliban Reach Zenith?," 85 National Defense 10 (Oct. 1, 2000).

113. Article 1 of Geneva III states "The High Contracting Parties undertake to respect and to ensure respect for the present Convention in all circumstances." *See also* Military and Paramilitary Activities (*Nicar. v. U.S.*), 1986 I.C.J. REP. 14, 14 (June 27) (holding that Geneva III applies in all circumstances regardless of the actions of the other party to the conflict). *See also, generally,* Theodor Meron, *The Humanization of Humanitarian Law,* 94 Am. J. Int'l L. 239, 248–249 (2000).

114. As the ICRC Commentaries on Article 1 state: "it is not merely an engagement concluded on a basis of reciprocity, binding each party to the contract only in so far as the other party observes its obligations. It is rather a series of unilateral engagements solemnly contracted before the world as represented by the other Contracting Parties. Each State contracts obligations 'vis-à-vis' itself and at the same time 'vis-à-vis' the others. The motive of the Convention is so essential for the maintenance of civilization that the need is felt for its assertion, as much out of respect for it on the part of the signatory State itself as in the expectation of such respect from all parties." ICRC *Commentaries to Article 1, Convention (III) relative to the Treatment of Prisoners of War, Geneva, 12 August 1949,* ICRC Database on Int'l Humanitarian Law (*available at* http://www.icrc.org./ihl.nsf/b466ed681ddfcfd241256739003e6368/49cfe5505d5912dlc12563ed00424cdd?Open Document). *See also* Geneva III, Art. 13.

115. George H. Aldrich, *The Taliban, Al Qaeda, and the Determination of Illegal Combatants,* 96 Am. J. Int'l L. 891, 895–96 (2002) (noting that North Korea and North Vietnam denied POW status to all American prisoners on the basis of the allegation that they were all war criminals).

116. Colin Powell apparently made remarks to this effect in a memo leaked to the press on January 27, 2002. *See* Editorial, *Bush's Call on Captives,* The Boston Globe, Jan. 29, 2002, at A10.

117. Legal commentators have argued that persons who have directly participated in the War in Afghanistan and who do not qualify as POWs under Geneva III (*i.e.,* detainees considered to be "unlawful combatants" by the U.S.) should automatically be considered "protected persons" under Geneva IV, unless other exceptions apply. *See, e.g.,* Michael Ratner, *Moving Away from the Rule of Law: Military Tribunals, Executive Detentions and Torture,* 24 Cardozo L. Rev. 1513, 1518–19 (2003) ("There is no gap between the two conventions"). Recent decisions of the International Criminal Tribunal for the Former Yugoslavia (ICTFY) have held that, "if an individual is not entitled to the protections of the Third Convention as a prisoner of war (or of the First or Second Conventions) he or she necessarily falls within the ambit of [Geneva IV]." *See The Prosecutor v. Delalic,* IT-96-21-T, at para. 271 (1998); *see also Prosecutor v. Tadic,* IT-94-I-A, 38 I.L.M. 158 (1999).

118. Such determination does not negate application of Common Article 3 to an "armed conflict not of an international character" or certain other provisions of international humanitarian law and the law of armed conflict.

119. The ICCPR, G.A. Res. 2200A (XXI), U.N. GAOR, 21st Sess., Supp. No. 16, at 52, U.N. Doc. A/6316, 999 U.N.T.S. 171 was adopted in 1966 and came into force in 1976. It was ratified by the United States in 1992, subject to a number of reservations, understandings and declarations. *See* 138 Cong. Rec. S4781-01 (1992).

120. Congressional ratification of the ICCPR with respect to the prohibition against cruel, inhuman or degrading treatment is subject to a reservation mirroring that taken by the U.S. under CAT: "The United States considers itself bound by Article 7 to the extent that 'cruel, inhuman, or degrading treatment or punishment' means the cruel and unusual treatment or punishment prohibited by the Fifth, Eighth and/or Fourteenth Amendments. . . ." *Id.*

121. *See Floyd Howell v. Jamaica,* Communication No. 798/1998 (20 January 1998), CCPR/C/79/D/798/1998; *Víctor Alfredo Polay Campos,* Communication No. 577/1994 (6 November 1997), CCPR/C/61/D/577/1994; *Dave Marais, Jr. v. Madagascar,* Communication No. 49/1979 (19 April 1979), U.N. Doc. Supp. No. 40 (A/38/40) at 141 (1983); *Raul Sendic Antonaccio v. Uruguay,* Communication No. R.14/63 (28 November 1979), U.N. Doc. Supp. No. 40 (A/37/40) at 114 (1982).

122. *See* Concluding Observations of the Human Rights Committee (Israel), CCPR/C/79/Add.93 (1998).

123. *See* General Comment 20, U.N. GAOR Hum. Rts. Comm., 47th Sess., Supp. No. 40, para. 9, U.N. Doc. A/47/40 (1992).

124. *Kindler v. Canada,* Communication No. 470/1991, Human Rights Committee, U.N. Doc. CCPR/C/48/D/470/1990 (1993).

125. *See, e.g., Poindexter v. Nash,* 333 F.3d 372, 379 (2d Cir. 2003); *Bannerman v. Snyder,* 325 F.3d 722, 724 (6th Cir. 2003); *Wesson v. U.S. Penitentiary Beaumont, TX,* 305 F.3d 343, 348 (5th Cir. 2002); *United States v. Duarte-Acero,* 296 F.3d 1277, 1283 (11th Cir. 2002); *Hain v. Gibson,* 287 F.3d 1224, 1243 (10th Cir. 2002); *United States v. Warden, FMC Rochester,* 286 F.3d 1059, 1063 (8th Cir. 2002);

Dutton v. Warden, FCI Estill, 2002 WL 255520, at *1 (4th Cir. 2002); *Lal v. Roe,* 2002 WL 31356505, at *1 (9th Cir. 2002); *Beazley v. Johnson,* 242 F.3d 248, 267 (5th Cir. 2001); *Kenan v. U.S.P. Lompac,* 2001 WL 1003213, at *1 n.1 (9th Cir. 2001); *Igartua De La Rosa v. United States,* 32 F.3d 8, 10 n.1 (1st Cir. 1994); *see also Beshli v. Dept. of Homeland Security,* 2003 WL 21693668, at *10 (E.D. Pa. July 22, 2003); *Macharia v. United States,* 238 F. Supp. 2d 13, 29-30 (D.D.C. July 30, 2002); *Reaves v. Warden, U.S.P.,* 2002 WL 535398, at *9 (M.D. Pa. Mar. 22, 2002); *Jama v. United States Immigration and Naturalization Service,* 22 F. Supp. 2d 353, 364–65 (D.N.J. 1998).

126. *See Kim Ho Ma v. Ashcroft,* 257 F.3d 1095, 1114 (9th Cir. 2001) (recognizing that an international prohibition exists against "prolonged and arbitrary detention" and citing, among other sources to ICCPR, Art. 9); *Martinez v. City of Los Angeles,* 141 F.3d 1373, 1383–84 (9th Cir. 1998) (same); *United States v. Romano,* 706 F.2d 370, 375 n.1 (2d Cir. 1983) (citing to ICCPR for articulation of rights of a person charged with a criminal offense); *Filartiga v. Peña-Irala,* 630 F.2d 876, 883–84 (2d Cir. 1980) (citing ICCPR as one example that international law universally rejects torture).

127. In ratifying the ICCPR, the U.S. Senate declared that "The United States. . .accepts the competence of the Human Rights Committee to receive and consider communications under Article 41 in which a State Party claims that another State Party is not fulfilling its obligations under the Covenant." *See supra* note 119.

128. *See* Optional Protocol to the International Covenant on Civil and Political Rights, 21 U.N. GAOR Supp. (No. 16) at 59, U.N. Doc. A/6316 (1966), 999 U.N.T.S. 302.

129. 1144 U.N.T.S. 123, *reprinted in* 9 I.L.M. 101 (1969).

130. *See Manrique v. Peru,* Report No. 56/98, Inter-Am. C.H.R., OEA/Ser.L/V/II.95 Doc. 7 rev. at 983 (1998).

131. *See, e.g., Request for Advisory Opinion OC-16, by the State of Mexico, of December 10, 1997,* OEA/Ser.L/V/III.39, Doc. 5, at para. 23(d) (1998); *Manrique v. Peru,* Report No. 56/98, Inter-Am. C.H. R., OEA/Ser.L/V/II.95 Doc. 7 rev. at 983, at paras. 87–88 (1998); *Congo v. Ecuador,* Report No. 63/99, Inter-Am. C.H.R., OEQ/Ser.L/V/II.95 Doc. 7 rev. at 475, at paras. 55–59 (1998); *Lucio Parada Cea, et al. v. El Salvador,* Report No. 1/99, Inter-Am. C.H.R., OEA/Ser.L/V/II.95 Doc. 7 rev. at 531, at para. 70 (1998).

132. *Villagran Morales et al. Case (the "Street Children" Case), Judgment of November 19, 1999,* Inter-Am. Ct. H.R. (Ser. C) No. 63, at para. 74 (1999).

133. *Loayza-Tamayo Case, Judgment of September 17, 1997,* Inter-Am. Ct. H.R. (Ser. C) No. 33, at para. 57 (1997).

134. The U.S. is not a signatory to the Inter-American Convention To Prevent and Punish Torture, O.A.S. Treaty Series No. 67. Article 2 of this Convention defines torture as "any act intentionally performed whereby physical or mental pain or suffering is inflicted on a person for purposes of criminal investigation, as a means of intimidation, as personal punishment, as a preventive measure, as a penalty, or for any other purpose. Torture shall also be understood to be the use of methods upon a person intended to obliterate the personality of the victim or to diminish his physical or mental capacities, even if they do not cause physical pain or mental anguish."

135. *See, e.g., Cantoral Benavides Case, Judgment of August 18, 2000,* Inter-Am. Ct. H.R. (Ser. C) No. 69, at paras. 43(a), 63(e)–(k), 104, 106 (2000); *Loayza-Tamayo Case, Judgment of September 17, 1997,* Inter-Am. Ct. H.R. (Ser. C) No. 33, at para. 58 (1997); *Castillo-Paez Case, Judgment of November 3, 1997,* Inter-Am. Ct. H.R. (Ser. C) No. 34, at para. 66 (1997); *Suarez-Rosero Case, Judgment of November 12, 1997,* Inter-Am. Ct. H.R. (Ser. C) No. 35, at para. 91 (1997).

136. *Cantoral Benavides Case, Judgment of August 18, 2000,* Inter-Am. Ct. H.R. (Ser. C) No. 69, at para. 100.

137. *See Fairen-Garbi and Solis Corrales Case, Judgment of March 15, 1989,* Inter-Am. Ct. H.R. (Ser. C) No. 6, at para 149 (1989); *Godinez-Cruz Case, Judgment of January 20, 1989,* Inter-Am. Ct. H.R. (Ser. C) No. 5, at para. 164 (1989); *Velazquez-Rodriguez Case, Judgment of July 29, 1988,* Inter-Am. Ct. H.R. (Ser. C) No. 4, at para. 156 (1988). In the *Suarez-Rosero* case, the Inter-American Court explained that incommunicado detention is "an exceptional measure" which can cause the detainee to suffer extreme psychological and moral injury. "[I]solation from the outside world produces moral and

psychological suffering in any person, places him in a particularly vulnerable position, and increases the risk of aggression and arbitrary acts in prisons." *Suarez-Rosero Case, Judgment of November 12, 1997,* Inter-Am. Ct. H.R. (Ser. C) No. 35, at para. 90 (1997).

138. *See Castillo-Petruzzi Case, Judgment of May 30, 1999,* Inter-Am. Ct. H.R. (Ser. C) No. 52, at para. 197 (1999).

139. *Coard, et al. v. United States,* Inter-Am. C.H.R. Report No. 109/99 (Sept. 29, 1999) ("*Coard*"). The *Coard* petitioners alleged that U.S. forces arrested them during the period in which it consolidated control over Grenada; that they were held incommunicado for many days; and that months passed before they were taken to a magistrate, or allowed to consult with counsel. "During this period petitioners were threatened, interrogated, beaten, deprived of sleep and food and constantly harassed." *Coard,* at para. 17. The petitioners alleged that their whereabouts were kept secret, and that requests by lawyers and others to meet with them were rejected. They also alleged that U.S. forces subjected them to threats and physical abuse—including threatening to hand the detainees over to Caribbean authorities and allowing Caribbean authorities to "soften" the detainees. *Coard,* at paras. 18–19.

140. *See supra* note 129, Art. 33.

141. *Id.,* Art. 41. The Commission has also been willing to apply other relevant legal standards, including the Geneva Conventions.

142. *Id.,* Arts. 44 and 46. The Inter-American Court also has competence with respect to matters relating to the fulfillment of the commitments made by the States Parties to the American Convention. *Id.,* Art. 33. Only States Parties and the Commission have the right to submit a case to the Inter-American Court, however, and only after the case has been considered by the Inter-American Commission. *Id.,* Art. 61.

143. A federal habeas corpus petition on behalf of named detainees at Guantánamo which was filed in parallel was dismissed for lack of jurisdiction because "the military base at Guantánamo Bay, Cuba is outside the sovereign territory of the United States." *Rasul v. Bush,* 215 F. Supp. 2d 55, 72 (D.D.C. 2002), *cert. granted,* 2003 WL 22070599 (U.S. Nov. 10, 2003).

144. *See* Rules of Procedure of the Inter-American Commission on Human Rights, Art. 25(1): "In serious and urgent cases, and whenever necessary according to the information available, the Commission may, on its own initiative or at the request of a party, request that the State concerned adopt precautionary measures to prevent irreparable harm to persons.").

145. *Ref. Detainees in Guantánamo Bay, Cuba Request for Precautionary Measures,* Inter-Am. C.H. R., Mar. 13, 2002, *reprinted in* 41 I.L.M. 532, 532. The Commission has ruled that OAS member states are subject to an international legal obligation to comply with a request for precautionary measures. *See Fifth Report on the Situation of Human Rights in Guatemala,* Inter-Am. C.H.R. OEA/Ser.L/V/II.111, Doc. 21 rev. (2001), at paras. 71–72 (2001); *Case 12.243,* Inter-Am. C.H.R. OEA/Ser.L/V/II.111, Doc. 21 rev. 1255 (2000), at para.–117.

146. 41 I.L.M. at 533.

147. *Id.*

148. *Id.,* at 534. The Inter-American Commission invited the U.S. to provide information concerning compliance with these precautionary measures. In response, the United States argued that: (i) the Commission did not have jurisdiction to apply international humanitarian law, particularly the Geneva Conventions, as well as customary international humanitarian law; (ii) the Commission lacks authority to request precautionary measures with respect to States which are not party to the American Convention; and (iii) in any event, precautionary measures are neither necessary nor appropriate because the detainees are not entitled to prisoner of war status, do not meet Geneva Convention criteria for lawful combatants and are, instead, enemy combatants. *See Response of the United States To Request For Precautionary Measures—Detainees in Guantánamo Bay, Cuba, reprinted in* 41 I.L.M. 1015, 1028–1030 (2002). The U.S. stated, however, that it "is providing the detainees with protections consistent with international humanitarian law." *Id.* at 1031. The U.S. also asserted that it had no obligation to convene a tribunal to determine the detainees' status, and that the detainees had no right to counsel or to have access to courts. *Id.* at 1034. The U.S. Response did not address interrogation techniques. However, on December 2, 2003, the Pentagon announced that U.S. citizen and Taliban soldier Yaser Esam Hamdi would be given access to a lawyer, "as a matter of discretion and military policy," but that the decision "should not be

treated as a precedent" and was "subject to appropriate security restrictions." *See* Associated Press Newswires, *Pentagon OKs Lawyer For Terror Suspect,* Dec. 3, 2003; Jerry Markon and Dan Eggen, *U.S. Allows Lawyer For Citizen Held as "Enemy Combatant"*, WASH. POST, Dec. 3, 2003, at A01.

149. *Ref. Detainees in Guantánamo Bay, Cuba Request for Precautionary Measures,* Inter-Am C.H.R., July 23, 2003, at 5.

150. In order for a state's practice to be recognized as customary international law, it must fulfill two conditions:

> Not only must the acts concerned amount to a settled practice, but they must also be such, or be carried out in such a way, as to be evidence of a belief that this practice is rendered obligatory by the existence of a rule of law requiring it. The need for such a belief, *i.e.,* the existence of a subjective element, is implicit in the very notion of the *opinion juris sive necessitas.* The States concerned must therefore feel that they are conforming to what amounts to a legal obligation.

North Sea Continental Shelf (*F.R.G. v. Den.*), 1969 I.C.J. 3, 44. *See also* Military and Paramilitary Activities (*Nicar v. U.S.*), 1986 I.C.J. 14, 14; R. JENNINGS & A. WATTS, OPPENHEIM'S INTERNATIONAL LAW, (9th ed. 1996); The Paquete Habana, 175 U.S. 677, 700 (1900) (cited with approval in *First Nat'l City Bank v. Banco Para El Comercio Exterior de Cuba,* 462 U.S. 611, 623 (1983)); *U.S. v. Yousef,* 327 F.3d 56, 92 (2d Cir. 2002).

151. GA Res. 3452 (XXX), U.N. GAOR, Supp. No. 34 at 91 (hereinafter the "Torture Resolution").

152. *See Report by the Special Rapporteur,* U.N. Economic and Social Council, E/CN.4/1986/15, at para. 3. The report details state practice and *opinio juris* with respect to national legislation prohibiting torture. *See also* HERMAN J. BURGERS & HANS SANELIUS, THE UNITED NATIONS CONVENTION AGAINST TORTURE AND OTHER CRUEL, INHUMAN OR DEGRADING TREATMENT OR PUNISHMENT (Martinus Nijhoff Publishers/Kluwer Academic Publishers 1988), at 1–12. The widespread ratification of regional human rights instruments such as the European Convention for the Protection of Human Rights and Fundamental Freedoms, the American Convention on Human Rights and the African Charter on Human and Peoples' Rights further reinforce the argument that torture is prohibited by customary international law.

153. *Report by the Special Rapporteur, id.,* at paras. 72, 82.

154. *See* RESTATEMENT (THIRD) OF FOREIGN RELATIONS LAW § 702 (1986). *See also Abebe-Jira v. Negewo,* 72 F.3d 844, 847 (11th Cir. 1996); *In re Estate of Ferdinand Marcos, Human Rights Litigation,* 25 F.3d 1467, 1475 (9th Cir. 1994); *Siderman de Blake v. Republic of Argentina,* 965 F.2d 699, 716 (9th Cir. 1992); *Cornejo-Barreto v. Seifert,* 218 F.3d 1004, 1006 (9th Cir. 2000); *Presbyterian Church of Sudan v. Talisman Energy, Inc.,* 244 F. Supp. 2d 289 (S.D.N.Y. 2003); *Mehinovic v. Vuckovic,* 198 Supp. 2d 1322 (N.D. Ga. 2002); *Doe v. Islamic Salvation Front,* 993 F. Supp. 3, 7 (D.D.C. 1998); *Doe v. Unocal,* 963 F. Supp. 880, 890 (C.D. Cal. 1997).

155. Vienna Convention on the Law of Treaties, 1969, Art. 53, 1155 U.N.T.S. 331.

156. *See, e.g.,* Universal Declaration of Human Rights, G.A. Res. 217, U.N. GAOR, 3d Sess., Art. 5, U.N. Doc. A/810 (1948) ("no one shall be subjected to torture or to cruel, inhuman or degrading treatment or punishment"); Declaration on the Protection of All Persons from Being Subjected to Torture and Other Cruel, Inhuman or Degrading Treatment or Punishment, G.A. Res. 3452, 30 U.N. GAOR, Supp. No. 34, U.N. Doc. A/10034 (1976), at Art. 3 ("Exceptional circumstances such as a state of war or a threat of war, internal political stability or any other public emergency may not be invoked as a justification of torture or other cruel, inhuman or degrading treatment or punishment."); ICCPR, *supra* note 119, at Art. 7 ("no one shall be subjected to torture or to cruel, inhuman or degrading treatment or punishment"); Additional Protocol I, *supra* note 21, at Art. 75; Protocol Additional to the Geneva Conventions of 12 August 1949, and Relating to the Protection of Victims of Non-International Armed Conflicts ("Additional Protocol II"), *reprinted in*16 I.L.M. 1442 (1977), at Art. 4; European Convention for the Protection of Human Rights and Fundamental Freedoms, 213 U.N.T.S. 221 (1950), at Art. 3 (declaring that torture and inhuman or degrading treatment or punishment is prohibited); American Convention, *supra* note 129, at Art. 5 (providing that every person retain the right to be free from torture and ill-treatment); African Charter on Human and Peoples' Rights, *reprinted in* 21 I.L.M. 58 (1981), at Art. 5 (prohibiting torture and ill-treatment).

157. Committee Against Torture, *Consideration of Reports Submitted by States Parties Under Article 19 of the Convention,* United States of America, U.N. Doc. CAT/C/28/Add.5 (2000) ("U.S. Report Under CAT"), at para. 6.
158. 28 U.S.C. § 1350.
159. *Id.*
160. 22 U.S.C. § 2152.
161. *See* Part I of this Report; U.S. Report Under CAT, at paras. 50, 301–348.
162. *See Abebe-Jira v. Negero,* 72 F.3d 844 (11th Cir. 1996), *cert. denied,* 519 U.S. 830 (1996); *Najarro de Sanchez v. Banco Central de Nicaragua,* 770 F.2d 1385 (5th Cir. 1985); *Xuncax v. Gramajo,* 886 F. Supp. 162 (D. Mass. 1995); *Paul v. Avril,* 901 F. Supp. 330 (S.D. Fla 1994).
163. *See* U.S. Dept. of State, Bureau of Democracy, Human Rights and Labor, *Country Reports on Human Rights Practices—2002* (for Brazil, Burma, China, Egypt, Israel and the occupied territories, Jordan, Kenya, Democratic People's Republic of Korea, Laos, Pakistan, Saudi Arabia, Togo, Turkey and Zimbabwe) (Mar. 31, 2003).
164. *Id.* (for Cameroon, Mongolia, Nigeria and Rwanda).
165. *See, e.g., Filartiga v. Peña-Irala,* 639 F.2d 876 (2d Cir. 1980) (allowing a torture claim to be prosecuted under the Alien Tort Claims Act, 28 U.S.C. § 1350); *see also Forti v. Suarez-Mason,* 672 F. Supp. 1531, 1541-43 (N.D. Cal. 1987) (recognizing torture and arbitrary detention as violations of customary international law, but finding that universal consensus regarding right to be free from cruel, inhuman and degrading treatment had not yet been established).
166. 213 U.N.T.S. 221.
167. *The Republic of Ireland v. The United Kingdom,* (1979–80) 2 E.H.R.R. 25.
168. *Id.*, at 30–31.
169. *Id.*, at 36.
170. *Id.*, at 25.
171. *Id.*, at 59.
172. *Id.*, at 25.
173. *Id.*, at 25.
174. *Id.*, at 75–76.
175. *Id.*, at 26.
176. *Id.*, at 26.
177. *Id.*, at 26.
178. *Id.*
179. *Id.*,, at 79–80. In separate annexed opinions, Judges Zekia, O'Donoghue and Evrigenis disagreed with the majority's ruling that the five practices did not amount to torture.

In the years since the *Republic of Ireland* decision, neither time nor the ever-expanding threat of terrorism has diminished the ECHR's commitment to maintaining an absolute prohibition against torture and inhuman or degrading treatment. In *Chahal v. United Kingdom,* Case No. 70/1995/576/662 (Nov. 15, 1996), for example, the ECHR rejected Great Britain's argument that national security considerations justified the deportation of an Indian citizen to India on grounds that he was active in extremist Sikh organizations in England and was suspected of planning terrorist and other violent acts in the country. Chahal argued that, if deported, he would be tortured in India. In ruling that Chahal's deportation by the United Kingdom would constitute a violation of Article 3 of the Convention, the ECHR stated:

> Article 3 enshrines one of the most fundamental values of democratic society. . . . The Court is well aware of the immense difficulties faced by States in modern times in protecting their communities from terrorist violence. However, even in these circumstances, the Convention prohibits in absolute terms torture or inhuman or degrading treatment or punishment, irrespective of the victim's conduct. Unlike most of the substantive clauses of the Convention and of Protocols Nos. 1 and 4, Article 3 makes no provision for exceptions and no derogation from it is permissible under Article 15 even in the event of a public emergency threatening the life of the nation.

Id., at 79. *See also Aksoy v. Turkey,* Case No. 100/1995/606/694 (Dec. 15, 1996), para. 62 (ruling that Turkish security forces' treatment of a detainee suspected of membership and activity on behalf of the PKK, a Kurdish militant organization operating against the Turkish government, constituted torture).

180. *Judgment Concerning The Legality Of The General Security Service's Interrogation Methods,* 38 I.L.M. 1471 (Sept. 9, 1999) (the "GSS Interrogation Methods Decision").

181. *Id.,* at 1472.

182. Excerpts printed in 23 Isr. L. Rev. 146 (1989).

183. *Id.,* at 184.

184. *Id.*

185. *Id.,* at 185.

186. *Id.,* at 186.

187. *GSS Interrogation Methods Decision,* 38 I.L.M. at 1477.

188. *Id.,* at 1474–76. The Israeli Government argued that such interrogation methods did not need to be outlawed because, before resorting to physical pressure against detainees, GSS interrogators are instructed to "probe the severity of the danger that the interrogation is intending to prevent; consider the urgency of uncovering the information presumably possessed by the suspect in question; and seek an alternative means of preventing the danger." *Id.,* at 1475. The Israeli Government also argued that directives respecting interrogation provide that in cases where shaking—considered the harshest interrogation method of those examined in the *GSS Interrogation Methods Decision*—is to be used, "the investigator must first provide an evaluation of the suspect's health and ensure that no harm comes to him." *Id.,* at 1475.

189. *Id.,* at 1480–81.

190. *Id.,* at 1482.

191. *Id.*

192. *Id.,* at 1482–84.

193. *Id.,* at 1483.

194. *Id.,* at 1485.

195. *Id.*

196. *Id.,* at 1486.

197. *Id.,* at 1487.

198. *Id.,* at 1486.

199. *Id.,* at 1481.

200. *See* 23 Isr. L. Rev., at 174.

201. CAT, Art. 2.

202. *GSS Interrogation Methods Decision,* 38 I.L.M. at 1481 (internal citations omitted).

203. *Id.,* at 1488.

THE IMPERIAL PRESIDENCY AND THE CONSEQUENCES OF 9/11

THE IMPERIAL PRESIDENCY AND THE CONSEQUENCES OF 9/11

Lawyers React to the Global War on Terrorism

VOLUME 2

Edited by James R. Silkenat and Mark R. Shulman

Foreword by Barry Kamins, Bettina B. Plevan,
E. Leo Milonas, and Evan A. Davis

PRAEGER SECURITY INTERNATIONAL
Westport, Connecticut · London

Library of Congress Cataloging-in-Publication Data

The imperial presidency and the consequences of 9/11 : lawyers react to the global war on terrorism / edited by James R. Silkenat and Mark R. Shulman.
v. cm.
Includes bibliographical references and index.
ISBN 0–275–99440–6 (set : alk. paper) — ISBN 0–275–99441–4 (vol 1 : alk. paper) — ISBN 0–275–99442–2 (vol 2 : alk. paper)
1. War and emergency powers—United States. 2. Terrorists—Legal status, laws, etc.—United States. 3. Prisoners of war—Legal status, laws, etc.—United States. 4. Detention of persons—Cuba—Guantánamo Bay Naval Base. 5. Trials (Genocide)—Iraq. 6. War on Terrorism, 2001– 7. Executive power—United States I. Silkenat, James R. II. Shulman, Mark R.
KF5060.I47 2007
342.73'062—dc22 2006100488

British Library Cataloguing in Publication Data is available.

Library of Congress Catalog Card Number: 2006100488
ISBN-10: 0–275–99440–6 (set code) ISBN-13: 978–0–275–99440-2 (set code)
0–275–99441–4 (Vol. 1) 978–0–275–99441-9 (Vol. 1)
0–275–99442–2 (Vol. 2) 978–0–275–99442-6 (Vol. 2)

First published in 2007

Praeger Security International, 88 Post Road West, Westport, CT 06881
An imprint of Greenwood Publishing Group, Inc.
www.praeger.com

Printed in the United States of America

The paper used in this book complies with the Permanent Paper Standard issued by the National Information Standards Organization (Z39.48–1984).

10 9 8 7 6 5 4 3 2 1

Contents

About the Editors and Contributors

EDITORS

JAMES R. SILKENAT is a partner in the firm of Arent Fox PLLC in New York City. He is a former Chair of the 16,000-member ABA Section of International Law and helps coordinate Arent Fox's international practice in New York, where he specializes in international finance, securities, and corporate law. He is also a former Chair of the ABA's Section Officers Conference and a member of the Executive Committee of the ABA Board of Governors. He has served for 15 years as a member of the American Bar Association House of Delegate and Chairs New York's Delegation in the ABA House of Delegates.

From 1980 to 1986, Mr. Silkenat was Legal Counsel for the International Finance Corporation, the private-sector-oriented affiliate of the World Bank in Washington, D.C., where he concentrated on privatization issues (including projects in China, Pakistan, Indonesia, Zimbabwe, and other countries). He has also handled significant privatization efforts in Australia, Peru, and Turkey. He is also the founder and former Chair of the ABA's Privatization Committee.

Mr. Silkenat received his J.D. from the University of Chicago Law School, where he was Editor of the *University of Chicago Law Review*. He also received an L.L.M. in International Law from New York University School of Law.

Mr. Silkenat was formerly Chair of the ABA Committee on the People's Republic of China and was the founder of the *China Law Reporter*. He has led Delegations to China for both the ABA and the Association of the Bar of the City of New York, and to the Common Market and Mexico for the ABA. He has also served as a Fellow of the National Endowment for the Humanities and as a Fellow in the U.S. State Department Scholar/Diplomat Program.

Mr. Silkenat is the Editor of *The Moscow Conference on Law and Bilateral Economic Relations, The Law of International Insolvencies and Debt Restructurings, The ABA Guide to Foreign Law Firms* (1988, 1993, 1999, and 2004 Editions), and *The ABA Guide to International Business Negotiations* (1994 and 2002 Editions). He is also the author of more than 100 articles on international law, finance, and public policy, and he has published articles in the *Harvard Law Review, Business Week,* the *New York Times,* and the *Stanford Law Review,* among other publications. He also served as Adjunct Professor of Law at Georgetown University Law Center, where he taught a graduate seminar on international project financing.

Mr. Silkenat also previously served as Chair of both The Lawyers Committee for Human Rights (now, Human Rights First) and The Council of New York Law Associates (now, The Lawyers Alliance for New York). He is a Life Fellow for the American Bar Foundation, has served as Chair of the Fellows of the American Bar Foundation, and is a member of the Council on Foreign Relations. Mr. Silkenat is also a former Chair of the International Human Rights Committee of the Association of the Bar of the City of New York, the City Bar's Task Force on International Legal Services, and the City Bar's Council on International Affairs.

Mr. Silkenat has particular expertise in the negotiation and drafting of international investment funds and international joint-venture agreements, Eurodollar and other international loan agreements, and related documentation, and he has worked on international mergers and acquisitions (including privatizations and restructurings) in both developing and developed countries.

MARK R. SHULMAN is Assistant Dean for Graduate Programs and International Affiliations and an Adjunct Professor of Law at Pace Law School. Until 2003, he practiced corporate law at the international firm of Debevoise & Plimpton.

Immediately prior to joining Pace, Mr. Shulman directed the Worldwide Security Program at the EastWest Institute. He has previously taught in the History Department at Yale University, at Columbia University's School of International and Public Affairs and at Columbia Law School, as well as the U.S. Air War College.

Mr. Shulman has published widely in the fields of history, law, and international affairs. Along with Sir Michael Howard and Professor George Andreopoulos, he edited *The Laws of War: Constraints on Warfare in the Western World.* He wrote *Navalism and the Emergence of American Sea Power, 1882–1893,* as well as numerous articles and book chapters. Mr. Shulman received his B.A. from Yale, a Masters degree from Oxford, and a Ph.D. in history from the University of California at Berkeley. He received his J.D. from Columbia where he served as Editor-in-Chief of the *Journal of Transnational Law,* on the board of which he continues to sit. He has also enjoyed Postdoctoral Fellowships at Yale and Georgetown and is a Visiting Scholar at Yale's International Security Program. He has also been a Visiting Research Scholar at the Naval War College.

He is currently Chair of the New York City Bar's International Human Rights Committee and a member of the City Bar's Council on International Affairs.

CONTRIBUTORS

JAMES J. BENJAMIN, JR. is a partner at Akin Gump Strauss Hauer & Feld LLP. Before joining Akin Gump, he served for more than five years as a federal prosecutor in the U.S. Attorney's Office for the Southern District of New York and he also served as a law clerk at the U.S. Supreme Court for Justices Lewis F. Powell Jr. and John Paul Stevens. He has published articles extensively in the *New York Law Journal,* his most recent article being titled "Rule 10b5-1 and Criminal Insider Trading Cases" (New York Law Journal, July 2004).

JOSEPH G. DAVIS is a partner in the Litigation Department of Willkie Farr & Gallagher LLP in Washington, D.C. Mr. Davis specializes in complex litigation and corporate compliance matters. Mr. Davis represents corporations and individuals in proceedings before federal and state courts and other tribunals. He is a graduate of Amherst College and the University of California at Berkeley School of Law (Boalt Hall).

NICOLE DELLER is a senior program officer at the World Federalist Movement-Institute for Global Policy and the Chair of the International Security Affairs Committee of the New York City Bar Association. Before joining WFM, Ms. Deller was a research associate and consultant for the Lawyers' Committee on Nuclear Policy and the Institute for Energy and Environmental Research.

MILES P. FISCHER is a lawyer in private practice in New York City. He is currently on the Board of Director-Advisors at the National Institute of Military Justice. He has also served as Chair on the Military Affairs and Justice Committee of the New York City Bar.

MARTIN S. FLAHERTY is Leitner Family Chair in International Human Rights and Professor of Law and Co-Director of the Joseph P. Crowley Program in International Human Rights at Fordham Law School in New York. He is a former Chair of the Committee on International Human Rights of the New York City Bar. He has published widely on constitutional law, foreign affairs, and international human rights in such journals as the *Columbia Law Review,* the *Yale Law Journal,* and the *University of Chicago Law Review.*

THOMAS H. MORELAND is a partner at Kramer Levin Naftalis and & Franklin LLP. He handles a wide variety of complex civil litigation matters in international and domestic arbitration. He has served as Vice President and Chair of the Executive Committee of the New York City Bar. He was also a founding member and currently serves as the Chairman of the Board of Volunteers of Legal Service, Inc., which facilitates pro bono service by lawyers in New York City.

ALAN R. ROTHSTEIN serves as General Counsel of the New York City Bar, where he coordinates the extensive law reform and public policy work of this 22,000-member Association. Prior to his 20 years with the Association, Rothstein was the Associate Director of Citizens Union and also practiced with the firm of Weil, Gotshal & Manges. Prior to earning his J.D. from New York University, Mr. Rothstein worked as an Economist in the environmental consulting field and for the New York City Economic Development Administration. Mr. Rothstein currently serves on the Board of Directors for Volunteers of Legal Service, Inc.

MARGARET L. SATTERTHWAITE is an Assistant Professor of Clinical Law and Faculty Director of the Center for Human Rights and Global Justice at New York University School of Law. She has written extensively in the field of international human rights law, and her most recent publications include "Fate and Whereabouts Unknown: Detainees in the 'War on Terror'" (*Center for Human Rights and Global Justice,* 2005) and "Crossing Borders, Claiming Rights: Using Human Rights Law to Empower Women Migrant Workers" (*Yale Human Rights & Development Law Journal,* 2005).

STEPHEN J. SHAPIRO is a lawyer in private practice in New York City. He is a past Chair of the Committee on Military Affairs and Justice of the New York City Bar.

DANIEL SILVERMAN serves as counsel for the Labor and Employment Group at Skadden Arps, Slate, Meagher & Flom LLP. Prior to joining Skadden, he had a distinguished career at the National Labor Relations Board where he acted in various capacities from trial attorney to the Regional Director at the New York City office. He is the Chairman of the Committee on Labor and Employment Law of the New York City Bar. Mr. Silverman also is as an Adjunct Professor at Cardozo Law School.

CLAUDIA SLOVINSKY has been an immigration and nationality attorney for over 20 years and heads her own law firm in New York City. She serves as the Chair of the Immigration and Nationality Committee of the New York City Bar and is a frequent lecturer on immigration issues both to the immigration bar and lay audiences. She also serves on the Board of the American Friends Service Committee Immigrant Rights Program, and is a member of the American Immigration Lawyers Association and the National Immigration Project of the National Lawyers Guild.

MARIANN SULLIVAN is the Deputy Chief Court Attorney for the New York State Appellate Division, First Department. She is the former Chair of the Committee on Legal Issues Pertaining to Animals of the New York City Bar and a current member of that Committee, as well as of the Special Committee on Animals and the Law of the New York State Bar Association. She co-authored "Foxes in the Henhouse: Animals, Agribusiness and the Law" (*Animal Rights: Current Debates and New Directions,* 2004).

CHAPTER 12

Dangerous Doctrine: The Attorney General's Unfounded Claim of Unlimited Authority to Arrest and Deport Aliens in Secret

PREFACE BY CLAUDIA SLOVINSKY

A major initiative of the Bush Administration, in the aftermath of the September 11 attacks, was the roundup of more than a thousand Muslim immigrants for routine visa violations. Many of these immigrants were detained for long periods of time, and actions were taken with regard to these immigrants in entirely secret proceedings. Attorney General John Ashcroft asserted the right to maintain secrecy of this entire class of proceedings and to withhold information that a particular alien is being detained.

The Association's Committees on Communications and Media Law and Immigration and Nationality Law prepared a joint report that examined the legal basis for the Attorney General's claim of authority and found that it plainly contradicts the Constitutional right of public access, "a right to attend, observe and report on government proceedings that is protected by the First Amendment." The imposed secrecy also circumvented statutory procedures, bypassing checks and balances that had been written into law, and increased the likelihood of erroneous removals.

> "Domestically, the danger is that in pursuit of security, we end up sacrificing crucial liberties, thereby weakening our common security, not strengthening it—and thereby corroding the vessel of democratic government from within."
>
> —UN Secretary-General Kofi Annan[1]

INTRODUCTION*

The September 11, 2001 attacks on the World Trade Center and the Pentagon triggered seismic changes in the American legal landscape, many driven by the Attorney General's effort to identify and deter future terrorist attacks. All nineteen individuals responsible for the attacks on 9/11 were foreigners. The United States Department of Justice ("DOJ") moved swiftly to question thousands of immigrants, and in the process arrested and detained hundreds of Muslims for routine visa violations. In a brazen claim of executive branch power, the Attorney General then asserted the authority to deport or remove immigrants completely in secret, denying

any right of the public to know what was being done and any power of the court to limit his exercise of authority.

The Attorney General claimed the power to designate any particular alien as being of "special interest," and thereby keep both the fact of the detention and the existence of any formal deportation or removal proceeding completely hidden from the public. While the extraordinary circumstances of 9/11 could well justify a need for extraordinary confidentiality in the investigation of suspected terrorists, the cloak of secrecy was invoked routinely for virtually every Muslim immigrant rounded-up for questioning in the aftermath of the events of 9/11. Even more alarming was the Attorney General's claim that he possessed the unilateral right to impose such secrecy over deportation hearings for any reason, or no reason at all.[2]

The Attorney General's claim of such sweeping executive branch power to act in secret is cause for great concern and plainly contradicts the constitutional right of public access—a right to attend, observe and report on government proceedings that is protected by the First Amendment. In the Attorney General's view, this First Amendment right does not extend to the executive branch at all, but in the *Pentagon Papers* case more than three decades ago, Justice Black emphasized that the First Amendment applies equally to the Executive, Legislative and Judicial branches: "The Bill of Rights changed the original Constitution into a new charter under which *no branch of government* could abridge the people's freedom of the press, speech, religion or assembly."[3] The Attorney General's approach fundamentally misconstrued the constitutional right of access, which is an integral and established element of the First Amendment. The Attorney General's position was properly rejected by the United States Courts of Appeals for both the Third and the Sixth Circuits.[4]

The secrecy imposed on deportation and removal proceedings raises additional issues for immigrants and immigration law. The unilateral actions taken by DOJ circumvent statutory procedures that Congress created specifically to remove suspected terrorists from the United States, bypassing checks and balances written into the law. Completely secret deportation hearings for immigrants from certain countries effectively deprive immigrants of access to counsel and due process of law in many cases, and increase the likelihood of erroneous removals. None of this can be monitored by the public or the press to protect against abuse.

Given the significant number of "special interest" immigrants that were held in federal detention facilities in New York,[5] and the presence in this city of the nation's leading news organizations, the Association of the Bar of the City of New York has a particular interest in both the treatment of the "special interest" immigrants and in safeguarding the right of the public and the press to attend deportation proceedings. Closing immigration hearings on a blanket basis, in the manner directed by the Attorney General, threatens to weaken the constitutional protection of access to essential government information, engender abuse, frighten the immigrant community, and ultimately "corrod[e] the vessel of democracy from within."

I. SECRET PROCEEDINGS: THE ATTORNEY GENERAL'S RESPONSE TO 9/11

The adverse implications for open government are illuminated by a review of steps taken by the Attorney General and the Department of Justice in September 2001, first in rounding up more than a thousand Muslim immigrants and then by attempting to change the legal rules that would apply to them.

A. The Round-up of Hundreds of Muslims

Soon after the attacks on the World Trade Center and the Pentagon, the FBI questioned and detained an estimated 1,200 individuals, mostly Muslim men.[6] Detentions were justified by

the initiation of immigration proceedings whenever any possible violation existed. Unlike typical immigration detentions, however, aliens arrested by the FBI after 9/11 were detained in secret—no information on an arrest was disclosed—and brought before immigration judges in secret hearings, held completely beyond the view of the public and the press.[7] Even the *existence* of the proceedings was withheld from public knowledge.

Many immigrants were held for weeks or months before being deported, having been designated by the Attorney General as "special interest" cases, a newly invented term without any basis in law; none was ever accused of any crime related to the 9/11 attacks.[8] Anyone with a possible connection to terrorism instead was held as a material witness or threatened with criminal prosecution. The hundreds of "special interest" deportations conducted in secret involved immigrants with no connection or information at all, who were unlucky enough to have been questioned by the FBI at a time when they had some visa problem. According to a *Los Angeles Times* report, administration officials acknowledged having used the immigration laws aggressively, "and they are proud of it."[9]

B. The Unilateral Imposition of Complete Secrecy

The Department of Justice, from the outset, sought to maintain complete control over all information relating to its terrorism investigation, and this included clamping a lid of secrecy around everything related to the immigrants rounded up by the Department. Guidelines previously issued by the Attorney General have long mandated that deportation hearings conducted by the Immigration and Naturalization Service ("INS") are to be open to the public, in almost all cases.[10] These guidelines reflect the long-standing practice of conducting such proceedings in public.[11] The guidelines do permit any given hearing to be closed "in the public interest," but the Department of Justice did not want to proceed on a case-by-case basis in closing the deportation hearings of aliens rounded up after 9/11. Therefore, on September 21, 2001, Chief Immigration Judge Michael Creppy of the Executive Office for Immigration Review[12] issued a directive, popularly known as "the Creppy Memo," ordering immigration judges to follow new procedures whenever the Attorney General of the United States deemed an immigrant to be "of special interest."[13]

Those new procedures, effective immediately, required hearings in all "special interest" cases to be closed completely—even to family members—and even the existence of the proceeding kept secret. There could be no public docket or release of any information, not even to confirm or deny the existence of a proceeding.[14]

The Creppy Memo did not explain what standard the Attorney General would use in designating certain cases as "special interest" cases. It was later revealed, however, that "special interest" cases invariably involved persons who were either Muslim or Arab from a selected set of countries, most of which were Middle Eastern.[15] "Special interest" immigrants were arrested and tried in secret, while the Government refused to reveal their names or whereabouts, and their family and friends were often unable to locate them. Even when the immigrants had attorneys, the Government in many cases refused to tell the attorneys their clients' whereabouts.[16] Lawyers reported that the "special interest" immigrants were being "denied legal counsel, held indefinitely without charges, suddenly moved to new locations, or kept in prison even after a judge orders release."[17]

In an apparently typical case, Malek Zeidan, a Syrian who worked as an ice cream truck driver, was arrested on February 1, 2002.[18] He had entered the United States more than a decade ago on a visa, and had stayed well beyond his period of admission. INS came across him accidentally in the course of investigating another case, and held him in detention for about forty (40) days before releasing him.[19] Ultimately, he was freed on bail, but his removal hearing

remained closed to the public. He had no known connections to terrorists of any kind, was not charged with a crime, and was apparently of so little danger to the safety of Americans that he was not kept in custody. His was labeled a "special interest" case, apparently for the sole reason that he is a Syrian national. When Mr. Zeidan sued to have his hearing opened to the public, DOJ suddenly redesignated his case so that it was no longer of "special interest," and avoided the legal challenge.[20]

Other "special interest" detainees have told similar tales. Mohammed Irshaid, a New York civil engineer, reported being arrested by federal agents, who accused him of being a terrorist, threw him in jail in Passaic, New Jersey, mistreated him badly, and then released him three weeks later, filing a minor immigration charge against him weeks after his release. Syed Jaffri, a Pakistani who had had a dispute with his Bronx landlord, reported being arrested, thrown into solitary confinement, beaten up, verbally abused, never advised of his right to a lawyer, and summarily deported (without his money or papers) to Canada after being held for six months.[21]

These examples reflect a larger pattern of improper behavior by Government agents in the wake of September 11.[22] Besides depriving the public of its constitutional right to know and monitor the conduct of government, the Creppy Memo operated to deprive immigrants of due process and their right to counsel. In deportation hearings aliens have the right to counsel, but, unlike in criminal court proceedings, the government is not obligated to provide immigrants with lawyers. Immigrants must locate, hire, and arrange to pay their own lawyers. Family members often must assist in locating an attorney, particularly if an immigrant is detained or unable to speak English. Even before September 11, this reality meant that many deportation proceedings were conducted with no one representing the immigrant, even though immigration law is often technical and complicated. The new rules imposed after 9/11 made this much worse and effectively prevented *pro bono* representation of detainees by volunteer attorneys.

Locked up in detention centers with only restricted access to the outside world, with their family and friends unable to obtain any information about when and where their relatives would be called before an administrative law judge, "special interest" immigrants found it uniquely difficult to obtain representation. Without a lawyer, and without access to their families and friends, many "special interest" immigrants were unable to offer a defense to the government's charges, and were unable or unwilling to appeal adverse rulings. As American Civil Liberties Union attorney Lee Gelernt described it, "special interest" immigrants were "literally [] sitting there all by themselves facing a trained INS prosecutor before a judge, often with language difficulties, while their liberty was at stake."[23] Given the adversarial nature of immigration court proceedings, neither the INS attorney nor the judge can be expected to look out for the interests of the immigrant, and the ability of immigrants to obtain fair hearings often depends on the public's knowledge of their cases—something the Creppy Memo expressly precluded.

II. THE CLAIM OF EXECUTIVE POWER TO ORDER SECRET DEPORTATION PROCEEDINGS

A. The Media's Challenge to Secrecy

The mandates for secret proceedings in cases designated by the Attorney General became the subject of two legal challenges by the press. In Michigan, the *Detroit Free Press* challenged its exclusion from a deportation hearing involving Rabih Haddad who had been detained for overstaying his visa.[24] Haddad's case gained attention because he was co-founder of an Islamic charity, the Global Relief Foundation, which had separately been accused by the Treasury Department of supporting terrorism and had its assets frozen.[25] By the time the *Detroit Free*

Press learned about the government's efforts to deport Haddad, three secret hearings had already been held.

In the meantime, two local papers in New Jersey, had been trying to obtain information about a large number of aliens who were arrested in that State after 9/11. Unable to learn anything about the status of these aliens, the papers filed a facial challenge to the Creppy Memo requiring all "special interest" proceedings to be secret.[26]

The two lawsuits brought by the press in Michigan and New Jersey framed the same issue: whether deportation hearings could be completely closed on the unilateral order of the Attorney General, without any review by a judge at any point. The newspapers argued that the blanket sealing of deportation hearings violated the First Amendment right of access to government proceedings, urging that a case by case inquiry was required to close specific deportation hearings. The newspapers also challenged the Attorney General's blanket approach to secrecy as ineffective in advancing security interests, because it barred the public from attending hearings before immigration judges, but left detainees free to disclose information to anyone they desired. Detainees actually connected to terrorist organizations were free to pass on information; only the public and press were kept in the dark.

B. The Overreaching Claim of Executive Power to Order Secrecy

The stated purpose for closing the deportation hearings was to avoid the possibility that potentially sensitive information would be disclosed to terrorists. Experts for the Department of Justice claimed that a blanket approach to secrecy was required because even routine information that appeared innocuous in isolation might prove valuable to terrorists as part of a broader "mosaic" of facts. For example, the Department was concerned that any details of how or why a "special interest" alien was detained "would allow the terrorist organizations to discern patterns and methods of investigation," and might reveal "what patterns of entry" to this country were most likely to succeed.[27]

Rather than simply claiming that these national security concerns justified secrecy in the cases designated by the Attorney General, the government took a far more extreme position to defend the actions by DOJ. The Government moved to dismiss the papers' claims for access by asserting that no constitutional right of access exists anywhere outside of Article III courts, suggesting that the right may even sweep no further than criminal proceedings.[28] This argument misstated both the constitutional source of the right of access and the Supreme Court's stated rationale in declaring the qualified right to be enforceable by the press and public.

The scope of the First Amendment right of access was defined by the Supreme Court in *Richmond Newspapers, Inc. v. Virginia,*[29] an appeal challenging the sealing of a whole criminal trial conducted in Virginia entirely in secret, under a statute that gave the judge discretion to do so. This secrecy was impermissible, Chief Justice Burger explained, because:

> [t]he explicit, guaranteed rights to speak and to publish concerning what takes place at a trial would lose much meaning if access to observe the trial could, as it was here, be foreclosed arbitrarily.[30]

The Court found a qualified right of public access to be implicit in the guarantees of free speech and press, just as the right of association, right of privacy, right to travel and the right to be presumed innocent are implicit in other provisions of the Bill of Rights.[31]

The *Richmond Newspapers* case "unequivocally holds that an arbitrary interference with access to important information is an abridgment of the freedoms of speech and of the press protected by the First Amendment."[32] The First Amendment right of access is an affirma tive individual right, enforceable by any member of the public or the press against abuse and over-reaching by those in power.[33]

DOJ sought to severely limit this Constitutional right, by theorizing that it does not extend to the "political branches" because Articles I and II of the Constitution supposedly contain their own specific "access" requirements (an unusual characterization of the President's obligation to report on "the State of the Union" and Congress' obligation to publish a "regular Statement and Account" of all public monies).[34] Given these express "access" obligations, DOJ contended, the Constitution must be read to foreclose other access obligations and "leave[ ] to the democratic processes" the regulation of the political branches.[35] This novel contention ignored that the Supreme Court located the right of public access in the First Amendment, which applies equally to all branches of government, and did so precisely because the access right is a necessary tool in the hands of voters if those "democratic processes" are to function effectively. As the Court put it in *Globe Newspaper Co. v. Superior Court,*[36] the First Amendment right of access to criminal trials is based upon,

> the common understanding that a 'major purpose of that Amendment was to protect the free discussion of governmental affairs'. By offering such protection, the First Amendment serves to ensure that the individual citizen can effectively participate in and contribute to our republican system of self-government.[37]

The DOJ's whole-cloth argument continued that the right of access supposedly had been found to exist in the judicial branch alone because the absence of any express "access" provision in Article III combined with the Sixth Amendment guarantee of a "public trial" together supported the inference of a right of access to judicial proceedings.[38] The *Richmond Newspapers* holding, however, had nothing to do with "access" obligations—missing or present—in Articles I through III. And, the Supreme Court just one year before *Richmond Newspapers* specifically rejected the notion that the Sixth Amendment creates any public right of access at all, finding the "public trial" guarantee to be an individual right extended only to criminal defendants.[39]

In short, DOJ was entirely off-base in claiming that administrative proceedings should not even be subject to evaluation under *Richmond Newspapers*. It argued that the Founders would never have contemplated any public access to the operations of administrative agencies.[40] In point of fact, "[t]he Framers, who envisioned a limited Federal Government, could not have anticipated the vast growth of the administrative state."[41] As the Supreme Court has explained, "formalized administrative adjudications were all but unheard of in the late 18th century and early 19th century."[42]

The Court has also explained that the "vast expansion" of administrative regulation through which the Government now operates is possible under our system only by adherence to certain "basic principles," and these include an obligation for quasi-judicial administrative proceedings generally to be "fair and open."[43] The Court long ago described a "fair and open" administrative hearing as:

> essential alike to the legal *validity* of administrative regulation and to the maintenance of public confidence in the value and soundness of this important governmental process. Such a hearing has been described as an "inexorable safeguard."[44]

This rationale has propelled the "prevailing" rule that administrative hearings are typically open, "if not by statutory mandate, then by regulation or practice."[45]

The DOJ finally argued that INS deportation proceedings should be exempt from the First Amendment right of access, even if it applies to some executive branch proceedings, because the "power to expel or exclude aliens" is a sovereign power,[46] characterizing the Creppy Memo as a "*bona fide* immigration regulation."[47] Yet, Congress also has broad power over the military but, under a *Richmond Newspapers* analysis, the right of access has been held to attach to court martial proceedings.[48] Congress, under Article II, Section 8, has power over "the subject of

Bankruptcies," yet access rights attach to bankruptcy proceedings, including creditors' meetings.[49] And, even accepting that Congress' plenary power over immigration is exceptionally broad, it is not exempt from constitutional constraints.[50] In the case of deportations, this means "the Government must respect the procedural safeguards of due process" in exercising its right to remove aliens.[51]

C. The Legal Framework That Was Available to Impose Necessary Secrecy

The DOJ's effort to create for the Executive branch a wholesale exemption from the First Amendment right of access is particularly problematic because it could readily have defended the need for secrecy after 9/11, without making this frontal assault on the right of access. DOJ had available other arguments to defend much of the secrecy it imposed, without advancing the extreme position that no right of access exists at all within the Executive branch. First, DOJ could more narrowly argue (and did successfully in the Third Circuit) that the right of access does not apply to deportation proceedings, in specific, because public access to such proceedings provides no structural benefit to the operation of government. In defining the scope of the right of access, the Supreme Court has said it only attaches to those government proceedings where there has been a tradition of openness that provides "structural" benefits to the operation of that proceeding.[52] This analysis requires a consideration of whether there exists a "tradition" of public access to a type of proceeding that carries "the favorable judgment of experience," and "whether public access plays a significant positive role in the functioning of the particular process in question."[53]

Second, DOJ could argue (and did as an alternative position) that "special interest" deportation proceedings properly could be closed because the right of access is a qualified right that must give way to legitimate national security concerns. Whether the qualified right of access may be restricted in a given instance is resolved by a consideration of four specific factors laid down by the Supreme Court in *Richmond Newspapers* and its progeny:

1. whether an open proceeding is substantially likely to prejudice another transcendent value;[54]
2. if so, whether any alternative exists to avoid that prejudice without limiting public access;[55]
3. if not, whether the limitation of access is narrowed (in scope and time) to the minimum necessary;[56] and
4. whether the limitation of access effectively avoids the prejudice it is intended to address.[57]

This four-part test requires only that a particularized showing be made to justify any denial of access on a case-by-case basis.[58]

In the two court challenges to the DOJ's imposition of total secrecy on the "special interest" deportation proceedings, both the Sixth Circuit and the Third Circuit rejected the Attorney General's breathtaking claim that the Executive branch was not bound by the First Amendment right of access. The Sixth Circuit, in *Detroit Free Press v. Ashcroft,*[59] faced an appeal of the district court's preliminary injunction striking down the closure of the "special interest" hearing of Rabih Haddad. Finding that DOJ's actions violated the First Amendment right of access, the opinion strongly endorsed the importance of openness as a check upon the abuse of governmental power:

> Today, the Executive Branch seeks to take this safeguard away from the public by placing its actions beyond public scrutiny. Against non-citizens, it seeks the power to secretly deport a class if it unilaterally calls them "special interest" cases. The Executive Branch seeks to uproot people's lives, outside the public eye, and behind a closed door. Democracies die behind closed doors. The First Amendment, through a free press, protects the people's right to know that their government acts fairly, lawfully, and accurately in deportation proceedings. When government begins closing doors, it selectively controls information

rightfully belonging to the people. Selective information is misinformation. The Framers of the First Amendment "did not trust any government to separate the true from the false for us." [Citation omitted] They protected the people against secret government.[60]

The court examined both the tradition of openness in deportation proceedings and the structural benefit of open deportation hearings. The court rejected the government's insistence that there must be a historical tradition dating back to the time "when our organic laws were adopted"[61] before a First Amendment right could be found. It noted that *Press-Enterprise II* and several circuit courts' holdings "relied exclusively on post-Bill of Rights history,"[62] and found that deportation proceedings had for the most part been conducted openly since the enactment of the first immigration statute in 1882.[63] The court said it "should look to proceedings that are similar in form and substance" and found that deportation hearings "'walk, talk and squawk' very much like a judicial proceeding" and are comparable to a statutory criminal sentencing statute authorizing removal.[64]

The Court of Appeals had little difficulty concluding that access would play "a significant positive role" in deportation proceedings—noting that "the press and the public serve as perhaps the only check on abusive government practices."[65] The court noted that additional benefits of public[66] proceedings included improved government performance, a "cathartic" effect on the community, the "perception of integrity and fairness," and a more informed public. The Government, according to the Court of Appeals, had not identified "one persuasive reason why openness would play a negative role in the process."[67] Thus, the Sixth Circuit found the right of access to attach to deportation proceedings.

Taking up the question of whether the qualified access right was overcome on the facts presented by the government, the court concluded it was not. Although the government had demonstrated a compelling interest in preventing the disclosure of information that might impede its ongoing anti-terrorism investigation, its blanket ban on access to all "special interest" hearings failed to satisfy two other requirements mandated by the First Amendment: that the closure order be narrowly tailored and that it be based on individualized "specific findings on the record so that a reviewing court can determine whether closure was proper and whether less restrictive alternatives exist."[68] The opinion characterized open deportation proceedings as a vital demonstration of democratic values "that Americans should not discard in these troubling times."[69]

The Third Circuit decided *North Jersey Media Group v. Ashcroft*[70] six weeks later, also rejecting the contention that the First Amendment right of access has no application to the Executive branch. In applying the two-prong test for determining whether the right of access attached specifically to deportation hearings, however, Chief Judge Becker took a strict view of the "tradition" requirement. Disagreeing with the Sixth Circuit, the Third Circuit majority noted that Congress had never explicitly guaranteed public access to deportation hearings, and viewed the "rebuttable presumption of openness" created by 1964 INS regulations to be too recent and too qualified to establish the type of "unbroken, uncontradicted history" of openness present in *Richmond Newspapers*.[71] Although Judge Becker considered a "1000-year history" unnecessary, he rejected the position that a court could rely solely on the "structural benefits" of open hearings in a given context, so long as there was no history of closed proceedings[72]—an approach taken in several Third Circuit cases involving modern criminal procedures.[73] Judge Becker concluded that a strict demonstration of a history of openness was required in order to "preserve administrative flexibility and avoid constitutionalizing ambiguous, and potentially unconsidered, executive decisions."[74]

With regard to the structural benefits prong of the test, the Third Circuit first noted that it "does not do much work" because no case had yet found an access request that satisfied the "experience" test, but failed the "logic" test.[75] It then read the *Press-Enterprise II* formulation

of "whether public access plays a significant positive role in the functioning of the particular process in question" to require an examination of the "flip side" of that inquiry: "the extent to which openness impairs the public good."[76] Judge Becker criticized the lower court for not fully crediting the declaration of the FBI's Counterterrorism Chief outlining how disclosure of seemingly minor and innocuous information about a deportation proceeding could be valuable to a person within a terrorist network, and could thwart the government's efforts to investigate and prevent future acts of violence.[77] In a confusing conclusion, however, the Court seemed to limit its analysis to "special interest" deportation hearings only. "On balance," stated Judge Becker, "we are unable to conclude that openness plays a positive role *in special interest deportation hearings* at a time when our nation is faced with threats of such profound and unknown dimension."[78]

In a vigorous dissent, Judge Sirica found that the two-step analysis for the existence of the First Amendment right was plainly satisfied. He found an adequate historical record of open proceedings, and relied on cases applying the Supreme Court precedents to civil trials as equally applicable given the similar procedures used at deportation hearings.[79]

The Supreme Court denied *certiorari* in the Third Circuit case,[80] and none was sought by the government from the Sixth Circuit ruling, so the split decision over the validity of the Creppy Memo stands for now. Both courts, however, squarely rejected the dangerous doctrine advanced by the Attorney General—that the Executive branch is exempt from any constitutional right of access. This extreme position is unsupportable in law or logic, and was properly denounced by the courts.

III. SHORTCOMINGS OF THE THIRD CIRCUIT APPROACH TO SECRET DEPORTATION HEARINGS

Departing from the approach of the Sixth Circuit, the Third Circuit accepted a blanket closure of "special interest" immigration hearings.[81] As noted, the Third Circuit rejected application of the right of access to deportation proceedings largely because it found a lack of evidence establishing a long history of open proceedings.[82] The Third Circuit approach is seriously flawed. *Press Enterprise II* establishes that it is not necessary to demonstrate a historical practice pre-dating our country's founding to find a constitutional right of access to a government proceeding.[83]

Indeed, few aspects of modern criminal prosecutions can boast a pedigree of public access dating back to the Founders and beyond, yet lower courts have widely found a right of access to phases of criminal proceedings that have no specific historical counterpart—such as plea hearings, pretrial suppression hearings, and motions for judicial disqualification.[84] Some courts have cited a consistent modern practice of openness as sufficient under the *Press Enterprise II* analysis, while others have concluded that the "favorable judgment of history" is not necessary where the structural benefits of openness are irrefutable.[85] For example, in *Seattle Times Co. v. United States District Court*,[86] the Ninth Circuit reasoned that introduction of new procedures that did not exist at common law by the Bail Reform Act of 1984, rendered "the historical tradition surrounding bail proceedings...much less significant."[87] As the Fifth Circuit similarly noted, First Amendment access rights "should not be foreclosed because these proceedings lack the history of openness relied on by the *Richmond Newspapers* court."[88]

The Third Circuit also went off the tracks with its analysis of the "structural benefits" inherent in the recognition of a qualified right of access to deportation hearings. This analysis is intended to focus on whether access plays a positive role in the functioning of the proceeding itself.[89] Because a deportation hearing is conducted in the form of a trial, the value of openness

to the "very process" itself is the same as in a judicial trial, and supports the existence of a constitutional right of access.

Immigration hearings are presided over by hearing officers, who are not judges but who are "neutral,"[90] and have authority to make binding decisions, subject only to limited review.[91] In fact, for most of the century, the hearing officers were INS employees,[92] but that structure was routinely criticized and, in 1983, the arrangement ended.[93] Although the hearing officer may take an active role in questioning a witness—as Federal Rule of Evidence 614 permits a judge to do during a civil trial—in practice, they rarely do so.[94]

Just like Article III judicial proceedings, immigration proceedings are adversarial.[95] Over time, the INS has developed a specialized staff of attorneys who are responsible for the prosecutorial functions of a removal or departure hearing, and these attorneys generally present the case to the hearing officer. An alien has a right to counsel in removal proceedings under the Fifth Amendment's due process clause, and the INS must also give the alien a list of attorneys in the area.[96]

Although the formal rules of evidence do not apply, INS regulations take care to ensure that only reliable evidence will be considered. Unauthenticated documents, hearsay, and other information that are not inherently trustworthy can be considered only after the hearing officer finds the specific evidence to be probative *and* reliable.[97] The different burdens of proof and levels of proof required track the structure of civil cases in Article III courts.[98]

The decisions made in immigration proceedings have a significant impact on the individual subject, usually far more than a civil lawsuit seeking only financial compensation. As a consequence, to ensure fairness and conformance with constitutional due process requirements, immigration proceedings, although conducted under the auspices of the executive branch's administrative apparatus, act and look very much like judicial proceedings.[99] In such a proceeding, the First Amendment right plainly exists. If a proceeding "walks, talks and squawks very much like a lawsuit...[i]ts placement within the Executive Branch cannot blind us to the fact that the proceeding is truly an adjudication."[100]

The Third Circuit not only misperceived the nature of the "structural benefits" analysis, it found that the standard was not satisfied because in a narrow category of deportation hearings —"special interest" cases involving national security—the public interest may be threatened by open hearings. This concern, however, does not address the value of openness of deportation hearings in general, but only the need to restrict openness in specific types of cases; and the question remains whether the Attorney General should have the unreviewable power of closure. This analysis should more appropriately have been applied to decide whether a particular proceeding *should* be closed, after concluding, as did the Sixth Circuit, that a qualified right of access to deportation hearings indeed exists. In this regard, the Sixth Circuit's conclusions about the value of access to deportation proceedings rests on much more solid constitutional ground than the Third Circuit's logically flawed approach of wholesale abdication to the Executive's whims.

The Third Circuit ridiculed the Sixth Circuit's statement that "democracies die behind closed doors," pointing out that the Constitutional Convention of 1787 was held behind closed doors, and that "is where democracy was born."[101] The Third Circuit's ridicule is inappropriate. The Constitutional Convention did not make determinations behind closed doors as to whether a particular individual should lose his life or liberty. In fact, making such decisions behind closed doors would have been anathema to the Founders, who would have called it a "Star Chamber," and who wrote the right to a speedy and public trial into the Bill of Rights. The Third Circuit judges, in questioning "how they could possibly rule against the government when national security and human lives were at stake,"[102] seem to have overlooked that

the lives of immigrants and the cohesion of immigrant families are at stake in immigration court hearings.

There are of course legitimate national security concerns that can come into play in deportation or removal hearings, and those concerns may well require closure of particular hearings. There is no logical reason, however, to conclude that there is no right of access to *any* deportation hearing, or even to sanction secret proceedings in an entire class of cases, upon the unsupported allegation that "national security" is implicated because an alien is from a particular country. Under traditional First Amendment principles, the Government should be required to make a case-by-case showing of why a particular hearing must be closed, and denied the power to close categories of hearing unilaterally.

IV. CLOSED HEARINGS CIRCUMVENT THE LAW, VIOLATE DUE PROCESS AND ARE BAD PUBLIC POLICY[103]

A. Closed Hearings Defeat the Purpose of the Alien Terrorist Removal Court

DOJ's policy of blanket closure of certain "special interest" immigration cases does an end-run around the existing statutory mechanism for deporting immigrants suspected of terrorist connections. In 1996, as part of the Illegal Immigration Reform and Immigrant Responsibility Act,[104] Congress enacted a statutory scheme to remove from the United States those persons suspected of being terrorists. Congress created a new court to hear these terrorist removal cases—the Alien Terrorist Removal Court.[105] Through these new procedures and this new court, Congress expanded the government's power to conduct deportation hearings with the use of secret evidence to target suspected terrorists.[106] The Alien Terrorist Removal Court, composed of five (5) United States district court judges appointed by the Chief Justice of the U.S. Supreme Court, is the proper court to be used to deport suspected terrorists.[107] The Court's rules create special protections for the rights of those brought within its jurisdiction.[108] To date, however, INS has chosen not to use this new court.[109]

Prior to 9/11, the INS[110] ignored this court, choosing instead to try persons suspected of being terrorists or linked to terrorists in regular deportation or removal proceedings.[111] At these proceedings, INS chose to introduce "secret evidence," which INS refused to show judges, aliens or their counsel. Often, when this "secret evidence" was later revealed, it proved to be so faulty as to cause the agency to become something of a laughingstock in the intelligence community.[112] In the post-September 11 world, DOJ has again attempted to disregard Congress's statutory scheme for deporting terrorists, instead invoking its regulatory powers to create secret proceedings for deporting immigrants. This end-run around existing statutes should not be allowed.

B. Closing Hearings Deprives Immigrants of Due Process

While immigration court proceedings are administrative, they implicate the most serious of interests—life and liberty.[113] An immigrant may face death in his native country, should he be deported. Certainly, at a minimum, he has a liberty interest. Under the venerable *Matthews v. Eldridge* test,[114] blanket closure of hearings is an unconstitutional violation of procedural due process because it serves to deprive immigrants of notice of the charges against them and a meaningful opportunity to be heard.

Mathews v. Eldridge requires that when the Government seeks to deprive persons of their life, liberty, or property, the Government must consider three distinct factors when determining how the deprivation may be carried out: first, the Government must consider the private interest that

will be affected by the official action; second, the risk of an erroneous deprivation of such interest through the procedures used, and the probable value, if any, of additional or substitute procedural safeguards; and finally, the government's interest, including the function involved and the fiscal and administrative burdens that the additional or substitute procedural requirement would entail.[115] In the case of immigration detainees, the private interest in preventing an improper deportation can be a matter of life and death. When secret hearings are held and an immigrant is deprived of the presence of her family, her witnesses, and her lawyer, there is a grave risk of an error; the value of additional procedural safeguards is great, and is also likely to save the Government time and money (for example, the involvement of a lawyer may clarify the facts more quickly). Third, while the Government's interest in deporting immigrants is often significant, there is little fiscal or administrative burden in requiring individual, case-by-case analysis of whether a hearing should be closed. Thus, the *Mathews v. Eldridge* test argues against the blanket hearing closure policy used by the DOJ after September 11.

It has become increasingly obvious, however, that the Government has paid scant attention, to the procedural due process rights of immigrants in the post-September 11 world. The media have reported that "the handling of Muslims arrested on immigration charges after September 11 has been fraught with delay and sloppy bookkeeping and that due process [has been] shortchanged..."[116] Immigrants have been held for months without being charged.[117] At least one detainee has died while in custody, apparently as a result of the stress of being detained.[118] "[D]etainees the government suspects least end up being held longest since they are low on the list of priorities. In the meantime, reputations are ruined, jobs are lost, families are kept apart, and lives are turned upside down."[119] While being held in detention, a number of detainees were abused.[120] The Office of the Inspector General of the Department of Justice issued a supplementary report at the end of 2003, after an in-depth investigation, concluding that "officers slammed detainees against the wall, twisted their arms and hands in painful ways, stepped on their leg restraint chains, and punished them by keeping them restrained for long periods of time."[121] Furthermore, it has become clear in recent months that immigration judges have been intimidated by the Attorney General, who has publicly commented on their decisions in an unprecedented and arguably unethical fashion.[122] Attorney General Ashcroft has fired members of the Board of Immigration Appeals with whose decisions he does not agree.[123] This biased behavior by the Attorney General threatens to further undermine the due process rights of immigrants.

Finally, the closed hearings policy has operated to deprive immigrants of witnesses needed for their cases, and has likely resulted in erroneous removals and deportations.

C. Closing Hearings Deprives Immigrants of Their Right to Counsel

Blanket closure of immigration hearings also deprives immigrants of their right to counsel, and is part of a disturbing Justice Department trend to hinder the right to counsel in general.[124] "There's been a concerted effort to cut defense lawyers out of the process, to make it impossible for people accused of terrorism offenses to mount an effective defense."[125]

As mentioned above, in an immigration court proceeding, if an alien wants a lawyer, she must find and pay for one herself, often while incarcerated and perhaps even unable to use a telephone. Even if the alien has an attorney, INS may ship the alien thousands of miles away from his attorney, without even notifying the attorney.[126] The alien is responsible for providing evidence to rebut the INS's claims, although such evidence might be in a faraway country, or come from US Government employees whom the INS will not produce to testify. Although rules officially exist to ensure procedural fairness, in reality, translations are frequently bad, shaky evidence is commonly admitted, and jaded immigration judges and INS attorneys with little

knowledge of the complicated politics of other nations can, without the guidance of counsel, make critical mistakes such as confuse one political group with another. Immigration law itself, in the words of the INS, is a "mystery and a mastery of obfuscation,"[127] and few immigrants can be expected to understand it or to appreciate their eligibility for relief. Access to counsel in immigration court is often the only chance an immigrant has to obtain justice—and perhaps prevent his own death.

Following the September 11 attacks, the Government has in many cases had a pattern and practice of denying "special interest" immigrants their right to counsel.[128] When giving immigrants lists of lawyers who can supposedly help with their cases, government officials have provided lists with bad phone numbers.[129] Lawyers have been told that they cannot accompany clients to interviews with the INS.[130]

Blanket closure of hearings deprives immigrants of access to counsel. When an immigrant is locked up, unable to contact his family, he often cannot obtain an attorney. If his family is unable to determine when and where his hearing will be, they cannot hire an attorney to be there to represent him. The Government will not provide him a free attorney. Because the Government itself is represented by an experienced attorney, and immigration court proceedings are adversarial, immigrants who are unrepresented by counsel are at a grave disadvantage.

D. Closing Hearings Can Injure Rather Than Protect National Security

The closure of hearings can actually hurt national security. The potential danger to national security posed by closed hearings is illustrated by the case of the Iraqi Six, a story that illustrates the grave consequences of unquestioning deference to Government requests for closed hearings.

In 1996, Saddam Hussein's troops rolled into Northern Iraq, attacking Kurdish allies of the United States. Kurdish opponents of the Iraqi regime were slaughtered. Belatedly, the US military evacuated some six thousand Iraqis and Kurds who had been associated with the Iraqi National Congress, taking the evacuees to Guam by military airlift. Among the evacuees were six men who would later earn the appellation "the Iraqi Six." Like their Kurdish and Iraqi compatriots, these men were interviewed on Guam by FBI agents, and later allowed to come to California. Once in California, they filed for political asylum, citing a well-founded fear of persecution by Saddam Hussein. After they filed for asylum, however, the US Immigration & Naturalization Service moved to deport them, claiming that classified evidence proved that the men were national security risks. INS said that secret evidence revealed that the men should be deported back to Iraq. INS refused to disclose the classified evidence to the men, or to their lawyers, despite the fact that one of their lawyers, R. James Woolsey, was the former Director of the Central Intelligence Agency.

If sent back to Iraq, the Iraqi Six faced certain death at the hands of Saddam Hussein. At the time of the hearings of the Iraqi Six, immigration hearings such as theirs were not closed. Although INS refused to allow the men or their lawyers to see the evidence in their cases, the hearings themselves were open. What happened during those hearings gives us a glimpse of what INS might do when no one—the press or the public—is there to watch. During the hearings of the Iraqi Six, the public learned that FBI agents with no prior experience dealing with Iraqi or Kurdish issues had interviewed the men after having had only a single 45-minute classified briefing on the situation in Iraq; translation problems caused the FBI to make critical mistakes in taking statements from the men; and FBI and INS agents collected allegations from other Iraqis, and then failed to investigate to see if the allegations were actually true. Government agents called these collections of allegations "evidence," classified them, refused to show them to the Iraqi Six or their lawyers, and used them as grounds for the "national security risk" charge. In addition, FBI and INS agents made appalling errors in interpreting evidence

in the case, including confusing thallium (rat poison) with valium (a common sedative), an error which caused them to determine that one of the men was a recreational drug user when instead he was a victim of poisoning by Iraqi intelligence agents. In another egregious error, an FBI interviewer thought that one man was lying because he described a trip to Baghdad in which he stayed with relatives who were Kurds. The FBI agent believed that no Kurds lived in Baghdad, although a quarter of Iraq's Kurds live there. The FBI agent was also unaware that Kurdish groups had engaged in negotiations with Saddam Hussein's regime. FBI agents mixed up family names with ethnic groups, and then said one man was lying because he failed to list his ethnic group as one of his names. INS failed to call as witnesses some key government employees—including at least one retired CIA agent—who could have cleared the men and testified how the men had helped the CIA. FBI and INS personnel had little understanding of the situation in Northern Iraq and the various struggles of the Kurdish people, and were thus unable to appreciate or evaluate the testimony they were hearing.

Media coverage of the deportation hearings of the Iraqi Six played a significant role in stopping their deportation and exposing these INS and FBI blunders. Under intense pressure, the Justice Department eventually declassified the evidence against the men. Once revealed publicly, the evidence proved to be shaky, unreliable, and in some cases, laughable. After having spent years in jail fighting deportation to Iraq, the men were eventually released. Today, these men are alive and well, and have helped the United States with the conflict in Iraq.

Were hearings like this held today, the men would no doubt be classified as "special interest" cases. The hearings would be closed to family, friends, and the press. Today, the press would not be allowed to expose the blunders of the FBI and the shaky nature of the INS's evidence. Under today's secret hearings, men like this would have no chance—they would have been sent back to their country long ago and might well be dead today.

Ironically, in cases like those of the Iraqi Six, media coverage also helps protect the national security of the United States. National security is harmed when shaky evidence is used to deport people who could help our country. National security is harmed even more if foreign governments or organizations know they can manipulate the INS into deporting a foreign government's enemies through secret tribunals. National security is further harmed by the United States developing a reputation, with both its own immigrant community and the world at large, of treating minorities (and typically Islamic minorities) unfairly through secret proceedings. The case of the Iraqi Six should be an example to us of one of the dangers of secret immigration hearings. While such hearings may speed the removal of aliens, they may also cover up abuses and mistakes, and lead ultimately to tragic results. As one writer recently noted, "the idea that openness can be more effective than secrecy in reducing risks has received too little attention."[131]

E. Closing Hearings Fosters Misconduct and Misinformation

Closed hearings are particularly pernicious because they presume the government will act professionally and accountably in the absence of any public scrutiny. Unfortunately, the historical record does not reflect that the Department is always professional and accountable when it operates without oversight. The Federal Bureau of Investigation and the Immigration & Naturalization Service, the two agencies most often involved in "special interest" immigration hearings, are particularly noteworthy for their poor record of respect for due process.

Throughout its history, but particularly during the 1950s and 1960s—a time when the nation was highly concerned about its security—the Federal Bureau of Investigation used illegal means to obtain information;[132] the FBI also used this information for political purposes unrelated to any national security threat.[133] Secrecy immunized the FBI's operations from public

scrutiny. In repeatedly breaking the law and covering up its behavior, the FBI used the same rationale offered today by Attorney General Ashcroft to justify the current blanket closures of immigration court hearings. In the 1950s and 1960s, those excuses proved to be fictitious:

> The FBI's interest in secrecy and in minimizing the attorney general's oversight role was not predicated on national security considerations or even the possibility that leaks might compromise legitimate security interests. [A] culture of lawlessness...shaped FBI policies...[S]ecrecy encouraged FBI officials to act independently, even insubordinately.[134]

This same danger is apparent today, as the FBI attempts to deal with the threat posed by al Qaeda terrorists. Although the Attorney General has argued that his Department is trustworthy even in the absence of any public scrutiny, there are indications that such confidence is misplaced. In 2002, the public learned that the FBI and Justice Department had systematically misled the judges of the nation's Foreign Intelligence Surveillance Court, providing misinformation to support *ex parte* requests for wiretaps and surveillance of terrorism suspects in about 75 cases.[135] More recently, the public learned that the Department of Justice had misreported the number of terrorism-related convictions it had obtained,[136] and may have exaggerated the number of terrorists present in the United States.[137] Finally, the Department of Justice's own Inspector General has documented serious abuses of immigrants that took place in connection with the post-September 11 mass arrests of Muslim men.[138]

Along with the FBI, the INS—the other key agency involved in immigration detainee cases—has not been a shining light in federal law enforcement circles, either.[139] Its inefficiency and ineptitude have become so notorious as to be a cliché. At least one lawmaker has called it the "agency from hell."[140] For years, news reports have told of corruption, mismanagement, and an agency culture that tramples on people's rights and tolerates racism and abuse.[141] There is no reason to think that the agency has suddenly been reformed post-September 11 such that it can be trusted to act properly in the absence of public scrutiny. Although the agency has now been absorbed into the new Department of Homeland Security, the employees remain largely the same.[142]

In connection with immigration detainees, the Department of Justice has repeatedly misled the public as to the reasons for its blanket policy. Attorney General Ashcroft himself first claimed that blanket closure of hearings was necessary because the "special interest" immigrants affected belonged to al Qaeda.[143] Later, Justice Department officials privately admitted that none of the immigration detainees were actually al Qaeda members. These errors in DOJ's reporting were ultimately revealed by the news media.[144] Perhaps not surprisingly, the DOJ has since sought even more opportunity to hide its operations from the media and the public.[145]

When DOJ "does not have sufficient management oversight and internal controls in place... to ensure the accuracy and reliability of its terrorism-related conviction statistics,"[146] it is highly unlikely that it has sufficient management oversight and internal controls over the designation of "special interest" administrative immigration cases, given that criminal cases have a much higher profile at the Department. Given the due process interests at stake in immigration court hearings, mismanagement and inefficiency should not be tolerated. There is no reason to think that mismanagement and inefficiency will disappear without public scrutiny.

F. Closing Hearings Alarms the Immigrant Community

The immigrant community has been terrified by the DOJ's new policies, including blanket closure of immigration hearings. Immigrants are leaving the United States, apparently from fear of this policy and others like it.[147] Ironically, this fear lessens the likelihood that immigrants

will come forward to help the Government win the war on terrorism. "By rounding up young Muslim men for questioning, or holding them indefinitely on minor immigration charges, the Justice Department may alienate precisely the people they need to blow the whistle on suspicious activity."[148]

G. DOJ Has Used a Fictitious Excuse to Close Hearings

The possibility of terrorists learning intelligence sources and methods from immigration court hearings is quite likely a pretext. In reality, the Government appears to prefer closed immigration hearings not because of any actual threat to national security posed by open hearings, but because closing hearings makes it easier to deport aliens. The pretextual nature of the Government's excuses for blanket closure of these hearings becomes apparent after one considers the information that has "leaked" out of "special interest" hearings. This information indicates that the Government may have misled the public about the reasons for closing these hearings. Matthew Purdy, a New York Times journalist, writes:

> One East Coast immigration judge, who asked that his name remain secret, said the secret cases were "just regular cases" and that he had heard no evidence of terrorism at the hearings. "I'm sure there are plenty of terrorists," he said. "I haven't seen any." He said the people he had seen "were at the wrong place at the wrong time."[149]

H. Closing Hearings is an Overbroad Response to the Problem of Deporting Terrorists

Events subsequent to the September 11 attacks have made it clear that the DOJ blanket policy of closing immigration court proceedings has been an overbroad response to the problem of terrorism.[150] The "special interest" policy has created a dragnet that has targeted many persons who have no connection whatsoever to terrorism. Many of these people have been deprived of liberty for months at a time and in a manner that undercuts the legitimacy of the Government's terrorism investigations. As one immigration attorney said, "If they're still holding people who clearly have no tie-in to September 11th, what does it say about the quality of the overall investigation?"[151]

I. Closing Hearings Makes America a Poor Example to the World

In the past, the United States Government has condemned other countries that resorted to secret hearings to try alleged terrorists. There is an obvious resemblance between the practice of holding secret immigration hearings and the former practices of totalitarian regimes. Now the United States Government is engaging in the behavior that it formerly condemned. It has become apparent that "an unknown number of detainees have simply disappeared into what amounts to a secret legal system."[152] Blanket closure of hearings is a poor example to the rest of the world, and undercuts the American role as an international model for how justice should be administered.

CONCLUSION

The Department of Justice's blanket closure of certain "special interest" immigration hearings has revealed the grave dangers inherent in such an approach. Immigration hearings are much like criminal trials, and often even more is at stake. Like criminal trials, immigration hearings should be open to public scrutiny, absent an individualized assessment that a particular hearing should be closed. Blanket closure of these hearings is not a weapon that the Government

needs in its war on terrorism, and it threatens to undermine our confidence in the workings of our government. Immigrants facing accusations that they are linked to terrorism should be afforded a right to free counsel and full due process. The Department of Justice should not be allowed to determine unilaterally whose hearings should be closed and whose should be open. The Sixth Circuit was emphatically correct that "democracies die behind closed doors."
Dated: May 25, 2004

NOTES

1. *Menace of Terrorism Requires Global Response, Says Secretary General, Stressing Importance of Increased United Nations Role,* United Nations Press Release SG/SM/8583 SC/7639, Jan. 20, 2003, *available at* http://www.un.org/Docs/sc/committees/1373/sgjan03.htm (last visited, Jan. 20, 2003).

* Sections of this report are drawn from a broader analysis of public access to administrative proceedings completed earlier by the Committee on Communications & Media Law. "If it Walks, Talks, and Squawks. . . First Amendment Right of Access to Administrative Adjudications: A Position Paper" (June 2004).

Committee on Immigration and Nationality Law: Claudia Slovinsky (chair), Cigdem Acar, Elisabeth Ames, Suzanne Christen, Rose Culson-Villazor, Sharon Finkel, Maurice Goldman, Amy Gottlieb, Dawn Pipek Guidone, Susanne Heubel, Katie Holbrook (adjunct), Janet Horn, Omar Jadwat, Allen E. Kaye, Jennifer Kim (adjunct), Julie Krasnogor, Christina LaBrie, Odaliz Martinez, Lynn Neugebauer, Udi Ofer, Jennifer Oltarsh, Sheldon Philip, Archi Pyati, Matilde Roman, Mario Russell, Dan Smulian, David Stern, Margaret Stock, Susan Taylor, Suzanne Tomatore, Evelyn Tucker, Gretchen Van Deusen, Cynthia Wachenheim, Elaine H. Witty (adjunct), Marianne C. Yang, and Sejal Zota.

Committee on Communications and Media Law: David A. Schulz (chair), Carolyn K. Foley (secretary), Stephanie Abrutyn, Robert D. Balin, Sandra Baron, Katherine M. Bolger, Dianne Brandi, Binta Nambi Brown, Eve Burton, Patricia A. Clark, Barbara Cohen, Cheryl L. Davis, R. Townsend Davis, Jonathan R. Donnellan, Sherri F. Dratfield, Jeremy Feigelson, Robert A. Feinberg, Bridgette Fitzpatrick, Stephen Fuzesi, Amy Glickman, Stuart D. Karle, Henry R. Kaufman, Edward J. Klaris, Daniel M. Kummer, Joel Kurtzberg, David E. McCraw, Joseph Miller, Amy L. Neuhardt, Lynn Oberlander, Lisa S. Pearson, Wesley R. Powell, Hon. Jed S. Rakoff (took no part in the preparation or consideration of this report), Elisa Rivlin, Hon. Robert Sack (took no part in the preparation or consideration of this report), Saul B. Shapiro, Charles R. Sims, David B. Smallman, Anke E. Steinecke, Miriam Stern, Suzanne L. Telsey, David H. Tomlin, Jack M. Weiss, Maura Jeanne Wogan, and Ira Wurcel.

2. *See, e.g.* Government's Brief on Appeal in *North Jersey Media Group Inc., v. Ashcroft,* 308 F.3d 198 (3d Cir. 2002), at 18–38, 2002 WL 32103548, at *15 (arguing that the Constitutional right to public access to governmental proceedings is limited to the 6th Amendment right to a public criminal trial) [hereinafter "Gov. Br. in North Jersey appeal".].

3. *New York Times Co. v. United States,* 403 U.S. 713, 716 (1971) (Black, J., concurring) (emphasis added).

4. *See Detroit Free Press v. Ashcroft,* 303 F.3d 681, 696 (6th Cir. 2002) ("we believe that there is a limited First Amendment right of access to certain aspects of the executive and legislative branches"), *reh'g en banc denied,* 2003 U.S. App. LEXIS 1278; *North Jersey Media Group, Inc. v. Ashcroft,* 308 F. 3d 198, 221 (3d Cir. 2002) (rejecting claim that right of access does not extend to executive branch, but holding that the public possesses no right of access specifically to deportation proceedings), *cert. denied,* 538 U.S. 1056 (2003).

5. *See* Tamara Audi, The Legal System: Secrecy Veils Arrests, Jailings in Terror Probe, The Detroit Free Press, Oct. 22, 2001, at 1A ("Lawyers in New York say people the government most suspects of being linked to terrorist organizations are sent to federal detention centers in New York. A hierarchy has developed, with the most serious suspects held in a Manhattan prison and lesser suspects in a Brooklyn prison. Those whom the government dismisses as having no connection to terrorism are sent to detention centers and courts in New Jersey. . . .").

6. *See Center for National Security Studies v. U.S. Dept. of Justice,* 331 F.3d 918, 921–22 (D.C. Cir. 2003) (over 700 individuals were detained on INS charges).

7. *See* David G. Savage, *Critics Say Terror Probe Bends Immigrations Laws,* LA Times, Sept. 10, 2002, at 17, available at http://mediaguidetoislam.sfsu.edu/intheus/pdfs/E_ABS_LATimes.pdf (last visited May 19, 2004).

8. *See id.* The only individual criminal charged by the United States in connection with the 9/11 attacks, Zacarias Moussaoui, was arrested on immigration law violations prior to the attacks. *See* John Bowman & Linda Ward, *Zacarias Moussaoui,* at http://www.cbc.ca/news/indepth/targetterrorism/backgrounders/moussaoui_zacarias.html (last modified July, 2002) (last visited May 20, 2004).

9. Savage, *supra* note 7.

10. Before the Homeland Security Act was adopted late in 2002, the INS was an agency within the Department of Justice, and guidelines promulgated by the Attorney General created a presumption of openness. *See* 8 C.F.R. § 246.16(a)(1965) ("Deportation hearings shall be open to the public, except that the special inquiry officer may, in his discretion and for the purpose of protecting witnesses, respondents, or the public interest, direct that the general public or particular individuals shall be excluded from the hearing in any specific case. Depending upon physical facilities, reasonable limitation may be placed upon the number in attendance at any one time, with priority being given to the press over the general public."); 8 C.F.R. § 3.27 (1997).

11. *E.g.,* Administrative Procedure in Government Agencies, Report of the Committee on Administrative Procedure, Appointed by the Attorney General, at the Request of the President, to Investigate the Need for Procedural Reform in Various Administrative Tribunals and to Suggest Improvements Therein, S. Doc. No. 77–8, 77th Cong., 1st Sess. at 68 (1941) (noting that administrative hearings are almost invariably public). *See also Pechter v. Lyons,* 441 F.Supp. 115, 117–18 (S.D.N.Y. 1977) (noting longstanding public policy that trials at which an individual's "life or liberty" is at stake be open).

12. The Executive Office for Immigration Review ("EOIR") is part of the United States Department of Justice. EOIR is responsible for all deportation and removal hearings. EOIR is independent of the Immigration & Naturalization Service ("INS"). *See BIA Interim Decisions,* last modified Feb. 18, 2004, *at* http://uscis.gov/graphics/lawsregs/biadec.htm (last visited May 19, 2004).

13. E-mail from Hon. Michael Creppy, Chief Immigration Judge, to All Immigration Judges and Court Administrators (Sept. 21, 2001, 13:20), *available* at http://news.findlaw.com/hdocs/docs/aclu/creppy092101memo.pdf (last visited May 29, 2004) [hereinafter, "The Creppy Memo"]. The Creppy Memo was immediately implemented, and its general terms were later made part of the Code of Federal Regulations. Protective Orders in Immigration Administrative Proceedings, 67 Fed. Reg. 36799 (May 28, 2002) (to be codified at 8 C.F.R. §§ 3.27, 3.31 & 3.46); see also Release of Information Regarding Immigration and Naturalization Service Detainees in Non-Federal Facilities, 67 Fed. Reg. 19508 (Apr. 22, 2002) (to be codified at 8 C.F.R. §§ 236.6 & 241.15).

14. In ordering the new procedures, the Chief Immigration Judge purported to be acting pursuant to the regulatory authority to close a specific proceeding "in the public interest." 8 C.F.R § 3.27 (2002).

15. *See e.g.,* Matthew Purdy, Our Towns; Their Right? To Remain Silenced, N.Y. Times, May 1, 2002, at B5 (recounting how an INS trial attorney told an immigration judge that a hearing was "special interest," and quoting a defense attorney as having said "That's a long way of saying he's Arab.").

16. *Inspector General Criticizes 9/11 Detentions,* 13 CQ Researcher No. 37, at 898 (Oct. 24, 2003), available at http://www.polisci.umn.edu/courses/fall2003/4303/001/kiosk/USAPatriotAct/CivilLiberties-CQ.pdf (last visited May 20, 2004).

17. Audi, *supra* note 5, at 1A.

18. Jim Edwards, Letter from Newark; keeping court proceedings secret at New Jersey immigration courts, The Nation Vol. 275 No. 19, Dec. 2, 2002, at 7; Rachel Elbaum, *Caught in the Dragnet: Arab-Americans swept up in the post-Sept. 11 maelstrom, at* http://www.msnbc.msn.com/id/3071555/ (last visited May 20, 2004).

19. *See id.*

20. *See North Jersey Media Group, Inc. v. Ashcroft,* 205 F.Supp.2d 288, 291 n.1 (D.N.J.), *rev'd,* 308 F.3d 198 (3d Cir. 2002), *cert. denied,* 538 U.S. 1056 (2003).

21. Steven Brill, After 145–46 & 404 (Simon & Schuster) (2003).

22. *See generally* U.S. Department of Justice, Office of the Inspector General, The September 11 Detainees: A Review of the Treatment of Aliens Held on Immigration Charges in Connection with the Investigation

OF THE SEPTEMBER 11 ATTACKS 195 (April 2003) (finding "significant problems" in the treatment of September 11 detainees), *available at* http://www.usdoj.gov/oig/special/0306/full.pdf (last visited May 20, 2004).

23. Remarks made at presentation to the Association of the Bar of the City of New York, September 18, 2002.

24. *See Detroit Free Press v. Ashcroft,* 303 F.3d 681 (6th Cir. 2002).

25. *See Global Relief Found., Inc. v. O'Neill,* 315 F.3d 748, 754-55 (7th Cir. 2002) (rejecting claim that government lacked authority to freeze the foundation's assets).

26. *See North Jersey Media Group, Inc. v. Ashcroft,* 308 F. 3d 198, 203-04 (3d Cir. 2002).

27. *Id.* at 203 (quoting from the appellant's papers).

28. Gov. Br. in North Jersey appeal, *supra* note 2, at 18–19.

29. 448 U.S. 555 (1980).

30. *Id.* 576–77 (plurality opinion by Burger, C.J.).

31. *See id.* at 577 (plurality opinion) ("the right of access to places traditionally open to the public... may be seen as assured by the amalgam of the First Amendment guarantees of speech and press" and as related to "the right of assembly"); *id.* at 585 (Brennan, J., concurring) ("the First Amendment—of itself and as applied to the States through the Fourteenth Amendment—secures such a public right of access to trail proceedings."); *id.* at 583 (Stevens, J., concurring) (stating that "an arbitrary interference with access to important information" abridges the First Amendment).

32. *Id.* (Stevens, J., concurring).

33. *E.g., Matter of Search of Office Suites for World and Islam Studies Enterprise,* 925 F.Supp. 738, 739 (M.D, Fla. 1996) ("The press has standing to challenge an order sealing court documents.").

34. Gov. Br. in North Jersey appeal, *supra* note 2, at 21–22.

35. *Id.* at 22.

36. 457 U.S. 596 (1982).

37. *Id.* at 604 (citation omitted). *See also, Richmond Newspapers, Inc.,* 448 U.S. at 587 (Brennan, J., concurring) ("But the First Amendment embodies more than a commitment to free expression and communicative interchange for their own sakes; it has a *structural* role to play in securing and fostering our republican system of self-government."); *Press-Enterprise Co. v. Superior Court,* 464 U.S. 501, 517 (1984) (Stevens, J., concurring) (stating that the right of access furthers the "core purpose" of assuring free communication about the functioning of government, quoting *Richmond Newspapers, Inc.,* 448 U.S. at 575 (plurality opinion) [herinafter, "Press-Enterprise I"].

38. Gov. Br. in North Jersey appeal, *supra* note 2, at 21.

39. *Gannett Co. v. DePasquale,* 443 U.S. 368 (1979); *see Press-Enterprise I,* 464 U.S. at 516 (Stevens, J., concurring) (stating that the right of public access to criminal trials is not founded upon "the public trial provision" of the Sixth Amendment); *United States v. Criden,* 675 F.2d 550 (3d Cir. 1982) (public has no rights of access under the Sixth Amendment).

40. Gov. Br. 23.

41. *Fed. Mar. Comm'n v. S. Carolina State Ports Auth.,* 535 U.S. 743, 755 (2002).

42. *Id.*

43. *Morgan v. United States,* 304 U.S. 1, 14 (1938).

44. (*Id.* citation omitted, emphasis added.).

45. *Fitzgerald v. Hampton,* 467 F.2d 755, 764 (D.C. Cir. 1972) *citing* Administrative Procedure in Government Agencies, Report of the Committee on Administrative Procedure, Appointed by the Attorney General, at the Request of the President, to Investigate the Need for Procedural Reform in Various Administrative Tribunals and to Suggest Improvements Therein, S. Doc. No. 77-8, 77th Cong., 1st Sess., (1941), *supra* note 11.

46. Gov. Br. in North Jersey appeal, *supra* note 2, at 48.

47. *Id.* at 18.

48. *E.g., United States v. Hershey,* 20 M.J. 433 (C.M.A. 1985); *United States v. Scott,* 48 M.J. 663, 665 (A. Ct. Crim. App. 1998) ("The right of public access to criminal trial applies with equal validity to trials by courts-martial.").

49. *In re Astri Inv. Mgmt.& Secs. Corp.*, 88 B.R. 730 (D. Md. 1988); *In re Symington,* 209 B.R. 678 (Bankr. D. Md. 1997).

50. *Zadvydas v. Davis,* 533 U.S. 678, 695 (2001) (Congress' plenary power over immigration "is subject to important constitutional limitations"); *Yamataya v. Fisher,* 189 U.S. 86, 99–100 (1903) (Congressional immigration authority is limited by the due process clause of the 5th Amendment).

51. *Galvan v. Press,* 347 U.S. 522, 531 (1954).

52. *E.g. Press-Enterprise Co. v. Superior Court,* 478 U.S. 1,8 (1986) (*"Pres- Enterprise II"*) (stating that many government processes operate best under public scrutiny).

53. *Id.*

54. *Globe Newspaper Co. v. Superior Court,* 457 U.S. 596, 606–607 (1982) (right of access must be weighed against risk of disclosure of sensitive information); *Press-Enterprise I,* 464 U.S. at 510.

55. *Press-Enterprise II,* 478 U.S. at 14; *Publicker,* 733 F.2d at 1070.

56. *Press Enterprise I,* 464 U.S. at 510; *United States v. Antar,* 38 F.3d 1348, 1363 (3d Cir. 1994) (stating that the court must ensure "that the limitation imposed is the least restrictive means possible.").

57. *Globe Newspaper,* 457 U.S. at 610; *In re Charlotte Observer,* 882 F.2d 850, 855 (4th Cir. 1989) ("Where closure is wholly inefficacious to prevent a perceived harm, that alone suffices to make it constitutionally impermissible."). The "effectiveness" factor flows from the proposition that First Amendment rights will not be abridged for an idle purpose. *See Nebraska Press Ass'n v. Stuart,* 427 U.S. 539 (1976) (rejecting a prior restraint in part because it might not have fulfilled its intended goal); *Smith v. Daily Mail Publ'g Co.,* 443 U.S. 97, 105 (1979 ("[e]ven assuming a state interest of the highest order, [the statute] does not accomplish its stated purpose.").

58. *Globe Newspaper,* 457 U.S. at 608.

59. 303 F.3d 681 (6th Cir. 2002).

60. *Id.* at 683.

61. *Id.* at 700 (quoting *Richmond Newspapers,* 448 U.S. at 569).

62. *Id.*

63. *Id.* at 701.

64. *Id.* (citing 8 U.S.C.A. § 1228(c) (2002)).

65. *Id.* at 703–04.

66. *Id.* at 704–05.

67. *Id.* at 705.

68. *Id.* at 707.

69. *Id.* at 711.

70. 308 F.3d 198 (3d Cir. 2002), *cert. denied,* 533 U.S. 1056 (2003).

71. *Id.* at 212.

72. *Id.* at 213.

73. *See e.g., United States v. Criden,* 675 F.2d 550, 555-57 (3d Cir.1982).

74. *North Jersey Media Group, Inc.*, 308 F.3d at 216.

75. *Id.* at 217.

76. *Id.* Judge Becker recognized that considering evidence of how open deportation hearings could threaten national security as part of the threshold inquiry into the existence of a presumptive access right created an "evidentiary overlap" with the "compelling government interest" analysis that is taken up to decide whether a proceeding could be closed, but felt that "the inquiries are not redundant because it is possible for openness to serve a positive role under a balanced logic prong even though the government has a compelling interest in closure. This would simply require that the policy rationales supporting openness be even more compelling than those supporting closure." *Id.* at 217 n. 13.

77. *Id.* at 218–19.

78. *Id.* at 220. (emphasis added).

79. *Id.* at 222 25 (Scirica, *J.*, dissenting).

80. *North Jersey Media Group, Inc. v. Ashcroft,* 123 S. Ct. 2215 (2003).

81. *North Jersey Media Grou, Inc. v. Ashcroft,* 308 F.3d 198 (3d Cir. 2002).

82. *Id.*

83. *See* 478 U.S. 1, 7-9; 478 U.S. at 21 (Stevens, J., dissenting) ("a common law right of access did not inhere in preliminary proceedings at the time the First Amendment was adopted").

84. *See, e.g., United States v. Haller,* 837 F.2d 84, 86 (2d Cir. 1988) (plea hearings "have typically been open to the public"); *Washington Post v. Robinson,* 935 F.2d 282, 288 (D.C. Cir. 1991) ("plea agreements have traditionally been open to the public"); *In re Providence Journal,* 293 F.3d 1, 9 (1st Cir. 2002) (documents submitted in criminal proceedings); *United States v. Presser,* 828 F.2d 340, 344 (6th Cir. 1987) *(Application of NBC)*(pretrial motion to disqualify judge, citing Sixth Circuit practice from 1924–1984).

85. *See, e.g., United States v. Cojab,* 996 F.2d 1404, 1407 (2d Cir. 1993) (pretrial hearing); *United States v. Criden,* 675 F.2d 550, 555 (3d Cir. 1982) ("societal interests" rather than historical analysis should determine First Amendment right of access to suppression hearing); *Id.* ("We do not think that historical analysis is relevant in determining whether there is a first amendment right of access to pretrial criminal proceedings").

86. 845 F.2d 1513, 1516 (9th Cir. 1988).

87. *See also United States v. Chagra,* 701 F.2d 354, 362-64 (5th Cir. 1983) (noting increased significance of bail procedures, citing the significance of Bail Reform Act of 1966); *Criden,* 550 F.2d at 555 ("We do not think that historical analysis is relevant to determining whether there is a first amendment right of access to pretrial criminal proceedings."). How the proceeding at issue is defined greatly affects the outcome of the historical analysis, and judges in several cases both in the Supreme Court and lower courts have differed on the proper approach. For example, although Justice Brennan in the majority opinion in *Globe Newspapers* alluded to the openness of criminal trials generally (*Globe Newspaper Co. v. Super. Court for County of Norfolk* 457 U.S. 596,605 (1982)), Chief Justice Burger in his dissent found the more relevant comparison in that case to be trials involving sex crimes against a minor, which he asserted were traditionally shielded from view. *Id. at,* 614 (Burger, C.J., dissenting). Similarly, there is little uniformity in geographical scope of judicial sources of "experience." Some courts have looked only at the "experience" of their own jurisdiction. *See, e.g., United States v. Presser,* 828 F.2d 340, 345 (6th Cir. 1987) *(Application of NBC)*. Others courts have looked beyond their own jurisdiction for guidance. *See, e.g., Rivera-Puig v. Garcia-Rosario,* 983 F.2d 311 (1st Cir. 1993). (although Puerto Rico typically held preliminary hearings in private, *Press Enterprise II* "refers to the experience in that type or kind of hearing throughout the United States, not the experience in only one jurisdiction").

88. *United States v. Chagra,* 701 F.2d 354, 363 (5th Cir. 1983).

89. *E.g., Richmond Newspapers v. Virginia,* 448 U.S. 555,587 (Brennan, J., concurring).

90. The Department of Justice has declined the extension of immigration proceedings to ALJs, perhaps because Supreme Court decisions permit it and DOJ can keep its hearing officers in closer check than ALJs. *See* Paul R. Verkuil, *Reflections Upon the Federal Administrative Judiciary,* 39 U.C.L.A. L. Rev. 1341, 1358-1360 (1992).

91. An alien may file a motion to reopen before the immigration judge or the Board of Immigration Appeals. 8 C.F.R. § 103.3 (2003). An alien may also appeal a removal order directly to the Court of Appeals, within 30 days of the removal order's issuance. 8 U.S.C.S. § 1252 (2004).

92. This practice was upheld in *Marcello v. Bonds,* 349 U.S. 302 (1955).

93. 8 C.F.R. § 1003 (2003). Confirming their judicial role in the deportation and removal process, responsibility for supervising immigration judges shifted to the Executive Office for Immigration Review and, more recently, to Bureau of Homeland Security under the Homeland Security Act.

94. *See* 8 U.S.C.S. § 1229 INA § 240(b)(1) (2003); 8 C.F.R. §§ 240.2 (2003). Note that this was redesigned and duplicated as chapter V, part 1240, Feb. 28, 2003, 68 F.R. § 9824; part 1240 was further amended to change reference citations, Mar. 5, 2003, 68 F.R. § 1240.2.

95. 8 U.S.C.S. 1229(a) (2004).

96. 8 U.S.C. S. §1229 (2004).

97. 8 C.F.R. § 240.7(a); *See Bustos-Torres v. INS,* 898 F.2d 1053, 1055–56 (5th Cir. 1990). *But see Cunanan v. INS,* 856 F.2d 1373, 1374–75 (9th Cir. 1988) (alien wife's affidavit excluded where INS had not attempted to produce her as a witness); *Iran v. INS,* 656 F.2d 469, 472–73 (9th Cir. 1981) (unauthenticated INS form and consulate letter inadmissible).

98. In most civil trials, the burden of proof on most issues is a "preponderance of the evidence." *See, e.g., Concrete Pipe & Prods. v. Constr. Laborers Pension Trust,* 508 U.S. 602, 622 (1993). In some

instances, however, the burden of proof is higher. *See New York Times v. Sullivan,* 376 U.S. 254 (1964) (requiring proof of actual malice by "clear and convincing" evidence). Similarly, in removal proceedings, burdens of proof vary depending on a variety of factors including whether the alien has been admitted into the United States. *See* INA § 204(c) (2003). The regulations now provide that:

> [T]he Service must first establish the alienage of the respondent. Once alienage has been established, unless the respondent demonstrates by clear and convincing evidence that he or she is lawfully in the United States pursuant to a prior admission, the *respondent* must prove that he or she is clearly and beyond a doubt *entitled to be admitted* to the United States and is not inadmissible as *charged.*

C.F.R. § 1240.8(c) (2003) (emphasis added). Although not explicit, the statute suggests that the INS must show that the person is an alien by "clear and convincing" evidence. INA § 240(c)(3)(A) (2003). Once the alien establishes admission or entitlement to admission, "the Service has the burden of establishing by clear and convincing evidence that, in the case of an alien who has been admitted to the United States, the alien is deportable. No decision on deportability shall be valid unless it is based upon reasonable, substantial, and probative evidence." *Id.*

99. *See generally,* Verkuil, *supra,* n.90.

100. *S. Carolina State Ports Auth. v. Fed. Mar. Comm'n,* 243 F.3d 165, 174 (4th Cir. 2001), *aff'd,* 535 U.S. 743 (2002) (holding that sovereign immunity bars claims under the Shipping Act).

101. Morning Edition: Whether the press and public should be allowed to attend deportation hearings (National Public Radio Broadcast, Sept. 18, 2002) (quoting Third Circuit judge Morton Greenberg). (transcript on file with Committee).

102. *Id.*

103. The following sections concerning issues of immigration law and policy are authored solely by the Committee on Immigration and Nationality Law.

104. Pub. L. 104-208, 110 Stat. 3009 (Sept. 30, 1996) (codified in scattered sections of 8 & 18 U.S.C.).

105. 8 U.S.C §§1531–1537 (2004).

106. *Id.* The use of secret evidence against foreigners suspected of being a danger to national security is not new, but dates back at least fifty (50) years to World War II. *See Knauff v. Shaughnessy,* 338 U.S. 537 (1950) (discussing the use of secret evidence against aliens during World War II).

107. *See* 8 U.S.C. § 1532 (2004).

108. *See* 8 U.S.C. §1534 (2004).

109. *See, generally,* Martin Schwartz, Niels Frenzen, & Mayra L. Calo, *Recent Developments on the INS's Use of Secret Evidence Against Aliens,* 2 IMMIGRATION & NATIONALITY LAW HANDBOOK 300-11 (2001 ed.).

110. The Immigration and Naturalization Service (INS), formerly an agency of the Department of Justice, has since been divided up, on March 1, 2003, with the creation of the Department of Homeland Security. The immigration prosecutorial functions are now with US Immigration and Customs Enforcement (USICE) while the Immigration Court and Board of Immigration Appeals remain with the Department of Justice.

111. *Id.* at 309 ("In recent years the INS has used secret evidence, with a few exceptions, primarily against Arabs and Muslims.").

112. *See, e.g.,* Andrew Cockburn, *The Radicalization of James Woolsey,* N. Y. Times, July 23, 2000 (describing how former CIA Director James Woolsey defended Iraqis whom INS attempted using "secret evidence") ("Finally free to read what the government had fought to conceal, he was astonished to discover that the case against his clients was, as he put it, 'a joke.'").

113. "[Deportation] may result also in loss of both property and life; or of all that makes life worth living." Ng Fung Ho v. White, 259 U.S. 276, 284 (1922).

114. 424 U.S. 319 (1976).

115. *Id.*

116. Jim Edwards, *Data Show Shoddy Due Process for Post-Sept. 11 Immigration Detainees: Some 'Special Interest List' inmates held for months without charges,* N.J. Law J., Feb. 4, 2002.

117. Id.

118. Somini Sengupta, *Ill-Fated Path to America, Jail & Death,* N.Y. Times, Nov. 5, 2001 (describing how a Pakistani detainee died of a heart attack after being inexplicably held in US jail after he agreed to depart the United States).

119. Audi, *supra* note 5.

120. Evan *Thomas* & Michael Isikoff, *Justice Kept in the Dark,* Newsweek, Dec. 10, 2001, at 37.

121. U.S. Department of Justice, Office of the Inspector General, Supplemental Report on September 11 Detainees' Allegations of Abuse at the Metropolitan Detention Center in Brooklyn, New York (December 2003).

122. For example, the Attorney General has issued a press release applauding the decision of an immigration judge to deny asylum to one particular Muslim male who was the subject of a "special interest" hearing. *See* Press Release, Department of Justice, Statement of Barbara Comstock, Director of Public Affairs, on the Haddad Asylum Decision (Nov. 22, 2002) (02-691) (available at http://www.usdoj.gov/opa/pr/2002/November/02_civ_691.htm.) The fact that the Attorney General would authorize the issuance of an official press release commenting on the Haddad case is troubling, because the Attorney General is the final administrative authority in asylum cases; his Department's commentary on the outcome of the case is akin to the Supreme Court issuing a press release applauding a U.S. District Court judge's decision in a case that is not yet final and may ultimately be appealed to the Supreme Court. Such behavior by the Supreme Court or other court would be deemed a violation of the Code of Conduct. Canon 3A(6) of the Code of Conduct for United States Judges provides that judges "should avoid public comment on the merits of a pending or impending action."

123. *See, e.g.* Ricardo Alonso-Zaldivar & Jonathan Peterson, *The Nation: 5 on Immigration Board Asked to Leave; Critics Call It a 'Purge,'* Los Angeles Times, Mar. 12, 2003, at 16 (quoting a Senate aide who said "This sends a signal to the remaining [members] that if you don't toe the line, you could be in jeopardy"); Lisa Getter & Jonathan Peterson, *The Nation: Speedier Rate of Deportation Rulings Assailed,* Los Angeles Times, Jan. 5, 2003, at 1 (describing Attorney General John Ashcroft's plan to clear administrative backlog with summary denials of appeals).

124. For example, the Justice Department has altered prison regulations to allow the government to eavesdrop on attorney-client conversations. *See, e.g.,* Jim Edwards, *No Secrets,* Miami Daily Bus. Rev., Aug. 29, 2002 at A9 (discussing "a lengthening line of laws, regulations and other measures that constrain attorneys representing those swept up in the [terrorism] probe").

125. Dan Christensen, *Secrets Within,* Miami Daily Bus. Rev., Mar. 12, 2003.

126. Audi *supra* note 5. ("When you're locked up in Tucson and transferred five times in three weeks and you're not given a phone, your right to counsel is rendered meaningless.").

127. *Metro: In Brief,* Wash. Post, Apr. 24, 2001, at B1 (quoting INS spokeswoman Karen Kraushaar as stating, "Immigration is a mystery and a mastery of obfuscation, and the lawyers who can figure it out are worth their weight in gold").

128. Brill, *supra* note 21, at 147 (recounting the story of a high-level Department of Justice meeting in which "someone in the room remarked that the government should not try too hard to make sure [aliens] could contact lawyers").

129. *Id.* ("Under INS rules, they were entitled to call a lawyer from jail, but the lists the INS provided of available lawyers invariably had phone numbers that were not in service").

130. Mark Bixler, *Right to Counsel Denied, Immigration Lawyers Say,* Atlanta J.-Const., Mar. 12, 2003, at 2E (recounting story of Iranian national whose lawyer was told that he could not accompany him to an INS interview).

131. Mary Graham, *The Information Wars: Terrorism Has Become a Pretext for a New Culture of Secrecy,* Atlantic Monthly, Sept. 2002, at 37.

132. *See* Select Comm. to Study Governmental Operations with Respect to Intelligence Activities, Intelligence Activities and the Rights ofAmericans, S. Rep. No. 755, at Book III 355 (1976) ("Before 1966, the FBI conducted over two hundred 'black bag jobs.' These warrantless surreptitious entries were carried out for intelligence purposes").

133. *See, e.g.,* G. Gordon Liddy, Will at 133 (1998) (describing how FBI Director J. Edgar Hoover had extensive files on various Washington politicians, which he used for political leverage).

134. Athan Theoharis, Chasing Spies: How the FBI Failed in Counterintelligence but Promoted the Politics of McCarythism in the Cold War Years 249–50 (2002).

135. Philip Shenon, *Secret Court Says F.B.I. Aides Misled Judges In 75 Cases,* N.Y. Times, Aug. 23, 2002, at A1.

136. U.S. Gen. Accounting Office, Justice Department: Better Management Oversight & Internal Controls Needed to Ensure Accuracy of Terrorism-Related Statistics, GAO-03-266 (Jan. 2003) (reporting that almost half of the convictions deemed "terrorism-related" by the Department of Justice were determined by GAO investigators to have been wrongly classified as such).

137. Patrick Howe, *FBI Agent Questions FBI's Terrorism Readiness if Iraq Attacked,* Associated Press, Mar. 6, 2003 (citing an agent's letter to FBI Director Robert Mueller in which she questions the evidence linking al Qaeda to Iraq and the truthfulness of a FBI statement claiming that there are 5,000 terrorists in the country).

138. Office of the Inspector Gen., *supra* note 22 and note 121.

139. *See, e.g.,* Brent Walth & Kim Christensen, *INS Bureaucracy, Blundering Create "The Agency from Hell,"* Oregonian, Dec. 11, 2000, at A01; Office of the Inspector Gen., U.S. Dep't of Justice, Immigr. & Naturalization Service Management of Property, Rep. No. 01-09 (Mar. 2001) (finding that "INS did not adequately account for property and that immediate corrective actions are necessary"); Thomas Alexander Aleinikoff et al., Immigration and Citizenship: Process and Policy 251 (4th ed. 1998) ("INS was once respected as a relatively well-run and efficient administrative agency... But as its tasks expanded and the statute and regulations became more complex,... [m]anagement systems became badly outmoded, and tales of long delays..., lost files, and poor morale... became distressingly common").

140. Walth & Christensen, *supra* note 139, at A01 (quoting Zoe Lofgren, D-Calif.).

141. *See, e.g.,* Kim Christensen et al., *Unchecked Power of the INS Shatters American Dream,* Oregonian, Dec. 10, 2000, at A01 (noting that "one in seven of the agency's 32,000 employees was the subject of an internal investigation in 1999").

142. *See, e.g.,* Philip Shenon, *Threats and Responses: Domestic Security; Ridge Discovers Size of Home Security Task,* N.Y. Times, Mar. 3, at A1.

143. *Terrorist Attack Investigation: Ashcroft Details Tally of Detainees, Other Developments,* Facts on File World News Dig., Nov. 27, 2001, at 932A1.

144. An article in the *Philadelphia Inquirer* first raised allegations that the DOJ was improperly reporting information about terrorism-related convictions. *See* Mark Fazlollah & Peter Nicholas, *U.S. Overstates Arrests in Terrorism: For Years, Officials Said, Cases That Should Not Have Been in that Category Were Included to Support Budget Requests,* Philadelphia Inquirer, Dec. 16, 2001, at A01. This article triggered the GAO investigation that confirmed the inaccurate reports.

145. Christensen, *supra* note 125, at A1 (reporting how the DOJ is apparently sealing all records relating to a civil lawsuit filed against the warden of a federal correctional institution by a since-released Muslim inmate).

146. U.S. Gen. Accounting Office, *supra* note 136.

147. Mae M. Cheng, *Uproot: Pakistanis Seek Refuge in Canada,* Newsday, Oct. 5, 2003, at A06 ("But after 9/11, they felt like they were targeted by authorities on the grounds that most are Muslim.... That has led them to Canada. Here, they are peaceful. They are comfortable.").

148. Thomas & Isikoff, *supra* note 120, at 37.

149. Purdy, *supra* note 15, at B5.

150. For example, many of the "special interest" detainees were Israeli Jews, a group that is highly unlikely to be a security threat to the United States. *See, e.g.,* John Mintz, *60 Israelis on Tourist Visas Detained Since Sept. 11; Government Calls Several Cases 'of Special Interest,' Meaning Related to Post-Attacks Investigation,* Wash. Post, Nov. 23, 2001, at A22 ("'It was obvious they mistook us' as Arabs from Israel," said an Israeli army veteran).

151. *Id.* at A22 (quoting attorney David Leopold, who represented several Israeli Jews who were held as "special interest" detainees, but were later released when the Government could produce no evidence connecting them to any terrorist activity).

152. Audi, *supra* note 5, at 1A.

CHAPTER 13

Letter from the Association President to U.S. Congressman Edward Markey re: HR 4674: The Proposed Legislation Seeking the End of U.S. Involvement in Extraordinary Rendition

PREFACE BY ALAN R. ROTHSTEIN

In the aftermath of 9/11 and the invasions of Afghanistan and Iraq, the United States government intensified its efforts to interrogate persons suspected of engaging in terrorist activities. The public soon came to learn of the Guantanamo detainee facility and of detainee centers in Iraq and those run by the Central Intelligence Agency around the world. The American public also became aware of the interrogation techniques that many claimed constituted torture or cruel, inhuman, or degrading treatment and of the efforts of lawyers in the Bush Administration to justify such actions as consistent with domestic and international law, an effort widely condemned both in this country and worldwide.

Much less has been made of the expansion of the use of "rendition" to conduct interrogations of terror suspects. Rendition is the transporting of an individual by a state to a foreign state without the use of legal process, such as extradition. While such transfers have been conducted for many years, the use has been primarily to subject the detainees to the legal processes of the country that receives the detainee. However, post-9/11, rendition has been used increasingly to transport an individual to a foreign country for interrogation. The particularly troublesome use of this technique is called "extraordinary rendition," the rendition of an individual to a foreign state in circumstances that make it more likely than not that the individual will be subjected to torture or other cruel, inhuman, or degrading treatment. We began to learn of cases like Maher Arar, a Canadian citizen detained by American authorities in the United States and rendered to Syria, a country in which torture is a documented practice (such documentation including that provided by the U.S. State Department). Though it was not well known at the time, U.S. agents had also been complicit in rendering Abu Omar, detained in Italy, to Egypt and Muhammed al-Zari and Ahmed Agiza, two individuals detained in Sweden, also to Egypt.

The Association of the Bar began a comprehensive study of the legality of the practice of extraordinary rendition, in concert with The Center for Human Rights

and Global Justice at New York University School of Law. As the study was nearing completion, Congressman Edward Markey (D–MA), a senior member of the House Homeland Security Committee, introduced a legislation designed to bar the United States from engaging in extraordinary rendition. The City Bar's letter expressed support for passage of this legislation, stressing that "extraordinary rendition" was a violation of international and domestic law.

Congressman Markey's bill was not enacted. However, he was in position to sharply and effectively oppose attempts to pass legislation to weaken the proscription against extraordinary rendition, which had been initially included in, but eventually dropped from, the bill introduced in late 2004 to implement recommendations of the 9/11 Commission.

August 4, 2004

Representative Edward J. Markey
United States House of Representatives
Washington, D.C. 20515

Dear Representative Markey:

I write on behalf of the Association of the Bar of the City of New York. The Association is an independent non-governmental organization of more than 22,000 lawyers, judges, law professors and government officials. Founded in 1870, the Association has a long history of dedication to human rights, notably through its Committee on International Human Rights, which investigates and reports on human rights conditions around the world.

The Association strongly supports H.R. 4674, your proposed legislation to end the extrajudicial transfer of individuals to countries in which they may be tortured or subjected to cruel, inhuman or degrading treatment or punishment—a practice known as "extraordinary rendition." The bill would reinforce prohibitions on extraordinary rendition that are already binding on the United States under international law. Laws banning the return or transfer of individuals to countries where they are likely to be tortured are articulated in a number of treaties to which the United States is a party. These include, most prominently, the United Nations Convention Against Torture and Other Forms of Cruel, Inhuman or Degrading Treatment or Punishment, and the International Covenant on Civil and Political Rights. By enacting the Foreign Affairs Reform and Restructuring Act of 1998, the United States reaffirmed its policy not to expel, extradite, or otherwise effect the involuntary return of any person to a country in which there are substantial grounds for believing the person would be in danger of being subjected to torture, regardless of whether the person is physically present in the United States.

The Association has been gravely concerned about the practice of extraordinary rendition since reports surfaced in the press in early 2002 alleging that the United States was involved in transferring individuals to countries in which torture is a documented practice. These reports, which have been supplemented in recent months by first-hand accounts of rendered individuals, such as Maher Arar, a Canadian citizen rendered to Syria from the United States, demonstrate the need for legislation like H.R. 4674.

The Association is currently preparing a report that will analyze the legal prohibitions on extraordinary rendition under domestic and international law. Our research has identified certain gaps in the enforcement of this legal obligation—gaps that your proposed legislation is aimed at closing. For example, while the regulations implementing domestic legislation offer protection from removal or extradition to torture-practicing countries to individuals present within the United States, no similar protection is afforded to individuals who are held by or

on behalf of the United States in other countries. With the enactment of H.R. 4674, however, such country-to-country transfers could be prohibited.

Because the bill clearly proscribes extraordinary rendition, rejects diplomatic assurances as insufficient, and creates crucial protections for those most at risk of being transferred to torture or cruel treatment, the Association strongly supports H.R 4674.

We thank you for your work to end the practice of extraordinary rendition, and hope that this important bill will be approved as soon as possible.

Respectfully,
Bettina B. Plevan
President, Association of the Bar of the City of New York

CHAPTER 14

Statement Opposing House 9/11 Bill

PREFACE BY CLAUDIA SLOVINSKY

When the 9/11 Commission appointed by President Bush completed its work in 2004, it submitted a series of legislative recommendations to Congress. When the House of Representatives developed legislation purportedly based on these recommendations, H.R. 10, it added a number of provisions that went well beyond the Commission's proposals to unduly expand executive power, undermine U.S. treaty obligations, and impose great hardships on many non-citizens. As with much 9/11-related legislation, H.R. 10 quickly gained momentum in Congress, and the combination of the speed and complexity of the legislation made it difficult to analyze. Several Association committees, however, identified sufficient problems with the bill to warrant the Association's urging Congress not to enact the legislation.

The Association's statement on H.R. 10 particularly flagged provisions which would have eliminated the protections afforded detainees from being sent to countries that engage in torture. The bill also would have imposed further draconian limitations on the rights of persons facing deportation or removal, including eliminating the authority of the courts to take certain actions. The statement further noted provisions that raised serious privacy concerns.

October 20, 2004

CITY BAR ASSOCIATION ISSUES STATEMENT OPPOSING HOUSE 9/11 BILL

The Association of the Bar of the City of New York joins the many organizations deeply concerned about the passage of HR 10 by the House and the possible legislation that will result from the House-Senate conference. Should the House bill prevail, there will be a major impact on our domestic law and our international treaty obligations. Many of these changes pose serious constitutional problems, negatively impact immigrant communities without gain in fighting terrorism, and have major implications with regard to Americans' privacy rights.

Specifically, the Association strongly opposes those provisions of the bill that violate our country's obligations under the Convention Against Torture and Other Cruel, Inhuman or Degrading Treatment (CAT), and other provisions that, while purporting to target only "terrorists," really undermine basic due process protections for *all* non-citizens.

Section 3032 allows for the removal of those accused of being terrorists to other countries known for their practice of torture upon a "diplomatic assurance" from that country that it will not torture that individual. Removal upon a diplomatic assurance from a country where torture is practiced is no assurance at all, especially when the law fails to provide a forum for disputing the reliability of such a finding or any mechanism to monitor the transfer of the individual to the country providing such assurance.

Equally troubling is the inclusion of immigrants with criminal convictions who have nothing to do with terrorism into the category of those who must be mandatorily detained even if they are granted some protection from removal under the immigration law.

The bill also generally makes CAT protection more difficult to obtain by all those who fear torture by requiring them to prove the likelihood of torture by "clear and convincing evidence." This is an evidentiary standard that even the most deserving applicants are unable to meet. The bill would further authorize the government to remove foreign nationals to countries that lack a functioning government, making it impossible to know whether they will suffer torture or other persecution upon their arrival. And the regulations which would be promulgated to effectuate this law would not be subject to judicial review.

The expanded group of those the House bill seeks to subject to expedited removal would deprive an even larger population of all due process rights. Immigrants living in the US as long as five years, often with US citizen families, would not be given any opportunity to present a valid defense to removal or to make a meritorious request for relief, including applications for withholding of removal based on a *likelihood* of persecution. This would clearly be in violation of the Refugee Convention to which the United States is a signatory.

The expansion of expedited removal would also be particularly problematic for battered immigrant women, a group Congress has previously singled out to especially protect when it passed the comprehensive scheme of federal protections for victims of domestic abuse in the Violence Against Women Act ("VAWA"). An expansion of expedited removal would allow batterers to more easily threaten their families with immediate deportation if they sought protection as well as discourage women from reporting abuse for fear of being deported. In addition, this provision could enable abusers to avoid prosecution for their crimes by getting their victims deported without any recourse or ability to seek help from police or victim services. Expansion of expedited removal under HR 10 would eviscerate these public policy interests and erase hard-won gains by law enforcement of the trust of immigrant communities.

Other provisions of HR 10 further curtail judicial review in some instances and prohibit it altogether in others, thereby denying non-citizens basic due process of law. The bill eliminates habeas corpus review of a variety of deportation decisions, including even review of the denial of protection under the Convention against Torture. The "Great Writ" of habeas corpus has been a long-standing safeguard against government error in the deportation of non-citizens. The Supreme Court has ruled that the availability of habeas corpus is essential to avoid "serious constitutional questions" in the face of statutes that seek to strip the federal courts' power to review unlawful government actions. *INS v. St. Cyr,* 533 U.S. 289, 314 (2001). HR 10's provisions, which would further restrict the already limited judicial review currently in the law, would result in prejudice because of unreviewable government misconduct and error, to tens of thousands of non-citizens who have nothing to do with terrorism and are, in many cases, integrated into our society as part of, and supporting, citizen and legal resident families.

In addition to drastically reduced judicial review, HR 10 also seeks to tie federal courts' hands by limiting the courts' power to grant stays of deportation, even in cases which involve asylum claims. The passage of this provision would burden the courts with emergency briefings and result in the automatic deportation of individuals with meritorious claims.

All of the above provisions fly in the face of the 9/11 Commission's admonition that the "border and immigration system of the United States must remain a visible manifestation of our belief in freedom, democracy, global economic growth, and the rule of law, yet serve equally well as a vital element of counterterrorism." We must remain faithful to the Commission's recommendations and effectively ensure our security without unduly abridging the most basic protections of due process for immigrants. If we do not rise to this challenge, legislation that is hastily passed into law today will render our immigration system even more dysfunctional, erode our democratic principles, and make us less secure tomorrow.

Other provisions HR 10 seeks to make law raise potentially serious concerns regarding privacy, by (a) allowing greater access to private personal information (for example, developing a system to provide employers with employees' criminal history information, including arrests, and not solely convictions), (b) establishing standards and a system that could serve as a method for creating a *de facto* national identification card system, and (c) creating a coordinated national computer system for tracking birth records. Traveler screening mechanisms using new techniques and approaches also are provided in this bill. While there is need for information and screening procedures in these times of heightened alert, the potential for error and misuse is great, as has been demonstrated repeatedly in our history. This potential is even more troubling as the data collected become ever more vast and inter-connected. Yet the legislation provides scant protection for the American people, largely delegating that issue to the very branch of government in which the power to collect and use the data reside.

We urge the House-Senate conference committee to reject the provisions of HR 10 and adopt the Senate version of the 9-11 Commission bill.

CHAPTER 15

Position Paper Regarding National Labor Relations Board Decision in IBM Case

PREFACE BY DANIEL SILVERMAN

The notion that terrorists can be anywhere in the United States has been an articulated underpinning of many of the Executive Branch's post-9/11 actions. It was even manifested in a National Labor Relations Board decision to which the Association's Labor and Employment Law Committee objected. In June 2004, the Board decided, in IBM Corp., 341 NLRB No. 148, that an employee not represented by a union could not have a co-worker present during an interview that may lead to disciplinary action. The concern, apparently, was that the co-worker would work in concert with, or coach, the employee such as to limit the employer's ability to obtain information relating to terrorism (perhaps the employee's terrorist activity) from the employee.

The Labor and Employment Law Committee saw the decision as a misconstruction of the National Labor Relations Act and expressed its belief "that the need to fully protect society from potential terrorist attacks does not include the need for employers to interrogate employees about matters that could lead to discipline without a representative present."

POSITION PAPER

On June 9, 2004, the National Labor Relations Board by a 3-2 vote reversed precedent and decided that employees who are not represented for purposes of collective bargaining by a labor organization do not have a right to have a co-worker present during an interview that may lead to discipline of the employee. *IBM Corp.,* 341 NLRB No. 148.

The Board said that a reconsideration of the existing law was required, in part, because the Board must now take into account both real and threatened terrorist attacks in light of the events of September 11, 2001 and its aftermath.

The Committee on Labor and Employment Law of the Association of the Bar of the City of New York (the "Committee")[1] strongly believes that the events of September 11 and the aftermath should not be used to justify the view adopted by the majority. To rely on such events in

determining the rights of employees have under the National Labor Relations Act distorts the legitimate decision making process and injects essentially political considerations into a matter of statutory construction. The Committee does not endorse the interpretation of the Act of either the majority or the dissenting opinions in *IBM,* but rather believes that the issue of employee rights in such circumstances should be decided on the application of traditional criteria of statutory construction.

Under the interpretation of the statute reversed in *IBM,* the employee's right to have a representative present when being questioned about a matter that could lead to discipline does not limit an employer's right to discharge an employee for misconduct. There is no requirement that the employer even conduct an investigation. The issue of representation only arises if the employer wishes to conduct the interview and to deny the employee his or her request to have another employee present.

Under NLRB law, the right of representation does not encompass a right to refuse to cooperate in the employer's investigation. A refusal to cooperate is itself a valid ground for discharge. There is no right of silence; an employee's refusal to fully answer the employer's questions can constitute a legitimate ground for discharge. If the investigation proceeds with the representative present, the representative may not in any way interfere with the employer's interrogation of the employee. There may be situations, of course, where the employees choice of representative cannot be accommodated either because of unavailability or because it is not appropriate for that person to act as representative in light of the information to be discussed. These matters should be decided on a case by case basis before the Board.

The role of the representative is to be in a position to assist the employee being interrogated in articulating the employee's position and in providing a witness to the interrogation.

The Committee believes that the need to fully protect society from potential terrorist attacks does not include a need for employers to interrogate employees about matters that could lead to discipline without a representative present. The employer's right to protect its business and the people connected with it is fully recognized by the Committee. The Committee appreciates that an employer must have the tools to carry out that responsibility fully and adequately. The role of a representative for an employee under suspicion is not changed, however, because the matter under investigation is related to terrorism. If the National Labor Relations Act, as properly interpreted, provides a right to have a representative present to assist the employee under suspicion, that right is in no way diminished because of a societal concern about terrorists activity, however valid. Indeed, it may be argued that the consequences of an investigation of potential terrorists activity increases the employee's need for representation. The Committee, however, expressly refrains from taking a position on the validity of the *IBM* decision. We merely reiterate that the threat of terrorism should not be used to modify the interpretations of a statute passed in 1935 with a purpose of regulating employer-employee relations. To rely on such concerns, distorts the debate and unnecessarily injects political considerations into a matter that should be decided on its legal merits and has no relevance to the question of whether the employee is or is not represented by a labor organization.

Dated: October 13, 2004

NOTE

1. The Committee is made up of labor, management and public sector representatives. Although all parties agree that the position set forth in this paper reflects the views of the Committee, certain members of the labor bar have additional views concerning the Board's decision to reverse precedent that are not expressed herein. Celeste J. Mattina, Regional Director of NLRB Region 2, abstained from the Committee's vote on this Position Paper.

CHAPTER 16

Torture by Proxy: International and Domestic Law Applicable to "Extraordinary Renditions"

PREFACE BY MARGARET L. SATTERTHWAITE

On December 26, 2002, the *Washington Post* published a story by Dana Priest and Barton Gellman that exposed the practice now known as "extraordinary rendition" through the words of an unnamed U.S. official. Attributing a source involved in sending suspects to other countries for interrogation, the story quoted the official as follows: "We don't kick the [expletive] out of them. We send them to other countries so they can kick the [expletive] out of them."[1] Although this comment contained all the elements of the practice, rendition did not become the focus of intense discussion for some time. Indeed, the practice remained largely in the shadows during the prisoner abuse scandals.

Similarly, the City Bar did not focus on rendition in its early work on torture. In its joint report on the meaning and application of international norms against torture, the Committees on International Human Rights and Military Affairs and Justice had only been able to make passing reference to rendition. The continuing—though periodic—reports about rendition that surfaced in the press during 2003 and 2004 led to the agreement that sustained analysis was needed. Through a collaborative project of the Committee on International Human Rights and the Center for Human Rights and Global Justice at NYU School of Law, a team of researchers, writers, and editors set out to comprehensively analyze rendition under international and domestic law.[2] After carefully examining the relevant regimes, we concluded that extraordinary renditions were contrary to both U.S. and international law.

The first challenge in preparing the report was defining the practice. To do so, we examined the history of the procedure known as "rendition to justice." This form of rendition had been authorized by a series of presidential directives dating to the Reagan era and involved the forcible capture of suspected terrorists by U.S. agents, followed by their transport to the United States to face criminal charges. Designed to gain personal jurisdiction over individuals who were in countries

where extradition procedures were non-existent or practically unavailable, these "snatches" were well known to those familiar with the Supreme Court case of *United States v. Alvarez-Machain*[3] or the D.C. Circuit case of *United States v. Yunis.*[4] While these earlier renditions to justice were designed to bring an individual to the United States to stand trial pursuant to recognized criminal charges, the new kind involved sending an individual to another country with an entirely different purpose. In short, what was "extraordinary" about the post-September 11 renditions was that they were aimed at interrogation and not trial and that they involved transfers to countries where torture was widespread or systematic.

We next debated the role of intent in our definition: was it the *purpose* of U.S. authorities to have an individual tortured in the receiving country? What evidence existed for such an allegation? Examining the media accounts, off-the-record statements by U.S. officials, and the factual circumstances of a series of renditions, we found there was insufficient evidence to clearly demonstrate that the United States actually had the purpose of subjecting individuals to torture. Moreover, our legal research revealed that this was unnecessary. The international prohibition on *refoulement*—sending an individual to a country where he or she faces a risk of torture—requires States to refrain from such transfers where this risk exists, regardless of the intent of the government. As a party to the Convention Against Torture, the International Covenant on Civil and Political Rights, and the Convention Relating to the Status of Refugees, the United States had accepted this rule numerous times. In implementing legislation, Congress had approved the rule and instructed agencies to follow and enforce it.

While we did not find evidence of an explicit intent to have individuals tortured, we decided to provide an analysis of the liability that would be attached if such an intent were proven. This seemed important given the allegations by investigative journalists that the rendition program was in fact aimed at having individuals interrogated under coercive conditions. Using standard federal criminal law doctrines, we examined the elements of the crimes of conspiracy and aiding and abetting in torture, concluding that extraordinary rendition could, when accompanied by the required mental element, entail serious crimes under U.S. law.

Two years later, many factual and policy questions remain about the extraordinary rendition program and process. Since our report was published, more than 20 alleged CIA agents have been made the subject of Italian indictments stemming from an extraordinary rendition they reportedly carried out in Milan; German officials are investigating the rendition of a German national apparently mistaken for a known terrorist suspect; and the Danish government has pledged to ensure that Danish airspace is not used for rendition operations. The impact of extraordinary renditions on diplomacy, on cooperative efforts aimed at bringing terrorists to justice, and on trust between American policy makers and the public remains uncertain. The law, on the other hand, is clear: the United States may not return individuals to countries where they are likely to face torture. *Torture by Proxy* provides the analysis needed to support this conclusion and shifts the burden back to those charged with enforcing that law.

Acronyms and Other References

9-11 Commission	National Commission on Terrorist Attacks Upon the United States
ABCNY	Association of the Bar of the City of New York
ACLU	American Civil Liberties Union
ATCA	Alien Torts Claims Act
AUMF	Authorization for Use of Military Force
BIA	Board of Immigration Appeals
CAT	Convention against Torture and Other Cruel, Inhuman or Degrading Treatment or Punishment
CAT Committee	Committee against Torture
CBP	of Customs and Border Protection, Department of Homeland Security
CCP	Crimes and Criminal Procedure
C.F.R.	Code of Federal Regulations
CIA	Central Intelligence Agency
CID	Cruel, inhuman or degrading
DCI	Director of Central Intelligence
DEA	Drug Enforcement Administration
DOD	Department of Defense
EOIR	Executive Office of Immigration Review
FARRA	Foreign Affairs Reform and Restructuring Act
FBI	Federal Bureau of Investigation
FOIA	Freedom of Information Act
FTCA	Federal Tort Claims Act
Geneva III	Geneva Convention (III) relative to the Treatment of Prisoners of War
Geneva IV	Geneva Convention (IV) relative to the Protection of Civilian Persons in Time of War
HRC	UN Human Rights Committee
INA	Immigration and Nationality Act
ICC	International Criminal Court
ICCPR	International Covenant on Civil and Political Rights
ICJ	International Court of Justice
ICRC	International Committee of the Red Cross
ICTR	International Criminal Tribunal for Rwanda
ICTY	International Criminal Tribunal for the former Yugoslavia
ILC	International Law Commission
MCM	Manual for Courts-Martial
MEJA	Military Extraterritorial Jurisdiction Act
NLRA	National Labor Relations Act
NSC	National Security Council
OAS	Organization of American States
PDD	Presidential Decision Directive
POW	Prisoner of war
Refugee Convention	Refugee Convention of 1951
TPA	Torture Victims Protection Act of 1991
UCMJ	Uniform Code of Military Justice
U.S.C.	United States Code

I. INTRODUCTION*

Since September 11, 2001, and especially in the aftermath of the wars in Afghanistan and Iraq, the United States has detained a large number of persons in various parts of the world for investigative purposes. Techniques used by U.S. authorities to interrogate these detainees have long been the subject of extensive criticism by human rights groups[5] and humanitarian agencies.[6] However, it was not until the military began receiving reports of mistreatment of detainees in Iraq, particularly at Abu Ghraib prison, that the Department of Defense began internal investigations into the conduct of army personnel.[7] These investigations and their results were kept away from the public eye until photographs depicting abuses at Abu Ghraib surfaced in media reports and information about the abuses became publicly available. At that time, the United States initiated investigations and congressional hearings into the abuses committed by U.S. officials. While the hearings focused on the mistreatment of prisoners at Abu Ghraib, members of Congress also questioned the scope of interrogation tactics generally used by U.S. actors.[8] This broader line of questioning has led to a widespread reconsideration of, and public debate over, the proper limits on interrogation in the "War on Terror." The standards relevant to defining clear limits—including federal law and human rights treaties (especially the UN Convention Against Torture[9])—have gained prominence, with arguments about the interpretation of the standards debated in print, during Congressional hearings, and on television.

Similarly, new attention has been focused on the variety of settings in which such abuses have occurred. "War on Terror" detainees have been held in military installations both inside and outside the United States (such as the Naval Consolidated Brig in Charleston, North Carolina, the U.S. naval base at Guantánamo Bay, Cuba, and the U.S. air force base in Bagram, Afghanistan), as well as reportedly being held in secret detention centers run by the Central Intelligence Agency (CIA) and other government agencies (including suspected secret sites on U.S. naval ships and at certain foreign bases or prisons[10]). The media, human rights organizations, and congressional bodies are currently investigating the abuses that have allegedly taken place in these detention centers. Internal probes have also been announced or acknowledged; at the time of this writing, investigations into detention practices and/or interrogation procedures had been concluded or were being conducted by personnel within the following agencies: the CIA, the Department of Homeland Security, and the Department of Defense.

Despite this flurry of attention, one U.S. "anti-terror" tactic has largely escaped sustained scrutiny by Congress and other oversight bodies,[11] and has not yet become the focus of public debate: the practice of "extraordinary rendition." For the purpose of this Report, Extraordinary Rendition is the transfer of an individual, with the involvement of the United States or its agents[12], to a foreign state in circumstances that make it more likely than not[13] that the individual will be subjected to torture or cruel, inhuman, or degrading treatment. As the term suggests, this "extraordinary" practice appears to be one form of what is an acknowledged practice—the covert rendition by U.S. officials of individuals suspected of involvement in terrorism to "justice"—*i.e.,* for trial or criminal investigation either to the United States or to foreign states. What is "extraordinary" about this more recent form of rendition is the role of torture and cruel, inhuman or degrading (CID) treatment reportedly involved in such transfers: U.S. officials reportedly are seeking opportunities to transfer terrorist suspects to locations where it is known that they may be tortured, hoping to gain useful information with the use of abusive interrogation tactics. At best, they appear to be turning a blind eye to abuses.

According to press reports, "regular" renditions—*i.e.,* transfers made without recourse to the regular legal procedures of extradition, removal, or exclusion, but not involving allegations of involvement in torture—have been occurring for more than a dozen years, and have included numerous transfers in the years leading up to September 11, 2001. According to reports,

however, the frequency of renditions increased significantly and their scope widened as the United States engaged in the "War on Terror."[14] Moreover, reports suggest that the pattern of renditions shifted during this time, focusing less on rendition to "justice" in the form of criminal investigation and trial in the United States or abroad, and more on interrogation—often in circumstances that indicate torture was at least a foreseeable possibility. As the former Director of the CIA's Counterterrorist Center J. Cofer Black stated during testimony before the House of Representatives and U.S. Senate Intelligence Committees, "there was a before 9/11 and there was an after 9/11. After 9/11 the gloves come off."[15]

This Report will assess the legality of the practice of Extraordinary Rendition under both U.S. and international law. The purpose of the Report is not to establish or verify facts concerning such transfers; that is a task better left to human rights organizations, international bodies, congressional oversight committees, and the U.S. government itself. Rather, using publicly available factual scenarios, this Report will describe the laws relevant to Extraordinary Renditions and the sanctions that may be applicable to individuals involved in such transfers. It will demonstrate that Extraordinary Rendition is prohibited by U.S. law, and is illegal under international human rights and humanitarian law. It will also explain that the U.S. government has an obligation to prevent Extraordinary Renditions, and to fully investigate, prosecute, and punish those responsible for such acts when they do occur. In addition to these duties to prevent and punish Extraordinary Rendition, the U.S. government may be liable under the international law of state responsibility for such transfers at the hands of its agents, and in some circumstances for the ill-treatment that occurs in states to which individuals are transferred, giving rise to the international legal obligation to immediately cease the practice and to remedy such abuses through restitution, compensation, and satisfaction.

II. EXECUTIVE SUMMARY

This joint Report of the International Human Rights Committee of the Association of the Bar of the City of New York and the Center for Human Rights and Global Justice at New York University School of Law analyzes the legal standards applicable to the practice of Extraordinary Rendition. The Report defines Extraordinary Rendition as the transfer of an individual, with the involvement of the United States or its agents, to a foreign state in circumstances that make it more likely than not that the individual will be subjected to torture or cruel, inhuman, or degrading treatment. The Report's main findings are that Extraordinary Rendition is an illegal practice under both domestic and international law, and that, consistent with U.S. policy against torture, the U.S. government is duty bound to cease all acts of Extraordinary Rendition, to investigate Extraordinary Renditions that have already taken place, and to prosecute and punish those found to have engaged in acts that amount to crimes in connection with Extraordinary Rendition.

The Report begins with an overview of the practice of Extraordinary Renditions as reported in the press; since Extraordinary Rendition appears to be a covert activity, the factual scenarios included in the Report have not been verified. Examples are given of cases in which the United States has allegedly been involved in transfers of individuals from inside the United States, from foreign states, and from U.S. military outposts to states well known to practice systematic or uncontrolled torture. The level of involvement of U.S. officials varies from case to case, but the facts in each example suggest that the United States is using this form of transfer as an interrogation technique in the "War on Terror." Indeed, while the use of Extraordinary Rendition has been denied in all official settings, officials speaking off the record have acknowledged the practice.

The Report next examines U.S. law to determine whether Extraordinary Renditions are, or could be, authorized by existing law or covert directives. After systematically considering the bases of authority for transfers of individuals by U.S. officials and the limits to that authority, the Report concludes that no publicly available statute, regulation, executive finding, directive or other action exists to authorize Extraordinary Rendition. Given the clear intent of Congress, expressed through legislation aimed at upholding U.S. obligations against torture and complicity in such abuse, and White House policy condemning torture, any purported authority to carry out Extraordinary Renditions would be an unauthorized derogation from U.S. law.

The Report then discusses the international law applicable to Extraordinary Rendition, including the Convention against Torture and Other Cruel, Inhuman or Degrading Treatment or Punishment; the International Covenant on Civil and Political Rights; the Geneva Conventions of 1949; and the Refugee Convention of 1951. The Report demonstrates that all of these treaties contain provisions preventing some aspects, or the entire practice, of Extraordinary Rendition. This Section concludes with a consideration of some guiding principles from international law on criminal liability that may be relevant in efforts to prosecute individuals who have been involved in Extraordinary Renditions. Standards explored include those governing complicity and conspiracy, the doctrine of command responsibility, and certain justifications and defenses available under international law. The Report then turns to the use of "diplomatic assurances"—promises made by governments not to torture or mistreat individuals who are being transferred into their custody. Because these promises are made only when the circumstances indicate that an individual is at risk of torture, and because there are no procedural safeguards allowing for their transparent implementation, the Report concludes that diplomatic assurances as currently used are ineffective.

The Report next demonstrates ways in which Extraordinary Rendition could leave the United States vulnerable to international liability under the doctrine of state responsibility. This Section explains that the U.S. government is required by international treaty law to prevent, investigate, prosecute, and punish acts amounting to Extraordinary Rendition. The Report concludes with a comprehensive examination of the U.S. criminal and civil statutes that are applicable to individuals involved in Extraordinary Rendition, demonstrating that such individuals may be open to criminal charges and/or civil liability for conspiracy and complicity in torture.

III. RECOMMENDATIONS

End the use of Extraordinary Rendition and take actions to remedy and compensate those harmed in Extraordinary Renditions.

- The president, the attorney general, the secretary of defense, and the secretary of homeland security should reject the practice of Extraordinary Rendition as contrary to U.S. and international law and policy.
- The United States should ensure that victims of Extraordinary Rendition are provided with adequate remedies.

Initiate formal investigations into the practice of Extraordinary Rendition.

- An independent commission, modeled on the National Commission on Terrorist Attacks Upon the United States (9-11 Commission) should be formed and charged with investigating Extraordinary Renditions.
- Congressional committees charged with oversight of the armed services, security and intelligence operations should fully investigate the practice of Extraordinary Rendition. Such investigations should

include an examination of the alleged authority for Extraordinary Renditions, and an accounting of how such practices came to be approved, if they were.

- The inspectors general of all relevant agencies, including the Central Intelligence Agency, the Federal Bureau of Investigation, the Department of Defense, and the Department of Homeland Security should investigate the involvement of their personnel and institutions in Extraordinary Rendition.
- Agencies with custody of documents concerning Extraordinary Rendition, including the Central Intelligence Agency, should declassify and make public such documents, and must comply with requests for documents pursuant to the Freedom of Information Act.
- The president should declassify Presidential Decision Directives and any other order or finding relevant to Extraordinary Renditions.
- The U.S. government should cooperate fully with the Canadian inquiry into the removal of Maher Arar.

Review and reform legislation and regulations relevant to Extraordinary Renditions.

- Congress should review and supplement the implementing legislation and accompanying regulations concerning the Convention against Torture to ensure that there are no gaps allowing for Extraordinary Rendition. Specifically, regulations should be promulgated by the relevant agencies to ensure that the obligation of *non-refoulement* set out in the Convention against Torture and the International Covenant on Civil and Political Rights, and implemented by the Foreign Affairs Reform and Restructuring Act of 1998, is enforced with respect to all detainees in the control or custody of U.S. actors, regardless of whether the person is physically present in the United States, as required by statute. The current failure to pass implementing legislation to this effect places relevant agencies at odds with their statutory duties.
- Congress should pass legislation modeled on H.R. 4674, drafted by Representative Markey, aimed at prohibiting Extraordinary Renditions.
- Congress should ensure that liability for complicity or conspiracy in torture is extended to civilian contractors working with U.S. armed forces, security personnel, or intelligence services.

Implement a moratorium on diplomatic assurances.

- The president, secretary of state, and attorney general should not rely upon diplomatic assurances as a means of negating the bar on transfers of those likely to face torture until and unless adequate safeguards have been implemented, including transparency, judicial review, and independent and effective monitoring.

Undertake criminal investigations into alleged acts of Extraordinary Rendition.

- Federal officials and military authorities should investigate individuals who may have been involved in acts that could amount to aiding and abetting or conspiracy to torture. Such investigations should include examination of officials involved in activities that could amount to aiding and abetting or conspiracy to torture, and should not be focused on only those lower level officials carrying out Extraordinary Renditions.
- Following such investigations, federal prosecutors and military officials should prosecute individuals concerning whom sufficient evidence exists to indict for aiding and abetting or conspiracy to torture.
- The United States should ensure that civil or military personnel involved in the custody, interrogation and treatment of any detainees be adequately trained and supervised in implementing the prohibition against torture and *refoulement*.

IV. EXTRAORDINARY RENDITIONS: AN OVERVIEW

A. Extraordinary Renditions—(Not) A New Phenomenon

No one knows for certain how many renditions (ordinary or extraordinary) have occurred because Congress is not notified about individual cases.[16] However, *Newsweek* reports that by 2004, the United States was running a covert charter airline moving CIA prisoners from one secret facility to another.[17] Usual destinations for rendered subjects are reported to be states such as Egypt, Jordan, Morocco, Saudi Arabia, Yemen, and Syria, all of which have been implicated by the U.S. State Department in using torture in interrogation.[18] The following examples of Extraordinary Renditions have been reported by various news sources. We are not in a position to verify or disprove these accounts; instead, they are offered here as examples of the practices to which we will apply our legal analysis:[19]

- In September 1995, U.S. intelligence agents reportedly picked up from Croatia one of Egypt's most wanted Islamic militants, placed him on a ship in the Adriatic Sea for interrogation, and subsequently turned him over to Egyptian authorities. His family believes he was executed in Egypt.[20]
- In 1998, U.S. agents reportedly transferred Tallat Fouad Qassem, a leader of the Islamic Group, an Egyptian extremist organization, to Egypt after he was picked up in Croatia. Egyptian lawyers said he was questioned aboard a U.S. ship off the Croatian coast before he was taken to Cairo, where a military tribunal had already sentenced him to death *in absentia*.[21]
- Also in 1998, CIA officers working with the Albanian police reportedly seized five members of Egyptian Islamic Jihad who were allegedly planning to bomb the U.S. embassy in Tirana. After three days of interrogation, the men were flown to Egypt, allegedly aboard a CIA-chartered plane; two of the men were put to death.[22]
- In October 2001, Jamil Qasim Aseed Mohammed, a Yemeni microbiology student, was allegedly flown from Pakistan to Jordan on a U.S.-registered Gulfstream jet after Pakistan's intelligence agency reportedly surrendered him to U.S. authorities at the Karachi airport. U.S. officials alleged that Aseed Mohammed was an Al Qaeda operative who played a role in the bombing of the USS *Cole*. The hand-over of the shackled and blindfolded Aseed Mohammed reportedly took place in the middle of the night in a remote corner of the airport, without the benefit of extradition or deportation procedures.[23]
- On December 18, 2001, Ahmed Agiza and Mohammed al-Zari were expelled from Sweden and transferred to Egypt. According to the reputable Swedish TV program Kalla Fakta, both men were flown on a Gulfstream V, a private jet alleged to be owned by a U.S. company and which reportedly is used mainly by the U.S. government.[24] Both were asylum seekers and the Swedish government had acknowledged that each had a well-founded fear of being persecuted if returned to Egypt. However, the men were excluded from refugee status based on secret evidence that they were associated with Islamist groups responsible for acts of terrorism.[25] To justify the expulsions, the Swedish government relied upon "diplomatic assurances" or formal guarantees from the Egyptian government that the two men would not be tortured and would have fair trials upon return. However, according to Human Rights Watch and a coalition of Swedish human rights groups, both men were tortured and ill-treated in Egyptian prisons upon transfer. Moreover, a trial monitor from Human Rights Watch provided a firsthand account of Agiza's re-trial by a military tribunal in April 2004 during which Agiza made serious allegations of torture and ill-treatment.[26] The re-trial was marred by numerous fair trial violations, proving a lack of compliance by the Egyptian authorities with their diplomatic assurances that Agiza would be granted a fair trial. Upon re-trial, Agiza was convicted again and sentenced to 25 years' imprisonment at hard labor. Kalla Fakta's report that the U.S. government was involved in the transfers of Agiza and al-Zari from Sweden to Egypt has been subsequently confirmed by the Swedish Ministry of Justice.[27]
- In January 2002, apparently based on information provided by the CIA, Indonesian authorities reportedly detained Muhammad Saad Iqbal Madni who is suspected by the CIA of having worked with Richard Reid (the "shoe-bomber").[28] According to a senior Indonesian official, a few days later, the Egyptian government formally asked Indonesia to extradite Iqbal, who carried an Egyptian as well as

a Pakistani passport.[29] The Egyptian request did not specify the crime, noting broadly that Egypt sought Iqbal in connection with terrorism. On January 11, 2002, allegedly without a court hearing or a lawyer, Iqbal was put aboard an unmarked U.S.-registered Gulfstream V jet and flown to Egypt.[30] A senior Indonesian official said that an extradition request from Egypt provided political cover to comply with the CIA's request. "This was a U.S. deal all along," the senior official said, "Egypt just provided the formalities."[31]

- On January 17, 2002, just a few hours after Bosnia's Supreme Court ordered the release from detention of several Algerian citizens for lack of evidence, Bosnian police handed them over to U.S. authorities, who reportedly flew them to Guantánamo Bay.[32] The Human Rights Chamber of Bosnia-Herzegovina subsequently noted that there was no evidence to suggest that "the hand-over of the [individuals] can be interpreted to be an extradition. In particular, the diplomatic note of 17 January 2002 from the U.S. embassy cannot be understood to be a valid extradition request of the United States of America. In this note, the U.S. embassy in Sarajevo advised the government of Bosnia and Herzegovina that it was prepared to assume custody of the six specified Algerian citizens and it offered to arrange to take physical custody of the individuals at a time and location mutually convenient."[33] The Chamber held that the transfer of the individuals to the custody of U.S. forces "without seeking and receiving any information as to the basis of the detention constitutes a breach of [Bosnia and Herzegovina's and the Federation of Bosnia and Herzegovina's] obligations to protect the [individuals] against arbitrary detention by foreign forces."[34]
- Also in 2002, U.S. immigration authorities, reportedly with the approval of then-Acting Attorney General Larry Thompson, authorized the "expedited removal"[35] of a Syrian-born Canadian citizen, Maher Arar, to Syria. U.S. authorities alleged that Arar had links to Al Qaeda.[36] While in transit at John F. Kennedy International Airport in New York in September 2002, Arar was taken into custody by officials from the FBI and Immigration and Naturalization Service (since reorganized into the Department of Homeland Security) and shackled.[37] Arar's requests for a lawyer were dismissed on the basis that he was not a U.S. citizen and therefore he did not have the right to counsel.[38] Officials repeatedly questioned Arar about his connection to certain members of Al Qaeda.[39] Arar repeatedly denied that he had any connections whatsoever to the named individuals.[40] Despite his denials, he remained in custody and was eventually put on a small jet that first landed in Washington, D.C., and then in Amman, Jordan.[41] Once in Amman, Arar was allegedly blindfolded, shackled and put in a van.[42] Arar was then transferred to Syria. Despite the fact that he is a Canadian citizen and has resided in Canada for seventeen years, Arar's pleas to return to Canada were ignored.[43] Upon reaching Syria, Arar was transferred to a prison where he was allegedly beaten for several hours and forced to falsely confess that he had attended a training camp in Afghanistan in order to fight against the United States.[44] Arar remained in Syria for ten months during which he was repeatedly beaten, tortured, and kept in a shallow grave.[45] Arar has subsequently been released and returned to Canada. No charges were ever filed against him in any of the countries involved in his transfer. Following intense public pressure, the Canadian government initiated a public inquiry into the circumstances surrounding Arar's transfer. The U.S. government has refused the invitation to participate in the Canadian inquiry. U.S. officials, speaking on condition of anonymity, have said that the Arar case fits the profile of what they called covert CIA Extraordinary Rendition—the practice of turning over low-level, suspected terrorists to foreign intelligence services, some of which are known to torture prisoners.[46]
- In October 2002, Australian citizen Mamdouh Habib was arrested in Pakistan and, reportedly at the request of the U.S. authorities, flown to Egypt where, allegedly, he was severely tortured.[47] Habib remained in Egypt for six months, after which he was transferred to Guantánamo where he has been detained since.[48]
- In 2003, Human Rights Watch urged the United States to abandon reported plans to send Uighur Chinese detainees held at Guantánamo Bay to China, where they were likely to face mistreatment and possibly torture.[49] China has a long and well-documented history of repression of Uighurs, a Muslim, Turkic-speaking community within China. The Chinese government has reportedly systematically tortured and otherwise mistreated suspected Uighur separatists. On August 12, 2004, speaking to Japanese journalists, Secretary of State Colin L. Powell stated that the U.S. government would not send Uighurs

to China and indicated that the United States was looking for third-party states willing to accept the Uighurs upon their release from Guantánamo Bay.[50]

B. Extraordinary Renditions—Cloaked in Secrecy

1. *"Off the Record": U.S. Involved in Extraordinary Renditions*

In statements made off the record, U.S. officials have admitted that the government has engaged in Extraordinary Renditions. In many instances, however, the officials (and the press) refer to the practice of transferring an individual, with the involvement of the United States (or its agents) to a foreign country in circumstances that make it more likely than not the individual will be subjected to torture or CID treatment as *rendition* (as opposed to Extraordinary Rendition).[51] As a technical matter, this Report makes a distinction between rendition and Extraordinary Rendition. Rendition is a covert procedure, also known as "rendition to justice," which is apparently authorized by a number of presidential directives, despite being itself a deviation from legally codified procedures for transfers of individuals. Extraordinary Rendition appears to be an unauthorized version of rendition. While rendition has been publicly acknowledged by U.S. officials, the existence of Extraordinary Rendition, which involves the risk of torture or CID treatment, has been formally denied by government officials.[52] The distinction between the two practices, however, is increasingly being blurred and media reports, as well as U.S. officials themselves, often do not differentiate between them when speaking off the record. Regardless of what classification is used, however, the practice described by the following U.S. officials off the record violates international and U.S. law and policy.

According to an unnamed senior U.S. intelligence official there have been "a lot of rendition activities" since September 11, 2001: "We are doing a number of them, and they have been very productive."[53] Similarly, in an interview with the *Washington Post,* an unnamed U.S. diplomat acknowledged that "[a]fter September 11, [renditions] have been occurring all the time. . . . It allows us to get information from terrorists in a way we can't do on U.S. soil."[54] According to another unnamed official, "[t]he temptation is to have these folks in other hands because they have different standards."[55] "Someone might be able to get information we can't from detainees," said another.[56] Another unnamed official who has been involved in rendering captives into foreign hands explained his understanding of the purpose of Extraordinary Renditions: "We don't kick the [expletive] out of them. We send them to other countries so they can kick the [expletive] out of them."[57] *Newsweek* reported that at a classified briefing for senators not long after September 11, 2001, then CIA Director George Tenet was asked whether Washington was planning to seek the transfer of suspected Al Qaeda detainees from governments known for their brutality. "Congressional sources" told *Newsweek* "that Tenet suggested it might be better sometimes for such suspects to remain in the hands of foreign authorities, who might be able to use more aggressive interrogation methods."[58] Most recently, on October 13, 2004, the Israeli newspaper *HaAretz* reported that the CIA runs a top-secret interrogation facility in Jordan, where at least 11 detainees who are considered Al Qaeda's most senior cadre are being held.[59] *HaAretz* relied on "international intelligence sources" who, according to the newspaper, "are considered experts in surveillance and analysis of Al-Qaida and are involved in interrogating the detainees."[60] *HaAretz* reported that detention of Al Qaeda suspects outside the United States "enables CIA interrogators to apply interrogation methods that are banned by U.S. law, and to do so in a country where cooperation with the United States is particularly close, thereby reducing the danger of leaks."[61]

Seymour M. Hersh, a well-respected journalist, asserts that Extraordinary Renditions form part of a special-access program (SAP) that was set up reportedly at the instigation of U.S.

Secretary of Defense Donald Rumsfeld and allegedly with the approval of President Bush and the National Security Advisor Condoleezza Rice.[62] The SAP allegedly recruited highly-trained commandos and operatives from U.S. elite forces (*e.g.* Navy SEALs, Delta Force and CIA paramilitary experts), who would be able to cross borders "without visas and could interrogate terrorism suspects deemed too important for transfer to the military's facilities at Guantànamo, Cuba. They carried out instant interrogations—using force if necessary—at secret detention centers scattered around the world."[63] Hersh alleges that the SAP was known in detail to few operatives and officials, although reportedly Secretary of Defense, Donald Rumsfeld, General Richard Myers, Chairman of the Joint Chiefs of Staff, and Dr. Stephen Cambone, the Under Secretary of Defense for Intelligence, were "completely read into the program."[64] According to a former intelligence official quoted by Hersh, the goal was to keep the operation protected: "We are not going to read more people than necessary into our heart of darkness. The rules are 'Grab whom you must. Do what you want.'"[65] The transfers of Ahmed Agiza and Mohammed Al-Zari from Sweden to Egypt, allegedly with the involvement of U.S. officials, were conducted as part of the SAP.[66]

In response to Hersh's reports, the Department of Defense issued a statement noting that "Mr. Seymour Hersh's upcoming book apparently contains many of the numerous unsubstantiated allegations and inaccuracies which he has made in the past based upon unnamed sources."[67] The Department of Defense response notes that investigations into detainee operations in Afghanistan, Iraq, "and elsewhere" are being or have been examined; however, the statement does not refute, or even address, *inter alia,* the existence of the SAP, the existence of secret detention centers, or the participation of the military and the CIA in Extraordinary Renditions.

Given the secrecy that surrounds Extraordinary Renditions, information about the practice is scarce. Although the CIA and other intelligence agents appear to be the main actors, immigration officials, FBI agents, military personnel (including elite Army forces), and contractors may also be involved.[68] According to news reports, transfers of individuals occur on U.S. chartered airlines,[69] but there appears to be no standard formula for dealing with individuals once they are rendered.[70] Sometimes, for instance in Saudi Arabia, U.S. officials allegedly "are able to observe through one-way mirrors the live investigations."[71] In other cases, according to a senior U.S. official, U.S. officials receive summaries of information obtained from interrogations after "feeding" the questions to foreign investigators.[72]

2. *"On-the-Record": U.S. Involved in "Renditions to Justice"*

On the record, U.S. government officials acknowledge only the existence of the practice of "rendition to justice"—a practice developed in the late 1980s when the technique was apparently created in order to allow U.S. law enforcement personnel to apprehend wanted individuals in "lawless" states like Lebanon during its civil war.[73] In the early 1990s, renditions to justice were allegedly exclusively law enforcement operations in which suspects were apprehended by covert CIA or FBI teams and brought to the United States or other states (usually the states having an interest in bringing the person to justice) for trial or questioning.[74] According to then FBI Director Louis J. Freeh, during the 1990s, the United States "successfully returned" thirteen suspected international terrorists to stand trial in the United States for completed or planned acts of terrorism against U.S. citizens.[75] Then CIA Director George Tenet testified that the CIA took part in over eighty renditions before September 11, 2001.[76]

The National Commission on Terrorist Attacks Upon the United States (9-11 Commission) explained the practice of renditions as a counter-terrorism measure and described the role of the CIA in the practice:

Under the presidential directives in the Clinton administration, [Presidential Decision Directive]-39 and PDD-62, the CIA had two main operational responsibilities for combating terrorism, rendition and disruption.... [I]f a terrorist suspect is outside of the United States, the CIA helps to catch and send him to the United States or a third country.... Overseas officials of the CIA, FBI and State Department may locate the terrorist suspect, perhaps using their own sources. If possible, they seek help from a foreign government. Though the FBI is often part of the process, the CIA is usually the main player, building and defining the relationships with the foreign government intelligence agencies and internal security services.[77]

George Tenet, in a written statement to the 9-11 Commission confirmed that:

CIA's policy and objectives statement for the FY 1998 budget submission prepared in early 1997 evidenced a strong determination to go on the offensive against terrorists. The submission outlined our Counterterrorist Center's offensive operations and noted the goal to "render the masterminds, disrupt terrorist infrastructure, infiltrate terrorist groups, and work with foreign partners."[78]

The interim staff report on diplomacy of the 9-11 Commission summed up the rendition process pre-September 11, 2001, as follows:

The role of diplomacy was to gain the cooperation of other governments in bringing terrorists to justice. PDD-39 stated: "When terrorists wanted for violation of U.S. law are at large overseas, their return for prosecution should be a matter of the highest priority and shall be a continuing central issue in bilateral relations with any state that harbors or assists them." If extradition procedures were unavailable or put aside, the United States could seek the local country's assistance in a rendition, secretly putting the fugitive in a plane back to America or some third country for trial.[79]

U.S. officials deny the existence of Extraordinary Renditions. According to a former covert field operations officer for the CIA, Mike Baker, torture was "not the point" of renditions; rather the "concept behind rendition is simply that moving the suspect to a third country, again, usually the origin of that suspect, will produce better cooperation, more information, as a result of normally such things as cultural affinity."[80]

In response to questioning by Senator Kennedy at the *Senate Armed Services Committee hearing regarding the mistreatment of Iraqi prisoners by some elements and certain personnel* (May 11, 2004), Dr. Stephen Cambone, Under Secretary of Defense for Intelligence, stated that he was not aware of any suspects "in DOD custody" who had been transferred to Saudi Arabia, Jordan, Morocco, or Syria for the purpose of gathering information. When asked by Senator Kennedy whether any suspects had been rendered for other purposes, Dr. Cambone replied: "If there are, I will come back to you and tell you. As best I know, there are not any persons under our custody that have been transferred."[81] Dr. Cambone also stated that to his knowledge, the United States has not been involved in turning over individuals "for torture and misbehavior —mistreatment."[82]

There is reason, however, to question such a statement from Dr. Cambone.[83] As recently as August 7, 2004, *The Oregonian* reported that a team of Oregon Army National Guard soldiers on duty in Iraq came across a walled compound in which the soldiers found dozens of Iraqi detainees who complained that they had been beaten, starved and deprived of water for three days.[84] According to the report, many of the Iraqis "including one identified as a 14-year-old boy, had fresh welts and bruises across their backs and legs."[85] The National Guard soldiers disarmed the Iraqi jailers and administered first aid to the prisoners.[86] However, when the highest-ranking U.S. officer on the scene radioed his superiors for instructions, he was told to return the prisoners to their abusers and immediately withdraw.[87] According to the news report, the U.S. embassy in Iraq confirmed the incident occurred and disclosed that the United States "raised questions about the...'brutality' with Iraq's interior minister."[88] This case represents an

instance of individuals in U.S. custody[89] being transferred to a state (*i.e.*, Iraq), pursuant to higher-command orders, under circumstances where it was clear that the individuals have been, and likely will continue to be, tortured. To our knowledge, Dr. Cambone has not publicly addressed the incident.

In a letter dated June 8, 2004 addressed to Senator Patrick Leahy, Defense Department General Counsel William Haynes stated: "Should an individual be transferred to another country to be held on behalf of the United States, or should we otherwise deem it appropriate, United States policy is to obtain specific assurances from the receiving country that it will not torture the individual being transferred to that country. We can assure you that the United States would take steps to investigate credible allegations of torture and take appropriate action if there were reason to believe that those assurances were not being honored."[90] Given that the process of obtaining diplomatic assurances is secret and not open to public scrutiny, it is impossible to verify Mr. Haynes' claim. However, in the case of Maher Arar, despite U.S. officials' insistence that they had received assurances in advance from Syria that Arar would not be mistreated, it has been determined by the Fact Finder in the Commission of Inquiry into the Actions of Canadian Officials in Relation to Maher Arar, that Arar was "subjected to torture in Syria."[91]

3. *Summary: United States Involved in Extraordinary Renditions*

Despite the formal denials of U.S. officials, off-the-record accounts as well as reports about rendered individuals suggest that Extraordinary Renditions do take place and, in fact, may be purposefully used as an interrogation technique. The practice appears to span a broad spectrum: from cases in which an individual is seized by U.S. officials and transferred by them to a third state known to use torture on detainees (*e.g.*, the 1998 case involving alleged seizure by the CIA in Albania of members of Egyptian Islamic Jihad who were subsequently transferred to Egypt, and the Arar case) to cases in which U.S. officials indirectly assist another state in transferring individuals to a third state that practices torture (*e.g.*, the case of Agiza and al-Zari who were transferred from Sweden to Egypt on a U.S.-chartered plane). Unfortunately, little additional information is available. According to news reports, the CIA's Inspector General has initiated an internal investigation into the agency's detention and interrogation practices in Iraq; however, it is not known whether renditions form part of that investigation.[92] No further information about the CIA's investigation is publicly available.[93] Nor is it known whether any other investigations with respect to individuals held at the so-called "secret detention facilities" are taking place. Other attempts to obtain additional information about renditions and Extraordinary Renditions have so far been without success. On January 9, 2004, the Office of the Inspector General of the Department of Homeland Security announced that he would review the reasons behind the removal of Maher Arar to Syria and look into general policies used by U.S. immigration officials to determine where to send non-immigrants who are removed. Unfortunately, the review's scope has been subsequently limited to an examination of the role of immigration officials only.[94] The United States has also refused to co-operate with the public inquiry being conducted by Canadian authorities into the case of Maher Arar.[95]

In October 2003 and May 2004, the American Civil Liberties Union (ACLU), jointly with other human rights organizations, filed Freedom of Information Act (FOIA) requests seeking records concerning the interrogation and treatment of detainees and the extrajudicial rendition of detainees to states known to use torture.[96] The Defense Department and other federal agencies, however, failed to release records, prompting the ACLU and its co-litigants to file a lawsuit in federal court.[97] Following a hearing on September 10, 2004 at which the government sought to delay release of documents until 2005, on September 15, federal Judge Alvin K. Hellerstein ordered the government to "produce or identify" the documents listed in the FOIA requests by

October 15, 2004.[98] A list of the documents produced at the time of this writing is available on the website of the ACLU.[99]

C. Extraordinary Renditions Violate U.S. Law

Given the secrecy surrounding Extraordinary Renditions and the formal denials by U.S. officials of the existence of the practice, it is difficult to ascertain what source of authority, if any, would provide the basis for U.S. engagement in Extraordinary Renditions. In this Section, we examine the U.S. legal standards that potentially could be applicable to Extraordinary Rendition. After a close examination of these potential sources of authority, we conclude that no publicly available statute, regulation, or executive finding, directive or other action exists to authorize Extraordinary Rendition. Given the clear intent of Congress, expressed through legislation aimed at upholding U.S. obligations against torture and complicity in such abuse, and the White House policy condemning torture, any purported authority to carry out Extraordinary Renditions would be an unauthorized derogation from U.S. law and policy.

1. Extraordinary Rendition and Existing Statutory Law (FARRA)

One of the most important pieces of U.S. legislation dealing with transfers of individuals is the Foreign Affairs Reform and Restructuring Act of 1998 (FARRA).[100] Regulations adopted pursuant to FARRA (FARRA Regulations) address transfers from the United States by virtue of extradition or removal, and include safeguards against removal and extradition of an individual to a country where he or she fears torture. The FARRA Regulations do not deal with transfers originating outside the United States and thus contain no authority for Extraordinary Renditions. However, given that fact that the FARRA Regulations prohibit the removal or extradition of an individual to a state where he or she is more likely than not to be subjected to torture, and given the FARRA policy statement that the "United States [shall] not...expel, extradite, or otherwise effect the involuntary return of any person to a country in which there are substantial grounds for believing the person would be in danger of being subjected to torture, *regardless of whether the person is physically present in the United States*,"[101] it can be inferred that Congress intended to prohibit any transfers (whether originating in the U.S. or elsewhere), with the involvement of U.S. officials, to states where the individual is more likely than not to be tortured.

A more detailed look at the FARRA Regulations supports this conclusion. For example, in the context of extradition,[102] according to the 2000 U.S. report to the Committee Against Torture regarding U.S. compliance with CAT, "in the United States, domestic law grants the Secretary of State discretion to decide whether to surrender a fugitive who has been found extraditable. This is a sufficient basis for the Secretary...to satisfy herself before she orders the surrender of the fugitive that he or she will not be tortured after extradition."[103]

Regulations concerning the removal of aliens from the United States, which are primarily found in the Code of Federal Regulations (C.F.R.) in Title 8, sections 208.16–208.18 and 1208.16–1208.18, prohibit the removal of aliens to states where they would more likely than not be subjected to torture.[104] For the purposes of these regulations, "torture" is understood to have the meaning prescribed in CAT Article 1, subject to the reservations, understandings, and declarations contained in the Senate's advice and consent to ratification of CAT.[105] Specifically, the regulations provide that where an individual subject to a removal order is more likely than not to be subjected to torture in the transferee state, such individual is eligible for a withholding or deferral of the removal order.[106] Aliens who are suspected of engaging in "terrorist activity," including those are suspected of providing material support to terrorist

organizations,[107] are removable and excludable from entry into the United States even if they face prospective persecution, including torture, abroad. They are not eligible for withholding of removal on CAT grounds, but are able nonetheless to apply for *a deferral of removal* pursuant to Title 8, section 208.17(a), which provides protection from transfer.[108]

Certain individuals seeking to enter the United States, including those having engaged in terrorist activities, may be inadmissible to the United States, and therefore may be summarily removed.[109] The decision regarding summary exclusion usually occurs at the border or airport when a Department of Homeland Security Bureau of Customs and Border Protection (CBP) officer *suspects* that an arriving alien is inadmissible on one of several grounds, including security or related grounds. However, even in those circumstances, the governing regulations provide that "[t]he Service shall not execute a removal order under this section [summary exclusion] under circumstances that violate...Article 3 of the Convention against Torture."[110]

Thus, while FARRA Regulations do not directly address Extraordinary Renditions, given that the regulations, and FARRA itself, are clear in their intent to offer protections to individuals against transfers to states where they are more likely than not to be subject to torture,[111] Congress must have intended to prohibit any practice that would forseeably result in torture, including Extraordinary Renditions.

2. *Extraordinary Rendition and the Courts*

Although U.S. courts have not addressed Extraordinary Renditions, they have dealt with *rendition*[112]—that is, extrajudicial transfers of individuals *from* third countries *to* the United States,—generally holding that such transfers (usually taking the form of abductions) do not preclude U.S. courts from exercising jurisdiction over the transferred individuals (the *Ker-Frisbie* doctrine).[113] U.S. courts, however, have been more reluctant to accept jurisdiction where extrajudicial transfers were accompanied by torture by or with the acquiescence of the United States. Thus, in *United States v. Toscanino*,[114] the Court of Appeals for the Second Circuit refused to exercise jurisdiction over an individual charged with conspiracy to import narcotics who was kidnapped by the U.S. government from Montevideo, bound, blindfolded, held incommunicado for eleven hours, deprived of food and water, and subsequently transferred to Brasilia where he was tortured for 17 days in the presence and with the participation of a member of the U.S. Bureau of Narcotics. Judge Mansfield, writing for the Second Circuit, stated:

> Society is the ultimate loser when, in order to convict the guilty, it uses methods that lead to decreased respect for the law....In light of these developments [in the protection of the rights of the accused] we are satisfied that the "Ker-Frisbie" rule cannot be reconciled with the Supreme Court's expansion of the concept of due process, which protects the accused against pretrial illegality by denying to the government the fruits of its exploitation of any deliberate and unnecessary lawlessness on its part. Although the issue in most of the cases forming part of this evolutionary process was whether evidence should have been excluded..., [w]here suppression of evidence will not suffice,...we must be guided by the underlying principle that the government should be denied the right to exploit its own illegal conduct,...and when an accused is kidnapped and forcibly brought within the jurisdiction, the court's acquisition of power over his person represents the fruits of the government's exploitation of its own misconduct....Faced with a conflict between the two concepts of due process, the one being the restricted version found in Ker-Frisbie and the other expanded and enlightened interpretation expressed in more recent decisions of the Supreme Court, we are persuaded that to the extent that the two are in conflict, the Ker-Frisbie version must yield.[115]

Although the courts have subsequently reaffirmed the *Ker-Frisbie* and confirmed that a court may exercise jurisdiction over an individual regardless of the method used to bring the

individual before the court,[116] those subsequent cases did not involve acts of torture of the abductee committed by or with the acquiescence of the U.S. officials.

3. *Extraordinary Rendition and Congress*

Congress has taken an even more assertive position than the courts against transfers in circumstances where the transferee was more likely than not to be subjected to torture. In 1998, in compliance with the ratification by the United States of CAT, Congress enacted FARRA, discussed above, in which it explicitly stated that "[i]t shall be the policy of the United States not to expel, extradite, or otherwise effect the involuntary return of any person to a country in which there are substantial grounds for believing the person would be in danger of being subjected to torture, *regardless of whether the person is physically present in the United States*."[117] Thus, Congress explicitly extended the principle of *non-refoulement* to persons who may be located *outside* the United States, although presumably limiting the operation of this policy to those within its jurisdiction. The extension of the *non-refoulement* policy is in line with recent interpretations of human rights standards, as discussed in Sections V.A.4 and Sections V.B. below. Congress has also implemented legislation criminalizing acts of torture *and* conspiracy to commit torture, once again evidencing its legislative intent against torture by proxy.[118] Because Extraordinary Rendition entails the transfer of individuals to states where they are more likely than not to be tortured, the practice is a clear violation of Congressional intent and U.S. policy.[119]

Congress has explicitly legislated on this issue; accordingly, any executive authorization for Extraordinary Rendition would be at "its lowest ebb."[120] The seminal case dealing with the legitimacy of executive actions vis-à-vis congressional will is *Youngstown Sheet & Tube Co. v. Sawyer*.[121] In that case, the Supreme Court set out a tripartite division of executive actions and their respective legitimacy, holding that (i) as a general matter, a president's power is at a maximum when exercised in a manner expressly authorized by Congress, (ii) a president's power is in a "zone of twilight" if taken in the absence of congressional authorization, and (iii) a president's power is at "its lowest ebb" when incompatible with congressional will.[122] The Supreme Court reaffirmed *Youngstown* in *Dames & Moore v. Regan*.[123] In light of Congress' enactment of FARRA, any purported presidential authority for Extraordinary Renditions would be incompatible with expressed congressional intent; accordingly, any executive action purporting to authorize Extraordinary Rendition very likely would be considered outside the scope of executive authority. In any event, as will be demonstrated below, based on publicly available information, no executive authority for Extraordinary Renditions exists.

4. *Extraordinary Rendition and the Executive Branch*

Extraordinary Renditions potentially implicate the Executive Branch's powers, including the president's specific powers to order covert actions as a commander-in-chief, and powers to make agreements with other nations.

(a) *The President's General Power as Commander-in-Chief*

The Constitution of the United States vests the power over national security matters primarily in the political branches—the Legislative and the Executive Branches of government.[124] The Constitution, however, separates congressional and presidential powers by vesting with Congress the power to declare war, and to "define and punish. . . .Offenses against the Law of Nations" and to "make Rules concerning Captures on Land and Water,"[125] and by vesting in the president the power to wage war as "Commander in Chief of the Army and the Navy of the United States, and of the Militia of the several States, when called into the actual Service

of the United States."[126] In addition, Article II, section 3 of the Constitution directs that the president "shall take Care that the Laws be faithfully executed," thus confirming that the president cannot act outside the scope of laws enacted by Congress. The principle of separation of powers also serves as a check on the exercise of presidential authority.

In the context of a war, it is less clear "to what extent Congress can control decisions of the President as Commander in Chief in the conduct of wars authorized by Congress."[127] Likewise, the question of the role of the courts in regulating the Executive Branch's power during war remains unsettled. Some commentators note that the Executive Branch has expanded by accretion its role in foreign affairs beyond its constitutionally enumerated powers.[128] Supreme Court cases throughout U.S. history, including the recently decided cases relating to detainees in the "War on Terror," make it clear that the power of the Executive Branch is not plenary.[129] The Executive Branch's wartime power is limited by the Constitution, by statutes,[130] and by treaty obligations.[131]

In April 2003, a Defense Department memo entitled "Detainee Interrogation in the Global War on Terrorism,"[132] drafted by the department's Working Group on Detainee Interrogation in the "War on Terror," took the position that the president, as Commander-in-Chief, is not bound by federal law and international treaties barring the use of torture. The memo asserted that

> Congress lacks authority...to set the terms and conditions under which the President may exercise his authority as Commander-in-Chief to control the conduct of operations during a war...Congress may no more regulate the President's ability to detain and interrogate enemy combatants than it may regulate his ability to direct troop movements on the battlefield. Accordingly, we would construe [the law] to avoid this constitutional difficulty and conclude that it does not apply to the President's detention and interrogation of enemy combatants....[133]

It is not clear to what extent the Bush Administration adopted this legal reasoning.[134] However, the memo failed to apply (or even mention) the *Youngstown* rule.[135] Congress has not only given its advice and consent to CAT, but has enacted legislative provisions implementing the treaty.[136] Under the *Youngstown* analysis, any presidential act that involves violations of U.S. treaty and statutory law very likely exceeds the scope of executive authority.[137] Because Extraordinary Renditions violate U.S. statutory law and binding treaty obligations,[138] presidential authorization for such practices very likely would be outside the scope of presidential authority.

The fact that Congress, after the attacks of September 11, 2001, granted the president broad powers to wage the "War on Terror," does not alter this calculus. The Authorization for Use of Military Force (AUMF), issued on September 18, 2001, authorized the president to "use all necessary and appropriate force against those nations, organizations, or persons he determines planned, authorized, committed, or aided the terrorist attacks" of September 11, 2001, and against those who "harbored such organizations or persons."[139] The U.S. government has contended that the AUMF and the Executive Branch's Article II constitutional powers provide blanket and unreviewable authorization for carrying out the "War on Terror."[140] In *Hamdi* and *Rasul*,[141] the Supreme Court rejected that stance. In *Hamdi,* the Court made clear that the AUMF did not give the government permission to indefinitely detain a suspect "for the purpose of interrogation."[142] The court did decide that the AUMF constitutes explicit congressional authorization for the detention of enemy combatants, but only because such detention was considered a "fundamental incident of war."[143] No such argument could apply to Extraordinary Renditions. No assertions have been made that this practice is a "fundamental incident of waging war;" instead, the U.S. government has formally denied that the practice takes place.[144]

(b) Presidential Power to Authorize Covert Actions and to Issue National Security Directives

Pursuant to the National Security Act of 1947,[145] the president has the authority to authorize covert actions upon a determination that "such an action is necessary to support identifiable foreign policy objectives of the United States and is important to the national security of the United States, which determination shall be set forth in a finding. . ."[146] The same statute explicitly provides that "[a] finding may not authorize any action that would violate the Constitution or any statute of the United States."[147] The president may also issue classified executive orders or directives on national security matters. Whether these directives have the force of law depends upon such factors as the president's authority to issue them, their conflict with constitutional or statutory provisions, and their promulgation in accordance with prescribed procedure.[148] As one commentator has pointed out, "[i]nherent in [the division of power] is the notion that the president must respect statutory commands even when they require a result contrary to his own policy preferences."[149] Accordingly, where there is a conflict between a presidential directive and a law enacted by Congress, agency heads must comply with the law.[150] Thus, for example, in *Chamber of Commerce v. Reich,*[151] the District of Columbia Circuit Court of Appeals declared illegal an executive order issued by President Clinton that directed federal agencies not to do business with contractors who hire permanent replacements for striking employees. The court, noting that the National Labor Relations Act (NLRA) permits the hiring of permanent replacements for strikers, concluded that an executive order to the contrary would upset the balance struck by Congress on an issue that "surely goes to the heart of United States labor relations policy."[152] Similarly, in *Building and Construction Trades Department v. Allbaugh,*[153] the court ruled illegal an executive order issued by President George W. Bush that prohibited federal contractors from using project labor agreements. The court held that the president lacked the authority under the Constitution and the Procurement Act to bar such agreements and that the executive order conflicted with the NLRA by prohibiting a practice that was considered legal under the Act.[154]

As detailed in Section IV.B.2 of this Report, a series of presidential decision directives (PDDs) apparently authorize transfers of suspected terrorists from foreign states to the United States. PDDs are National Security Council documents that announce presidential decisions and guide policy implementation. They range from the publicly available to the highly classified. According to the testimony of then-FBI Director Louis Freeh, "[t]he rendition process is governed by PDD-77, which sets explicit requirements for initiating this method for returning terrorists to stand trial in the United States."[155] This directive remains classified. Because many of the potentially relevant PDDs (including PDD-77) remain classified, the full scope of the relevant PDDs' authority is unknown. U.S. officials and the 9-11 Commission have also referred to PDD-39, entitled "U.S. Policy on Counterterrorism," signed on June 21, 1995 following the bombing of the federal building in Oklahoma City, in circumstances that indicate this PDD may also be implicated in rendition.[156] Since this PDD is available only in highly redacted form, any specific provisions applicable to renditions are not publicly known. The Commission's interim staff report on intelligence policy states that "under the presidential directives in the Clinton Administration, PDD-39 and PDD-62, the CIA had two main operational responsibilities for combating terrorism, rendition and disruption."[157] Based on available information, it seems that this directive dealt with the transfers of suspected terrorists *to* the United States outside of formal extradition channels, rather than renditions *from* the United States or *from* a third state to another foreign state. A General Accounting Office report found that PDD-62, signed in May 1998, "reaffirmed PDD-39 and further articulated responsibilities for specific agencies."[158]

Although the scope of various presidential directives is unknown, because Extraordinary Renditions violate U.S. statutory law, and, as will be demonstrated in subsequent Report Sections, treaty law (which is considered to be supreme law of the land under the Constitution), it is unlikely that any PDD explicitly purports to authorize Extraordinary Rendition. Moreover, under U.S. law, Congress could have authorized departure from international obligations of the United States. However, not only did it not do so, but by enacting FARRA and sections 2340 and 2340A of the U.S. Code, Congress reaffirmed United States' commitment to CAT and to the *jus cogens* norm of the prohibition against torture. Without congressional authorization, it is unlikely that executive orders can be issued in violation of the international obligations of the United States. Accordingly, any PDD authorizing Extraordinary Rendition very likely would be outside the scope of presidential authority.

(c) Presidential Power to Make International Agreements

The president has authority to make international agreements "dealing with any matter that falls within his independent powers under the Constitution."[159] However, as stated above, pursuant to Article III of the Constitution, the president has the duty to "take Care that the Laws be faithfully executed" (take care clause).[160] Thus, under the "take care" clause, as well as in accordance with U.S. jurisprudence, the president likely would be prohibited from making international agreements that contravene the laws of the United States by permitting or aiding torture.[161] In addition, any order permitting the transfer of individuals to other states in circumstances that constitute complicity, participation, or assistance in CID treatment would also contravene stated administration policies that detainees in the "War on Terror" be "treated humanely, without any adverse distinction based on race, color, religion, gender, birth, wealth, or any similar criteria."[162]

5. Extraordinary Rendition and the CIA

Because Extraordinary Renditions appear to be covert operations the existence of which is formally denied by the U.S. government, and because information about the operations of the CIA is similarly not available to the public, it is difficult to ascertain whether anything in the mandate of (or regulations governing) the CIA could be interpreted to authorize Extraordinary Renditions. This Section provides an overview of the scope of authorization of the CIA activities based on publicly available information and analyzes the practice of Extraordinary Renditions in light of that information.

The CIA was established and granted its general powers under the National Security Act of 1947.[163] It was first given authority to conduct covert operations by National Security Council (NSC) Directive 10/2, issued on June 18, 1948.[164] This authority has been reaffirmed and elaborated upon in several NSC directives and executive orders.

Provisions governing the CIA specify, among other things, how the CIA could use secret funds (a specific budget item to be allocated by the Director of Central Intelligence (DCI) as needed without normal accounting review), granted the CIA the right to borrow personnel from other government agencies, allowed the agency to ignore immigration laws, and gave the DCI the right to determine which of the agency's activities and documents should be kept secret.[165] It is noteworthy that the CIA's powers to override immigration laws are restricted to those affecting the *admission* of aliens. Specifically, section 403h provides that:

> Whenever the Director, the Attorney General, and the Commissioner of Immigration and Naturalization shall determine that the admission of a particular alien into the United States for permanent residence is in the interest of national security or essential to the furtherance of the national intelligence mission, such alien and his immediate family shall be admitted to the United States for permanent residence without

regard to their inadmissibility under the immigration or any other laws and regulations, or to the failure to comply with such laws and regulations pertaining to admissibility. . . .[166]

No similar authority, however, is given to the CIA in respect of a *removal* of individuals from the United States. Thus, because the Act explicitly includes the admission but not the removal of aliens, one can infer that congressional intent was *not* to grant the CIA powers to override laws governing *removal* of aliens.

Generally, CIA operations are subject to oversight by congressional intelligence committees. However, alternative oversight is provided for highly classified actions: if the president determines that it is essential to limit access to a finding to meet extraordinary circumstances affecting vital interests of the United States, the finding may be reported to the chairpersons and ranking minority members of the congressional intelligence committees, the Speaker and minority leader of the House of Representatives, the majority and minority leaders of the Senate, and such other member or members of the congressional leadership as may be included by the president.[167]

There are apparently CIA regulations in place that explicitly prohibit the use of or participation in torture by CIA officers. According to a *Washington Post* article, "the CIA's authoritative Directorate of Operations instructions, drafted in cooperation with the general counsel, tells case officers in the field that they may not engage in, provide advice about or encourage the use of torture by cooperating intelligence services from other countries."[168] However, the same article reports that "the CIA, in practice, is using a narrow definition of what counts as 'knowing' that a suspect has been tortured: 'If we're not there in the room, who is to say?' said one official conversant with recent reports of renditions."[169] Since these regulations are not publicly available, it is not possible to analyze their consistency with U.S. and international law, or to determine whether they would appear to authorize Extraordinary Renditions. However, based on publicly available information, no authority for Extraordinary Renditions can be found in the CIA governing documents. This is not surprising given that the practice of Extraordinary Rendition is inherently contrary to both U.S. and international law.

V. EXTRAORDINARY RENDITIONS VIOLATE INTERNATIONAL LAW

In this Section of the Report, we consider in detail the international legal standards applicable to Extraordinary Renditions.[170] The United States is party to international human rights and humanitarian law treaties that prohibit both torture and the transfer of individuals to states where they are in danger or at risk of torture. Specifically, the United States is a party to the UN Convention against Torture and Other Cruel, Inhuman or Degrading Treatment or Punishment,[171] the International Covenant on Civil and Political Rights,[172] the Geneva Conventions of 1949,[173] and the Refugee Convention of 1951.[174] Each treaty prohibits torture, a prohibition that has become a non-derogable norm under international law. To varying degrees, the treaties also prohibit cruel, inhuman, or degrading (CID) treatment; the differences among the treaties reflect the open-textured nature of the definition of CID treatment. Either directly or indirectly (*i.e.,* through the jurisprudence or commentary of courts or treaty or regional bodies charged with interpreting a particular treaty), each of these treaties includes another norm: the prohibition against the *refoulement,* or transfer, of an individual to another state where that individual faces the danger or risk of torture. Although these treaties may differ in their particulars, together with customary international law, they prohibit (and, in some instances, require the United States to criminalize) each of the different examples of Extraordinary Renditions described in Section IV.A. of this Report.

CAT prohibits both torture and CID treatment. It also explicitly prohibits the *refoulement* of individuals to states where there is a "substantial likelihood" that they "may be in danger of" torture.[175] The ICCPR prohibits torture and CID, but its *refoulement* protection is broader than that of CAT: as interpreted by the Human Rights Committee, the ICCPR prohibits the *refoulement* of individuals to states where they may be "at risk of" either torture or CID (or both). Geneva Convention (III) and Geneva Convention (IV) prohibit both torture and the inhuman treatment of prisoners of war and civilians classified as "protected persons" in the context of armed conflict. The transfer of a prisoner of war (POW) to a state where the POW is likely to be tortured or inhumanely treated is a violation of Geneva III. The unlawful transfer of a civilian classified as a "protected person" to such a state has harsher consequences—the transfer is a "grave breach" under Geneva IV, and is a criminal act. The Refugee Convention may also afford protection against torture and *refoulement* to individuals with a "well-founded fear of persecution" on specific enumerated grounds.

Under CAT, the prohibition against *refoulement* to torture requires both an objective assessment of the conditions in the state to which an individual may be transferred, and a subjective assessment of the danger particular to the individual. CAT protections apply when these assessments lead to a substantial likelihood of a danger of torture that is greater than "mere suspicion," but the likelihood does not have to rise to the level of "high probability." CAT protections, which apply to all types of transfers (including expulsion and extradition) are the most protective of any of the treaties to which the United States is a party. In order for ICCPR protections to apply, the individual must face a "real risk" of danger. This standard has also been interpreted to contain a subjective and an objective assessment, although the "real risk" standard is higher that the CAT "in danger of" threshold.[176]

Although the assessment whether a particular allegation of *refoulement* to torture meets the subjective component of both the CAT and the ICCPR tests must be made on a case-by-case basis, each alleged instance of Extraordinary Rendition described earlier in Section IV.A. meets the objective component. According to the U.S. Department of State's own annual human rights reports, each of the states to which individuals have allegedly been transferred is known to the United States as having a history of torture of detainees. Many of these states have also been identified by the United States as states that commonly use torture against individuals detained for alleged security reasons or because they are suspected of terrorism.

CAT, the ICCPR and the Geneva Conventions have each been interpreted to require that states investigate and criminalize torture by their own officials and those acting at the officials' direction. Under CAT, the requirement to criminalize acts of torture or complicity or participation in torture is directly imposed by the treaty itself, and, in the context of Extraordinary Renditions, applies to acts by U.S. state actors (or non-state actors acting with the consent or acquiesence of a state actor) that take place in territory under U.S. jurisdiction (interpreted to include territory over which the United States has factual control), acts on board of U.S.-registered ships or aircraft, or acts by U.S. state actors (or non-state actors acting with the consent or acquiescence of a state actor) anywhere in the world.[177]

The ICCPR has been interpreted to require a state party to prevent, punish, investigate and redress harm caused by acts of both torture and CID treatment, and complicity to torture and CID treatment, by state actors and by private parties. Failure to investigate and prosecute may result in liability on the part of the state itself. The scope of applicability of ICCPR protections is similar to CAT, but has been interpreted more broadly to include state responsibility for violations of an individual's ICCPR protections (i) in the physical territory of the state or (ii) that may be imputed to the state if the individual was in the power or effective control of the state (even if outside its territory) or if the violations were committed by state actors, regardless of where they

took place.[178] The protections of the Geneva Conventions apply in situations of armed conflict, and to individuals who qualify as "protected persons" under the Conventions.

The breadth of these criminalization provisions and interpretations is a reflection of the importance placed by the community of nations on the anti-torture prohibition. Each of the cases of alleged Extraordinary Rendition described above must therefore be investigated and, if there are reasonable grounds for belief that torture was committed, or that U.S. agents or nationals were complicit in transferring an individual to a state where the person was tortured, the United States must prosecute. As described in greater detail below, the failure by a state party to investigate and prosecute allegations of torture and complicity in torture may itself give rise to a breach by the United States of its obligations under CAT and the ICCPR.

This Report focuses on the United States' obligations pursuant to the international treaties to which it is a party, primarily CAT and the ICCPR, as well as the Geneva Conventions and the Refugee Convention. Given the importance of international standards in interpreting U.S. domestic law[179] as reflected in part by recent U.S. Supreme Court decisions in which the court has explicitly looked to international law for guidance[180] in interpreting those obligations, we consider the commentary and decisions by the Committee against Torture (CAT Committee)[181] and the Human Rights Committee,[182] the bodies charged respectively by CAT and the ICCPR with interpreting each treaty, monitoring compliance by states with the treaty, and, if applicable, considering individual petitions. The primary treatise on CAT, which was written by two of the principal drafters of the convention and which includes analysis of the CAT *travaux préparatoires,* also provides assistance in interpreting CAT.[183]

An additional international legal instrument that applies to the United States through its membership in the Organization of American States (OAS) is the American Declaration on the Rights and Duties of Man.[184] We also look briefly to the American Convention on Human Rights (American Convention), which the United States signed on June 1, 1997, but has not yet ratified.[185]

In addition to the U.S. treaty obligations, we look to *jus cogens*[186] norms by which the United States is bound. The prohibition against torture has been universally recognized as a customary international law norm[187] and as a *jus cogens* norm applicable in times of war and peace, from which no derogation is permitted.[188] In *The Paquete Habana,* the U.S. Supreme Court recognized that customary international law applies to the U.S. domestic sphere.[189] As discussed in greater detail below, the prohibitions against torture and *refoulement* are specifically articulated in international law in numerous treaties (including treaties to which the United States is a party), in state practice (including that of the United States) and in the works of scholars.

The United States is not alone in facing the threat of terrorism both within its borders and against its citizens and interests abroad. The experience of other states and regions that have, and still are, facing the threat of terrorism offers useful guidance. Other sources we therefore look to include the European Convention for the Protection of Human Rights and Fundamental Freedoms[190] (as interpreted by the European Court of Human Rights). Finally, this Report briefly examines the international criminal law standards that have been applied to prosecutions of individuals for violations of the anti-torture prohibition.

A. The United States Is Obligated to Prevent Extraordinary Renditions under the UN Convention Against Torture

CAT defines and prohibits torture and conduct that is considered cruel, inhuman or degrading,[191] prohibits the transfer or *refoulement* of a person to a state that would subject the person to torture,[192] and requires the United States to prevent, investigate and criminalize direct,

complicitous or other participation in torture by state actors and also non-state actors acting with the consent or acquiescence of a state actor.[193]

1. *CAT Prohibits Torture and Cruel, Inhuman or Degrading Treatment*

As the Convention's preamble notes, at the time of CAT's formulation, torture and CID treatment were already prohibited by Article 5 of the Universal Declaration of Human Rights,[194] Article 7 of the ICCPR,[195] and also by the UN General Assembly's Declaration on the Protection of All Persons from Being Subjected to Torture and Other Cruel, Inhuman or Degrading Punishment.[196] Unlike any of these instruments, though, CAT specifically defines torture as

> any act by which severe pain or suffering, whether physical or mental, is intentionally inflicted on a person for such purposes as obtaining from him or a third person information or a confession, punishing him for an act he or a third person has committed or is suspected of having committed, or intimidating or coercing him or a third person, or for any reason based on discrimination of any kind, when such pain or suffering is inflicted by or at the instigation of or with the consent or acquiescence of a public official or other person acting in an official capacity. It does not include pain or suffering arising only from, inherent in or incidental to lawful sanctions.[197]

CAT makes it clear, therefore, that the torture prohibition includes conduct undertaken for the purposes of obtaining information by state actors, or by other persons acting with the consent or acquiescence of a state actor.[198]

CAT does not define CID, but the jurisprudence of the CAT Committee makes clear that CID punishment or treatment is on a continuum with torture, through Article 16, which requires ratifying states to prevent "other actors of cruel, inhuman or degrading treatment or punishment which do not amount to torture."[199] Article 16 further imposes on ratifying parties the same obligations with respect to investigation of allegations of CID treatment as the parties have with respect to investigation of torture allegations.[200]

2. *CAT Prohibits the Transfer of Individuals to States Where They May Be in Danger of Torture*

CAT's prohibition against the transfer of individuals to states where they are in danger of torture is absolute and unqualified. CAT Article 3(1) states: "No State Party shall expel, return ("*refouler*") or extradite a person to another State where there are substantial grounds for believing that he would be in danger of being subjected to torture."[201] The scope of the CAT prohibition against *refoulement* was broadly drafted in order to apply to (i) transfers to any other state where an individual is in danger of torture; (ii) all persons in danger of torture upon transfer; and (iii) all types of transfers (including, for example, deportations or transfers pursuant to extradition treaties).

(a) Prohibition Against Transfers to Subsequent States

According to the CAT Committee, "the phrase 'another State' in article 3 refers to the State to which the individual concerned is being expelled, returned or extradited, as well as to any State to which the author may subsequently be expelled, returned or extradited."[202] Burgers and Danelius state that Article 3 "makes it clear that a State is not only responsible for what happens in its own territory, but it must also refrain from exposing an individual to serious risks outside its territory by handing him or her over to another State from which treatment contrary to [CAT] might be expected."[203]

(b) Standards for Determining Application of Non-refoulement *Obligation to Persons in Danger of Torture*

The CAT *non-refoulement* obligation applies to all individuals who "would *be in danger of* being subjected to torture" (emphasis added) and not just to individuals who *would be tortured* upon transfer.[204] The focus is on future danger that could occur. CAT further provides that to determine whether "substantial grounds for believing that [an individual] would be in danger of being subjected to torture" exist, "the competent authorities shall take into account all relevant considerations including, where applicable, the existence in the State concerned of a consistent pattern of gross, flagrant or mass violations of human rights."[205] In commentary and decisions, the CAT Committee has provided guidance on interpretation of the *non-refoulement* standard, and the considerations that should be taken into account in assessing the danger of torture.

First, the CAT Committee has interpreted "substantial grounds" to mean that "the risk of torture must be assessed [by the State Party and the Committee] on grounds that go beyond mere theory or suspicion. However, the risk does not have to meet the test of being highly probable."[206] The CAT Committee therefore interprets the "substantial grounds" threshold at a lesser level than that used by the United States: the United States ratified CAT subject to an understanding that it would interpret the CAT Article 3 phrase, "where there are substantial grounds for believing that he would be in danger of being subjected to torture," as used in article 3 of the Convention, to mean "if it is more likely than not that he would be tortured."[207]

Second, the CAT Committee has determined that the "substantial grounds for belief" requirement incorporates both (i) an objective assessment of the conditions in the state to which an individual is to be transferred,[208] and (ii) a subjective assessment of the danger of torture to the individual facing a transfer.[209] Thus, the CAT Committee has determined that applicants should not be returned to states where reports of conditions indicated the danger of torture and where the state of return was not a party to CAT.[210] For example, in *Khan v. Canada,* the Committee found that because Pakistan was not a party to CAT, the petitioner's return would not only put him in danger of torture, but would strip him of any possibility of applying for protection under CAT.[211] On the other hand, the fact that the state of return is a party to CAT does not preclude a finding that a particular person may be at risk of torture in that state.[212]

According to press reports, the United States has transferred individuals for interrogation to states including Egypt, Jordan, Syria, Saudi Arabia, Morocco, Yemen, and Egypt. These are all nations that the U.S. Department of State itself has identified as practitioners of torture on detainees, including as an interrogation method, in State Department human rights reports for each of 2001, 2002, and 2003. The United States thus has knowledge that the objective prong of the "substantial grounds for belief" test is likely satisfied in alleged cases of Extraordinary Rendition to each of these states:

- **Egypt.** In its 2003 report, the State Department found "there were numerous, credible reports that security forces tortured and mistreated detainees" and that "torture and abuse of detainees by police, security personnel, and prison guards remained frequent." The "[p]rincipal methods of torture reportedly employed by the police and [security services] included victims being: stripped and blindfolded; suspended from a ceiling or doorframe with feet just touching the floor; beaten with fists, whips, metal rods, or other objects; subjected to electrical shocks; and doused with cold water. Victims frequently reported being subjected to threats and forced to sign blank papers for use against the victim or the victim's family in the future should the victim complain of abuse. Some victims, including male and female detainees and children reported that they were sexually assaulted or threatened with rape themselves or family members."[213]

- **Jordan.** In its 2003 report, the State Department stated that "police and security forces sometimes abuse detainees physically and verbally during detention and interrogation, and allegedly also use torture. Allegations of torture are difficult to verify because the police and security officials frequently deny detainees timely access to lawyers, despite legal provisions requiring such access. The most frequently alleged methods of torture include sleep deprivation, beatings on the soles of the feet, prolonged suspension with ropes in contorted positions, and extended solitary confinement."[214]
- **Morocco.** In its 2003 report, the State Department stated that "[t]he law prohibits torture, and the Government denied the use of torture; however, some members of the security forces tortured or otherwise abused detainees."[215]
- **Syria.** In its 2003 report, the State Department stated that former prisoners and human rights groups report "that torture methods include administering electrical shocks; pulling out fingernails; forcing objects into the rectum; beating, sometimes while the victim is suspended from the ceiling; hyperextending the spine; and using a chair that bends backwards to asphyxiate the victim or fracture the victim's spine....Although torture occurs in prisons, torture is most likely to occur while detainees are being held at one of the many detention centers run by the various security services throughout the country, and particularly while the authorities are attempting to extract a confession or information regarding an alleged crime or alleged accomplices."[216]
- **Saudi Arabia.** In its 2003 report, the State Department stated that "there were credible reports that the authorities abused detainees, both citizens and foreigners. Ministry of Interior officials were responsible for most incidents of abuse of prisoners, including beatings, whippings, and sleep deprivation. In addition, there were allegations of torture, including allegations of beatings with sticks and suspension from bars by handcuffs. There were reports that torture and abuse were used to obtain confessions from prisoners. Canadian and British prisoners that were released during the year reported that they had been tortured during their detention.....The Government continued to refuse to recognize the mandate of the UN Committee against Torture to investigate alleged abuses. A government committee established in 2000 to investigate allegations of torture still had not begun functioning at year's end."[217]
- **Yemen.** In its 2003 report, the Department of State stated that "[Security forces continued to arbitrarily arrest, detain, and torture persons. The Government sometimes failed to hold members of the security forces accountable for abuses....The Constitution is ambiguous regarding the prohibition of cruel or inhuman punishment, and members of the security forces tortured and otherwise abused persons in detention. Arresting authorities were known to use force during interrogations, especially against those arrested for violent crimes. Detainees in some instances were confined in leg-irons and shackles, despite a 1998 law outlawing this practice."[218]

(c) Types of Transfers to Which Non-refoulement *Obligation Applies*

CAT Article 3's scope is broad and intended to encompass all transfers. The original draft of Article 3(1) referred to expulsion and *refoulement* only; the reference to extradition was added so that Article 3 would "cover all measures by which a person is physically transferred to another state."[219] Because of the breadth of this scope, concerns were raised during the drafting of CAT that the *non-refoulement* obligation could conflict with states' obligations under existing extradition treaties. According to a report of the Working Group on CAT, set up by the UN Commission on Human Rights:

> Some delegations indicated that their States might wish, at the time of signature or ratification of the Convention or accession thereto, to declare that they did not consider themselves bound by Article 3 of the Convention, in so far as that article might not be compatible with obligations towards States not Party to the Convention under extradition treaties concluded before the date of the signature of the Convention.[220]

Thus, states were aware of and on notice that a reservation or declaration regarding the primacy of extradition treaties over the CAT prohibition against *refoulement* could be made at the time of CAT ratification. Indeed, the initial version of CAT sent by President Reagan to

the Senate for ratification included the reservation (intended to be included in the ratification instrument) that "[t]he U.S. does not consider itself bound by Article 3 insofar as it conflicts with the obligations of the United States toward States not a party to the Convention under bilateral extradition treaties with such states."[221] This proposed reservation was not included in the final U.S. ratification and no such declaration was made by any state. The scope of the *non-refoulement* obligation therefore covers transfers of individuals to states with which the United States has extradition treaties and which may subject the individual to the danger of torture. These include states to which Extraordinary Renditions are reported to have been made, such as Pakistan,[222] Egypt, and Jordan.[223]

(d) Development of International Law on Non-refoulement

CAT Article 3's prohibition of *refoulement* is based in part on the jurisprudence of the European Commission of Human Rights,[224] interpreting the European Convention for the Protection of Human Rights and Fundamental Freedoms (European Convention).[225] The jurisprudence of the European Commission, and subsequently that of the European Court of Human Rights, therefore is instructive and is evidence that the prohibition against *refoulement* to a state where an individual is in danger of torture is a broadly accepted international norm.

The European Convention does not contain an explicit prohibition against *refoulement.* However, Article 3 of the Convention provides that "[n]o one shall be subjected to torture or to inhuman or degrading treatment or punishment." The European Court has interpreted Article 3 to encompass a prohibition against *refoulement,* based on what it expressly identifies as a set of shared norms: the "common heritage of political traditions, ideals, freedom and the rule of law" of the states party to the European Convention.[226]

In the seminal case of *Soering v. United Kingdom,* the European Court of Human Rights held that the extradition to the United States of a German citizen accused of murder in the United States and arrested in the United Kingdom would be a violation of Article 3 of the European Convention. The court emphasized the absolute, non-derogable prohibition on torture and of other inhuman or degrading treatment and held that:

> Article 3 makes no provision for exceptions and no derogation from it is permissible in time of war or other national emergency. This absolute prohibition of torture and of inhuman or degrading treatment or punishment under the terms of the Convention shows that Article 3 enshrines one of the fundamental values of the democratic societies making up the Council of Europe. It is also to be found in similar terms in other international instruments such as the 1966 International Covenant on Civil and Political Rights and the 1969 American Convention on Human Rights and is generally recognised as an internationally accepted standard.[227]

The court then examined whether the European Convention's Article 3 prohibition against torture and CID treatment also applied to the extradition of an individual to a state where the individual was at substantial risk for torture or CID treatment. The court concluded that it did:

> The fact that [CAT] should spell out in detail a specific obligation attaching to the prohibition of torture does not mean that an essentially similar obligation is not already inherent in the general terms of Article 3 of the European Convention. It would hardly be compatible with the underlying values of the Convention, that "common heritage of political traditions, ideals, freedom and the rule of law" to which the Preamble refers, were a Contracting State knowingly to surrender a fugitive to another State where there were substantial grounds for believing that he would be in danger of being subjected to torture, however heinous the crime allegedly committed.... [I]n the Court's view this inherent obligation not to extradite also extends to cases in which the fugitive would be faced in the receiving State by a real risk of exposure to inhuman or degrading treatment or punishment proscribed by that Article.[228]

The European Court subsequently confirmed its decision and extended its holdings to any kind of forced removal or transfer of an individual where there were substantial grounds to believe the person would face torture or ill-treatment.[229]

That the prohibition against *refoulement* to states where an individual faces the danger of torture is a broadly accepted norm is also shown in part by the large number of treaties that incorporate the prohibition, and the number and variety of states that have ratified them.[230] CAT has been ratified by an overwhelming majority of states.[231] The states that have not signed or ratified CAT are states that have yet to recognize fully the prohibition against torture in their own domestic law or practice. The practice of the states that have ratified or signed CAT also supports the conclusion that the *non-refoulement* principle embodied in CAT is widely accepted and enforced.[232]

A number of multinational or regional treaties ratified or enacted before CAT also support the status of *non-refoulement* as a principle of international law, and show that the protection afforded by the principle has expanded over time. As discussed in greater detail below, the Refugee Convention includes a prohibition against *refoulement* that specifically protects refugee who meet certain qualifications.[233] The United States is obligated to comply with the Refugee Convention through its accession to the 1967 Protocol, including the prohibition against *refoulement*. In the Americas, both the 1978 American Convention on Human Rights[234] and the 1987 Inter-American Convention to Prevent and Punish Torture[235] include prohibitions of *refoulement*. Article 13 of the Inter-American Torture Convention provides that:

> Extradition shall not be granted nor shall the person sought be returned when there are grounds to believe that his life is in danger, that he will be subjected to torture or to cruel, inhuman or degrading treatment, or that he will be tried by special or ad hoc courts in the requesting States.[236]

In Africa, regional treaties containing a *non-refoulement* standard include the Convention Governing the Specific Aspects of Refugee Problems in Africa[237] and the African [Banjul] Charter on Human and Peoples' Rights.[238] Finally, the prohibition against *refoulement* is often recognized by scholars as a norm of customary international law.[239]

3. *CAT Requires States Parties to Prevent, Prosecute and Punish Torture and Complicity to Torture*

CAT Article 4 requires that acts of torture must be treated as offenses under the criminal laws of the states party to the convention and "[t]he same shall apply to an attempt to commit torture and *to an act by any person which constitutes complicity or participation in torture*."[240] Article 1's definition of acts of torture includes the phrase "inflicted by or at the instigation of or with the consent or acquiescence of a public official or other person acting in an official capacity."[241] Burgers and Danelius note that the breadth of the phrase was intended to encompass an offender who was "not directly connected with any public authority but that the authorities have hired him to help gather information or have at least accepted or tolerated his act."[242] Read together, these provisions require the United States to criminalize (i) direct acts of torture; (ii) complicity in torture; (iii) attempted torture; and (iv) aiding and abetting torture when committed by officials or non-state actors under the direction or with the consent or acquiescence of a state actor.[243] Depending on their degree of involvement in Extraordinary Renditions, U.S. officials and (U.S. or foreign) non-state actors acting with the consent or acquiescence of a U.S. official could therefore be liable directly for torture or complicity to torture, and could also incur liability for complicity, attempt, or aiding and abetting torture through the facilitation of the transfer or *refoulement* of an individual to a state where that individual is in danger of torture.[244]

Acts of torture by state actors or those acting with their consent or acquiescence may also render a state directly liable. According to Burgers and Danelius, "[i]f torture is performed by a public agency, such as the security police, the government of the country has no defence under [CAT] in saying that it was unaware of the act or even disapproved of it once it was informed."[245] Failure to investigate and prosecute could also constitute violations of CAT on the part of the state. CAT Article 6 obligates a state to investigate (if circumstances warrant), assert jurisdiction over, and take into custody an individual who is alleged to have committed torture or is complicit in or has participated in torture, and investigate the circumstances surrounding the allegations.[246] CAT Article 7 incorporates into CAT the obligation to prosecute or extradite in cases of violations of the prohibition against torture.[247]

In addition, CAT requires the United States to train fully persons "who may be involved in the custody, interrogation or treatment of any individual subjected to any form of arrest, detention or imprisonment," including civil or military law enforcement and medical personnel, in the prohibition against torture.[248] CAT also requires the United States to review systematically and on an on-going basis, the rules and practices regarding the custody and interrogation of detainees in order to prevent any cases of torture.[249] If there are reasonable grounds to believe that torture has occurred in any territory subject to U.S. jurisdiction, the United States must ensure a prompt and impartial investigation, and also ensure that any alleged victim has timely recourse to an impartial authority that will examine allegations of torture.[250] Victims of torture by U.S. actors must have access to redress and compensation through the U.S. legal system.[251] In the context of alleged Extraordinary Renditions, therefore, the United States must ensure that civil or military personnel involved in the custody, interrogation, and treatment of any detainees be trained in the prohibition against torture. The United States must also promptly investigate allegations of Extraordinary Rendition by U.S. actors, or those acting with their consent or acquiescence, and provide recourse and compensation to any individual who is found to have been Extraordinarily Rendered.

4. *Scope of Application of CAT Standards Under International Law*

Together, CAT's prohibitions against torture and *refoulement,* and its criminal enforcement provisions, require the United States (i) to prohibit torture and complicity in torture and to punish acts of state actors (or non-state actors acting with their consent or acquiescence) that violate these prohibitions; (ii) to exercise criminal jurisdiction over such acts of torture and complicity in torture; and (iii) to prohibit the *refoulement* of individuals to states where they are in danger of torture. If, after fulfilling its obligation to investigate allegations of Extraordinary Rendition, the United States finds there is a reasonable basis to believe alleged Extraordinary Renditions occurred, the United States must exercise criminal jurisdiction over, and prosecute, U.S. officials, or individuals acting with their consent or acquiescence, who may have been involved in such Extraordinary Renditions that could amount to complicity in torture.

(a) Scope of Obligations Regarding Torture

To implement CAT Article 4's requirement that each state party criminalize torture, attempted torture, and an act by "any person which constitutes complicity or participation in torture," CAT mandates that each state party "shall" establish jurisdiction over torture and complicity to torture:

(i) When the offenses are committed in any territory under its jurisdiction or on board a ship or aircraft registered in that State;

(ii) When the alleged offender is a national of that State;

(iii) When the victim is a national of that State if that State considers it appropriate.[252]

In addition, CAT Article 5(2) requires each state party to establish jurisdiction over these offenses when the alleged offender is "present in any territory under its jurisdiction" and the state party choses not to extradite the alleged offender to another state party with jurisdiction.[253] Finally, CAT permits the exercise of "any criminal jurisdiction exercised in accordance with" the domestic laws of the state party.[254] Together, these CAT provisions constitute a mandatory system of universal jurisdiction over criminal acts of torture and complicity in torture.[255]

The Vienna Convention on the Law of Treaties requires that a treaty must be interpreted "in accordance with the ordinary meaning to be given to the terms of the treaty in their context and in light of its object and purpose."[256] Read in conjunction with each other, the plain language of the CAT torture prohibition, the requirement of criminalization of complicity or participation in torture, and the jurisdictional provisions, result in a positive obligation for the United States to assert jurisdiction over the following:

(i) any act that violates CAT's torture prohibitions "in any territory over which [the United States] has jurisdiction";

(ii) any act of torture or complicity to torture that occurs on a U.S.-registered ship or aircraft;[257]

(iii) any act by a U.S. state actor, or a U.S. national acting with the consent or acquiescence of a U.S. state actor, who either directly engages in torture, or is complicit in torture, regardless of the state in which the action(s) take place;

(iv) acts of a national of any other state who, acting with the consent or acquiescence of a U.S. state actor, either directly engages in torture, or is complicit in torture, and is present in "any territory under [U.S.] jurisdiction," and whom the United States decides not to extradite; and

(v) any person over whom, or act over which, jurisdiction is permissible under the provisions of U.S. domestic law.

There is a dearth of case law and CAT Committee guidance on the content of the phrase "territory under its jurisdiction" as used in CAT. According to Burgers and Danelius, this phrase was intended to extend to "territories under military occupation, to colonial territories and to any other territories over which a State has factual control."[258] This interpretation of "territory under its jurisdiction" also applies to the other CAT provisions that incorporate the territorial jurisdictional requirement.[259] The legislative history of the CAT ratification into U.S. domestic law indicates that the Senate had a narrower interpretation of the scope of "territory under its jurisdiction," stating that it referred to "all places that the State Party controls as a governmental authority, including ships and aircraft registered in that State."[260] In its formal instrument of CAT ratification, however, the United States did not make a reservation or other declaration reflecting this narrower understanding. For a discussion of the interpretation of precisely the same phrase used in the ICCPR's jurisdictional provisions, see Section V.B.2. below.

(b) Scope of Obligations Regarding Non-refoulement

Given the object and purpose of CAT, the *non-refoulement* obligation should be applied not only to prohibit transfers by the United States of an individual from its own territory to another state where the individual is in danger of torture, but also to (i) the transfer of an individual located outside the United States but under the control of the United States or its agents, and (ii) the transfer of an individual from a second state to any subsequent state in which the individual faces the danger of torture. CAT Article 4's criminalization requirement does not apply

directly to violations of the *refoulement* prohibition. However, actions taken by a U.S. state actor or a non-state actor acting with the consent or acquiescence of a state actor to transfer or *refoule* an individual to another state where the individual is in danger of torture may constitute enough state involvement to result in liability for torture or complicity in torture.

5. *The United States' Implementation of CAT*

(a) Ratification

The United States ratified CAT in October 1994, with certain reservations, understandings and declarations, and enacted a new federal law to implement the requirements of the CAT relating to acts of torture committed outside the United States.[261] The United States is thus bound by CAT, subject to its reservations, understandings and declarations, as well as the international law norms that CAT codifies.[262]

Under U.S. implementing legislation and regulations, "acquiescence" that amounts to conspiracy or complicity to torture may result in liability for a U.S. state actor.[263] Thus, persons operating under the color of law do not necessarily need to engage directly in acts of torture to be culpable for them. For a public official to acquiesce to an act of torture, that official must, "prior to the activity constituting torture, have *awareness* of such activity and thereafter breach his or her legal responsibility to intervene to prevent such activity."[264] Subsequent U.S. jurisprudence and administrative decisions have recognized that "willful blindness" by officials to torture may constitute "acquiescence" under CAT,[265] but acquiescence does not occur when a government is aware of third-party torture but is unable to stop it.[266] In addition, mere noncompliance with applicable legal procedural standards does not *per se* constitute torture.[267] With respect to the provisions of CAT Article 3, which prohibits *refoulement* of persons to states where substantial grounds exist for believing the person would be subjected to torture, the United States declared its understanding that this requirement refers to instances in which it would be "more likely than not" that the alien would be tortured.[268]

The U.S. Initial CAT Report[269] states that the United States "has long been a vigorous supporter of the international fight against torture" and that "[torture] is categorically denounced as a matter of policy and as a tool of state authority."[270] The report further provides that prior to the enactment of the legislation implementing CAT, "the Department of State relied on the law and practice of the United States to provide authority for declining to extradite a fugitive to another State party where there are substantial grounds to believe he would be in danger of being subjected to torture."[271]

(b) Criminalization of Torture

The U.S. obligation under CAT Articles 4 and 5 to criminalize and assert jurisdiction over acts of torture and complicity to torture is described in detail in Section V.A.3. above. Subsequent to its ratification of CAT, the United States enacted section 2340A of the U.S. criminal code to criminalize acts of torture occurring outside its territorial jurisdiction.[272] Pursuant to section 2340A, any person who commits or attempts to commit an act of torture outside the United States is subject to a fine and/or imprisonment for up to twenty years, except in circumstances where death results from the prohibited conduct, in which case the offender may be subject to imprisonment or death.[273] Persons who conspire to commit an act of torture outside the United States are generally subject to the same penalties faced by those convicted of committing torture, except that in the case of conspiracy, the death penalty does not apply.[274] The United States asserts jurisdiction over these actions when (i) the offender is a national of the United States or (ii) the offender is present in the United States, irrespective of the nationality of the

victim or offender.[275] Sections 2340 and 2340A are discussed in more detail in Section VIII. A.1. below.

(c) FARRA Regulations

As part of its commitment to implement CAT, the United States, through the enactment of FARRA, required relevant agencies to promulgate regulations effectuating FARRA provisions.[276] The FARRA Regulations broadly address three categories of people: (i) individuals subject to "summary exclusion" (also known as "expedited removal"), (ii) individuals subject to removal orders, and (iii) individuals subject to extradition orders. The scope of CAT protection varies both among and within these categories.

(i) Summary Removal

Broadly speaking, an individual arriving to the United States may be summarily removed if the individual is found inadmissible pursuant to sections 212(a)(6)(C) or 7 of the INA (i.e., lack of required documents or misrepresentation)[277] or if the individual is viewed as a threat to national security.[278] In the latter case, if an immigration officer suspects that an arriving individual appears to be inadmissible under section 212(a)(3)(A) (other than clause (ii)), (B), or (C) of the INA (i.e., based on terrorism-related grounds),[279] the immigration officer is required to order the removal of the individual and report the action promptly to the district director.[280] The district director then forwards the report to the regional director for further action.[281] The regional director may deny any further inquiry or hearing by an immigration judge.[282] The decision of the regional director is final and there is no administrative appeal.[283] FARRA Regulations section 235.8(b)(4) provides that the "Service shall not execute a removal order under this section under circumstances that violate section 241(b)(3) of the Act [i.e., restrictions on removal to a country where the individual's life or freedom would be threatened] or Article 3 of the Convention Against Torture." However, no guidance is provided regarding when, how and by whom the determination of a CAT claim would take place. In fact, the same section explicitly states that provisions of part 208[284] "relating to consideration or review by an immigration judge, the Board of Immigration Appeals, or an asylum officer shall not apply."[285] Thus, the scope of CAT protection in the case of individuals arriving to the United States and *suspected* of being a threat to national security is unclear. Moreover, to the extent that some protocol for determination of CAT claims exists, lack of any review makes it impossible to evaluate the compliance of such a protocol with the protections afforded by CAT.

(ii) Removal

CAT-based procedures for individuals who are *not* subject to summary exclusion proceedings at the U.S. border are better-defined. In such cases, the determination of a CAT claim is made by an immigration judge.[286] Generally, an applicant for non-removal under CAT Article 3 has the burden of proving that it is "more likely than not" that he or she would be tortured if removed to the proposed state.[287] If credible, the applicant's testimony may be sufficient to sustain this burden without additional corroboration.[288] In assessing whether it is "more likely than not" that an applicant would be tortured if removed to the proposed state, all evidence relevant to the possibility of future torture is required to be considered, including, *inter alia,* (i) evidence of past torture inflicted upon the applicant; (ii) a pattern or practice of gross human rights violations within the proposed state of removal; and (iii) other relevant information regarding conditions in the state of removal.[289] For purposes of ascertaining a pattern of gross violations, substantial weight is generally given to the Country Reports on Human Rights Practices issued annually by the U.S. Department of State.[290] The Board of Immigration Appeals (BIA), the appellate administrative body within the Executive Office for Immigration Review, has recognized that evidence concerning the likelihood of torture must be particularized; evidence of

torture of similarly situated individuals is insufficient alone to demonstrate that it is more likely than not that an applicant would be tortured if removed to a proposed state.[291]

If the immigration judge considering a CAT application determines that an individual is more likely than not to be tortured in the state of proposed removal, the individual is entitled to protection under CAT.[292] Generally, protection will be granted through the withholding of removal, unless the person falls within one of the categories of aliens described in section 241 (b)(3)(B) of the INA, in which case the person will be denied the withholding of removal (although the person could seek to have his or her removal deferred).

(iii) Extradition

In the context of extradition, pursuant to Criminal Code sections 3184 and 3186, the secretary of state is the U.S. official responsible for the final determination of whether to surrender an alleged fugitive to a foreign state by means of extradition.[293] The regulations pertaining to extradition quote Article 3 of CAT,[294] and specify that "in order to implement the obligation assumed by the United States pursuant to Article 3 of the Convention, the State Department considers the question of whether a person facing extradition from the United States 'is more likely than not' to be tortured in the State requesting extradition when appropriate in making this determination."[295] Using the language of CAT Article 3, the regulations stipulate that in making this determination, the authorities must take into account "all relevant considerations including, where applicable, the existence in the State concerned of a consistent pattern of gross, flagrant or mass violations of human rights."[296]

Generally, a decision to certify a detainee as extraditable is made initially by a judicial officer, and then the decision is presented to the secretary of state. If the individual subject to an extradition order asserts that he or she will be subject to torture in the state of extradition, "appropriate policy and legal offices review and analyze information relevant to the case in preparing a recommendation to the Secretary as to whether or not to sign the surrender warrant."[297] Even if the individual does not make a claim pursuant to CAT, the State Department will give consideration "to the requesting country's human rights record, as set forth in the annual Country Reports on Human Rights Practices, from the perspective of Article 3 [of CAT]."[298]

Decisions of the secretary of state concerning surrender of alleged fugitives for extradition "are matters of executive discretion not subject to judicial review."[299] The regulations further provide that

> pursuant to FARRA Section 2242(d), notwithstanding any other provision of law, no court shall have jurisdiction to review these regulations, and nothing in Section 2242 shall be construed as providing any court jurisdiction to consider or review claims raised under the convention or Section 2242, or any other determination made with respect to the application of the policy set forth in Section 2242(a), except as part of the review of a final order of removal pursuant to Section 242 of the INA.[300]

The regulations note that section 242 is not applicable to extradition.[301]

Although the enactment of FARRA was a laudable step towards implementing CAT, the regulatory framework for implementation of the *non-refoulement* obligation of CAT and of FARRA suffers from certain deficiencies, including a lack of clear procedural guidelines for determination of CAT claims (in the context of summary removal proceeding for individuals deemed by an immigration officer to be inadmissible on possible terrorism-related grounds) and lack of administrative or judicial review in cases of summary removals and extraditions.[302] In those cases, therefore, there appears to be nothing to prevent arbitrary decisions and no procedural safeguards to ensure compliance with U.S. obligations under CAT and FARRA.

In addition, there appears to be a gap in the implementation of FARRA's policy directive to apply the principle of *non-refoulement* regardless of whether the person is physically present in the United States. The United States has enunciated a clear policy "not to expel, extradite,

or *otherwise effect* the involuntary return of any person to a country in which there are substantial grounds for believing the person would be in danger of being subjected to torture, *regardless of whether the person is physically present in the United States*."[303] Congress evinced its intent to extend U.S CAT obligations to certain acts outside the United States through the enactment into the U.S. Code of sections 2340 and 2340A, which criminalize the act of and complicity in torture if the act *occurs outside the U.S. territory*.[304] However, neither the regulations governing extradition nor those governing removal proceedings under FARRA are designed to apply to persons being transferred by, or with the complicity of, U.S. actors *outside the United States* to third states. This failure to regulate against *refoulement* abroad not only represents a failure of regulatory agencies to comply with the directives of FARRA, but also constitutes a breach of the U.S. international obligation to implement and comply fully with the provisions of CAT.

B. The United States Is Obligated to Prevent Extraordinary Renditions under the ICCPR

1. *The ICCPR Prohibits Torture, CID Treatment, and Refoulement*

The International Covenant on Civil and Political Rights, to which the United States is a party,[305] explicitly prohibits both torture and CID treatment: "No one shall be subjected to torture or to cruel, inhuman or degrading treatment or punishment."[306]

Although the ICCPR does not contain a direct prohibition against Extraordinary Rendition, the Human Rights Committee has interpreted Article 7 to require that states party to the ICCPR "must not expose individuals to the danger of torture or cruel, inhuman or degrading treatment or punishment upon return to another country by way of their extradition, expulsion or *refoulement*.[307] The Human Rights Committee also interprets ICCPR Article 2's obligation on a state party "to respect and to ensure to all individuals within its territory and subject to its jurisdiction the rights recognized" by the Covenant as including a *non-refoulement* obligation:[308]

> [ICCPR Article 2's] obligation requiring that States Parties respect and ensure the Covenant rights of all persons in their territory and all persons under their control entails an obligation not to extradite, deport, expel or otherwise remove a person from their territory, where there are substantial grounds for believing that there is a real risk of irreparable harm, such as that contemplated by article[]. . . 7 of the Covenant, either in the country to which removal is to be effected or in any country to which the person may subsequently be removed.[309]

Consistent with this interpretation, the Human Rights Committee has previously held that "[i]f a State party extradites a person within its jurisdiction in circumstances such that as a result there is a real risk that his or her rights under the Covenant will be violated in another jurisdiction, the State party itself may be in violation of the Covenant."[310] According to the Human Rights Committee, the state party "would itself be in violation of the Covenant if it handed over a person to another State in circumstances in which it was foreseeable that torture would take place. The foreseeability of the consequence would mean that there was a present violation by the State party, even though the consequence would not occur until later on."[311]

The Human Rights Committee has provided only limited guidance on the factors that would constitute a "real risk" of a violation of the ICCPR prohibition against torture, CID treatment or *refoulement*.[312] Legal commentators have noted, however, that the Committee's terminology tracks that of the European Court of Human Rights, and that ICCPR Article 7 should be interpreted in light of the court's jurisprudence interpreting Article 3 of the European Convention.[313] That jurisprudence shows that the "real risk" standard requires a higher showing than CAT's "in

danger of" standard.[314] Legal commentators argue that the European Court of Human Rights (and thus the ICCPR) standard is more stringent than that of CAT because the European Convention and ICCPR provide for *non-refoulement* protection over a broader range of abuse—including both torture and CID treatment or punishment—than CAT, which protects only against *refoulement* to torture.[315]

An additional basis for the ICCPR *non-refoulement* obligation may be found in the principle that, with the exception of a tiny subset of citizenship rights, states parties to the ICCPR may not distinguish between rights afforded to their own citizens and those extended to aliens. The Human Rights Committee has clarified that states may not discriminate between their own citizens and aliens in relation to the state's "territory and subject to its jurisdiction."[316] According to the Committee, "the general rule is that each one of the rights of the Covenant must be guaranteed without discrimination between citizens and aliens. Aliens receive the benefit of the general requirement of non-discrimination in respect of the rights guaranteed in the Covenant, as provided for in article 2 thereof."[317] Included among the rights of aliens under ICCPR is that "[t]hey must not be subjected to torture or to cruel, inhuman or degrading treatment or punishment.... If lawfully deprived of their liberty, they shall be treated with humanity and with respect for the inherent dignity of their person. Aliens are entitled to equal protection by the law. There shall be no discrimination between aliens and citizens in the application of these rights."[318]

2. *Scope of Application of ICCPR Standards under International Law*

The Human Rights Committee has interpreted both Article 7's prohibition against transfer of an individual to a state where he or she faces a real risk of torture or CID treatment or punishment,[319] and Article 2's "respect and ensure" obligation as requiring state parties to prevent, investigate, and punish or remedy violations both by state agents and non-state actors, under that state's domestic laws.[320] Failure to protect individuals against such violations may engage the international responsibility of the state party.[321]

Examples of instances in which the Human Rights Committee has found a state party to be responsible for violations of the ICCPR generally encompass: (i) violations that occur within the physical territory of the state,[322] and (ii) violations that otherwise are imputable to the state. Under the jurisprudence of the Human Rights Committee, acts that may be imputed to the state include the following: (a) violations of an individual's ICCPR protections when that individual is in the "power or effective control" of a state, even if outside the territory of that state;[323] (b) acts within a state's territory that have the effect of violating the individual's ICCPR protections, even if these effects occur outside the territory of that state;[324] (c) acts by state officials or agents of the state (including civilian contractors) that violate an individual's ICCPR protections, no matter where those acts occur;[325] and (d) violations of the state's obligation to "take appropriate measures or to exercise due diligence to prevent, punish, investigate and redress the harm caused by" ICCPR violations by state actors or private persons or entities.[326] The Human Rights Committee explicitly found that Article 7 requires states party to take measures against ICCPR violations by private persons to "ensure that private persons or entities do not inflict torture or cruel, inhuman or degrading punishment on others within their power."[327] In addition to these specific instances, other acts imputable to the State under general international law rue of attribution may come to light which amount to violations of the ICCPR.

Although further factual development of the allegations of U.S. involvement in Extraordinary Renditions is necessary, based on the Human Rights Committee's jurisprudence, the United States could be liable for acts of torture or CID treatment or complicity to torture or CID treatment by state actors or private persons in each of the instances of alleged Extraordinary

Rendition described above in Section IV.A. above. In addition, the United States could be liable for the *refoulement* of an individual under the control of the United States, or from territory under U.S. control (e.g a secret detention facility)[328] to any other state where the person faces "a real risk" of torture or CID treatment, regardless of whether the person is actually subjected to ill treatment.[329]

The requirement that the United States investigate and prosecute allegations of Extraordinary Renditions is mandated by the terms of the Covenant, as interpreted by the Human Rights Committee. In order to ensure the effective application of ICCPR Article 7's protection against torture, CID treatment, and *refoulement,* the Human Rights Committee requires that state parties investigate allegations of breaches of the protections in the treaty, including those against torture, CID treatment, and *refoulement,* to bring offenders to justice in the case of criminal violations, and to provide appropriate remedies.[330] States are obligated not only to investigate and prosecute, but also to submit periodic reports that include information about training and instruction of state agents and medical personnel on ICCPR protections.[331] A failure by the state party to take any of these actions could itself give rise to a separate breach of the ICCPR by the state.[332] Finally, the Human Rights Committee has interpreted the Article 7 protections in conjunction with the Article 2(3) obligation to provide appropriate remedies as requiring state parties to provide effective complaint procedures and remedies under domestic law for breaches of Article 7.[333]

3. *The United States' Implementation of the ICCPR*

The U.S. Senate ratified the ICCPR on April 2, 1992, and the ICCPR came into force for the United States on September 8, 1992.[334] The instrument of ratification contained certain declarations, reservations, and understandings, including a declaration that ICCPR Articles 1 through 27 were not self-executing (*i.e.,* that these provisions must be implemented by domestic legislation).[335] Even though the United States has ratified the ICCPR with the express declaration that it is not self-executing and has not implemented the ICCPR into domestic legislation, the United States is nonetheless under an obligation to enact legislation to give effect to any international agreement to which it is a party.[336] That obligation is included explicitly in Article 2 of the ICCPR, which requires states party to implement and enforce the protections of the ICCPR.[337] Finally, the United States will be liable for violations of the ICCPR regardless of its failure to pass implementing legislation.

C. The Geneva Conventions' Prohibitions of Extraordinary Renditions

The four Geneva Conventions of 1949 codify a vast array of international humanitarian law standards on the treatment of prisoners of war and civilians during armed conflict and in occupied territories.[338] The protections afforded by the Geneva Conventions apply to (i) the actions of a High Contracting Party in territory under its control during an armed conflict, (ii) the actions of a High Contracting Party outside territory under its control, but which are taken in connection with an armed conflict, and (iii) to individuals falling within specified categories and classified as "protected persons."[339] The Conventions also apply "to all cases of partial or total occupation of the territory of a High Contracting Party, even if the occupation meets with no armed resistance."[340] A High Contracting Party to the Conventions is bound by their terms with respect to other states accepting and applying the Geneva Conventions.[341] The Geneva Conventions' protections have been interpreted to extend to individuals detained during the war in Afghanistan (though not without controversy), and also the U.S. war in, and occupation of, Iraq.[342] As discussed below, the Geneva Conventions' applicability to individuals captured

by the United States in situations other than these two conflicts and held, for example, in so-called secret detention facilities is open to question. Of course, all detainees held by the United States—regardless of where or when they were captured or of their status—are entitled to humane treatment and the protection of human rights law, including CAT and the ICCPR.

1. *Geneva III Protections*

Under Geneva III, "combatants" are entitled to POW status if they are members of the armed forces (other than medical personnel, chaplains,[343] spies or saboteurs). The specific requirements for combatant/POW status are set forth in Article 4 of Geneva III.[344] If there is any doubt as to whether captured persons meet Article 4's criteria for POW status, such persons are entitled to interim POW status until a "competent tribunal" determines their legal status.[345] A detailed discussion of the debate over the U.S. failure to establish such tribunals, the status and adequacy of the tribunals currently underway, and the U.S. categorization of detainees in the course of the war in Afghanistan as "enemy combatants" or "security detainees" to whom Geneva Convention protections do not apply is beyond the scope of this Report, but is discussed in detail in the HR Standards Report at pages 3–8 and 39–47, and at the HR Standards Supplement at pages 3–12.[346]

Briefly, Geneva III mandates that POWs be treated humanely at all times. This includes freedom from physical and mental torture, acts of violence, intimidation and insult, and exposure to public humiliation.[347] Pursuant to Article 14, POWs also "are entitled in all circumstances to respect for their persons and their honour. . . . [and] shall retain the full civil capacity which they enjoyed at the time of their capture." With respect to interrogation in particular, Article 17 of Geneva III provides: "No physical or mental torture, nor any other form of coercion, may be inflicted on prisoners of war to secure from them information of any kind whatever. Prisoners of war who refuse to answer may not be threatened, insulted, or exposed to any unpleasant or disadvantageous treatment of any kind." As discussed in greater detail below, in Section V. C.1., the torture or inhumane treatment of POWs is classified as a "grave breach" of Geneva III, obligating the United States to investigate and prosecute any such torture as a war crime.[348]

Geneva III also mandates that POWs may not be transferred to other states unless those states are also parties to Geneva III, and will fully protect the rights of such POWs (including the protections against torture or inhuman treatment). Although the unlawful transfer of POWs to a third state is not classified as a "grave breach," Geneva III provides that if POW protections are not to be afforded by the third state, the Detaining Power is obligated to take back custody of the POW and intern the POW in a place where his or her rights will be respected.[349]

Thus, under Geneva III, the United States may be required to investigate and prosecute as a war crime any allegations of Extraordinary Rendition of POWs in which U.S. agents may have been complicit to torture. If a POW has been transferred to a third state where he or she has been subjected to torture, the United States, as the original transferring Power, must take effective measures to correct the situation or seek the return of the POW.

2. *Geneva IV Protections*

Geneva IV applies in international armed conflicts to the same extent as Geneva III. It covers "protected persons," defined as "those who, at a given moment and in any manner whatsoever, find themselves, in case of a conflict or occupation, in the hands of a Party to the conflict or Occupying Power of which they are not nationals."[350] "Protected persons" do not, however, include "[n]ationals of a State which is not bound by the Convention," "[n]ationals of a neutral State who find themselves in the territory of a belligerent State" and "nationals of a co-

belligerent State. . . while the State of which they are nationals has normal diplomatic representation in the State in whose hands they are."[351] The term "protected persons" includes persons detained as spies or saboteurs as well as persons suspected of engaging in activities hostile to the security of the Occupying Power, with some limitations.[352] The fact that a person may have unlawfully participated in a conflict does not deprive that person of Geneva IV's protections against torture, inhumane treatment and unlawful transfer.[353] These Geneva IV protections would thus extend to individuals (who are not POWs covered by Geneva III) detained during the wars in Afghanistan and Iraq, and would protect them against torture, inhumane treatment and against transfer to other states where they may be subject to torture.

Like POWs under Geneva III, "protected persons" under Geneva IV cannot be subjected to coercive interrogation tactics. Specifically, Article 31 of Geneva IV provides that "[n]o physical or moral coercion shall be exercised against protected persons, in particular to obtain information from them or from third parties." Article 32 further provides that "any measure of such a character as to cause physical suffering or extermination of protected persons" is prohibited and that "[t]his prohibition applies not only to murder, torture, corporal punishments, mutilation and medical or scientific experiments not necessitated by the medical treatment of a protected person, but also to any other measures of brutality, whether applied by civilian or military agents."

Geneva IV contains detailed rules regarding the internment, transfer and deportation of civilians.[354] Article 45 specifically provides that:

> Protected persons shall not be transferred to a Power which is not a party to the Convention. . . .
>
> Protected persons may be transferred by the Detaining Power only to a Power which is a party to the present Convention and after the Detaining Power has satisfied itself of the willingness and ability of such transferee Power to apply the present Convention. If protected persons are transferred under such circumstances, responsibility for the application of the present Convention rests on the Power accepting them, while they are in its custody. Nevertheless, if that Power fails to carry out the provisions of the present Convention in any important respect, the Power by which the protected persons were transferred shall, upon being so notified by the Protecting Power, take effective measures to correct the situation or shall request the return of the protected persons. Such request must be complied with.
>
> In no circumstances shall a protected person be transferred to a country where he or she may have reason to fear persecution for his or her political opinions or religious beliefs.

As discussed in greater detail below, in Section V.C.2., both the torture or inhuman treatment and the "unlawful deportation or transfer or unlawful confinement of a protected person" are classified as "grave breaches" of Geneva IV, obligating the United States to investigate and prosecute any such transfer as a war crime.[355]

It is unclear whether Geneva IV would apply to individuals detained outside the United States (and not Iraqi or Afghan nationals captured during the wars in Iraq or Afghanistan, respectively) as part of the "War on Terror," including individuals detained at the U.S. secret detention facilities. First, in the context of the so-called war against terrorism, the United States is not engaged in international armed conflict with another state during the course of which these individuals were detained. Second, without a status hearing (which have now begun in the case of detainees at Guantánamo only, and whose procedural adequacy has been called into question by military lawyers and human rights groups) it is not possible to determine whether a particular individual is an interned civilian to whom Geneva IV would apply. As noted above, however, regardless of whether Geneva IV protections apply, transfer of any of these individuals to states where they are in danger of torture would still clearly be prohibited under human rights treaties.

By its terms, Geneva IV ceases to apply "on the general close of military operations" in the case of an international conflict or, in the case of "occupied territory," "one year after the

general close of military operations," or as long thereafter as the occupying power exercises the "functions of government."[356] But the questions of when military operations have ended or when a territory is no longer occupied are often not easily answered. For example, whether military operations have reached a "general close" and whether the United States constituted an Occupying Power after the establishment of the Karzai government in June 2002, and its recognition by the UN Security Council, are questions open to controversy. Similarly, U.S. military operations in Iraq are on-going, and, even though governing authority was in many respects transferred to the interim Iraqi Government on June 28, 2004, with the approval of the UN Security Council and the subsequent recognition of the new government by numerous nations, the United States continues to hold some of the powers of government, including legal and physical control over prisoners. Thus, the ability of some civilians captured in Afghanistan or Iraq to claim "protected person" status under Geneva IV today is subject to additional debate.[357] However, regardless of the characterization of the current conflicts in Afghanistan and Iraq, torture and CID treatment of civilian detainees from the war or ongoing conflict in Afghanistan and Iraq is not permitted, whether or not they qualify as "protected persons" under Geneva IV. All such persons are still entitled to the protections of international human rights law and to humane treatment under Common Article 3 and Article 75 of Additional Protocol I.

3. *Additional Geneva Convention Protections*

Detained civilians captured in situations of international or non-international armed conflict who do not fall within the definition of "protected persons" in Geneva IV are nevertheless covered by Article 3 common to all four Geneva Conventions."[358] Common Article 3, which applies to armed conflict of any kind—international and non-international—is recognized as part of customary international law.[359] Pursuant to Common Article 3, detainees "shall in all circumstances be treated humanely" and prohibits the following acts "at any time and in any place whatsoever": "violence to life and person, in particular murder of all kinds, mutilation, cruel treatment and torture;" and "outrages upon personal dignity, in particular humiliating or degrading treatment."[360] Common Article 3 also provides that the "wounded and sick shall be collected and cared for."[361] Common Article 3 does not address the transfer of detainees.

4. *The Geneva Conventions Require High Contracting Parties to Investigate and Prosecute Torture and Complicity to Torture as War Crimes*

Common Articles 50, 51, 130, and 147 of the Geneva Conventions define specific "grave breaches" of the Geneva Conventions as war crimes.[362] Included in the grave breaches provisions is "willful killing, torture or inhuman treatment" of POWs and civilians qualified as "protected persons."[363] Geneva IV, applicable to civilians, also includes as a "grave breach" the "unlawful deportation or transfer or unlawful confinement of a protected person."[364] States are required to investigate allegations of "grave breach" violations and to prosecute, or extradite to another state that will prosecute, perpetrators of "grave breaches."[365] The Geneva Conventions require criminal sanctions to be imposed on people who either directly commit "grave breaches," or order "grave breaches" to be committed.[366] The obligation to prosecute or extradite is absolute and non-derogable. It applies regardless of the nationality of the perpetrator or of the victim and also regardless of the place where the "grave breach" was committed.[367] "Grave breaches" of the Geneva Conventions are a part of customary international law.[368] Geneva Conventions Common Article 3 is also part of the customary international law, and violations of Common Article 3 have also been interpreted as requiring criminal sanctions.[369]

Recently, the statute for the ICTY incorporated the language of the Geneva Convention grave breaches provisions and authorized the tribunals to prosecute individuals "committing or ordering to be committed" crimes including torture or inhuman treatment as set out under the Geneva Conventions.[370] The statute for the ICTR reflects the fact that, unlike the war in the former Yugoslavia, the conflict in Rwanda was at all times a non-international armed conflict and criminalizes violations of Geneva Convention Common Article 3, including, specifically "violence to life, health and physical or mental well-being of persons, in particular murder as well as cruel treatment such as torture, mutilation or any form of corporal punishment."[371]

5. *The United States' Implementation of the Geneva Conventions*

The United States signed the Geneva Conventions on December 8, 1949 and ratified them on February 8, 1955.[372] The United States has applied the prohibitions and protections of the Geneva Conventions (and those of its predecessor treaties) since at least the Nuremberg Tribunals following the Second World War, including during the Vietnam War, and the Persian Gulf War of 1990. The provisions of the Geneva Conventions are also reflected in U.S. domestic statutes, including the Uniform Code of Military Justice, applicable to all military personnel.[373] However, it was not until 1996 that the Geneva Conventions were formally implemented into domestic legislation through the War Crimes Act of 1996. The War Crimes Act provides, in pertinent part:

(a) Offense.—Whoever, whether inside or outside the United States, commits a war crime, in any of the circumstances described in subsection (b), shall be fined under this title or imprisoned for life or any term of years, or both, and if death results to the victim, shall also be subject to the penalty of death.

(b) Circumstances.—The circumstances referred to in subsection (a) are that the person committing such war crime or the victim of such war crime is a member of the Armed Forces of the United States or a national of the United States (as defined in section 101 of the Immigration and Nationality Act).

(c) Definition.—As used in this section the term '"war crime"' means any conduct: (1) defined as a grave breach in any of the international conventions signed at Geneva 12 August 1949, or any protocol to such convention to which the United States is a party; which constitutes a violation of common Article 3 of the international conventions signed at Geneva, 12 August 1949, or any protocol to such convention to which the United States is a party and which deals with non-international armed conflict.[374]

D. The Refugee Convention's Prohibitions of Extraordinary Renditions

Extraordinary Rendition may also, in the case of transfer of individuals who seek asylum in the United States, violate the provisions of the Refugee Convention.[375] Article 33(1) of the Refugee Convention prohibits the expulsion or *refoulement* of any person to a state "where his life or freedom would be threatened on account of his race, religion, nationality, membership in a particular social group or political opinion."[376] The Refugee Convention does not refer to torture or to CID treatment or punishment, but rather applies to any person who "owing to well-founded fear of being persecuted for reasons of race, religion, nationality, membership of a particular social group or political opinion, is outside the country of his nationality and is unable, or owing to such fear, is unwilling to avail himself to the protection of that country."[377] Thus the Refugee Convention's protections are both narrower and broader than those of CAT. CAT prohibits *refoulement* of *any* individual to *any* state where that individual faces the danger of torture, regardless of the reason for the danger or the purpose of the torture.[378] The Refugee Convention's protections extend only to individuals who face persecution in their home state (or state of habitual residence) on one of the five enumerated grounds. On the other hand, CAT

applies to prohibit torture by state actors or individuals acting with the consent or acquiescence of state actors, while the Refugee Convention has been interpreted to include persecution by civilians, if the persecution is tolerated by state authorities or if state authorities are unable to prevent it.[379]

Also unlike CAT's *non-refoulement* prohibition, which is absolute and permits no exceptions, the Refugee Convention contains certain exceptions that prohibit a person from obtaining refugee status, or protection against *refoulement,* even if the person has a well-founded fear of persecution on one of the five enumerated grounds. Article 33(2) limits the *non-refoulement* protection by providing that a person who has been recognized as a refugee may not be protected against *refoulement* if "there are reasonable grounds for regarding [him] as a danger to the security of the country in which he is, or who, having been convicted...of a particularly serious crime, constitutes a danger to the community of that country."[380] Article 1F of the Refugee Convention also states that the Convention shall not be applicable to a person if:

(a) He has committed a crime against peace, a war crime, or a crime against humanity . . .;

(b) He has committed a serious non-political crime outside the country of refuge prior to his admission to that country as a refugee;

(c) He has been guilty of acts contrary to the purposes of the United Nations.[381]

The United States could seek to justify the *refoulement* of an asylum seeker to his or her home country based on these exceptions to applicability of the Refugee Convention. Still, to the extent that an individual seeking asylum to the United States is returned by the United States to his or her home state (or any another state) where that person is in danger of torture, U.S. obligations under CAT and the ICCPR would be violated.

E. Guidance Provided by International Law on Criminal Liability

Torture is universally proscribed. The community of states has recognized the egregiously transgressive nature of torture, and international human rights and humanitarian law treaties include provisions that either directly criminalize torture (for example, through the "grave breaches" provisions of the Geneva Conventions), or require that states party criminalize torture in their domestic legal regimes (for example CAT, or the ICCPR, as interpreted by the Human Rights Committee). Individuals acting either as agents of a state, or as private actors, can be held accountable for torture as an international crime.[382] Reflecting the seriousness of the offense of torture, an evolving body of international law also requires criminalization and prosecution of ancillary acts, such as complicity to, and aiding and abetting, torture. This body of law is reflected in multilateral treaties that set out legal standards and a basis for criminal sanctions, and also in the norms of customary international law.[383] Although not all of this body of law is directly binding on the United States, it offers useful guidance to the United States in interpreting its own obligations under the treaties to which it is party, and a set of principles, applied by international courts and tribunals, that the United States should follow in its domestic prosecutions of alleged acts of torture or conspiracy in torture.

In this Section, we look therefore to the International Criminal Court statute[384] and the statutes and decisions of the criminal tribunals for Yugoslavia[385] and Rwanda[386] for guidance and comparison to the bases for prosecution (and defenses) under international criminal law. The United States is not a party to the Rome Statute, but was actively involved in the negotiations of the provisions of that statute.[387] The provisions of the Rome Statute relating to the responsibility of civilian and military state actors for violations of international law reflect the most recent understanding by the community of states of the norms allowing for prosecutions

of crimes under international law.[388] In the future, the decisions of the ICC (with or without U.S. participation) will form and further the development of international criminal law and provide guidance as to its interpretation and application. The United States was actively involved in the negotiation and drafting of the statutes of the ICTY and the ICTR. Although by their terms applicable only to the "armed conflict" in the former Yugoslavia[389] and the "widespread or systematic attack" in Rwanda,[390] both the statutes and the body of the tribunals' jurisprudence on prosecutions of numerous individual defendants reflect the most recent international jurisprudence on individual liability for "grave breaches" of the Geneva Conventions,[391] war crimes, including torture, and crimes against humanity, including systematic torture. A general discussion of certain key developments in international criminal law follows.

1. *Complicity, Conspiracy, and Aiding and Abetting*

The requirement of criminalization of complicity under CAT is not unusual in international law. Accomplice liability has been recognized in international criminal law since at least the post-World War II Nuremberg Trials.[392] More recently, the ICTY and ICTR statutes have criminalized acts by individuals who plan, instigate, order, commit or otherwise aid or abet in the planning, preparation or execution of a crime.[393]

In a case involving complicity to torture, the ICTR undertook a comparative review of criminal civil and common law systems and held that an accomplice may be tried (i) for complicity in a crime even if the principal perpetrator is unidentified or if the principal perpetrator's guilt cannot be proven, and (ii) even if the accomplice has not "wished" that the principal offense be committed.[394] According to the Chamber, "anyone who knowing of another's criminal purpose, voluntarily aids him or her in it, can be convicted of complicity even though he regretted the outcome of the offence."[395] Accomplice liability does require the predicate showing that the accused's actions had a "direct and substantial effect" on the commission of the offense. According to the ICTY, a substantial effect is shown "if the criminal act most probably would not have occurred in the same way had not someone acted in the role that the accused in fact assumed."[396]

Liability for planning or conspiring to commit acts that violate international criminal law as set out in treaties or customary international law has also long been a basis for prosecution beginning during the Nuremberg tribunals and culminating in the recent case law of the ICTY and the ICTR.[397] More recently, however, the Rome Statute provisions governing co-perpetrator liability do not expressly include conspiracy as a basis for prosecution.[398] A basis for prosecution on grounds similar to conspiracy may be Rome Statute Article 25(3)(d) which establishes criminal liability for an individual who "contributes to the commission or attempted commission of. . .a crime by a group of persons acting with a common purpose."[399] The contribution must be intentional and must either: (a) be made with the aim of furthering the criminal activity or criminal purpose of the group, where such activity or purpose involves the commission of a crime within the jurisdiction of the court; or (b) be made in the knowledge of the intention of the group to commit the crime.

Aiding and abetting liability has also been recognized under customary international law.[400] In the *Tadic* case, the ICTY laid out the basis for accomplice liability for aiding and abetting an international crime:

> The most relevant sources for such a determination are the Nuremberg war crimes trials, which resulted in several convictions for complicitous conduct. While the judgments generally failed to discuss in detail the criteria upon which guilt was determined, a clear pattern does emerge upon an examination of the relevant cases. First, there is a requirement of intent, which involves awareness of the act of participation coupled with a conscious decision to participate by planning, instigating, ordering, committing, or otherwise aiding

and abetting in the commission of a crime. Second, the prosecution must prove that there was participation in that the conduct of the accused contributed to the commission of the illegal act.[401]

Tadic recognized three types of joint activity that could subject a perpetrator to liability for the acts of others: (i) co-defendants, acting pursuant to a common design, who possess the same criminal intention;[402] (ii) members of military or administrative units acting pursuant to a joint plan[403] and with "knowledge of the nature of the system of ill-treatment and intent to further the common design of ill-treatment;"[404] (iii) where the accused possesses "the intention to take part in a joint criminal enterprise and to further. . .the criminal purposes of that enterprise" and the offenses committed by members of the group are foreseeable.[405] According to the ICTY, intent in instances of action pursuant to a joint plan may be shown "either directly or as a matter of inference from the nature of the accused's authority within the camp or organizational hierarchy."[406]

In the *Furundzija* judgment, the ICTY considered torture as a crime against humanity even in the absence of an armed conflict and suggested that the mere presence of a superior may be enough to constitute participation by that superior for complicity and also aiding and abetting liability:

[P]resence, when combined with authority, can constitute assistance in the form of moral support, that is, the actus reus of the offence. The supporter must be of a certain status for this to be sufficient for criminal responsibility. . . .In sum, the Trial Chamber holds the legal ingredients of aiding and abetting in international criminal law to be the following: the actus reus consists of practical assistance, encouragement, or moral support which has a substantial effect on the perpetration of the crime. The mens rea required is the knowledge that these acts assist the commission of the offence. This notion of aiding and abetting is to be distinguished from the notion of common design, where the actus reus consists of participation in a joint criminal enterprise and the mens rea required is intent to participate.[407]

Prosecution for accomplice and co-conspirator liability for international crimes such as torture is clearly established in international law.

2. *Status of Certain Defenses to Criminal Liability under International Law*

Just as the evolving body of international criminal law provides guidance on criminalization and prosecution of acts of torture and complicity to torture, so too does it provide guidance on the status of certain defenses to criminal liability under international law. It is clear that the Bush Administration is cognizant of and concerned about the availability of defenses to prosecutions for violations of CAT and U.S. laws that either implement CAT or otherwise include prohibitions against torture and complicity to torture. The Bush Administration's memos concerning the possible use of torture in interrogations include a focus on the possible defenses that may be asserted, including the superior orders defense, and the defenses of duress and necessity.[408] Although U.S. domestic criminal and military law will govern any prosecution of, and defenses available to, individual involvement in Extraordinary Renditions,[409] it is important to note that certain of the defenses that the Bush Administration memos argue may be asserted are unavailable under international law. To provide comparison and guidance for future prosecutions of alleged Extraordinary Renditions, therefore, it useful to describe briefly the status of certain defenses to the crime of torture and complicity to torture, under international law.

(a) The Doctrine of Command Responsibility

Criminal liability under international law has been interpreted to expand beyond those individuals who directly take part in the action and includes individuals throughout the chain of command. The doctrine of command responsibility has been recognized since the International

Military Tribunal at Nuremberg, which held that persons in *de facto* or *de jure* control are responsible for the acts of those under their power.[410] Codified in Articles 86 and 87 of Protocol 1 of the Geneva Conventions (1977), the doctrine has since been cemented in the decisions of the ICTY and ICTR. Under the doctrine, military superiors who ordered or planned international crimes, and those who knew or should have known that they were occurring may be held criminally liable for the crimes. As discussed below, a civilian superior may also be held criminally responsible for international crimes, depending on the individual's position in the chain of command and the individual's ability to prevent and punish the offense.

(i) Individual Criminal Responsibility of Commanders

As a preliminary matter, any superior who was involved in the commission of a criminal act may be individually liable. Thus any official who planned, ordered,[411] instigated, committed or otherwise aided and abetted in the planning, preparation or execution of a crime is individually responsible for that crime. This principle is recognized in the Geneva Conventions,[412] and the attribution of liability is codified in Article 7(1) of the ICTY Statute, Article 6(1) of the ICTR Statute, and Article 25(3)(b) of the Rome Statute.[413] Both the Rome Statute, in Article 27(1), and the ICTR Statute, in Article 6(2), further state that individual criminal responsibility shall apply to all persons regardless of any official capacity.[414] The position of an individual as Head of State or as a responsible government official is irrelevant in prosecutions before international courts or tribunals.[415]

(ii) Command Responsibility

Both civilian and military superiors may be held responsible for the criminal acts of subordinates even if they did not actually order the subordinate to commit the acts. Article 28 of the Rome Statute, Article 6(3) of the ICTR Statute, and Article 7(3) of the ICTY statute make clear that superiors may be held criminally liable under the doctrine of command responsibility.[416] The doctrine extends to civilian leaders to the extent they have a degree of effective control[417] similar to military commanders such that the exercise of de facto authority has the trappings of de jure authority.[418] Under the decisions of the ICTY and the ICTR, the main factors in determining a civilian superior's liability are (a) whether there is a *de jure* or *de facto* chain of command;[419] and (b) whether the superior has the *material ability* to prevent and punish the offenses.[420]

The three elements international criminal tribunals have held are necessary for a military superior to be held responsible for crimes committed by subordinates are: (1) the existence of a superior-subordinate relationship of effective control between the accused and the perpetrator of the crime, (2) the knowledge, or constructive knowledge, of the accused that the crime was about to be committed or had been committed, and (3) the failure of the accused to take the necessary and reasonable measures to prevent or stop the crime or to punish the perpetrator.[421]

An accused may argue that a superior-subordinate relationship did not exist since such a relationship is an essential element if an individual is to be held responsible under command responsibility.[422] However, the concept of a superior-subordinate relationship is not limited to a formal military command structure in international criminal prosecutions, and international tribunals look at both *de jure* and *de facto* power to control.[423] What is determinative is effective control to prevent or punish the criminal acts.

The second element for showing command responsibility requires that the superior either knew or had reason to know that subordinates were about to commit or had committed a crime.[424] Actual knowledge may be proven through direct or circumstantial evidence, and the evidence required may differ based on the position of authority and distance from the crimes. While responsibility is not based on strict liability, an individual's command position *per se* is a significant indication that the individual knew about the crimes.[425] It is not necessary to prove

actual knowledge if the superior "had some general information in his possession which would put him on notice."[426] Further, it is not required that the superior acquainted himself with the information, but just that it was provided or available to him.[427] Ignorance arising from the negligent failure to carry out a duty to inform oneself of the actions of subordinates will not constitute a defense.[428] Superiors who know or should have known about a crime have a duty to prevent or punish that crime using all necessary and reasonable measures that are feasible and use every means in their power. The degree of effective control over subordinates will determine what is required.[429]

(iii) Superior Orders Defense

Under the superior orders defense, a subordinate who is legally obligated to follow the orders of his or her superiors is not liable for carrying out those orders. This defense is unavailable in customary international law and given the absolute prohibition against torture, would not likely excuse conspiracy to commit torture.

Article 8 of the London Charter establishing the Nuremberg International Military Tribunal explicitly prohibited the superior orders defense, and this prohibition has generally become accepted in international law.[430] The defense was clearly rejected in the trial of Adolf Eichmann, where the court noted that such an approach had "become general in all civilized nations."[431] More recently, international instruments have explicitly required that states exclude the defense from their criminal law. Article 2(3) of CAT states that, "An order from a superior officer or a public authority may not be invoked as a justification of torture."[432] The Human Rights Committee has also recommended that states party to the ICCPR revoke the superior orders defense for violations of the ICCPR.[433] Similarly, Article 6(4) of the ICTR Statute and Article 7(4) of the ICTY Statute state that, "the fact that an accused person acted pursuant to an order of a Government or of a superior shall not relieve him or her of criminal responsibility."[434] While superior orders may be taken into account as a mitigating factor when considering punishment, these instruments make clear that they do not absolve an individual of criminal responsibility.[435]

Unlike other instruments, the Rome Statute does leave open the possibility of a defense of superior orders, but not one that would apply in cases of torture or complicity to torture. Article 33 of the Rome Statute provides that the defense is not available for offenses that are commonly known to be unlawful.[436] Thus the superior orders defense is available only when the individual was legally bound to obey the orders and the person did not know that the orders were unlawful. Further, the orders must not have been manifestly unlawful. Torture is manifestly unlawful and, like murder and genocide, it is a crime that every individual must be presumed to know is illegal and thus cannot be excused by superior orders.

(b) Duress and Necessity

Duress and necessity are related defenses where the accused argues that criminal acts are justified because the accused faced an imminent threat to his or her life. Under common law, necessity is seen as a defense when the accused is required to choose between two evils and must choose the lesser evil. Duress under common law is seen as an excuse.

The defenses should not be available for violations of CAT.[437] CAT Article 2(2) makes clear that, "no exceptional circumstances whatsoever, whether a state of war or a threat or war, internal political instability or any other public emergency, may be invoked as a justification of torture."[438] The prohibition against torture is a norm that is not derogable even in times of public emergency.[439] This provision makes clear that there can be no threat compared to which torture is a lesser harm. Moreover, the harm that is caused by torture is definite whereas the benefits gained by torture are difficult to measure and often negligible. Torture is carried out to collect information, but often fails to produce actionable intelligence. The

criminal laws of most nations prohibit the use of information obtained from torture or abusive interrogation.[440]

Moreover, torture is rarely, if ever, carried out in an attempt to avoid a truly imminent threat. Under international law, an imminent harm must be known and specific[441] and an assertion that an individual may have information about a possible future attack is unlikely to fulfill this requirement. Legal interrogation, surveillance and intelligence techniques may be employed to gather the same information that officials hope to gather through torture.

Finally, duress and necessity are clearly inapplicable in cases where an individual is rendered to face torture as a form of punishment for past actions or to gather information related to previously committed attacks. The defenses require that the crime be committed with the intent of avoiding future harm. Any torture where the focus is on past events is clearly missing the required mental element.

(c) Self-Defense

While self-defense is recognized in international law, it applies narrowly, to excuse illegal conduct carried out to protect oneself or another person against an imminent unlawful use of force.[442] International law excuses reasonable acts to protect oneself as long as they are proportionate to the degree of danger, but an individual's involvement in a defensive operation does not constitute a ground for the excuse. The doctrine is most clearly laid out in Article 31(1)(c) of the Rome Statute, which states:

> A person shall not be criminally responsible if, at the time of that person's conduct. . . The person acts reasonably to defend himself or herself or another person or, in the case of war crimes, property which is essential for the survival of the person or another person or property which is essential for accomplishing a military mission, against an imminent and unlawful use of force in a manner proportionate to the degree of danger to the person or the other person or property protected. The fact that the person was involved in a defensive operation conducted by forces shall not in itself constitute a ground for excluding criminal responsibility under this subparagraph.[443]

The ICTY has also emphasized that "involvement of a person in a defensive operation does not, in itself, constitute a ground for excluding criminal responsibility."[444] These sources make clear that it is not a defense to argue, for example, that in conspiring to commit torture, an individual is protecting his or her state from terrorist attack.

F. Extraordinary Renditions in the Context of the "War on Terror" Violate International Law

There is an inherent tension between the need to obtain potentially life-saving information through interrogation of terrorist suspects and the legal requirement of upholding the anti-torture standards in the treaties to which the United States is a party. Still, "condoning torture under any circumstances erodes one of the most basic principles of international law and human rights and contradicts our values as a democratic state."[445] Torture harms not only the detainees, but also interrogators and our society. The universal condemnation of the abuses that have come to light at Abu Ghraib prison and other U.S. detention facilities in Iraq and Afghanistan have damaged this nation's standing in the community of nations, and have served to fuel the enmity of those who seek to harm U.S. citizens and U.S. interests domestically and abroad. Extraordinary Renditions may be one step removed from the direct torture of detainees by U.S. agents, but to condone any level of U.S. involvement in the interrogation by torture of detainees remains wrong and immoral. This position is reflected in international law, which, as discussed above, prohibits both torture and complicity to torture, including, as discussed below, in the context of terrorism and national security emergencies.

1. *The Prohibition Against Torture Is Absolute and Non-Derogable*

Article 2(2) of CAT provides that "No exceptional circumstances whatsoever, whether a state of war or a threat of war, internal political instability or any other public emergency, may be invoked as a justification of torture."[446] The absolute nature of this prohibition was specifically included in CAT to distinguish freedom from torture as one of "the few fundamental rights of the individual" from which no derogation is permitted under international law, even in times of war or other emergency.[447] After the terror attacks of September 11, 2001, as the United States geared up its "War on Terror," the CAT Committee issued a statement in which it condemned the terror attacks, expressed "profound condolences to the victims, who were nationals of some 80 countries, including many States parties to [CAT]," but reminded states of the non-derogable nature of CAT obligations.[448] The CAT Committee highlighted the obligations contained in article 2 (prohibition of torture under all circumstances), article 15 (prohibiting confessions extorted by torture being admitted in evidence, except against the torturer), and article 16 (prohibiting CID treatment or punishment). The Committee added that these provisions must be observed in all circumstances, and expressed confidence that "whatever responses to the threat of international terrorism are adopted by States parties, such responses will be in conformity with the obligations undertaken by them in ratifying the Convention against Torture."[449]

Unlike CAT, each of the ICCPR, the European Convention and the American Convention contains provisions permitting certain derogations from human rights obligations in specific circumstances.[450] Each of these conventions is clear, however, that certain rights are always non-derogable. Paradigmatic among these is the prohibition against torture.[451] Even derogation from other rights is only permitted in the special circumstances and according to the specified limits defined in each of the three treaties. Under the ICCPR, any such measures must be of exceptional character,[452] strictly limited in time[453] and to the extent required by the exigencies of the situation,[454] subject to regular review,[455] consistent with other obligations under international law, and must not involve discrimination.[456] Each of the three treaties further requires that formal notice be given to the secretary-general of the United Nations or the relevant regional organization, detailing which provisions a state has derogated from and the reasons for such derogation.[457] Thus, in 2001, when its anti-terrorism legislation was adopted, the United Kingdom filed notices of derogation under the ICCPR[458] and the European Convention.[459] The United States has filed no such notice of derogation under the ICCPR or any other human rights or humanitarian law treaty to which it is a party.

Like CAT's non-derogability provision, the Geneva Conventions' obligation to investigate and prosecute individuals who are alleged to have committed "grave breaches" of the Geneva Conventions is not derogable. Thus Geneva III's prohibition against torture and inhumane treatment of POWs and Geneva IV's prohibition against torture, inhumane treatment and unlawful transfers of civilians to states where they may be subject to Geneva Convention violations apply during war – surely the greatest of national security emergencies.[460] Moreover, even though Geneva IV contains a national security exception to the applicability of "protected person" status,[461] in no circumstance does this exception permit a High Contracting Party to commit "grave breaches" as defined in Art. 147, which includes torture or inhuman treatment and willfully causing great suffering or serious injury to body or health.[462] To the extent that any physical or moral coercion (otherwise prohibited by Article 31 of Geneva IV) might fall below the level of "grave breach," the ICRC commentary to the derogations contained in Article 5 of Geneva IV, involving persons engaged in activities hostile to the security of the state, notes that:

> [W]idespread application of the Article may eventually lead to the existence of a category of civilian internees who do not receive the normal treatment laid down by the Convention but are detained under conditions which are almost impossible to check. It must be emphasized most strongly, therefore, that Article 5 can only be applied in individual cases of an exceptional nature, when the existence of specific charges makes it almost certain that penal proceedings will follow. This Article should never be applied as a result of mere suspicion.[463]

2. *Application of the Prohibition Against Torture and Refoulement in the Context of Terrorism or National Security Risk*

The CAT Committee has specifically addressed the *non-refoulement* of asylum seekers and other foreigners in the context of a state party's concerns that a claimant may present a security risk:

> [T]he test of article 3 of the Convention is absolute. Whenever substantial grounds exist for believing that an individual would be in danger of being subjected to torture upon expulsion to another State, the State party is under obligation not to return the person concerned to that State. The nature of the activities in which the person concerned engaged cannot be a material consideration when making a determination under article 3 of the Convention.[464]

The CAT Committee's holding is echoed by the Human Rights Committee's comment on the link between removal, expulsion or *refoulement* of non-nationals and torture, in its General Comment No. 20 on article 7 of the ICCPR:

> States parties must not expose individuals to the danger of torture or cruel, inhuman or degrading treatment or punishment upon return to another country by way of their extradition, expulsion or *refoulement*.[465]

The Human Rights Committee has acknowledged "the difficulties that the State Party faces in its prolonged fight against terrorism, but recalls that no exceptional circumstances whatsoever can be invoked as a justification for torture, and expresses concern at the possible restrictions of human rights which may result from measures taken for that purpose."[466]

The European Court of Human Rights has also addressed the principle of *non-refoulement* to the danger of torture in the context of terrorism and national security, and determined that the prohibition against *refoulement* is based on "one of the most fundamental values of democratic society,"[467] and may not be violated even on national security grounds.[468] In *Chahal v. United Kingdom*,[469] The government of the United Kingdom claimed that the petitioner was a threat to the United Kingdom's national security, refused his claim for asylum and issued a deportation order. The Court found that Chahal would be in danger of ill-treatment if sent to India, and stated that the absolute nature of Article 3 applied to expulsion cases. With respect to the United Kingdom's claim that the petitioner posed a threat to its national security, the Court stated that:

> The Court is well aware of the immense difficulties faced by States in modern times in protecting their communities from terrorist violence. However, even in these circumstances, the Convention prohibits in absolute terms torture or inhuman or degrading treatment or punishment, irrespective of the victim's conduct. . . . The prohibition provided by Article 3 against ill-treatment is equally absolute in expulsion cases. Thus, whenever substantial grounds have been shown for believing that an individual would face a real risk of being subjected to treatment contrary to Article 3 if removed to another State, the responsibility of the Contracting State to safeguard him or her against such treatment is engaged in the event of expulsion. . . . In these circumstances, the activities of the individual in question, however undesirable or dangerous, cannot be a material consideration.[470]

The Inter-American Court of Human Rights has similarly held that the prohibition against torture is a *jus cogens* norm, which prohibits an individual from return to a country where that person is likely to be tortured, even if the individual is suspected of terrorist activities.[471]

These cases provide guidance to the United States in its necessary task of striking a balance between the need to address the threat of terrorism and the "fundamental values of democratic society." International law uniformly provides that regardless of whether the transfer of a person occurs as part of an extradition request and regardless of any exceptional circumstances such as efforts to combat terrorism or another threat against national security, the anti-torture and *non-refoulement* principles would be violated if, as a result of such transfer, the person could be subjected to torture or other ill-treatment.

VI. DIPLOMATIC ASSURANCES

Despite the prohibitions against torture and *refoulement* to torture under CAT and the ICCPR, so-called "diplomatic assurances" have been used by the United States as well as certain European states and Canada as a basis for the transfer of alien detainees or asylum seekers to states where the individual faces the risk or danger of torture.[472] Specifically in the United States, regulations implementing CAT provide that if assurances are obtained by the secretary of state from the government of a specific state "that an alien would not be tortured there if the alien were removed to that country" and such assurances are forwarded to the attorney general or the secretary of the Department of Homeland Security, the official to whom this information is forwarded shall determine, in consultation with the secretary of state, whether such assurances are "sufficiently reliable" to permit the alien's removal to that state without violating U.S. obligations under Article 3 of CAT.[473] Diplomatic assurances were apparently obtained by the United States in at least one case of alleged Extraordinary Rendition (the Maher Arar case, discussed below). It is not clear whether they have been obtained in other cases because the U.S. State and Justice Departments and the Department of Homeland Security are not required to make public their use of diplomatic assurances.

In this Section, we examine the legality of diplomatic assurances under international and U.S. law and conclude that although diplomatic assurances arguably fall under a "grey area"—neither envisioned nor prohibited by the international treaties to which the United States is a party—as currently implemented, they violate the strict letter and the object and purpose of these treaties. We also briefly consider examples of the use of diplomatic assurances to determine their effectiveness. We conclude that diplomatic assurances, as implemented, are inadequate safeguards against torture for two fundamental reasons: (i) diplomatic assurances are unilaterally employed by the Executive Branch without judicial or administrative review or any opportunity for the transferred detainee to challenge their basis, and (ii) they are tools of diplomacy without means of effective monitoring and enforcement.

A. Legality of Diplomatic Assurances under International and Domestic Law

International Law Applicable to Diplomatic Assurances

Use of diplomatic assurances as a permissible basis for the transfer of an individual to another state falls into a grey area under international law. CAT (and other treaties containing the torture prohibition) neither envisions nor prohibits the use of diplomatic assurances. Arguably, a receiving state's diplomatic assurance could be one of the "relevant conditions" to be taken into account under CAT Article 3 in the determination of whether there are substantial grounds to believe that an individual is "in danger of" torture upon transfer to a receiving state. On the other hand, the prohibition against torture under the strict letter of CAT, the ICCPR, the Geneva Conventions and under customary international law is absolute and non-derogable. CAT, the ICCPR and, as applicable in specific contexts, the Geneva Conventions and the Refugee

Convention also prohibit the *refoulement* of an individual to a state where the person faces the risk or danger of torture.

Diplomatic assurances are most likely used where conditions in the proposed receiving state present a risk of torture to the individual to be transferred: otherwise, diplomatic assurances would be unnecessary. The United States, along with other states party to CAT, the ICCPR, the Geneva Conventions and the Refugee Convention, must interpret and implement its obligations under these treaties "in accordance with the ordinary meaning to be given to the terms of the treaty in their context and in light of its object and purpose."[474] If a risk or danger of *refoulement* to torture exists, then the use of diplomatic assurances is a circumvention of the absolute prohibition against torture and *refoulement* to torture—the creation of "an island of legality, in a sea of illegality."[475]

Diplomatic assurances were addressed by the UN Special Rapporteur on Torture in a July 2002 interim report to the UN General Assembly. Specifically focusing on the prohibition of torture in the context of counter-terrorism measures, the Special Rapporteur called on states not to extradite any individual "unless the Government of the receiving country has provided an unequivocal guarantee to the extraditing authorities that the persons concerned will not be subjected to torture or any other forms of ill-treatment upon return, and that a system to monitor the treatment of the persons in question has been put into place with a view to ensuring that they are treated with full respect for their human dignity."[476] The Special Rapporteur recommended a two-pronged test to assess the reliability of diplomatic assurances. First, according to the Special Rapporteur, diplomatic assurances must be "unequivocal" before the transfer of an individual took place—the diplomatic assurances must leave no doubt that torture or ill-treatment will not occur. Second, the Special Rapporteur required a "monitoring" system, agreed upon in advance between the transferring state and the state offering assurances, to ensure that, upon return, the individual contined to be protected from torture or CID treatment. As described below, however, the monitoring mechanism has, in practice, proved to be an inadequate safeguard.

2. *U.S. Law Applicable to Diplomatic Assurances*

Under U.S. law, if diplomatic assurances satisfactory to the attorney general are provided, an alien detainee's claims for protection under CAT Article 3 "shall not be considered further by an immigration judge, the Board of Immigration Appeals, or an asylum officer" and the alien may be removed.[477] The detainee has no opportunity to challenge the attorney general's determination, and the attorney general's decision is not subject to any judicial or administrative review.

Deferral of removal may also be terminated on the basis of diplomatic assurances following the same procedure. The regulations specifically provide that "[a]t any time while deferral of removal is in effect the Attorney General may determine whether it should be terminated based on diplomatic assurances forwarded by the secretary of state pursuant to the procedures in 8 C.F.R. §208.18(c)."[478]

There is no mention of diplomatic assurances in the section of the regulations dealing with CAT claims made in the context of summary exclusion.[479] The process and standards for determining a CAT claim in summary exclusion proceedings are unclear, and the only restriction articulated is the prohibition of removal where it would violate CAT Article 3. Given the broad discretion granted to the Executive Branch, and the extent to which removal in this context is shielded from review or any form of judicial scrutiny, it is unclear and probably unlikely that the U.S. government even seeks to obtain diplomatic assurances in summary exclusion cases. Even assuming there are procedures for considering the CAT claim of a summarily removable

individual suspected of terrorist activities, there is a danger that an immigration officer may simply determine that it is unlikely that the individual would be tortured upon his or her return.

Although there is also no mention of diplomatic assurances in the regulations dealing with the application of CAT in the context of extradition,[480] C.F.R. section 95.3(b) provides that once the secretary of state has received "review and analysis" from relevant policy and legal offices in relation to a CAT claim, he or she may decide "to surrender the fugitive to the requesting State, to deny surrender of the fugitive, or to surrender the fugitive *subject to conditions*" (emphasis added). Such conditions would appear to include diplomatic assurances and other executive agreements between states.

B. Examples of Uses of Diplomatic Assurances

In the United States, the use of diplomatic assurances is not made public and it is not possible to determine how many people have been transferred to other states from the United States, or from territories or detention facilities under its jurisdiction, on the basis of diplomatic assurances. As the case of Maher Arar demonstrates, however, diplomatic assurances have recently been used in the context of at least one reported Extraordinary Rendition from the United States.[481]

Arar, a Syrian-born Canadian citizen, was allegedly detained by U.S. officials while in transit at John F. Kennedy Airport to Canada.[482] He was not seeking to enter the United States.[483] Without any apparent authority, Arar was held in U.S. detention for two weeks and interrogated during this time about his alleged affiliation with terrorist groups, including Al Qaeda.[484] During his detention, Arar was informed that he had been designated by the secretary of state as a member of a foreign terrorist organization.[485] Arar was given no meaningful opportunity to challenge this designation.[486] Apparently without notification to his lawyer, Arar was then flown to Jordan, where he was interrogated and beaten by Jordanian authorities.[487] The Jordanian authorities then turned him over to Syria, where he was held in prison for ten months.[488] The United States reportedly received diplomatic assurances from Syria that he would not be tortured.[489] During the time he spent in Syria, Arar alleges that he was tortured: "Syrian authorities regularly beat him on the palms, hips, and lower back, using a two-inch thick electric cable."[490] Arar alleges that, as a result of torture, he made and signed false confessions about his participation in terrorist training in Afghanistan; Arar states that, in fact, he has never been to Afghanistan.[491]

Although Arar was visited by Canadian consular officials during his detention in the Syrian prison, Syrian security officers reportedly threatened him with additional torture if he complained about his treatment.[492] Arar reportedly kept silent from October 23, 2002 to August 14, 2003, when apparently "unable to bear the mistreatment any longer, Mr. Arar yelled out to a Canadian Consular official that he had been tortured and was being kept in a grave."[493] Arar was released to Canadian authorities in October 2003, without charges brought against him.[494]

According to a Syrian diplomat in Washington, after extensive investigation, Syrian authorities found no link between Arar and Al Qaeda.[495] Arar was released, according to this official, as a gesture of goodwill to Canada, and because Syrian officials could not substantiate any allegations against him.[496] Of note, Canada has begun a public inquiry to determine what role, if any, Canadian officials played in his transfer to Syria.

The Arar case and media reports raise concern that even if the United States is obtaining diplomatic assurances, it may not be doing so in good faith. Arar alleges that U.S. authorities provided Syrian authorities with suggested topics to be covered during interrogation, and that Syrian authorities provided the United States with information coerced from him.[497] Similarly, at least one media report indicates that U.S. intelligence and law enforcement officials have

seized and rendered purported terror subjects from one foreign state to another state that the United States knows to employ torture as an interrogation technique. The United States has reportedly provided to these intelligence forces lists of questions that it wants answered.[498] In the context of such alleged practices, diplomatic assurances from countries that the United States knows to practice torture do not appear to be a good faith compliance by the Executive Branch towards U.S. obligations under international and domestic law.

In a detailed report on diplomatic assurances, Human Rights Watch provides a number of examples of the use of diplomatic assurances in Europe.[499] The report shows, among other things, the inadequacy of the post-assurance monitoring mechanism used by European states as a safeguard against torture. For example, in the case that was the subject of *Shamayev and 12 Others v. Georgia and Russia*,[500] the Russian government offered diplomatic assurances to the European Court of Human Rights itself, after thirteen Chechens were extradited to Russia by Germany. These diplomatic assurances included the right to access to the detainees by the European Court.[501] In violation of these assurances, the Russian government subsequently denied access to the detainees to a fact-finding mission from the European Court.[502]

Another instructive example in the Human Rights Watch report is the case of Ahmed Agiza and Mohammed al-Zari. Agiza and al-Zari were Egyptians seeking asylum in Sweden. Both were expelled from Sweden to Egypt in December 2001, despite the Swedish authorities' reported acknowledgement that they had a well-founded fear of persecution in Egypt.[503] Before expulsion, Swedish authorities reportedly obtained diplomatic assurances from Egypt that the men would not be subjected to torture or ill-treatment, would receive a fair trial, and would not be sentenced to death.[504] After return, Swedish representatives did not visit the men for five weeks, and they were reportedly held "in incommunicado detention" during that time.[505] Although visits subsequently occurred, Swedish authorities were always accompanied by Egyptian authorities.[506] Based on subsequent investigation, Human Rights Watch and Swedish journalists report there is credible evidence that the men were tortured in Egypt.[507] Significantly, Swedish journalists found that the men had been transported to Egypt on a U.S.-registered plane, with the involvement of U.S. agents.[508] After Swedish journalists reported the allegations of torture by Egyptian authorities, the Swedish vice foreign minister stated "[t]his is so ominous that we have prepared a visit to Cairo, on a high political level from the Swedish side, to take up this question with representatives of the Egyptian security service. And of the Egyptian government."[509] The vice foreign minister acknowledged that Egypt had not acted in accordance with its diplomatic assurances.[510]

Finally, in the one known case in which the United States reportedly obtained diplomatic assurances, involving Maher Arar's transfer to Syria, there is no indication that the United States sought to monitor Syria's compliance with its assurances. To the contrary, Arar alleges that the United States suggested to Syrian security agents topics to be covered during interrogation, and that Syrian security agents provided to U.S. agents information obtained from Arar as a result of torture.[511]

C. In Practice, Diplomatic Assurances Are Inadequate Safeguards Against Torture

Even if diplomatic assurances are permissible under international law, their implementation in practice raises significant doubts about their reliability as a means of safeguarding against the danger or risk of torture to an individual.

First, the use of diplomatic tools as a means of compliance with the prohibition against torture is limited. Although U.S. foreign service officers often perform valuable work monitoring and advocating against human rights violations in the states to which they are posted, their role is of necessity restricted by the need to maintain diplomatic, trade, and commercial relations of

significance to the United States. In turn, the danger exists that the Executive Branch will seek diplomatic assurances in return for other concessions, such as military or economic assistance. Diplomats, including the secretary of state, are subject to political pressure and are able in turn to exert it.

Second, monitoring mechanisms have been shown to be inadequate. In large part, this is because torture is conducted in secret and regimes that use torture have become adept at hiding it. As the Human Rights Watch report on diplomatic assurances notes, in countries where torture is widespread and systematic, it is practiced within the walls of prisons and detention facilities rarely open to scrutiny by independent, well-trained monitors.[512] Prison guards and other prison personnel are trained in torture methods that leave few external marks and are also trained to intimidate prisoners into silence.[513] In addition, prison medical personnel are often complicit in covering up torture.[514] Moreover, the HRW Diplomatic Assurances report notes, in such countries governments routinely deny access to independent monitors or experts in detecting signs of torture, and in many instances state authorities may not have effective control over the forces perpetrating acts of torture.[515] Indeed, governmental authorities in countries where torture is systematic routinely deny the existence of torture at all.[516] In those circumstances, the dangers of relying on diplomatic assurances as a safeguard against torture are apparent. As the Human Rights Watch report notes, "[w]here governments routinely deny that torture is practiced, despite the fact that it is systematic or widespread, official assurances cannot be considered reliable."[517]

The inadequacies inherent in current monitoring mechanisms are apparent from the United States' own internal investigations. As the investigation into the Abu Ghraib torture scandal by U.S. Army Major General Antonio Taguba revealed, military guards at the prison moved a group of detainees around the prison to hide them from a visiting ICRC delegation.[518] Recent investigatory reports by General Paul A. Kern and former Secretary of Defense James R. Schlesinger, have raised congressional concern about so-called ghost detainees held by the CIA.[519] Unlike some of the states to which it has allegedly Extraordinarily Rendered individuals, the United States does not have a history and practice of systemic torture. Still, these examples reveal the relative ease by which the monitoring mechanism may be circumvented.

Third, even if diplomatic assurances themselves are permissible under international law, the unfettered discretion the Executive Branch exercises in seeking diplomatic assurances and making the unilateral decision to transfer an individual pursuant to those assurances leaves the individual with no due process protection or the safeguard of judicial oversight. This procedural shortcoming likely violates international law. The United States has an obligation to provide detainees in its custody an effective opportunity to challenge the reliability and adequacy of diplomatic assurances. This obligation is grounded in CAT Article 3 (prohibiting torture and CID) and Article 2 (requiring state parties to implement judicial and administrative measures to prevent torture); and ICCPR Article 7 (prohibiting torture and CID) and Article 2(1) (interpreted by the Human Rights Committee as requiring state parties "to respect and to ensure" ICCPR protections through prevention and provision of judicial or administrative review).

CAT requires each state party to enact legislative and administrative measures to prevent torture.[520] Interpreting these obligations, the CAT Committee has expressed particular concern about instances in which individuals are transferred to third states without the right of appeal.[521] In *Arana v. France,* an individual was convicted in France for links to the Basque separatist group ETA and sought by Spanish police on suspicion that he was an ETA leader. Spain sought deportation from France through an administrative procedure, whereby the detainees would be exchanged between the two nations' police forces, without judicial oversight or intervention. The CAT Committee found violations of CAT Article 3, as well as violations of due-process

rights because the handover of the detainee by the French police to the Spanish police was not subject to judicial oversight:

> The deportation was effected under an administrative procedure, which the Administrative Court of Pau had later found to be illegal, entailing a direct handover from police to police. . . . At the time of the consideration of the [previous] report. . ., the Committee expressed its concern at the practice whereby the police hand over individuals to their counterparts in another country. . . without the intervention of a judicial authority and without any possibility for the author to contact his family or his lawyer. That meant that a detainee's rights had not been respected and had placed the author in a situation where he was particularly vulnerable to possible abuse. The Committee recognizes the need for close cooperation between States in the fight against crime and for effective measures to be agreed upon for that purpose. It believes, however, that such measures must fully respect the rights and fundamental freedoms of the individuals concerned.[522]

Although U.S. regulations governing diplomatic assurances include a determination by the Executive Branch, there is no similar oversight or intervention by a neutral judicial authority.

In a 2002 case,[523] the Canadian Supreme Court examined the adequacy of procedural safeguards in the use of diplomatic assurances in light of CAT Article 3(1)'s, and held that, "[g]iven Canada's commitment to the CAT, we find that. . . the phrase 'substantial grounds' raises a duty to afford an opportunity to demonstrate and defend those grounds."[524] The court further added that "[w]here the Minister is relying on written assurances from a foreign government that a person would not be tortured, the refugee must be given an opportunity to present evidence and make submissions as to the value of such assurances."[525] While this case is of course not legally binding on the United States, it offers useful guidance on the interpretation of U.S. CAT obligations.

Article 2 of the ICCPR defines the scope of the legal obligations undertaken by the United States as a party to the ICCPR.[526] The Human Rights Committee has interpreted Article 2's "respect and ensure" language as incorporating the obligation on a state to provide judicial or administrative review.[527] Moreover, paragraph 1 of Article 2(3) of the ICCPR requires that an individual claiming a remedy for violation of his rights under the ICCPR shall have an accessible and effective remedy determined by competent judicial, administrative or legislative authorities.[528] At no stage in the U.S. diplomatic assurance process is there any opportunity for an individual to present evidence to a judicial or administrative authority that diplomatic assurances may be inadequate, or to seek a remedy for rendition. Moreover, it does not appear that there is any mechanism for the United States to seek the return of an individual who, in violation of diplomatic assurances, is tortured by the receiving state.

VII. STATE RESPONSIBILITY

As discussed in detail in this Report, Extraordinary Renditions violate numerous provisions of CAT, the ICCPR, and the Geneva Conventions.[529] The United States is a party to all of these treaties and, as such, is bound by them as a matter of international law.[530] In the Extraordinary Rendition context, the United States has three major obligations: the duty to refrain from engaging in or facilitating torture, the duty to refrain from transferring an individual when there is a risk that the individual may face torture (the *non-refoulement* obligation), and the duty to prevent such violations and remedy them once they have occurred.

The Articles on State Responsibility for Internationally Wrongful Acts (ILC Articles)[531] establish the "basic rules of international law concerning the responsibility of states for their internationally wrongful acts."[532] The ILC Articles are secondary rules of international law—that is, they do not speak to or interpret the content of states' primary obligations, which are contained in treaties and customary law; rather, they "provide the framework for determining

whether the consequent obligations of each State have been breached, and with what legal consequences. . . ."[533] For a wrongful act to result in some form of international liability on the part of a state, two elements must be established: (i) the conduct must constitute a breach of an international legal obligation in force for that state at that time, and (ii) the conduct in question must be attributable to the state.[534] In this Section of the Report, we first consider the actions that would amount to breaches of U.S. obligations with respect to Extraordinary Renditions under the treaties to which it is a party. We then discuss the standards under which conduct is attributable to the United States.

A. U.S. Conduct Constitutes a Breach of International Law in Relation to Extraordinary Renditions

This subsection of the Report outlines the types of U.S. conduct that could amount to a breach of international law in relation to Extraordinary Renditions under CAT, the ICCPR, and the Geneva Conventions. These obligations are binding even though the United States has ratified both CAT and ICCPR with the express understanding that they are not self-executing. The United States is in fact under a binding international obligation to give effect to any international agreement to which it is a party.[535] Failure to enact or enforce such legislation or other procedures will itself amount to a violation of the treaties to which the United States is a party, and provides no excuse for the additional violations flowing from that failure.[536]

1. *Refoulement Constitutes a Breach of International Law*

The United States' involvement in the process of Extraordinary Rendition directly violates its *non-refoulement* obligations as set out in CAT and the ICCPR.[537] CAT explicitly prohibits the transfer or *refoulement* of a person to a country where the individual may be in danger of torture.[538] The ICCPR includes a similar prohibition: the Human Rights Committee has interpreted ICCPR Article 7 to include a prohibition against *refoulement* to states where the individual may be at risk of torture or CID treatment.[539] The wrongful act of *refoulement* is the transfer itself in the face of risk:[540] state responsibility attaches even if the individual is never tortured or subject to CID treatment.

2. *Complicity in Torture Constitutes a Breach of International Law*

Participation in Extraordinary Rendition may amount to a breach of the United States' international obligations to refrain from engaging in acts that amount to complicity or participation in torture. The prohibition against torture is absolute and enshrined in both CAT and the ICCPR.[541] CAT requires states to criminalize complicity or participation in torture.[542] Under CAT Article 4, states must ensure that both "an attempt to commit torture" and "an act by any person which constitutes complicity or participation in torture" is a criminal offense.[543] State actors who are complicit in torture engage the responsibility of the state.

3. *The Failure to Prevent or Remedy Torture or CID Treatment Constitutes a Breach of International Law*

The failure of the United States to prevent torture or *refoulement* and to remedy these abuses once they have occurred amounts to a violation of international law. Under CAT, the United States is required to train civil or military personnel involved in the custody, interrogation and treatment of any detainees in the prohibition against torture.[544] The United States must ensure that any allegation of torture or CID treatment by U.S. officials is fully and impartially

investigated by a competent authority.[545] The United States must also criminalize and assert mandatory jurisdiction over direct, complicitous, or other participation in torture by state actors.[546] Victims of torture by U.S. actors must have access to redress and compensation through the U.S. legal system.[547] Failure to train, investigate, prosecute, and provide redress and compensation could, by the terms of CAT, constitute a violation by the United States.

Article 2 of the ICCPR requires states party "to respect and to ensure" to all individuals the rights set out in the ICCPR, "to give effect to" those rights through legislation, and to provide "an effective remedy" for those rights.[548] The Human Rights Committee's authoritative General Comments on the ICCPR have interpreted the "respect and ensure" language, the "give effect to" language, and the "effective remedy" language of ICCPR Article 2 to require the criminalization of violations of Article 7's prohibitions against torture, by (i) state actors acting in their official capacity, or outside their official capacity or in a private capacity,[549] and (ii) private parties, which could include contractors determined to be non-state actors or agents.[550] In addition, according to the Human Rights Committee, both the failure to investigate allegations of violations of the ICCPR and the failure to bring perpetrators to justice could amount to a breach of the ICCPR by a state party.[551]

The Human Rights Committee has applied these interpretations in cases arising under the ICCPR's individual complaints mechanism, the First Optional Protocol. In the seminal case of *Irene Bleier Lewenhoff & Rosa Valino de Bleier v. Uruguay* concerning arbitrary arrests, torture, and disappearances in Uruguay in the late 1970s, the Human Rights Committee found that Uruguay had a duty to investigate allegations including violations of ICCPR Article 7 (prohibiting torture), Article 9 (arbitrary detention), and Article 10(1) (humane treatment of prisoners), to prosecute those responsible for ICCPR violations, and to pay reparation.[552] Similarly, the Human Rights Committee has found that in response to allegations of torture, Zaire was "under a duty to...conduct an inquiry into the circumstances of [the victim's] torture, to punish those found guilty of torture and to take steps to ensure that similar violations do not occur in the future."[553]

The Geneva Conventions require the United States to investigate allegations of "grave breach" violations of the Geneva Conventions and to prosecute or extradite to another state that will prosecute, perpetrators of "grave breaches."[554] Common Articles 50, 51, 130, and 147 of the Geneva Conventions define specific "grave breaches" as war crimes. Included in the "grave breaches" provisions is "willful killing, torture or inhuman treatment" of POWs and civilians qualified as "protected persons."[555] Geneva IV, applicable to civilians, also includes as a "grave breach" the "unlawful deportation or transfer or unlawful confinement of a protected person."[556] The obligation to prosecute "grave breaches" is absolute and non-derogable. It applies regardless of the nationality of the perpetrator or of the victim and also regardless of the place where the "grave breach" was committed.[557] Thus, in the Extraordinary Rendition context, the United States would be in breach of the Geneva Conventions if it fails to investigate and prosecute (i) the torture or complicity to torture of POWs and civilian detainees by U.S. actors or those acting at their direction, and (ii) the unlawful transfer of civilian detainees to third states where those detainees will be subject to torture.

B. Acts Attributable to the United States in the Context of Extraordinary Rendition

The second part of the state responsibility analysis asks whether or not a particular act is attributable to the state; in other words, what constitutes an "'act of state' for the purposes of state responsibility."[558] While the United States might intend to shield itself from liability by "outsourcing" torture, under international law, the U.S. may be held responsible for acts of torture committed by private actors and even by a third state subsequent to rendering.

1. *The United States is Liable for the Authorized and Unauthorized Actions of its Officials, Including the Armed Forces, CIA, and FBI*

Under the general rules of attribution, a state faces responsibility for an alleged wrongful act if that act was carried out by the state through its many organs and officials. Article 4 explains that:

> The conduct of any State organ shall be considered an act of that State under international law, whether the organ exercises legislative, executive, judicial or any other functions, whatever position it holds in the organization of the State, and whatever its character as an organ of the central government or of a territorial unit of the State.

Thus, involvement of the U.S. military, the CIA, and the FBI in violations of international law would render the United States itself liable for such violations. The ILC Articles specify that a state cannot elude responsibility by demonstrating that the act in question was not authorized. The state can still be held responsible for the conduct of "an organ of a State or of a person or entity empowered to exercise elements of the governmental authority" even if the entity "exceed[ed] its authority or contravene[d] instructions."[559] Arguments that "rogue" CIA officers are behind Extraordinary Renditions, for example, would not shield the United States from responsibility under international law.

2. *The United States is Liable for the Actions of Individuals or Groups Acting under its Instructions, Direction, or Control, Including Private Actors*

ILC Article 8 provides that:

> The conduct of a person or group of persons shall be considered an act of State under international law if the person or group of persons is in fact acting on the instructions of, or under the direction or control of that State in carrying out the conduct.[560]

The commentary to this article indicates that there are two main circumstances in which the conduct of private entities may be attributable to the state: (a) "where State organs supplement their own action by recruiting or instigating private persons or groups who act as 'auxiliaries' while remaining outside the official structure of the State," or (b) "where private persons act under the State's direction or control."[561]

In discussing the applicable test regarding the degree of control necessary to attribute the acts of private entities to a state, the commentaries to the ILC Articles examine the standard articulated in the International Court of Justice's (ICJ) judgment in *Military and Paramilitary Activities in and against Nicaragua v. United States*.[562] That case concerned the covert and overt involvement of the United States in supporting the *contra* rebel forces in Nicaragua in the 1980s. The ICJ held that by training, arming, financing, and supplying the *contras*,[563] the United States had breached a number of its customary international law obligations, including its obligation not to use force against another state and its obligation not to intervene in the affairs of another state.[564] However, the ICJ rejected Nicaragua's claim that, for legal purposes, the *contras* should be considered an organ or agent of the U.S. government such that the United States should be held responsible for violations, including the murder of non-combatants, committed by the *contras*.[565] The ICJ stated:

> The Court does not consider that the assistance given by the United States to the *contras* warrants the conclusion that these forces are subject to the United States to such an extent that any acts they have committed are imputable to that State. It takes the view that the *contras* remain responsible for their acts, and that the United States is not responsible for the acts of the *contras*, but for its own conduct vis-à-vis Nicaragua, including conduct related to the acts of the contras.[566]

The ICJ refused to attribute the actions of the *contras* to the United States absent a finding of *effective control* (as opposed to "general control," which was held by the court to be present) by the United States of the *contra* forces at the specific times that the violations were committed.[567]

In *Prosecutor v. Tadic,* the ICTY carved out an exception to the standard enunciated by the ICJ in the *Nicaragua* case. Distinguishing two kinds of cases encompassed by the *Nicaragua* test, the *Tadic* court concluded that the *Nicaragua* test was applicable to inquiries about individuals or groups of individuals, but inappropriate when examining the actions of an organized armed faction. When examining organized paramilitary groups, the Court set out the following test:

> In order to attribute the acts of a military or paramilitary group to a State, it must be proved that the State wields overall control over the group, not only by equipping and financing the group, but also by coordinating or helping in the general planning of its military activity. Only then can the State be held internationally accountable for any misconduct of the group. However, it is not necessary that, in addition, the State should also issue, either to the head or to members of the group, instructions for the commission of specific acts contrary to international law.[568]

The ICTY thus limited the use of the ICJ's standard of effective control during a particular act to situations where the "issue is whether a *single* private individual or a *group that is not militarily organized* has acted as a *de facto* State organ when performing a specific act."[569]

Under either the ICJ's *Nicaragua* test for effective control or the ICTY's subsequent formulation of that test in *Tadic,* the United States could be held liable for Extraordinary Renditions carried out by private individuals (or groups) acting under its direction and control. Private contractors who have been hired by various organs of the United States to perform functions on behalf of those organs (*e.g.,* investigation or interrogation of detainees, transfer or transport of detainees) may incur the responsibility of the United States to the extent that they act under the direction and control of the agencies by which they are employed.[570] While the United States would also be responsible for the acts of armed groups acting under its overall control, this scenario is less applicable in the context of Extraordinary Renditions.[571]

3. *The United States May Be Liable for the Actions of Organs of a Foreign State Acting under its Direction and Control*

ILC Article 6 states that:

> The conduct of an organ placed at the disposal of a State by another State shall be considered an act of the former State under international law if the organ is acting in the exercise of elements of the governmental authority of the State at whose disposal it is placed.

According to the commentaries to the ILC Articles, the condition that the organs of the third state be "placed at the disposal" of a state is a strictly construed requirement. The organs of the third state must be acting under the "exclusive direction and control" of the former state, not just acting "on instructions."[572] The commentaries further state that "mere aid or assistance offered by organs of one State to another" would not give rise to liability under this article.[573] Accordingly, the United States may be liable for acts of torture or mistreatment committed by foreign officials in the country to which an individual is rendered if such officials are acting under the exclusive direction and control of U.S. actors. The level of control the United States may have over foreign officials in the context of Extraordinary Renditions is a factual inquiry that may only be conclusively determined after the United States conducts investigations of alleged renditions in accordance with its international law obligations. Given reports of the existence of U.S. secret detention facilities abroad, and the possible use of foreign officials as

agents in U.S.-directed interrogations, there is reason to believe that the requisite direct control may exist in the context of Extraordinary Renditions.

4. *The United States May Be Liable for Knowingly Assisting in the Unlawful Acts of a Foreign State*

ILC Articles 16 and 17 establish ways in which a state might be derivatively responsible for the acts of another state. As the commentaries to the ILC Articles note, "the essential principle is that a State should not be able to do through another what it could not do itself."[574]

Article 16 establishes responsibility for aiding or assisting in the commission of an internationally wrongful act:

> A State which aids or assists another State in the commission of an internationally wrongful act by the latter is internationally responsible for doing so if: (a) that State does so with knowledge of the circumstances of the internationally wrongful act; and (b) the act would be internationally wrongful if committed by that State.[575]

Under this article, a state is responsible to the extent of the aid or assistance given.[576] While the text of the article itself provides two conditions for attribution, namely awareness of the act and that the act constitute a violation of an international obligation of the aiding state, the commentaries appear to add an intent requirement.[577] The aid or assistance need not have been essential to the performance of the wrongful act, but the assistance must have "contributed significantly" to that act.[578]

The commentary for Article 16 lists "facilitating the abduction of persons on foreign soil" as an example of a situation where state responsibility for the acts of another state would attach.[579] More generally, the commentaries are clear that liability could arise from the provision of material aid to a state for the purpose of facilitating a human rights violation. In such a situation, the commentaries advise that a fact-intensive inquiry is needed to determine whether the aiding state was "aware of and intended to facilitate the commission of the internationally wrongful act."[580] Thus, for example, liability may attach to the United States for Extraordinary Rendition (to the extent of its assistance) in situations where the United States provided intelligence, personnel, or, as in the Swedish case,[581] the aircraft that facilitated the illegal abduction of detainees with the intent to aid in violation either of the principle of *non-refoulement* (*e.g.,* in the Swedish case) or any other provision of CAT, the ICCPR, Geneva Conventions, or customary international law.

Finally, the United States may be found internationally responsible under ILC Article 17, which provides:

> A State which directs and controls another State in the commission of an internationally wrongful act by the latter is internationally responsible for that act if: (a) that State does so with knowledge of the circumstances of the internationally wrongful act; and (b) the act would be wrongful if committed by that State.[582]

While under ILC Article 16 a state is liable only to the extent of the assistance offered, under ILC Article 17, a state that directs and controls another state in the commission of a wrongful act is responsible for the act itself.[583] State responsibility under Article 17 is historically associated with international dependency relationships between imperial and colonial states.[584] In modern times, Article 17 may apply in a situation where a state controls the activities of another state as a result of occupation, or through a treaty or other, less formal, international agreement. In the context of Extraordinary Renditions, this provision could apply to the extent that the United States has directed or controlled interrogations in, for example, Afghanistan or Iraq (both nations that the United States has occupied, and that have historically practiced torture

as a means of interrogation by security forces) or other states that resort to torture or CID treatment. In such situations, the United States may derive responsibility for acts of torture or mistreatment committed during those interrogations.

C. A Note on Adjudicating State Responsibility

A full discussion of the process by which a state may be found liable by a court for internationally wrongful acts attributable to it is beyond the scope of this Report. Even though the venues for bringing suit against the United States may be limited, the United States, as a matter of international law, remains bound by its treaty obligations and may be considered responsible for violating the prohibition of *non-refoulement* and the rule against torture when it extraordinarily renders a suspected terrorist.[585] A breach of an international obligation, regardless of whether it results in litigation, has serious consequences for the victims of that violation, for the standing of the United States in the international community, and for the development of international human rights generally.

In brief, a state may be found liable though a suit brought either by another state, or by an individual.[586] For actions by states suing other states, suits may be brought at the International Court of Justice or through a relevant system of arbitration, provided that jurisdictional requirements are met. The ICJ may only adjudicate a dispute when the states concerned have consented to its jurisdiction.[587] The United States revoked its general consent to ICJ jurisdiction in the 1980s, and the ICJ only has jurisdiction to adjudicate a claim involving the United States if the United States grants it permission in that case, or if the case involves a dispute over a treaty to which the United States is a party and which contains a clause granting the ICJ jurisdiction over disputes arising from that treaty.[588] Of the treaties discussed in this Report—CAT, the ICCPR, the Refugee Convention and the Geneva Conventions—only CAT contains such a clause;[589] however, the United States, in its reservations to CAT, declared that it does not consider itself bound by that clause.[590] The United States did reserve the right to permit ICJ jurisdiction or some other dispute resolution mechanism in a given case. Thus, for any nation to bring a claim at the ICJ under one of these treaties against the United States, the United States would have to consent to the jurisdiction of the ICJ to adjudicate that particular dispute. Considering that the United States has historically been reluctant to submit to the jurisdiction of the ICJ, such permission would be unlikely.[591] In the absence of jurisdiction, the ICJ may issue a non-binding advisory opinion "on any legal question at the request of whatever body may be authorized by or in accordance with the Charter of the United Nations to make such a request."[592]

For an *individual* who has suffered torture as a result of Extraordinary Rendition seeking to sue the United States for international law claims, the only possible international forum would be the Inter-American Commission and Court on Human Rights because the United States has not accepted the jurisdiction of the international treaty-monitoring bodies established under the ICCPR or CAT to hear individual claims under those treaties. The Inter-American Commission on Human Rights is the principal organ created under the OAS Charter to promote the observance and protection of human rights in the Americas.[593] The United States has signed but not ratified the American Convention on Human Rights. Nevertheless, the United States is a member of the OAS, and Article 44 of the American Convention allows the Inter-American Commission on Human Rights to hear complaints by individuals against states if those states are members of the OAS.[594] If a state (such as the United States) has not ratified the American Convention, the Commission will examine any such claims under the American Declaration of the Rights and Duties of Man.[595]

The possibility of bringing a suit against a U.S. official in a U.S. court for torture that occurred overseas seems to have been foreclosed by the recent Supreme Court ruling in the case of *United States v. Alvarez-Machain.*[596] In that case, a Mexican doctor alleged that the United States was liable for false arrest after the Drug Enforcement Administration (DEA) arranged for other Mexican nationals to abduct him and bring him to the United States to face charges for the murder of a DEA agent.[597] After the doctor was acquitted, he brought suit against the United States under the Federal Tort Claims Act (FTCA), which authorizes suit "for...personal injury...caused by the negligent or wrongful act or omission of any employee of the Government while acting within the scope of his office or employment."[598] The Supreme Court held that the case fell under an exception to the FTCA which precludes a claim "arising in a foreign country."[599] More broadly, the court ruled that the "FTCA's foreign country exception bars all claims based on any injury suffered in a foreign country...."[600] In the Extraordinary Rendition context, the alleged torture occurs in a foreign state, and so suit under the FTCA may be barred.[601]

VIII. INDIVIDUAL LIABILITY UNDER DOMESTIC LAW

The following Section discusses the parameters of individual liability for commission or participation in torture. This Section does not focus on the actions of individuals that amount to illegal *refoulement,* since the conduct amounting to *refoulement* has not in itself been made the subject of criminal penalties. Instead, the focus is on legal accountability for indirect participation in torture, including by way of *refoulement.*

A. Participation in Extraordinary Renditions May Result in Criminal Liability

Acts of Extraordinary Renditions may be sanctioned by the Torture Act of 2000[602] and the Uniform Code of Military Justice.[603] Moreover, the Military Extraterritorial Jurisdiction Act of 2000[604] provides a jurisdictional basis for prosecution of military and certain civilian personnel for acts committed outside the United States that would be criminal if committed in the United States.

1. *Acts of Extraordinary Rendition May Amount to Conspiracy to Commit Torture and/or Aiding and Abetting in the Commission of Torture Pursuant to the Torture Act of 2000*

(a) Jurisdiction

In order to comply with CAT's provisions requiring each ratifying country to criminalize acts of torture (including attempts to commit torture and complicity in torture), the United States enacted into U.S. Code sections 2340 and 2340A.[605] Section 2340A(a) makes it a criminal offense for any person "outside the United States [to] commit...or attempt...to commit torture." In addition, section 2340A, as amended by the USA Patriot Act,[606] codifies the offense of conspiracy to commit torture.

Section 2340A extends jurisdiction to military members, civilian employees of the United States, as well as contract employees, and generally applies to acts committed by U.S. nationals "outside of the United States."[607] The Ronald W. Reagan National Defense Authorization Act for Fiscal Year 2005 amends section 2340(3) to define the "United States" as "the several States of the United States, the District of Columbia, and the commonwealths, territories, and possessions of the United States."[608]

(b) Offense

In addition to criminalizing direct acts of torture, section 2340A(c) provides that "a person who *conspires* to commit [torture] shall be subject to the same penalties (other than the penalty of death) as the penalties prescribed for the offense, the commission of which was the object of the conspiracy." (emphasis added) Torture is defined as an "act committed by a person acting under the color of law specifically intended to inflict severe physical or mental pain or suffering (other than pain or suffering incidental to lawful sanctions) upon another person within his custody or physical control."[609] "Severe mental pain or suffering" is defined as the prolonged mental harm caused by or resulting from—

(A) the intentional infliction or threatened infliction of severe physical pain or suffering;

(B) the administration or application, or threatened administration or application, of mind-altering substances or other procedures calculated to disrupt profoundly the sense or the personality;

(C) the threat of imminent death, or

(D) the threat that another person will imminently be subjected to death, severe physical pain or suffering, or the administration or application of mind-altering substances or other procedures calculated to disrupt profoundly the sense or personality.[610]

This definition of torture was intended to track the definition set forth in CAT, taking into account the reservations, understandings and declarations made by the United States as part of its ratification.[611]

No cases have been brought to date under section 2340. However, guidance as to the meaning of "torture" under U.S. law can be gleaned from cases interpreting the Alien Tort Claims Act of 1789 (ATCA),[612] and the Torture Victim Protection Act of 1991 (TPA).[613] Thus, for example, courts have found that the following acts constitute torture: subjecting detainees to interrogation sessions lasting 14 hours,[614] beating with hands,[615] threatening with death,[616] and using techniques to exacerbate pain or injury.[617]

Section 2340 requires that the act must be "specifically intended" to inflict severe physical or mental pain or suffering. Generally, if specific intent is required, the prosecution must show that the defendant intended the illegal consequences of his actions. In *United States v. Newiswender,*[618] the Court noted that in order to establish that the defendant had "specific intent to obstruct justice" "the defendant need only have had knowledge or notice that success [in his act] would have likely resulted in an obstruction of justice. Notice is provided by the reasonable foreseeability of the natural and probable consequences of one's acts."[619] The Court further added that this rule "is grounded upon sound policy for. . .a rule focusing on foreseeable, rather than intended consequences operates in sensible and fair fashion to deter the conduct sought to be avoided and to punish those whose actions are blameworthy, even though undertaken for purposes that may or may not be culpable."[620]

As will be demonstrated below, in certain circumstances, acts of Extraordinary Rendition may amount to a crime of conspiracy to commit torture and/or to the crime of aiding and abetting in the commission of torture.[621]

(i) Conspiracy

Section 2340A has not been litigated before the courts. As a result, there is no jurisprudence on the scope of the crime of conspiracy to commit torture. Guidance, however, can be gleaned from the general federal conspiracy statute (18 U.S.C. §371), the Model Penal Code, and state jurisprudence. The following analysis draws on each of these sources.

(A) *Federal Conspiracy Statute.* Under 18 U.S.C. §371 (the crime of defrauding the United States), the government must establish beyond a reasonable doubt: 1) that two or more people

agreed to pursue an unlawful objective; 2) that the defendant voluntarily agreed to join the conspiracy; and 3) that one or more members of the conspiracy committed an overt act in furtherance of the conspiracy.[622] With respect to the third requirement, however, courts have held that where a statute does not provide for a requirement of an overt act (as is the case in section 2340A), no proof of an overt act for the conspiratorial objective is required.[623] In addition, an overt act may not be required if the contemplated crime is serious, likely of completion, or likely to encourage future criminal activity.[624] Even where an overt act is required, it is generally viewed merely as evidence of the offense and not an element of proof.[625]

(B) *The Model Penal Code*. The Model Penal Code[626] provides that a person is guilty of conspiracy with another person to commit a crime if "with the purpose of promoting or facilitating its commission he: (a) agrees with such other person or persons that they or one or more of them will engage in conduct which constitutes such crime or an attempt or solicitation to commit such crime, or (b) agrees to aid such other person or persons in the planning or commission of such crime or of an attempt or solicitation to commit such crime."[627] An agreement is an essential element of conspiracy. However, the agreement does not need to be written, nor is it necessary that an oral agreement be made.[628] Mere tacit understanding suffices.[629] As the Supreme Court stated in *Iannelli v. United States,*[630] "[t]he agreement need not be shown to have been explicit. It can instead be inferred from the facts and circumstances of the case."[631]

Under U.S. law, the crime of conspiracy usually requires intent to conspire as well as intent to achieve an unlawful or criminal result.[632] The latter intent need not be so particular that the conspirator has in mind a particular time, place, victim, etc., but at least must relate to a particular type of criminal activity.[633] Where the objective of conspiracy is itself a crime, it has been held that "at least the degree of criminal intent necessary for the substantive offense itself" is required to prove the conspiracy charge.[634] Intent may be inferred from circumstantial evidence. Thus, for example, a supplier who furnishes equipment which he *knows* will be use to commit a serious crime may be deemed from that knowledge alone to have intended to produce the result.[635] Although some courts have allowed for a defense of "good faith" to be a defense to conspiracy,[636] other courts have rejected this defense, usually by resort to the general rule that ignorance of the criminality of one's conduct is no defense.[637]

(ii) Accomplice Liability

Section 2 of Title 18, provides that

> (a) Whoever commits an offense against the United States or aids, counsels, commands, induces or procures its commission, is punishable as a principal.
> (b) Whoever willfully causes an act to be done which if directly performed by him or another would be an offense against the United States, is punishable as a principal.[638]

The Courts have generally accepted that section 2 applies to the entire U.S. criminal code.[639] Accordingly, section 2 is applicable to the crime of torture codified in section 2340.

Generally, one may become an accomplice by acting to induce another through threats or promises,[640] by words or gestures of encouragement,[641] or by providing others with the plan for the crime.[642] Thus, for example, furnishing of weapons,[643] supplies,[644] or instrumentalities[645] to be used in committing the crime has been considered rendering of assistance. As the court in *State ex rel. Martin v. Tally*[646] stated:

> The assistance given...need not contribute to the criminal result in the sense that but for it the result would not have ensued. It is quite sufficient if it facilitated a result that would have transpired without it. It is quite enough if the aid merely renders it easier for the principal actor to accomplish the end intended by him and the aider and abetter, though in all human probability the end would have been attained without it.

Although mere presence at the scene of the crime is not enough,[647] it is sufficient assistance that the accomplice is standing by at the scene of the crime ready to give some aid if needed,[648] provided that the principal is aware of the accomplice's intentions.[649]

The accomplice must intentionally encourage or assist the commission of the crime, in the sense that his purpose is to encourage or assist another in the commission of a crime as to which the accomplice has the requisite mental state.[650] Thus, for example, an accomplice is not guilty of first degree murder unless he acted with premeditation and deliberation (because first degree murder requires a deliberate and premeditated killing).[651] However, there is some authority to support the proposition that an individual may become an accomplice by giving encouragement or assistance *with the knowledge* that it will promote or facilitate a crime.[652] As a practical matter, in a case of a completed act of torture, the same mental state that supports the crime of conspiracy (*see* Section VIII.A.1.b.i. above) will also support the offense of complicity.

According to media and off-the record statements by officials, some Extraordinary Renditions to states like Syria, Egypt, Saudi Arabia, Yemen, and Morocco may have the purpose of subjecting the rendered person to interrogations with harsh methods that amount to torture or to CID treatment. According to some reports, U.S. officials may provide transportation, supply interrogation questions, and may even be present during the interrogation. Information obtained during such interrogations is allegedly relayed back to the U.S. officials. Under such circumstances, it is possible to contend that U.S. officials implicated in the Extraordinary Rendition could be charged under section 2340A(a) and/or (c). Thus, for example, under the *Newiswender* rule, a deliberate transfer of an individual to a state where it is reasonably foreseeable that the individual would be tortured, could result in criminal liability on the grounds of conspiracy in the commission of torture under section 2340A(c) and an accomplice liability to the commission of torture under sections 2 and 2340A(a).

In circumstances where diplomatic assurances that rendered individuals will not be tortured are used, it could be argued that U.S. officials lack the intent to conspire to commit, or to aid in the commission of, torture. However, the Department of State reports on human rights practices have consistently revealed systematic uses of torture in detentions and interrogations by states to which individuals have allegedly been Extraordinarily Rendered. The reliability of diplomatic assurances in the face of such systemic use of torture is suspect.[653] Thus, Extraordinary Renditions to such states may demonstrates deliberate avoidance of knowledge, potentially allowing for prosecution under the theory of willful blindness.

2. *The Uniform Code of Military Justice (UCMJ) May Be Used as a Sanction Against Extraordinary Renditions*

(a) Jurisdiction

The UCMJ[654] regulates the conduct of all persons serving in the U.S. Armed Forces and certain civilians accompanying such personnel.[655] Its purpose is to "promote justice, to assist in maintaining good order and discipline in the armed forces, to promote efficiency and effectiveness in the military establishment, and thereby to strengthen the national security of the United States."[656]

As a jurisdictional matter, the UCMJ applies worldwide,[657] and persons subject to the UCMJ include any U.S. service member[658] as well as certain civilians "[i]n time of war. . . serving with or accompanying an armed force in the field"[659] and POWs.[660] The scope of the applicability of the UCMJ to civilians has been narrowed by the courts over the years. Although courts' interpretations of the terms "serving," "accompanying," and "in the field" suggest a broad application, the "time of war" requirement is construed narrowly when applied to civilians.[661] Thus, for example, the Supreme Court held that during peacetime the UCMJ does not apply to

discharged personnel.[662] The UCMJ also cannot be used to try dependents of military personnel in noncapital cases.[663] Nor can the UCMJ be used to try civilian employees (either in capital or noncapital cases).[664] As recently as 1998, the Court of Appeals for the Armed Forces[665] analyzed the propriety of the application of the UCMJ to civilians and stated:

> As a matter of constitutional law, the Supreme Court has held that Congress may not extend court-martial jurisdiction to cover civilians who have no military status in peacetime, even if they are accompanying United States forces overseas as employees or dependents.[666]

Jurisprudence in this area generally focuses on the application of the UCMJ to civilian contractors and civilian dependents of service members.[667] No cases directly address whether CIA operatives (other than military personnel detailed to the CIA) conducting para-military operations with the regular armed forces or interrogations within a military base are considered civilians for purposes of UCMJ application. However, in *Reid v. Covert,* the Supreme Court stated, "[e]ven if it were possible, we need not attempt here to precisely define the boundary between 'civilians' and members of the 'land and naval Forces.' We recognize that there might be circumstances where a person could be 'in' the armed services...even though he had not formally been inducted into the military or did not wear a uniform."[668]

(b) Offense

The UCMJ comprises a set of criminal laws, which include many crimes punished under civilian law (*e.g.,* assault, manslaughter, murder, rape, etc.). It also provides procedures for courts martial and for matters relating to detention and questioning of persons subject to the UCMJ. Article 55 of the UCMJ provides that:

> Punishment by flogging, or by branding, marking, or tattooing on the body, or any other cruel or unusual punishment, may not be adjudged by any court-martial or inflicted upon any person subject to this chapter. The use of irons, single or double, except for the purpose of safe custody, is prohibited.[669]

Article 55 is unique in its specific definition of "cruel or unusual punishment" as a standard for treatment.[670] While most military courts have followed the Supreme Court's analytical framework of protections under the Eighth Amendment as they pertain to cruel and unusual punishment,[671] several military courts have found that Article 55 provides greater protections than those given under the Eighth Amendment.[672] It is notable that Article 55 applies at least the equivalent of the protection afforded by the Eighth Amendment even if the victim is not otherwise entitled to constitutional rights (*e.g.,* a non-citizen apprehended and detained outside the United States and arguably not entitled to such rights).[673]

Other potentially relevant provisions include the offenses of cruelty and maltreatment (10 U.S.C. §893) and offenses under punitive articles corresponding to the normal criminal definitions of murder (10 U.S.C. §918), manslaughter (10 U.S.C. §919) and assault. Also of particular interest are the offenses of dereliction of duty (10 U.S.C. §892), which applies to personnel who know of offenses by others and fail to report them, and failure to obey orders and dereliction of duty (separate offenses under 10 U.S.C. §892). Such offenses have been the basis of investigations and charges in connection with the conduct at Abu Ghraib and other recently alleged abuses of military detainees.

In addition, section 934 of Article 134 provides that

> Though not specifically mentioned in this chapter, all disorders and neglects to the prejudice of good order and discipline in the armed forces, all conduct of a nature to bring discredit upon the armed forces, and crimes and offenses not capital, of which persons subject to this chapter may be guilty, shall be taken cognizance of by a general, special, or summary court-martial, according to the nature and degree of the offense, and shall be punished at the discretion of that court.

Article 134 makes punishable acts in three categories of offenses not specifically covered in any other article of the UCMJ: Clause 1 offenses involving disorders and neglect to the prejudice of good order and discipline; Clause 2 offenses involving conduct of a nature to bring discredit upon the armed forces; and Clause 3 offenses entailing non-capital crimes or offenses that violate Federal law. Thus, the UCMJ effectively provides a basis for the prosecution of military personnel in courts-martial for the offense of torture in violation of 18 U.S.C. § 2340.

In order to successfully charge an individual under Clauses 1 and 2 of this Article, the government must show: (i) that the accused did or failed to do certain acts; and (ii) that, under the circumstances, the accused's conduct was to the prejudice of good order and discipline in the armed forces or was of a nature to bring discredit upon the armed forces.[674] Under Clause 1, the acts must be directly prejudicial to good order and discipline, rather than remotely so. Under Clause 2, discredit is interpreted to mean "injure the reputation of," and encompasses conduct that brings the service "into disrepute or which tends to lower it in public esteem."[675] With respect to Clause 3 offenses, as a general rule, any offense created by Federal statute may be prosecuted as an Article 134 offense.[676] Thus, a service member whose conduct is alleged to violate 18 U.S.C. § 2340A could be prosecuted under Article 134 of the UCMJ, as a Clause 3 violation, although charges in courts martial are usually brought under the UCMJ's punitive offenses rather than generally applicable criminal statutes. Moreover, multiple counts alleging Article 134 violations also could be brought in such a situation, because such conduct could be construed as prejudicial to good order and discipline and/or of a nature to bring discredit upon the armed forces.[677]

The UCMJ also provides for an offense of conspiracy by any person subject to the UCMJ "with any other person to commit an offense under [UCMJ]" "if one or more of the conspirators does an act to effect the object of the conspiracy."[678] Conspiracy is punishable by a court-martial. Accordingly, the UCMJ can be used to prosecute conspiracy to commit the prohibited acts, including both acts of torture and cruelty, making its scope potentially larger than the federal torture statute.

3. *The Military Extraterritorial Jurisdiction Act (MEJA) May Provide Jurisdiction for Prosecution of Involvement in Extraordinary Renditions*

To date there have been virtually no cases that rely on MEJA.[679] In February 2004, proposed regulations under MEJA were issued for comment, but, to date, they have not become final. The first case filed under MEJA, in June 2004, involved an alleged murder by a spouse of an Air Force officer stationed abroad.[680] The case resulted in a conviction.[681]

(a) Jurisdiction

Section 3261(a) of MEJA provides that

> Whoever engages in conduct outside the United States that would constitute an offense punishable by imprisonment for more than 1 year if the conduct had been engaged in within the special maritime and territorial jurisdiction of the United States –
>
> (1) while employed by or accompanying the Armed Forces outside the United States; or
>
> (2) while a member of the Armed Forces subject to chapter 47 of title 10 (the Uniform Code of Military Justice),
>
> shall be punished as provided for that offense.

The provisions of MEJA do not apply if a foreign government, in accordance with jurisdiction recognized by the United States, has prosecuted or is prosecuting the person for the offense; however, the United States may nonetheless prosecute such person under MEJA if approval for the prosecution is granted by the attorney general or the deputy attorney general.[682]

The report analyzing MEJA prepared by the House of Representatives' Judiciary Committee makes it clear that the reference to "the special maritime and territorial jurisdiction of the United States" includes those "acts that would be a Federal crime regardless of where they are committed in the United States, such as the drug crimes in title 21."[683] The term "employed by the Armed Forces outside the United States" means "(A) employed as a civilian employee of the Department of Defense (including a nonappropriated fund instrumentality of the Department), as a Department of Defense contractor (including a subcontractor at any tier), or as an employee of a Department of Defense contractor (including a subcontractor at any tier); (B) present or residing outside the United States in connection with such employment; and (C) not a national of or ordinarily resident in the host nation."[684] The term "accompanying the Armed Forces outside the United States" means

(A) a dependent of (i) a member of the Armed Forces, (ii) a civilian employee of the Department of Defense (including a nonappropriated fund instrumentality of the Department), or (iii) a Department of Defense contractor (including a subcontractor at any tier) or an employee of a Department of Defense contractor (including a subcontractor at any tier)

(B) residing with such member, civilian employee, contractor, or contractor employee outside the United States; and

(C) not a national of or ordinarily resident in the host nation.[685]

The Ronald W. Reagan National Defense Authorization Act for Fiscal Year 2005, amends section 3267(1)(A) to extend MEJA jurisdiction to –

(i) a civilian employee of –

(I) the Department of Defense...; or

(II) any other Federal agency, or any provisional authority, to the extent that such employment relates to supporting the mission of the Department of Defense overseas;

(ii) a contractor (including a subcontractor at any tier) of –

(I) the Department of Defense...; or

(II) any other Federal agency, or any provisional authority, to the extent such employment relates to supporting the mission of the Department of Defense overseas; or

(iii) an employee of a contractor (or a subcontractor at any tier) of –

(I) the Department of Defense...; or

(II) any other Federal agency, or any provisional authority, to the extent such employment relates to supporting the mission of the Department of Defense overseas.[686]

MEJA does not apply to members of the Armed Forces who are subject to the UCMJ, unless such individuals cease to be subject to UCMJ (for example, if they had been discharged from the Armed Forces after commission of the act in question but before charges were brought) or unless they have committed an offense with one or more other defendants, at least one of whom is not subject to the relevant chapter.[687]

Where conduct violates both section 3261 and another federal statute having extraterritorial application (other than the UCMJ), "the Government may proceed under either statute."[688] In cases where conduct violates both section 3261 and the UCMJ, the Department of Defense has the exclusive right to prosecute, provided that the offender is not part of a conspiracy or other illegal activity with civilians. If a military member is indicted with a civilian, MEJA allows the government to prosecute the military member in federal court.[689] This remains

the case even if a federal judge later orders that the military and civilian defendants be tried separately.[690]

(b) Offense

MEJA was intended to be broad in scope and to cover crimes found in Titles 18 and 21 of the U.S. Code (*e.g.*, murder, rape, assault, etc.) as well as crimes under other federal statutes that provide for criminal liability.[691] Even though many of these statutes refer to crimes that take place within the United States, the language used in the MEJA includes these crimes within its scope. Accordingly, MEJA can be used to prosecute individuals for conspiracy to commit torture under section 2340A as well as for common law crimes such as conspiracy to commit, or aiding and abetting in commission of, assault, sexual assault, manslaughter, and murder.

As explained above, with the requisite *mens rea,* instances of Extraordinary Renditions may amount to aiding and abetting in the commission of torture, assault, sexual assault, and, where death results, manslaughter or murder. Accordingly, those officials who fall within the jurisdiction of MEJA can be prosecuted for participation in these crimes under the appropriate MEJA provisions.

B. Defenses to Criminal Liability Generally Are Inapplicable to Most Cases of Extraordinary Renditions

Under certain circumstances, the defenses of necessity, self-defense, or superior orders may be available to those charged in connection with Extraordinary Renditions. However, as explained in more detail below, such defenses are inapplicable to most instances of Extraordinary Renditions.

Necessity and self-defense are related defenses that involve admission to the illegal act but which seek to justify the act because the individual prevented greater harm by committing the crime. As a preliminary matter, it should be noted that the arguments set out below that seek to justify Extraordinary Rendition under the defenses of necessity and self-defense run counter to the right of the individual who has been Extraordinarily Rendered to be presumed innocent until proven guilty, and rest on the assumption that the person in custody has actionable information of an imminent terrorist attack. In reality, this scenario is far from guaranteed and in many cases those sent to face torture provide no information to confirm that they know of terrorist activity.

Both defenses have been historically applied whenever an individual's belief that his or her action will prevent future harm can be shown to have been reasonable. It could be argued that if the belief that the person in custody possessed information about a future attack was reasonable, then the fact that that person did not actually posses such information is not relevant. However, the change from a presumption of innocence standard to a reasonableness standard seems to disproportionately favor the state in this context given the extreme consequences of Extraordinary Rendition and the state action involved.

1. *Necessity*

Necessity is a traditional defense to criminal liability that was raised by now-Judge Jay S. Bybee, formally Assistant Attorney General in the Justice Department, in a memo entitled *Re: Standards of Conduct for Interrogation under 18 U.S.C. §§2340-2340A*. Despite the memo's assertion to the contrary, it remains an open question as to whether federal courts have the authority to recognize a necessity defense that is not statutorily provided.

The Supreme Court has discussed the availability of the defense of necessity in the federal context without rejecting or accepting it, and has stated that the applicability of the defense to

federal crimes is questionable since such crimes are defined by statute and not by common law. In *United States v. Bailey,*[692] the court rejected a claim of necessity on the grounds that a legal alternative existed. While the court noted that Congress legislates against the background of the common law and may have considered a necessity defense, it refused to balance harms as the defense would require, explaining that "we are construing an Act of Congress, not drafting it." In *United States v. Oakland Cannabis Buyers' Cooperative,*[693] the court again refused to decide whether necessity could ever be a defense when a federal statute did not provide for it. While the court admitted that it had discussed the possibility of the defense in *Bailey,* it made clear that the earlier case had not settled the question. The Court reiterated its view that, "whether, as a policy matter, an exemption should be created is a question for legislative judgment, not judicial inference."[694]

Since sections 2340 and 2340A are silent on the issue of necessity, it is unclear whether the defense would apply. It could be argued that, given the gravity of torture, had Congress intended any exception to the blanket prohibition, it would have included the parameters of such an exception. Absent express intent, it could be argued that courts should not insert such a defense into the federal criminal statute.[695]

Whether the defense of necessity would be available to a member of the Armed Forces is even more questionable. Neither the UCMJ nor the Manual explicitly allow for the defense. The Manual only provides for a defense of "coercion or duress."[696] The U.S. Court of Appeals for the Armed Forces and its predecessor court have considered necessity but have yet to apply it or explicitly allow it. In *United States v. Rockwood,*[697] the court stated that there may be an unusual situation in which consideration might be given to the defense. In both *Rockwood* and *United States v. Washington,*[698] a more recent case in which the court also declined to recognize the defense, the court emphasized the importance of order, explaining that the essence of military duty is the subordination of individual interest and sacrifice. It implied that the defense of necessity would be less applicable in the military setting than in the civilian context.[699]

The defense of necessity could be available to individuals charged under MEJA.[700] However, in that context, the necessity defense would justify only illegal conduct that the actor believed was necessary to avoid harm to himself or to another. The defense of necessity has three general requirements, all of which must be satisfied: (i) the actor must have intended to avoid the greater harm, (ii) the harm avoided must be greater than the harm done, and (iii) there must have been no alternative which would have caused less harm than the harm actually caused. In principle, there is no limit to the type of harm that may be justified by the defense and, in general, it can apply even to intentional homicide.[701] It is for the trier of fact, not the defendant, to determine whether the harm done by the defendant was less than the harm that was avoided.[702]

The first requirement of the defense could be satisfied only if an Extraordinary Rendition was carried out in an attempt to avoid a terrorist attack. The intent requirement holds that a person may not commit a crime for an impermissible reason and then justify it afterwards by pointing to the fact that a greater harm just happened to be avoided. The intent to avoid future harm must be the reason why the crime was committed. Thus, the defense would be inapplicable in cases were an individual was rendered to face torture as a form of punishment for past actions or to gather information related to previously committed attacks.[703]

Moreover, to justify Extraordinary Rendition, the court would have to determine that the harm avoided by such practice is greater than the harm resulting from it. In this objective inquiry, the court acts as a legislature, balancing the two harms and deciding whether the individual's decision was consistent with societal values.[704] Accordingly, the defense is unavailable when the legislature has made the determination of values and has made clear that violation of a statute cannot be outweighed by the harm avoided. The memos produced for the Bush

Administration have suggested that the harm avoided by preventing a future terrorist attack would outweigh the harm caused by torturous interrogation.[705] However, as demonstrated by the fact that the anti-torture norm is largely recognized to have achieved the status of *jus cogens,* a court is likely to find that torture is so inherently harmful that nothing can outweigh it. Both CAT and section 2340A make clear that society considers the harm caused by torture to be great, and the White House has repeatedly reaffirmed that "United States stands against and will not tolerate torture and that the United States remains committed to complying with its obligations under [CAT]."[706] Moreover, the harm that is caused by torture is definite whereas the benefits gained by torture are difficult to measure and often negligible. U.S. officials themselves have acknowledged that torture is an ineffective means of producing reliable intelligence.[707] Accordingly, the harm alleged as being prevented as a result of Extraordinary Renditions is unlikely to outweigh the harm caused to the "rendered" individual.

Even if the purpose of Extraordinary Renditions was to avoid greater harm, the defense requires that there be no alternative to the action taken. Courts have interpreted this requirement strictly, holding the defense inapplicable when any legal or less harmful option was available.[708] Thus, this requirement will be satisfied only in the unlikely event that no alternative to Extraordinary Rendition is available.

Further, to rely on the necessity defense, the harm avoided must be known and specific. Some state statutes further require that the threatened harm be imminent and state that the defense only applies in emergency situations.[709] In this regard, courts have held that "the possibility of harm at an indeterminate date in the future is insufficient."[710] An assertion that an individual may have information about a possible future attack is unlikely to fulfill this requirement. It could be argued, however, that the "threatened harm is imminent" in a situation where U.S. officials are aware of a specific threat but unaware of its operational details. It could be further argued that the ongoing "War on Terror" adds further urgency to uncovering such details. However, while the current environment may be described as an ongoing emergency, the necessity defense is only available if all legal options for halting a known, specific, and imminent threat are taken before Extraordinary Rendition. Although terrorist groups may be continually plotting attacks, this does not satisfy the imminence requirement. Thus, unless U.S. officials are truly dealing with a "ticking bomb" scenario, the necessity defense is unlikely to be applicable to most instances of Extraordinary Renditions.[711] It is submitted that the purposes of the necessity defense are validly effected by appropriate use of prosecutorial discretion in those rare cases where it might apply.

2. *Self-Defense and Defense of Others*

The doctrine of self-defense justifies the use of force to prevent unlawful bodily harm to oneself, provided that the force is necessary to avoid the bodily harm. The doctrine of defense of others is a related defense that allows for the use of force to protect another person and has the same requirements as self-defense.[712] Although self-defense and defense of others could be asserted against a charge of complicity to commit torture, it is doubtful whether these defenses can be used as defenses against a charge of conspiracy.[713] In the context of military law, self-defense and the defense of others are allowable defenses only for charges of homicide or assaults.[714] Even if such defenses were available, because, like necessity, self-defense and defense of others are common law defenses, they raise the same issue of applicability to federal law. Thus, self-defense and defense of others are unlikely to be available as defenses against conspiracy charges. In any event, self-defense in the context of Extraordinary Renditions can be understood as a personalized version of the social defense of necessity and should

be subject to the same limitations. Accordingly, neither self-defense nor the defense of others is likely to be a successful means for negating charges of participation in Extraordinary Renditions.

3. *Superior Orders*

An individual charged with complicity (or conspiracy) to commit torture under sections 2340A(a) or (c), or for crimes under military law may argue that he or she should be immune from liability because a superior ordered the Extraordinary Rendition. This defense is not available to civilians or CIA contractors facing federal charges. Similarly, a person may not plead the defense of superior orders to avoid liability in tort. In holding that an unconstitutional order or practice is actionable under 42 U.S.C. §1983, Chief Justice Marshall laid down the principle that "instructions cannot change the nature of the transaction, nor legalize an act."[715]

The defense of superior orders, however, is available to a member of the Armed Forces charged under military laws. The rationale for this defense lies in the importance of order and discipline in the military setting. Indeed, for a subordinate to question an order may amount to insubordination for which the individual could be criminally charged. Accordingly, following superior orders provides a defense except in instances of palpable illegality, *i.e.,* where the order is so manifestly beyond the legal power of the commander as to give no doubt as to its illegality. The Manual for Courts-Martial formalizes the defense. It states "it is a defense to any offense that the accused was acting pursuant to orders unless the accused knew the orders to be unlawful or a person of ordinary sense and understanding would have known the orders to be unlawful."[716]

The defense does not justify obviously illegal acts, such as a conduct that is obviously a war crime.[717] Indeed, the Department of the Army Field Manual states:

> The fact that the law of war has been violated pursuant to an order of a superior authority, whether military or civil, does not deprive the act in question of its character of a war crime, nor does it constitute a defense in the trial of an accused individual, unless he did not know and could not reasonably have been expected to know that the act ordered was unlawful.[718]

The central issue is whether a person of ordinary sense and understanding would know that the order was illegal. In *U.S. v. Calley,*[719] the court upheld a finding that the order to kill non-combatant civilians in My Lai, Vietnam, was so clearly unlawful that it did not justify the murders. The court emphasized the "ordinary sense and understanding" standard and stated that Calley must be presumed to know that he could not lawfully kill the people involved.[720]

Because of their training, all U.S. soldiers have been informed of the Geneva Conventions, which make clear that the torture of individuals is illegal. In *Calley* the court stated that, "[w]hether Lieutenant Calley was the most ignorant person in the United States Army in Vietnam, or the most intelligent, he must be presumed to know that he could not kill the people involved here."[721] Like murder, torture is a crime that every soldier must be presumed to know is illegal and thus is a crime that cannot be excused by superior orders. However, not every soldier can be presumed to know whether a certain individual would be subjected to torture if transferred to a particularly country, or that a particular conduct constitutes torture. Accordingly, the defense may be available to those soldiers who have no reason to believe (and no knowledge suggesting otherwise) that the individual whom they were ordered to transfer to a third country is more likely than not to be tortured on there. On the other hand, defense of superior orders may be *un*available in circumstances of Extraordinary Rendition to a military official who knows that torture of the transferred individuals is foreseeable.

C. U.S. Officials Participating in Extraordinary Rendition May Face Civil Liability for their Involvement in the Practice

In certain circumstances, U.S. officials participating in Extraordinary Renditions may be subject to civil liability. The ability to bring a lawsuit against a U.S. official, however, is subject to certain limitations. If the attorney general certifies that "the defendant employee was acting within the scope of his office or employment at the time of the incident out of which the claim arose...the United States shall be substituted as the party defendant."[722] This provision effectively removes "the potential personal liability of Federal employees for common law torts committed within the scope of their employment, and would instead provide that the exclusive remedy for such torts is through an action against the United States under the [FTCA]."[723]

Although generally, sovereign immunity precludes civil suits against the federal government, the Federal Tort Claims Act (FTCA) provides a limited waiver of the government's sovereign immunity, stating that the government can only be sued "under circumstances where the United States, if a private person, would be liable to the claimant in accordance with the law of the place where the act or omission occurred."[724] The federal government will not be liable for:

> Any claim arising out of assault, battery, false imprisonment, false arrest, malicious prosecution, abuse of process, libel, slander, misrepresentation, deceit, or interference with contract rights: *Provided, That, with regard to acts or omissions of investigative or law enforcement officers of the United States Government, the provisions of this chapter and section 1346(b) this title shall apply* to any claim arising, on or after the date of the enactment of this proviso, out of assault, battery, false imprisonment, false arrest, abuse of process, or malicious prosecution.[725]

An "investigative or law enforcement officer" is "any officer of the United States who is empowered by law to execute searches, to seize evidence, or to make arrests for violations of Federal law."[726] In certain circumstances, military officials (particularly the military police) may be considered "investigative or law enforcement officers."[727]

1. *Alien Tort Claims Act (ATCA)*

ATCA extends the jurisdiction of U.S. district courts to "any civil action by an alien for a tort only, committed in violation of the law of nations or a treaty of the United States." The courts have consistently recognized that ATCA establishes a forum where plaintiffs can seek redress for violations of international law.[728] Most recently, in *Sosa v. Alvarez-Machain et al.,*[729] the Supreme Court stated that "[t]he jurisdictional grant [of ATCA] is best read as having been enacted on the understanding that the common law would provide a cause of action for the modest number of international law violations with a potential for personal liability at the time." The court noted, however, that any claim based on the present-day law of nations must "rest on a norm of international character accepted by the civilized world and defined with a specificity comparable to the features of [violation of safe conducts, infringement of the rights of ambassadors, and piracy.]"[730]

The tort pled under ATCA must be "definable, obligatory (rather than hortatory) and universally condemned."[731] To satisfy this specificity requirement, the following is required: (i) no state condones the act in question, and there is a recognizable "universal" consensus of prohibition against it; (ii) there are sufficient criteria to determine whether a given action amounts to the prohibited act and thus violates the norm; and (iii) the prohibition against it is non-derogable and therefore binding at all times upon all actors.[732]

Torture is actionable under ATCA (as well as under TPA, discussed below)[733] and courts have allowed ATCA suits to proceed based on theories of conspiracy and aiding and abetting of torture.[734] Torture practices in countries of rendition, such as Egypt, Syria, Lebanon, Saudi

Arabia, and Morocco, amount to egregious, universally condemnable acts, which are prohibited both by customary and statutory international law. Conspiracy to commit or aiding and abetting the commission of acts of torture in such countries through the rendition of individuals by U.S. officials could, therefore, give rise to civil liability under ATCA.

2. *Torture Victims Protection Act (TPA)*

The Torture Victims Protection Act of 1991 (TPA) was signed into law in 1992 and was appended to the U.S. Code as a note to section 1350. The TPA provides that "[a]n individual who, under actual or apparent authority, or color of law, of any foreign nation – (1) subjects an individual to torture shall, in a civil action, be liable for damages to that individual; or (2) subjects an individual to extrajudicial killing shall, in a civil action, be liable for damages to the individual's legal representative, or to any person who may be a claimant in an action for wrongful death." The Senate Judiciary Committee has stated that, consistent with international law, "responsibility for torture, summary execution, or disappearances extends beyond the person or persons who actually committed those acts; anyone with higher authority who authorized, tolerated or knowingly ignored those acts is liable for them," thus evidencing that TPA is intended to apply to those complicit in acts of torture.[735] Moreover, U.S. courts have held that a private actor who conspires with a government official can be considered to act "under color of law."[736] By analogy, a U.S official who conspires with or aids a foreign perpetrator who acts under apparent authority of a foreign government may be considered to act "under color of foreign law" and thus may be held liable under the TPA.[737]

IX. CONCLUSION

This Report concludes that both international and domestic law prohibit the practice of Extraordinary Rendition. Despite these clear standards, allegations of such transfers have surfaced repeatedly in the press and in the reports of human rights and humanitarian organizations. The United States should demonstrate its opposition to this practice by initiating formal inquiries into Extraordinary Renditions, investigating cases in which U.S. officials or their agents may have committed criminal acts, and implementing a moratorium on the use of diplomatic assurances in torture cases. Far from being an acceptable tool in the "War on Terror," Extraordinary Renditions are illegal and constitute a perversion of justice that must be exposed and brought to an end.

October 29, 2004

NOTES

1. Dana Priest & Barton Gellman, *U.S. Decries Abuse but Defends Interrogations; 'Stress and Duress' Tactics Used on Terrorism Suspects Held in Secret Overseas Facilities,* THE WASHINGTON POST, Dec. 26, 2002, at A1.

2. The work of Hina Shamsi and Angelina Fisher, the principal authors and researchers on the report, should be recognized here.

3. *United States v. Alvarez-Machain,* 504 U.S. 655 (1992).

4. *See United States v. Yunis,* 859 F.2d 953, at 957 (D.C. Cir. 1988) (describing arrest), *and* 924 F.2d 1086 (D.C. Cir. 1991) (upholding jurisdiction to try Yunis).

* **The Association of the Bar of the City of New York Committee on International Human Rights:** Martin S. Flaherty (chair; member of the Committee who participated in the preparation of the Report), Jeanmarie Fenrich (secretary), Patricia C. Armstrong (member of the Committee who participated in the preparation of the Report), Nicole A. Barrett, Hon. Deborah A. Batts (took no part in preparation or consideration of this Report), Aarthi Belani (student member; member of the Committee who participated in

the preparation of the Report), Amy Christina Cococcia, Eric O. Darko (member of the Committee who participated in the preparation of the Report), Linda Ford, Douglas C. Gray, Alice H. Henkin, Sharon K. Hom, Miranda B. Johnson (student member), Mamta Kaushal, Elise B. Keppler, Katharine Lauer, Sara E. Lesch, Marko C. Maglich, Nina Massen, Sam Scott Miller, David Eli Nachman, Elena Dana Neacsu (member of the Committee who participated in the preparation of the Report), Dyanna C. Pepitone, Christina Marie Posa, Robert J. Quinn, Marny A. Requa, Margaret L. Satterthwaite (member of the Committee who participated in the preparation of the Report), Hina Shamsi (member of the Committee who participated in the preparation of the Report), Mark R. Shulman, Liza May Velazquez, and Katherine Zeisel (student member; member of the Committee who participated in the preparation of the Report).

Acknowledgments: The Committee and the Center for Human Rights and Global Justice at NYU School of Law thank the following people for their work and/or assistance in the preparation of the Report: Project director: Margaret Satterthwaite, Center for Human Rights and Global Justice, NYU School of Law; Principal authors and researchers: Angelina Fisher, Center for Human Rights and Global Justice, NYU School of Law; Hina Shamsi, Member, ABCNY International Human Rights Committee; Contributing authors: Bassina Farbenblum, American Civil Liberties Union; Yael Fuchs, Columbia University School of Law (student); David Lisson, University of Toronto School of Law (student); Research assistance was provided by: Aarthi Belani, Institute for International Law and Justice, NYU School of Law (student); James Boeving, Columbia University School of Law (student); Elena Dana Neacsu, Columbia University School of Law; Allison Young, Georgetown University School of Law (student); Advice on the Report, or aspects of it, was provided by: Paul Chevigny, NYU School of Law; Julia Hall, Human Rights Watch; Smita Narula, Center for Human Rights and Global Justice, NYU School of Law; Steven McPherson Watt, Center for Constitutional Rights; Substantive review and comment on the Report was provided by: Natasha Balendra, Center for Human Rights and Global Justice, NYU School of Law; John Cerone, New England School of Law; Paul Chevigny, NYU School of Law; James Cockayne, Institute for International Law and Justice, NYU School of Law (student); Olivier De Schutter, NYU School of Law; Miles P. Fischer, Chair, ABCNY Military Affairs and Justice Committee; Martin S. Flaherty, Fordham University School of Law; Chair, ABCNY International Human Rights Committee; Scott Horton, Patterson, Belknap, Webb & Tyler, LLP; Chair, ABCNY International Law Committee; Sidney Rosdeitcher, Paul, Weiss, Rifkind, Wharton & Garrison LLP; Chair, ABCNY Civil Rights Committee; Claudia Slovinsky, Law Offices of Claudia Slovinsky; Chair, ABCNY Immigration and Nationality Law Committee; Principal copyeditor: Patricia Armstrong, Center for Human Rights and Global Justice, NYU School of Law; Copyediting assistance: Eric O. Darko, International Center for Transitional Justice; Elena Dana Neacsu, Columbia University School of Law; NYU School of Law students: Marissa Alternelson, Ahmen Ghappour, Andrew Hagan, Bryan D. Kreyes, Erika Mae de Castro Lorenzana, Peter Nelson, Matthew Scott, Matthew Shrumpf, Derek Soler, and Kathy Zeisel; Fordham University School of Law students: Lauren Attard, Kristen Hiensch, Brian Honermann, Jason N. Visco, and Nicole Washienko; Web and distribution assistance: Larissa Annoual, Vilas Dhar, and Joanna Pozen.

We are also grateful to Nicole Barrett and Sullivan & Cromwell LLP, Sam Scott Miller and Orrick, Herrington & Sutcliffe LLP, and Sidney Rosdeitcher and Paul, Weiss, Rifkind, Wharton & Garrison LLP for summer associate assistance on aspects of the Report.

5. *See, e.g.*, Amnesty Int'l., *USA: Memorandum to the U.S. Government on the Rights of People in U.S. Custody in Afghanistan and Guantánamo Bay* (April 2002), *available at* http://web.amnesty.org/library/index/engamr510532002 (last visited Oct. 25, 2004); Amnesty Int'l., *Iraq: Memorandum on Concerns Relating to Law and Order* (July 2003), *available at* http://web.amnesty.org/library/Index/ENGMDE141572003 (last visited Oct. 25, 2004); *and* Human Rights Watch, *U.S.: Reports of Torture of Al Qaeda Suspects* (Dec. 27, 2002), *available at* http://www.hrw.org/press/2002/12/us1227.htm (last visited Oct. 25, 2004).

6. The International Committee of the Red Cross, which has a special status under international law as the guardian of international humanitarian law, issued a number of reports concerning ill-treatment of prisoners held by the United States, one of which was made public in the wake of the Abu Ghraib revelations. *See* International Committee of the Red Cross, *Report of the International Committee of the Red Cross (ICRC) on the Treatment by the Coalition Forces of Prisoners of War and other Protected Persons by*

the Geneva Conventions in Iraq During Arrest, Internment and Interrogation (Feb. 2004), *available at* http://www.derechos.org/nizkor/us/doc/icrc-prisoner-report-feb-2004.pdf (last visited Oct. 25, 2004).

7. A number of investigations have been conducted by the Department of Defense into the abuses at Abu Ghraib, with many of the reports now publicly available. *See, e.g.,* Maj. Gen. Antonio M. Taguba, *Article 15-6 Investigation of the 800th Military Police Brigade* (February 2004) (Taguba Report), *available at* http://www.npr.org/iraq/2004/prison_abuse_report.pdf (last visited Oct. 25, 2004); Department of the Army Inspector General, *Detainee Operations Inspection* (July 2004), *available at* http://www.globalsecurity.org/military/library/report/2004/daig_detainee-ops_21jul2004.pdf (last visited Oct. 25, 2004); Lt. Gen. Anthony R. Jones & Maj. Gen. George Fay, *Investigation of Intelligence Activities at Abu Ghraib* (August 2004), *available at* http://www.informationclearinghouse.info/article6784.htm (last visited Oct. 25, 2004); *and* Independent Panel to Review Department of Defense Detention Operations, Final Report (August 2004), *available at* http://www.defenselink.mil/news/Aug2004/d20040824finalreport.pdf (last visited Oct. 25, 2004). It is now undisputed that U.S. military personnel committed acts that amounted to torture, and to cruel, inhuman or degrading (CID) treatment or punishment. General Taguba's report on the abuses at Abu Ghraib prison concludes that "between October and December 2003, at the Abu Ghraib Confinement Facility (BCCF), numerous incidents of sadistic, blatant, and wanton criminal abuses were inflicted on several detainees. This systemic and illegal abuse of detainees was intentionally perpetrated by several members of the military police guard force. . . ." Taguba Report, at 16. Acts of abuse included "(a) Punching, slapping, and kicking detainees; jumping on their naked feet; (b) videotaping and photographing naked male and female detainees; (c) forcibly arranging detainees in various sexually explicit positions for photographing; (d) forcing detainees to remove their clothing and keeping them naked for several days at a time; (e) forcing naked male detainees to wear women's underwear; (f) forcing groups of male detainees to masturbate themselves while being photographed and videotaped; (g) arranging naked male detainees in a pile and then jumping on them; (h) positioning a naked detainee on a MRE Box, with a sandbag on his head, and attaching wires to his fingers, toes, and penis to simulate electric torture; (i) writing "I am a Rapest" (sic) on the leg of a detainee alleged to have forcibly raped a 15-year old fellow detainee, and then photographing him naked; (j) placing a dog chain or strap around a naked detainee's neck and having a female soldier pose for a picture; (k) a male MP guard having sex with a female detainee; (l) using military working dogs (without muzzles) to intimidate and frighten detainees, and in at least one case biting and severely injuring a detainee; (m) taking photographs of dead Iraqi detainees." Taguba Report, at 16–18. Other acts reported by the detainees who were found to be credible by General Taguba include (a) breaking chemical lights and pouring the phosphoric liquid on detainees; (b) threatening detainees with a charged 9mm pistol; (c) pouring cold water on naked detainees; (d) beating detainees with a broom handle and a chair; (e) threatening male detainees with rape; (f) allowing a military police guard to stitch the wound of a detainee who was injured after being slammed against the wall in his cell; (g) sodomizing a detainee with a chemical light and perhaps a broom stick; (h) using military working dogs to frighten and intimidate detainees with threats of attack, and (i) in one instance actually biting a detainee." *Id.*

8. *See, e.g., Hearing on Allegations of Mistreatment of Iraqi prisoners Before the Senate Armed Services Committee,* 108th Cong. (May 2004), *available at* http://armed-services.senate.gov/ (last visited Oct. 25, 2004).

9. United Nations Convention Against Torture and Other Cruel, Inhuman or Degrading Treatment or Punishment, *opened for signature* December 10, 1984, G.A. Res. 39/46, 39 UN GAOR Supp. No. 51, at 197, UN Doc. A/RES/39/708 (1984), *entered into force* June 26, 1987, 1465 U.N.T.S. 85, 23 I.L.M. 1027 (1984), *as modified,* 24 I.L.M. 535, *available at* http://www.ohchr.org/english/law/cat.htm (last visited Oct. 24, 2004) (CAT). The United States ratified CAT in October 1994, and CAT entered into force with respect to the United States on November 20, 1994. The instrument of ratification contained certain declarations, reservations, and understandings relevant to U.S. obligations addressed in this Report, including a declaration that CAT Articles 1 through 16 were not self-executing (*i.e.,* that these provisions must be implemented by domestic legislation). *See* United Nations Treaty Collection: Declarations and Reservations, *available at* http://www.unhchr.ch/html/menu3/b/treaty12_asp.htm (last visited Oct. 9, 2004). Other declarations, reservations and understandings are discussed below in the relevant Sections of this Report detailing U.S. CAT obligations. A reservation generally is a unilateral statement, made by a state when

signing, ratifying, accepting, approving or acceding to a treaty that purports to exclude or to modify the legal effect of certain provisions of the treaty in their application to that State. Vienna Convention on the Law of Treaties, concluded May 23, 1969, 1155 U.N.T.S. 331, 333, *entered into force* Jan. 27, 1980 (Vienna Convention), art. 2 para. 1(d). Section 2 of the Vienna Convention contains a regime on reservations which, together with the definitional article (Article 2(1)(d)), determines what constitutes a reservation, the criteria it must meet to be permissible, and the effect it will have, both in the event that it is accepted by other contracting states and in the event that it is not. Under international law, reservations are invalid if they "are incompatible with the object and purpose" of the treaty. Vienna Convention, art. 19 para. (c). A number of states have objected to the United States' reservations concerning specific provisions of CAT as contrary to the object and purpose of the Convention. *See* Declarations and Reservations of Finland (objecting to the United States' reservation to article 16), Netherlands (considering the United States' reservation to articles 1 and 16 to be contrary to the object and purpose of the Convention), Sweden (explaining that it does not consider the United States' reservation to article 16 to be valid or effective), *available at* http://www.ohchr.org/english/law/cat-reserve.htm (last visited Oct. 25, 2004). The Committee Against Torture, authorized under CAT to monitor compliance with the Convention, has called on the United States to "withdraw its reservations, interpretations and understandings relating to the Convention." *Summary record of the first part of the 431st meeting: Slovenia, United States of America,* Committee Against Torture, UN Doc. CAT/C/SR.431 (2000). Also relevant to these discussions but less frequently invoked is the International Covenant on Civil and Political Rights, G.A. Res. 2200A (XXI), UN GAOR, 21st Sess., Supp. No. 16, at 52, UN Doc. A/6316 Dec. 16, 1966, *entered into force* 23 March 1976, 999 U.N.T.S. 171 *available at* http://www.ohchr.org/english/law/ccpr.htm (last visited Oct. 24, 2004) (ICCPR). As with CAT, the U.S. instrument of ratification of the ICCPR contained certain declarations, reservations, and understandings, including a declaration that ICCPR Articles 1 through 27 were not self-executing. *See* International Covenant on Civil and Political Rights, Declarations, Reservations and Understandings made by the United States, *available at* http://www.unhchr.ch/tbs/doc.nsf/887ff7374eb89574c1256a2a0027-ba1f/80256404004ff315c125638b005f309e?OpenDocument (last visited Oct. 24, 2004). *See* discussion in Section V.B for more on the relevant substantive norms binding the United States under the ICCPR.

10. *See generally* Human Rights First, *Ending Secret Detentions* (June 2004) (discussing secret detention facilities suspected to exist on, *inter alia,* U.S. Naval ships, including the USS *Bataan* and the USS *Peleliu,* and inside foreign prisons such as the Al Jafr prison in Jordan), *available at* http://www.humanrightsfirst.org/us_law/PDF/EndingSecretDetentions_web.pdf (last visited Oct. 25, 2004); Human Rights Watch, *The United States "Disappeared": The CIA's Long-Term "Ghost Detainees"* (Oct. 2004), *available at* http://www.hrw.org/backgrounder/usa/us1004/ (last visited Oct. 25, 2004).

11. This practice, however, is beginning to draw the attention of at least some members of Congress. *See, e.g.,* the questioning of Dr. Stephen A. Cambone, Under Secretary of Defense for Intelligence, by Senator Kennedy during the Senate Armed Services Committee hearing regarding the mistreatment of Iraqi prisoners. *Hearing on Allegations of mistreatment of Iraqi prisoners Before the Senate Armed Services Committee,* 108th Cong. (May 2004) (statement by Dr. S.A. Cambone, Under Secretary of Defense for Intelligence) (Cambone Statement). On June 23, 2004, Congressman Markey (Mass.) introduced legislation to stop the extra-judicial practice of sending terrorism suspects to foreign governments known to engage in torture. For the full text of the Markey bill, *see* http://www.house.gov/markey/Iraq.htm#LOC (last visited October 25, 2004).

12. Although this Report focuses mainly on cases in which U.S. actors are actually involved in the transfer of an individual, Extraordinary Rendition may be also considered to have occurred where an individual is placed in the custody of a foreign government at the direction of the U.S. government without U.S. officials ever being physically involved in the seizure or transfer. *See., e.g., Omar Abu Ali ex. rel Ahmed Abu Ali v. Ashcroft,* Case No. 1:04-CV-01258 JDB (D.D.C. filed July 28, 2004) (lawsuit alleging that Abu Ali was arrested and detained by Saudi Arabian officials at the request of the United States and that the respondents, acting under color of law violated U.S. law by engaging in the practice of "rendition to torture, namely placing an individual in the custody of a foreign government for purposes of interrogation in connection with suspected terrorist activities where harsh forms of interrogation are employed."), complaint *available at* http://www.humanrightsusa.org/modules.php?op=modload&name=News&file=article&sid=13 (last visited Oct. 25, 2004).

13. This Report uses the "more likely than not" standard for assessing an individual's risk upon transfer because it is the test that the United States employs when assessing that risk. By using this standard, the Report intends to examine the set of transfers that would be illegal under U.S. law, while acknowledging that this approach excludes cases of Extraordinary Rendition that could be technically legal under federal law, but would violate international human rights law that is binding on the United States. The relevant human rights treaties contain significantly more protective standards concerning the level of risk of torture or CID treatment that an individual faces upon transfer. The standard under CAT requires the presence of "substantial grounds for believing [the individual] would be in danger of being subjected to torture" upon transfer. CAT, *supra* note 9, art. 4(1). The ICCPR has been authoritatively interpreted to prohibit transfer in cases where there are "substantial grounds for believing that there is a real risk of irreparable harm" from torture or CID treatment. Human Rights Committee, General Comment 31, *Nature of the General Legal Obligation on States Parties to the Covenant,* U.N. Doc. CCPR/C/21/Rev.1/Add.13 (2004) (HRC General Comment 31). The United States has codified a standard that is more stringent, requiring that it be "more likely than not" that an individual will face torture upon transfer. For a discussion of U.S. law implementing CAT, *see* Section V.A.5. For a discussion of CAT standards, *see* Section V.A. for a discussion of ICCPR standards, *see* Section V.B.

14. On September 13, 2001, the Sunday Tribune (Ireland) reported that upon learning that 15 of the 19 hijackers involved in the September 11, 2001 attacks were from Saudi Arabia, President Bush met with the Saudi Ambassador to the United States, Prince Bandar bin Sultan. During the meeting, President Bush reportedly told Ambassador Bandar that if any Al Qaeda operatives were captured "if we can't get them to co-operate, we'll hand them over to you." *See* Diarmuid Doyle, *Which Ones Are the Bad Guys, Then? The US's Contempt for the Rights of Its Prisoners Puts Saddam to Shame,* The Sunday Tribune (Ireland), Mar. 30, 2003.

15. *Hearing Before the Joint Investigation of the House and Senate Intelligence Committees,* 107th Cong. (Sept. 26, 2002), (statement of Cofer Black, former Chief of the Counterterrorist Center, Central Intelligence Agency), *available at* http://intelligence.senate.gov/0209hrg/020926/witness.htm (last visited Oct. 25, 2004).

16. According to intelligence officials, Congress, which oversees the CIA, knows of only the broad authority to carry out renditions, but is not informed about individual cases. Kareem Fahim, *The Invisible Men,* Village Voice , Apr. 6, 2004, at 37.

17. Jon Barry et al., *The Roots of Torture,* Newsweek, May 24, 2004, at 36.

18. *See, e.g.,* U.S. Dep't. of State Country Reports on Human Rights Practices (2003) *available at* http://www.state.gov/g/drl/rls/hrrpt/2003/27938.htm (report on Syria) (last visited Oct. 25, 2004); http://www.state.gov/g/drl/rls/hrrpt/2003/27930.htm (report on Jordan) (last visited Oct. 25, 2004); http://www.state.gov/g/drl/rls/hrrpt/2003/27934.htm (report on Morocco) (last visited Oct. 25, 2004); http://www.state.gov/g/drl/rls/hrrpt/2003/27937.htm (report on Saudi Arabia) (last visited Oct. 25, 2004); http://www.state.gov/g/drl/rls/hrrpt/2003/27942.htm (report on Yemen) (last visited Oct. 25, 2004). Reportedly, during the Clinton Administration, renditions of suspected terrorists to Egypt had been stopped after repeated complaints about the Egyptian government's brutal interrogation methods. More recently, however, when asked about complaints about human rights abuses in the countries alleged to be destination countries for rendered suspects, one Bush Administration official replied: "You can be sure that we are not spending a lot of time on that now." Peter Beinart, *Outsourcing,* The New Republic , May 31, 2004, at 6.

19. This list is not exhaustive. Factual information used in this Report is based solely on reports published by reputable mainstream media sources.

20. Anthony Shadid, *America Prepares the War on Terror; U.S., Egypt Raids Caught Militants,* Boston Globe, Oct. 7, 2001, at A1.

21. *U.S. Bypasses Law in Fight against Terrorism,* International Herald Tribune, Mar. 12, 2002; Rajiv Chandrasekaran & Peter Finn, *U.S. Behind Secret Transfer of Terror Suspects,* Washington Post, Mar. 11, 2002, at A1.

22. *U.S. Bypasses Law in Fight against Terrorism,* International Herald Tribune, Mar. 12, 2002; Rajiv Chandrasekaran & Peter Finn, *U.S. Behind Secret Transfer of Terror Suspects,* Washington Post, Mar. 11, 2002, at A1.

23. *U.S. Bypasses Law in Fight against Terrorism,* INTERNATIONAL HERALD TRIBUNE, Mar. 12, 2002; Rajiv Chandrasekaran & Peter Finn, *U.S. Behind Secret Transfer of Terror Suspects,* WASHINGTON POST, Mar. 11, 2002, at A1.

24. *The Broken Promise,* (TV4 Kalla Fakta Broadcast, May 17, 2004) (English transcript *available at* http://hrw.org/english/docs/2004/05/17/sweden8620.htm (last visited Oct. 25, 2004)) (TV4 Kalla Fakta Broadcast); *see also* SEYMOUR HERSH, CHAIN OF COMMAND 54 (HarperCollins, 2004) (HERSH, CHAIN OF COMMAND).

25. In 1999, Agiza had been tried and convicted in absentia by an Egyptian military tribunal for terrorism-related acts. It remains unclear on what grounds al-Zari was expelled from Sweden and then imprisoned in Egypt. He was released from a Cairo prison in October 2003 without charge or trial, but remains under constant surveillance and is routinely summoned for interrogations. Human Rights Watch, *"Empty Promises:" Diplomatic Assurances No Safeguard against Torture* (April 2004), *available at* http://hrw.org/reports/2004/un0404/index.htm (last visited Oct. 25, 2004) (HRW Diplomatic Assurances Report).

26. Human Rights Watch, *Sweden: Torture Inquiry Must be Under U.N. Auspices; Independent Panel Must Probe Abuses by Sweden, Egypt and U.S. Operatives* (May 2004), *available at* http://www.hrw.org/english/docs/2004/05/27/sweden8621_txt.htm (last visited Oct. 25, 2004).

27. Craig Whitlock, *A Secret Deportation of Terror Suspects; 2 Men Reportedly Tortured in Egypt,* WASHINGTON POST, July 25, 2004, at A1.

28. *U.S. Bypasses Law in Fight Against Terrorism, supra* note 21; Chandrasekaran & Finn, *supra* note 21.

29. *U.S. Bypasses Law in Fight Against Terrorism, supra* note 21; Chandrasekaran & Finn, *supra* note 21.

30. *U.S. Bypasses Law in Fight Against Terrorism, supra* note 21; Chandrasekaran & Finn, *supra* note 21; Dana Priest & Joe Stephens, *Secret World of U.S. Interrogation: Long History of Tactics in Overseas Prisons Is Coming to Light,* WASHINGTON POST, May 11, 2004, at A1.

31. Chandrasekaran & Finn, *supra* note 21; *U.S. Bypasses Law in Fight Against Terrorism, supra* note 21.

32. Priest & Stephens, *supra* note 30.

33. *Boudellaa et al. v. Bosnia and Herzegovina and the Federation of Bosnia and Herzegovina,* Cases Nos. CH/02/8679, CH/02/8689, CH/02/8690 and CH/02/8691, Human Rights Chamber for Bosnia and Herzegovina, Oct. 2002, para. 227.

34. *Id.* para. 233. The Human Rights Chamber noted that "[c]onsidering the broad interpretation of the term jurisdiction, this obligation arises even if under the Dayton Peace Agreement [Bosnia and Herzegovina and the Federation of Bosnia and Herzegovina] had no direct jurisdiction over U.S. forces stationed in Bosnia and Herzegovina." *Id.*

35. *See* Section V.A.5(c) of this Report for more detail on the procedure of "expedited removal," also referred to as "summary removal."

36. For additional information on the case of Maher Arar, *see* http://www.maherarar.ca/.

37. According to a lawsuit filed by Arar against Attorney General John Ashcroft and other U.S. officials, Larry D. Thompson (then Acting Attorney General), J. Scott Blackman (then Regional Director of the Immigration and Naturalization Services for the Eastern District), Edward J. McElroy (formerly District Director for the Immigration and Naturalization Services for the New York City District and presently District Director of U.S. Immigration and Customs Enforcement), Robert Mueller (Director of the Federal Bureau of Investigation), and others, unlawfully detained and interrogated Arar for thirteen days. Complaint and Demand for Jury Trial, filed with the U.S. District Court, Eastern District of New York in *Arar v. Ashcroft, et al., available at* http://www.ccr-ny.org/v2/legal/september_11th/docs/ArarComplaint.pdf (last visited Oct. 25, 2004) (Arar v. Ashcroft).

38. *Id.*

39. *Id.* paras. 31, 33.

40. *Id.* para. 38.

41. *Id.* para. 49.

42. *Id.*

43. *Id.* paras. 53, 62.

44. *Id.*

45. *Id.* para 61; *see also* Priest & Stephens, *supra,* note 30.

46. DeNeen, L. Brown & Dana Priest, *Deported Terror Suspect Details Torture in Syria; Canadian's Case Called Typical of CIA,* Washington Post, Nov. 5, 2003, at A1. Gar Pardy, one of Canada's most senior diplomats at the time, stated that, "The fact that you went looking for assurances, which is reflected here, tells you that even in the minds of people who made this decision... I mean, there were some second thoughts." 60 Minutes II, *His Year in Hell* (Jan. 21, 2004) *available at* http://www.cbsnews.com/stories/2004/01/21/60II/main594974.shtml (last visited Oct. 25, 2004).

47. *The Trials of Mamdouh Habib* (SBS, Dateline, July 7, 2004) (transcript *available at* http://www6.sbs.com.au/dateline/index.php?page=archive&daysum=2004-07-07# (last visited Oct. 25, 2004)).

48. Joint Press Release, Attorney-General The Hon. Daryl Williams AM QC MP and Minister for Foreign Affairs and Trade The Hon. Alexander Downer MP, Mamdouh Habib in United States Custody (Apr. 18, 2002), *available at* http://www.ag.gov.au/www/attorneygeneralhome.nsf/0/49DF56AF955E312CCA256B9F007F44FA?OpenDocument (last visited Oct. 25, 2004); *The Trials of Mamdouh Habib* (SBS, Dateline, July 7, 2004) (transcript *available at* http://www6.sbs.com.au/dateline/index.php?page=archive&daysum=2004-07-07# (last visited Oct. 25, 2004)).

49. Human Rights Watch, *U.S.: Don't Send Detainees Back to China* (Nov. 26, 2003), *available at* http://www.hrw.org/press/2003/11/us112603.htm (last visited Oct. 25, 2004). *See also* Center for Constitutional Rights (CCR), *Inter-American Commission on Human Rights Asked to Take Urgent Action Regarding Reports of Torture Used on "Terrorism Detainees"* (Feb. 11, 2003) (CCR asked, *inter alia,* the Commission to take measures to stop the transfer of prisoners to third party states where torture is permitted), *available at* http://www.ccr-ny.org/v2/newsroom/releases/pReleases.asp?ObjID=OUMbKGaiNu&Content=195 (last visited Oct. 25, 2004).

50. U.S. Dept. of State, Office of the Spokesman, Interview: Secretary of State Colin L. Powell Roundtable with Japanese Journalists (Aug. 12, 2004) ("The Uighurs are not going back to China, but finding places for them is not a simple matter, but we are trying to find places for them. And we are trying to find places for them, and, of course, all candidate countries are being looked at."), *available at* http://www.usconsulate.org.hk/uscn/state/2004/081201.htm (last visited Oct. 25, 2004).

51. *See* Section IV.B.2 of this Report for an additional discussion of the distinction between *rendition* and *Extraordinary Rendition.*

52. *See* Cambone Statement, *supra* note 11.

53. Brown & Priest, *supra* note 46. It is not clear whether the reference is to "renditions" or Extraordinary Renditions.

54. Duncan Campbell, *September 11: six months on: U.S. sends suspects to face torture,* Guardian (London), Mar. 12, 2002, at 4.

55. Brown & Priest, *supra* note 46.

56. *Id.*

57. Dana Priest & Barton Gellman, *U.S. Decries Abuse but Defends Interrogations; 'Stress and Duress' Tactics Used on Terrorism Suspects Held in Secret Overseas Facilities,* Washington Post, Dec. 26, 2002, at A1; Ken Coates, *A Season of Cruelty,* Morning Star, Mar. 10, 2003, at 7. *See also A Review of the State Department Country Reports on Human Rights Practices: Hearing Before the Committee on International Relations, Subcommittee on International Terrorism, Nonproliferation and Human Rights,* 108th Cong. (April 30, 2003) (statement of Alexandra Arriaga, Director of Government Relations, Amnesty International) *available at* http://wwwc.house.gov/international_relations/108/arri0430.htm (last visited Oct. 25, 2004).

58. John Barry, Michael Hirsh & Michael Isikoff, *The Roots of Torture,* Newsweek, May 24, 2004, at 26.

59. Yossi Melman, *CIA Holding AL-Qaida suspects in secret Jordanian lockup,* HaAretz, Oct. 13, 2004, *available at* http://haaretzdaily.com/hasen/spages/488039.html (last visited Oct. 25, 2004).

60. *Id.*

61. *Id.*

62. Hersh, Chain of Command, *supra* note 24, at 16, 17, 47, 49–50; Seymour M. Hersh, *The Gray Zone,* The New Yorker, May 24, 2004.

63. Hersh, Chain of Command, *supra* note 24, at 50.

64. Hersh, Chain of Command, *supra* note 24, at 51.

65. *Id.*

66. Hersh, Chain of Command, *supra* note 24, at 53–54.

67. Press Release, U.S. Department of Defense, *Department of Defense Statement on Seymour Hersh Book,* Sept. 10, 2004, *available at* http://www.defenselink.mil/releases/2004/nr20040910-1240.html (last visited Oct. 25, 2004).

68. There is anecdotal evidence that the Army's elite DELTA force as well as Navy SEALS may also be involved in Extraordinary Renditions. Hersh, Chain of Command, *supra,* note 24, at 50.

69. Barry, Hirsh & Isikoff, *supra* note 58; TV4 Kalla Fakta Broadcast, *supra* note 24.

70. Coates, *supra* note 57.

71. *Id.; see also* Priest & Gellman, *supra* note 57.

72. Coates, *supra* note 57; Priest & Gellman, *supra* note 57.

73. Kareem Fahim, *The Invisible Men,* Village Voice, Apr. 6, 2004, at 37.

74. Brown & Priest, *supra* note 46. One U.S. official, speaking on condition of anonymity, characterized such renditions as follows: "These are not abductions, these are renditions. If [the detainees] are wanted by foreign governments and there is concern that they are involved in terrorist activities, the idea is to render them to justice." Anthony Shadid, *America Prepares the War on Terror; U.S., Egypt Raids Caught Militants,* Boston Globe, Oct. 7, 2001, at A1.

75. *U.S. Counterterrorism Policy: Hearing Before the Senate Judiciary Committee,* 106th Cong. (Sept. 1998) (statement by Louis J. Freeh, Director of Federal Bureau of Investigation), *available at* http://www.fas.org/irp/congress/1998_hr/98090302_npo.html (last visited Oct. 25, 2004) (Freeh Statement). This figure includes the renditions of two suspects in the August 7, 1998, bombing of the U.S. embassy in Nairobi, Mohamed Rashed Daoud Al-'Owhali and Mohamed Sadeek Odeh. All of the examples given by Freeh involved renditions of suspects *to* the United States in order to stand trial.

76. *Counterterrorism Policy: Hearing Before the National Commission on Terrorist Attacks Upon the United States* (March 24, 2004) (statement by George Tenet, former Director of Central Intelligence), *available at* http://www.9-11commission.gov/archive/hearing8/9-11Commission_Hearing_2004-03-24.htm (last visited Oct. 25, 2004) (Tenet Statement to 9-11 Commission). It is not clear which transfers were included in this number, but it would appear that this number encompasses both transfers to the United States and those to other states.

77. *National Commission on Terrorist Attacks Upon the United States: Staff Statement 7, available at* http://news.findlaw.com/hdocs/docs/terrorism/911comm-ss7.pdf (last visited Oct. 25, 2004); *see also Counterterrorism Policy: Hearing Before the National Commission on Terrorist Attacks Upon the United States* (March 24, 2004) (statement by Christopher Kojm, Testimony of the Deputy Executive Director, National Commission on Terrorist Attacks Upon the United States, and former Deputy Assistant Secretary of State), *available at* http://www.9-11commission.gov/archive/hearing8/9-11Commission_Hearing_2004-03-24.pdf (last visited Oct. 25, 2004) (Kojm Statement).

78. Tenet Statement to 9-11 Commission, *supra* note 76.

79. *Formulation and Conduct of U.S. Counterterrorism Policy: Hearing Before the National Commission on Terrorist Attacks Upon the United States (Interim Report)* (Mar. 23, 2004), *available at* http://www.9-11commission.gov/archive/hearing8/9-11Commission_Hearing_2004-03-23.pdf (last visited Oct. 25, 2004).

80. *Is the U.S. Subcontracting for Torture?* Interview by Jonathan Mann and Susan Candiotti, CNN, with Mike Baker, a former covert field operations officer for the CIA, and Barbara Olshansky, assistant legal director, Center for Constitutional Rights (Nov. 12, 2003).

81. Cambone Statement, *supra* note 11.

82. *Id.*

83. *See, e.g.,* Hersh, Chain of Command, supra note 24, at 51–52 (claiming that Dr. Cambone was an instrumental figure in the SAP); Hersh, Gray Zone, supra note 62 (same).

84. Mike Francis, *Ordered to Just Walk Away,* The Oregonian, Aug. 7, 2004, *available at* http://www.oregonlive.com/special/oregonian/iraq/index.ssf?/base/front_page/1091880082213032.xml (last visited Oct. 25, 2004); *see also U.S. troops ordered to ignore prisoner abuses,* The Advertiser, Aug. 9, 2004.

85. Francis, *supra* note 84.

86. *Id.*

87. *Id.*

88. *Id.*

89. According to the news report, National Guard soldiers disarmed the jailors and took control of the prisoners. *Id.*

90. *See* Human Rights Watch, *U.S.: Don't Send Detainees Back to China* (Nov. 26, 2003), *available at* http://www.hrw.org/press/2003/11/us112603.htm (last visited Oct. 25, 2004).

91. *See* Commission of Inquiry into the Actions of Canadian Officials in Relation to Maher Arar, *Report of Professor Stephen J. Toope Fact Finder* (Oct. 14, 2005) *available at* http://www.ararcommission.ca/eng/ToopeReport_final.pdf (last visited June 14, 2006), at 23. See further *Arar v. Ashcroft, supra* note 37, paras. 50–63 (outlining Arar's treatment in Syria). Diplomatic assurances were also obtained by Sweden from Egypt in connection with the expulsion of Ahmed Agiza and Mohammed al-Zari.

92. Bradley Graham & Josh White, *General Cites Hidden Detainees,* Washington Post, Sept. 10, 2004, at A24; Dana Priest, *Torture: The Legal Road to Abu Ghraib and Beyond,* panel organized by The Center on Law and Security, N.Y.U. Law School (Sept. 23, 2004) (notes on file with the International Human Rights Committee, ABCNY).

93. Dana Priest, *Torture: The Legal Road to Abu Ghraib and Beyond, supra* note 92.

94. Letter from Clark Kent Ervin, Inspector General, U.S. Department of Homeland Security, to Congressman John Conyers, Jr. (Jan. 9, 2004) (on file with the International Human Rights Committee, ABCNY); Letter from Clark Kent Ervin, Inspector General, U.S. Department of Homeland Security, to Steven Watt, Center for Constitutional Rights (Aug. 30, 2004) (on file with the International Human Rights Committee, ABCNY) (stating that "we will not review the involvement of other agencies such as the Department of Justice, Federal Bureau of Investigation, Central Intelligence Agency, and the Department of State").

95. Press Release, Commission of Inquiry into the Actions of Canadian Officials in Relation to Maher Arar, U.S. declines to directly cooperate with Arar Commission of Inquiry, (Sept. 21, 2004); *U.S. Won't Help Arar Inquiry*, CBC Ottawa (Sept. 22, 2004), *available at* http://ottawa.cbc.ca/regional/servlet/View?filename=ot_arar20040922 (last visited Oct. 25, 2004).

96. Press Release, American Civil Liberties Union "The Public Should Know Of Our Government's Treatment of Individuals Captured And Held Abroad," Judge Says, (Sept. 15, 2004), *available at* http://www.aclu.org/SafeandFree/SafeandFree.cfm?ID=16465&c=281 (last visited Oct. 25, 2004).

97. *Id.*

98. *Id.* Documents that are not produced must be identified in a list that includes the author, addressee, date and subject matter. Documents that cannot be identified because of their classification status must be produced in a log to the court. The government must also supply the ACLU with a list called a "Vaughn index" stating its justification for withholding documents. *Id.*

99. ACLU, *Records Released in Response to Torture FOIA Request, available at* http://www.aclu.org/torturefoia/released/ (last visited Oct. 25, 2004). One of the released documents is a letter sent by William H. Taft, IV, legal advisor for the Department of State, to Christophe Girod, Head of Delegation, International Committee of the Red Cross (ICRC). The letter, dated May 11, 2004, was in response to the concern expressed by the ICRC about the transfer for prosecution of seven nationals of the Russian Federation from Guantanamo Bay to Russia. Taft reiterates the U.S. policy "not to expel, return ("*refouler*") or extradite individuals to other countries where it believes it is "more likely than not" that they will be tortured." He proceeds to say, however, that "[b]efore transfer from Guantanamo to the control of another government, United States policy is to obtain specific assurances from the receiving country that it will provide human treatment and not torture the individual to be transferred. In determining whether it is "more likely than not" that an individual would be tortured, the United States takes into account the treatment the individual is likely to receive upon transfer, including inter alia the expressed commitments of officials from the receiving country." Letter from William H. Taft, IV, legal adviser, Department of

State, to Christophe Girod, Head of Delegation, International Committee of the Red Cross (May 11, 2004), *available at* http://www.aclu.org/torturefoia/released/State_Dept_ltr_051104.pdf (last visited Oct. 25, 2004). Taft concludes that the U.S. government obtained "assurances from senior Russian authorities that the detainees will be treated humanely in accordance with Russian law and obligations." *Id.* It is surprising that the U.S. government would find such assurances from Russian authorities credible, given that the U.S. State Department Country Report for 2003 unequivocally finds that "There were credible reports that [Russian] law enforcement personnel frequently engaged in torture, violence, and other brutal or humiliating treatment and often did so with impunity." U.S. Dep't of State Country Reports on Human Rights Practices (2003): Russia, *available at* http://www.state.gov/g/drl/rls/hrrpt/2003/27861.htm (last visited Oct. 25, 2004). The 2002 State Department report also noted that while the Russian Constitution prohibits torture, violence, and other brutal or humiliating treatment or punishment "there were credible reports that law enforcement personnel frequently engaged in these practices to coerce confessions from suspects and that the Government often did not hold officials accountable for such actions. Neither the law nor the Criminal Code defines torture; it is mentioned only in the Constitution. As a result, it was difficult to charge perpetrators. The only accusation prosecutors could bring against the police was that they exceeded their authority or committed a simple assault. Prisoners' rights groups, as well as other human rights groups, documented numerous cases in which law enforcement and correctional officials tortured and beat detainees and suspects. Human rights groups described the practice of such abuse as widespread. Numerous press reports indicated that the police frequently beat persons with little or no provocation or used excessive force to subdue detainees." *Id.*

100. Foreign Affairs Reform and Restructuring Act of 1998, Pub. L. No. 105-277, div. G, Title XXII, § 2242.

101. FARRA, *supra* note 100, §1242(a) (emphasis added).

102. Generally, under the law of the United States, extradition to another state takes place pursuant to a duly ratified extradition treaty. The exceptions are (i) extradition to the international tribunals for the former Yugoslavia and Rwanda (Act Feb. 10, 1996, P.L. 104-106, Div A, Title XIII, Subtitle E, § 1342, 110 Stat. 486); (ii) extradition of non-U.S. nationals who have committed crimes of violence against a U.S. national in foreign countries in certain circumstances (18 U.S.C. §3181 with note, §3184); and extradition to Palau, the Marshall Islands and the Federated States of Micronesia pursuant to a legislative executive agreement (48 U.S.C.S. § 1901).

103. Committee Against Torture, Consideration of Reports Submitted by States Parties Under Article 19 of the Convention; Initial reports of States parties due in 1995: United States of America, CAT/C/28/Add.5, Feb. 8, 2000, available at http://www.unhchr.ch/tbs/doc.nsf/(Symbol)/CAT.C.28.Add.5.En?OpenDocument (last visited Oct. 24, 2004) (U.S. Initial CAT Report).

104. The Department of Homeland Security has primary day-to-day authority to implement and enforce these regulations. The Department of Justice, through the Executive Office of Immigration Review (EOIR) has adjudicative authority over some detention and removal decisions.

105. 8 C.F.R. §208.18(a). For a description of U.S. reservations and declarations, *see* Section V.A.5(a) of this Report. For a discussion of the legality under international law of United States' reservations and declarations, *see* note 9, *supra*.

106. 8 C.F.R. §208.16(c)(4).

107. Such individuals are considered a security threat covered under section 241(b)(3)(B) of the Immigration and Nationality Act (INA). Act June 27, 1952, ch. 477, 66 Stat. 163, *as amended* 8 U.S.C. §1101 *et seq*. Terrorist activity does not include material support if the secretary of state or attorney general, following consultation with the other, concludes in his sole discretion (which is not subject to a review) that the definition of "terrorist activity" does not apply. *Id.* § 212(a)(3)(B).

108. *See* INA *supra* note 107, §§237(a)(4)(B) (2004), 241(b)(3)(B) (2004), 8 U.S.C. §§1227(a)(4)(B) (2000), 1231(b)(3)(B) (2000). Aliens to be designated as engaging in "terrorist activity" include those who, acting as an individual or part of an organization, (1) commit or incite to commit, under circumstances indicating an intention to cause death or serious bodily injury, a terrorist activity; (2) prepare or plan a terrorist activity; (3) gather information on potential targets for a terrorist activity; (4) solicit funds for a terrorist activity or organization, unless it can be demonstrated that the alien did not know and should not reasonably have known that solicitation would further terrorist activity; (5) solicit any individual for

terrorist activity or membership, unless it can be demonstrated that the alien did not know and should not reasonably have known that solicitation would further terrorist activity; or (6) commit an act that the actor knows, or reasonably should know, affords material support to the terrorist organization, including providing a safe house, transportation, communications, funds, transfer of funds or other material financial benefit, false documentation or identification, weapons, explosives, or training. CRS Report for Congress, "The UN Convention Against Torture: Overview of U.S. Implementation Policy Concerning the Removal of Aliens," *available at* http://fpc.state.gov/documents/organization/31351.pdf (last visited Oct. 25, 2004) (CRS Report); *See* INA §212(a)(3)(B) (2004), 8 U.S.C. §1182(a)(3)(B) (2000).

109. INA, *supra* note 107, §212(a)(3) (2004); § 235(c).

110. 8 C.F.R. §235.8(4). Those held for summary removal who are not suspected of terrorism and fear persecution or torture if returned can apply for a "credible fear" interview, which if positive, entitles the individual to a full hearing before an immigration judge. INA *supra* note 107, §208.30.

111. As discussed in Section V.A.5(c) of the Report, protections that are offered under FARRA do not comply fully with the obligations of the United States under CAT.

112. *See* Sections IV.B.1. and IV.B.2. of this Report.

113. *See, e.g., Ker v. Illinois,* 119 U.S. 436 (1886) (extrajudicial kidnapping from Peru of an individual for purposes of bringing him to trial in the United States on charges of larceny and embezzlement did not deprive the U.S. court of jurisdiction to try the defendant in the United States); *Frisbie v. Collins,* 342 U.S. 519, 522–23 (1952) (reaffirming the *Ker* doctrine, the court stated that "[t]here is nothing in the Constitution that requires a court to permit a guilty person rightfully convicted to escape justice because he was brought to trial against his will."); *United States v. Alvarez-Machain,* 504 U.S. 655 (1992) (Supreme Court sustained the jurisdiction of a U.S. court to try a Mexican national who was brought to the United States through abduction rather than pursuant to the extradition treaty between the United States and Mexico).

114. 500 F.2d 267 (2d Cir. 1974), *reh'g denied,* 504 F.2d 1380 (2d Cir. 1974). On remand, the court found "[no] credible evidence which would indicate any participation on the part of the United States officials prior to the time the defendant arrived in this country. Nor is there any evidence which shows that the abduction was carried out at the direction of United State officials." *United States v. Toscanino,* 398 F. Supp. 916, 917.

115. 500 F.2d at 274–75. *Cf. United States v. Lira,* 515 F.2d 68 (2d Cir. 1975), *cert. denied,* 423 U.S. 847 (1975). In *Lira,* the prisoner was charged with narcotics offenses and alleged that he had been arrested, taken to a local police station (and then to Chilean Naval Prison), tortured, forced to sign a decree expelling him from Chile, and subsequently sent to New York accompanied by of U.S. DEA agents and the Chilean police. Accepting jurisdiction, the Court distinguished *Lira* from *Toscanino* on the grounds that "the evidentiary hearing produced no proof that representatives of the United States participated or acquiesced in the alleged misconduct of the Chilean officials." *Id.* at 70.

116. *See, e.g., United States v. Alvarez-Machain, supra* note 113; *United States v. Best,* 304 F.3d 308 (3rd Cir. 2002).

117. FARRA, *supra* note 100, §1242(a) (emphasis added).

118. For a discussion of this legislation, *see* Section VIII.A.1. of this Report. For a more detailed description of U.S. ratification of CAT and the ICCPR, including descriptions of reservations and declarations, *see* Sections V.A.5. and V.B. of this Report.

119. In October 2004, Rep. Dennis Hastert introduced a bill (H.R. 10) a provision of which (section 3032) removes those suspected as terrorists from any protection against transfer to other countries known for their practice of torture. Indeed, under this provision, there would be no protection against such transfer even if it was for the specific purpose of interrogation under torture. This provision was denounced by human rights groups as well as by the White House. *See* Executive Office of the President, Statement of Administration Policy: H.R. 10-9/11 Recommendations Implementation Act Oct. 7, 2004). The bill has been subsequently amended by Rep. Hostettler. The Hostettler amendment provides that when dealing with suspected terrorists who "would threaten the national security or endanger the lives and safety of the American people" the secretary of homeland security may, in his or her "unreviewable discretion" determine that such individuals are specially dangerous aliens and should be detained until they are removed. Amendment to H.R. 10, offered by Rep. Hostettler (Oct. 4, 2004). The amendment further states

that if such an alien has been granted any other protection under the immigration law restricting the alien's removal, such alien shall be detained and diplomatic assurances will be sought prior to the removal. The amendment, although still inconsistent with the United States' obligations under CAT, nonetheless evidences that members of Congress are resistant to authorizing blanket transfers to countries where an individual is more likely than not to be subject to torture.

120. *Youngstown Sheet & Tube Co. v. Sawyer,* 343 U.S. 579, 637–638 (1952).

121. *Id.*

122. *Id.* at 635–38.

123. 453 U.S. 654 (1981).

124. *Hamdi v. Rumsfeld,* 124 S. Ct. 2633, 2637 (2004) ("[O]ur Constitution recognizes that core strategic matters of warmaking belong in the hands of those who are best positioned and most politically accountable for making them").

125. U.S. Const. art. I, §8.

126. U.S. Const. art. II, §2.

127. Restatement (Third) of the Foreign Relations Law of the U.S., §1, Reporters Note 3 (1987) (Restatement).

128. Louis Henkin, Foreign Affairs and the Constitution 38 (Oxford University Press 1972) (Henkin).

129. For a thorough review of cases addressing the scope of the president's wartime powers, *see* The Association of the Bar of the City of New York: Committee on Federal Courts, The Indefinite Detention of "Enemy Combatants": Balancing Due Process and National Security in Context of the War on Terror (Feb. 6, 2004, revised Mar. 18, 2004), *available at* http://www.abcny.org/pdf/1C_WL06!.pdf (ABCNY, *Indefinite Detention Report*) (last visited Oct. 25, 2004).

130. *See, e.g.,* 18 U.S.C. § 4001(a) (2000) (Non-Detention Act, barring imprisonment or detention of a citizen "except pursuant to an Act of Congress"). *See also Hamdi v. Rumsfeld,* 124 S. Ct. 2633, 2641 (2004). As explained in the concurring opinion of Justices Souter and Ginsburg, Congress enacted this statute to guard against another episode like the WWII internments of citizens of Japanese ancestry.

131. *See Hamdi, supra* note 130, at 2637 (relying on Article 118 of the Geneva Convention (III) Relative to the Treatment of Prisoners of War, Aug. 12, 1949 [1955] 6 U.S.T. 3406, T.I.A.S. No. 3364, for the proposition that detention of combatants may last no longer than active hostilities).

132. Pentagon, Working Group Report on Detainee Interrogation in the Global War on Terrorism: Assessment of Legal, Historical, Policy, and Operational Considerations (Apr. 4, 2003), *available at* http://www.ccr-ny.org/v2/reports/docs/PentagonReportMarch.pdf (last visited Oct. 25, 2004).

133. *Id.* at 21.

134. The Bush Administration later disavowed an August 1, 2002 Department of Justice memo that served as the basis of many of the conclusions in the April 4, 2003 document. Jay S. Bybee, Office of Legal Counsel of the Department of Justice, *Re: Standards of Conduct for Interrogation Under 18 U.S.C. §§23440-23440A* (Aug. 1, 2002), *available at* http://www.washingtonpost.com/wp-srv/nation/documents/dojinterrogationmemo20020801.pdf (Bybee Memorandum) (last visited Oct. 25, 2004). The crux of this memo was an attempt to narrow what constitutes torture under U.S. law. The Working Group's memo, however, has not been repudiated. Mike Allen & Susan Schmidt, *Memo on Interrogation Tactics Is Disavowed: Justice Document Had Said Torture May Be Defensible,* Washington Post, June 23, 2003, at A1.

135. *See* Section IV.C.3 of this Report.

136. Congress enacted FARRA, which regulates transfers from the United States, as well as 18 U.S.C. §§ 2340 and 2304A, which criminalize torture and conspiracy to commit torture.

137. During a White House press briefing held on June 22, 2004, White House Legal Counsel Alberto Gonzales dismissed discussions in Bybee memorandum of the scope of the president's power as Commander-in-Chief as "unnecessary," "irrelevant," and "overbroad," and stated that the United States will follow its treaty obligations and U.S. law, both of which prohibit the use of torture. Press Briefing, White House Counsel Judge Alberto Gonzales, June 22, 2004, *available at* http://www.whitehouse.gov/news/releases/2004/06/20040622-14.html (last visited Oct. 25, 2004).

138. *See* Section V.A.5(c) of this Report for a discussion of FARRA and Section VIII.A.1. for a discussion of Sections 2340 and 2340A. *See generally* Sections IV.C. and V of this Report.

139. Authorization for Use of Military Force, Pub. L. No. 107-40, 115 Stat. 224 (Sept. 18, 2001). *See* ABCNY, *Indefinite Detention Report, supra* note 129, at 65–66.

140. *See, e.g., Hamdi,* 124 S. Ct., *supra* note 130 at 2636, Brief for Respondents (Solicitor General Theodore Olson arguing that the president has the power to detain "enemy combatants" during wartime, and that this authority is subject to only a deferential standard of review by the courts); Reply Brief for the Petitioner at 12–13, *Rumsfeld v. Padilla,* 124 S. Ct. 2711 (2004) (asserting that the president has authority to detain an "enemy combatant" under his Commander in Chief powers and Congress's Authorization).

141. *Rasul et al. v. Bush,* 159 L. Ed. 2d 548 (2004); *Hamdi,* 124 S. Ct *supra* note 130.

142. *Hamdi,* 124 S. Ct., *supra* note 130 at 2641.

143. *Id.* at 2640–41.

144. *See* Sections IV.B.1 and IV.B.2. of this Report.

145. 50 U.S.C. §301 *et. seq.* (2004).

146. 50 U.S.C. §413(b) (2004). The National Security Act of 1947 created the National Security Council, and directed the NSC, subject to the direction of the president, *inter alia,* to: "a) assess and appraise the objectives, commitments and risks of the United States in relation to our actual and potential military power, in the interest of national security, for the purposes of making recommendations to the president in connection therewith; and b) consider policies on matters of common interest to the departments and agencies of the government concerned with national security, and...make recommendations to the president in connection therewith." J.S. Lay & R.H. Johnson, ORGANIZATIONAL HISTORY OF THE NATIONAL SECURITY COUNCIL DURING THE TRUMAN AND EISENHOWER ADMINISTRATIONS, at 3 (Washington, D.C.: National Security Council, 1960).

147. 50 U.S.C. §413(a)(5) (2004).

148. Harold C. Relyea, Specialist in American National Government, Government Division, *Report for Congress: Presidential Directives: Background and Overview,* Feb. 10, 2003, *available at* http://www.fas.org/irp/crs/98-611.pdf (last visited Oct. 25, 2004).

149. Robert V. Percival, *Presidential Administrations and Administrative Law: Presidential Management of the Administrative State: The Not-So-Unitary Executive,* 51 DUKE L. J. 963 (2001).

150. *Id.*

151. *Chamber of Commerce of the U.S. v. Reich,* 74 F.3d 1322 (D.C. Cir. 1996).

152. *Id.* at 1337.

153. *Building and Const. Trades Dept., AFL-CIO v. Allbaugh,* No. 01-0902, 2001 WL 1381197, at *18, 20 (D.D.C. Nov. 7, 2001).

154. *Id.*

155. Freeh Statement to 9-11 Commission, *supra* note 75.

156. *Formulation and Conduct of U.S. Counterterrorism Policy: Hearing Before the National Commission on Terrorist Attacks Upon the United States (Interim Report),* (Mar. 23, 2004), *available at* http://www.9-11commission.gov/archive/hearing8/9-11Commission_Hearing_2004-03-23.pdf (last visited Oct. 25, 2004); GOVERNMENT ACCOUNTABILITY OFFICE, COMBATING TERRORISM: ISSUES TO BE RESOLVED TO IMPROVE COUNTERTERRORISM OPERATIONS, (May 1999) (Washington, D.C.: U.S. General Accounting Office, 1999), at 3, *available at* http://www.gwu.edu/~nsarchiv/NSAEBB/NSAEBB55/gaonsiad-99-135.pdf (last visited Oct. 25, 2004) ("After the bombing of a federal building in Oklahoma City, Oklahoma, the President issued Presidential Decision Directive (PDD) 39 in June 1995, which enumerated responsibilities for federal agencies in combating terrorism, including domestic incidents.").

157. Kojm Statement, *supra* note 77.

158. GOVERNMENT ACCOUNTABILITY OFFICE, COMBATING TERRORISM: ISSUES TO BE RESOLVED TO IMPROVE COUNTERTERRORISM OPERATIONS, *supra* note 156.

159. RESTATEMENT, *supra* note 127, at §303(4) (sole executive agreements).

160. U.S. CONST. art. III, § 2.

161. Under the "later in time" rule, sole executive agreements may be superseded by subsequent domestic legislation. A clear congressional prohibition on Extraordinary Rendition would thus override any such agreements.

162. Military Order, "Detention, Treatment, and Trial of Certain Non-Citizens in the War Against Terrorism," (Nov. 13, 2001), *available at* http://www.deathpenaltyinfo.org/article.php?scid=33&did=224 (last visited Oct. 25, 2004).

163. 50 U.S.C. §§401 *et. seq.*

164. National Security Council Directive 10/2, June 18, 1948, *printed in* Foreign Relations, 1945–1950, Emergence of the Intelligence Establishment (United States Government Printing, 1996) Document 292 (NSC 10/2). *See Note on U.S. Covert Actions, in* Foreign Relations 1964–1968, Volume XXVI, Indonesia; Malaysia-Singapore; Philippines, Released by the Office of the Historian of the U.S. Department of State, *available at* http://www.state.gov/r/pa/ho/frus/johnsonlb/xxvi/4440.htm (last visited Oct. 25, 2004). NSC 10/2 defines "covert" operations as all activities "which are conducted or sponsored by this Government against hostile foreign states or groups or in support of friendly states or groups but which are so planned and executed that any U.S. Government responsibility is not evident to unauthorized persons and that if uncovered the US Government can plausibly disclaim any responsibility for them." NSC 10/2. The precise definition of covert operations has differed among administrations, although not in material ways. *See* David Isenberg, *The Pitfalls of U.S. Covert Operations,* CATO Policy Analysis No. 118 (April 7, 1989), *available at* http://www.cato.org/pub_display.php?pub_id=1645 (last visited Oct. 25, 2004).

165. *See, e.g.,* 50 U.S.C. §403(f), (g), (h).

166. 50 U.S.C. §403h.

167. 50 U.S.C. §413(b).

168. Priest & Gellman, *supra* note 57.

169. *Id.*

170. As we noted in the Introduction and Overview Sections, this Report, including this international law discussion, addresses the different instances of Extraordinary Rendition and not renditions *per se,* which are beyond the scope of this Report.

171. CAT, *supra* note 9.

172. ICCPR, *supra* note 9.

173. Convention for the Amelioration of the Condition of the Wounded and the Sick in Armed Forces in the Field, Aug. 12, 1949, *entered into force* Oct. 21, 1950, *6 U.S.T. 3217,* 75 U.N.T.S. 31, *available at* http://www.icrc.org/ihl.nsf/7c4d08d9b287a42141256739003e636b/fe20c3d903ce27e3c125641e004a92f3 (last visited Oct. 24, 2004) (Geneva I); Convention for the Amelioration of the Condition of Wounded, Sick, and Shipwrecked Members of Armed Forces at Sea, Aug. 12, 1949, *entered into force* Oct. 21, 1950, *6 U.S.T. 3217,* 75 U.N.T.S. 85, *available at* http://www.icrc.org/ihl.nsf/7c4d08d9b287a42141256739003e636b/44072487ec4c2131c125641e004a9977 (last visited Oct. 24, 2004) (Geneva II); Convention Relative to the Treatment of Prisoners of War, Aug. 12, 1949, *entered into force* Oct. 21, 1950. *6 U.S.T. 3316,* 75 U.N.T.S. 135, *available at* http://www.icrc.org/ihl.nsf/7c4d08d9b287a42141256739003e636b/6fef854a3517b75ac125641e004a9e68 (last visited Oct. 24, 2004) (Geneva III); Convention Relative to the Protection of Civilian Persons in Times of War, Aug. 12, 1949, *entered into force* Oct. 21, 1950, *6 U.S.T. 3516,* 75 U.N.T.S. 287, *available at* http://www.icrc.org/ihl.nsf/7c4d08d9b287a42141256739003e636b/6756482d86146898c125641e004aa3c5 (last visited Oct. 24, 2004) (Geneva IV) (together, Geneva Conventions).

174. Convention Relating to the Status of Refugees, *opened for signature* July 28, 1951, *19 U.S.T. 6259, 6261,* 189 U.N.T.S. 150, 152, *entered into force* Apr. 22, 1954, *available at* http://www.ohchr.org/english/law/refugees.htm (last visited Oct. 24, 2004) (Refugee Convention). Although the United States did not ratify the Refugee Convention, it is a party to it through its accession to the 1967 Protocol Relating to the Status of Refugees, *opened for signature* Jan. 31, 1967, *19 U.S.T. 6223,* 606 U.N.T.S. 267, *entered into force* Oct. 1967, *available at* http://www.ohchr.org/english/law/protocolrefugees.htm (last visited Oct. 24, 2004) (1967 Protocol), which adopted and extended the Refugee Convention's protections. Also relevant is the American Declaration of the Rights and Duties of Man, May 2, 1948, OEA/ser. L./V/II.23, doc. 21 rev. 6, (1979), *available at* http://www.iachr.org/Basicos/basic2.htm (last visited Oct. 9, 2004) (American Declaration). The American Declaration was adopted by the Ninth International Conference of the OAS held at Bogota, Columbia, March 30–May 2, 1948, and applies to the United States through its membership in the Organization of American States (OAS). The Inter-American Court of

Human Rights has determined that the American Declaration is a source of international obligation for the United States and other OAS member states that are not parties to the American Convention on Human Rights, based upon Articles 3, 16, 51, 112, and 150 of the OAS Charter. *See* Inter-Am. Court H.R., Advisory Opinion OC-10/89, *Interpretation of the American Declaration of the Rights and Duties of Man Within the Framework of Article 64 of the American Convention on Human Rights,* July 14, 1989, Ser. A No. 10 (1989), paras. 35–45.

175. The *refoulement* of individuals to states where they are in danger of CID treatment is not explicitly prohibited.

176. A likely explanation for the higher ICCPR threshold is that the ICCPR has been interpreted to extend the *non-refoulement* protection over a broader range of abuse—including both torture *and* CID treatment or punishment—than CAT, which on its face protects only against *refoulement* to torture.

177. CAT, *supra* note 9, art. 5(1). For a detailed discussion of the scope of CAT's application, *see* Section V.A.4.

178. For a detailed discussion of the scope of the ICCPR's application, *see* Section V.B.2.

179. *Murray v. The Charming Betsy,* 6 U.S. (2 Cranch) 64, 118 (1804) (a statute "ought never to be construed to violate the law of nations, if any other possible construction remains"). *See also United States v. P.L.O.,* 695 F. Supp. 1456, 1468 (S.D.N.Y. 1988) (noting "the lengths to which our courts have sometimes gone in construing domestic statutes so as to avoid conflict with international agreements..."); *INS v. St. Cyr,* 533 U.S. 289 (2001).

180. *Lawrence v. Texas,* 539 U.S. 558, 123 S.Ct. 2472 (2003); *Hamdi v. Rumsfeld,* 124 S. Ct. at 2641 (citing to international treaties for "clearly established" principles of the laws of war).

181. The Committee against Torture is the monitoring body created by the states party to CAT. CAT, *supra* note 9, arts. 17–24. It is charged with: (i) considering and commenting on country reports submitted under CAT (art. 19); (ii) the ability to inquire into an individual state's practices with regard to torture if it receives "reliable information" of "well-founded indications" that torture is being practiced in the territory of the state (art. 20); (iii) resolving inter-State disputes (art. 21); and (iii) determining individual complaints (art. 22). The Committee Against Torture "is not an appellate, a quasi judicial or an administrative body, but rather a monitoring body created by the States parties themselves with declaratory powers only." Committee Against Torture, General Comment 1, *Communications concerning the return of a person to a State where there may be grounds he would be subjected to torture (article 3 in the context of article 22),* U.N. Doc. A/53/44, annex IX at 52 (1998), *reprinted in* Compilation of General Comments and General Recommendations Adopted by Human Rights Treaty Bodies, U.N. Doc. HRI/GEN/1/Rev.6 at 279 (2003) (CAT Article 3 Comment), para. 9. The United States is bound by the Article 20 inquiry procedure, and has entered a declaration accepting the Article 21 interstate complaint procedure. *See* United Nations Treaty Collection: Declarations and Reservations, *available at* http://www.unhchr.ch/html/menu3/b/treaty12_asp.htm (last visited Oct. 9, 2004). The United States has not accepted the competence of the CAT Committee under Article 22 to receive and consider complaints on behalf of individuals subject to U.S. jurisdiction who claim to be victims of a CAT violation. *Id.*

182. The Human Rights Committee is the most authoritative source, at the international level, of interpretations of a state's obligations under the ICCPR. Pursuant to the ICCPR, *supra* note 5. The Human Rights Committee is empowered to: (i) receive state party reports and comment on those reports (art. 40 (4)); (ii) rule on complaints filed by a state party that another state party is not fulfilling its obligations under the Covenant (art. 41); and (iii) rule on complaints filed by individuals "who claim that any of their rights enumerated in the Covenant have been violated and who have exhausted all available domestic remedies" Optional Protocol to the International Covenant on Civil and Political Rights, G.A. Res. 2200A (XXI), 21 U.N. GAOR Supp. (No. 16) at 59, U.N. Doc. A/6316 (1966), 999 U.N.T.S. 302, *entered into force* March 23, 1976, *available at* http://www.ohchr.org/english/law/ccpr-one.htm (last visited Oct. 24, 2004). In ratifying the ICCPR, the U.S. Senate declared that "The United States...accepts the competence of the Human Rights Committee to receive and consider communications under Article 41 in which a State Party claims that another State Party is not fulfilling its obligations under the Covenant." *See* 138 Cong. Rec. S4781-01 (daily ed., April 2, 1992).

183. *See* J. Herman Burgers & Hans Danelius, The United Nations Convention Against Torture: A Handbook on the Convention Against Torture and Other Cruel, Inhuman, or Degrading Treatment or

Punishment (1988). Pursuant to the Vienna Convention on the Law of Treaties, if a treaty term is "ambiguous or obscure," "recourse may be had to supplementary means of interpretation, including the preparatory work of the treaty and the circumstances of its conclusion." The Vienna Convention on the Law of Treaties, *opened for signature* May 23, 1969, *entered into* force Jan. 27, 1980, art. 32, 1155 U.N.T.S. 331, *available at* http://www.un.org/law/ilc/texts/treaties.htm (last visited Oct. 24, 2004) (Vienna Convention), art 32. The Vienna Convention has not been ratified by the United States, but the provisions relied upon in this Report are considered to codify customary international law. The Vienna Convention has been treated as authoritative by the U.S. Department of State and several courts of appeal. *See* Maria Frankowska, *The Vienna Convention Before the United States Courts,* 28 Va. J. Int'l L. 281 (1988).

184. American Declaration, *supra* note 174.

185. American Convention on Human Rights, Nov. 22, 1969, KAV 2305, 9 ILM 673 (1970), O.A.S. Treaty Series No. 36, art. 5, P 2, OEA/Ser. L./V/II.23 doc. rev. 2, art. 5 *entered into force* July 18, 1978, *available at* http://www.cidh.org/Basicos/basic3.htm (last visited Oct. 25, 2004) (American Convention).

186. A *jus cogens* norm is defined in the Vienna Convention as "accepted and recognized by the international community of states as a whole as a norm from which no derogation is permitted and which can be modified only by a subsequent norm of general international law having the same character." Vienna Convention, *supra* note 183, art. 53.

187. "Customary international law results from a general and consistent practice of states followed by them from a sense of legal obligation." Restatement, *supra* note 127, at §102 (2). The Restatement specifies that "[i]nternational agreements create law for the states parties thereto and may lead to the creation of customary international law [for states which are not parties] when such agreements are intended for adherence by states generally and are in fact widely accepted." *Id.* §102(3). The Restatement includes "torture or other cruel, inhuman or degrading treatment or punishment" as a violation of customary international law. *Id.* §702(d). Customary international law is part of the common law of the United States and is considered to control if there is no contrary treaty, statute or executive act. U.S. Const., art. III, § 8; *Filartiga v. Pena-Irala,* 630 F.2d 876, 880 (2d Cir. 1980).

188. *Siderman de Blake v. Republic of Argentina,* 965 F.2d 699, 714, 717 (9th Cir. 1992), *cert. denied* 507 U.S. 1017, 113 S. Ct. 1812 (1993) (quoting Vienna Convention definition of *jus cogens* and noting that the prohibition against torture by state actors has "the force of a *jus cogens* norm"). *See also Kadic v. Karadzic, 70* F.3d 232 (2d Cir. 1996) (holding that torture is a violation of customary international law and upholding a civil suit against the leader of the Bosnian Serbs under the Torture Victim Protection Act of 1991); *In re Estate of Ferdinand E. Marcos Human Rights Litigation,* 978 F.2d 493, 499 (9th Cir. 1992) (finding that official torture violates customary international law); *Filartiga v. Pena-Irala,* 630 F.2d at 881, 883-84, 887 (2d Cir. 1980) (holding that torture is a violation of "the law of nations"); *Forti v. Suarez-Mason,* 672 F. Supp. 1531, *1541* (N.D. Cal. 1987) (following *Filartiga* and finding a universal proscription against official torture); Inter-Am. Comm'n H. R., *Report on the Situation of Human Rights of Asylum Seekers within the Canadian Refugee Determination System* OEA/Ser.L/V/II.106, Doc. 40 rev., February 28, 2000, para.154 (prohibition against torture is a *jus cogens* norm); *Prosecutor v. Furundzija,* Case No. No. IT-95-17/1-T, Judgment (ICTY Trial Chamber December 10, 1998) (recognizing prohibition against torture as *jus cogens* norm); *R. v. Bow Street Metropolitan Stipendiary Magistrate, Ex parte Pinochet Ugarte (No. 3),* [1999] 2 W.L.R. 827 (H.L.) (same); Restatement, *supra* note 127, at cmt. n, (the prohibitions against torture and CID treatment and punishment have the status of *jus cogens* norms).

189. *The Paquete Habana,* 175 U.S. 677, 700 (1900).

190. European Convention for the Protection of Human Rights and Fundamental Freedoms, 213 U.N.T.S. 222, *opened for signature* Nov. 4, 1950, *entered into force* Sept. 3, 1953, *as amended by* Protocols Nos 3, 5, 8, and 11 which *entered into force* on 21 September 1970, 20 December 1971, 1 January 1990, and 1 November 1998 respectively, *available at* http://www.echr.coe.int/Convention/webConvenENG.pdf (last visited Oct. 24, 2004) (European Convention).

191. CAT, *supra* note 9, art. 1.

192. *Id.* art. 3.1.

193. *Id.* art. 4.1.

194. Universal Declaration of Human Rights, G.A. Res. 217, UN GAOR, 3d Sess., UN Doc. A/810 (1948) art. 5, *available at* http://www.unhchr.ch/udhr/lang/eng.htm (last visited Oct. 24, 2004)

(providing that "no one shall be subjected to torture or to cruel, inhuman or degrading treatment or punishment").

195. ICCPR, *supra* note 9, art. 7 ("no one shall be subjected to torture or to cruel, inhuman or degrading treatment or punishment").

196. Declaration on the Protection of All Persons from Being Subjected to Torture and Other Cruel, Inhuman or Degrading Treatment or Punishment, G.A. res. 3452 (XXX), annex, 30 U.N. GAOR Supp. (No. 34) at 91, U.N. Doc. A/10034 (1975), *available at* http://www.ohchr.org/english/law/declarationcat.htm (last visited Oct. 24, 2004).

197. When ratifying CAT, the United States specified its understanding concerning the scope of "torture." *See* United Nations Treaty Collection: Declarations and Reservations, *available at* http://www.unhchr.ch/html/menu3/b/treaty12_asp.htm (last visited Oct. 9, 2004). The understanding is discussed in Association of the Bar of the City of New York, *Human Rights Standards Applicable to the United States' Interrogation of Detainees,* April 2004 (HR Standards Report) *available at* http://www.abcny.org/pdf/HUMANRIGHTS.pdf (last visited Oct. 6, 2004), at 20–21. Acts that the CAT Committee has held constitute torture are discussed in greater detail in the HR Standards Report, pages 16–17.

198. *See also* Burgers & Danelius, *supra* note 183, at 119 ("It is important to note. . .that the primary purpose of [CAT] is to eliminate torture committed by or under the responsibility of public officials for purposes connected with their public functions. Precisely because the public interest is sometimes seen in such cases as a justification, the authorities may be reluctant to suppress these practices."). For a discussion of liability of state actors, *see* Section VIII. of this Report.

199. In its ratification of CAT, the U.S. reservation to Article 16 of CAT provides that the United States considers itself bound by Article 16 only insofar as CID treatment is understood to mean "the cruel, unusual and inhumane treatment or punishment prohibited by the Fifth, Eighth and Fourteenth Amendments." *See* United Nations Treaty Collection: Declarations and Reservations, *available at* http://www.unhchr.ch/html/menu3/b/treaty12_asp.htm (last visited Oct. 25, 2004). For further discussion of the interpretation of this reservation, *see* HR Standards Report, *supra* note 197, at 27–30. Acts that the CAT Committee has found to constitute CID treatment or punishment are discussed in greater detail in the HR Standards Report, *supra* note 197, at 18–19.

200. CAT, *supra* note 9, article 16(1) provides:

> 1. Each State Party shall undertake to prevent in any territory under its jurisdiction other acts of cruel, inhuman or degrading treatment or punishment which do not amount to torture as defined in article 1, when such acts are committed by or at the instigation of or with the consent or acquiescence of a public official or other person acting in an official capacity. In particular, the obligations contained in articles 10, 11, 12 and 13 shall apply with the substitution for references to torture of references to other forms of cruel, inhuman or degrading treatment or punishment.
> 2. Each State Party shall include this prohibition in the rules or instructions issued in regard to the duties and functions of any such person.

See Section V.A.3. of this Report, discussing CAT articles 10, 11, 12 and 13.

201. The CAT *non-refoulement* obligation prohibits transfers to states where an individual is in danger of torture, and not transfers to states where the individual faces the danger of CID treatment or punishment. This was a deliberate choice on the part of the drafters who were concerned that although "torture" could be defined with specificity, a definition of CID treatment or punishment was less easily specified. Burgers & Danelius, *supra* note 183, at 70, 74, 122–23. As discussed below, however, the Human Rights Committee has interpreted the ICCPR (to which the United States is also a party), to impose the prohibition against *refoulement* to states where an individual faces the danger of CID treatment as well as the danger of torture. The United States should also be guided by the jurisprudence of the European Court of Human Rights and its Commission, interpreting Article 3 of the European Convention, *supra* note 190. Article 3 of the European Convention prohibits torture and CID treatment or punishment but does not include a prohibition against *refoulement.* Nevertheless, the European Court and the European Commission have interpreted European Convention Article 3 to prohibit transfers to states in which an individual may be subjected to torture or to CID treatment or punishment. *See Soering v. United Kingdom,* 161 Eur. Ct. H.R. (ser. A) (1989).

202. CAT Article 3 Comment, *supra* note 181, para. 2.

203. Burgers & Danelius, *supra* note 183, at 125.

204. This standard has a lower threshold than the Refugee Convention's *refoulement* prohibition, which requires a showing of a "well-founded fear of persecution." *See* Section V.D. below.

205. CAT, *supra* note 9, art. 3(2).

206. CAT Article 3 Comment, *supra* note 181, para. 6.

207. *See* United Nations Treaty Collection: Declarations and Reservations, *available at* http://www.unhchr.ch/html/menu3/b/treaty12_asp.htm (last visited Oct. 25, 2004).

208. Among the sources of information the CAT Committee will consider is whether the state to which an individual may be returned is "one in which there is evidence of a consistent pattern of gross, flagrant or mass violations of human rights." CAT Article 3 Comment, *supra* note 181, para 8.

209. According to the CAT Committee, "The grounds for belief are subjective to the individual in danger of being tortured." *Id.* para. 7. To assess a particular individual's risk, the CAT Committee will look to whether the individual has engaged in activity "within or outside the State concerned which would appear to make him/her particularly vulnerable to the risk of being placed in danger of torture were he/she to be expelled, returned or extradited to the State in question." *Id.* para 8. *See also Mutombo v. Switzerland,* Communication No. 13/1993, Committee Against Torture, U.N. Doc. A/49/44 at 45 (1994) (applicant for CAT relief must show that the risk of torture is specific to that individual).

210. *See Mutombo v. Switzerland,* Communication No. 13/1993, Committee Against Torture, U.N. Doc. A/49/44 at 45 (1994); *Khan v. Canada,* Communication No. 15/1994, Committee Against Torture, U.N. Doc. A/50/44 at 46 (1994).

211. *Khan v. Canada,* Communication No. 15/1994, Committee Against Torture, U.N. Doc. A/50/44 at 46 (1994).

212. *Alan v. Switzerland,* Communication No. 21/1995, Committee Against Torture, UN Doc. CAT/C/16/D/21/1995 (1996).

213. U.S. Dep't. of State Country Reports on Human Rights Practices 2003: Egypt, *available at* http://www.state.gov/g/drl/rls/hrrpt/2003/27926.htm ("The Constitution prohibits the infliction of "physical or moral harm" upon persons who have been arrested or detained; however, torture and abuse of detainees by police, security personnel, and prison guards remained common and persistent. The November, 2002 session of the Committee Against Torture noted a systematic pattern of torture by the security forces. . . .") (last visited Oct. 9, 2004). *See also* U.S. Dep't. of State Country Reports on Human Rights Practices 2002: Egypt, *available at* http://www.state.gov/g/drl/rls/hrrpt/2002/18274.htm (same) (last visited Oct. 9, 2004) *and* U.S. Dep't. of State Country Reports on Human Rights Practices 2001: Egypt, *available at* http://www.state.gov/g/drl/rls/hrrpt/2001/nea/8248.htm (same) (last visited Oct. 9, 2004).

214. U.S. Dep't. of State Country Reports on Human Rights Practices 2003: Jordan, *available at* http://www.state.gov/g/drl/rls/hrrpt/2003/27930.htm (last visited Oct. 9, 2004). *See also* U.S. Dep't. of State Country Reports on Human Rights Practices 2002: Jordan, *available at* http://www.state.gov/g/drl/rls/hrrpt/2002/18279.htm (same) (last visited Oct. 9, 2004), *and* U.S. Dep't. of State Country Reports on Human Rights Practices 2001: Jordan, *available at* http://www.state.gov/g/drl/rls/hrrpt/2001/nea/8266.htm (same) (last visited Oct. 9, 2004).

215. U.S. Dep't. of State Country Reports on Human Rights Practices 2003: Morocco, *available at* http://www.state.gov/g/drl/rls/hrrpt/2003/27934.htm (last visited Oct. 9, 2004). *See also* U.S. Dep't. of State Country Reports on Human Rights Practices 2002: Morocco, *available at* http://www.state.gov/g/drl/rls/hrrpt/2002/18284.htm (same) (last visited Oct. 9, 2004), *and* U.S. Dep't. of State Country Reports on Human Rights Practices 2001: Morocco, *available at* http://www.state.gov/g/drl/rls/hrrpt/2001/nea/8277.htm (same) (last visited Oct. 9, 2004).

216. U.S. Dep't. of State Country Reports on Human Rights Practices 2003: Syria, *available at* http://www.state.gov/g/drl/rls/hrrpt/2003/27934.htm (last visited Oct. 9, 2004). *See also* U.S. Dep't. of State Country Reports on Human Rights Practices 2002: Syria, *available at* http://www.state.gov/g/drl/rls/hrrpt/2002/18289.htm (same) (last visited Oct. 9, 2004), *and* U.S. Dep't. of State Country Reports on Human Rights Practices 2001: Syria, *available at* http://www.state.gov/g/drl/rls/hrrpt/2001/nea/8298.htm (same) (last visited Oct. 9, 2004).

217. U.S. Dep't. of State Country Reports on Human Rights Practices 2003: Saudi Arabia, *available at* http://www.state.gov/g/drl/rls/hrrpt/2003/27937.htm. *See also* U.S. Dep't. of State Country Reports on Human Rights Practices 2002: Saudi Arabia, *available at* http://www.state.gov/g/drl/rls/hrrpt/2002/18288.htm (same) (last visited Oct. 9, 2004), *and* U.S. Dep't. of State Country Reports on Human Rights Practices 2001: Saudi Arabia, *available at* http://www.state.gov/g/drl/rls/hrrpt/2001/nea/8296.htm (same) (last visited Oct. 9, 2004).

218. U.S. Dep't. of State Country Reports on Human Rights Practices 2003: Yemen *available at http://www.state.gov/g/drl/rls/hrrpt/2003/27942.htm* (last visited Oct. 25, 2004).

219. Burgers & Danelius, *supra* note 183, at 126. The reference to *refoulement* originates in, but differs from, Article 33 of the Refugee Convention, which states that "No Contracting State shall expel or return ("*refouler*") a refugee in any manner whatsoever to the frontiers of territories where his life or freedom would be threatened on account of his race, religion, nationality, membership of a particular social group or political opinion." Refugee Convention, *supra* note 174. But, whereas the Refugee Convention protects only persons who meet one of five specified categories that form a basis for persecution under the Refugee Convention, CAT was intended to apply to "any person who, for whatever reason, is in danger of being subjected to torture if handed over to another country." Burgers & Danelius, *supra* note 183, at 125.

220. U.N. Doc. E/CN.4/1367, para. 18, *cited in* Burgers & Danelius, *supra* note 183, at 126–27.

221. S. Treaty Doc. No. 100–20, at iii, 9–14 (1988) (adding that "This reservation would eliminate the possibility of conflicting treaty obligations. This is not to say, however, that the United States would ever surrender a fugitive to a State where he would actually be in danger of being subjected to torture. Pursuant to his discretion under domestic law, and existing treaty bases for denying extradition, the Secretary of State would be able to satisfy himself on this issue before surrender.").

222. U.S. Dep't. of State Country Reports on Human Rights Practices 2003: Pakistan , *available at* http://www.state.gov/g/drl/rls/hrrpt/2003/27950.htm ("The Constitution and the Penal Code prohibit torture and other cruel, inhuman, or degrading treatment; however, security forces regularly tortured, and otherwise abused persons. Police routinely used force to elicit confessions. Human rights observers suggested that, because of widespread torture by the police, suspects usually confessed to crimes regardless of their actual culpability; the courts subsequently at times dismissed such confessions...Over the years, there have been allegations that common torture methods included: beating; burning with cigarettes; whipping the soles of the feet; sexual assault; prolonged isolation; electric shock; denial of food or sleep; hanging upside down; forced spreading of the legs with bar fetters; and public humiliation.") (last visited Oct. 9, 2004); the State Department Reports for Egypt and Jordan are described above in notes 213 and 214 respectively, and the text accompanying those footnotes.

223. 18 U.S.C. §3181 (2002) (listing countries with which the United States has extradition treaties).

224. According to Burgers and Danelius (who participated in the drafting of CAT and whose authoritative text on the treaty includes discussion of the CAT *travaux préparatoires*), CAT Article 3 was "inspired by the case law of the European Commission of Human Rights with regard to Article 3 of the European Convention....The Commission has considered that the prohibition of torture and inhuman or degrading treatment in article 3 of the European Convention does not only oblige a State to prevent torture within its own territory, but also to refrain from handing a person over to another State where he might, with some degree of probability, be subjected to torture." Burgers & Danelius, *supra* note 183, at 125; *see also id.* at 125–128 (describing European Commission case law and the negotiations and discussions among states that lead to the final version of CAT Article 3, incorporating the European Commission's interpretation of Article 3 of the European Convention).

225. European Convention, *supra* note 190.

226. *Soering v. United Kingdom,* 161 Eur. Ct. H.R. (ser. A) (1989), para. 88.

227. *Id.*

228. *Id.*

229. *Cruz Varas v. Sweden,* 201 Eur. Ct. H.R. (ser. A) (1989) paras. 69–70 (holding that European Convention Article 3's prohibition against a state's transfer of an individual to another state where the person will face a real risk of torture or CID treatment applies to expulsions as well as extraditions); *Vilvarajah and Others v. United Kingdom,* 215 Eur. Ct. H.R. (ser. A) (1991) para 103 (same).

230. To determine whether a principle included in international treaties is a part of customary international law, U.S. courts will look to, *inter alia,* the "relative influence of [non-ratifying or signatory states] in international affairs. *Flores,* 343 F.3d at 163. States that are not party to CAT include: Angola, the Bahamas, Barbados, Bhutan, Brunei Darussalam, the Central African Republic, Democratic People's Republic of Korea, the Dominican Republic, Gambia, Guinea-Bissau, India, Madagascar, Nauru, Nicaragua, Pakistan, San Marino, Sao Tome and Principe, Thailand and Sudan. For a full list of states that are not party to CAT, *see* http://www.unhchr.ch/tbs/doc.nsf/newhvstatbytreaty?OpenView&Start=1&Count=250&Expand=1.1#1.1 (last visited Oct. 24, 2004). Many of these states have a relatively low profile in international affairs. Significantly, many of these states have committed themselves to the *non-refoulement* principle by ratifying other treaties that include the principle, including, for example, the African Union Convention Governing the Specific Aspects of Refugee Problems in Africa, *concluded on* Sept. 10, 1969, *entered into force* June 20, 1974, 1001 U.N.T.S. 45 (ratified by 44 states to date). For ratification status of these treaties, *see* Office of the United Nations High Commissioner for Human Rights, Status of Ratifications of the Principal International Human Rights Treaties, *available at* http://www.unhchr.ch/pdf/report.pdf (Status of Ratifications) (last visited Oct. 25, 2004).

231. As of June 9, 2004, CAT had been ratified by 136 states and signed by 12 additional states. Only two states, the United States and Germany, entered reservations to Article 3. *See* Status of Ratifications, *supra* note 230, and http://www.unhchr.ch/tbs/doc.nsf/Statusfrset?OpenFrameSet (last visited Oct. 9, 2004). Neither reservation indicates an intent to derogate from CAT's *non-refoulement* requirement. The U.S. ratification of CAT states its understanding that Article 3.1's requirement of "substantial grounds" to mean "if it is likely than not that he would be tortured." *Id.* Germany declared its opinion that Article 3 expressed an obligation on the part of a state, which was met by existing German domestic law. *Id.*

232. Fifty-four states have recognized the competence of the Committee against Torture to receive and process individual communications concerning those states' practices under CAT Article 22. *See* Status of Ratifications, *supra* note 230.

233. *See* Section V.D.

234. Article 22(8) of the American Convention states that "In no case may an alien be deported or returned to a country, regardless of whether or not it is his country of origin, if in that country his right to life or personal freedom is in danger of being violated because of his race, nationality, religion, social status, or political opinion." However, Article 27 of the American Convention allows a state to derogate from Article 22 (and other provisions) during "times of war or other public emergency that threaten the independence and security of the State party." *See* American Convention, *supra* note 185.

235. O.A.S. Treaty Series No. 67, *entered into force* February 28, 1987, *reprinted in* Basic Documents Pertaining to Human Rights in the Inter-American System, OEA/Ser.L.V/II.82 doc.6 rev.1 at 83 (1992), *available at* http://www.oas.org/juridico/english/Treaties/a-51.html (last visited Oct. 24, 2004).

236. Unlike CAT and the European Court of Human Rights' case law on *refoulement,* the Inter-American Convention threshold for knowledge of likelihood of torture is not "substantial" grounds, but rather, *any* ground for belief that a person will be subject to torture or CID treatment.

237. The Convention Governing the Specific Aspects of Refugee Problems in Africa, *adopted* 1974, *entered into force* June 20, 1974, 1001 U.N.T.S. 45, *available through* http://www.africa-union.org/home/Welcome.htm (last visited Oct. 24, 2004), art. 2(3) ("No person shall be subjected by a Member State to measures such as rejection at the frontier, return or expulsion, which would compel him to return to or remain in a territory where his life, physical integrity or liberty would be threatened....").

238. *Adopted* 26 June 1981, *entered into force* Oct. 21, 1986, OAU Doc. CAB/LEG/67/3, Rev. 5, *reprinted in* 21 I.L.M. 58 (1982), *available through* http://www.africa-union.org/home/Welcome.htm (last visited Oct. 24, 2004), art. 2(3) ("No person shall be subjected by a Member State to measures such as rejection at the frontier, return or expulsion, which would compel him to return or to remain in a territory where his life, physical integrity or liberty would be threatened for the reasons set out in Article I, paragraphs 1 and 2").

239. GUY S. GOODWIN-GILL, INTERNATIONAL LAW AND THE MOVEMENT OF PERSONS BETWEEN STATES 141 (1978); G. STENBERG, "NON-EXPULSION AND *NON-REFOULEMENT:* THE PROHIBITION AGAINST REMOVAL OF REFUGEES WITH SPECIAL REFERENCE TO ARTICLES 32 AND 33 OF THE 1951 CONVENTION RELATING TO THE STATUS OF REFUGEES (1989); Martin A. Rogoff, *Interpretation of International Agreements by Domestic Court and the Politics of*

International Treaty Relations: Reflections on Some Recent Decisions of the United States Supreme Court, 11 Am. U.J. Int'l L. & Pol'y 559, 579 (1996); David Weissbrodt and Isabel Hörtreitere, *The Principle of Non-refoulement: Article 3 of the Convention Against Torture and Other Cruel, Inhuman or Degrading Treatment or Punishment in Comparison with the Non-refoulement Provisions of Other International Human Rights Treaties,* 5 Buff. Hum. Rts. L. Rev., 1, 7 (1999); Arthur Helton, *Applying Human Rights Law in U.S. Asylum Cases,* 3 Int'l Civ. Liberties Rep. 1, 2 (2000); A. Montavon-McKillip, *CAT Among Pigeons: The Convention Against Torture, A Precarious Intersection Between International Human Rights Law and U.S. Immigration,* 44 Ariz. L. Rev. 247, 269 (2002).

240. CAT, *supra* note 9, art. 4 (emphasis added).

241. *Id.,* art. 1 ("For the purposes of this Convention, the term 'torture' means any act. . .inflicted by or at the instigation of or with the consent or acquiescence of a public official or other person acting in an official capacity.").

242. Burgers & Danelius, *supra* note 183, at 120.

243. Burgers & Danelius, *supra* note 183, at 120, 129, 130.

244. For a discussion of individual criminal liability under U.S. law, *see* Section VIII.A.

245. Burgers & Danelius, *supra* note 183, at 120.

246. Article 6 of CAT, *supra* note 9, provides:

1. Upon being satisfied, after an examination of information available to it, that the circumstances so warrant, any State Party in whose territory a person alleged to have committed any offense referred to in article 4 is present shall take him into custody or take other legal measures to ensure his presence. The custody and other legal measures shall be as provided in the law of that State but may be continued only for such time as is necessary to enable any criminal or extradition proceedings to be instituted.
2. Such State shall immediately make a preliminary inquiry into the facts.
3. Any person in custody pursuant to paragraph 1 of this article shall be assisted in communicating immediately with the nearest appropriate representative of the State of which he is a national, or, if he is a stateless person, with the representative of the State where he usually resides.
4. When a State, pursuant to this article, has taken a person into custody, it shall immediately notify the States referred to in article 5, paragraph 1, of the fact that such person is in custody and of the circumstances which warrant his detention. The State which makes the preliminary inquiry contemplated in paragraph 2 of this article shall promptly report its findings to the said States and shall indicate whether it intends to exercise jurisdiction.

247. CAT Article 7(1) provides: "1. The State Party in the territory under whose jurisdiction a person alleged to have committed any offense referred to in article 4 is found shall in the cases contemplated in article 5, if it does not extradite him, submit the case to its competent authorities for the purpose of prosecution." CAT, *supra* note 9.

248. *Id.,* art. 10:

1. Each State Party shall ensure that education and information regarding the prohibition against torture are fully included in the training of law enforcement personnel, civil or military, medical personnel, public officials and other persons who may be involved in the custody, interrogation or treatment of any individual subjected to any form of arrest, detention or imprisonment.
2. Each State Party shall include this prohibition in the rules or instructions issued in regard to the duties and functions of any such person.

Unlike other CAT provisions (e.g. those imposing obligations on states party to review interrogation methods and techniques (art. 11), investigate allegations of torture and CID (art. 12), adjudicate allegations of torture or CID by an individual (art. 13)), Article 10's obligations are not based on the state party's jurisdiction over the territory in which its agents may be conducting interrogations. *See also* art. 16(1).

249. *Id.,* art. 11 ("Each State Party shall keep under systematic review interrogation rules, instructions, methods and practices as well as arrangements for the custody and treatment of persons subjected to any form of arrest, detention or imprisonment in any territory under its jurisdiction, with a view to preventing any cases of torture.").

250. *Id.,* art. 12 ("Each State Party shall ensure that its competent authorities proceed to a prompt and impartial investigation, wherever there is reasonable ground to believe that an act of torture has been committed in any territory under its jurisdiction.") and art. 13 ("Each State Party shall ensure that any individual who alleges he has been subjected to torture in any territory under its jurisdiction has the right to complain to, and to have his case promptly and impartially examined by, its competent authorities. Steps shall be taken to ensure that the complainant and witnesses are protected against all ill-treatment or intimidation as a consequence of his complaint or any evidence given.").

251. *Id.,* art. 14:

1. Each State Party shall ensure in its legal system that the victim of an act of torture obtains redress and has an enforceable right to fair and adequate compensation, including the means for as full rehabilitation as possible. In the event of the death of the victim as a result of an act of torture, his dependants shall be entitled to compensation.
2. Nothing in this article shall affect any right of the victim or other persons to compensation which may exist under national law.

252. *Id.*, art. 5(1). The broadest basis of jurisdiction in the context of Extraordinary Renditions is that of Article 5(1)(b), requiring that the United States exercise criminal jurisdiction over a U.S. national who directly participates in, or is complicit or otherwise participates in torture. According to the U.S. CAT ratification legislative history, implementing jurisdictional legislation was required only for this provision and for the Article 5(2) requirement that the United States extend its criminal jurisdiction over foreign offenders who commit torture abroad and are later found in a territory under U.S. jurisdiction. Sen. Exec. Rpt. 101-30, Resolution of Advice and Consent to Ratification (1990). This domestic legislation was enacted as 18 U.S.C. §2340A(a).

253. Article 5(2) can be seen as a basis for the assertion of universal jurisdiction, but this article does not obligate a state to establish jurisdiction over an alleged offender who is not within its territory. CAT, *supra* note 9.

254. *Id.*, art. 5(3) ("This Convention does not exclude any criminal jurisdiction exercised in accordance with internal law.").

255. Burgers & Danelius, *supra* note 183, at 3.

256. Vienna Convention, *supra* note 183, art. 31(1).

257. In addition, if the requisite *mens rea* element is met for any participating U.S. official or non-state actor, (*see* Section VIII.A. of this Report), an argument could be made that the United States is required to assert jurisdiction if U.S.-registered ships or aircraft are used to transfer an individual to any state where the individual faces the danger of torture.

258. Burgers & Danelius, *supra* note 183, at 131.

259. *Id.*, at 133. These provisions include CAT Articles 6 (requiring a state party in whose territory an individual is alleged to have committed a violation of CAT Article 4 to take that individual into custody, after ascertaining that the circumstances so warrant, in order to investigate the allegations) and 7 (requiring a state party either to extradite or prosecute an individual alleged to have committed a violation of CAT Article 4, who is in a territory under the jurisdiction of the state party).

260. S. Treaty Doc. No. 100-20, at 5, 9–14 (1988).

261. 18 U.S.C. §2340 *et seq*. Domestic legislation was required because the Senate's advice and consent to CAT ratification was subject to the declaration that CAT was not self-executing. Sen. Exec. Rpt. 101-30, Resolution of Advice and Consent to Ratification (1990). (Ratification Resolution) One of the reservations was with respect to CAT Article 16, which requires states to prevent lesser forms of cruel and unusual punishment that do not constitute torture. According to the reservation, the United States considered itself bound to Article 16 to the extent that such cruel, unusual, and inhuman treatment or punishment

was prohibited by the Fifth, Eighth, and/or Fourteenth Amendments to the U.S. Constitution. *Id.; see also* CRS Report, *supra* note 108.

262. *See* note 9 of this Report.

263. Ratification Resolution, *supra* note 261, at II.(1)(b); *see also* Section VIII.A. of this Report.

264. Ratification Resolution, *supra* note 261, at II.(1)(b).

265. *See, e.g., Zheng v. Ashcroft,* 332 F.3d 1186 (9th Cir. 2003) (declaring that the correct inquiry in deciding whether a Chinese immigrant was entitled to relief from removal from the United States under CAT was not whether Chinese officials would commit torture against him, but whether public officials would turn a blind eye to the immigrant's torture by specified individuals); *Ontunez-Turios v. Ashcroft,* 303 F.3d 341 (5th Cir. 2002) (upholding Board of Immigration Appeals' deportation order, but noting that "willful blindness" constitutes acquiescence under CAT); *Bullies v. Nye,* 239 F.Supp. 2d 518 (M.D. Pa. 2003) (under CAT implementing regulations, acquiescence by government to torture by non-governmental agents requires either willful acceptance by government officials or at least turning a blind eye); *see also Pascual-Garcia v. Ashcroft,* 73 Fed.Appx. 232 (9th Cir. 2003) (holding that relief under CAT does not require that torture will occur while victim is in the custody or physical control of a public official).

266. *See, e.g., Moshud v. Blackman,* 68 Fed. Appx. 328 (3rd Cir. 2003) (denying alien's claim to reopen removal proceedings to assert a CAT claim based on her fear of female genital mutilation in Ghana, because although the practice was widespread, the Ghanian government had not acquiesced to the practice because it had been made illegal and public officials had condemned the practice); *Matter of S-V-,* 22 I&N Dec. 1306 (BIA 2000) (holding that protection under CAT does not extend to persons fearing entities that a government is unable to control).

267. Ratification Resolution, *supra* note 261, at II.(1)(e). *See also* CRS Report, *supra* note 104, at 5.

268. Ratification Resolution, *supra* note 261, at II.(2). This is the standard commonly used by the United States in determining whether to withhold removal for fear of persecution. *See INS v. Stevic,* 467 U.S. 407, 429–30 (1984); *See also* CRS Report, *supra* note 108, at 6.

269. U.S. Initial CAT Report, *supra* note 103, para. 5.

270. *Id.* The same sentiment was expressed by President Bush on the United Nations International Day in Support of Victims of Torture: "The United States is committed to the world-wide elimination of torture and we are leading this fight by example." President George W. Bush, Statement by the President on the United Nations International Day in Support of Victims of Torture (June 26, 2003) (transcript *available at* http://www.whitehouse.gov/news/releases/2003/06/20030626-3.html (last visited Oct. 25, 2004).

271. U.S. Initial CAT Report, *supra* note 103, para. 165.

272. 18 U.S.C., §2340A(a).

273. *Id.*

274. *Id.*

275. 18 U.S.C. §2340A(b).

276. FARRA, *supra* note 100, §2242(b).

277. 8 C.F.R. §235.3. Section 212(a)(6)(C) of the INA provides: Except as otherwise provided in this Act, aliens who are inadmissible under the following pragraphs are ineligible to receive visas and ineligible to be admitted to the United States:. . .

(i) Any alien who, by fraud or willfully misrepresenting a material fact, seeks to procure (or has sought to procure or has procured) a visa, other documentation, or admission into the United States or other benefit provided under this Act is inadmissible;

(ii) (I) Any alien who falsely represents, or has falsely represented, himself or herself to be a citizen of the United States for any purpose or benefit under this Act (including section 274A) or any other Federal or State law is inadmissible.(II) In the case of an alien making a representation described in subclause (I), if each natural parent of the alien (or, in the case of an adopted alien, each adoptive parent of the alien) is or was a citizen (whether by birth or naturalization), the alien permanently resided in the United States prior to attaining the age of 16, and the alien reasonably believed at the time of making such representation that he or she was a citizen, the alien shall not be considered to be inadmissible under any provision of this subsection based on such representation.

(iii) Waiver authorized.-For provision authorizing waiver of clause (i), see subsection (I).

Section 212(a)(7) of the INA enumerates required documentation for entry to the United States.

278. 8 C.F.R. §235.8.

279. Section 212(a)(3)(A) of the INA provides, in relevant part: "Any alien who a consular officer or the Attorney General knows, or has reasonable ground to believe, seeks to enter the United States to engage solely, principally, or incidentally in: (i) any activity (I) to violate any law of the United States relating to espionage or sabotage or (II) to violate or evade any law prohibiting the export from the United States of goods, technology, or sensitive information, . . . or (iii) any activity a purpose of which is the opposition to, or the control or overthrow of, the Government of the United States by force, violence, or other unlawful means, is inadmissible." INA Section 212(a)(3)(B) provides, in relevant part and with certain exceptions that the following people are ineligible for entry to the United States: "Any alien who (I) has engaged in a terrorist activity, (II) a consular officer or the Attorney General knows, or has reasonable ground to believe, is engaged in or is likely to engage after entry in any terrorist activity (as defined in clause (iv)), (III) has, under circumstances indicating an intention to cause death or serious bodily harm, incited terrorist activity, (IV) is a representative (as defined in clause (v)) of (aa) a foreign terrorist organization, as designated by the Secretary of State under section 219, or (bb) a political, social or other similar group whose public endorsement of acts of terrorist activity the Secretary of State has determined undermines United States efforts to reduce or eliminate terrorist activities, (V) is a member of a foreign terrorist organization, as designated by the Secretary under section 219, or is inadmissible. An alien who is an officer, official, representative, or spokesman of the Palestine Liberation Organization is considered, for purposes of this Act, to be engaged in a terrorist activity. (VI) has used the alien's position of prominence within any country to endorse or espouse terrorist activity, or to persuade others to support terrorist activity or a terrorist organization, in a way that the Secretary of State has determined undermines United States efforts to reduce or eliminate terrorist activities, or (VII) is the spouse or child of an alien who is inadmissible under this section, if the activity causing the alien to be found inadmissible occurred within the last 5 years." Section 212(a)(3)(C) provides, with certain exceptions, that "[a]n alien whose entry or proposed activities in the United States the Secretary of State has reasonable ground to believe would have potentially serious adverse foreign policy consequences for the United States is inadmissible."

280. 8 C.F.R. §235.8(a). For a detailed description of summary exclusion procedures, *see* CRS Report, *supra* note 108. If possible, the relevant officer or judge must take a brief statement from the alien, and the alien must be notified of the actions being taken against him and of his right to submit a written statement and additional information for consideration by the attorney general, who has authority to assess whether grounds exist to exclude the alien. INA §235(c)(2)(B). If the attorney general concludes, on the basis of confidential information, that the alien is inadmissible on security or terror-related grounds and the release of such information would be prejudicial on security or safety grounds, the CBP regional director is authorized to deny any further inquiry as to the alien's status and either order the alien removed or order disposal of the case as the director deems appropriate. *See* 8 C.F.R. § 235.8(b)(1). If the alien's designation as inadmissible is based on non-confidential information, however, the regional director has discretion to either conduct a further examination of the alien concerning his admissibility or to refer the alien's case to an immigration judge for a hearing prior to ordering removal. 8 C.F.R. § 235.8(b)(2). The regional director's written, signed decision must be served to the alien unless it contains confidential information prejudicial to U.S. security, in which case the alien shall be served a separate written order indicating disposition of the case, but with confidential information deleted. 8 C.F.R. § 235.8(b)(3).

281. 8 C.F.R. §235.8(a).

282. 8 C.F.R. §235.8(b).

283. 8 C.F.R. §235.8(c).

284. FARRA Regulations section 208.30 provides that "the Service has exclusive jurisdiction to make credible fear determinations [for individuals inadmissibile on terrorist-related grounds], and the Executive Office for Immigration Review has exclusive jurisdiction to review such determinations." 8 C.F.R. §208.30. It also specifies procedures for making a determination of credible fear claims.

285. 8 C.F.R. §235.8(b)(4).

286. 8 C.F.R. §208.16(4).

287. 8 C.F.R. § 208.16(c)(2).
288. *Id.*
289. 8 C.F.R. § 208.16(c)(3).
290. *See, e.g., In Re S- V-,* 22 I.&N Dec. 1306, 2000 WL 562836 (B.I.A. 2000), *overuled on other grounds, Zheng v. Ashcroft,* 332 F.3d 1186 (9th Cir. 2003); *In re M-B-A,* 231 I.&N Dec. 474, 2002 WL 31201697 (B.I.A. 2002).
291. *See Matter of M-B-A,* 23 I&N Dec. 474 (BIA 2002).
292. 8 C.F.R. §208.16(c)(4).
293. 22 C.F.R. §95.2(b).
294. 22 C.F.R. § 95.2(a)(1).
295. 22 C.F.R. § 95.2(b).
296. 22 C.F.R. § 95.2(a)(2).
297. U.S. Initial CAT Report, *supra* note 103, para. 167.
298. *Id.*
299. 22 C.F.R. § 95.4.
300. *Id.*
301. *Id.* In *Cornejo-Barreto v. Seifert,* 218 F.3d 1004 (9th Cir. 2000), the Ninth Circuit's stated that individuals who fear torture upon return to a state of extradition may present a habeas claim under the general habeas statute, 22 U.S.C. §2241, alleging violation of CAT, following the secretary of state's decision to return the alien. Subsequently, the Ninth Circuit held that its statement in *Cornejo* was advisory and nonbinding. *Cornejo-Barreto v. Seifert,* 379 F.3d 1075 (9th Cir. 2004). However, more recently the Court agreed to a rehearing *en banc.* 2004 WL (9th Cir. Oct. 19, 2004).
302. Generally, judicial appeal or review is available for any action, decision, or claim raised under CAT only insofar as it is part of a review of a final order of alien removal pursuant to INA section 242. 8 U.S.C. §1231.
303. FARRA, *supra* note 100, §2242 (emphasis added).
304. *Cf. Sale v. Haitian Centers Council Inc.,* 509 U.S. 155, 183, 113 S.Ct. 2549, 2565 (1993) (rejecting argument that the *non-refoulement* protections of Article 33 of the Refugee Convention had extraterritorial applicability to prevent *refoulement* of Haitians intercepted by U.S. officials on the high seas and holding that "a treaty cannot impose uncontemplated extraterritorial obligations on those who ratify it through no more than its general humanitarian intent."). The case was then brought before the Inter-American Commission on Human Rights, which stated that Article 33 of the Refugee Convention is not subject to geographical limitations. *Haitian Centre for Human Rights v. United States,* Case No. 10.675, Inter-Am. C.H.R. 51/95, OEA/ser.L/V./II.95 doc. 7 rev. at 550 (1997).
305. The ICCPR, *supra* note 9, was ratified by the United States in 1992, subject to a number of reservations, understandings and declarations. *See* 138 Cong. Rec. S4781-01 (1992). As it would later do in its ratification of CAT, the United States sought to protect its interpretation of its international obligations in accordance with domestic jurisprudence and ratified the ICCPR with the reservation that "the United States considers itself bound by article 7 to the extent that 'cruel, inhuman or degrading treatment or punishment' means the cruel and unusual treatment or punishment prohibited by the Fifth, Eighth, and/or Fourteenth Amendments to the Constitution of the United States." *See* International Covenant on Civil and Political Rights, Declarations, Reservations and Understandings made by the United States, *available at* http://www.unhchr.ch/tbs/doc.nsf/0/80256404004ff315c125638b005f309e?OpenDocument (last visited Oct. 25, 2004).
306. ICCPR, *supra* note 9, art. 7.
307. Human Rights Committee, General Comment 20, *Article 7,* UN Doc. A/47/40 (1992) *reprinted in* Compilation of General Comments and General Recommendations Adopted by Human Rights Treaty Bodies, U.N. Doc. HRI\GEN\1\Rev.1 at 30 (1994), (HRC General Comment 20), para. 9.
308. ICCPR, *supra* note 9, art. 2(1) states: "Each State Party to the present Covenant undertakes to respect and to ensure to all individuals within its territory and subject to its jurisdiction the rights recognized within the present Covenant, without distinction of any kind such as race, colour, sex, language, religion, political or other opinion, national or social origin, property, birth or other status."

309. HRC General Comment 31, *supra* note 13, para. 12; *see also* HRC General Comment 20, *supra* note 307, para. 9.

310. *Kindler v. Canada,* Communication No. 470/1991, Human Rights Committee, UN Doc. CCPR/C/48/D/470/1991 (1993), para. 13.1.

311. *Ng v. Canada,* Communication No. 469/1991, Human Rights Committee, UN Doc. CCPR/C/49/D/469/1991 (1994), para. 6.2.

312. *See, e.g., Mrs. G. T. v. Australia,* Communication No. 706/1996, UN Doc. CCPR/C/61/D/706/1996 (1997), para. 8.4 ("A real risk is to be deduced from the intent of the country to which the person concerned is to be deported, as well as from the pattern of conduct shown by the country in similar cases.").

313. Weissbrodt & Hörtreitere, *supra* note 239, at 44–45 (citing Ralf Alleweldt, *Schutz Vor Abschiebung Bei Drohender Folter Oder Unmenschlicher Oder Erniedrigender Behandlung Oder Strafe: Refoulement-Verbote Im Volkerrecht Und Im Deutschen Recht Unter Besonderer Berucksichtigung Von Artikel 3 Der Europaischen Menschenrechtskonvention Und Artikel 1 Des Grundgesetzes* [*Protection Against Expulsion In The Case of Threat of Torture or Inhuman or Degrading Treatment or Punishment*], *and* MANFRED NOWAK, THE UN COVENANT ON CIVIL AND POLITICAL RIGHTS: CCPR COMMENTARY 131 et seq. (1993)).

314. *See Chahal v. United Kingdom,* 23 Eur. Ct. H.R. 413 (ser. A) (1996), para. 79–82, 87–107 (in case where the United Kingdom sought to expel asylum seeker based on assertion that he was a threat to national security, the Court insisted on absolute nature of Article 3 protections even in the face of an alleged threat to national security, including in the context of expulsion cases, and found that despite an improvement in human rights conditions in India, abuses by security forces continued and the asylum seeker faced a "real risk" of ill-treatment by those forces if returned to India); *Soering v. United Kingdom,* 11 EHRR 439, 161 Eur. Ct. H.R. (ser. A) (1989) paras. 91, 96, 99 (assessment of "real risk" includes assessment of conditions in the state to which the individual is to be extradited, including the likelihood that the particular individual will be subject to ill-treatment in the receiving state that would violate Article 3); *Cruz Varas v. Sweden,* 201 Eur. Ct. H.R. (ser. A) (1991) paras. 70, 77 to 86 (even though individual asserted he had been tortured upon his previous forced transfer to Chile by Sweden, where political conditions in Chile had changed at the time of potential subsequent expulsion, and where the individual's assertion of torture were not substantiated and deemed to lack credibility by the Court, there were no substantial grounds for belief that he faced a real risk of treatment prohibited by European Convention Article 3); *Vilvarajah and Others v. United Kingdom,* 215 Eur. Ct. H.R. (ser. A) (1991) at paras. 140–44 (requiring that the "real risk" be current and subjectively be faced by the individual; evidence of mass violations of human rights, "random" acts of torture against the population by security forces, or evidence of prior torture suffered by applicants did not suffice to show such a real risk).

315. Weissbrodt & Hörtreitere, *supra* note 239, at 1, 50, 55–56.

316. Human Rights Committee, General Comment No. 15, *The Position of Aliens under the Covenant, reprinted in* Compilation of General Comments and General Recommendations Adopted by Human Rights Treaty Bodies, U.N. Doc. HRI\GEN\1\Rev.1 at 18 (1994), (HRC General Comment 15), para. 1 ("Reports from States parties have often failed to take into account that each State party must ensure the rights in the Covenant to "all individuals within its territory and subject to its jurisdiction" (art. 2, para. 1). In general, the rights set forth in the Covenant apply to everyone, irrespective of reciprocity, and irrespective of his or her nationality or statelessness."). *See also* Human Rights Committee, General Comment No. 18, *Non-Discrimination, reprinted in* Compilation of General Comments and General Recommendations Adopted by Human Rights Treaty Bodies, U.N. Doc. HRI\GEN\1\Rev.1 at 26 (1994) (HRC General Comment 18), para. 1 ("Non discrimination, together with equality before the law and equal protection of the law without any discrimination, constitute a basic and general principle relating to the protection of human rights. Thus, article 2, paragraph 1, of the International Covenant on Civil and Political Rights obligates each State party to respect and ensure to all persons within its territory and subject to its jurisdiction the rights recognized in the Covenant without distinction of any kind, such as race, colour, sex, language, religion, political or other opinion, national or social origin, property, birth or other status.").

317. HRC General Comment 15, *supra* note 316, para. 2.

318. *Id.,* para. 7.

319. HRC General Comment 20, *supra* note 307, para. 8 ("The Committee notes that it is not sufficient for the implementation of article 7 to prohibit such treatment or punishment or to make it a crime. States parties should inform the Committee of the legislative, administrative, judicial and other measures they take to prevent and punish acts of torture and cruel, inhuman and degrading treatment in any territory under their jurisdiction.").

320. *Id.* para. 2 ("It is the duty of the State party to afford everyone protection through legislative and other measures as may be necessary against the acts prohibited by article 7, whether inflicted by people acting in their official capacity, outside their official capacity or in a private capacity."); HRC General Comment 31, *supra* note 13, para. 8 ("The Covenant cannot be viewed as a substitute for domestic criminal or civil law. However the positive obligations on States Parties to ensure Covenant rights will only be fully discharged if individuals are protected by the State, not just against violations of Covenant rights by its agents, but also against acts committed by private persons or entities that would impair the enjoyment of Covenant rights in so far as they are amenable to application between private persons or entities. . . . States are reminded of the interrelationship between the positive obligations imposed under article 2 and the need to provide effective remedies in the event of breach under article 2, paragraph 3. The Covenant itself envisages in some articles certain areas where there are positive obligations on States Parties to address the activities of private persons or entities. . . . It is also implicit in article 7 that States Parties have to take positive measures to ensure that private persons or entities do not inflict torture or cruel, inhuman or degrading treatment or punishment on others within their power."); *see also* HRC General Comment 20, *supra* note 307, at para. 13 ("States parties should indicate when presenting their reports the provisions of their criminal law which penalize torture and cruel, inhuman and degrading treatment or punishment, specifying the penalties applicable to such acts, whether committed by public officials or other persons acting on behalf of the State, or by private persons. Those who violate article 7, whether by encouraging, ordering, tolerating or perpetrating prohibited acts, must be held responsible.").

321. HRC General Comment 31, *supra* note 13, para. 8 ("There may be circumstances in which a failure to ensure Covenant rights as required by article 2 would give rise to violations by States Parties of those rights, as a result of States Parties' permitting or failing to take appropriate measures or to exercise due diligence to prevent, punish, investigate or redress the harm caused by such acts by private persons or entities.").

322. ICCPR, *supra* note 9, art. 2(1); *see also* Concluding Observations of the Human Rights Committee, Cyprus, UN Doc. CCPR/C/79/Add.88, para 3 (1998) (Cyprus not obligated to apply ICCPR protections to territory over which it did not exercise control because of occupation by another state). *But see* Concluding Observations of the Human Rights Committee, Bosnia and Herzegovina, UN Doc. CCPR/C/79/Add.14, para 4 (1992) (Republic of Bosnia-Herzegovina legally responsible for acts in territory over which it had factual and effective control, and also other parts of its territory). Professor Dominic McGoldrick sees this decision as "best understood in the context of Bosnia's newly attained statehood." Dominic McGoldrick, *Extraterritorial Application of the International Covenant on Civil and Political Rights, in* EXTRATERRITORIAL APPLICATION OF HUMAN RIGHTS TREATIES (FONS COOMANS AND MENNO T. KAMMINGA, eds., 2004), 50.

323. HRC General Comment 31, *supra* note 13, para. 10 ("States Parties are required by article 2, paragraph 1, to respect and to ensure the Covenant rights to all persons who may be within their territory and to all persons subject to their jurisdiction. This means that a State party must respect and ensure the rights laid down in the Covenant to anyone within the power or effective control of that State Party, even if not situated within the territory of the State Party. . . . [T]he enjoyment of Covenant rights is not limited to citizens of States Parties but must also be available to all individuals, regardless of nationality or statelessness, such as asylum seekers, refugees, migrant workers and other persons, who may find themselves in the territory or subject to the jurisdiction of the State Party. This principle also applies to those within the power or effective control of the forces of a State Party acting outside its territory, regardless of the circumstances in which such power or effective control was obtained, such as forces constituting a national contingent of a State Party assigned to an international peace-keeping or peace-enforcement operation.") and para. 12 ("article 2's obligation requiring that States Parties respect and ensure the Covenant rights of all persons in their territory and all persons under their control entails an obligation not to extradite, deport, expel or otherwise remove a person from their territory, where there are substantial grounds for believing

that there is a real risk of irreparable harm); *see also* Concluding Observations of the Human Rights Committee, Belgium, UN Doc. CCPR/C/79/Add.99 (1998), para. 14 (expressing concern about actions of Belgian soldiers in Somalia, and acknowledging that Belgium recognized the applicability of ICCPR to those actions); Concluding Observations of the Human Rights Committee, Croatia, UN Doc. CCPR/C/79/Add.15 (1992), paras. 7 and 10 (noting that Croatia was responsible for ICCPR violations in areas of Bosnia-Herzegovina under the control of Croatian military).

324. *Ng v. Canada,* Communication No. 469/1991, Human Rights Committee, UN Doc. CCPR/C/49/D/469/ 1991 (1994), para. 6.1 (extradition of applicant from Canada to the United States where the applicant could face the death penalty could violate Article 7 and render Canada liable for ICCPR violation because "if a State party takes a decision relating to a person within its jurisdiction, and the necessary and foreseeable consequence is that this person's rights under the Covenant will be violated in another jurisdiction, the State party itself may be in violation of the Covenant."); *see also Kindler v. Canada,* Communication No. 470/1991, Human Rights Committee, UN Doc. CCPR/C/48/D/470/1991 (1993) (same); *Lopez Burgos v. Uruguay,* Communication No. R.12/52, Human Rights Committee, UN Doc. Supp. No. 40 (A/36/40) at 176 (1981), paras. 12.1–12.3 (in case involving the kidnapping of Uruguayan from Argentina by Uruguayan "security and intelligence forces," Human Rights Committee held that Article 2 (1) "does not imply that the State party concerned cannot be held accountable for violations of rights under the Covenant which its agents commit upon the territory of another State, whether with the acquiescence of the Government of the State or in opposition to it.....[I]t would be unconscionable to so interpret the responsibility under Article 2 of the Covenant as to permit a State party to perpetrate violations of the Covenant on the territory of another State, which violations it could not perpetrate on its on territory."); *Celiberti v. Uruguay,* Communication No. R.13/56, Human Rights Committee, UN Doc. Supp. No. 40 (A/36/40) at 185 (1981). Based on the reasoning applied by the Human Rights Committee in these cases, Professor McGoldrick thinks it makes no difference if the applicant had not been a Uruguayan national —it is the acts of arrest and abduction that violate ICCPR protections and bring the individual into the jurisdiction of the state committing those acts. McGoldrick, *supra* note 322, at 62.

325. *Ng v. Canada,* Communication No. 469/1991, UN Doc. CCPR/C/49/D/469/1991 (1994), para. 6.1; *Kindler v. Canada,* Communication No. 470/1991, Human Rights Committee, UN Doc. CCPR/C/48/D/470/1991 (1993); *Lopez Burgos v. Uruguay,* Communication No. R.12/52, Human Rights Committee, UN Doc. Supp. No. 40 (A/36/40) at 176 (1981), paras. 12.1–12.3; *Celiberti v. Uruguay,* Communication No. R.13/56, Human Rights Committee, UN Doc. Supp. No. 40 (A/36/40), at 185 (1981).

326. HRC General Comment 31, *supra* note 13, para. 8 ("[T]he positive obligations on States Parties to ensure Covenant rights will only be fully discharged if individuals are protected by the State, not just against violations of Covenant rights by its agents, but also against acts committed by private persons or entities that would impair the enjoyment of Covenant rights in so far as they are amenable to application between private persons or entities....States are reminded of the interrelationship between the positive obligations imposed under article 2 and the need to provide effective remedies in the event of breach under article 2, paragraph 3. The Covenant itself envisages in some articles certain areas where there are positive obligations on States Parties to address the activities of private persons or entities.").

327. *Id.* ("It is also implicit in article 7 that States Parties have to take positive measures to ensure that private persons or entities do not inflict torture or cruel, inhuman or degrading treatment or punishment on others within their power.").

328. For a detailed discussion of the scope of extraterritorial application of the ICCPR, *See* McGoldrick, *supra* note 322.

329. HRC General Comment 31, *supra* note 322, para. 12 ("article 2's obligation requiring that States Parties respect and ensure the Covenant rights of all persons in their territory and all persons under their control entails an obligation not to extradite, deport, expel or otherwise remove a person from their territory, where there are substantial grounds for believing that there is a real risk of irreparable harm").

330. *Id.*, at paras. 15, and 18 ("Where the investigations referred to in paragraph 15 reveal violations of certain Covenant rights, States Parties must ensure that those responsible are brought to justice. As with failure to investigate, failure to bring to justice perpetrators of such violations could in and of itself give rise to a separate breach of the Covenant. These obligations arise notably in respect of those violations

recognized as criminal under either domestic or international law, such as torture and similar cruel, inhuman and degrading treatment (article 7).").

331. HRC General Comment 20, *supra* note 307, para. 10.

332. *Id.* para. 18.

333. *Id.*, para. 14; *see also* HRC General Comment 31, *supra* note 13, at para. 7 ("Article 2 requires that States Parties adopt legislative, judicial, administrative, educative and other appropriate measures in order to fulfill their legal obligations.").

334. *See* 138 Cong. Rec. S4783-84 (daily ed. Apr. 2, 1992); United Nations Treaty Collection: Declarations and Reservations, *available at* http://www.unhchr.ch/html/menu3/b/treaty12_asp.htm (last visited Oct. 25, 2004).

335. *See* International Covenant on Civil and Political Rights, Declarations, Reservations and Understandings made by the United States, *available at* http://www.unhchr.ch/tbs/doc.nsf/887ff7374eb89574c1256a2a0027ba1f/80256404004ff315c125638b005f309e?OpenDocument (last visited Oct. 25, 2004).

336. *See* U.S. Const. art. VI, §2 ("This Constitution and the laws of the United States which shall be made in pursuance thereof, and all treaties which shall be made under the authority of the United States, shall be the supreme law of the land); *see also* Restatement, *supra* note 127, at cmt. H ("If an international agreement. . . is non-self-executing, the United States is under an international obligation to adjust its laws and institutions as may be necessary to give effect to the agreement."); Louis Henkin, *Treaties in a Constitutional Democracy,* 10 Mich. J. Int'l L. 406, 425 (1989) ("The international obligation of the United States under a treaty is immediate, whether a treaty is self-executing or not. . . . [T]he United States has an obligation to enact necessary legislation promptly so as to enable it to carry out its obligations under the treaty.").

337. *See also* ICCPR, *supra* note 9, art. 50 ("the provisions of the present Covenant shall extend to all parts of federal states without any exceptions or limitations.").

338. Geneva Conventions, *supra* note 173.

339. Emanuela-Chiara Gillard, *International Humanitarian Law and Extraterritorial State Conduct, in* Extraterritorial Application of Human Rights Treaties, (Fons Coomans and Menno T. Kamminga eds., 2004), 27. Common Article 2 of the Geneva Conventions provides that the Conventions are applicable to any "declared war or any other armed conflict between two or more High Contracting Parties even though the state of war has not been recognized." Geneva Conventions, *supra* note 173, art. 2. An influential source of interpretation of the Geneva Conventions is the International Committee of the Red Cross's Commentary on the Geneva Conventions, which states that "any difference arising between two States and leading to the intervention of armed forces is an armed conflict within the meaning of Article 2, even if one of the Parties denies the existence of a state of war." ICRC Commentary on the Geneva Convention Relative to the Protection of Civilian Persons in Time of War, 20 (J.S. Pictet ed., 1958). In addition, Common Article 3 of the Geneva Conventions applies "in case of armed conflict not of an international character occurring in the territory of one of the High Contracting Parties." Geneva Conventions, *supra* note 173, art. 3.

340. *See* Geneva Conventions, *supra* note 173, art. 2.

341. *Id.*

342. For a discussion of the standards used to determine a state's "occupation" by another state, *see* Association of the Bar of the City of New York, *Supplement to the Report on Human Rights Standards Applicable to the United States' Interrogation of Detainees* (2004) (HR Standards Supplement), *available at* http://www.abcny.org/pdf/ABCNY-InterrogationReportSupp.pdf (last visited Oct. 24, 2004), at 5.

343. Both medical personnel and chaplains may, however, still be entitled to POW protections under Geneva III even though they are not entitled to POW status. *See* Geneva III, *supra* note 173, art. 33.

344. Article 4 of Geneva III, *supra* note 173, provides, in part:

> Prisoners of war, in the sense of the present Convention, are persons belonging to one of the following categories, who have fallen into the power of the enemy:

1. Members of the armed forces of a Party to the conflict as well as members of militias or volunteer corps forming part of such armed forces.
2. Members of other militias and members of other volunteer corps, including those of organized resistance movements, belonging to a Party to the conflict and operating in or outside their own territory, even if this territory is occupied, provided that such militias or volunteer corps, including such organized resistance movements, fulfill the following conditions:

   (a) That of being commanded by a person responsible for his subordinates;

   (b) That of having a fixed distinctive sign recognizable at a distance;

   (c) That of carrying arms openly;

   (d) That of conducting their operations in accordance with the laws and customs of war.
3. Members of regular armed forces who profess allegiance to a government or an authority not recognized by the Detaining Power.

Articles 43 and 44 of Additional Protocol I set out the circumstances in which an individual may be considered a prisoner of war in conflicts governed by that protocol.

345. *See* Geneva III, *supra* note 173, art. 5; *see also,* U.S. Dept. of Army, Field Manual 27-10, *Law of Land Warfare,* art. 71 (1956); U.S. Dept. of Army, Regulation 190-8 Military Police, *Enemy Prisoners of War, Retained Personnel, Civilian Internees and Other Detainees,* §1-5 (a)(2) (1997). Under U.S. military regulations, a "competent tribunal" pursuant to Article 5 of Geneva III consists of three commissioned officers. The regulations also require that persons whose status is to be determined: be advised of their rights; be permitted to attend all open sessions, call witnesses, question witnesses called by the tribunal; and, be permitted (but not compelled) to testify or otherwise address the tribunal and be provided with an interpreter. The regulations provide for the tribunal's determination of a detainee's status in closed session by a majority vote and require a preponderance of the evidence to support the tribunal's finding. *See* Erin Chlopak, *Dealing with the Detainees at Guantànamo Bay: Humanitarian and Human Rights Obligations Under the Geneva Conventions* 9 Hum Rts. Br. 6, 8 (2002).

346. This Report notes, however, that pursuant to Geneva III, *supra* note 173, art. 118, POWs are required to be "released and repatriated without delay after the cessation of active hostilities." If detainees captured during the Afghan conflict and the war in, and occupation of, Iraq are POWs (but have not been adjudicated as such), continued detention, without charge, constitutes a breach of Article 118, unless such persons are detained in compliance with Geneva IV relating to detention of civilians (*e.g.* pursuant to Article 5 with respect to security detainees and Article 42 permitting internment "if the security of the Detaining Power makes it absolutely necessary.").

347. Specifically, Article 13 of Geneva III, *supra* note 173, provides:

> Prisoners of war must at all times be humanely treated. Any unlawful act or omission by the Detaining Power causing death or seriously endangering the health of a prisoner of war in its custody is prohibited, and will be regarded as a serious breach of the present Convention. In particular, no prisoner of war may be subjected to physical mutilation or to medical or scientific experiments of any kind which are not justified by the medical, dental or hospital treatment of the prisoner concerned and carried out in his interest.
>
> Likewise, prisoners of war must at all times be protected, particularly against acts of violence or intimidation and against insults and public curiosity.

348. *Id.,* arts. 130 and 131.

349. Article 12 of Geneva III, *id.,* provides:

> Prisoners of war are in the hands of the enemy Power, but not of the individuals or military units who have captured them. Irrespective of the individual responsibilities that may exist, the Detaining Power is responsible for the treatment given them.

> Prisoners of war may only be transferred by the Detaining Power to a Power which is a party to the Convention and after the Detaining Power has satisfied itself of the willingness and ability of such transferee Power to apply the Convention. When prisoners of war are transferred under such circumstances, responsibility for the application of the Convention rests on the Power accepting them while they are in its custody.
>
> Nevertheless if that Power fails to carry out the provisions of the Convention in any important respect, the Power by whom the prisoners of war were transferred shall, upon being notified by the Protecting Power, take effective measures to correct the situation or shall request the return of the prisoners of war. Such requests must be complied with.

350. Geneva IV, *supra* note 173, art. 4.

351. *Id.*

352. Specifically, Article 5 of Geneva IV, *id.*, provides:

> Where in occupied territory an individual protected person is detained as a spy or saboteur, or as a person under definite suspicion of activity hostile to the security of the Occupying Power, such person shall, in those cases where absolute military security so requires, be regarded as having forfeited rights of communication under the present Convention.
>
> In each case, such persons shall nevertheless be treated with humanity and, in case of trial, shall not be deprived of the rights of fair and regular trial prescribed by the present Convention. They shall also be granted the full rights and privileges of a protected person under the present Convention at the earliest date consistent with the security of the State or Occupying Power, as the case may be.

353. A debate exists as to whether persons who have directly participated in the war in Afghanistan hostilities and who do not qualify as POWs under Geneva III (*i.e.*, detainees considered to be "unlawful combatants" by the United States) should automatically be considered "protected persons" under Geneva IV, unless other exceptions apply. Recent decisions of the International Criminal Tribunal for the Former Yugoslavia have held that, "if an individual is not entitled to the protections of the Third Convention as a prisoner of war (or of the First or Second Conventions) he or she necessarily falls within the ambit of [Geneva IV]." *See Prosecutor v. Delalic,* Case No. IT-96-21-T, Judgment, (ICTY Trial Chamber November 16, 1998), para. 271; *see also Prosecutor v. Tadic,* Case No. IT-94-1-A, Judgment, (ICTY Appeals Chamber, July 15, 1999). For a further discussion of the standards applicable to the determination of a "protected person" under Geneva IV, and the Bush Administration's designation of certain detainees as "enemy combatants," *see* HR Standards Supplement, *supra* note 342, at 3–5 and 9–10.

354. Geneva IV, *supra* note 173, arts. 41 and 42 (civilians may be interned only where "absolutely necessary"), art. 43 (internment order must be reconsidered upon the civilian's request, "as soon as possible by an appropriate court or administrative board" and periodically "at least twice yearly"), art. 45 (civilians may be transferred only to a Detaining Power that is a party to the Convention), art. 78 (civilian internment authorized only for "imperative reasons of safety"), arts. 79–126 (rules on treatment of civilian internees), arts. 127–28 (rules on transfers of internees), arts. 132–35 (rules on repatriation of civilian internees).

355. *Id.*, arts. 147 and 148. Article 49 of Geneva IV, *id.*, prohibits "[i]ndividual or mass forcible transfer, as well as deportations of protected persons from occupied territory to the territory of the Occupying Power or to that of any other country, occupied or not,...regardless of their motive." Geneva IV, *supra* note 173, art. 49. It has recently been reported that the CIA has secretly transferred detainees from Iraq for interrogations under authority of a draft legal opinion dated March 19, 2004 and authored by Jack Goldsmith, then Assistant Attorney General of the Department of Justice's Office of Legal Counsel. *See* Dana Priest, *Memo Lets CIA Take Detainees Out of Iraq: Practice is Called Serious Breach of Geneva Conventions,* Washington Post, Oct. 24, 2004, at A1; *see also* Jack Goldsmith, Office of Legal Counsel of the Department of Justice, *Re: Permissibility of Relocating Certain "Protected Persons" from Occupied Iraq,* (draft dated March 19, 2004), available at http://www.washingtonpost.com/wp-srv/nation/documents/doj_memo031904.pdf (last visited Oct. 26, 2004) (Goldsmith Memo). According to Bush Administration officials, the Goldsmith Memo "establishes an important exception to public assertions by the Bush administration since March 2003 that the Geneva Conventions applied comprehensively to

prisoners taken in the conflict in Iraq." Douglas Jehl, *U.S. Action Bars Right of Some Captured in Iraq,* N.Y. Times, Oct. 26, 2004, at A1. The memo reasons that Article 49's protection against forcible transfer and deportation is not available to "illegal aliens" in Iraq. Goldsmith Memo at 2–8. The memo also reasons that Article 49's protections do not apply to transfers of either "protected persons" or of what the memo calls "illegal aliens" for the purposes of interrogations because such transfers do not apply to persons who have either been accused of an offense or who have not been accused but are removed only "temporarily" for interrogation as opposed to being "permanently uprooted" from their homes. *Id.* at 9–14. The memo's reasoning ignores the plain language of Article 49. Moreover, as the authoritative ICRC Commentary to Geneva IV states, Article 49's "prohibition is absolute and allows of no exceptions, apart from those stipulated in paragraph 2 [which authorizes *evacuation* as a preventative measure only in circumscribed instances for the *protection* of "protected persons."]" ICRC, Commentary on the Geneva Convention Relative to the Protection of Civilian Persons in Time of War, 278 (J.S. Pictet ed., 1958).

356. *Id.* art. 6.

357. The authoritative ICRC has not asserted that either Afghanistan after June 2002, or Iraq after June 2004, was occupied within the meaning of Geneva IV.

358. Detained civilians captured in situations of armed conflict governed by Additional Protocol I to the Geneva Conventions are also protected by article 75(2) of that instrument. *See* Protocol I Additional to the Geneva Conventions of Aug. 12, 1949, *opened for signature* Dec. 12, 1977, U.N. Doc. A/32/144, Annex I, *reprinted in* 1125 U.N.T.S. 3; 16 I.L.M. 1391 (Additional Protocol I), *available at* http://www.icrc.org/ihl.nsf/7c4d08d9b287a42141256739003e636b/f6c8b9fee14a77fdc125641e0052b079 (last visited Oct. 24, 2004). Although the United States is not a party to Additional Protocol I, it is generally acknowledged that relevant sections of Protocol I constitute either binding customary international law or good practice, in particular the minimum safeguards guaranteed by Article 75(2). *See* Michael J. Matheson, *Remarks on the United States Position on the Relation of Customary International Law to the 1977 Protocols Additional to the 1949 Geneva Conventions, reprinted in The Sixth Annual American Red Cross-Washington College of Law Conference on International Humanitarian Law: A Workshop on Customary International Law and the 1977 Protocols Additional to the 1949 Geneva Conventions,* 2 Am. U. J. Int'l L. & Pol'y 415, 425–6 (1987).

359. *See, e.g., Military and Paramilitary Activities in and against Nicaragua* (*Nicar. v. U.S.*), 1986 I.C.J. 14 (June 27, 1986) (*Nicaragua case*), paras. 218–20 (affirming that Common Article 3 is part of customary international law); *Prosecutor v. Tadic,* Case No. IT-94-1, Decision on the Defence Motion for Interlocutory Appeal on Jurisdiction, (ICTY Appeals Chamber, Oct. 2, 1995) para. 98 ("[S]ome treaty rules have gradually become part of customary law. This holds true for common Article 3 of the 1949 Geneva Conventions. . . ."); *Prosecutor v. Kunarac et. al.,* Case Nos. IT-96-23 and IT-96-23/1, Judgement, (ICTY Appeals Chamber, June 12, 2002) para. 68 (Common Article 3 "is indeed regarded as being part of customary international law."); *Prosecutor v. Blaškić,* Case No. IT-95-14, Judgment, (ICTY Trial Chamber, March 3, 2000) para. 166 ("Common Article 3 must be considered a rule of customary international law."); *Prosecutor v. Naletilic and Martinovic,* Case No. IT-98-34, Judgment, (ICTY Trial Chamber, March 31, 2003) para. 228 ("It is . . . well established that [C]ommon Article 3 has acquired the status of customary international law."). *See also* Theodor Meron, *The Geneva Conventions as Customary Law,* 81 Am. J. Int'l L. 348 (1987).

360. Geneva Conventions, *supra* note 173, art. 3. Additional Protocol I, *supra* note 358, article 75 also provides protection against ill-treatment in conflicts that are governed by that instrument:

> The following acts are and shall remain prohibited at any time and in any place whatsoever, whether committed by civilians or by military agents:
>
> (a) Violence to the life, health or physical or mental well-being of persons, in particular:
>
> (i) Murder;
>
> (ii) Torture of all kinds, whether physical or mental;
>
> (iii) Corporal punishments; and
>
> (iv) Mutilations

(b) Outrages on personal dignity, in particular, humiliating and degrading treatment, enforced prostitution, and any form of indecent assault.

361. Geneva Conventions, *supra* note 173, art. 3.

362. Article 85(2) of Additional Protocol I, *supra* note 358, also includes a "grave breaches" provision, and extends "grave breaches" protections beyond those in the Geneva Conventions to include, among others, "(1) Persons who have taken part in hostilities and have fallen into the power of an adverse Party (defined by Additional Protocol I as including combatants and prisoners of war); (2) Refugees and stateless persons in the power of an adverse Party; (3) The wounded, sick, and shipwrecked of the adverse Party; and (4) Medical or religious personnel, medical units or medical transports which are under the control of the adverse Party and protected under the Protocol (see Article 8 for definitions)."

363. Geneva I, art. 50; Geneva II, art. 51; Geneva III, art. 130; Geneva IV, art. 147, *supra* note 173. Geneva III Article 130 states: "Grave breaches....shall be those involving any of the following acts, if committed against persons or property protected by the Convention: willful killing, torture or inhuman treatment, including biological experiments, willfully causing great suffering or serious injury to body or health, compelling a prisoner of war to serve in the forces of the hostile Power, or willfully depriving a prisoner of war of the rights of fair and regular trial prescribed in this Convention."

364. Geneva IV, *supra* note 173, art. 147. Geneva IV's grave breaches provision refers to "persons... protected by the present Convention," as opposed to "protected persons" The full text of the Article states: "Grave breaches...shall be those involving any of the following acts, if committed against persons or property protected by the present Convention: willful killing, torture or inhuman treatment, including biological experiments, willfully causing great suffering or serious injury to body or health, unlawful deportation or transfer or unlawful confinement of a protected person, compelling a protected person to serve in the forces of a hostile Power, or willfully depriving a protected person of the rights of fair and regular trial prescribed in the present Convention, taking of hostages and extensive destruction and appropriation of property, not justified by military necessity and carried out unlawfully and wantonly."

365. Geneva I, art. 51, Geneva II, art. 52, Geneva III, art. 131, Geneva IV, art. 148, *supra* note 173.

366. Geneva I, art. 49, Geneva II, art. 50, Geneva III, art. 129, Geneva IV, art. 146, *supra* note 173.

367. Geneva III, art. 129; Geneva IV, art. 146, *supra* note 173.

368. United Nations Secretariat, *Report of the Secretary-General Pursuant to Paragraph 2 of Security Council Resolution 808,* U.N. SCOR, 3175th mtg., U.N. Doc. S/25704 (1993), at 9, para. 35, *reprinted in* 32 I.L.M. 1163 (1993) (grave breaches of the Geneva Conventions, genocide, and other crimes against humanity are undoubtedly a part of customary international law). This Report was approved by the U.N. Security Council. S.C. Res. 827, U.N. SCOR, 48th Sess., 3217th mtg. at 6, U.N. Doc. S/RES/827 (1993), *reprinted in* 32 I.L.M. 1203 (1993).

369. *Prosecutor v. Tadic,* Case No. IT-94-1, Decision on the Defense Motion for Interlocutory Appeal on Jurisdiction, (ICTY Appeals Chamber, Oct. 2, 1995) para. 128–129 (individuals who violate the laws of war, including Common Article 3, may incur individual criminal responsibility under international law).; *Prosecutor v. Mucic et al.,* Case No. IT 96 21, Judgment, (Appeals Chamber, Feb. 20, 2001) para. 162, 171 ("[T]he fact that common Article 3 does not contain an explicit reference to individual criminal liability does not necessarily bear the consequence that there is no possibility to sanction criminally a violation of this rule. The [International Military Tribunal at Nuremberg] indeed followed a similar approach, as recalled in the *Tadic* Jurisdiction Decision when the Appeals Chamber found that a finding of individual criminal responsibility is not barred by the absence of treaty provisions on punishment of breaches. The Nuremberg Tribunal clearly established that individual acts prohibited by international law constitute criminal offences even though there was no provision regarding the jurisdiction to try violations....The Appeals Chamber is unable to find any reason of principle why, once the application of rules of international humanitarian law came to be extended (albeit in an attenuated form) to the context of internal armed conflicts, their violation in that context could not be criminally enforced at the international level."); *Prosecutor v. Blaškić,* Case No. IT-95-14 (Trial Chamber), March 3, 2000, para. 176 ("[C]ustomary international law imposes criminal responsibility for serious violations of Common Article 3."); *see also* U.S. Dept. of Army, Field Manual 27-10, "Law of Land Warfare", art. 499 ("The term 'war crime' is the technical expression for a violation of the law of war by any person or persons, military or civilian. Every

violation of the law of war is a war crime.") and 506 (1956); United Kingdom *Manual of Military Law, Part 111* (1958), para. 626 ("all other violations of the [Geneva] Conventions, not amounting to "grave breaches", are also war crimes).

370. Statute of the International Criminal Tribunal for the Former Yugoslavia, art. 2, May 25, 1993, S.C. Res. 827, U.N. SCOR, 48th Sess., 3217th mtg., at 1–2, U.N. Doc. S/RES/827 (1993), *amended by* S.C. Res. 1166, U.N. SCOR, 53rd Sess., 3878th mtg., U.N. Doc. S/RES/1166 (1998), *amended further by* S.C. Res. 1329, U.N. SCOR, 55th Sess., 4240th mtg., U.N. Doc. S/RES/1329 (2000), *amended further by* S. C. Res. 1411, U.N. SCOR, 57th Sess., 4535th mtg., U.N. Doc. S/RES/1411 (2002), *available at* http://www.un.org/icty/basic/statut/stat2000.htm (last visited Oct. 25, 2004) (ICTY Statute).

371. Statute of the International Criminal Tribunal of Rwanda, art. 4, U.N. SCOR, 48th Sess., 3217th mtg., U.N. Doc. S/Res/955 (1994) *amended by* S.C. Res. 978, U.N. SCOR, 50th Sess., 3504th mtg., U.N. Doc. S/RES/978 (1995), *amended further by* S.C. Res. 1165, U.N. SCOR, 53rd Sess., 3877th mtg., U.N. Doc. S/RES/1165 (1998), *amended further by* S.C. Res. 1329, U.N. SCOR, 55th Sess., 4240th mtg., U.N. Doc. S/RES/1329 (2000), *available at* http://www.ictr.org/ENGLISH/Resolutions/955e.htm (last visited Oct. 25, 2004) (ICTR Statute).

372. Status of Ratification of the Geneva Conventions, United States, *available at* http://www.icrc.org/ihl.nsf/db8c9c8d3ba9d16f41256739003e6371/d6b53f5b5d14f35ac1256402003f9920?OpenDocument (last visited Oct. 25, 2004).

373. 10 U.S.C. §§801-941 (1994 & Supp. IV 1999); *see* Section VIII.A.2. of this Report.

374. Pub. L. No. 104-192 (codified at 18 U.S.C. §§ 2401, 2441, Aug. 21, 1996, 110 Stat. 2104, Sec. 2401); renumbered Sec. 2441, Public Law 104-294, title VI, Sec. 605(p)(1), Oct. 11, 1996, 110 Stat. 3510; amended by Public Law 105-118, title V, Sec. 583, Nov. 26, 1997, 111 Stat. 2436.

375. Refugee Convention, *supra* note 174. Although the United States did not ratify the Refugee Convention, it is a party to it through its accession to the 1967 Protocol, *supra* note 174, which adopted and extended the Refugee Convention protections. Formal procedures for granting asylum and withholding of deportation in accordance with the Refugee Convention were first enacted into domestic law through amendments to the Immigration and Nationality Act, 8 U.S.C. §1101 *et seq.,* and by the Refugee Act of 1980, Pub. L. No. 96-212, 94 Stat. 102 (1980). Subsequent U.S. legislation that contains provisions relating to Refugee Convention protections include: the Immigration Act of 1990, Pub. L. 101-649, 104 Stat. 4978; the Illegal Immigration Reform and Immigrant Responsibility Act of 1996, Pub. L. No. 104-208, 110 Stat. 3009 (codified at 8 U.S.C.A. 1231(b)(3)); and the Antiterrorism and Effective Death Penalty Act of 1996, Pub. L. 104-132 (Apr. 24, 1996).

376. The *non-refoulement* obligation in the Refugee Convention is thus not limited to persons in danger of torture, as it is under CAT Article 3, but is concerned with the larger category of ill-treatment that constitutes "persecution" under the Refugee Convention.

377. Refugee Convention, *supra* note 174, art. 1(A)(2); *see also* 1967 Protocol, *supra* note 174, art. 1 (2). In *I.N.S. v. Cardoza-Fonseca,* the Supreme Court held that the principal focus of the test of "well-founded fear" was on the applicant's subjective beliefs: as long as an objective situation is established by the evidence, it need not be shown that the situation will probably result in persecution; it is enough that persecution is a reasonable possibility. 480 U.S. 421, 107 S. Ct. 1207 (1987).

378. CAT Article 1, *supra* note 9, lists certain reasons that torture may be perpetrated, but this list is not exhaustive.

379. United Nations High Commissioner for Refugees, Handbook On Procedures And Criteria For Determining Refugee Status Under The 1951 Convention And The 1967 Protocol Relating To The Status of Refugees, U.N. Doc. HCR/1P/4/Eng/REV.2 (1992) (UNHCR Handbook), para. 65.

380. Refugee Convention, *supra* note 174, art. 33(2).

381. *Id.,* art. 1F. The UNHCR has cautioned that application of this exclusion clause to a person who otherwise meets the definition of a "refugee" would only be justified if the crime was particularly severe, and that the authorities must balance the degree of persecution feared by the applicant against the severity of the crime. UNHCR Handbook, *supra* note 379, paras. 38 and 156. For a detailed discussion of these provisions, *see* Kathleen M. Keller, *A Comparative and International Law Perspective on the United States (Non) Compliance with its Duty of Non-Refoulement,* 2 Yale Hum. Rts. & Dev. L.J. 183, 190 (1999); Joan

Fitzpatrick, *Rendition and the War Against Terrorism: Guantanamo and Beyond,* 25 Loy. L.A. Int'l & Comp. L. Rev. 457, 473 (2003).

382. 1 Oppenheim's International Law 148 (Robert Jennings & Arthur Watts eds., 9th ed. 1992); M. Cherif Bassiouni, Crimes Against Humanity in International Law 514 (1999); John W. Bridge, The Case for an International Court of Criminal Justice and the Formulation of International Criminal Law, in International Courts for the Twenty-First Century 213, 223 (Mark W. Janis ed., 1992); David Stoelting, *Status Report on the International Criminal Court,* 3 Hofstra L. & Pol'y Symp. 233, 252 (1999).

383. *See, e.g., Filartiga v. Pena-Irala,* 630 F.2d 876, 880 (2d Cir. 1980) ("In light of the universal condemnation of torture in numerous international agreements, and the renunciation of torture as an instrument of official policy by virtually all of the nations of the world (in principle if not in practice), we find that an act of torture committed by a state official against one held in detention violates established norms of the international law of human rights. . . .").

384. Rome Statute of the International Criminal Court, July 17, 1998, U.N. Doc. A/CONF.183/9 (1998), 37 I.L.M. 999 (Rome Statute), *available at* http://www.un.org/law/icc/statute/romefra.htm (last visited Oct. 25, 2004).

385. ICTY Statute, *supra* note 370.

386. ICTR Statute, *supra* note 371.

387. *See generally,* the materials of the United Nations Preparatory Committee on the Establishment of an International Criminal Court, *available at* http://www.un.org/law/icc/prepcomm/prepfra.htm and http://www.iccnow.org/documents/prepcom/ (last visited Oct. 25, 2004).

388. More that 120 states voted for the Rome Statute. Currently, 139 states have signed the Rome Statute, and 94 have ratified it. *See* http://untreaty.un.org/ENGLISH/bible/englishinternetbible/partI/chapterXVIII/treaty10.asp and http://www.iccnow.org/countryinfo/worldsigsandratifications.html (last visited Oct. 7, 2004).

389. ICTY Statute, *supra* note 370, art. 5.

390. ICTR Statute, *supra* note 371, art. 3 (the statute specifies that crimes for which individuals may be prosecuted must be "against any civilian population on national, political, ethnic, racial, or religious grounds").

391. ICTY Statute, *supra* note 370 art. 2 (including torture and inhumane treatment among the enumerated "grave breaches").

392. Report of the International Law Commission to the General Assembly, [1950] 2 Y.B. Int'l L. Comm'n 374–78, U.N. Doc. A/CN.4/SER.A/1950 (Nuremberg Principles), Principle VII (establishing complicity in the commission of a crime). The Nuremberg Principles were adopted by the U.N. General Assembly in 1950. *See* G.A. Res. 177(II)(a), U.N. GAOR, 2d Sess., Supp. No. 12, at 11–14, U.N. Doc. A/1316 (1950). *See also* Agreement for the Prosecution and Punishment of the Major War Criminals of the European Axis (Charter of the International Military Tribunal), 58 Stat. 1544, E.A.S. No. 472, 82 U.N.T.S. 280 *entered into force* August 8, 1945 (Nuremberg Charter) art. 6 (accomplice liability for participation in formulation or execution of a common plan or conspiracy to commit a crime; liability of particular accomplice extends to acts performed by all other accomplices).

393. ICTY Statute, *supra* note 370, art. 7(1); ICTR Statute, *supra* note 371, art. 6(1) (same). *See also* Convention on the Prevention and Punishment of the Crime of Genocide, 78 U.N.T.S. 277, *entered into force* Jan. 12, 1951, (Genocide Convention) *available at* http://www.ohchr.org/english/law/genocide.htm (last visited Oct. 24, 2004) art. III(e) (complicity in genocide). *See also* International Law Commission, *Draft Code of Crimes Against the Peace and Security of Mankind: Texts of and Commentaries to Articles 1–20,* U.N. GAOR, 51st. sess., Supp. No. 10, U.N. Doc. A/51/10 (1996), *reprinted in* 18 HUM. RTS. L.J. 96 (1997) (ILC Draft Code of Crimes) (liability under article 2(3)(d) (liability for knowingly aiding, abetting or otherwise assisting, directly and substantially, in the commission of such a crime, including providing the means for its commission).

394. *Prosecutor v. Akayesu,* Case No. ICTR-96-4-T, Judgment, (ICTR Trial Chamber Sept. 2, 1998).

395. *Id.* para. 539.

396. *Prosecutor v. Tadic,* Case No. IT-94-1-T, Judgment, (ICTY Chamber II May 7, 1997), para. 688, *aff'd.,* Case No. IT-94-1-A, (ICTY Appeals Chamber July 15, 1999).

397. Nuremberg Charter, *supra* note 392, art. 6; Nuremberg Principles, *supra* note 392, Principle VI (liability for conspiracy to commit an offense); *see also* Genocide Convention, *supra* note 393, Art. III (b) (conspiracy to commit genocide); ICTY Statute, *supra* note 370, art. 7 (1) (liability for planning); ICTR Statute, *supra* note 371, art. 6 (1) (same); ILC Draft Code of Crimes, *supra* note 393, art. 2(3)(e) (liability for direct participation in planning or conspiracy to commit a crime that actually occurs).

398. Article 25 of the Rome Statue does not specifically include conspiracy, although it creates liability for committing a crime individually or jointly; ordering, soliciting, or inducing "the commission of such a crime which in fact occurs or is attempted"; and, aiding, abetting, or otherwise assisting in the commission of a crime "or its attempted commission, including providing the means for its commission." Rome Statute, *supra* note 384, art. 25(3)(a)-(c).

399. *Id.* art. 25(3)(d).

400. *Prosecutor v. Tadic,* Case No. IT-94-1-T, Judgment, (ICTY Chamber, May 7, 1997) paras. 662 and 669 (aiding and abetting liability is "beyond any doubt customary law").

401. *Id.* para. 674.

402. *Prosecutor v. Tadic,* Case No. IT-94-1A, Judgment, (ICTY Appeals Chamber, July 15, 1999) para. 196.

403. *Id.* para. 202.

404. *Id.* para. 220.

405. *Id. See also Prosecutor v. Krstic,* Case No. IT-98-33-T, Judgment, (ICTY Trial Chamber Aug. 2, 2001) paras. 601–613 (summarizing jurisprudence of ICTY and ICTR on individual criminal liability and co-perpetrator crimes as follows: "Planning" means that one or more persons design the commission of a crime at both the preparatory and execution phases; "Instigating" means prompting another to commit an offense; "Aiding and abetting" means rendering a substantial contribution to the commission of a crime; and "Joint criminal enterprise" liability is a form of criminal responsibility…implicitly included Article 7 (1) of the Statute. It entails individual responsibility for participation in a joint criminal enterprise to commit a crime.)

406. *Prosecutor v. Tadic,* Case No. IT-94-1A, Judgment, (ICTY Appeals Chamber, July 15, 1999) para. 220.

407. *See Prosecutor v. Furundzija,* Case No. IT-95-17/1, Judgment, (ICTY Trial Chamber Dec. 10, 1998) paras. 207, 209, 235 (footnotes omitted).

408. *See, e.g.,* Bybee Memorandum, *supra* note 134, at 39–44.

409. *See* Section VIII.A. of this Report.

410. In an early case applying the doctrine of command responsibility, the U.S. Supreme Court held that a military commander could be liable for crimes by his troops even if he possessed only *de jure* control and had ceded or delegated *de facto* control. *Yamashita v. U.S.,* 327 U.S. 1, 16, 35 (1946). *See also United States v. Von Leeb,* 11 Trials of War Criminals Before the Nuremberg Military Tribunals Under Control Law No. 10, 1, 462 (1950); *United States v. List,* 11 Trials of War Criminals Before the Nuremberg Military Tribunals Under Control Law No. 10, 759, 1230 (1951); *United States v. von Weizsaecker,* 11 Trials of War Criminals Before the Nuremberg Military Tribunals Under Control Law No. 10, 308 (1952).

411. "Ordering" entails a person in a position of authority using that position to convince or instruct another to commit the offense. *See Prosecutor v. Krstic,* Case No. IT-98-33, Judgment, (ICTY Trial Chamber, Aug. 2, 2001) para. 601; *Prosecutor v. Akayesu,* Case No. ICTR-96-4-T, Judgment, (ICTY Trial Chamber, Sept. 2, 1998) para. 483. An order may be explicit or implicit and need not be given directly to the person who performs the offense. *Prosecutor v. Blaškić,* Case No. IT-95-14, Judgment, (ICTY Trial Chamber, Mar. 3, 2000) para. 281–82. No formal or legal superior-subordinate relationship need exist so long as the accused possessed the authority to order. *Prosecutor v. Kordic and Cerkez,* Case No. IT-95-14/2, Judgment, (ICTY Trial Chamber, Feb. 26, 2001).

412. Geneva I, art 49, Geneva II, art. 50; Geneva III, art. 129; Geneva IV, art. 146, *supra* note 173.

413. ICTY Statute, *supra* note 370; ICTR Statute, *supra* note 371; Rome Statute, *supra* note 384.

414. *See also* ILC Report, art. 2(3)(b) and art. 6 ("The fact that a crime against the peace and security of mankind was committed by a subordinate does not relieve his superiors of criminal responsibility if they knew or had reason to know, in the circumstances at the time, that the subordinate was committing or

was going to commit such a crime and if they did not take all necessary measures within their power to prevent or suppress the crime.").

415. Nuremberg Principles, *supra* note 392, Principle III ("The fact that a person who committed an act which constitutes a crime under international law acted as Head of State or responsible Government official does not relieve him from responsibility under international law."). *See also Prosecutor v. Milosovic,* Case No. IT-99-37, Indictment of May 22, 1999 paras. 55–89 (responsibility for crimes as head of state based on allegations of *de jure* and *de facto* position of command); *Prosecutor v. Milosovic,* Case No. IT-99-37-I, Amended Indictment of June 29, 2001, paras. 27–34 (same); *Prosecutor v. Taylor,* Case No. SCSL-03-I, Indictment of March 3, 2003; *R v. Bow Street Metropolitan Stipendiary Magistrate, ex parte Pinochet Ugarte* (No. 3), 2 W.L.R. 827 (H.L. 1999) (holding that General Augusto Pinochet could not claim official immunity for torture after Chile had signed the UN Convention Against Torture); *see also Case Concerning the Arrest Warrant of 11 April 2000* (*Democratic Republic of the Congo v. Belgium*) 441 I.L.M. 536 (2002) (holding that, under customary international law, heads of state and other senior ministers may be immune from prosecution in domestic courts, but may be prosecuted at an international criminal tribunal with jurisdiction).

416. ICTY Statute, *supra* note 370; ICTR Statute, *supra* note 371; Rome Statute, *supra* note 384. The Human Rights Committee has also interpreted the nature of the legal obligation of ICCPR Article 2 to include a prohibition against the recognition of official immunity: "no official status justifies persons who may be accused of responsibility for [ICCPR] violations being held immune from legal responsibility." HRC General Comment 31, *supra* note 13, para. 15.

417. *Prosecutor v. Delali,* Case No. IT-96-21-T, Judgment, (ICTY Trial Chamber, Nov. 16, 1998) para. 346; *Prosecutor v. Akayesu,* Case No. ICTR-96-4-T, Judgment (ICTR Trial Chamber, Sept. 2, 1998) para. 491.

418. *Prosecutor v. Mucic et al.,* Case No. IT-96-21, Judgment, (ICTY Appeals Chamber Feb. 20, 2001), paras. 192–94, 256; *Prosecutor v. Blaškić,* Case No. IT-95-14, Judgment, (ICTY Trial Chamber Mar. 3, 2000), paras. 300–302; *Prosecutor v. Kayishema and Ruzindana,* Case No. ICTR-95-1-T, Judgment, (ICTR Trial Chamber May 21, 1999), paras. 217–231; *Prosecutor v. Bagilishema,* Case No. ICTR-95-1A-T, Judgment, (ICTR Trial Chamber June 7, 2001) para. 39; *Prosecutor v. Delalic,* Case No. IT-96-21-T, Judgment, (ICTY Trial Chamber Nov. 16, 1998), paras. 355–57, 363; *Prosecutor v. Aleksovski,* Case No. IT-95-14/1, Judgment, (ICTY Trial Chamber June 25, 1999), paras. 75, 78.

419. See I. Bantekas, *The Contemporary Law of Superior Responsibility,* 93 AJIL 580, 581, 584 (1999).

420. *Prosecutor v. Delalic,* Case No. IT-96-21-T, Judgement, (ICTY Trial Chamber Nov. 16, 1998), para. 378; *Prosecutor v. Aleksovski,* Case No. IT-95-14/1, Judgment, (ICTY Trial Chamber June 25, 1999), para. 81; *Prosecutor v. Blaškić,* Case No. IT-95-14-T, Judgment, (ICTY Trial Chamber Mar. 3, 2000), paras. 302, 325.

421. *Prosecutor v. Kordic and Cerkez,* Case No. IT-95-14/2, Judgment, (ICTY Trial Chamber Feb. 26, 2001), para. 401, *Prosecutor v. Blaškić,* Case No. IT-95-14-T, Judgment, (ICTY Trial Chamber Mar. 3, 2000), para. 294; *Prosecutor v. Bagilishema,* Case No. ICTR-95-1A-T, Judgment, (ICTR Trial Chamber June 7, 2001), para. 38.

422. *Prosecutor v. Kunarac et al.,* Case Nos. IT-96-23 and IT-96-23/11, Judgment, (ICTY Trial Chamber Feb. 22, 2001), para. 369.

423. *Prosecutor v. Mucic et al.,* Case No. IT-96-21, Judgment, (ICTY Appeals Chamber Feb. 20, 2001), paras. 192–94, 256; *Prosecutor v. Kayishema and Ruzindana,* Case No. ICTR-95-1-T, Judgment, (ICTR Trial Chamber May 21, 1999), paras. 217–231; *Prosecutor v. Bagilishema,* Case No. ICTR-95-1A-T, Judgment, (ICTR Trial Chamber June 7, 2001), para. 39.

424. *Prosecutor v. Akayesu,* Case No. ICTR-96-4-T, Judgment, (ICTR Trial Chamber Sept. 2, 1998), para. 476; *Prosecutor v. Blaškić,* Case No. IT-95-14-T, Judgment, (ICTY Trial Chamber Mar. 3, 2000), para. 307.

425. *Prosecutor v. Blaškić,* Case No. IT-95-14-T, Judgment, (ICTY Trial Chamber Mar. 3, 2000), para. 308; *Prosecutor v. Kordic and Cerkez,* Case No. IT-95-14/2, Judgment, (ICTY Trial Chamber Feb. 26, 2001), para. 428; *Prosecutor v. Bagilishema,* Case No. ICTR-95-1A-T, Judgment, (ICTR Trial Chamber June 7, 2001), paras. 44–46.

426. *Prosecutor v. Mucic et al.,* Case No. IT-96-21, Judgment, (ICTY Appeals Chamber Feb. 20, 2001), para. 222.

427. *Id.,* paras. 222–241.

428. *Prosecutor v. Blaškić,* Case No. IT-95-14-T, Judgment, (ICTY Trial Chamber Mar. 3, 2000), para. 332; *Prosecutor v. Kayishema and Ruzindana,* Case No. ICTR-95-1-T, Judgment, (ICTR Trial Chamber May 21, 1999); *see also* Additional Protocol I, *supra* note 358, art. 86(2) (imposing "penal or disciplinary responsibility" on superiors who "knew or had information which should have enabled them to conclude in the circumstances at the time, that a subordinate was committing or was going to commit such a breach of the Conventions or of this Protocol and if they did not take all feasible measures within their powers to prevent or repress the breach.").

429. *Prosecutor v. Bagilishema,* Case No. ICTR-95-1A-T, Judgment, (ICTR Trial Chamber June 7, 2001), paras. 47–50; *Prosecutor v. Blaškić,* Case No. IT-95-14-T, Judgment, (ICTY Trial Chamber Mar. 3, 2000), paras. 294, 335; *Prosecutor v. Kordic and Cerkez,* Case No. IT-95-14/2, Judgment (ICTY Trial Chamber Feb. 26, 2001), paras. 441, 445.

430. Nuremberg Judgment, at 42 ("The provisions of this article are in conformity with the law of all nations. That a soldier was ordered to kill or torture in violation of the international law of war has never been recognized as a defense to such acts of brutality."); *see also* Nuremberg Principles, *supra* note 392, Principle IV ("The fact that a person acted pursuant to order of his Government or of a superior does not relieve him from responsibility under international law, provided a moral choice was in fact possible to him").

431. *A.G. of the Government of Israel v. Adolf Eichmann,* (Dec. 12, 1961) 36 International Review 18, 20 (1968).

432. CAT, *supra* note 9.

433. HRC General Comment 31, *supra* note 13, para. 15. ("impediments to the establishment of legal responsibility should also be removed, such as the defense of obedience to superior orders").

434. ICTR Statute, *supra* note 370; ICTY Statute, *supra* note 371.

435. *Prosecutor v. Erdemovic,* Case No. IT-96-22, Judgment, (ICTY Appeals Chamber Nov. 29, 1996), para. 54.

436. Article 33 states:

1. The fact that a crime within the jurisdiction of the Court has been committed by a person pursuant to an order of a Government or of a superior, whether military or civilian, shall not relieve that person of criminal responsibility unless:

   (a) The person was under a legal obligation to obey orders of the Government or the superior in question;

   (b) The person did not know that the order was unlawful; and

   (c) The order was not manifestly unlawful.

437. *See also* Rome Statute, *supra* note 384, art. 31(1)(d):

> The conduct which is alleged to constitute a crime within the jurisdiction of the Court has been caused by duress resulting from a threat of imminent death or of continuing or imminent serious bodily harm against that person or another person, and the person acts necessarily and reasonably to avoid this threat, provided that the person does not intend to cause a greater harm than the one sought to be avoided. Such a threat may either be: (i) Made by other persons; or (ii) Constituted by other circumstances beyond that person's control.

438. CAT, *supra* note 9.

439. *See* discussion *supra* at Section V.F.2.

440. *See, e.g., Haynes v. Washington,* 373 U.S. 503, 514–515 (1963) (involuntary confession inadmissible).

441. Rome Statute, *supra* note 384, art. 31(1)(d).

442. Wayne R. LaFave, Criminal Law (3d ed. 2000), §5.7. (LaFave)

443. Rome Statute, *supra* note 384.

444. *Prosecutor v. Kordic and Cerkez,* Case No. IT-95-14/2 (Trial Chamber, February 26, 2001), paras. 448–452.

445. HR Standards Report, *supra* note 197, at 10.

446. CAT, *supra* note 9.

447. Burgers & Danelius, *supra* note 183, at 124.

448. Committee against Torture, UN Doc. No. CAT/C/XXVII/Misc.7, Nov. 22, 2001; *see also* Committee Against Torture U.N. Doc. No. A/52/44, para. 258 (1997) ("[A] State party to the Convention [against Torture]...is precluded from raising before [the] Committee [against Torture] exceptional circumstances as justification for acts prohibited by article 1 of the Convention. This is plainly expressed in article 2 of the Convention."); Committee Against Torture, U.N. Doc. No. A/51/44, paras. 180–222 (1997), Inquiry under Article 20 (same).

449. Committee against Torture, UN Doc. No. CAT/C/XXVII/Misc.7, Nov. 22, 2001. Similarly, although not binding under international law, a resolution specifically focusing on the need to protect human rights and fundamental freedoms while countering terrorism was adopted for the first time by the General Assembly on 18 December 2002 (UN Doc. No. A/RES/57/219). It affirmed that states must ensure that any measure taken to combat terrorism complies with their obligations under international law, in particular international human rights, refugee and humanitarian law.

450. ICCPR, *supra* note 9, art. 4(1); European Convention, *supra* note 190, art. 15; American Convention, *supra* note 185, art. 27(1). The most common exception is for conditions of "public emergency," such as in Article 4 of the ICCPR, *supra* note 9, which states:

> In time of public emergency which threatens the life of the nation and the existence of which is officially proclaimed, the States Parties to the present Covenant may take measures derogating from their obligations...to the extent strictly required by the exigencies of the situation, provided that such measures are not inconsistent with their other obligations under international law....

451. European Convention, *supra* note 190, art. 15(2); American Convention, *supra* note 185, art. 27 (2); ICCPR, *supra* note 9, art. 4 (limits on derogation); HRC Comment 20, *supra* note 307, para. 3, ("The text of article 7 allows of no limitation. The Committee also reaffirms that, even in situations of public emergency such as those referred to in article 4 of the Covenant, no derogation from the provision of article 7 is allowed and its provisions must remain in force."); Human Rights Committee, General Comment 29, *States of Emergency (article 4),* U.N. Doc. CCPR/C/21/Rev.1/Add.11 (2001) (HRC General Comment 29) para. 7 ("Article 4, paragraph 2, of the Covenant explicitly prescribes that no derogation from the following articles may be made:...article 7 (prohibition of torture or cruel, inhuman or degrading punishment, or of medical or scientific experimentation without consent)..."); *see also Aksoy v. Turkey,* ECHR, 18 December 1996 (para. 62) ("Article 3, as the Court has observed on many occasions, enshrines one of the fundamental values of democratic society. Even in the most difficult of circumstances, such as the fight against organised terrorism and crime, the Convention prohibits in absolute terms torture or inhuman or degrading treatment or punishment. Unlike most of the substantive clauses of the Convention..., Article 3 makes no provision for exceptions and no derogation from it is permissible under Article 15 even in the event of a public emergency threatening the life of the nation.").

452. CCPR/C/79/Add.76, para. 25 (1997) ("The Committee...expresses its concern that the resort to declarations of states of emergency is still frequent and seldom in conformity with article 4, paragraph 1, of the Covenant, which provides that such declaration may be made only when the life and existence of the nation is threatened").

453. CCPR/CO/76/EGY, para. 6 (2002); CCPR/CO/71/SYR, para. 6 (2001); CCPR/C/79/Add.93, para. 11 (1998) ("The Committee is disturbed by the fact that the state of emergency proclaimed...in 1981 is still in effect, meaning that the State party has been in a semi-permanent state of emergency ever since. The State party should consider reviewing the need to maintain the state of emergency.").

454. CCPR/C/79/Add.42, para. 9 (1995) ("The Committee deplores the lack of clarity of the legal provisions governing the introduction and administration of the state of emergency...which would permit derogations contravening the State party's obligations under article 4, paragraph 2, of the Covenant.").

455. CCPR/C/79/Add.76, para. 38 (1997) ("Constitutional and legal provisions should ensure that compliance with article 4 of the Covenant can be monitored by the courts"); CCPR/C/79/Add.56, para. 13 (1995) ("[The Human Rights Committee] is...concerned that courts do not have the power to examine the legality of the declaration of emergency and of the different measures taken during the state of emergency").

456. The European Court of Human Rights has interpreted Article 15 of the European Convention (which contains language almost identical to ICCPR Article 4(1)'s national emergency exception) to hold that, to qualify as a public emergency, the danger must be actual or imminent, the effects must involve the whole nation, the danger must threaten the continuance of the organized life of the community, and that the danger must be so exceptional that normal measures under the Convention that permit maintenance of public safety, health and order, are inadequate. *The Greek Case,* 1969 Y.B. EUR. CONV. ON HUM. RTS. 511, P153 (Eur. Comm'n on Hum. Rts.) (resolution).

457. CCPR/CO/72/GTM, para. 11 (2001) ("The state party should ensure that its constitutional provisions for emergency situations are compatible with article 4 of the Covenant. It should also comply with the obligation to notify the other states parties through the intermediary of the secretary-general of the United Nations in all cases when an emergency situation is declared and to inform them of the provisions from which it has derogated and of the reasons for the derogation"); ICCPR, *supra* note 9, art. 4(3); European Convention, *supra* note 190, art. 15(3); American Convention, *supra* note 185, art. 27(3).

458. United Kingdom, *Notice of Derogation from the ICCPR, available at* http://www.bayefsky.com/./html/uk_t2_ccpr.php (last visited October 27, 2004).

459. United Kingdom, *Notice of Derogation from the ECHR, available at* http://www.legislationline.org/view.php?document=55973 (last visited October 27, 2004).

460. Geneva III, arts. 2, 130 and 131; Geneva IV, arts. 2, 146 and 147, *supra* note 173.

461. Article 5 of Geneva IV provides: "Where in the territory of a Party to the conflict, the latter is satisfied that an individual protected person is definitely suspected of or engaged in activities hostile to the security of the State, such individual person shall not be entitled to claim such rights and privileges under the present Convention as would, if exercised in the favour of such individual person, be prejudicial to the security of such State." Geneva IV, *supra* note 173, art. 5.

As drafted (*i.e.,* the use of the words "the latter"), it would appear that the national security derogation is available only to the State on whose territory the conflict is occurring (*i.e.,* in the War in Afghanistan, only Afghanistan would be able to take a national security derogation under Article 5). The ICRC has not made a definitive statement on whether this provision would be interpreted to apply to any party to the conflict.

462. *See* Geneva IV, *supra* note 173, art. 146.

463. ICRC, Commentary on the Geneva Convention Relative to the Protection of Civilian Persons in Time of War, 51 (J.S. Pictet ed., 1958).

464. *Paez v. Sweden,* Communication No. 39/1996, Committee Against Torture, U.N. Doc. CAT/C/18/D/39/1996 (1997).

465. HRC General Comment No. 20, *supra* note 307, para. 9.

466. Conclusions and recommendations of the Committee against Torture, Egypt, U.N. Doc. CAT/C/CR/29/4 (2002), para. 4.

467. *Chahal v. United Kingdom,* 23 Eur. Ct. H.R. 413 (ser. A) (1996), para. 79.

468. *Tomasi v. France,* 15 Eur. Ct. H.R. 1 (Ser. A) (1992), para. 1 15 ("The requirements of the investigation and the undeniable difficulties inherent in the fight against crime, particularly with regard to terrorism, cannot result in limits being placed on the protection to be afforded in respect of the physical integrity of individuals.").

469. 23 Eur. Ct. H.R. 413 (ser. A) (1996).

470. *Id.* paras. 79–80. *See also Ahmed v. Austria,* 24 Eur. H.R. Rep. 278, 287 and 291 (1997) (even individuals that a transferring state classifies as "undesirable or dangerous" may not be extradited or transferred to a state "where substantial grounds have been shown for believing that the person concerned faces a real risk of being subjected to torture.").

471. Inter-Am. Court H.R., OEA/Ser.L/V/II.106, Doc. 40 rev., February 28, 2000 (para. 154). ("[T]he prohibition of torture as a norm of *jus cogens*—as codified in the American Declaration generally, and Article 3 of the UN Convention against Torture in the context of expulsion—applies beyond the terms of

the 1951 [Refugee] Convention. The fact that a person is suspected of or deemed to have some relation to terrorism does not modify the obligation of the State to refrain from return where substantial grounds of a real risk of inhuman treatment are at issue.").

472. Diplomatic assurances are used in other contexts as guarantees against ill-treatment, such as an agreement made by a receiving state to a transferring state that an individual extradited or otherwise removed will not be subject to the death penalty. *See* HRW Diplomatic Assurances Report, *supra* note 25, at 3, fn.2. A discussion of the broader uses of diplomatic assurances is beyond the scope of this Report, which focuses on what Human Rights Watch has described as the "novel practice" of using diplomatic assurances in the context of torture. *Id.*

473. 8 C.F.R. §235.8(c)(1), (2).

474. Vienna Convention, *supra* note 182, art. 31(1);

475. Interview of Julia Hall, Counsel and Senior Researcher, Europe and Central Asia Division, Human Rights Watch, June 14, 2004, Notes on file with the ABCNY International Human Rights Commitee.

476. Interim report of the Special Rapporteur on Torture, Theo van Boven, to the General Assembly A/57/173, July 2, 2002. The Special Rapporteur subsequently submitted a report to the General Assembly in July 2003, report to the reaffirming the absolute nature of the principle of *non-refoulement*. Report by the Special Rapporteur on Torture, Theo van Boven, to the United Nations General Assembly, U.N. Doc. No. A/58/120, July 3, 2003.

477. 8 C.F.R. §208.18(c)(3).

478. 8 C.F.R. §208.17(f).

479. 8 C.F.R. §235.8; *see also* Section V.A.5.c.i. of this Report.

480. 22 C.F.R. §95.

481. *See Arar v. Ashcroft, supra* note 37; *see also* Brown & Priest, *supra* note 47. Diplomatic assurances were also reportedly requested by the United States from Saudi Arabia, in the 1999 case of Hani Abdel Rahim Sayegh, suspected of involvement in the Khobar Towers bombing in Saudi Arabia. *Oversight hearing on "Immigration Relief Under the Convention Against Torture for Serious Criminals and Human Rights Violators": Hearing Before the Subcommittee on Immigration, Border Security, and Claims of the House Judiciary Committee*, 108th Cong. (July 11, 2003) (statement of Regina Germain, Esq.) *available at* http://www.house.gov/judiciary/germain071103.htm (last visited Oct. 25, 2004). Sayegh was returned to face trial and possible execution if convicted. *Id.*

482. *Arar v. Ashcroft, supra* note 37, paras. 11, 25–26.

483. *Arar v. Ashcroft, supra* note 37, para. 26.

484. *Arar v. Ashcroft, supra* note 37, paras. 31, 33.

485. *Arar v. Ashcroft, supra* note 37, para. 38.

486. *Id.*

487. *Arar v. Ashcroft, supra* note 37, para. 49.

488. *Arar v. Ashcroft, supra* note 37, para. 50.

489. DeNeen L. Brown, *Canadian Sent to Middle East Files Suit,* Washington Post, Nov. 25, 2003, at A25.

490. *Arar v. Ashcroft, supra* note 37, para. 51.

491. *Arar v. Ashcroft, supra* note 37, paras. 53 and 62.

492. *Arar v. Ashcroft, supra* note 37, para. 61.

493. *Id.*

494. *Arar v. Ashcroft, supra* note 37, para. 64.

495. *Arar v. Ashcroft, supra* note 37, para. 65.

496. *Id.*

497. *Arar v. Ashcroft, supra* note 37, paras. 55–56.

498. Priest & Gellman, *supra* note 57.

499. HRW Diplomatic Assurances Report, *supra* note 25, at 21–36.

500. Application No. 36378/02, Oct. 4, 2002.

501. HRW Diplomatic Assurances Report, *supra* note 25, at 24.

502. *Id.* at 25.

503. *Id.* at 34.

504. *Id.*
505. *Id.* at 35.
506. *Id.*
507. *Id.;* TV4 Kalla Fakta Broadcast, *supra* note 24.
508. TV4 Kalla Fakta Broadcast, *supra* note 24.
509. *Id.*
510. *Id.*
511. *Arar v. Ashcroft, supra* note 37, paras. 55–56.
512. HRW Diplomatic Assurances Report, *supra* note 25, at 4.
513. *Id.*
514. *Id.*
515. *Id.*
516. *Id.*
517. *Id.*
518. Taguba Report, *supra* note 7.
519. Graham & White, *supra* note 94; *see also* HRW Report, *supra* note 10; Dana Priest, *Memo Lets CIA Take Detainees Out of Iraq; Practice Is Called Serious Breach of Geneva Conventions,* WASHINGTON POST, Oct. 24, 2004, at A1.
520. *See* CAT, *supra* note 9, art. 2(1) ("Each State Party shall take effective legislative, administrative, judicial or other measures to prevent acts of torture in any territory under its jurisdiction") *and* Article 2(2) ("No exceptional circumstances whatsoever...may be invoked as a justification of torture.").
521. Committee Against Torture, *Concluding Observations*, Sweden, U.N. Doc. CAT/C/XXVIII/CONCL.1, para. 6 (2002) ("The Committee [against Torture]...records its concern at the following:...(b) The Special Control of Foreigners Act, known as the anti-terrorism law, allows foreigners suspected of terrorism to be expelled under a procedure which might not be in keeping with the Convention, because there is no provision for appeal.").
522. *Arana v. France,* Case No. 63/1997, Committee Against Torture, views adopted on 9 November 1999, para. 11.5.
523. *Manickavasagam Suresh v. The Minister of Citizenship and Immigration and the Attorney General of Canada (Suresh v. Canada),* 2002, SCC 1. File No. 27790, January 11, 2002 *available at* http://www.lexum.umontreal.ca/csc-scc/en/pub/2002/vol1/html/2002scr1_0003.html (last visited Oct. 25, 2004).
524. *Id.* para. 119.
525. *Id.* para. 123.
526. Article 2 provides, in pertinent part:

> 2(1): Each State Party to the present Covenant undertakes to respect and to ensure to all individuals within its territory and subject to its jurisdiction the rights recognized in the present Covenant, without distinction of any kind, such as race, colour, sex, language, religion, political or other opinion, national or social origin, property, birth or other status.
> 2(2): Where not already provided for by existing legislative or other measures, each State Party to the present Covenant undertakes to take the necessary steps in accordance with its constitutional processes and with the provisions of the present Covenant, to adopt such legislative or other measures as may be necessary to give effect to the rights recognized in the present Covenant.
> 2(3): Each State Party to the present Covenant undertakes:
> 1. To ensure that any person whose rights or freedoms as herein recognized are violated shall have an effective remedy, notwithstanding that the violation has been committed by persons acting in an official capacity; to ensure that any person claiming such a remedy shall have his rights thereto determined by competent judicial, administrative or legislative authorities, or by any other competent authority provided for by the legal system of the State, and to develop the possibilities of judicial remedy[.]

527. HRC General Comment 31, *supra* note 13, para. 12.

528. The Human Rights Committee has interpreted ICCPR Article 2(1) as applicable both to persons within a state's territory and also within the state's "power or effective control." HRC General Comment 31, *supra* note 13, para. 10; *see also id*. para. 15.

529. *See* Sections V.A, B, and C of this Report.

530. *See Sosa v. Alvarez-Machain* at *74 ("the [ICCPR] does bind the U.S. as matter of international law. . ."). Article 26 of the Vienna Convention, which codifies the fundamental international law principle of *pacta sunt servanda,* that is, that agreements must be observed, states that "[e]very treaty in force is binding upon the parties to it and must be performed by them *in good faith.*" Vienna Convention, *supra* note 183, art. 26 (emphasis added).

531. The ILC Articles were adopted by the International Law Commission on August 9, 2001, commended to governments by a resolution of the General Assembly on December 12, 2001, and are reproduced in full, together with the International Law Commission's Commentaries in JAMES CRAWFORD, THE INTERNATIONAL LAW COMMISSION'S ARTICLES ON STATE RESPONSIBILITY: INTRODUCTION, TEXT AND COMMENTARIES (2002) (ILC Articles and Commentaries). For the text of the articles and their commentaries without a critical introduction, *see* http://www.un.org/law/ilc/texts/State_responsibility/responsibilityfra.htm (last visited Oct. 25, 2004).

532. ILC Articles and Commentaries, *supra* note 531, at 74.

533. *Id.,* at 75.

534. ILC Articles and Commentaries, *supra* note 531, art. 2, at 81.

535. Vienna Convention, *supra* note 183, at arts. 26 and 27.

536. *Id.*

537. *See* Sections V.A. and B. of this Report. Of course, the United States would also face liability for any torture directly committed by its military or intelligence personnel.

538. CAT, *supra* note 9, art. 3(1).

539. HRC General Comment 20, *supra* note 307. As demonstrated in Section V. above, the different treaties contain slightly different standards concerning the level of risk that must be present to trigger the obligation not to transfer an individual who fears torture or CID.

540. The CAT standard requires the presence of "substantial grounds for believing [the individual] would be in danger of being subjected to torture" upon transfer. CAT, *supra* note 9, at art. 4(1). The Human Rights Committee has interpreted the ICCPR to prohibit transfer in cases where there are "substantial grounds for believing that there is a real risk of irreparable harm." HRC General Comment No. 31, *supra* note 13, para. 12. The United States has codified a standard that is more stringent, requiring that it be "more likely than not" that an individual will face torture upon transfer. *See* Section V.A.5. of this Report. Under international law, the United States is responsible for violations of the treaty standards, regardless of federal law. *See* Vienna Convention, *supra* note 183, at arts. 26 and 27.

541. CAT, *supra* note 9, arts. 1, 2(2); ICCPR, *supra* note 9, arts. 7, 4(2).

542. CAT, *supra* note 9, art. 4(1).

543. CAT, *supra* note 9.

544. *Id.* arts. 10, 11 and 12.

545. *Id.* arts. 10, 11, 12 and 16.

546. *Id,* arts. 4.1, 6 and 7.

547. *Id.* art. 14.

548. Article 2 of the ICCPR *supra* note 9 provides:

1. Each State Party to the present Covenant undertakes to respect and to ensure to all individuals within its territory and subject to its jurisdiction the rights recognized in the present Covenant, without distinction of any kind, such as race, color, sex, language, religion, political or other opinion, national or social origin, property, birth or other status.
2. Where not already provided for by existing legislative or other measures, each State Party to the present Covenant undertakes to take the necessary steps, in accordance with its constitutional processes and with the provisions of the present Covenant, to adopt such legislative or other measures as may be necessary to give effect to the rights recognized in the present Covenant.

3. Each State Party to the present Covenant undertakes:

(a) To ensure that any person whose rights or freedoms as herein recognized are violated shall have an effective remedy, notwithstanding that the violation has been committed by persons acting in an official capacity;

(b) To ensure that any person claiming such a remedy shall have his right thereto determined by competent judicial, administrative or legislative authorities, or by any other competent authority provided for by the legal system of the State, and to develop the possibilities of judicial remedy;

(c) To ensure that the competent authorities shall enforce such remedies when granted.

549. ICCPR, *id.* art. 2(3)(a) (ensuring that a person whose rights have been violated is entitled to an effective remedy "notwithstanding that the violation has been committed by persons acting in an official capacity."). HRC General Comment 20, *supra* note 307, para. 2 ("The aim of the provisions of article 7 of the International Covenant on Civil and Political Rights is to protect both the dignity and the physical and mental integrity of the individual. It is the duty of the State party to afford everyone protection through legislative and other measures as may be necessary against the acts prohibited by article 7, whether inflicted by people acting in their official capacity, outside their official capacity or in a private capacity. The prohibition in article 7 is complemented by the positive requirements of article 10, paragraph 1, of the Covenant, which stipulates that 'All persons deprived of their liberty shall be treated with humanity and with respect for the inherent dignity of the human person.'")

550. HRC General Comment 31, *supra* note 13, para. 8 ("The article 2, paragraph 1, obligations are binding on States Parties and do not, as such, have direct horizontal effect as a matter of international law. The Covenant cannot be viewed as a substitute for domestic criminal or civil law. However the positive obligations on States Parties to ensure Covenant rights will only be fully discharged if individuals are protected by the State, not just against violations of Covenant rights by its agents, but also against acts committed by private persons or entities that would impair the enjoyment of Covenant rights in so far as they are amenable to application between private persons or entities.... It is also implicit in article 7 that States Parties have to take positive measures to ensure that private persons or entities do not inflict torture or cruel, inhuman or degrading treatment or punishment on others within their power."); *see also* HRC General Comment 20, *supra* note 307, para. 13 ("States parties should indicate when presenting their reports the provisions of their criminal law which penalize torture and cruel, inhuman and degrading treatment or punishment, specifying the penalties applicable to such acts, whether committed by public officials or other persons acting on behalf of the State, or by private persons. Those who violate article 7, whether by encouraging, ordering, tolerating or perpetrating prohibited acts, must be held responsible.").

551. HRC General Comment 31, supra note 13, para. 15. ("There may be circumstances in which a failure to ensure Covenant rights as required by article 2 would give rise to violations by States Parties of those rights, as a result of States Parties' permitting or failing to take appropriate measures or to exercise due diligence to prevent, punish, investigate or redress the harm caused by such acts by private persons or entities. States are reminded of the interrelationship between the positive obligations imposed under article 2 and the need to provide effective remedies in the event of breach under article 2, paragraph 3. The Covenant itself envisages in some articles certain areas where there are positive obligations on States Parties to address the activities of private persons or entities").

552. *Irene Bleier Lewenhoff and Rosa Valiño de Bleier v. Uruguay,* Communication No. 30/1978, Human Rights Committee, U.N. Doc. CCPR/C/OP/1 at 109, para. 13.3 (1985); *see also Alberto Grille Motta v. Uruguay,* Communication No. 11/1977, Human Rights Committee, U.N. Doc. CCPR/C/OP/1 at 54, para. 14 (1984); *William Torres Ramirez v. Uruguay,* Communication No. 4/1977 (26 January 1978), Human Rights Committee, U.N. Doc. CCPR/C/OP/1 at 4, para. 16 (1984); *Edgardo Dante Santullo Valcada v. Uruguay,* Communication No. 9/1977, Human Rights Committee, U.N. Doc. CCPR/C/OP/1 at 43, para. 11 (1984); *Anthony McLeod v. Jamaica,* Communication No. 734/1997, U.N. Doc. CCPR/C/59/D/734/1997 (3 June 1998).

553. *Tshitenge Muteba v. Zaire,* Communication No. 124/1982 (25 March 1983), Human Rights Committee, U.N. Doc. Supp. No. 40 (A/39/40) at 182 (1984); *see also John Khemraadi Baboeram at al. v. Suriname,* Communication No. 146/1983 and 148 to 154/1983, Human Rights Committee, U.N. Doc. Supp.

No. 40 (A/40/40) at 187, para. 13.2 (1985) (same with respect to extra-judicial executions); *Maria del Carmen Almeida de Quinteros and Elena Quinteros Almeida v. Uruguay,* Communication No. 107/1981, U.N. Doc. Supp. No. 40 (A/38/40) at 216 (1983) (same with respect to forced abductions by state agents). Regional courts have also interpreted similar "ensure and respect" and "right to remedy" language in regional conventions and treaties to incorporate a state's obligation to investigate and prosecute conventional violations. For example, the Inter-American Commission on Human Rights has interpreted the American Convention's Article 1(1) duty to "ensure and respect" and Article 25 "right to a remedy" duty to include the obligation to investigate and prosecute responsible individuals in cases of torture or disappearance. Case No. 6586 Inter-Am. C.H.R. 91, OEA/ser.L./V/II/61, doc. 22 rev. 1 (1983), at 93; *see also Gary Hermosilla et. al.,* Case No. 10.843, Inter-Am C.H.R. (1988). The European Court of Human Rights has also interpreted the "right to a remedy" language of Article 13 of the European Convention to include the obligation to investigate and prosecute. *See McCann and others v. United Kingdom,* 324 Eur. Ct. H.R. 31 (ser. A) (1995). *See* European Convention, supra note 190, art. 13, which provides that "[e]veryone whose rights and freedoms as set forth in this Convention are violated shall have an effective remedy before a national authority notwithstanding that the violation has been committed by persons acting in an official capacity."

554. Geneva I, art. 51, Geneva II, art. 52, Geneva III, art. 131, Geneva IV, art. 148, *supra* note 173.

555. Geneva I, art. 50, Geneva II, art. 51, Geneva III, art. 130, Geneva IV, art. 147, *supra* note 173.

556. Geneva IV, *supra* note 173, art. 147,

557. Geneva III, art. 129, Geneva IV, art. 146, *supra* note 173.

558. *See* ILC Articles and Commentaries, *supra* note 531, at 82 (art. 2, cmt. 5). Chapter II of the ILC Articles sets out the general rules by which a wrongful act might be attributed to a state.

559. ILC Articles and Commentaries, *supra* note 531, at 106 (art. 7).

560. ILC Articles and Commentaries, *supra* note 531, at 110 (art. 8).

561. ILC Articles and Commentaries, *supra* note 531, at 110 (art. 8, cmts. 1 & 2).

562. *Nicaragua case, supra* note 359; ILC Articles and Commentaries, *supra* note 531, at 110–111 (art. 8, cmt. 4).

563. *Id.* para. 108.

564. *Id.* para. 211, 238.

565. *Id.* para 115.

566. *Id.* para 116.

567. *Id.* para 115. Some commentators have suggested that by not holding the United States responsible for the acts of the *contras,* the ICJ set the legal standard for attribution too high. *See, e.g.,* Mark Gibney, Katarina Tomasevski and Jens Vedsted-Hansen, *Transnational State Responsibility for Violations of Human Rights,* 12 Harv. Hum. Rts. J. 267, 285–87 (Spring 1999). The article argues that the "ICJ's notion of 'control' is premised on very transitional notions of state-sovereignty and power relations between nation-states, where one country attempts to rule or dominate another. This approach, however, will miss most of what presently governs relations between and among states." *Id.* at 286.

568. *Prosecutor v. Tadic,* Case No. IT-94-1-A, Judgment, (ICTY Trial Chamber, July 15, 1999), paras. 131, 137.

569. *Id.* (emphasis added).

570. Possible liability of civilian contractors is discussion in Sections V.E. and VIII.A. of this Report.

571. Some commentators have suggested that the threshold for attribution of the acts of private parties to a state appears to have been lowered significantly post-September 11, 2001. Subsequent to the attacks in New York, Washington, and Pennsylvania, the United States asserted the right to act in self-defense against Afghanistan because the Taliban regime had *supported and harbored* leaders of the Al Qaeda terrorist network. D. Jinks, *State Responsibility for Sponsorship of Terrorists and Insurgent Groups: State Responsibility for the Acts of Private Armed Groups,* 4 Chi. J. Int'l L. 83. The Bush Administration did not allege that Al Qaeda acted on behalf of the Taliban, or that the Taliban played any direct role in, or had any direct knowledge of, the planning or execution of the attacks; instead it attributed the acts of Al Qaeda to Taliban simply because the Taliban had *harbored and supported* the group. *Id.* The attribution was without regard to whether Afghanistan in fact exercised "effective control" (or "overall control") over

the group. The UN Security Council, North Atlantic Treaty Organization, and the OAS expressly or tacitly endorsed the U.S. position. *Id.*

572. ILC Articles and Commentaries, *supra* note 531, at 103 (art. 6, cmt. 2).

573. ILC Articles and Commentaries, *supra* note 531, at 103 (art. 6., cmt. 3).

574. ILC Articles and Commentaries, *supra* note 531, at 154 (art. 17, cmt. 8).

575. ILC Articles and Commentaries, *supra* note 531, at 148 (art. 16).

576. ILC Articles and Commentaries, *supra* note 531, at 148 (art. 16).

577. *See, e.g.,* ILC Articles and Commentaries, *supra* note 531, at 149 (art. 16, cmt. 3) ("the aid or assistance must be given with a view to facilitating the commission of that act"), cmt. 5 ("A State is not responsible for aid or assistance under article 16 unless the relevant State organ *intended,* by the aid or assistance given, to facilitate the occurrence of the wrongful conduct. . . .") (emphasis added).

578. ILC Articles and Commentaries, *supra* note 531, at 149 (art. 16, cmt. 5).

579. ILC Articles and Commentaries, *supra* note 531, at 148 (art. 16, cmt. 1).

580. ILC Articles and Commentaries, *supra* note 531, at 150 (art. 16, cmt. 9).

581. *See* Sections IV.A. and VI. of this Report.

582. ILC Articles and Commentaries, *supra* note 531, at 152 (art. 17).

583. ILC Articles and Commentaries, *supra* note 531, at 152 (art. 17, cmt. 1).

584. ILC Articles and Commentaries, *supra* note v, at 152 (art. 17, cmt. 2).

585. *Cf. Armed Activities on the Territory of the Congo* (New Application: 2002) (*Democratic Republic of the Congo v. Rwanda*), 2002 I.C.J. 126 (July 10, 2002) ("whether or not States accept the jurisdiction of the Court, they remain in any event responsible for acts attributable to them that violate international law").

586. In reality, states rarely resort to lawsuits for resolving international disputes. The more common modes of recourse include protests or claims and negotiations through diplomatic channels. *See* John F. Murphy, *Civil Liability for the Commission of International Crimes as an Alternative to Criminal Prosecution,* 12 HARV. HUM. RTS. J. 1 (1999).

587. Statute of the International Court of Justice, Oct. 24, 1945, 59 Stat. 1031, T.S. No. 993 (ICJ Statute), art. 36. States may manifest their consent in three ways: through special agreement relating to the single case at issue; through a clause in a treaty (known as a "jurisdictional clause") giving the ICJ authority to adjudicate a dispute relating to the interpretation or application of a given treaty; or through a unilateral declaration recognizing the jurisdiction of the Court as compulsory, in relation to any other State accepting the same obligation (known as an "optional clause.") *See also* the website of the ICJ, *at* http://www.icj-cij.org/icjwww/ibasicdocuments/ibasictext/ibasic_whobringcases.html (last visited Oct. 25, 2004).

588. J.G. Merrills, INTERNATIONAL DISPUTE SETTLEMENT 126–129 (1998).

589. CAT, *supra* note 9, art. 30(1).

590. *See* Declarations and Reservations of the United States of America, *available at* http://www.ohchr.org/english/law/cat-reserve.htm (last visited Oct. 25, 2004).

591. For an overview of the efforts of the U.S. government to insulate itself from liability in international fora, *see, e.g.,* John Quigley, *American Style in International Human Rights Adjudication,* 19 OHIO ST. J. ON DISP. RESOL. 249 (2003).

592. ICJ Statute, *supra* note 575, art. 65.

593. Dinah L. Shelton, *The Inter-American Human Rights System,* in GUIDE TO INTERNATIONAL HUMAN RIGHTS PRACTICE, 119 (Hurst Hannum ed., 2d ed. 1992).

594. By ratifying the Charter of the OAS, the United States accepted the competence of the Inter-American Commission on Human Rights to hear petitions concerning its alleged violations of human rights. *See* Charter of the Organization of American States, 119 U.N.T.S. 3, *entered into force* December 13, 1951; amended by Protocol of Buenos Aires, 721 U.N.T.S. 324, O.A.S. Treaty Series, No. 1-A, *entered into force* Feb. 27, 1970; amended by Protocol of Cartagena, O.A.S. Treaty Series, No. 66, 25 I.L.M. 527, *entered into force* Nov. 16, 1988; amended by Protocol of Washington, 1-E Rev. OEA Documentos Oficiales OEA/Ser.A/2 Add. 3 (SEPF), 33 I.L.M. 1005, *entered into force* September 25, 1997; amended by Protocol of Managua, 1-F Rev. OEA Documentos Oficiales OEA/Ser.A/2 Add.4 (SEPF), 33 I.L.M. 1009, *entered into force* January 29, 1996.

595. O.A.S. Res. XXX, adopted by the Ninth International Conference of American States (1948), reprinted in Basic Documents Pertaining to Human Rights in the Inter-American System, OEA/Ser.L.V/II.82 doc.6 rev.1 at 17 (1992).

596. *Sosa v. Alvarez-Machain, U.S. v. Alvarez-Machain,* 124 S. Ct. 2739 (2004).

597. *Id.*

598. 28 U.S.C. §1346(b)(1).

599. *Alvarez-Machain,* 124 S. Ct. 2739 at 16, 36, *referring to* 28 U.S.C. § 2690(k). In its opinion, the Supreme Court rejected the so-called "headquarters doctrine" that the Ninth Circuit had applied when it ruled on the case. Under the headquarters doctrine, the U.S. may be liable for an act that took place in another country if the wrongdoing originated in the U.S. but had its "operative effect in another country." *Alvarez-Machain* at *17, citing *Sami v. U.S.,* 617 F.2d 755, 762 (CADC 1979) (refusing to apply § 2680(k) where a communique sent from the United States by a federal law enforcement officer resulted in plaintiff's wrongful detention in Germany).

600. *Alvarez-Machain,* 124 S. Ct at 36.

601. The FTCA might still provide a cause of action in instances where the torture occurred in a U.S. facility overseas, such as in the Guantánamo detention facility. *See Rasul et al. v. Bush,* 159 L. Ed. 2d 548 (2004). *See* Section VIII.B., for a discussion of possible claims under Alien Tort Claims Act of 1789 and the Torture Victim Protection Act of 1991.

602. 18 U.S.C. §§2340, 2340A, and 2340B.

603. Pub. L. No. 81-506, 64 Stat. 107-49 (*as subsequently amended*), 10 U.S.C. §801 *et seq.*

604. Pub. L. No. 106-523, 18 U.S.C. § 3261, 114 Stat. 2488.

605. 18 U.S.C. §§2340 and 2340A. The Senate Committee on the Judiciary acknowledged the relationship of 18 U.S.C. §2340 to CAT and the Torture Victim Protection Act in a 2002 report. *See* S. REP. NO. 107-44 (2002), 10–11.

606. Uniting and Strengthening America by Providing Appropriate Tools Required to Intercept and Obstruct Terrorism Act of 2001, Pub. L. No. 107-56, 115 Stat. 272 (2001) (USA Patriot Act).

607. U.S.C. §§2340A(a). Section 2340(3) defined the "United States" as including "all areas under the jurisdiction of the United States including any of the places described in sections 5 and 7 of this title and section 46501(2) of title 49." The USA Patriot Act broadened the scope of section 7, extending jurisdiction under that section to foreign diplomatic, military and other facilities. By cross-reference, these places would have been excluded from the reach of section 2340A. *But see* note 608.

608. H.R.4200, 108th Cong. §1089 (2004).

609. 18 U.S.C. §2340.

610. 18 U.S.C. §2340.

611. *See* Sen. Rep. 103-107; for a discussion of the legality under international law of the United States' reservation, understanding and declarations with respect to ratification of CAT, *see supra* note 9.

612. 28 U.S.C. §1350. ATCA states that "[t]he district courts shall have original jurisdiction of any civil action by an alien for a tort only, committed in violation of the law of nations or a treaty of the United States."

613. Torture Victim Protection Act of 1991, Mar. 12, 1992, P.L. 102-256, 106 Stat. 73, *enacted* as a note to 28 U.S.C. §1350. The TPA provides that: "[a]n individual who, under actual or apparent authority, or color of law, of any foreign nation – (1) subjects an individual to torture shall, in a civil action, be liable for damages to that individual; or (2) subjects an individual to extrajudicial killing shall, in a civil action, be liable for damages to the individual's legal representative, or to any person who may be a claimant in an action for wrongful death." *Id.* §2(a). *See also* S. REP. No. 102-249 (1991) (stating that the TPA would "carry out the intent of the Convention Against Torture and Other Cruel, Inhuman or Degrading Treatment or Punishment, which was ratified by the U.S. Senate on October 27, 1990").

614. *Xuncax v. Gramajo,* 886 F. Supp. 162, 170 (D. Mass 1995).

615. *Tachiona v. Mugabe,* 234 F. Supp.2d 401, 420-423 (S.D.N.Y. 2002); *Cabiri v. Assasie-Gyimah,* 921 F. Supp. 1189, 1191, 1196 (S.D.N.Y. 1996); *Abebe-Jira v. Negewo,* 72 F.3d 844, 845 (11th Cir. 1996).

616. *Abebe-Jira v. Negewo,* 72 F.3d 844, 845 (11th Cir. 1996).

617. *Id.*

618. 590 F.2d 1269 (4th Cir. 1979).

619. Deliberate avoidance of knowledge does not preclude a finding of intent with respect to the conspiracy. *See, e.g., United States v. Richardson,* 14 F.3d 666, 671–72 (1st Cir. 1994) (willful blindness instruction to the jury is appropriate when defendant intentionally avoids gaining knowledge of the obvious); *United States v. Mancuso,* 42 F.3d 836, 846 (4th Cir. 1994) (knowledge of a fact may be inferred from willful blindness to existence of that fact); *United States v. Whittington,* 26 F.3d, 456, 463 (4th Cir. 1994) (willful blindness instruction to the jury is appropriate when defendants go to "great lengths to insulate [themselves] from the fraud perpetrated"); *United States v. Faulkner,* 17 F.3d, 745, 767–78 (5th Cir. 1994) (deliberate ignorance instruction is appropriate when defendant claims lack of guilty knowledge but evidence supports inference of deliberate indifference); *United States v. Gonzalez,* 933 F.2d 417, 422 (7th Cir. 1991) (same).

620. *See also, People v. Lauria,* 59 Cal. Rptr. 628, 623 (Cal. Ct. App., 1967), (inferring intent from knowledge: the "element of intent may be proved either by direct evidence, or by evidence of circumstances from which an intent to further a criminal enterprise by supplying lawful goods or services may be inferred. Direct evidence of participation, such as advice from the supplier of legal goods or services to the user of those goods or services on their use for illegal. . . . But in cases where direct proof of complicity is lacking, intent to further the conspiracy must be derived from the sale itself and its surrounding circumstances in order to establish the supplier's express or tacit agreement to join the conspiracy."); *See generally,* LAFAVE, *supra* note LAFAVE, §5.7.

621. Syria, Egypt, Saudi Arabia, and other states to which the United States is alleged to have Extraordinarily Rendered individuals are known to employ interrogation techniques that unequivocally amount to torture. *See, e.g.,* U.S. DEP'T. OF STATE COUNTRY REPORTS ON HUMAN RIGHTS PRACTICES 2001: SYRIA, *available at* http://www.state.gov/g/drl/rls/hrrpt/2001/nea/8298.htm (last visited Oct. 25, 2004) ("there was credible evidence that security forces continued to use torture. During the year, . . . numerous cases of torture in custody [were reported], including the case of two Kurdish leaders, Marwan Uthman and Hasan Saleh, who were arrested in December 2002 for organizing a demonstration. . . . Former prisoners and detainees, as well as the SHRC, reported that torture methods included administering electrical shocks; pulling out fingernails; forcing objects into the rectum; beating, sometimes while the victim is suspended from the ceiling; hyperextending the spine; bending the detainees into the frame of a wheel and whipping exposed body parts; and using a chair that bends backwards to asphyxiate the victim or fracture the victim's spine. Torture was most likely to occur while detainees were being held at one of the many detention centers run by the various security services throughout the country, particularly while the authorities were attempting to extract a confession or information "); U.S. DEPARTMENT OF STATE, COUNTRY REPORTS ON HUMAN RIGHTS PRACTICES – 2003: LEBANON, *available at* http://www.state.gov/g/drl/rls/hrrpt/2003/27932.htm (last visited Oct. 26, 2004) ("The Government acknowledged that violent abuse usually occurred during preliminary investigations conducted at police stations or military installations, in which suspects were interrogated without an attorney. Such abuse occurred despite laws that prevented judges from accepting any confession extracted under duress"); U.S. DEPARTMENT OF STATE, COUNTRY REPORTS ON HUMAN RIGHTS PRACTICES – 2003: EGYPT, *available at* http://www.state.gov/g/drl/rls/hrrpt/2003/27926.htm (last visited Oct. 26, 2004) ('there were numerous, credible reports that security forces tortured and mistreated detainees. Human rights groups believed that the SSIS, police, and other Government entities continued to employ torture. Torture was used to extract information, coerce the victims to end their oppositionist activities, and to deter others from similar activities. Reports of torture and mistreatment at police stations remained frequent."); U.S. DEPARTMENT OF STATE, COUNTRY REPORTS ON HUMAN RIGHTS PRACTICES – 2003: SAUDI ARABIA, *available at* http://www.state.gov/g/drl/rls/hrrpt/2003/27937.htm (last visited Oct. 26, 2004) ("there were credible reports that the authorities abused detainees, both citizens and foreigners. Ministry of Interior officials were responsible for most incidents of abuse of prisoners, including beatings, whippings, and sleep deprivation. In addition, there were allegations of torture, including allegations of beatings with sticks and suspension from bars by handcuffs. There were reports that torture and abuse were used to obtain confessions from prisoners. . . . Canadian and British prisoners that were released during the year reported that they had been tortured during their detention.")

622. *United States v. Loe,* 262 F.3d 427 (5th Cir. 2001).

623. *United States v. Sassi,* 966 F.2d 283 (7th Cir. 1992) (while general federal conspiracy statute specifically requires overt act, several specific conspiracy statutes, including 21 U.S.C.A. § 846, do not so

specify, and as to them proof of overt act unnecessary); *State v. D'Ingianni,* 47 So. 2d 731 (1950); *Martin v. State,* 19 So. 2d 488 (Miss.1944); *State v. Condrey,* 562 S.E.2d 320 (S.C. 2002). Even those statutes that do contain an overt act requirement provide that an act need not be done by all conspirators and the act need not be criminal or unlawful in itself. *Braverman v. United States,* 317 U.S. 49 (1942); *Castro v. United States,* 296 F.2d 540 (5th Cir. 1961); *State v. Heitman,* 629 N.W.2d 542 (2001); *McCann v. State,* 606 S.W.2d 897 (Tex. Ct. App. 1980).

624. LaFave, *supra* note 442, §6.5(c); American Law Institute Model Penal Code Official Draft, 1962, §5.03(5) (Model Penal Code).

625. *Yates v. United States,* 354 U.S. 298 (1957); LaFave, *supra* note 442, §6.5(c).

626. The Model Penal Code is not binding law. However, it has been very influential and numerous court opinions cite to the Model Penal Code as persuasive authority for the interpretation of an existing statute or in the exercise of a court's occasional power to formulate a criminal law doctrine. *See, e.g., U.S. v. Crowley,* 318 F.3d 401 (2nd Cir. 2003); *United States v. Bussey,* 507 F.2d 1096, 1098 (9th Cir. 1974).

627. Model Penal Code, *supra* note 608, §5.03(1).

628. *American Tobacco Co. v. United States,* 328 U.S. 781 (1946); *United States v. Amiel,* 95 F.3d 135 (2d Cir. 1996); *State v. Gillespie,* 336 S.W.2d 677 (Mo. 1960); *Burk v. State,* 848 P.2d 225 (Wyo. 1993).

629. *United States v. Hartley,* 678 F.2d 961 (11th Cir. 1982); *State v. Mapp,* 585 N.W. 2d 746 (Iowa 1998); *O'Neill v. State,* 296 N.W. 96 (Wisc. 1941); *Martinez v. State,* 943 P.2d 1178 (Wyo. 1997).

630. 420 U.S. 770 (1975).

631. *See also,* LaFave, *supra* note 442, §6.4(d).

632. *Id.* at 275–276.

633. LaFave, *supra* note 442, §6.4(e).

634. *U.S. v. Lichenstein,* 610 F.2d 1272 (5th Cir. 1980); *McDonald v. State,* 454 So. 2d 488 (Miss. 1984).

635. *People v. Lauria,* 59 Cal. Rptr. 628, 623 (Cal. Ct. App. 1967) (dictum).

636. *People v. Powell,* 63 N.Y. 88 (NY 1875); *Commonwealth v. Gormleym,* 77 Pa. Super. 298 (1921); *Landen v. United States,* 299 F. 75 (6th Cir. 1924).

637. *See generally,* LaFave, *supra* note 442, §6.4

638. 18 U.S.C. §2.

639. *Breeze v. United States,* 398 F.2d 178 (10th Cir. 1968) (holding that 18 U.S.C. §2 is applicable to entire U.S. criminal code, so that 18 U.S.C. §1381, relating to harboring, concealment, protection or assistance of deserter from Armed Forces of United States should be read and construed in like manner as if 18 U.S.C. §2 were part of it); *United States v. Mucciante,* 21 F.3d 1228, 1234 (2nd Cir. 1994) ("an aiding and abetting charge is arguably implicit in every indictment….The Federal aiding and abetting statute, 18 U.S.C. 2, does not penalize conduct apart from the substantive crime with which it is coupled."); *see also United States. v. Sabatino,* 943 F.2d 94 (1st Cir. 1991) (same effect).

640. *State v. Scott,* 68 A. 258 (1907).

641. *United States v. Whitney,* 229 F.2d 1296 (10th Cir. 2000); *Alonzi v. People,* 597 P.2d 560 (Colo. 1979).

642. *State v. Haddad,* 456 A.2d 316 (Conn. 1983); *Commonwealth v. Richards,* 293 N.E. 2d 854 (Mass. 1973).

643. *Commonwealth v. Richards,* 293 N.E. 2d 854 (Mass. 1973).

644. *Malatkofski v. United States,* 179 F.2d 905 (1st Cir. 1950) (supplying money for bribe).

645. *United States v. Eberhardt,* 417 F.2d 1009 (4th Cir. 1969) (provided own blood to be poured on selective service files).

646. 15 So. 722 (Ct. 1893) *, 86–87.

647. The defendant was not an accomplice where he "stood by" while the mother killed the child but neither actually aided the mother in the acts of abuse nor "counsel[ed], command[ed] or encourage[d] her." *Pope v. State,* 396 A.2d 1054 (Md. 1979).

648. *Commonwealth v. Morrow,* 296 N.E. 2d 468 (Mass. 1973); *Skidmore v. State,* 115 N.W. 288 (Neb. 1908).

649. LaFave, *supra* note 442, §6.7(a).

650. *Id.* §6.7(b).

651. *Id.* §6.7(c).

652. *Id.* §6.7(d); *see also Backun v. United States,* 112 F.2d 635 (4th Cir. 1940); *United States v. Giovannetti,* 919 F.2d 1223 (7th Cir. 1990) (willful blindness suffices as a mental state for accomplice liability). *Cf. United States v. Peoni,* 100 F.2d 401 (2d Cir. 1938).

653. For a more detailed discussion of unreliability of diplomatic assurances, *see* Section VI of this Report.

654. 10 U.S.C. §§801–941 (1994 & Supp. IV 1999).

655. 10 U.S.C.A. §802 (1994). The term "armed forces" is defined in section 101(a)(4) to mean the "Army, Navy, Air Force, Marine Corps, and Coast Guard," 10 U.S.C. §101(a)(4) (1994).

656. MANUAL FOR COURTS-MARTIAL, UNITED STATES (2002 ed.) (The Manual). The Manual is issued by the President as a regulation under authority granted by Congress under Article 3 of the UCMJ.

657. 10 U.S.C. §805.

658. 10 U.S.C. §802.

659. 10 U.S.C. §802(a)(10).

660. 10 U.S.C. §802(a)(9). The UCMJ does not define the term POW. Thus it is uncertain whether "POW" in the UCMJ has the same meaning as in Geneva III.

661. *United States v. Averette,* 19 U.S.C.M.A. 363, 365–66, 41 C.M.R. 363, 365-–66 (1970) (the phrase "in time of war" is limited to "a war formally declared by Congress"; even though the Vietnam conflict "qualified as a war as that word is generally used and understood[,]...such a recognition should not serve as a shortcut for a formal declaration of war, at least in the sensitive area of subjecting civilians to military jurisdiction"). *Cf. United States v. Anderson,* 17 U.S.C.M.A. 588, 589, 38 C.M.R. 386, 387 (1968) (U.S. involvement in Vietnam conflict "constitutes a 'time of war'...within the meaning of" Article 43(a) of the UCMJ, which provides that there is no statute of limitations over certain offenses committed "in time of war").

662. *United States ex rel Toth v. Quarles,* 350 U.S. 11 (1955).

663. *Kinsella v. Singleton,* 361 U.S. 234, 248 (1960).

664. *Grisham v. Hagen,* 361 U.S. 278, 279 (1960); *McElroy v. Guagliardo,* 361 U.S. 281, 286 (1960)

665. The Court of Appeals for the Armed Forces (formerly the Court of Military Appeals) is a civilian Article I court hearing appeals from the intermediate appellate courts for each of the Army, Navy (and Marines) and Air Force, subject to possible appeal to the U.S. Supreme Court.

666. *Willenbring v. Neurauter,* 48 M.J. 152, 157, 1998 CAAF LEXIS 43 (C.A.A.F. 1998).

667. *See, e.g., Robb v. United States,* 456 F.2d 768 (Ct. Cl. 1972) (civilian engineer employed by U.S. Navy in Vietnam was not subject to the UCMJ); *Reid v. Covert,* 354 U.S. 1 (1957) (no jurisdiction over civilian dependents of service members stationed overseas in peacetime for capital offenses).

668. *Reid v. Covert,* 354 U.S. 1, 22 (1957). As described below, the Military Extraterritorial Jurisdiction Act of 2000 eliminated some of the gap in jurisdiction resulting from *Reid v. Covert* by conferring jurisdiction on federal courts over certain civilians accompanying the armed forces abroad.

669. 10 U.S.C. §855. The protections of Article 55 apply to "any person subject to" the UCMJ. As stated previously, the UCMJ applies to "prisoners of war," at least as defined in the Geneva Conventions, which probably includes persons whose status is in doubt pending resolution by a competent tribunal, and would apply to unlawful combatants charged with offenses under the UCMJ under 10 U.S.C. § 818.

670. The Articles of War preceding the UCMJ prohibited "cruel and unusual punishment," but the phrase was changed to "cruel *or* unusual punishment" in Article 55 (emphasis added). *See* Articles of War 41, Manual for Courts-Martial, U.S. Army, 1929 at 212, and 1949 at 284. The legislative history of Article 55 provides no rationale why the word "and" was changed to "or." *United States v. White,* 54 M. J. 469, 2001 CAAF LEXIS 497 (C.A.A.F. 2001).

671. *See United States v. Kinsch,* 54 M.J. 641, 2000 CCA LEXIS 237 (A.C.C.A. 2000). *See also* HR Standards Report, *supra* note 197.

672. *See United States v. Wappler,* 2 C.M.A. 393, 9 C.M.R. 23, 1953 CMA LEXIS 897 (C.M.A. 1953); *United States v. White,* 54 M.J. 469, 473 2001 CAAF LEXIS 497 (C.A.A.F. 2001); *United States v. Avila,* 53 M.J. 99, 2000 CAAF LEXIS 569 (C.A.A.F. 2000).

673. Compare the federal criminal civil rights statutes, 18 U.S.C. §§241 and 242, and the civil statute 42 U.S.C. §1983, all of which apply only where the victim is entitled to constitutional rights.

674. The Manual, *supra* note 656, para. 60.b (1-2).

675. *Id.* para. 60.c (3).

676. *United States v. Perkins,* 47 C.M.R. 259 (Ct. of Mil. Rev. 1973). According to the Manual, however, the doctrine of preemption "prohibits application of Article 134 to conduct covered by Articles 80 through 132. For example, larceny is covered in Article 121, and if an element of that offense is lacking – for example, intent – there can be no larceny or larceny type offense, either under Article 121 or, because of preemption, under Article 134." The Manual, para. 60.c (5)(a). In effect, Article 134 may not be employed to salvage a charge where the charge could not be sustained under the substantive offense provisions of the UCMJ or Federal statute. Accordingly, conduct which violated Article 55 discussed above or any other substantive provision of the UCMJ could not be charged under Article 134. These remain alternative, not cumulative provisions.

677. *United States v. Perkins,* 47 C.M.R. 259, 263–264 (Ct. of Mil. Rev. 1973); HR Standards Report, *supra* note 197.

678. 10 U.S.C.A. §881.

679. The Military Extraterritorial Jurisdiction Act of 2000, Pub. L. No. 106-553; 18 U.S.C.S. § 3261, added Nov. 22, 2000, P.L. 106-523, §2(a), 114 Stat. 2488.

680. Jessica Ioigo, *In first use of jurisdiction act, USAF spouse to be tried in husband's death,* Stars and Stripes (European Edition), June 5, 2003, *available at* http://cndyorks.gn.apc.org/caab/articles/usafspousetobetried.htm (last visited Oct. 25, 2004).

681. *Californian convicted of killing husband at U.S. base in Turkey,* Associated Press, Oct. 15, 2004, *available at* http://www.mercurynews.com/mld/mercurynews/news/local/states/california/the_valley/9930855.htm?1c (last visited Oct. 25, 2004). No details of the case are available as of the time of this writing.

682. 18 U.S.C.S. §3261(b).

683. H.R. REP. No. 106-788, pt. 1, at 19 (2000), 14–15 & n.27, *available at* http://thomas.loc.gov/cgi-bin/cpquery/T?&report=hr778p1&dbname=cp106& (House Report) (last visited Oct. 25, 2004).

684. 18 U.S.C.S., §3267.

685. 18 U.S.C.S., §3267.

686. H.R. 4200, 108th Cong. §1088 (2004).

687. 18 U.S.C.S. §3261(d). Retired personnel, as distinguished from discharged personnel, remain subject to the UCMJ and may be recalled to active duty for purposes of being tried by court martial.

688. House Report, *supra* note 683, at 15 n.28 (citing *United States v. Batchelder,* 442 U.S. 114 (1979)).

689. *Id.*, at 16. The House Report stated that the provision "is designed to allow the Government to try the military member together with a non-military co-defendant in a United States Court." *Id.*

690. MEJA §3261, 114 Stat. 2488. Because section 3261(d)(2) only requires that the military member be indicted, or an information filed against him, together with another person, this element of the crime will be satisfied even if the judge approves a motion for separate trials. Of course, in such a situation, Justice could agree to dismiss the complaint against the military member so that the Department of Defense could proceed against him or her by court-martial, but nothing in the statute requires this.

691. G.R. Schmitt, *Closing the Gap in Criminal Jurisdiction Over Civilians Accompanying the Armed Forces Abroad—A First Person Account of the Creation of the Military Extraterritorial Jurisdiction Act of 2000,* 51 Cath. U.L. Rev. 55 (2001).

692. 444 U.S. 394, 415–416 (1980).

693. 532 U.S. 483, 490 (2001).

694. *Id.* (quoting *United States v. Rutherford,* 442 U.S. 544, 559 (1979)).

695. Note that the Bybee Memorandum makes a similar argument but in reverse. Judge Bybee suggests that because Congress did not include provisions from CAT that explicitly prohibit the defense of necessity, Congress implicitly allowed the defense. Bybee Memorandum, *supra* note 134.

696. The Manual, *supra* note 656, Rule 916(h).

697. 52 M.J. 58 (C.M.A. 1999).

698. 57 M.J. 394 (C.M.A. 2002).

699. Note that in the context of military justice, the defense has traditionally been examined through the prism of a subordinate's refusal to follow a superior order. In the Extraordinary Rendition context the situation may be reversed however, and the accused might raise the defense to justify following the order.

700. Because MEJA incorporates crimes under Title 18 and 21, presumably it incorporates the applicable defenses as well.

701. LaFave, *supra* note 442, §5.4(d).

702. *See, e.g., United States v. Coupez,* 603 F.2d 1347 (9th Cir. 1979) and state statutes such as N.Y. Penal Law §35.05.

703. It may be assumed that the defense is likely to assert that individual's intent was to avoid future harm. However, only in the ticking bomb scenario where the purpose of an Extraordinary Rendition is to gather information to prevent an imminent future terrorist attack is it likely that this requirement of the defense will be met.

704. *See, e.g., People v. Gray,* 150 Misc. 2d 852, 856–857 (N.Y. Crim. Ct. 1991).

705. *See* Bybee Memorandum, *supra* note 134.

706. Alberto Gonzalez, Counsel to the President, *The President's Stance on Torture,* The Washington Post, Oct. 5, 2004, A24, *available at* http://www.washingtonpost.com/wp-dyn/articles/A7245-2004Oct4.html?referrer=emailarticlepg (last visited Oct. 25, 2004).

707. *See, e.g.,* D. Filkins, *General Says Less Coercion of Captives Yields Better Data,* New York Times, Sept. 7, 2004.

708. *See e.g., Bailey,* 442 U.S. at 635; *United States v. Arellano-Rivera,* 244 F.3d 1119 (9th Cir. 2001); *Regina v. Dudley & Stephens,* L.R. 14 Q.B.D. 273 (1884).

709. LaFave, *supra* note 442, §5.4(d); *see, e.g.,* N.Y. Penal Law §35.05.

710. *State v. Howley,* 128 Idaho 874 (Idaho 1996).

711. *See* e.g., *Public Committee Against Torture in Israel et. al. v. The State of Israel,* HCJ 5100/94 (1999) (restricting the application of the defense of necessity in cases of torture during interrogation).

712. LaFave, *supra* note 442, §5.8.

713. *State of Connecticut v. Robert Dejesus,* 260 Conn. 466 ("...defense counsel suggested that self-defense does apply to the mens rea element of the offense of conspiracy to commit murder. In any event, we are unaware of any authority that supports the defendant's request at trial for an instruction on self-defense as to the charge of conspiracy to commit murder...."); *Richmond v. Commonwealth,* 255 Ky. 758 (Whitley Circuit Court, 1934).

714. Manual, *supra* note 638, Rule 916(e).

715. *Little v. Barreme* 6 U.S. 170, 179 (1804).

716. Manual, *supra* note 638, Rule 916(d).

717. *See United States of America v. Otto Ohlendorf, et al.,* Case No. 9, IV Trials of War Criminals before the Nuremberg Military Tribunals, at 1,470.

718. Army Field Manual 27-10; The Law of Land Warfare, July 1976.

719. 22 U.S.C.M.A. 534, 544 (U.S.C.M.A. 1973).

720. *See also, U.S. v. Griffen,* 39 C.M.R. 586, (A.B.R. 1968); *U.S. v. Kinder* 14 C.M.R. 742 (A.F.B.R. 1954) (superior orders did not provide defense to homicide when soldiers followed orders to shoot prisoners).

721. *Calley,* 22 U.S.C.M.A., at 544.

722. 28 U.S.C. S 2679(d)(1).

723. H.R. Rep. No. 100-700, 100th Cong., at 4 (1988). According to the legislative history, the term "common law tort" "embraces not only those state law causes of action predicated on the 'common' or case law of the various states, but also encompasses traditional tort causes of action codified in state statutes that permit recovery for acts of negligence." *Id.* at 6.

724. 28 U.S.C. §1346(b).

725. 28 U.S.C. §2680(h). FTCA is limited by other exceptions pursuant to which the government is not subject to suit, such as the discretionary function exception, which bars a claim "based upon the exercise or performance or the failure to exercise or perform a discretionary function or duty on the part of a federal

agency or an employee of the Government, whether or not the discretion involved be abused." 28 U.S.C. S 2680(a).

726. 28 U.S.C. §2680(h).

727. *See, e.g., Kennedy v. United States,* 585 F. Suppl. 1119 (1984) (under 28 U.S.C.S. §2680(h), government is liable for tortuous conduct of the military police amounting to assault and battery and false arrest). *Contrast Solomon v. United States,* 559 F.2d 309 (5th Cir. 1977) (security employees of a military exchange are not investigative or law enforcement officers within the meaning of section 2680(h)); *DeLong v. United States,* 600 F.Supp. 331 (D. Alaska 1984) (marine guards are not law enforcement officers within the meaning of section 2680(h).) Section 2680(k) precludes liability for any "claim arising in a foreign country." However, an argument can be made that a claim for conspiracy and/or aiding and abetting in the commission of torture originates in the United States, even though "its operative effect" takes place in a foreign country. *See, e.g. Richard v. United States,* 369 U.S. 1 (1962). *But see* notes 596–601 and accompanying discussion.

728. *Filartiga v. Pena-Irala,* 630 F.2d 876 (2nd Cir. 1980); *Abebe-Jira v. Negewo,* No. 93-9133 (10th Cir. 1996) ("the Alien Tort Claims Act establishes a federal forum where courts may fashion domestic common law remedies to give effect to violations of customary international law").

729. *Sosa v. Alvarez-Machain, U.S. v. Alvarez-Machain,* 124 S. Ct. 2739 (2004).

730. Reference to these three crimes stems from Supreme Court's analysis of legislative history of ATCA. The court looked to Blackstone's definition of the law of nations, which listed the three specific offenses. The Court stated that "[i]t was this narrow set of violations of the law of nations, admitting of a judicial remedy and at the same time threatening serious consequences in international affairs, that was probably on minds of the men who drafted [ATCA] with its reference to tort." *Id.* at 2756.

731. *Fortin v. Suarez-Mason,* 672 F. Supp. 1531, 1539–41 (N.D. Cal. 1987).

732. *Aldana v. Fresh Del Monte Produce, Inc.,* 305 F. Supp. 2d 1285 (D. Fla. 2003); *Xuncax v. Gramajo,* 886 F.Supp. 162, 184 (D. Mass. 1995).

733. *Filartiga v. Pena-Irala,* 630 F.2d 876 (2nd Cir. 1980); *Aldana v. Fresh Del Monte Produce, Inc.,* 305 F. Supp. 2d 1285 (D. Fla. 2003); *Presbyterian Church of Sudan v. Talisman Energy, Inc.,* 244 F. Supp. 2d 289 (S.D.N.Y. 2003).

734. Presbyterian Church of Sudan v. Talisman Energy, Inc., 244 F. Supp. 2d 289 (S.D.N.Y. 2003).

735. S. Rep. No. 249, 102d Cong., 1st Sess., at 4–5 (1991), at 8–9; see *also Estate of Ferdinand E. Marcos Human Rights Litigation,* MDL No. 840 (D. Haw.).

736. *See, e.g., Dennis v. Sparks,* 449 U.S. 24, 27–29 (1980) (nongovernmental witness could act "under color of law" by conspiring with the prosecutor or other state officials); *Adickes v. S.H. Cress & Co.,* 398 U.S. 144, 152 (1970) ("The involvement of a state official in such a conspiracy plainly provides the state action essential to show a direct violation of petitioner's Fourteenth Amendment equal protection rights, whether or not the actions of the police were officially authorized, or lawful); *Monroe v. Pape,* 365 U.S. 167 (1961); *see also United States v. Classic,* 313 U.S. 299, 326 (1941); *Screws v. United States,* 325 U.S. 91, 107–11 (1945); *Williams v. United States,* 341 U.S. 97, 99–100 (1951). Moreover, a private party involved in such a conspiracy, even though not an official of the State, can be liable under § 1983. 'Private persons, jointly engaged with state officials in the prohibited action, are acting "under color" of law for purposes of the statute. To act "under color" of law does not require that the accused be an officer of the State. It is enough that he is a willful participant in joint activity with the State or its agents,' *United States v. Price,* 383 U.S. 787, 794 (1966).").

737. It should be noted that it is not clear whether TPA would apply to actions of U.S. armed forces. *See* President George H.W. Bush, Statement on Signing the Torture Victim Protection Act of 1991 (Mar. 12, 1992) ("I must note that I am signing the bill based on my understanding that the Act does not permit suits for alleged human rights violations in the context of United States military operations abroad or law enforcement actions. . . . I do not believe it is the Congress' intent that H.R. 2092 should apply to United States Armed Forces or law enforcement operations, which are always carried out under the authority of United States law.").

CHAPTER 17

Letter from the Association President to the Honorable Alberto Gonzales re 9/11 Issues

PREFACE BY ALAN R. ROTHSTEIN

The nomination of Alberto Gonzales to be Attorney General raised a number of issues regarding Judge Gonzales's performance as Counsel to the President. In particular, Judge Gonzales was widely perceived as coordinating the strategy that resulted in a series of memoranda justifying the Bush Administration's break with traditional U.S. norms regarding interrogation and torture of detainees. This letter was directed to the nominee and requested responses in a number of areas relating to the detention policies, application of the Geneva Conventions, and public release of documents relevant to legal policy formulation.

December 22 , 2004

The Honorable Alberto Gonzales
Counsel to the President
The White House
1600 Pennsylvania Avenue, NW
Washington, DC, 20500

Dear Judge Gonzales:

I am writing on behalf of the Association of the Bar of the City of New York. The Association is an independent non-governmental organization with a membership of more than 22,000 lawyers, judges, law professors and government officials, principally from New York City but also from throughout the United States and from 50 other countries. Founded in 1870, the Association has a long history of engagement in issues of legal policy of concern to the profession and has been a continuous advocate of the Rule of Law at home and around the world. The Association has been a long-standing advocate of international humanitarian law. Indeed, one century ago officers of the Association represented the United States at the Hague conferences which produced an important forerunner to the Geneva Conventions. Today we remain committed to the preservation of this legacy.

Let me begin by congratulating you on your nomination as Attorney General of the United States. In contrast to our policy regarding the judiciary, the Association has no historical

practice of taking positions on nominations to the Executive Branch or the Department of Justice. Nonetheless, as one of the nation's largest voluntary bar organizations, we have been following your nomination process with interest, with special attention to maintaining our government's highest traditions in promoting the Rule of Law both domestically and internationally. Toward these ends, we hope that we will be able to assist you in your capacity as the nation's chief law enforcement officer. Where appropriate, we also hope to share our views, as we have traditionally done, with regard to important legal matters of the day.

Accordingly, the Association desires to take the opportunity of your appointment to raise with you several issues concerning legal positions in connection with the United States' response to the attacks of September 11. As a lawyers' organization based in New York City, no one is more sensitive than we are to the dangers posed by terrorist attacks on our soil. At the same time, we believe that our government's responses to these and related threats must accord with applicable law. For this reason the Association has published numerous major reports assessing measures taken in the war on terror in light of legal safeguards protecting civil liberties and international human rights. By contrast, numerous memoranda from within the Bush Administration that have appeared in the press over the past year take a contrary position. We believe that these memoranda include some rather unorthodox views concerning the applicability of the Geneva Conventions and other important international conventions, as well as the domestic legislation intended to enforce them. In consequence, we invite you to make clear your own position on the matters that these memoranda raise. We do so with the conviction that your views as Attorney General will reflect established U.S. positions on civil liberties and international law, rather than the extreme positions that the memoranda in many instances take.

1. PRESIDENTIAL AUTHORITY TO IGNORE STATUTES AND CONVENTIONS.

As an initial matter, various memoranda drafted in the White House Counsel's Office, the Department of Justice, and the Department of Defense suggest that the Anti-Torture Act, the War Crimes Act, and various international treaties that the United States has ratified, including the Geneva Conventions and the Convention Against Torture, would be unconstitutional if applied to limit the President's authority in treating detainees and in undertaking military operations more generally. This novel view runs counter to well-settled interpretations based on constitutional history, structure, and text, not least of which are grants of authority to Congress under Article I, sec. 8, cls. 10–11 of the United States Constitution. Such view also ignores the framework established by the Supreme Court in *Youngstown Sheet & Tube Co. v. Sawyer* and *Dames & Moore v. Regan*. We at the Association respectfully urge that you endorse the bedrock principle that the President is subject to the constitutional checks and balances of the other branches, including with regard to military and foreign affairs. In particular, we hope that you will be prepared to enforce Federal statutes and apply U.S. treaty obligations on the treatment of detainees regardless of any contrary thinking in the Executive Branch.

2. AUTHORITY FOR EXTREME INTERROGATION TECHNIQUES

We understand that on your request the Office of Legal Counsel prepared a memorandum discussing the standards for interrogation of detainees under U.S. law as well as the Convention Against Torture, the Statute of the International Criminal Court, and other international obligations. This request resulted in an August 1, 2002 memorandum drafted by William Bybee and John Yoo. Press accounts have reported that this memo was solicited in connection with a White

House request to use harsh, new interrogation practices on a particular detainee. No subsequent action by the White House appears as of record. We would appreciate your views as to whether it is legally appropriate to authorize the Secretary of Defense, the Director of the CIA, or any other Executive official to undertake any of the extreme interrogation methods that the analysis offered by Judge Bybee and Professor Yoo deemed acceptable.

3. CLARIFICATION OF THE "TORTURE MEMORANDA"

Third, we at the Association would likewise be reassured were you to make clear that your own position as Attorney General will reject the analysis and conclusions that the Bybee/Yoo memorandum and the highly derivative Department of Defense Working Group Report of April 4, 2003 put forward. Among other things, these documents argue that in order to count as "torture" within the meaning of 28 USC § 2340 (the "U.S. Anti-Torture Statute"), physical pain must be "equivalent in intensity to the pain accompanying serious physical injury, such as organ failure, impairment of bodily function, or even death." This position is unprecedented and is contrary to the plain language of the U.S. Anti-Torture Statute as well as the Torture Victim Protection Act. It is also contrary to the language and purpose of the Convention Against Torture, consequent interpretations by international and foreign courts, and the understanding accorded it by monitoring bodies, chief among them the International Committee of the Red Cross.

4. EXTRAORDINARY RENDITIONS

Fourth, the Association has further, serious concerns on the topic of so-called "extraordinary renditions." This term refers to numerous, well-documented instances of U.S. involvement in extrajudicial transfers of terrorist suspects to countries where there is a serious risk that detainees will be subjected to torture or cruel, inhuman, or degrading treatment. Reported examples of U.S. involvement in this practice include the transfer of a Canadian citizen, Maher Arar, from the United States to Syria, and of Australian Citizen Mamdouh Habib from Pakistan to Egypt and then to Guantanamo. The practice of extraordinary rendition is a clear and unequivocal violation of international law, and is contrary to U.S. law and policy. We urge you make clear that, as Attorney General, you will condemn this practice and enforce all domestic and international measures that prohibit it.

5. APPLICATION OF THE GENEVA CONVENTIONS IN THE GLOBAL WAR ON TERROR

Fifth, our members would be appreciative if you would clarify your position on the Geneva Conventions in light of your draft memorandum dated January 25, 2002 and since made public. We understand this document to have often been quoted out of context in an inflammatory fashion. That document nonetheless does advise the President that he could determine that the main provisions of the Geneva Conventions do not apply with respect to members of al Qaeda and the Taliban on the grounds that Afghanistan was a "failed state" and that the Taliban do not qualify as regular forces, and in addition, that the President could suspend their operation. The memorandum further argues that to the extent that the main body of the Geneva Conventions do not apply, minimum protections of Common Article 3 are inapplicable to the Afghan conflict. Especially when read in conjunction with a memorandum drafted by John Yoo and Robert Delahunty dated January 9, 2002, this position is apparently based on the mistaken understanding

that Common Article 3 applies only to nationals involved in a conventional civil war not involving more than one nation. This position cannot be squared with the Conventions' history or consistent interpretation by bodies such as the ICRC, as well as the International Criminal Tribunals for the former Yugoslavia and Rwanda. We invite you to share with the public your actual views on these positions, and more generally your position about the applicability of the Geneva Conventions.

6. MILITARY COMMISSIONS

Sixth, we seek to know what your position as Attorney General will be with regard to military commissions. Unlike courts martial, military commissions of the type authorized by the Presidential Military Order of November 13, 2001 and elaborated by the Department of Defense Military Commission Order No. 1 of 2002, lack fundamental due process guarantees. Moreover, as recently determined by the United States District Court for the District of Columbia in *Hamdan v. Rumsfeld,* the current military commissions lack such bedrock due process safeguards as the right to confront witnesses. Conversely, the Association has high confidence in the existing United States courts martial, which we believe comply with United States and international law standards applicable to such proceedings. As Attorney General, would you be at least prepared to reconsider the omission of key due process safeguards lacking in the military commissions as currently constituted?

7. PUBLIC RELEASE OF DOCUMENTS RELEVANT TO LEGAL POLICY FORMULATION

Finally, we at the Association believe that transparency promotes informed public assessment and decisionmaking. Accordingly, we urge that you provide as complete an account as possible of both the Administration's legal position and supporting analysis with reference to the issues that are outlined above. Such an account would include a more complete disclosure of documents both prior and subsequent to the memoranda referred to in this letter, as well as similar memoranda that have also been made public. A complete and relevant disclosure would also include any and all documents seeking and granting authorization for the practices that this letter discusses. Such disclosure, we believe, is far preferable to the piecemeal press leaks that we have seen in the past year for all concerned.

In his opinion in *Hamdi v. Rumsfeld,* Justice Scalia declared, "Many think it not only inevitable but entirely proper that liberty give way to security in times of national crisis—that, at the extremes of military exigency, *inter arma silent leges*. Whatever the general merits of the view that war silences law or modulates its voice, that view has no place in the interpretation and application of a Constitution designed precisely to confront war and, in a manner that accords with democratic principles, to accommodate it." We at the Association agree. We would add, moreover, that this conclusion extends to our nation's commitment to international law. We are hopeful that, if confirmed as Attorney General of the United States, you will maintain these fundamental American traditions as well. We are likewise hopeful that in your current capacity as the President's nominee to that post you will do so by publicly addressing the matters I have raised in this letter.

Sincerely,
Bettina B. Plevan
President,
Association of the Bar
of the City of New York

CHAPTER 18

Statement of the Association with Respect to Release or Transfer of Detainees at Guantanamo Bay Naval Station

PREFACE BY ALAN R. ROTHSTEIN

News reports that the U.S. government was about to transfer many prisoners from the Guantanamo Naval Base to their home countries gave the Association concern. In the following statement, the Association cautioned that, in transferring prisoners, the Administration must avoid sending them to countries where there was a reasonable expectation that they would be tortured. Such "rendition" of detainees would violate the Convention Against Torture. While it is unusual for the Association to issue a cautionary statement such as this, doing so was necessary as the Bush Administration did not seem to acknowledge the legal issues that would be triggered by a transfer of prisoners on the large scale that had been reported.

January 14, 2005

The Association of the Bar of the City of New York takes note of press reports suggesting that the United States intends to "release or transfer hundreds of prisoners" from facilities now maintained at Guantanamo Bay Naval Station, Cuba. To the extent the United States proposes to release or transfer prisoners into the hands of other sovereign nations, the Association notes that such action is subject to applicable United States law and policy, and in particular to the limitations contained in article 3 of the Convention Against Torture and Other Cruel, Inhuman and Degrading Treatment and the statement of policy in the Foreign Affairs Reform and Restructuring Act of 1998.[1]

Detainees should not be released or transferred to other sovereigns without affording detainees an opportunity to challenge any rendition to a power which has a reputation for torture and as to which the detainee can credibly assert the fear that he will be subject to torture. Association President Bettina Plevan stated "Press accounts over the past two years detail a remarkable number of cases in which U. S. Government agents appear to have turned detainees over to Governments with a reputation for torture in circumvention of the laws which limit or preclude this practice. While the U. S. Government has the right to modify its logistical arrangements on Guantanamo and to move detainees to other locations in its custody, its right to render these

detainees to other nations is subject to the limitations of U.S. and international law governing renditions."

For a fuller expression of the basis for its concerns, the Association refers to its report, "Torture by Proxy: International and Domestic Law Applicable to 'Extraordinary Renditions'" which may be found on the Association's website, www.abcny.org.

NOTE

1. "It shall be the policy of the United States not to expel, extradite, or otherwise effect the involuntary return of any person to a country in which there are substantial grounds for believing the person would be in danger of being subjected to torture, regardless of whether the person is physically present in the United States." Pub. L. No. 105-277, sec. 2242(a).

CHAPTER 19

Letter from the Association President to Representative Edward Markey re HR 952: The Proposed Bill Seeking to End U.S. Involvement in Extraordinary Rendition

PREFACE BY ALAN R. ROTHSTEIN

Representative Edward Markey (D–MA) has been a leader in opposing the practice of "extraordinary rendition," the extrajudicial transfer or return of persons to countries where torture or other inhuman treatment of persons occurs. The Association's letter supported H.R. 952, Representative Markey's proposed legislation to ban this practice. The letter argued that "extraordinary rendition" is prohibited by both domestic and international law and commended this effort to end the "odious practice" of extraordinary rendition.

February 24, 2005

Representative Edward J. Markey
United States House of Representatives
Washington, D.C. 20515

Dear Representative Markey:

The Association of the Bar of the City of New York strongly supports H.R. 952, which you introduced on February 17, 2005. Your proposed bill seeks to end the United States' direct or indirect use of "extraordinary rendition," the extra-judicial transfer or return of persons to countries where torture or other inhuman treatment of persons occurs. Extraordinary rendition is prohibited by both domestic and international law, and we commend your efforts to end this odious practice.

The Association is an independent non-governmental organization of more than 22,000 lawyers, judges, law professors and government officials. Founded in 1870, the Association has a long history of dedication to human rights, notably through its Committee on International Human Rights, which investigates and reports on human rights conditions around the world. In October 2004, the Association issued a report entitled *Torture by Proxy: International and Domestic Law Applicable to "Extraordinary Renditions,"* which presented an in-depth legal analysis of extraordinary rendition and related practices. The report, which the Association issued jointly with the Center for Human Rights and Global Justice (CHRGJ) at New York

University School of Law, concluded that extraordinary renditions clearly violate both United States and international law.[1]

Your bill comes at a critical time. Recent reports indicate that agents of the United States' intelligence community have been and are practicing extraordinary rendition, often as an interrogation technique, and, in fact, use of extraordinary rendition appears to be on the rise. Your proposed legislation would reinforce prohibitions on extraordinary rendition that are already binding on the United States under international law by unequivocally requiring that transfers of individuals to other countries occur with full due process guarantees and in conformity with United States' international obligations. The bill would clarify that extraordinary renditions are unequivocally prohibited—no matter where they take place, and no matter whether they are conducted by a government agency or by a contractor of such an agency. The bill would also prevent officials from circumventing the prohibitions against extraordinary rendition by obtaining an "assurance" from a foreign government that it will not torture or ill-treat a specific person who is being transferred to its custody. (Available evidence indicates that assurances obtained from governments of states where torture is known to occur are highly unreliable.) Importantly, your bill would permit transfers to countries where there are substantial grounds for believing that torture or cruel, inhuman, or degrading treatment is commonly used only where the Secretary of State has certified to specified Congressional committees that the receiving government has ended all acts of torture or cruel, inhuman, or degrading treatment, and that there is a verifiable mechanism that assures the United States that a person transferred to the requesting government will not be tortured or subjected to cruel, inhuman, or degrading treatment. Finally, your bill would fill in certain gaps in domestic law that have facilitated the continued use of extraordinary renditions by government agents in contravention of the United States' obligations under international law.

We thank you for your work to end the practice of extraordinary rendition and hope that this important bill will be taken up and passed as soon as possible.

Respectfully,
Bettina B. Plevan

NOTE

1. The full text of the report is available on the Association's website, www.abcny.org.

CHAPTER 20

Letter from the Association President to Honorable Arlen Specter and Honorable Patrick Leahy re: Nomination of William J. Haynes II to a Seat on the U.S. Court of Appeals for the 4th Circuit

PREFACE BY ALAN R. ROTHSTEIN

When William J. Haynes II, General Counsel of the Department of Defense, was nominated for a seat on the Fourth Circuit Court of Appeals, the Association felt it important to advise the Senate Judiciary Committee of the need to question Mr. Haynes regarding his actions with respect to the development of the government's legal analysis underpinning its treatment of detainees. This letter developed some concerns regarding Mr. Haynes's actions as Defense Department Counsel, particularizes those concerns, and sets forth lines of questioning that would address those concerns. Mr. Haynes's nomination was withdrawn in January 2007.

March 4, 2005

Hon. Arlen Specter
Chair, Committee on the Judiciary
United States Senate
Washington, DC 20510
Hon. Patrick Leahy
Ranking Member, Committee on the Judiciary
United States Senate
Washington, DC 20510

Nomination of William J. Haynes II

Dear Senators Specter and Leahy:

I am writing on behalf of the Association of the Bar of the City of New York. The Association is an independent non-governmental organization with a membership of more than 22,000 lawyers, judges, law professors and government officials, principally from New York City but also from throughout the United States and from 50 other countries. Founded in 1870, the Association has a long history of engagement in issues of legal policy of concern to the profession and has been a continuous advocate of the Rule of Law at home and around the world. The Association has been a long-standing advocate of international humanitarian law. Indeed, one century ago officers of the Association represented the United States at the Hague conferences

which produced an important forerunner to the Geneva Conventions. Today we remain committed to the preservation of this legacy.

I am writing to you with respect to the President's nomination of Mr. William J. Haynes II, who currently serves as General Counsel of the Department of Defense ("DOD"), to a seat on the United States Court of Appeals for the Fourth Circuit. The Association does not, as a matter of policy, take positions on nominees for federal courts outside of the Second Circuit and the Supreme Court, and thus is not taking a position with regard to Mr. Haynes' nomination. Nevertheless, in the course of the Association's work on questions concerning detention and interrogation policy for the Global War on Terror, and arrangements for the creation of military commissions to try detainees, the Association has communicated with Mr. Haynes, and has developed some concerns regarding his actions as DOD General Counsel. We hope that the Judiciary Committee can take these concerns into account in the review process in eliciting comments and clarifications from Mr. Haynes.

(1) *Assurances Concerning Torture, and Cruel, Inhuman and Degrading Treatment.* In correspondence to Senator Leahy dated June 25, 2003, Mr. Haynes furnished assurances that the United States does not "permit, tolerate or condone" torture as defined in the Federal anti-torture statute. He further provided assurance that United States policy is to treat all detainees consistent with its commitment not to use "cruel, inhuman and degrading treatment ("CID")" as precluded in article 16 of the Convention Against Torture. A copy of this correspondence was furnished to the Association in response to an inquiry that raised similar concerns to those voiced in Senator Leahy's letter of June 2, 2003 to Condoleezza Rice. Documents subsequently surfacing, including in particular the Department of Defense Working Group Report and a November 27, 2002 memorandum from Mr. Haynes to the Secretary of Defense cause us to question these assurances. In particular, it appears that the administration adopted a posture qualifying the application of the commitment not to use CID in DOD detention facilities, notably including Guantánamo. We believe that Mr. Haynes' views on the legal standards applicable should be explored and that he should have an opportunity to explain the apparent discrepancies between his assurances and the internal policy formulation process he oversaw.

(2) *Specific Advice Concerning Use of Interrogation Techniques.* Mr. Haynes issued a memorandum to the Secretary of Defense dated November 27, 2003 in which he recommended approval of a series of "extreme" interrogation techniques, while limiting the general application of the most aggressive techniques.[1] The approved extreme techniques included threats to kill a detainee's family members, waterboarding, forced nudity and the use of dogs to induce stress. The Secretary of Defense apparently relied upon Mr. Haynes' recommendation in approving the techniques in question. The Secretary of Defense subsequently rescinded this approval. The list of techniques approved by Mr. Haynes raise profound questions of compliance with United States law, including the Uniform Code of Military Justice, as well as policy articulated by the Congress, policy statements of the President, and assurances given by Mr. Haynes. We believe that Mr. Haynes should be given an opportunity to explain his reasoning in issuing this memorandum and the entire policy formulation process associated with it.

(3) *Commander-in-Chief Authority.* Mr. Haynes commissioned the preparation of a special Working Group Report on Detainee Interrogations (the "Working Group Report") and provided guidance in its preparation. The Working Group Report, issued on April 4, 2003, contains a discussion of commander-in-chief authority which includes the assertion that applicable "constitutional principles preclude an application of Section 2340A [the anti-torture statute] to punish officials for aiding the President in exercising his exclusive constitutional authorities."[2] The discussion is legally incompetent, particularly in that it fails to cite passages of the Constitution (art. I, sec. 8, cls. 10–11) which contradict this conclusion, or to discuss controlling Supreme

Court precedent which dictate a contrary conclusion, most significantly *Youngstown Sheet & Tube Co. v. Sawyer*. We believe that Mr. Haynes should explain his reaction to the quoted statement and why he apparently accepted the report and allowed authorized its further dissemination notwithstanding the professional incompetence that characterizes it. Alternatively, if Mr. Haynes stands by the position taken by the Working Group, he should explain the legal rationale and authority for that position, which would be helpful in understanding his views on the separation of powers.

(4) *Definition of Torture.* The Working Group Report also contains an extensive passage defining torture in an impermissibly restrictive fashion. This language appears largely derived from a memorandum issued by Jay Bybee at the Department of Justice to Alberto Gonzales dated August 1, 2002. This memorandum has since been repudiated by the Department of Justice and replaced by a memorandum dated December 30, 2004. We believe Mr. Haynes should explain his role in the redefinition of torture contained in the Working Group Report, the subsequent withdrawal of the Bybee memorandum, and how it is that the Working Group Report stayed in place in light of that withdrawal and subsequent repudiation.

(5) *Availability of Specific Defenses.* The Working Group Report also discusses at length the availability of certain criminal law defenses as possible bases for the avoidance of criminal law liability by interrogators applying new interrogation guidelines. The defenses discussed include necessity, self-defense, military law enforcement action and superior orders. This discussion also appears substantially derived from the withdrawn and repudiated Department of Justice memorandum. Mr. Haynes should explain his reaction to the Working Group's claim of the availability of certain defenses.

(6) *"Unlawful Combatant."* From several documents, it appears that Mr. Haynes embraced a concept of "unlawful combatants" as individuals who are outside the scope of the Geneva Conventions, and, essentially without legal protections of any kind. While precedent does support a concept of "unlawful combatants," the suggestion that such individuals lack protection under the Geneva Conventions and other law seems highly questionable, and a number of district courts have declined to follow it. Some of those cases appear headed for the Fourth Circuit (*e.g., Padilla v. Rumsfeld,* decided earlier this week). We believe it would be useful for Mr. Haynes to explain his views on this issue. Considering Mr. Haynes' advocacy of the "unlawful combatant" concept and his position as counsel to a party, we believe it important to clarify his intention to recuse himself from cases in which this issue is raised.

(7) *Military Commissions.* Mr. Haynes played a key role in DOD arrangements for the creation of a special Military Commission to try detainees in the Global War on Terror pursuant to the President's Military Order. The Association and the American Bar Association have previously articulated reservations concerning these arrangements, which appear to us to undermine the basic due process assurances provided by the United States' exemplary court martial system. Mr. Haynes should explain why he believes derogations from the court martial system were necessary and appropriate and why they were adopted after minimal consultation with the Judge Advocates of the services and without consultation with Congress.

(8) *Public Release of Documents Relevant to Legal Policy Formulation.* Finally, we at the Association believe that transparency promotes informed public assessment and decision making. Accordingly, we urge that you secure as complete an account as possible of both Mr. Haynes' legal position and supporting analysis with respect to the issues identified above. Such an account would include a more complete disclosure of documents both prior and subsequent to the memoranda referred to in this letter, as well as similar memoranda that have also been made public. A complete and relevant disclosure would also include any and all documents seeking and granting authorization for the practices that this letter discusses. Such

disclosure, we believe, is far preferable for all concerned to the piecemeal press leaks that we have seen in the past year.

I wish to stress that the Association has not undertaken a review of Mr. Haynes' performance in prior positions, including as General Counsel at DOD or of his qualifications generally, nor does the Association express any view as to his suitability to serve as a federal judge. However, we feel strongly that the public interest would be served by a full inquiry into the matters identified above as his qualifications are reviewed by the Committee.

Respectfully submitted,
Bettina B. Plevan

NOTES

1. By "extreme interrogation techniques" we mean techniques beyond the scope authorized in *Department of the Army Field Manual 34-52* (1992), which is widely accepted as a legally correct statement of the rules governing interrogation as required by the Law of Armed Conflict.
2. Reproduced in Greenberg & Drahtel, eds., *The Torture Papers* at 304 (2005).

CHAPTER 21

Letter from the Association President to Honorable Pat Roberts and Honorable John D. Rockefeller IV re: Hearings on Patriot Act Reauthorization and Revision

PREFACE BY ALAN R. ROTHSTEIN

The Senate Select Committee on Intelligence, in its consideration of whether to reauthorize the USA PATRIOT Act, determined to hold closed hearings on the bill to the public. This letter protests this process and also expresses its opposition to Section 213 of the bill, which would expand the FBI's powers to issue administrative subpoenas requiring production of any records either relevant to an authorized investigation or to protect against international terrorism. This provision would effectively eliminate the PATRIOT Act's requirement that orders seeking production of such records be issued only through an application to a judge of the U.S. Foreign Intelligence Surveillance Court or a specially designated magistrate.

June 3, 2005

The Honorable Pat Roberts
Chairman
Senate Select Committee on Intelligence
109 Hart Senate Office Building
Washington, District of Columbia 20510
The Honorable John D. Rockefeller IV
Vice Chairman
Senate Select Committee on Intelligence
531 Hart Senate Office Building
Washington, District of Columbia 20510

Re: Hearings on Patriot Act Reauthorization and Revision

Dear Senators Roberts and Rockefeller:

I write on behalf of The Association of the Bar of the City of New York. The Association is a professional association of over 22,000 attorneys in New York City and throughout the United States and numerous foreign countries. Founded in 1870, the Association has long been committed to protecting, preserving, and promoting civil liberties, civil rights, and the democratic process. Through its standing committees, including those on Civil Rights, Immigration Law,

Federal Legislation and International Human Rights, the Association has long had an interest in the need to balance the fundamental interests of civil liberties and individual freedom with the needs of national security and to assure that concerns for national security do not unnecessarily or unduly undermine guarantees of civil liberties that are the hallmark of our constitutional democracy and a beacon to the world.

The Association is writing to express its grave concerns about the Committee's decision to hold hearings closed to the public on a bill to reauthorize and expand provisions of P.L. 107-56, the law known as the PATRIOT Act. The interests implicated by the PATRIOT Act and by its modification and possible expansion are of vital concern to the American people as they affect the very core of our nation's commitment to individual freedoms and civil liberties. The very decision to hold hearings on these matters in secret and without public scrutiny is itself a severe blow to fundamental democratic values.

While the Association is concerned about a number of the provisions in the current PATRIOT Act and the proposed revisions you are considering, we single out one proposed provision which the Association vigorously opposes to illustrate the intense need for public involvement and oversight of the legislative process pertaining to these matters: Section 213 of the proposed bill you are considering entitled "Administrative Subpoenas in National Security Investigations."

The proposed Section 213 would expand the powers granted under the current Section 215 of the PATRIOT Act by enabling the Federal Bureau of Investigation to issue administrative subpoenas requiring "the production of any records or other materials that are relevant to an authorized investigation...to protect against international terrorism or clandestine intelligence activities." This proposal would effectively eliminate the current requirement that orders under Section 215 requiring production of such records only be issued through application to a judge of the Foreign Intelligence Surveillance Act court ("FISA court") or a specially designated U.S. magistrate. The effect of the proposed revision would be to give the FBI the power to issue such orders on its own initiative with no prior judicial supervision. The Association vigorously opposes this proposal because it has the potential for serious abuse and grave and unwarranted intrusions into rights guaranteed by the First and Fourth Amendments to the Constitution.

As you know, Section 215, as it now exists, is the subject of intense controversy and concern. It has the potential for unprecedented intrusions into individual privacy, for example, by authorizing the production of library records and prevents public scrutiny of any abuses because it prohibits recipients of 215 orders from disclosing their existence. The Association submits that the proposed expansion of Section 215—permitting the FBI to issue subpoenas requiring such production without prior judicial review—exacerbates these concerns and is wholly unnecessary. Any encroachment on civil liberties and individual privacy should be undertaken only where there is an overriding showing of need. While investigative powers are essential to effectively addressing the threat of terrorism, there has been no demonstration that the very limited judicial review required by Section 215 has hindered the government's ability to carry out intelligence investigations.

Given the extraordinary nature of the PATRIOT Act powers, and the fact that it was rapidly enacted in response to 9/11, now is the time that Congress should be revisiting its provisions and carefully evaluating their necessity. In particular, consideration should be given to amending Section 215 in a manner that restores the checks and balances on the exercise of governmental authority that are central to our democracy. While the present bill would allow for very limited judicial review *after* the FBI subpoena has been issued through a challenge by its recipient, pre-issuance judicial review is particularly critical in the context of the broad records requests envisioned by the proposed Section 213. The current Section 215 forbids the recipient to disclose receipt of the subpoena and the proposed expansion also would permit the FBI to forbid

disclosure by the recipient (with the exception of disclosing it to an attorney to obtain legal advice). As a result, persons whose records are held by a business or institution that has received a subpoena will be unaware that the subpoena was issued and thus will have no opportunity to challenge its validity. Instead, under the proposed bill, only the third party recipient of the subpoena will be empowered to raise such a challenge. Because these third-party recipients are immunized from liability for compliance with the subpoena, they will have little incentive to undertake the burden of challenging the subpoena to protect the interest of persons whose records are covered by the subpoena. Assuming that non-disclosure is warranted for a given investigation, it is imperative that the judiciary, entrusted with protecting the liberty interests of the public, provide a check on potential abuses of these investigative powers before the subpoena issues.

Similarly, because the imposition of a non-disclosure requirement affects both the First Amendment rights of subpoena recipients, and the Fourth Amendment rights of notice and challenge for persons whose records are covered by the subpoenas, the burden should be on the government to demonstrate to the court the need for non-disclosure in each situation. Requiring the FBI to aver that non-disclosure is compelled by national security interests, with no judicial scrutiny of that averment, does not provide a satisfactory check on potential abuse.

The Association is aware that proponents of the present bill have asserted that granting administrative subpoena power in the context of anti-terrorism efforts is no different from the powers already used in areas, such as some criminal investigations, where the national interest is considerably weaker. We believe this comparison is inapposite. In these other contexts, subpoenas are used for clearly defined purposes and to obtain limited types of records. Under the proposed legislation, however, the subpoenas must only be related to "an investigation to protect against international terrorism." Such investigations can be far-reaching and can encompass legal, as well as illegal, activity. In the case of foreign nationals, such investigations can also be based solely upon the exercise of First Amendment rights. Moreover, administrative subpoenas issued in intelligence investigations can also apply to entire databases or files and need not pertain to the records of a particular subject. Hence, as long as the FBI merely determines in its own judgment, that records are relevant to an investigation to "protect against international terrorism" it could demand records of such activities as books checked out of libraries or attendance at meetings or conferences encompassing persons having nothing to do with any wrongful conduct. Another critical difference is that in the criminal context, notice is provided to the subject of the subpoena, typically at the time of its issuance, and the subject is afforded an opportunity to judicially challenge its validity. As discussed earlier, neither the PATRIOT Act nor the proposed bill would offer such notice and an opportunity to challenge the subpoena.

The administrative subpoena issue is only one of a number of serious issues raised by the proposed bill that affect the civil liberties and rights of all Americans. The Association, therefore, strongly urges that your committee hearings be opened to the public so that all can be made aware of the serious issues at stake. To the extent that legitimate security interests are affected by the Committee's deliberations, they should be accommodated in a manner that preserves an open democratic process to the greatest extent possible. Deliberating over these issues in secret only heightens the legitimate concerns of our citizenry over the encroachment of intelligence powers into individual privacy and civil liberties.

Sincerely,
Bettina B. Plevan

CHAPTER 22

Hamdan v. Rumsfeld: *The City Bar's Amicus Brief Challenging Military Commissions*

PREFACE BY JAMES J. BENJAMIN, JR.

In October 2001, less than a month after the 9/11 attacks, the war on terror began in earnest with the U.S. assault against the Taliban in Afghanistan. Most Americans have supported that campaign, but there has been disagreement on the proper way to treat captured enemy combatants, some of whom are suspected of complicity in terrorism. Most would agree that such prisoners, if alleged to have taken part in terrorism or other atrocities, should be tried in due course. If they are found to have violated the law, they should be punished. And if the violations are serious, the punishments should be severe.

But when and where should these trials occur? How should the trials function? What sort of evidence should be considered? What if any protections should be afforded to the defendants? What role should the federal courts play in assuring fair process? In short, how should we reconcile our desire to see the guilty receive severe punishment with our commitment to fairness? As we sort through these questions, we must remember that our decisions may end up affecting the fate of own soldiers and sailors who fall into enemy hands during this open-ended global conflict.

The Bush Administration has taken an uncompromising and aggressive stance on these questions. In November 2001, the President issued a military order authorizing the creation of military commissions to try and punish enemy combatants captured in the war on terrorism. Military commissions have been part of our nation's history back to the Revolutionary War, and the Supreme Court has repeatedly upheld the legitimacy of these "common law war courts." But in March 2002, the Defense Department issued regulations governing the military commissions that are unprecedented. The Defense Department's regulations permit the presiding officer to

- exclude the defendant from the courtroom based on national security considerations;
- preclude the defendant from even knowing what evidence has been admitted against him if it implicates national security; and

- receive evidence of dubious probative value, including anonymous unsworn statements with multiple layers of hearsay.

Military commissions may impose severe sentences, including death. There is only very limited judicial review of the trial or the sentence.

For a criminal lawyer and former prosecutor like myself,[1] these rules are amazing. A "trial" based on secret evidence, from which the defendant has been excluded, with no meaningful standards governing the evidence that can be admitted, and with very limited judicial review, is alien to the our justice system. It is an invitation to mistakes or worse. There is no precedent for it in our history.

In July 2003, the government announced its intention to invoke these procedures against a prisoner named Salim Hamdan, who was detained at Guantanamo Bay, Cuba. Hamdan sought a writ of *habeas corpus* in federal court in Washington, D.C., arguing that the procedures to be used at his trial failed to satisfy Common Article 3 of the Geneva Conventions of 1949. That treaty provision, which the United States ratified in 1955, mandates that a person captured in a conflict may be punished only after trial "before a regularly constituted court affording all the judicial guarantees which are recognized as indispensable by civilized peoples." Hamdan argued that the Defense Department regulations violate this minimal requirement.

The District Court agreed. It granted the writ and enjoined Hamdan's trial. On appeal, the D.C. Circuit reversed and ordered Hamdan's trial to proceed. The Supreme Court granted certiorari and, in a landmark decision, struck down the military tribunals as incompatible with the Geneva Conventions and the statutes that govern military justice.

My law firm was privileged to represent the City Bar as an *amicus curiae* before the D.C. Circuit and the Supreme Court (at both the cert stage and on the merits). Our argument was straightforward—we said that the Geneva Conventions were enforceable in a *habeas corpus* action, that Common Article 3 of the Geneva Conventions applied to Hamdan's case, and that the military tribunals to be used against Hamdan failed to satisfy the minimal requirements of Common Article 3. Although the D.C. Circuit had rejected these arguments, the Supreme Court majority adopted them, and they are now the law of the land.

The future of the Guantanamo detainees remains unclear. As of late Summer 2006, it seems likely that Congress will intervene and, after hearings and debate, establish trial procedures for the detainees. In my view, this is as it should be. There are no easy answers to the questions about how detainees should be tried. But in my view, those questions should be answered through the political process.

It is my hope that Congress respects the guarantees of Common Article 3, which are themselves part of the law of war. Common Article 3 does not require much in the way of procedural rights—it clearly does not require, for example, that prisoners such as Hamdan are entitled to a full criminal trial. But elemental fairness requires that prisoners be afforded basic protections such as the right to be present at trial and to confront the evidence in a meaningful way. To do otherwise—to permit a secret trial with anonymous evidence—is to invite abuse and betray the very principles that distinguish us from those against whom we are fighting.

INTEREST OF *AMICI CURIAE* AND SOURCE OF AUTHORITY TO FILE[2]

The Association of the Bar of the City of New York ("ABCNY") is a professional association of over 22,000 attorneys. Founded in 1870, ABCNY has long been committed to studying, addressing, and promoting the rule of law and, when appropriate, law reform. Through its many standing committees, ABCNY educates the bar and public about legal issues relating to the war on terrorism, the pursuit of suspected terrorists, and the treatment of detainees.

The Human Rights Institute of the International Bar Association (the "IBA"), headquartered in London, England, helps to promote, protect and enforce human rights under a just rule of law, and works to preserve the independence of the judiciary and legal profession worldwide. Founded in 1995, the Institute now has more than 7,000 members. The Institute was established by the IBA, which was created in 1947 to support the establishment of law and the administration of justice worldwide, and is composed today of 20,000 individual lawyers and over 195 Bar Associations and Law Societies.

While they embrace the necessity of apprehending and punishing those responsible for terrorist acts and preventing future acts of terrorism, *amici* believe that the Administration's cramped interpretation of the four Geneva Conventions of 1949 (the "Conventions") is incompatible with the United States' treaty obligations. *Amici* submit this brief to present the Court with authority regarding the proper application of Common Article 3 of the Conventions in the context of this case.[3]

INTRODUCTION AND SUMMARY OF ARGUMENT

For more than a half-century, the Geneva Conventions have stood as bulwarks, safeguarding minimum standards of humanity against wartime abuses. Common Article 3, so called because it is common to all four Conventions, establishes minimum protections that must be afforded to all persons captured in a military conflict in a contracting party's territory. Among those protections is the requirement that a detainee may be punished only after a trial before a "regularly constituted court affording all the judicial guarantees which are recognized as indispensable by civilized peoples." Geneva Convention Relative to the Treatment of Prisoners of War, Aug. 12, 1949 ("Geneva III"), art. 3, 6 U.S.T. 3316 (same text in other three 1949 Conventions).

Strict adherence to Common Article 3 is imperative not only to ensure that the United States government refrains from inflicting unjust punishments on enemy detainees (punishments which can include the death penalty or life imprisonment), but also to protect United States servicemembers from mistreatment when *they* fall into the hands of hostile forces. As the District Court astutely observed, when the government makes novel arguments that the Conventions do not apply to the war on terror, its conduct "can only weaken the United States' own ability to demand application of the Geneva Conventions to Americans captured during armed conflicts abroad." *Hamdan v. Rumsfeld,* 344 F. Supp. 2d 152, 163 (D.D.C. 2004). To reduce the peril faced by our Nation's soldiers and sailors who fall into enemy hands, and to vindicate the rule of law against overreaching by the Executive Branch, we urge this Court to hold that the proposed trial of petitioner before a Military Commission violates Common Article 3. Our argument incorporates three points.

First, as recognized by Judge Williams in his concurring opinion below, the protections of Common Article 3 extend to all persons, including petitioner, who are captured during hostilities in Afghanistan. By its terms, Common Article 3 applies to any "armed conflict not of an international character." Geneva III, art. 3, 6 U.S.T. 3316. Although the other articles of the Conventions apply, more narrowly, only in *international* conflicts "between two or more of

the High Contracting Parties," *see* Geneva III, art. 2, 6 U.S.T. 3316 (same text in other three 1949 Conventions), Common Article 3 was intended as a "gap filler" for all other conflicts. Common Article 3's expansive language thus extends to *all* conflicts on the territory of signatory nations other than those between sovereign nations who have signed the Conventions. Contrary to the conclusion reached by the majority of the D.C. Circuit panel below, there is no "carve-out" for conflicts between signatories and non-state actors such as al Qaeda.

Second, the Military Commission convened to try petitioner violates Common Article 3. Notwithstanding the enormous power that the Military Commission wields—including the power to sentence petitioner to imprisonment for any term up to life or even death—the Commission is not a "regularly constituted court" as required by Common Article 3. It was created by the Executive Branch alone, is part of a regime of "special tribunals" targeted against alleged terrorists, vests extraordinarily broad discretion in the hands of the Commission members and their Executive Branch superiors, and can be changed or abolished at the Executive's whim. In addition, procedural rules governing Military Commissions fail to afford "all the judicial guarantees which are recognized as indispensable by civilized peoples." Some of the rules are nothing less than shocking to any observer familiar with the justice system in the United States. Under the rules:

- A prisoner can be excluded from the courtroom, during trial, based on anything the presiding officer or the Secretary of Defense deems to be a matter of national security. His assigned military defense counsel is prohibited from sharing with him any evidence that is received in his absence. As a result, a prisoner could be sentenced to prison, or even executed, without knowing on what grounds he had been found guilty.
- A Military Commission may receive anonymous unsworn statements, including statements embodying multiple levels of hearsay, whose sources a defendant cannot confront or impeach.
- Prisoners may be detained indefinitely before being charged or tried.
- The Military Commission's judgment may be finalized only after review by the President or the Secretary of Defense, both of whom have already made clear their view that the guilt of the Guantanamo detainees is a foregone conclusion.

Third, petitioner may invoke the protections of Common Article 3 in this habeas corpus proceeding. As made clear by this Court's precedents dating back to the late eighteenth century, treaties—which are part of the "supreme Law of the Land" under our Constitution—must be judicially applied as the rule of decision in a case with a proper jurisdictional foundation as long as two conditions are met: (1) the treaty is "self-executing" (*i.e.,* it is judicially enforceable without the need for any implementing legislation); and (2) the treaty protects individual rights. Here, because both conditions are satisfied, petitioner is entitled to judicial enforcement of his rights under Common Article 3.

ARGUMENT

I. Common Article 3 Protects Petitioner and Others Captured During the Conflict in Afghanistan

As made clear by the plain language of the Geneva Conventions, the Conventions' overall structure, the authoritative Red Cross drafting history, and relevant decisions from lower courts and international tribunals, Common Article 3 applies to the conflict in Afghanistan. Before discussing the universal applicability of Common Article 3, we provide background on the Geneva Conventions of 1949.

A. Common Article 3 of the Geneva Conventions of 1949

In 1949, soon after the horrors of World War II, representatives of 61 nations met in Switzerland to consider revisions to the existing 1929 Geneva Conventions. The delegates drafted four separate treaties guaranteeing protections to (1) wounded and sick soldiers in the field; (2) wounded, sick and shipwrecked sailors; (3) prisoners of war; and (4) civilians. The four 1949 Conventions are commonly referred to by number; *i.e.,* the "First Geneva Convention" and so forth. The United States ratified all four of the 1949 Conventions in 1955. As of December 2005, almost 200 states, including Afghanistan, had ratified the Conventions.

Common Article 3 of the 1949 Conventions provides in relevant part as follows:

> In the case of armed conflict not of an international character occurring in the territory of one of the High Contracting Parties, each Party to the conflict shall be bound to apply, as a minimum, the following provisions:
>
> (1) Persons taking no active part in the hostilities, including members of armed forces who have laid down their arms and those placed 'hors de combat' by sickness, wounds, detention, or any other cause, shall in all circumstances be treated humanely, without any adverse distinction founded on race, colour, religion or faith, sex, birth or wealth, or any other similar criteria. To this end, the following acts are and shall remain prohibited at any time and in any place whatsoever with respect to the above-mentioned persons:
>
> (a) violence to life and person, in particular murder of all kinds, mutilation, cruel treatment and torture;
>
> (b) taking of hostages;
>
> (c) outrages upon personal dignity, in particular humiliating and degrading treatment;
>
> (d) the passing of sentences and the carrying out of executions without previous judgment pronounced by a regularly constituted court, affording all the judicial guarantees which are recognized as indispensable by civilized peoples.
>
> (2) The wounded and sick shall be collected and cared for.

See Geneva III, art. 3, 6 U.S.T. 3316.

Common Article 3, which is described in the official Red Cross Commentaries as "one of [the] most important Articles" in the Conventions, *see* International Committee of the Red Cross, *Commentaries to the Convention (I) For the Amelioration of the Conditions of the Wounded and Sick in Armed Forces in the Field* 38 (1949), represented a dramatic innovation over the prior 1929 Conventions. *See id.* (Common Article 3 "marks a new step forward" and is "an almost unhoped for extension" of the prior Conventions).[4] For the first time, Common Article 3 established rules governing the humane treatment of persons captured in non-international conflicts. *See generally id.* at 38–48. Further, in contrast to the 1929 Conventions, which only guaranteed regularized court process before punishment for misconduct occurring while in captivity, *see Application of Yamashita,* 327 U.S. 1, 21–23 (1946), Common Article 3 guarantees adequate legal process before a detainee may be subjected to *any* punishment, including for misconduct occurring before his capture.

In 1997, the terms of Common Article 3 were incorporated into federal criminal law by the War Crimes Act, which makes it a felony for U.S. military personnel or U.S. nationals to engage in conduct "which constitutes a violation of common Article 3 of the international conventions signed at Geneva, 12 August 1949." 18 U.S.C. § 2441(c)(3). Additionally, the Third and Fourth Geneva Conventions (each of which includes Common Article 3) were incorporated as required conduct for the Armed Services by Army Regulation 190-8 (and identical regulations for the other Services) adopted on October 1, 1997. That regulation provides in Section 1-5(a)(3) that punishment of detainees "known to have, or suspected of having, committed serious offenses will be administered [in accordance with] GPW [the Third Geneva Convention], GC [the Fourth Geneva Convention], the Uniform Code of Military Justice and the Manual for Courts Martial."

Army Regulation 190-8, *available at* http://www.au.af.mil/au/awc/awcgate/law/ar190-8.pdf, at § 1-5(a)(3) (1997) ("AR 190-8").

B. *Common Article 3 Applies to the Conflict in Afghanistan*

In the decision below, two judges on the D.C. Circuit panel held that the 1949 Conventions are inapplicable to this case because they do "not apply to al Qaeda and its members." *Hamdan v. Rumsfeld,* 415 F.3d 33, 41 (D.C. Cir. 2005). The panel majority reasoned that the "Convention appears to contemplate only two types of armed conflicts," "international conflicts" (to which the broad panoply of Geneva Convention protections apply) and "civil war[s]" (to which only the more limited protections of Common Article 3 apply). *Id.* Accepting the government's argument that the war against al Qaeda in Afghanistan does not fit within either of these categories, the panel majority concluded that the Geneva Conventions do not apply to petitioner's case. *Id.* at 41–42.

The panel majority's decision departs from the plain language of Common Article 3 and is at odds with that provision's negotiating history and with the way it has been interpreted by lower courts and international tribunals. In addition, as explained by Judge Williams in his separate opinion, the panel majority's interpretation cannot be squared with the structure and purpose of the 1949 Conventions, which make it clear that Common Article 3 was intended to apply to all conflicts "between a signatory and a non-state actor" such as al Qaeda. 415 F.3d at 44 (Williams, J., concurring).

As the majority itself acknowledged, the bulk of the Conventions, conferring protections surpassing those of Common Article 3, apply to "international" conflicts. As the majority also recognized, Common Article 2 of the Conventions assigns that term a specific meaning: conflicts "between two or more of the High Contracting Parties." *Hamdan,* 415 F.3d at 41 (quoting Conventions at art. 2). Accordingly, as Judge Williams reasoned (and the majority failed to apprehend), the phrase "conflict not of an international character" refers simply to conflicts involving non-signatories to the Conventions.[5] If, as the D.C. Circuit majority concluded, the conflict with al Qaeda is not "international" because it is separate from the conflict with the Taliban in Afghanistan, then it clearly falls within this expansive definition of "conflict[s] not of an international character." *See id.* at 44 (Williams, J., concurring). Any other reading of Common Article 3 would require inexplicably different conceptions of the term "international" in Articles 2 and 3.

This reading is confirmed by the negotiating history of Common Article 3. As the Commentaries explain, the Red Cross initiated consideration of Common Article 3 by submitting draft language that would have extended the full protection of the Conventions to "all cases of armed conflict which are not of an international character, especially cases of civil war, colonial conflicts, or wars of religion. . . ." International Committee of the Red Cross, *Commentaries to the Convention (IV) Relative to the Protection of Civilian Persons in Time of War* (hereinafter "ICRC Commentaries (IV)") 30 (1949). There was, however, "almost universal opposition to the application of the Convention, with all its provisions," to non-international conflicts, even when the Conference delegates proposed compromises "limiting the number of cases in which the Convention was to be applicable." *Id.* at 32. A solution was found, however, when the French delegation suggested drafting Common Article 3 so that its substantive protections would be limited, rather than the types of conflicts to which they applied. *Id.* Thus, the deliberations over the Article were based on the understanding that its provisions "were to be equally applicable to civil and to international wars." *Id.* at 33.

Given this text and history, it is clear that Common Article 3 was intended to serve as a baseline for *all* armed conflicts. Since the rest of the Conventions, with their stronger protections,

cover international conflicts, all conflicts are governed at a minimum by the protections of this Article. *Id.* at 38 ("Representing, as [Common Article 3] does, the minimum which must be applied in the least determinate of conflicts, its terms must a fortiori be respected in the case of international conflicts proper, when all the provisions of the Convention are applicable").

As Judge Williams recognized in his concurring opinion, the structure of the Conventions does not allow for the gap in coverage envisioned by the D.C. Circuit majority. A non-state actor cannot sign a treaty, and therefore cannot be party to an "international" conflict under Article 2. *Hamdan,* 415 F.3d at 44 (Williams, J., concurring). Common Article 3 was drafted to provide minimal protection for those who had no protection before: stateless combatants. *Id.* "Thus the words 'not of an international character' are sensibly understood to refer to a conflict between a signatory nation and a non-state actor." *Id.* Although a civil war is one example of a conflict involving a non-state actor, it does not follow that Common Article 3 is confined *only* to civil wars, as the panel majority mistakenly concluded. Moreover, even if Common Article 3 is deemed ambiguous in this regard, the panel majority's construction should be rejected under the longstanding canon that treaties must be interpreted liberally to protect individual rights. *See United States v. Stuart,* 489 U.S. 353, 368 (1989) ("'[e]ven where a provision of a treaty fairly admits of two constructions, one restricting, the other enlarging, rights which may be claimed under it, the more liberal interpretation is to be preferred'") (quoting *Bacardi Corp. of Am. v. Domenech,* 311 U.S. 150, 163 (1940) (alteration in original)); *see also Nielsen v. Johnson,* 279 U.S. 47, 52 (1929); *Asakura v. City of Seattle,* 265 U.S. 332, 342 (1924); *Hauenstein v. Lynham,* 100 U.S. 483, 487 (1879).

Lower courts have recognized Common Article 3's universal applicability. In *Mehinovic v. Vuckovic,* 198 F. Supp. 2d 1322, 1351 (N.D. Ga. 2002), a case against a former Bosnian Serb police officer who perpetrated acts of torture during the Yugoslav conflict, the district court found the defendant liable, under the Alien Tort Claims Act, for violating Common Article 3. The court noted that the conflict in the former Yugoslavia had been recognized as international in character, but nevertheless held that the standards of Common Article 3 are broadly applicable "to any armed conflict, whether it is of an internal or international character." *Id.* at 1351 n.39 (internal quotations omitted). *See also Kadic v. Karadzic,* 70 F.3d 232, 243 (2d Cir. 1995) (under Common Article 3, "all 'parties' to a conflict... are obliged to adhere to these most fundamental requirements of the law of war").

International tribunals have also embraced the universal application of Common Article 3.[6] In *Military and Paramilitary Activities In And Against Nicaragua (Nicar. v. U. S.),* 1986 I.C.J. 14 (June 27) ("*Nicaragua*"), the International Court of Justice considered claims arising from the conflict in Nicaragua. Noting the difficulty of characterizing the underlying conflict as internal (as a Nicaraguan civil war) or international (because of the allegation of U.S. involvement), the I.C.J. concluded that "[b]ecause the minimum rules applicable to international and to non-international conflicts are identical... [t]he relevant principles are to be looked for in the provisions of Article 3." *Id.* at ¶ 219. More recently, the International Tribunal for the Prosecution of Persons Responsible for Serious Violations of International Humanitarian Law Committed in the Territory of the Former Yugoslavia since 1991 ("ICTFY") considered whether the Yugoslavian conflict was international or non-international, and concluded, citing *Nicaragua,* that the "character of the conflict is irrelevant" because Common Article 3 reflects "'elementary considerations of humanity' applicable under customary international law to any armed conflict, whether it is of an internal or international character." *Prosecutor v. Tadic,* Case No. IT-94-1, Decision on the Defence Motion for Interlocutory Appeal on Jurisdiction, ¶ 102 (ICTFY Appeals Chamber Oct. 2, 1995) ("*Tadic*"). The ICTFY subsequently reaffirmed this ruling in *Prosecutor v. Delalic,* Case No. IT-96-21, Judgement, ¶ 140–50 (ICTFY Appeals Chamber

Feb. 20, 2001); *see also Prosecutor v. Furundzija,* Case No. IT-95-17/1, Judgment, ¶ 138 (ICTFY Trial Chamber Dec. 10, 1998) (Common Article 3 "is applicable both to international and internal armed conflicts").

II. The Military Commission Convened Against Petitioner Violates Common Article 3

A. The Military Commission Convened to Try Petitioner Is Not a "Regularly Constituted Court" as Required by Common Article 3

Common Article 3 mandates that prisoners may be punished only after trial by a "regularly constituted court." The Commentaries provide little insight into this provision, stating only that Common Article 3 was intended to ban "'summary' justice" while leaving "intact the right of the State to prosecute, sentence and punish according to the law." ICRC Commentaries (IV) at 39. In a somewhat different context, however, the Commentaries make clear that the requirement of a "regularly constituted" court "definitely excludes all special tribunals." *Id.* at 340 (discussing Article 66 of the Fourth Convention, which mandates that civilians be punished by "properly constituted, non-political military courts"). Geneva Convention (IV) Relative to the Protection of Civilian Persons in Time of War, Aug. 12, 1949, art. 66, 6 U.S.T. 3516. The Commentary to Article 66 further states that "it is the ordinary military courts of the Occupying Power which will be competent. Such courts will, of course, be set up in accordance with the recognized principles governing the administration of justice." ICRC Commentaries (IV) at 340.

In this case, the Military Commissions were established pursuant to the President's Military Order dated November 13, 2001 (the "November 13 Order"), *see* 66 Fed. Reg. 57,833, as well as the Defense Department's Military Commission Order No. 1 ("MCO 1"), as amended most recently on August 31, 2005, see http://www.defenselink.mil/news/Sep2005/d20050902order.pdf.[7] The November 13 Order makes clear that the Military Commissions are "special tribunals" set up to punish individuals specifically identified by the President. Indeed, § 2(a) of the November 13 Order mandates that an individual may be tried by Military Commission only if the President personally determines that there is reason to believe that the individual is a member of al Qaeda, has participated in terrorism, or has harbored a terrorist. *See* 66 Fed. Reg. 57,834. Because the Military Commissions are thus vested with jurisdiction only in cases that are specially designated on an *ad hoc* basis, they stand in contrast to regularized tribunals, such as general courts-martial, which possess jurisdiction over a broad class of persons, including detainees who are not prisoners of war. *See* 10 U.S.C. § 818 (jurisdiction of general courts-martial).

Further, although the Military Commissions are cloaked in the forms of legality, drawing their authority from orders listed in the Federal Register and the Code of Federal Regulations, in fact they vest members of the Executive Branch with breathtaking discretion. Under the Military Commission rules, the President and/or his subordinates enjoy power to decide:

- Which individuals should be tried by a Military Commission, *see* 66 Fed. Reg. 57,834 and MCO 1 § 3 (A);
- Whether to exclude members of the public, the press, civilian defense counsel, or even the defendant himself from a trial based on "national security interests," *see* MCO 1 § 6(B)(3);
- Whether to receive evidence at trial, provided only that it must be deemed to "have probative value to a reasonable person" in order to be admitted, *see id.* at § 6(D)(1);

- Whether to issue protective orders that preclude the defendant and civilian defense counsel from seeing certain of the prosecution's evidence, *see id.* at § 6(D)(5)(b); and
- What sentence to impose upon conviction, including "death, imprisonment for life or for any lesser term," or other sentences, *see* 66 Fed. Reg. 57,834; MCO 1 §§ 6(G), 6(H)(6).

Further, the rules governing Military Commissions are subject to change at the sole discretion of the Executive Branch either by way of formal amendment, *see, e.g.,* MCO 1 § 11 ("The Secretary of Defense may amend this Order from time to time"), or if the Secretary of Defense exercises an open-ended power to circumvent the rules, *see id.* § 1 ("Unless otherwise directed by the Secretary of Defense. . . the procedures prescribed herein shall and no others shall govern" trials before Military Commissions). Taken together, these provisions amount to a massive and unilateral assertion of authority by the Executive Branch to select, try, and punish prisoners under Military Commissions. As such, the Commissions are not a "regularly constituted court" and thus fail to satisfy the basic requirement of Common Article 3.[8]

B. Common Article 3 Entitles Petitioner to Basic Judicial Safeguards Recognized in International Law and This Court's Longstanding Precedents

Even if the Military Commissions are deemed "regularly constituted courts," their highly irregular procedural rules fail to afford "all the judicial guarantees which are recognized as indispensable by civilized peoples" as separately required by Common Article 3. This latter provision was inserted with the intention that signatory nations should "surround the administration of justice with safeguards aimed at eliminating the possibility of judicial errors." ICRC Commentaries (IV) at 39. The precise contours of the Common Article 3 safeguards were delineated in Article 75 of Protocol I to the Conventions, which was adopted in 1977 ("Article 75"). Protocol Additional to the Geneva Conventions of 12 August 1949, and relating to the Protection of Victims of International Armed Conflicts (Protocol 1), June 8, 1977, art. 75, 1125 U.N.T.S. 3; *see also* ICRC, *Commentaries to the Protocol Additional to the Geneva Conventions of 12 August 1949, and relating to the Protection of Victims of International Armed Conflicts (Protocol I)* 878 (1977) ("Protocol I Commentaries"). Although the United States did not adopt Protocol I because of objections to other provisions, "it does regard the provisions of Article 75 as an articulation of safeguards to which all persons in the hands of an enemy are entitled." William H. Taft, IV, *The Law of Armed Conflict After 9/11,* 28 Yale J. Int'l L. 319, 322 (2003); *see also* Conference, *The Sixth Annual American Red Cross-Washington College of Law Conference on International Humanitarian Law,* 2 Am. J. Int'l L. & Pol'y 415, 427 (1987) (remarks of U.S. Dep't of State Legal Adviser Michael J. Matheson that the U.S. supports "the fundamental guarantees contained in article 75"). Therefore, to comport with Common Article 3, the Military Commissions must satisfy the provisions of Article 75, which include:

(1) prompt judicial proceedings;

(2) the right to be tried in one's presence;

(3) the right to not be compelled to testify against himself;

(4) the right to cross-examine witnesses against him and to provide witnesses on his behalf; and

(5) release from detention with the minimum delay possible as soon as the circumstances justifying the arrest have ceased to exist.

Article 75 at ¶ 4.[9]

These guarantees are deeply rooted in our own Constitutional traditions. For example, in *Crawford v. Washington,* 124 S. Ct. 1354, 1363 (2004), this Court admonished that the rights enshrined in the Sixth Amendment's Confrontation Clause have historically been considered "indispensable conditions" and "founded on natural justice" (internal quotations omitted). Another "principle of natural justice" is the right of the accused to be present at his trial. *Windsor v. McVeigh,* 93 U.S. 274, 277 (1876); *see also Lewis v. United States,* 146 U.S. 370, 372 (1892) (absence of defendant at his own trial is "contrary to the dictates of humanity") (internal quotations omitted). This Court has also declared that keeping evidence, favorable or not, from the eyes of the accused violates fundamental precepts of fairness. *See, e.g., Brady v. Maryland,* 373 U.S. 83, 88 (1963) (withholding of favorable evidence from an accused "does not comport with standards of justice"); *Joint Anti-Fascist Refugee Comm. v. McGrath,* 341 U.S. 123, 170–71 n. 17 (1951) ("[t]he plea that evidence of guilt must be secret is abhorrent to free men") (internal quotations omitted).

Because the safeguards demanded by Common Article 3 (as spelled out in Article 75) are universally recognized as bedrock requirements of any civilized justice system, it is hardly surprising that they have been incorporated into the international tribunals established since the passage of Protocol I. These tribunals have tried defendants, including ex-Serbian president Slobodan Milosevic, accused of the most heinous crimes, including genocide. *See generally* Statute of the ICTFY, S.C. Res. 827, U.N. SCOR, 48th Sess., 3217th mtg. at 6, U.N. Doc. S/RES/827 (May 25, 1993) ("ICTFY Statute") at art. 20–21; Statute of the International Criminal Tribunal for Rwanda, S.C. Res. 955, U.N. SCOR, 49th Sess., 3453d mtg. at 3, U.N. Doc. S/RES/955 (Nov. 8, 1994) ("ICTR Statute") at art. 19–20; The European Convention on Human Rights, Nov. 4, 1950, art. 5–6, 213 U.N.T.S. 221 ("ECHR").

MCO 1 fails to meet the requirements of Common Article 3 in four respects: (1) it allows petitioner to be unwillingly excluded from his trial; (2) it permits the tribunal to eviscerate petitioner's ability to cross-examine adverse witnesses; (3) it has permitted petitioner to be detained for years before trial; and (4) it fails to provide an impartial and independent tribunal. We address each of these points in turn.

1. Right to Be Present at Trial

Although the Commission rules nominally recognize petitioner's right to be present at his tribunal, MCO 1 at § 5(K), that right yields if the Commission closes the proceedings to petitioner and his Civilian Defense Counsel based on anything the Presiding Officer or Secretary of Defense deems to be a matter of national security. *Id.* at § 6(B)(3). The Presiding Officer may exclude petitioner upon an *ex parte* presentation by the prosecution. *Id.* This rule violates petitioner's "right to be tried in his presence." Article 75 at ¶ 4(e); *see also* ICCPR art. 14 at ¶ 3(d); ICTFY Statute art. 21 at ¶ 4(d); ICTR Statute art. 20 at ¶ 4(d). Petitioner's exclusion also neutralizes his right to cross-examine witnesses by preventing him from observing them and conferring with his counsel. Article 75 at ¶ 4(g); *see also* ICCPR art. 14 at ¶ 3(e); ICTFY Statute art. 21 at ¶ 4(e); ICTR Statute art. 20 at ¶ 4(e); ECHR art. 6 at ¶ 3(d).

Compounding this violation is the Commission's ability to offer evidence, under the rubric of "Protected Information," against petitioner without his ever knowing about it. *See* MCO 1 at § 6 (D)(5). Although any admitted evidence must be seen by Detailed Defense Counsel, *id.* at §6(D)(5)(b)(iii), Detailed Defense Counsel is not permitted to share the content of that evidence with petitioner or Civilian Defense Counsel. "Thus, for example, testimony may be received from a confidential informant, and petitioner will not be permitted to hear the testimony, see the witness's face, or learn his name." *Hamdan,* 344 F. Supp. 2d at 168. The consequences of such secret evidence are dire: petitioner could be sentenced to a lengthy prison term, or even executed, without ever knowing on what grounds he has been found guilty.

The fact that Detailed Defense Counsel can be present at all stages of the trial does not cure the problem of petitioner's exclusion. "The perception that confrontation is essential to fairness has persisted over the centuries because there is much truth to it." *Coy v. Iowa,* 487 U.S. 1012, 1019 (1988). The District Court's ruling adhered to this principle, noting the need for counsel to be able to turn to his client and ask, "Did that really happen? Is that what happened?" *Hamdan,* 344 F. Supp. 2d at 168 (internal quotations omitted). *See also* Protocol I Commentaries at 883 ("the important thing is that the defendant is present at the sessions where the prosecution puts its case, when oral arguments are heard, etc. In addition, the defendant must be able to hear the witnesses and experts [and] to ask questions himself"). The government has not provided a single instance of a past tribunal, whether court proceeding or military commission, that has allowed for the involuntary exclusion of a defendant for any reason other than disruption of proceedings. The Uniform Code of Military Justice does not allow for such measures. 10 U.S.C. § 839(b); *United States v. Daulton,* 45 M.J. 212, 219 (C.A.A.F. 1996).

2. Right to Cross-Examine Adverse Witnesses

The Commissions' rules compromise petitioner's confrontation and cross-examination rights beyond excluding him unwillingly from the courtroom. *See* Article 75 at ¶ 4(g); *see also* ICCPR art. 14 at ¶ 3(e); ICTFY Statute art. 21 at ¶ 4(e); ICTR Statute art. 20 at ¶ 4 (e); ECHR art. 6 at ¶ 3(d). The Commission is allowed to consider any evidence it deems probative "including, but not limited to, testimony from prior trials and proceedings, sworn or unsworn written statements, physical evidence, or scientific or other reports." MCO 1 at § 6 (D)(3). Thus, even if petitioner is present, the Commission may receive anonymous unsworn statements whose sources petitioner cannot confront or impeach. This is exactly the situation the Supreme Court found an affront to historical concepts of natural justice in *Crawford,* 541 U.S. at 49. Furthermore, the military commissions in *Madsen v. Kinsella,* 343 U.S. 341 (1952), on which the government has often relied, explicitly guaranteed the defendant the rights to be present at her proceeding and to cross-examine adverse witnesses without qualification. *Id.* at 358 n.24.

3. Right to Prompt Judicial Proceedings

Petitioner has endured an unconscionably lengthy pre-trial detention. He was brought to Guantanamo in June 2002, and the decision to try him by military commission was made over a year later in July 2003, but he was not charged until after another full year, in July 2004. Common Article 3's promptness requirement does not countenance such delays. Indeed, the Protocol I Commentaries establish a *10 day* time limit for being informed of charges. Protocol I Commentaries at 876–77.

International law entitles the accused to be "promptly informed of any charges against him" and "to trial within a reasonable time." ICCPR art. 9 at ¶ 2, 3; *see also* Article 75 at ¶ 3, 4(a); ICTFY Statute art. 21 at ¶ 4(a), 4(c); ICTR Statute art. 20 at ¶ 4(a), 4(c); ECHR art. 6 at ¶ 1, 3 (a). As the Supreme Court has emphasized, unreasonable delay in proceedings not only subjects an accused to the harm of a lengthy pretrial confinement, but impairs the accused's defense "by dimming memories and loss of exculpatory evidence." *Doggett v. United States,* 505 U.S. 647, 654 (1992). None of the military tribunals previously encountered by this Court involved detention as prolonged as petitioner's. *Madsen,* 343 U.S. at 343–44 (defendant charged a day after arrest and tried six months later); *Yamashita,* 327 U.S. at 5 (defendant charged within a month of capture and tried two weeks later); *Ex parte Quirin,* 317 U.S. 1, 7–8 (1942) (defendants charged within three weeks of capture and tried less than a week later).

4. Right to Be Tried by an Independent and Impartial Tribunal

Finally, the Commissions are not an "independent and impartial tribunal" as required by Common Article 3. ICCPR art. 14 at ¶ 1; UDHR art. 10; ECHR art. 6 at ¶ 1. The Commission members are appointed by the Secretary of Defense, and can be removed at any time for "good cause." MCO 1 at § 4(A)(1)–(3). Once the Commission renders a decision, the case passes automatically to a Review Panel, which either recommends a disposition to the Secretary of Defense or remands the case to the Commission for further proceedings. *Id.* at § 6(H)(4). The Secretary of Defense, in turn, either forwards the case to the President with a recommended disposition or remands the case to the Commission for further proceedings. *Id.* at § 6(H)(5). The President may approve or disapprove the recommendation; change the conviction to one of a lesser included offense; mitigate, commute, defer or suspend the sentence imposed; or delegate his final authority to the Secretary of Defense. *Id.* at § 6(H)(6). Although the President or Secretary of Defense cannot change a "Not Guilty" finding to "Guilty," a "Not Guilty" disposition will not take effect until it is finalized by the President or Secretary of Defense. *Id.* at § 6(H)(2).[10]

As the foregoing structure makes clear, the Commissions are under the control of the President and Secretary of Defense. But these two individuals have already asserted that the Guantanamo detainees are guilty. For example, the President has unequivocally said of the Guantanamo detainees: "these are killers." Press Release, President Meets with Afghan Interim Authority Chairman (Jan. 28, 2002), http://www.whitehouse.gov/news/releases/2002/01/20020128-13.html. The Secretary of Defense, meanwhile, has called the Guantanamo detainees "among the most dangerous, best-trained, vicious killers on the face of the Earth." Jess Bravin, Jackie Calmes & Carla Anne Robbins, *Status of Guantanamo Bay Detainees Is Focus of Bush Security Team's Meeting,* Wall St. J., Jan. 28, 2002, at A16; *see also* Transcript, Defense Department Briefing (Jan. 22, 2002), http://www.globalsecurity.org/military/library/news/2002/01/mil-020122-usia01.htm (quoting Secretary of Defense as calling Guantanamo detainees "committed terrorists" who "have been found to be engaging on behalf of the al Qaeda"). The government can offer no precedent for a military tribunal operating under such an overt bias. To the contrary, the later German saboteur tribunals in World War II were modified so that they would be *more* independent than earlier tribunals had been. *See* Louis Fisher, *Nazi Saboteurs on Trial* 140–43 (Univ. Press of Kansas 2003).

III. Petitioner's Rights under Common Article 3 Are Enforceable in Federal Court

In the decision below, the Court of Appeals erroneously concluded that petitioner's rights under the Geneva Conventions cannot be enforced in federal court. The Court of Appeals reached this decision based largely upon its reading of this Court's decision in *Johnson v. Eisentrager,* 339 U.S. 763 (1950). In doing so, the Court of Appeals mistakenly conflated two distinct questions: (1) whether the Conventions provide a private right of action (*i.e.,* whether a private litigant can gain federal jurisdiction solely by claiming a violation of the Conventions), and (2) whether the rights guaranteed by the Conventions are judicially enforceable (*i.e.,* whether a litigant can invoke the Conventions as the rule of decision in a case with an independent jurisdictional foundation). The first of these questions, which was addressed in *Eisentrager,* is not relevant here. Petitioner does not rely on the Conventions for a "private right of action," as he has independently gained access to the federal courts by way of his habeas petition. The answer to the second question, informed by numerous decisions of this Court dating back to the 1700s, is plainly "yes." Because Common Article 3 protects individual rights and is self-executing (*i.e.,* it is judicially enforceable without the need for any implementing legislation), it can and should supply the rule of decision in petitioner's case.

A. *This Court Has Consistently Enforced Treaties That Protect Individual Rights and Are Self-Executing*

As the Supremacy Clause of the Constitution declares in relevant part, "all Treaties made, or which shall be made, under the Authority of the United States, shall be the supreme Law of the Land." U.S. Const. art. VI, cl. 2. In the early days of our nation's history, Chief Justice Marshall proclaimed that "where a treaty is the law of the land, and as such affects the rights of parties litigating in court, that treaty as much binds those rights and is as much to be regarded by the court as an act of congress." *United States v. Schooner Peggy,* 5 U.S. 103, 110 (1801). He later explained, in *Foster v. Neilson,* 27 U.S. 253, 314 (1829), *overruled in part by United States v. Percheman,* 32 U.S. 51 (1833), that this tenet of American law enshrined "a different principle" than that followed in Great Britain. In Britain, a treaty was considered "*not* a legislative act," and was therefore "carried into execution by the sovereign power of the respective parties to the instrument." *Id.* at 314 (emphasis added). In the United States, in contrast, a treaty is "to be regarded in courts of justice as equivalent to an act of the legislature, whenever it operates of itself without the aid of any legislative provision." *Id.; accord United States v. Rauscher,* 119 U.S. 407, 417–18 (1886). Over the years, this Court has enforced treaty provisions if those provisions require no implementing legislation to make them effective, and has used the term "self-executing" to describe such provisions. *See, e.g., Whitney v. Robertson,* 124 U.S. 190, 194 (1888) ("If the treaty contains stipulations which are self-executing, that is, require no legislation to make them operative, to that extent they have the force and effect of a legislative enactment").

This Court has a long history of finding treaty provisions self-executing, and therefore judicially enforceable in favor of individual litigants, when those provisions confer rights upon individuals. For example, in *Chew Heong v. United States,* 112 U.S. 536, 538 (1884), a Chinese laborer was detained by the Executive Branch when he attempted to re-enter the U.S. after traveling to Hawaii. The alien in *Chew Heong* (who accessed the federal courts by means of a habeas petition) argued that his detention violated an 1880 treaty between China and the United States declaring that "Chinese laborers who are now in the United States shall be allowed to go and come of their own free will and accord." *Id.* at 538, 542. The Court observed that the 1880 treaty "operate[d] of itself without the aid of legislation," and therefore "while in force constitute[d] a part of the supreme law of the land." *Id.* at 540. Accordingly, the Court enforced the alien's "right to go from and return to the United States at pleasure" as "secured by [the] treaty." *Id.* at 539–40.

Two years later, this Court similarly enforced a treaty as providing the rule of decision in *Rauscher.* There, the United States prosecuted a defendant on a charge of "cruel and unusual punishment" after extraditing him from Great Britain on a murder charge. 119 U.S. at 409. The defendant appealed on the grounds that the governing extradition treaty required that he be tried only for the crime for which he was extradited. *Id.* The *Rauscher* Court noted that the Constitution had departed from the British norm of exclusive diplomatic enforcement of treaties. *Id.* at 417–18. The Court then concluded that because the extradition treaty was "the supreme law of the land," the Court was "bound to take judicial notice, and to enforce in any appropriate proceeding the rights of persons growing out of that treaty." *Id.* at 419. Based on this reasoning, the Court held that the treaty conferred upon the defendant the right to be tried only for the charge underlying his extradition. *Id.* at 433.

The turn of the century brought no change to the Court's view on judicial enforcement of treaty provisions protecting individual rights. In *Asakura,* 265 U.S. at 339–40, a Japanese national challenged a city ordinance restricting pawn-brokering to U.S. citizens, relying on a

1911 treaty between Japan and the U.S. guaranteeing each country's citizens the "liberty to enter, travel and reside in the territories of the other to carry on trade...upon the same terms as native citizens and subjects." The Court unanimously held that the 1911 treaty "operates of itself without the aid of any legislation, state or national," and would therefore "be applied and given authoritative effect by the courts." *Id.* at 341. After interpreting the term "trade" to encompass pawn-brokering, the Court vindicated the petitioner's rights under the treaty and enjoined the city from enforcing the ordinance against him. *Id.* at 343–44.

Shortly after World War II, in a decision that is highly probative here, this Court treated the 1949 Conventions' predecessors, the 1929 Geneva Conventions, as judicially enforceable. In *Yamashita,* which arose out of the trial of a top Japanese general by a military commission following the Japanese surrender, the defendant challenged the tribunal's procedural rules, which permitted it to receive into evidence depositions, affidavits, hearsay, and opinion evidence in a manner that would not be permitted in a criminal trial in a U.S. court. *See* 327 U.S. at 6. Although the Court rejected the defendant's argument on the merits, it gave full consideration to his contention that the procedures used by the military commission were impermissible under the 1929 Geneva Conventions. *See Yamashita,* 327 U.S. at 23.[11]

The foregoing decisions stand alongside many other precedents in which this Court has enforced the treaty rights of private litigants. None of these precedents dealt with treaties containing specific language regarding self-execution or judicial enforcement, and all of them belie the contention that enforcement of treaties is exclusively a matter for sovereign negotiation. *See, e.g., Ware v. Hylton,* 3 U.S. 199, 239 (1796) (enforcing British citizens' right to collect a debt under peace treaty provision stating that "creditors, on either [the American or British] side ...shall meet with no lawful impediment to the recovery of the full value...of all bona fide debts, heretofore contracted"); *Hauenstein,* 100 U.S. at 486 (enforcing Swiss national's right to proceeds from property of Virginian decedent under treaty provision giving Swiss nationals the right to sell inherited property and "the liberty at all times to withdraw and export the proceeds thereof"); *Johnson v. Browne,* 205 U.S. 309, 319 n.† (1907) (granting writ of habeas corpus to prisoner extradited from Canada for different crime than the one he was sentenced for, because extradition treaty stated that no extradited defendant "shall be triable or be tried for any crime or offense...other than the offense for which he was surrendered"); *Jordan v. Tashiro,* 278 U.S. 123, 126 n.1 (1928) (enforcing Japanese national's right to set up corporation under same treaty provisions as in *Asakura*); *Nielsen,* 279 U.S. at 50 (enforcing Danish national's right to succeed to property without paying inheritance tax imposed on nonresident aliens under treaty provision guaranteeing that a Danish person's property within the U.S. would be taxed no more heavily than if it were owned by an American citizen); *Kolovrat v. Oregon,* 366 U.S. 187, 191 n.6 (1961) (enforcing Yugoslavian national's right to inherit from American decedent under treaty provision giving Serbian citizens the right to acquire property in the U.S. as if they were American citizens).

In each of these cases, the Court enforced treaty provisions in order to vindicate the individual rights conferred by the respective treaties. Additionally, in each case, those individual rights were conferred in terms that could be given effect without additional legislative action (*i.e.,* in "self-executing" provisions). In the *Head Money Cases,* 112 U.S. 580 (1884), this Court recognized that treaties bearing both of these characteristics should be judicially enforced. Specifically, the Court noted that a treaty may:

> contain provisions which confer certain rights upon the citizens or subjects of one of the nations residing in the territorial limits of the other, which partake of the nature of municipal law, and which are capable of enforcement as between private parties in the courts of the country....A treaty, then, is a law of the land as an act of congress is, whenever its provisions prescribe a rule by which the rights of the private citizen

or subject may be determined. And when such rights are of a nature to be enforced in a court of justice, that court resorts to the treaty for a rule of decision for the case before it as it would to a statute.

112 U.S. at 598–99; *see also Foster,* 27 U.S. at 307 (observing that the judiciary should not resolve disputes purely between sovereigns, but that "its duty commonly is to decide upon individual rights"); Restatement (Third) of the Foreign Relations Law of the United States § 111, Rep. n.5 (1987) ("Restatement") ("agreements that can be readily given effect by executive or judicial bodies, federal or State, without further legislation, are deemed self-executing, unless a contrary intention is manifest").

B. *Common Article 3 Protects Individual Rights and Is Self-Executing*

In this case, Common Article 3 bears both characteristics that were identified in the *Head Money Cases* as the criteria for judicial enforcement: it protects individual rights and is capable of stand-alone implementation by a court.

First, by its own terms Common Article 3 explicitly confers rights upon individuals, including prohibitions against discrimination based on "race, colour, religion or faith, birth or wealth, or any other similar criteria"; against "murder of all kinds, mutilation, cruel treatment and torture"; and, most relevant here, "the passing of sentences and the carrying out of executions without previous judgment pronounced by a regularly constituted court affording all the judicial guarantees which are recognized as indispensable by civilized peoples." Common Article 3 at cl. 1, 1(a), 1(d). Common Article 3 employs mandatory language, stipulating that detainees "*shall* in all instances be treated humanely" and mandating that signatory nations "*shall be prohibited*" from engaging in specified types of misconduct. *Id.* at cl. 1 (emphasis added). This Court has repeatedly enforced treaties with this sort of mandatory language. *See, e.g., Ware,* 3 U.S. at 239; *Chew Heong,* 112 U.S. at 538; *Asakura,* 265 U.S. at 340.

Second, the rights conferred by Common Article 3 are judicially enforceable without additional legislation. As an initial matter, courts plainly are competent to enforce Common Article 3. Congress recognized this proposition as recently as 1997, when it incorporated Common Article 3 into federal criminal law in the War Crimes Act. *See* 18 U.S.C. § 2441(c)(3) (making it unlawful for U.S. nationals to engage in conduct "which constitutes a violation of common Article 3 of the international conventions signed at Geneva, 12 August 1949"). Furthermore, the ratification process compellingly demonstrates that Common Article 3 is capable of enforcement without implementing legislation.

The Senate Report accompanying the ratification of the Conventions in 1955 stated broadly that "it appears that very little in the way of new legislative enactments will be required to give effect to the provisions contained in the four [Geneva] conventions." S. Exec. Rep. No. 84–9, at 30–31 (1955). The Senate Report selected a handful of articles from the Conventions—Common Article 3 not among them—and designated those articles in need of implementing legislation. *Id.* As the Restatement of Foreign Relations makes clear, the Senate's conclusion is powerful evidence that the provision is self-executing. *See* Restatement at § 111 Rep. n.5. ("[I]f the Executive Branch has not requested implementing legislation and Congress has not enacted such legislation, there is a strong presumption that the treaty has been considered self-executing by the courts. (This is especially so if some time has elapsed since the treaty has come into force.)"). Indeed, if the Senate had wished to render the Conventions non-self-executing, it would have done so explicitly, as it did with the more recently enacted ICCPR. *See* 138 Cong. Rec. S4784 (Apr. 2, 1992) (ratifying the ICCPR subject to the declaration that "the provisions of Articles 1 through 27 of the Covenant are not self-executing"); *accord Sosa v. Alvarez-Machain,* 542 U.S. 692, 728 (2004). Furthermore, the fact that a scant minority of the provisions

in the 1949 Conventions were viewed as non-self-executing can hardly support an argument that the Conventions are non-self-executing *in toto,* especially when the Senate took affirmative steps to enact implementing legislation for the 1949 Conventions where it understood such legislation to be required. *See* Restatement at § 111 cmt. h ("[s]ome provisions of an international agreement may be self-executing and others non-self-executing"); *see also Fok Young Yo v. United States,* 185 U.S. 296, 303 (1902) (finding one provision of 1880 treaty between China and the U.S. to be self-executing and another provision non-self-executing).

C. *In the Decision Below, the Court of Appeals Misread* Eisentrager

In holding that the Geneva Conventions are not judicially enforceable, the D.C. Circuit misread this Court's decision in *Eisentrager*. *See* 415 F.3d at 39–40 (discussing *Eisentrager*). *Eisentrager* was a putative habeas corpus action brought by German partisans who were captured during hostilities in China, convicted by a military commission in China, and repatriated to Germany to serve their sentences. *See* 339 U.S. at 765–67. Noting the lack of any precedent for a habeas petition brought by an alien enemy who was not present, at any relevant time, on United States territory, the Court held that the petitioners could not bring an action in federal court. *Id.* at 790–91.

Toward the end of *Eisentrager,* the Court addressed the prisoners' arguments that their convictions by the military commission in China were invalid under the 1929 Geneva Conventions. On the merits, the Court rejected the argument. 339 U.S. at 789–90.[12] In footnote 14, the Court noted that the prisoners did retain "right[s] which the military authorities are bound to respect" under the 1929 Conventions; *i.e.,* proper treatment as captives, but stated that the prisoners lacked the ability to enforce their treaty rights in federal court because "responsibility for observance and enforcement of these rights is upon political and military authorities." *Id.* at 789 n.14. In the decision below, the Court of Appeals placed great reliance on footnote 14, holding that it "leads to the conclusion that the 1949 Geneva Convention cannot be judicially enforced." 415 F.3d at 39.

But the Court of Appeals failed to recognize that footnote 14 followed inexorably from the holding in *Eisentrager* that the prisoners lacked the ability to *bring any challenge* in U.S. courts to their trial or punishment. With no independent right of action to justify their presence in federal court, the *Eisentrager* petitioners were not permitted to rely on the treaty as their sole basis for filing suit. This holding has no application here, where petitioner has an independent basis for filing his claim in federal court: his statutory right, recognized in *Rasul v. Bush,* 542 U.S. 466 (2004), to seek a petition for a writ of habeas corpus. Far more germane than the *Eisentrager* footnote is *Yamashita,* which the Court of Appeals did not discuss or even cite in its discussion of treaty enforceability. As *Yamashita* makes clear, and as this Court's treaty jurisprudence establishes, the Geneva Conventions can and should serve as the rule of decision in a properly filed habeas corpus action such as this one.

CONCLUSION

For the reasons stated, this Court should reverse the judgment of the Court of Appeals.

Respectfully Submitted,
James J. Benjamin, Jr.
Nancy Chung
Amit Kurlekar
Laura S. Lucas

Steven M. Pesner
Shannon Shah
AKIN GUMP STRAUSS HAUER & FELD LLP
590 Madison Avenue
New York, New York 10022
Attorneys for Amici Curiae Association of the Bar of the City of New York and International Bar Association

NOTES

1. Mr. Benjamin is a partner in the New York office of Akin Gump Strauss Hauer & Feld, LLP and a former Assistant U.S. Attorney in the Southern District of New York. He wishes to acknowledge the support of Akin Gump and the indispensable assistance of his colleagues at the firm, especially Nancy Chung, Amit Kurlekar, Laura Lucas, Steve Pesner, and Shannon Shah.

2. All parties have consented to this filing. Counsel for a party did not author this brief in whole or in part. No person or entity, other than the *amici curiae,* their members, or their counsel made a monetary contribution to the preparation and submission of this brief.

3. *Amici* express no view with respect to the merits of petitioner's case, including his alleged membership in al Qaeda and his guilt or innocence on the charges that have been filed against him.

4. These Commentaries are "widely recognized as a respected authority on interpretation of the Geneva Conventions. The authors of the Commentary were primarily individuals intimately involved with the revision of the Convention of 1929 and the drafting of the present Conventions." *United States v. Noriega,* 808 F. Supp. 791, 795 n.6 (S.D. Fla. 1992).

5. The philosopher Jeremy Bentham, credited with coining the term "international," defined it to encompass "mutual transactions between sovereigns as such," meaning that a non-"international" conflict would be any conflict not between sovereign states. Mark Weston Janis, *The American Tradition of International Law: Great Expectations 1789–1914* 13–14 (Oxford University Press 2004) (quoting Jeremy Bentham, *An Introduction to the Principles and Morals of Legislation* 296 (Burns and Hart eds. 1970)).

6. Although international jurisprudence is not binding upon this Court, we respectfully submit that the international decisions in favor of Common Article 3's applicability are persuasive authority, especially in light of this Court's statement that it "should give respectful consideration to the interpretation of an international treaty rendered by an international court with jurisdiction to interpret such." *Breard v. Greene,* 523 U.S. 371, 375 (1998).

7. An earlier version of MCO 1 was codified at 32 C.F.R. § 9.

8. We do not argue that *all* military commissions would fail to satisfy the "regularly constituted court" requirement of Common Article 3. Rather, we argue only that *these* Military Commissions fail to do so because they are focused selectively on cases chosen by the Executive and because the formation, structure, and operation of these Military Commissions rests on such an enormous assertion of authority by the Executive Branch.

9. The requirements of Article 75 are also embodied in subsequent international covenants respecting human rights, such as Articles 9 and 14 of the International Covenant on Civil and Political Rights ("ICCPR"), Mar. 23, 1976, 999 U.N.T.S. 171. In 1992, the U.S. ratified the ICCPR. In addition to encompassing the specific protections listed in Article 75, the ICCPR incorporates a general guarantee of an "independent and impartial tribunal." *Id.* at art. 14. This last provision echoes Article 10 of the Universal Declaration of Human Rights, G.A. Res. 217 A(III), U.N. GAOR 3, U.N. Doc. A/810 at 73 (1948) ("UDHR"), which the U.S. government has recognized as a charter of inalienable human rights. *See, e. g.,* U.S. Dep't of State Statement on Human Rights, http://www.state.gov/g/drl/hr/ ("a central goal of U.S. foreign policy has been the promotion of respect for human rights, as embodied in the Universal Declaration of Human Rights").

10. On December 31, 2005, shortly before the deadline for filing this brief, the President signed into law the National Defense Authorization Act for Fiscal Year 2006, H.R. Con. Res. 1815 (2005) (enacted)

("NDAA"). Section 1092 of the NDAA establishes limited jurisdiction in the D.C. Circuit to review final decisions of Military Commissions. *See id.* at § 1092(d)(3). The practical effect of this new statute is uncertain. It is unknown, for example, what standards the D.C. Circuit will employ in choosing to exercise its discretionary jurisdiction in cases in which the defendant has been sentenced to a term of imprisonment of less than 10 years, *see id.* at § 1092(d)(3)(B)(ii), or what standard of review will be used in cases where the D.C. Circuit does exercise jurisdiction. Given the government's consistent effort to "push the envelope" by asserting Executive authority as aggressively as possible, we anticipate that the government will seek to resist substantive judicial review of Military Commission decisions under the new statute. In any case no judicial review is triggered until the Executive gives final approval to the Commission's judgment, meaning that the timing of review is ultimately at the discretion of the Executive.

11. On the merits, finding that the 1929 Conventions only regulated procedures before imposing punishment for offenses committed during a prisoner's period of captivity, the Court concluded that the receipt of hearsay and opinion evidence at Yamashita's trial did not violate the treaty. *Id.* at 23. *Yamashita*'s holding on the merits became obsolete with the passage of the 1949 Conventions, which as noted above extended procedural protections far beyond the now-defunct 1929 Conventions. In particular, in contrast to the 1929 Conventions, Common Article 3 regulates the procedures that must be observed before a prisoner may be punished for *any* offense, not merely for offenses committed during the time of captivity. *Compare, e.g.*, Geneva III, art. 3, 6 U.S.T. 3316 *with* Geneva Convention Relative to the Treatment of Prisoners of War, Jul. 27, 1929, 47 Stat. 2021.

12. As was the case in *Yamashita, Eisentrager* applied the now-obsolete 1929 Geneva Conventions, so the Court's substantive analysis is not relevant to the instant case. *See supra* n.11.

CHAPTER 23

The Prevention and Prosecution of Terrorist Acts: A Survey of Multilateral Instruments

PREFACE BY NICOLE DELLER

The project that led to the publication of *The Prevention and Prosecution of Terrorist Acts: A Survey of Multilateral Instruments* began in the months after 9/11 when the New York City Bar began reflecting on the impact of the terrorist attacks on domestic and international law. Specifically, this Committee* was interested in the question of how the United States would use international law to combat international terrorism.

Prior to and soon after the 9/11 attacks, there was a dramatic shift in U.S. foreign policy from reliance on one of the most established frameworks for international relations, the international treaty system, toward more *ad hoc* and less formalized arrangements. In the early months of the Bush Administration, the United States "unsigned" the Rome Statute of the International Criminal Court, rejected the Kyoto Protocol to the United Nations Framework Convention on Climate Change, withdrew from the Anti-Ballistic Missile Treaty, entered into an arms reduction treaty that is neither irreversible nor verifiable, and halted nearly completed negotiations on a protocol to strengthen the monitoring and verification of the Biological Weapons Convention. The Bush Administration's criticisms of the existing system of treaties and conventions were that they are unverifiable and unenforceable and that many governments join with no intention of complying, while only the "good guys" take their treaty obligations seriously. Proponents of the international treaty system warned that U.S. exceptionalism would erode the many successes brought about by the system of collective norms and obligations codified in these treaties in the areas of arms control and collective security.

As the United States undertook a broader strategy for combating terrorism, the City Bar's International Security Affairs Committee asked whether the United States would approach international obligations regarding terrorism as it had other international security instruments. This Report was drafted in part to demonstrate the many ways that the United States would not be able to "go it alone" in the fight against terrorism. The United States depends on the political will and strengthened legal systems of all countries to ensure prosecution of terrorist acts, to prevent

transfer of materials that can be used in terrorist activities, and to dismantle the complex web of financing criminal activity that fuels al Qaeda and other terrorist networks.

While the following Report highlights the numerous existing international frameworks that would be valuable for U.S. policy, in preparing it the Committee also monitored the development of new policies and arrangements. One major trend is the expanded reliance on the Security Council as a body to develop and enforce anti-terrorism laws. Soon after 9/11, the UN Security Council, for the first time, passed anti-terrorism resolutions that required all states to make changes in their legal systems. Security Council Resolution 1367 required states to criminalize terrorist activities and to freeze terrorist funds. It created an oversight body, still in its early stages, to build capacity and to ensure compliance with this mandate. Similarly, Security Council Resolution 1540 was aimed at preventing non-state actors from acquiring weapons of mass destruction (WMD) and mandated the adoption of appropriate measures, including national criminal laws, to prevent acquisition of and trafficking in WMD and their delivery systems.

At the same time, the United States engaged in more flexible political arrangements to accomplish its objectives. In 2003, the United States launched the Proliferation Security Initiative, a political arrangement whereby states agree that, using their own laws and resources, they will coordinate with other governments to halt or avert shipments of WMD-related items. Activities may include boarding and searching ships and seizure of equipment, in countries' territorial waters or possibly on the high seas. This system may very well reach the limits of what is permitted under international law. Here and elsewhere, the United States must confront how the international legal system should adapt to the changing demands of security.

Ultimately, combating terrorism requires both capacity and political will. The United States, working with its allies and through the United Nations, is helping to build capacity on many fronts. Mobilizing political will poses the greater challenge. That will requires that governments accept the legitimacy of the international system in which they are called upon to participate. That means the system must be seen as fair. So, a key question arises for the United States: Is it committed to an international system that imposes obligations equally on all members? During the five years since the 9/11 attacks, the United States has relied heavily on international legal mechanisms in its anti-terrorist activities. Yet, as this Report documents, there is evidence that the United States places a premium on ensuring the flexibility of its actions while also strengthening the ability to impose measures on other countries. The Report reflects a weakening of important international agreements on disarmament and non-proliferation, including the Non-Proliferation Treaty.[1] As the possible combination of weapons of mass destruction and terrorism is one of the greatest U.S. national security fears, the ambivalent attitude toward an international legal system to combat WMDs may pose a threat to the U.S. agenda.

New York City Bar
Standing Committee on International Security Affairs
June 2006

The events of September 11, 2001 are etched in Americans' minds. The large-scale attacks occurring on U.S. territory brought home the imperative of preventing terrorism here and abroad, especially in light of the risk that future attacks might be perpetrated with nuclear or

other weapons of catastrophic effect. In the years since then, casualties from international terrorism have remained high, largely due to attacks in South Asia and the Middle East.[2]

This report demonstrates that a framework of treaty-based regimes and other international initiatives and programs plays a valuable role in preventing terrorism, and should be strengthened and supported. It is an essential part of a broader campaign that includes intelligence coordination, border security, domestic law enforcement and emergency preparedness.

First, the framework articulates and solidifies the norm that terrorism is a wholly impermissible form of political conduct. The importance of entrenching this norm was well stated by Undersecretary of Defense Douglas Feith:

> Our ultimate goal is to change the international environment regarding terrorism—instead of tolerance, [to] an international norm of renunciation and repudiation of terrorism. As I said, we want the world to view terrorism as it views piracy, slave trading or genocide—activities universally repudiated by respectable people. This is not an abstract, philosophical, academic point, but a strategic purpose of great practical significance.[3]

Second, the framework provides tools to prevent terrorists from acquiring weapons of mass destruction (WMD). Among the tools are treaties[4] banning WMD, programs to secure materials and weapons in Russia and elsewhere, and an initiative to prevent and interdict shipment of WMD-related items. The 9/11 Commission placed great emphasis on the need to succeed in this effort, stating that "al Qaeda has tried to acquire or make weapons of mass destruction for at least ten years. There is no doubt the United States would be a prime target. Preventing the proliferation of these weapons warrants a maximum effort. . . ."[5]

Third, the framework provides mechanisms to bring terrorists to justice, including treaties requiring the prosecution or extradition of persons alleged to have committed terrorist acts, and international tribunals.

There are of course problems in working through international institutions, laws, and initiatives. For example, treaties banning WMD may give rise to unwarranted complacency that certain states are in fact complying with the bans. The United Nations—or more accurately, the states working through the UN—has been notoriously slow in arriving at a definition of terrorism. This report fully addresses these and other problems, concerns, and criticisms, indicating when they are justified and what can be done about it.

Part I of the report surveys the conventions on terrorism, the treaties that require prosecution or extradition of suspected terrorists and those that require other anti-terrorism measures relating to finance and to security of nuclear facilities. Part II addresses anti-terrorism efforts in the UN context, including the negotiation of a comprehensive convention on terrorism and the adoption of a Security Council resolution requiring all states to take measures to suppress and prevent terrorism. Part III discusses the potential contribution of the International Criminal Court and other international tribunals to the prosecution of suspected terrorists. Part IV describes the array of international measures relevant to preventing terrorist acquisition of WMD, including WMD treaties, a Security Council resolution, export control arrangements, programs to secure materials and weapons, and the initiative to prevent shipment of WMD-related items.

I. CONVENTIONS ON TERRORISM

(A) Treaties in Force

Twelve multilateral treaties relating to terrorism have entered into force in the last forty years. The United States is a party to all of them.[6]

(1) 1963 Tokyo Convention on Offenses and Certain Other Acts Committed on Board Aircraft[7]

This treaty does not define specific offenses; it broadly covers "(a) offences against penal law" and "(b) acts which, whether or not they are offences, may or do jeopardize the safety of the aircraft or of persons or property therein or which jeopardize good order and discipline on board." The state of registration of the aircraft is deemed to have jurisdiction over these acts and must enact legislation or other measures to ensure its ability to prosecute. The Tokyo Convention *inter alia* provides authority for the commander of the aircraft to take necessary measures to protect the aircraft and requires states to permit the aircraft to land and to take custody of the perpetrator when necessary.

Many of the acts that fall within the scope of this treaty are also addressed in more detail in the aviation-related treaties described below.

(2) 1970 Hague Convention for the Suppression of Unlawful Seizure of Aircraft[8]

This treaty covers the prosecution of individuals accused of committing hijackings using force, threat of force, or any other form of intimidation. It also covers accomplices and attempted hijackings. State parties agree to adopt legislation making these acts punishable by "severe penalties." States are required to take measures to establish jurisdiction over acts committed in their territory and in aircraft registered to them. States must also take measures to establish jurisdiction over alleged offenders located in their territory and either prosecute or extradite them.

The Hague Convention improves on the Tokyo Convention by detailing specific unlawful acts and requiring prosecution or extradition and the administration of "severe penalties."

(3) 1971 Montreal Convention for the Suppression of Unlawful Acts Against the Safety of Civil Aviation[9]

This treaty covers violent acts against persons on board that are likely to endanger flight safety, destruction of the aircraft, damage to the aircraft that is likely to endanger flight safety, and destruction or damage of air navigation facilities. It also covers accomplices and attempted acts. Like the 1970 Hague Convention, the Montreal Convention requires states to adopt severe penalties against these offenses and to take measures to exercise jurisdiction over acts committed in their territory and in aircraft registered to them. States must also take measures to establish jurisdiction over alleged offenders located in their territory and either prosecute or extradite them.

The distinction between the Hague and Montreal Conventions is that the Hague Convention is aimed at acts of hijackings, whereas the Montreal Convention covers bombings and other violent acts that are likely to cause an aircraft to crash.

(4) 1973 Convention on the Prevention and Punishment of Crimes Against Internationally Protected Persons, Including Diplomatic Agents[10]

This treaty covers violent acts (such as assassination or other attacks) against heads of state and representatives of government and international organizations that are protected under international law. Attempted acts and accomplices are also covered. States are required to make the crimes punishable by appropriate penalties in relation to the gravity of the crime. States must take measures to establish jurisdiction over acts committed in their territory, by their nationals and when the victim is a protected person acting on behalf of the state. States must

also establish jurisdiction over suspected offenders located in their territory and prosecute or extradite them.

(5) 1979 Convention Against the Taking of Hostages[11]

This treaty defines the offense of hostage-taking as "seiz[ing] or detain[ing] and threaten[ing] to kill, to injure or to continue to detain another person...in order to compel a third party...to do or abstain from doing any act as an explicit or implicit condition for the release of the hostage." Attempted acts and accomplices are also covered. It requires states to make the crimes punishable by appropriate penalties given the gravity of the crime and to take measures to establish jurisdiction over offenses committed in their territory, by their nationals and, where appropriate, when hostages are their nationals. States must also establish jurisdiction over suspected offenders located in their territory and prosecute or extradite them.

(6) 1980 Convention on the Physical Protection of Nuclear Material[12]

This convention sets standards for the protection of nuclear material being used for peaceful purposes. It applies mainly to material in international transport. States agree that they will only export or import nuclear material if they are assured of certain physical protections as laid out by the convention. States are required to criminalize acts including the theft of nuclear material, fraudulent acquisition of nuclear material, acts without lawful authority that constitute "the receipt, possession, use, transfer, alteration, disposal or dispersal of nuclear material and which cause[] or [are] likely to cause death or serious injury to any person or substantial damage to property," and threats to use nuclear material to cause injury to any person or substantial damage to property. States must take measures to establish jurisdiction for offenses that occur in their territory or by their nationals. States must also establish jurisdiction over suspected offenders located in their territory and prosecute or extradite them.

On July 8, 2005, delegates from 89 countries agreed to fundamental changes that will substantially strengthen the Convention on the Physical Protection of Nuclear Material (CPPNM). IAEA Director-General Mohamed ElBaradei welcomed the agreement, stating that: "This new and stronger treaty is an important step towards greater nuclear security by combating, preventing, and ultimately punishing those who would engage in nuclear theft, sabotage or even terrorism. It demonstrates that there is indeed a global commitment to remedy weaknesses in our nuclear security regime."[13] The amended CPPNM requires states parties to protect nuclear facilities and material in peaceful domestic use, storage and transport. It will also provide for expanded cooperation among States regarding rapid measures to locate and recover stolen or smuggled nuclear material, mitigate any radiological consequences of sabotage, and prevent and combat related offenses. The new rules will come into effect once they have been ratified by two-thirds of the 112 states parties of the Convention, expected to take several years.

(7) 1988 Protocol for the Suppression of Unlawful Acts of Violence at Airports Serving International Civil Aviation[14]

This protocol extends the provisions of the 1971 Montreal Convention to acts of violence at airports serving international civil aviation.

(8) 1988 Rome Convention for the Suppression of Unlawful Acts Against the Safety of Maritime Navigation[15]

This convention was drafted largely in response to the 1985 *Achille Lauro* hijacking to address terrorist acts aboard ships. Offenses under the treaty include seizure of control of a ship

by threat or use of force; violent acts against persons on board a ship (passengers or crew) that are likely to endanger the safety of its navigation, destruction of a ship or damage likely to endanger the safety of its navigation and damage to maritime navigation facilities. It covers attempted acts and accomplices. It does not apply to ships used for military purposes. It requires states to take measures to establish jurisdiction over offenses committed in their territory, on ships flying their flag and by their nationals. States must also establish jurisdiction over suspected offenders located in their territory and prosecute or extradite them.

(9) 1988 Protocol for the Suppression of Unlawful Acts Against the Safety of Fixed Platforms Located on the Continental Shelf[16]

This protocol, which supplements the 1988 Rome Convention, creates a legal regime similar to that which applies to international aviation. This protocol provides for the prosecution of violent acts committed against fixed platforms located on the continental shelf, which are defined as structures attached to the sea bed for "exploration or exploitation of resources or for other economic purposes."

(10) 1991 Convention on the Marking of Plastic Explosives for the Purpose of Detection[17]

This convention was drafted largely in response to the 1988 explosion of a Pan Am flight over Lockerbie, Scotland. Recognizing the role that plastic explosives have played in terrorist bombings, this convention requires states to mark plastic explosives with a detection agent that will enhance their detectability. States are required to take measures (which may be penal, but are not required to be) to prohibit and prevent the manufacture of unmarked plastic explosives in their territory. To the extent that states' police or military retain unmarked plastic explosives, they must be marked, consumed or destroyed within 15 years.

(11) 1997 Convention for the Suppression of Terrorist Bombings[18]

This convention defines the offense of terrorist bombings as delivering, placing, discharging or detonating an explosive or other lethal device in, into or against a place of public use, a state or government facility, a public transportation system or an infrastructure facility with the intent to cause death or serious bodily injury; or cause extensive destruction where the destruction results in or is likely to result in major economic loss. States must adopt necessary legislation to make these acts criminal. States are required to take measures to establish jurisdiction for offenses committed in their territory and by their nationals and may establish jurisdiction in other instances, including offenses committed against their nationals and their government facilities. States must also establish jurisdiction over suspected offenders located in their territory and prosecute or extradite them.

(12) 1999 Convention for the Suppression of the Financing of Terrorism[19]

Noting that the number and seriousness of terrorist attacks depend on obtaining funding, this treaty criminalizes the financing of terrorism. The offense of financing of terrorism is defined as providing or collecting funds intended to be used to carry out: (a) an act which constitutes an offense under specified terrorism-related treaties (the treaties listed above, with the exception of the 1963 Tokyo Convention and the 1991 Convention on Plastic Explosives) or (b) "any other act intended to cause death or serious bodily injury to a civilian, or to any other person not taking an active part in hostilities in a situation of armed conflict, when the purpose of such

act, by its nature or context, is to intimidate a population, or to compel a Government or an international organization to do or to abstain from doing any act."

It is notable that clause (b) of the definition of financing terrorism comes closer to defining "terrorism" than any provision contained in the other 11 treaties. The treaty requires states to adopt penal legislation to prosecute individual offenders and also to hold legal entities liable for offenses committed on their behalf. States are required to take appropriate measures for the identification, detection, and freezing or seizure of any funds used or allocated for financing terrorism, or that are proceeds from terrorism. States must take measures to establish jurisdiction for offenses committed in their territory and by their nationals. There are other instances for which a state may establish jurisdiction, including when an offense is directed toward a state's territory or nationals. States must also establish jurisdiction over suspected offenders located in their territory and prosecute or extradite them.

(B) 2005 International Convention for the Suppression of Acts of Nuclear Terrorism

A recent development in the network of anti-terrorism treaties was the adoption of a convention addressing terrorist acts using, threatening to use, or aiming to use nuclear weapons or radiological bombs or involving damage to a nuclear reactor or facility. It also encourages States to cooperate in preventing terrorist attacks by sharing information and assisting each other in connection with criminal investigations and extradition proceedings. On April 13, 2005, the General Assembly adopted the treaty, and it opened for signature on September 14. It will enter into force when ratified by 22 states. Under its provisions, alleged offenders must be either extradited or prosecuted. It excludes activities of armed forces during an armed conflict, while also providing that it does not address the issue of the legality of the use or threat of use of nuclear weapons by states.

(C) Assessing the Anti-Terrorism Treaty Regime

The value that most of these treaties bring to the fight against terrorism is that they require states to take action against terrorist acts or actors within their territories and to ensure that their legal systems, particularly their criminal codes, are equipped to address these crimes. There have been some successes associated with these treaties. For example, in 1986, John F. Murphy, an expert on international terrorism, noted a general decline in aircraft hijacking "due in part to the preventive techniques mandated by [the International Civil Aviation] conventions and now employed both in airports and aboard aircraft."[20] Although the author observed that hijackings were on the rise again because hijackers were learning to avoid the security devices, he found that "[t]here is also ample evidence that hijackers have been submitted for prosecution either in the states where they have been found or in states to which they have been extradited. The [International Civil Aviation] conventions appear to have played a useful role in support of these prosecutions."[21]

The treaties on terrorism, however, are limited in what they are able to accomplish. They largely focus on prosecution, not prevention.[22] Due to their *ad hoc* nature, there are gaps in what they cover. For example, they do not extend to assassinations of non-official professionals such as businessmen and journalists and do not specifically criminalize attacks against water supplies, public buses or trains.[23] Most are far from universal, meaning that many states have not adopted them. They do not create any regulatory bodies to monitor implementation or ensure states' compliance. No sanctions exist for states parties that refuse to extradite or prosecute terrorists or that harbor terrorists. Several of the treaties are weakened by failure to reach acts that are committed solely within one state's territory and are inconsistent as to whether they permit

refusal of extradition of suspects based on grounds of political acts.[24] The following discussion details some of the attempts being made to address gaps in this treaty system.

Since the September 11, 2001 terrorist attacks, progress has been made on the goal of universal ratification of the anti-terrorism treaties. In September 2001, the Security Council passed Resolution 1373, which requires states to take a series of actions to combat terrorism (discussed below).[25] It also calls upon states to become parties to the twelve international terrorism conventions and to increase cooperation in the fight against terrorism. The Counter-Terrorism Committee (CTC), the committee created to monitor implementation of Resolution 1373, is contributing to states' efforts to become parties to all twelve instruments. The CTC has been identifying those states that need assistance with the ratification process and working to ensure such states receive help from appropriate assistance providers. Prior to Resolution 1373, only a few states had ratified all 12 anti-terrorism conventions. After two years, over 40 states had done so.[26]

Efforts to improve the treaty regime continue within the United Nations, with the General Assembly continuing to negotiate a comprehensive convention on terrorism—including a definition of terrorism—and the Security Council passing resolutions aimed at strengthening member states' anti-terrorism laws. These are discussed below.

II. UNITED NATIONS ACTIVITIES ON TERRORISM

(A) The Efforts to Create a Comprehensive Terrorism Convention

As noted above, because most of the terrorism-related treaties were drafted in response to highly visible terrorist acts, they address only specific acts of terrorism and neglect others. A comprehensive terrorism convention would end this piecemeal response. In his survey of terrorism-related treaties, *International Terrorism: Multilateral Conventions and Documents,* international law scholar M. Cherif Bassiouni observed:

> A comprehensive convention which combines all existing conventions pertaining to terrorism into a single updated text would significantly advance the overall objectives of these conventions. Such a comprehensive text would contribute to the elimination of overlaps, gaps and ambiguities which currently exist in the [existing] conventions. It would also eliminate the need to consult multiple legal sources in order to enforce State Party obligations. If this piecemeal subject-matter approach trend continues, there is no end to the number of conventions likely to be developed over the years to come, and there is no hope to make the legal mechanisms contained within each convention more effective.[27]

International terrorism scholar John F. Murphy also concluded that a global convention to "define international terrorism, make it an international crime, subject all state parties to the 'extradite or prosecute' formula and provide for other forms of cooperation" would be ideal.[28]

Since 1996, an *ad hoc* committee created by the United Nations General Assembly ("GA") in 1996 and open to all UN members has been negotiating a draft comprehensive convention on terrorism. As elaborated by the *ad hoc* committee, the comprehensive convention would define terrorism and require states to criminalize terrorist acts and take measures to establish jurisdiction over terrorist acts.[29] Two main issues have stalled completion of the draft: (1) whether acts committed by persons engaged in the struggle against "foreign occupation" (*e.g.,* Palestinian attacks in Israel) should be considered acts of terrorism, and (2) whether the acts of states' armed forces, which are already subject to the law of armed conflict during wartime, should be covered by this convention, *i.e.,* whether acts committed by armed forces may be treated as terrorist acts under this convention.[30]

(B) The Definition of Terrorism

The debate over the definition of terrorism, particularly whether the definition of terrorism should exclude resistance against foreign occupation, reflects the often-heard adage that one state's terrorist is another state's freedom fighter. It is a tension that has existed since the UN's first attempts at addressing terrorism in the early 1970s.[31] At that time, there was a larger degree of tolerance for the position that politically motivated acts, particularly those committed in resistance to foreign occupation, did not constitute terrorism. As Professor Malvina Halberstam observes, this was demonstrated in a 1972 General Assembly (GA) resolution relating to terrorism that established an *Ad Hoc* Committee on Terrorism but at the same time "reaffirm [ed] the inalienable right to self-determination and independence of all peoples under colonial and racist regimes and other forms of alien domination and uph[eld] the legitimacy of their struggle, in particular the struggle of national liberation movements."[32] That resolution did not even condemn terrorism, and it was not until 1985 that the GA passed a resolution unequivocally condemning "as criminal, all acts, methods and practices of terrorism wherever and by whomever committed."[33]

In 2005, efforts to reach a definition on terrorism were re-energized as part of the UN reform process leading to a 2005 summit of world leaders. The Secretary-General and a panel of high-level experts convened for the purpose of making recommendations on global security challenges both urged that a definition of terrorism be included in the Summit outcome.[34] Negotiations were not successful in reaching an agreement on a definition of terrorism. Instead, the 2005 Summit Outcome Document "condemned terrorism in all its forms" and stressed "the need to make every effort to reach an agreement on and conclude a comprehensive convention on international terrorism during the sixtieth session of the General Assembly."[35]

The Security Council, especially since the September 11 attacks, has also condemned terrorism on numerous occasions and worked towards a definition as well. In 2004, Security Council Resolution 1566 stated that "criminal acts, including against civilians, committed with the intent to cause death or serious bodily injury, or taking hostages, with the purpose to provoke a state of terror in the general public or in a group of persons or particular persons, intimidate a population or compel a government or an international organization to do or to abstain from doing any act, which constitute offences within the scope of and as defined in the international conventions and protocols relating to terrorism, are under no circumstances justifiable by considerations of a political, philosophical, ideological, racial, ethnic, religious or other similar nature...."[36]

While the General Assembly and the Security Council have condemned terrorism regardless of its motives, there are many member states that oppose this construct of terrorism as unfairly imposed by powerful states and in ignorance of the types of "terrorism" that powerful states wage on repressed states. Libya raised this issue in the 2001 General Assembly debates, speaking on behalf of the Arab Group:

> We cannot condemn terrorism and fight it when it hits one country and turn a blind eye when it hits other countries. It is unacceptable to label as terrorism the struggle of peoples to protect themselves or to attain their independence, while at the same time ignoring real terrorism and its many faces—such as occupation...[37]

It is this fundamental disagreement that poses a serious obstacle to achieving a definition.[38] Nevertheless, progress has been made since 9/11 to develop a system to improve states' capacity to prevent and prosecute terrorist acts, particularly through rules imposed by the Security Council.

(C) Security Council Resolutions

(1) Pre-9/11

The Security Council is uniquely qualified to respond to terrorism and to require states to take measures addressing terrorism. Under Chapter VII of the UN Charter, once the Security Council determines the existence of a threat to international peace and security—and the Council has determined that acts of international terrorism do constitute such a threat[39]—states are required to comply with the measures that the Security Council determines are appropriate to meet this threat. In addition to condemning certain specific acts of terrorism, the Security Council has passed a number of resolutions aimed at denying certain individuals and groups the means to carry out terrorist acts and requiring states to take action against such individuals and groups. For example, Resolution 1267 called for Afghanistan's Taliban regime to stop providing sanctuary and training for international terrorists and to cooperate with efforts to bring indicted terrorists to justice.[40] Resolution 1267 ordered the Taliban to turn over Osama bin Laden to authorities in a state where he had been indicted, such as the United States, or to another state where he would be arrested and prosecuted. It banned flights to Afghanistan, directed states to freeze funds that related to properties owned by the Taliban, and created a committee to oversee implementation of these sanctions. These measures were augmented by Resolution 1333 of December 2000, which included sanctions against the sale of military equipment to the Taliban.[41]

The sanctions regime created under Resolution 1267 has continued to function following the overthrow of the Taliban, by targeting specific individuals and entities for sanctions regardless of their physical whereabouts. All states are required to freeze the assets, prevent transit through their territory, and prevent the supply of arms and military equipment to individuals and entities designated by a Security Council committee established for this purpose (the '1267 Committee').[42] The 1267 Committee, comprised of all Security Council members, maintains and updates the list of Taliban or Al Qaeda-related individuals and entities that are subject to sanctions, and monitors state compliance with these sanctions.

(2) Post-9/11

The September 11, 2001 terrorist attacks brought a new level of urgency to the issue of terrorism in the United States and the United Nations. The UN Security Council responded to the September 11 attacks in Resolution 1368, passed the following day. The Security Council has the authority to take actions including authorizing use of military force to respond to threats to peace and security, and Resolution 1368 noted the Security Council's "readiness to take all necessary steps" to respond to the attacks. The resolution also recognized "the inherent right of individual or collective self-defence in accordance with the [UN] Charter," thus reaffirming the principle articulated in UN Charter Article 51 that "[n]othing in the...Charter shall impair the inherent right of individual or collective self-defence if an armed attack occurs against a Member of the United Nations, until the Security Council has taken measures necessary to maintain international peace and security." When the United States invaded Afghanistan in its search for the perpetrators of the 9/11 attacks, it did not request authorization from the Security Council. This decision was generally accepted as consistent with this right to self-defense and the terms of Resolution 1368.

The most far-reaching Security Council response to the 9/11 terrorist attacks was adopted on September 28, 2001 at the behest of the United States. Resolution 1373 *requires* all states to take a series of actions: criminalize the act of providing or collecting funds to be used to carry

out terrorist attacks; freeze all funds of individuals or entities with ties to terrorist activities; refrain from supporting entities or persons involved with terrorism, including the elimination of the supply of weapons to terrorists; and deny terrorists safe haven and ensure their prosecution. As described by John Negroponte, the U.S. Ambassador to the United Nations at the time the resolution passed, Resolution 1373 "generat[ed] a worldwide juridical transformation."[43] Unlike the twelve terrorism conventions, which are only binding on states that ratify them, Resolution 1373, as a decision of the Security Council, binds all states.[44]

As a result, all states, regardless of whether they had consented to do so in any of the terrorism treaties, are by virtue of Resolution 1373 obligated "to prevent and suppress terrorist attacks and take action against perpetrators of such attacks" and to transform their national legislation to criminalize terrorist financing. The obligations set forth in Resolution 1373 are of unlimited duration and can only be terminated by a subsequent Security Council resolution.[45] As described by one international legal scholar, with Resolution 1373, "the United Nations Security Council broke new ground by using, for the first time, its Chapter VII powers under the Charter to order all states to take or to refrain from specified actions in a context not limited to disciplining a particular country."[46]

Resolution 1373 ushered in a new era for the Security Council acting as global lawmaking body. In April 2004, the Security Council passed Resolution 1540, which requires states to adopt laws and other control measures to prevent the acquisition of weapons of mass destruction by non-state actors, discussed in Part V of this Report.[47] Like Resolution 1373, it establishes a sub-committee to monitor state implementation. Security Council Resolution 1566 sets forth a definition of terrorism (without labeling it as such) and called on all states to "ensure that such acts are punished by penalties consistent with their grave nature."[48] Most recently, Resolution 1624, passed by a Security Council meeting of heads of state during the September 2005 Summit, creates a legal prohibition on incitement to commit terrorist acts.[49]

(D) The Counter-Terrorism Committee

(1) Functions of the CTC

Resolution 1373 called for the creation of the CTC, composed of all Security Council member states, to monitor the implementation of its measures and increase states' capabilities to fight terrorism. States are required to report to the CTC on the measures they have taken to implement the Resolution. These reports form the basis of the CTC's work; experts employed by the CTC review the reports and ask follow-up questions to be answered by states in additional reports.[50] The CTC received initial reports from all 191 countries.

The CTC's assessment of states' capabilities is separated into three stages. The first stage is to ensure that states have the necessary legislation in place to address all aspects of Resolution 1373, with a particular focus on combating the financing of terrorism.[51] The CTC recognized that legislation is a "key issue because without an effective legislative framework States cannot develop executive machinery to prevent and suppress terrorism, or bring terrorists and their supporters to justice."[52] The second stage focuses on improving states' executive machinery to best implement counter-terrorism legislation, for example, ensuring that states have in place effective intelligence and police to monitor and apprehend those involved in terrorist activities. The third stage focuses on "the implementation of the above legislation and executive machinery to bring terrorists and their supporters to justice."[53] Measures may include cooperation on the exchange of information and judicial cooperation to prosecute terrorists.

The CTC is not itself able to provide assistance to improve states' anti-terrorism capabilities. It works as a switchboard to connect assistance providers with states seeking assistance. One

tool offered by the CTC is its database, the CTC Directory of Counter-Terrorism Information and Sources of Assistance, which offers information on standards, best practices and sources of assistance in the area of counter-terrorism.[54] The CTC also maintains a "Matrix of Assistance Requests" that provides an overview of assistance needs, and information on assistance programs.[55]

(2) Revitalizing the CTC

The early assessment of the CTC was that it was helping to build the political will to combat terrorism but that it lacked the infrastructure to sustain itself. On the positive side, as noted above, it significantly increased membership in the 12 anti-terrorism conventions. Reports to the CTC revealed that a large number of states did not have any legislation tailored to counter terrorism and are now revising their laws. However, the political will to implement this resolution has faded. Three years after the adoption of Resolution 1373, 78 states had failed to meet their latest reporting requirements.[56]

A January 2004 report of the Chair of the Counter-Terrorism Committee highlighted the problems in implementing Resolution 1373 and in particular the difficulties of the CTC's role. The report determined, among other things, that the CTC needed to play a more proactive role in assessing states' needs, needed to better monitor provision of assistance, including with field missions, and needed greater coordination and cooperation with regional, subregional and international organizations.[57] The Counter-Terrorism Committee then submitted a proposal for changes to the CTC's structure.[58]

In March 2004, the Security Council endorsed the CTC's reform proposals and unanimously adopted a "reform plan" in Resolution 1535.[59] It is described as "revitalizing" the CTC to strengthen its ability to help states implement their obligations under Resolution 1373.[60] The Committee was restructured to contain an Executive Directorate (hereinafter "CTED"), meaning that the Committee now has a full-time staff of professionals working on its agenda. It was declared operational in December 2005.[61] The CTED is committed to facilitating state assistance and developing a set of best practices for state implementation of counter terrorism efforts. The CTC has also adopted guidelines and procedures for conducting visits to member states, so as to better monitor implementation of Resolution 1373 and to identify more effectively the technical assistance needs of states.[62] The absence of such procedures had been considered a major impediment to the effectiveness of the Committee.

(3) Assessing the CTC

Even with its revitalization, there are limits as to what the CTC may accomplish. It is a reporting body, not a sanctions body. It is aimed at long-term and cooperative efforts, not challenging states' violations. It is therefore better suited to address states that are willing but unable to improve their national capabilities to fight terrorism than those states that are unwilling to fight terrorism. The CTC may report issues of non-compliance to the Security Council, which must then decide what tools it should bring to bear against states that fail to properly implement the terms of Resolution 1373.

The fact that Resolution 1373 does not include a definition of terrorism had left some ambiguities as to what acts states' legislation must cover. Resolution 1566 clarified this ambiguity with the inclusion of a definition of terrorist acts that states must take measures to prevent and prosecute.

The fundamental limitation of the CTC is that it depends on the political will of its member states. States must be willing to maintain their commitments and use these tools to prevent

terrorist acts and apprehend suspected terrorists. Despite its limitations, the CTC nevertheless has an important role to play in strengthening states' capacities to combat terrorism. The exchange of information between state governments and the CTC has generated an unprecedented amount of data on counter-terrorism capacities and practices. The Committee is best-positioned to coordinate the delivery of technical assistance by international and regional organizations and donor states to those requesting it. As the demand for assistance continues to increase, the CTC's function in this regard will become increasingly important.[63] The Committee is also best-positioned to improve coordination and cooperation among the many international and regional bodies concerned with counter-terrorism. Improving performance in these areas will allow the CTC to fulfill its mandate more effectively.[64]

Another important challenge for the United Nations is ensuring that states respect human rights in preventing and suppressing terrorism. The question of how to strike the right balance between protection of human rights and anti-terrorism efforts of terrorism is beyond the scope of this report. It is noteworthy, however, that the actions taken at the UN immediately after 9/11 did not affirm human rights norms in the context of combating terrorism while more recent UN-initiatives to counter terrorism now incorporate human rights language.

Resolution 1373, for example, was criticized for failing to refer to states' duties to respect human rights in the fight against terrorism and the lack of a mandate for the CTC to consider human rights implications of counter terror efforts.[65] The Security Council subsequently began to incorporate normative expressions that human rights be respected in the context of combating terrorism. Security Council Resolutions 1456 , 1535 and 1624 require states to "ensure that any measures to combat terrorism comply with all their obligations under international law, and [to] adopt such measures in accordance with international law, in particular international human rights, refugee, and humanitarian law." The World Summit Outcome included a similar statement.[66] The Counter-terrorism Executive Directorate also now includes a human rights expert.

III. INTERNATIONAL TRIBUNALS TO PROSECUTE TERRORIST ACTS

Many of the terrorism-related treaties described above are aimed at strengthening states' legal systems to improve their ability to bring terrorists to justice in a national legal system. But there may be incidents where a compelling interest exists for the prosecution of terrorists in an international forum, for example, when a large-scale terrorist attack directly affects a number of states or implicates citizens from a number of countries. For those crimes, there are several possible international tribunals where prosecutions could take place.

(A) The International Criminal Court

On July 1, 2002, the International Criminal Court (ICC) came into existence.[67] It was created by a treaty, the Rome Statute of the International Criminal Court, that has been ratified by over 100 states,[68] and is the world's first permanent court empowered to prosecute individuals. The ICC is distinct from the International Court of Justice, the principal judicial organ of the UN, which handles disputes among *states*. The ICC has jurisdiction over crimes against humanity, war crimes and genocide, as well as aggression if and when agreement is reached upon its definition.[69] As a precondition for jurisdiction, crimes must be a) committed on the territory of a state party (or a state that has provided consent to the court's jurisdiction); b) committed by a citizen of a state party (or a state that has provided consent to the court's jurisdiction); or c) referred to the ICC by the UN Security Council. The ICC provides complementary jurisdiction to national courts. That is, the court will act only in cases where the relevant state is either unwilling or unable to exercise jurisdiction.

Acts of terrorism are not crimes *per se* under the ICC statute,[70] but large-scale terrorist attacks of the type and magnitude that occurred on September 11, 2001 would likely fall within the definition of crimes against humanity, which are covered under the ICC statute.[71] The possibility of the ICC trying terrorist acts has been confirmed by the ICC's chief prosecutor Luis Moreno Ocampo. Mr. Ocampo noted that the court's jurisdiction would cover acts on the scale of the 9/11 attacks, provided that the acts satisfy the preconditions for the ICC's jurisdiction (stated above).[72] The 9/11 attacks themselves may not be brought before the ICC because they took place before the ICC statute came into effect on July 2, 2002.

Currently, the United States is actively opposed to the ICC and does not endorse the use of the ICC to prosecute terrorists. The primary objection to the ICC is the fear that it will be used for politically-motivated prosecutions against American soldiers or politicians.[73] Proponents of the court deny that this is a credible risk, arguing that there are sufficient safeguards in place to prevent politically motivated prosecutions.[74]

President Clinton signed the Rome Statute, but simultaneously noted that he did not intend to seek its ratification.[75] In May 2002, the Bush administration revoked the U.S. signature of the Rome Statute.[76] Meanwhile, Congress passed legislation to block U.S. cooperation with and support for the Court, known as the American Servicemembers Protection Act (the ASPA).[77] The ASPA also blocks military funding—in the form of International Military Education Training funds and Foreign Military Financing funds—to states that are parties to the ICC unless those states enter into agreements where they undertake not to send U.S. citizens to the ICC or if the President waives this requirement based on national security.[78] In 2004, Congress added restrictions on economic assistance—in the form of Economic Support Funds—to the ASPA's restrictions on military funding in legislation known as the Nethercutt Amendment.[79]

Despite the U.S. government's general opposition to the ICC, Congress did recognize that the ICC could contribute to bringing terrorists and other international criminals to justice. Thus, the ASPA includes a clause (the Dodd Amendment) that states: "Nothing in this title shall prohibit the United States from rendering assistance to international efforts to bring to justice Saddam Hussein, Slobodan Milosovic, Osama bin Laden, other members of Al Qaeda, leaders of Islamic Jihad, and other foreign nationals accused of genocide, war crimes or crimes against humanity."[80] This amendment recognizes that the ICC may play a role in prosecuting terrorists in the future, and the United States does not want to foreclose the possibility of involvement in such prosecutions. The sponsor of the amendment, Senator Chris Dodd, stated:

> I cannot believe, I do not want to believe, that if we apprehend, through the international community, people I have just mentioned on [the amendment's] list, that under this bill we would be prohibited from assisting in the prosecution of Osama bin Laden, the Islamic Jihad, Saddam Hussein, and other members of the terrorist community in the world.[81]

David Scheffer, former U.S. Ambassador at Large for War Crimes Issues, observed that the possibility of using the ICC to prosecute terrorists is a powerful reason to consider supporting the court: "If only in its own self-interest, the United States will want to collaborate with its allies and friends around the world and explore the utility of the ICC as a potent judicial weapon in the war against terrorism."[82]

Notwithstanding its objections to the ICC, in March 2005 the U.S. abstained rather than vetoed a Security Council referral to the ICC Prosecutor to investigate atrocities in Darfur.[83] Adopted by a vote of 11 in favor, none against, with 4 abstentions (Algeria, Brazil, China, United States), the resolution accommodated the United States by deciding that officials or personnel from a contributing State outside the Sudan which was not a party to the Rome Statute would be subject to the exclusive jurisdiction of that contributing State. The United States refrained from vetoing the resolution based on the need for the international community to work

together in order to end the climate of impunity in the Sudan, and because the resolution provided protection from investigation or prosecution for United States nationals.

(B) *Ad Hoc* International Tribunals

Another international legal option that may be available to the United States for the prosecution of terrorists is the creation of an *ad hoc* tribunal established by the UN Security Council.

There is precedent for the establishment of Security Council-based *ad hoc* tribunals to prosecute crimes against humanity in the International Criminal Tribunal for the Former Yugoslavia and the International Criminal Tribunal for Rwanda.[84] Both tribunals were created by the Security Council acting under its Chapter VII authority[85] to prosecute persons responsible for serious violations of international humanitarian law in the two territories. The Security Council could create a similar tribunal to address serious terrorist acts.[86] Unlike the ICC, an *ad hoc* tribunal would have the ability to prosecute crimes that took place prior to July 1, 2002, the date that the jurisdiction of the ICC took effect. Also, it would likely have more political appeal to the United States than the ICC because such a court would have a limited mandate (tied to a certain act or series of acts) and would be overseen by the Security Council, a body in which the U.S. wields veto power. Such a court would therefore not risk the prosecution of US military personnel or government officials.

Some international law and human rights advocates have supported the use of international tribunals for the prosecution of suspected terrorists apprehended by the United States during the invasion of Afghanistan who are being held in Guantanamo Bay.[87] However, the use of international courts has been rejected by the Bush administration, which instead proceeded with trials in domestic courts and military commissions established by President Bush after 9/11 to try suspected terrorists.[88]

The post-9/11 policies of detaining and trying terrorists have been substantially eroded through challenges in the U.S. courts. The detention of suspected terrorists held in U.S. custody, whether or not for trial by military tribunals, was limited by a pair of decisions handed down by the Supreme Court in June 2004. The Court held that detainees could invoke the writ of habeas corpus to challenge their detentions, meaning that their detentions are open to review in U.S. courts.[89] The Court stopped short of declaring a right of all detainees to a full criminal trial, instead holding that they are entitled to "a meaningful opportunity to contest the factual basis for [their] detention before a neutral decisionmaker," in accordance with due process of law.[90]

Subsequently, the use of the military commissions established by the Bush Administration to try suspected terrorists was rejected by the Supreme Court in Hamdan v. Rumsfeld[91] This case concerned a Guantanamo detainee, Salim Ahmed Hamdan, a Yemeni who was allegedly Osama bin Laden's driver in Afghanistan. The Supreme Court ruled that the tribunals did not meet the requirements of the Geneva Conventions and the U.S. Uniform Code of Military Justice for failing to confer certain protections to the accused, including the right to be present, equivalent to those provided by courts martial for U.S. military personnel.[92] The Armed Services Committees of the Senate and the House of Representatives held hearings in July 2006 to consider amendments to the Uniform Code of Military Justice in order to permit military commissions to proceed.[93] It is not known what legislation, if any, will emerge

The decision to use military tribunals had been harshly criticized by human rights activists and many international legal experts. The president of the American Society of International Law at the time of the announcement, Anne-Marie Slaughter, defended the use of international tribunals for these detainees: "The difference between military commissions and an international tribunal is the sanction and legitimacy of the global community. An international tribunal would demonstrate the depth of international solidarity against terrorism."[94] On the

other hand, Ruth Wedgwood, international law professor and advisor to the Department of Defense on military tribunals, observed that preference for military tribunals over international *ad hoc* tribunals is partly because the *ad hoc* tribunals do not have the ability to handle a volume of cases and will not offer sufficient protection for sensitive intelligence information.[95] Others have suggested expanding the mandate of existing *ad hoc*tribunals to allow for the prosecution of terrorists.[96]

It is clear even in this brief review of US policy that the United States has not embraced the use of international tribunals to prosecute terrorists. Indeed, this is one of the most controversial uses of international legal mechanisms for American policy makers. Even with the rejection of the US military tribunals, the possibility of international tribunals does not appear to be an option in the near term. Nevertheless, employing international tribunals to dispense international justice is no longer only an ideal, and prosecution of past and future terrorist acts in a variety of international legal forums is a real option.

IV. MULTILATERAL INSTRUMENTS ADDRESSING WEAPONS OF MASS DESTRUCTION

The December 2002 United States *National Strategy to Combat Weapons of Mass Destruction* reflects how closely this administration links proliferation of WMD with the threat of terrorism: "[T]errorist groups are seeking to acquire WMD with the stated purpose of killing large numbers of our people and those of our friends and allies—without compunction and without warning." The report goes on to name a number of international regimes that are intended to control access to and prevent use of WMD. The White House expressed the goals of strengthening and ensuring compliance with these instruments, creating new regimes to serve these goals and "cultivat[ing] an international environment that is more conducive to nonproliferation."[97] Nonproliferation can be achieved by enhancing measures "that seek to dissuade or impede proliferant states and terrorist networks, as well as to slow and make more costly their access to sensitive technologies, material and expertise."

Describing the successes of treaties and export control regimes, the Director of the State Department's Office of Chemical, Biological, and Missile Nonproliferationsaid:

> These efforts have impeded progress in missile and [chemical and biological weapons] programs of concern—among other things causing delays, forcing the use of elaborate and time-consuming procurement networks, and compelling reliance on older and sometimes less effective technology. They have established a global political and legal barrier against the spread of WMD and led to unprecedented international inspections of nuclear and chemical weapons programs. Each has recorded a number of successes and each faces unique challenges.[98]

The relevant instruments described below range from multilateral treaties to less formal cooperative export control groups and codes of conduct.

(A) WMD Treaties

The primary purpose of these instruments is to address state actions. However, they also contain provisions that are useful in improving states' abilities to block terrorists' access to WMD and their precursors.

(1) 1968 Nuclear Nonproliferation Treaty[99]

Nuclear weapons and facilities pose several distinct risks in connection with terrorism. There is a risk that a state engaged in developing or acquiring nuclear weapons or materials will sell or

transfer them to terrorists. There is a risk that terrorists will steal a nuclear weapon. Another risk is terrorist diversion of nuclear materials from a nuclear facility or during transit to manufacture a radiological weapon (a dirty bomb), which disperses radioactive material rather than creating a nuclear explosion. If sufficiently resourced and organized, there is a risk that terrorists will obtain fissile materials and then build a nuclear explosive device. There is also a risk that the nuclear facilities themselves will be attacked and disperse radioactive material.

The Nuclear Nonproliferation Treaty (NPT) and its monitoring agency, the International Atomic Energy Agency (IAEA), address these threats in a variety of ways. With respect to states transferring weapons to terrorists, the NPT prohibits nuclear weapon states (China, France, Russia, the United Kingdom and the United States) from transferring to any recipient whatsoever nuclear weapons or nuclear explosive devices or control over such weapons. The non-nuclear weapon states agree not to develop nuclear weapons or accept their transfer. All states are entitled to use nuclear energy for peaceful purposes. All but four states take part in this regime.[100]

In order to ensure that NPT non-nuclear weapon states are not diverting nuclear energy programs for use in weapons, they are required to accept comprehensive safeguard agreements relating to their peaceful nuclear activities with oversight from the IAEA. Pursuant to these safeguards, the IAEA conducts inspections that, among other things, verify records and inventories.

(a) IAEA Measures to Combat Terrorism

After 9/11, the IAEA added initiatives and expanded existing programs to better guard against terrorism, many of which are set forth in its "Action Plan on Combating Nuclear Terrorism," published in March 2002.[101] The focus areas of the action plan are prevention, detection and response.

The IAEA issues recommendations to help states improve the physical protection of their nuclear materials and facilities.[102] It also monitors and works to combat the illicit trafficking in nuclear material. It maintains a database on illicit trafficking and offers training to member states' customs and police officials. Since 1993, the IAEA database has recorded "approximately 630 confirmed incidents of trafficking in nuclear or other radioactive material."[103] Training is also offered to strengthen states' systems for accountancy and control of nuclear materials. Finally, the IAEA also promotes the development of national legislation and adherence to related international agreements and guidelines.[104]

Although the IAEA continues to evolve in the face of heightened fears of nuclear terrorism, its mandate is limited. The recommendations regarding protection of nuclear materials and facilities are only recommendations; unlike the safeguard agreements, they are not binding obligations. Under the existing system, the ultimate responsibility for intra-state security of nuclear materials is not in the hands of the IAEA but with states themselves. As with the CTC, the success of these initiatives depends on the capabilities and the will of states.

(b) Nuclear Fuel Cycle Technology

Non-nuclear weapon states regard the acquisition of technology to produce plutonium and enriched uranium to power nuclear reactors as their right under the NPT, should they choose to exercise it. However, the same technology can also produce materials for weapons. In the wake of revelations about the Pakistan-based nuclear proliferation network led by nuclear metallurgist A.Q. Khan, the North Korean denial of IAEA monitoring of its fissile materials production capabilities, and concerns that Iran may be seeking a nuclear weapons capability, proposals have emerged to control the spread of uranium enrichment and plutonium reprocessing technology. One of the drivers for this trend is the desire to limit access of terrorists to the

materials. About a dozen countries, including those possessing nuclear arms, now have such technology.

One proposed course of action is for exporting countries to deny the technology to additional states, as called for by President Bush. The G-8 responded to President Bush's call by declaring a moratorium on supply to non-possessing states, but the far larger Nuclear Suppliers Group has yet to take any action. A second course is indicated by IAEA Director-General Mohamed ElBaradei's call for "working towards multilateral control over the sensitive parts of the nuclear fuel cycle—enrichment, reprocessing, and the management and disposal of spent fuel."[105] While this proposed approach has received favorable comment from states and others, its implementation does not seem imminent.

(c) The Role of Disarmament

The NPT goes beyond establishing a monitored nonproliferation regime; it also includes a commitment to disarmament made by the nuclear weapon states. Article VI states: "Each of the Parties to the Treaty undertakes to pursue negotiations in good faith on effective measures relating to cessation of the nuclear arms race at an early date and to nuclear disarmament, and on a treaty on general and complete disarmament under strict and effective international control." Although that language intentionally left the nuclear weapon states' commitment vague and indefinite, in recent years, states parties have clarified what the obligation entails, and the nuclear weapons states have agreed to arms control/disarmament measures.[106] Nuclear weapons states most recently made such commitments in the Final Declaration of the NPT 2000 Review Conference.[107] They include the entry into force of the Comprehensive Test Ban Treaty, negotiating a treaty to ban production of fissile material for nuclear weapons, and making the reduction and elimination of nuclear arsenals irreversible and verified.

If these steps are taken by all nuclear weapon states, they will also help to reduce and secure nuclear materials and explosives that would be available for acquisition or diversion by terrorists. In recent years, though, the nuclear weapons states, and particularly the United States, have backpedaled on the 2000 commitments. The May 2005 NPT Review Conference failed to reach any agreement, in large part due to deep division over the current status of the commitments.[108] The breakdown of the Review Conference was followed by the failure to agree on any measures or even language regarding non-proliferation and disarmament of nuclear and other weapons of mass destruction at the September 2005 World Summit.[109] One consequence has been an inability to advance action on widely agreed non-proliferation goals like enhancing the inspection powers of the IAEA, or to take on the difficult task of coming to agreement on proposals to control the spread of nuclear fuel cycle technology.

(2) 1972 The Biological Weapons Convention[110]

Parties to this treaty (the "BWC") are prohibited from developing, acquiring or retaining microbial or other biological agents or toxins in quantities that have no justification for prophylactic, protective or other peaceful purposes or means of delivery of these agents or toxins. States are prohibited from transferring the prohibited items to any recipient whatsoever, directly or indirectly, and may not assist or encourage "any State, group of States or international organizations" to manufacture or acquire these items. States must also enact laws to prohibit the development or possession of bioweapons and equipment in their territory.

This treaty contains the basic framework to address biological weapons, but it lacks the necessary measures to restrain states from acquiring or using bioweapons and to ensure that states are protecting against terrorist bioweapons activity in their jurisdictions. The BWC contains

no mechanisms to monitor compliance. It does not require states to prosecute people who are found to be violating the treaty's prohibitions.

Between 1994 and 2001, BWC parties worked to fill in some of the gaps in the BWC with the negotiation of a protocol, a legally binding regime of declarations and inspections. It also would have required states to adopt criminal laws to prosecute individuals engaged in bioweapon activity. In July 2001, however, the United States put an end to the creation of this or any additional legally binding mechanism. The United States explained that it rejected the protocol because it would be ineffective (largely because of the difficulty in detecting small quantities of biological agents) and would compromise national security and commercial proprietary information.[111] As a substitute for the protocol, states parties, led by U.S. proposals, are considering ways to strengthen the convention through non-legally binding measures. Proposals include adopting legislation to criminalize offenses, devising a procedure to clarify and resolve compliance concerns on a voluntary basis, drafting a code of conduct for scientists, strengthening national security measures for handling toxins, and enhancing international response capabilities.[112]

There are no current plans to add to the BWC the type of monitoring regime that exists for chemical and nuclear weapons. Many arms control experts have pointed to the need to resume efforts toward a binding multilateral arrangement. Although such a protocol would not be able to detect all cheaters, supporters argue that it would offer benefits of increased transparency, deterrence and provide international standards and oversight.[113]

(3) 1993 Chemical Weapons Convention[114]

States parties to the Chemical l Weapons Convention (the "CWC") agree never to develop, acquire or use chemical weapons or transfer them to anyone, and those with stockpiles agree to destroy them. Each state party must declare the contents of its stockpiles and allow routine inspection of "dual-use" chemicals and facilities that could be used in a prohibited manner. The CWC prohibits the transfer of the most dangerous chemicals to non-member states.

The CWC creates a legal mechanism to help prevent chemical terrorism. The monitoring and accounting of chemicals and facilities help to deny terrorists' access and deter potential diversions. States are required to ensure the physical security of their chemical facilities. Also, with the requirement that states enact criminal laws prohibiting individuals within their jurisdiction from producing, transferring and using chemical weapons, states are better able to investigate and prosecute chemical weapons-related terrorist activities. The regime includes a mechanism for challenge inspections in the event that one state suspects that another state is violating its provisions. This mechanism would be useful in the event a member country had permitted someone in its jurisdiction to acquire chemical weapons.[115]

Implementation of these provisions is conducted with assistance from the Organization for the Prohibition of Chemical Weapons ("OPCW"). The OPCW's mission includes ensuring the destruction of member states' chemical weapons and the prevention of their re-emergence, providing protection and assistance against chemical weapons, encouraging international cooperation in the peaceful uses of chemistry and working for the universal ratification of the CWC.

In order to be most effective against terrorism, the CWC requires progress in a number of areas. It has not achieved universality, that is, many states are not yet members, and some states outside the CWC regime are suspected of developing weapons programs. There are concerns that some member states are attempting to develop chemical weapons. Challenge inspections have not yet been exercised. One reason, according to the United States, is that the OPCW is currently incapable of conducting the work required in a challenge inspection.[116] Expressing a

commitment to strengthen the organization and improve its management, the United States led a successful movement to change OPCW's leadership in 2002.

(4) Summary Regarding WMD Treaties

The NPT, BWC and CWC are not directly targeted at terrorists, but rather aim to address state behavior. They can make a significant contribution in regard to terrorism because they prohibit transfer of materials to terrorists and criminalize possession of WMD materials. The ability of these treaties to succeed in curbing terrorists' acquisition of weapons of mass destruction depends to a large extent on the willingness of states to adhere to their treaty commitments. Universal adoption of the treaties is needed. At this time, there are a number of significant states outside of these regimes.[117]

The NPT and CWC, which include established declaration and inspection regimes, have the most potential for detecting illicit transfers to either terrorist groups or other states outside the treaty regime. The BWC, on the other hand, is in need of further strengthening to be an effective tool against transfers of bioweapons to terrorists.

(B) Security Council Resolution on WMD and Non-State Actors

In an address to the General Assembly in September 2003, President Bush stated:

> Today, I ask the U.N. Security Council to adopt a new anti-proliferation resolution. This resolution should call on all members of the U.N. to criminalize the proliferation of weapons—weapons of mass destruction, to enact strict export controls consistent with international standards, and to secure any and all sensitive materials within their own borders. The United States stands ready to help any nation draft these new laws, and to assist in their enforcement.[118]

Led by the United States, in April 2004, the Security Council adopted Resolution 1540, which seeks to prevent "non-state actor" acquisition of, or trafficking in, WMD weapons-related equipment, materials, and delivery systems.[119] The term "non-state actor" refers not only to terrorists, but also to unauthorized state officials and to businesses. The reasons for this scope are illustrated by the Pakistan-based nuclear proliferation network led by nuclear metallurgist A.Q. Khan. The Pakistani government maintains that it did not authorize Khan's activities, and businesses from several countries around the world contributed to the Khan network. Acting under Chapter VII of the Charter, the Security Council *required* every state in the world to prohibit non-state actor acquisition of and trafficking in WMD weapons and related items. It also mandated the adoption of appropriate measures—national criminal laws, export controls, border controls, law enforcement efforts, physical security and materials accounting techniques—to prevent such acquisition and trafficking.

In some ways the resolution added new obligations for states, for example regarding export controls and border controls. Also, previously there had been no explicit requirement under the NPT and the Biological Weapons Convention that acquisition of and trafficking in nuclear and biological weapons be made criminal by national legislation. In other ways the resolution reinforced existing obligations and also applied them to the relatively few countries not party to the NPT and the biological and chemical weapons conventions. There is a parallel between Resolution 1540 and the Resolution 1373, described above, in that both are aimed at revising states' legal systems to respond to terrorist activities, both impose mandatory requirements on all states, and both establish a committee made up of all members of the Security Council to implement the resolution.[120]

(C) Export Controls

Export control regimes are made up of groups of states that agree to "restrict the sale of goods to certain countries or to ensure that safeguards or end-use guarantees are applied to the export and sale of sensitive technologies and materials."[121] The United States regards these regimes as crucial to the fight to keep dangerous materials out of the hands of so-called rogue states and terrorists.

Although these arrangements cover many of the same materials that are regulated under the treaties listed above, the goals of these regimes differ from those of treaties. A treaty regulating a potentially dangerous material generally establishes a comprehensive ban on the maintenance or use of that material for hostile purposes and establishes an accounting or inspection regime for the peaceful use of these materials. In contrast, export control regimes are not legally binding at the international level; they involve a grouping of countries that do not restrict their own use of the subject material but voluntarily agree to limit, through legislation and regulation, transfers to foreign nationals, entities and states not meeting certain criteria (for example, acceptance of IAEA safeguards) or otherwise deemed untrustworthy. Export controls are often able to control a broader scope of dual-use materials, including software, lab equipment and other technology that not covered by the treaties.

The export control regimes described below have made efforts post 9-11 to strengthen their controls against terrorist acquisition of the subject materials.

(1) Australia Group

One export control group that is specifically mentioned in the U.S. *National Strategy to Combat Weapons of Mass Destruction* is the Australia Group. The Australia Group is an "informal network of countries that consult on and harmonise their national export licensing measures on [chemical and biological weapon] items."[122] The group is made up of thirty-three participants from Europe, North America, and Asia that apply licensing measures to the export of specified chemicals, biological agents, and dual-use chemical and biological manufacturing facilities and equipment. These export controls are aimed at both curbing proliferation and also "allow[ing] legitimate trade to prosper in an unfettered manner and promot[ing] peaceful economic development everywhere."[123] Since 9/11, the Australia Group has revised its export restrictions to include items that would be useful to terrorists rather than states.[124]

(2) The Missile Technology Control Regime

Formed in 1987, the MTCR restricts the export of delivery systems (and related technology) capable of carrying a 500-kilogram payload for a distance of at least 300 kilometers and systems capable of delivering weapons of mass destruction. Its group of thirty-three participants largely overlaps with the countries that make up the Australia Group.[125] The members agree to a set of guidelines for the export of a list of materials. Some transfers are prohibited; others are subject to the satisfaction of specific conditions or the provision of certain assurances. The director of the State Department's Office of Chemical, Biological and Missile Nonproliferation described the value of this regime: "MTCR Partners' vigorous enforcement of export controls consistent with the MTCR Guidelines and Annex continues to make it more difficult for proliferators to get items for their missile programs, increasing the cost, time, and effort required."[126]

The MTCR is now placing more emphasis on combating the risk of missile components and components falling into the hands of terrorism. At the 2002 plenary meeting of the MTCR, the partner states agreed to study possible changes to better address this risk, and in 2003, announced some revisions to the guidelines, including a national "catchall requirement" that

would "provide a legal basis to control the export of items that are not on a control list, when such items are destined for missile programs."[127]

(3) The Nuclear Suppliers Group

The Nuclear Suppliers Group (NSG) is made up of forty states that have the ability to supply items designed for nuclear use, that adhere to non-proliferation arrangements (such as the NPT), and that have national policies to implement export controls. The aim of the group is "to contribute to prevention of the proliferation of nuclear weapons through export controls of nuclear-related material, equipment, software and technology, without hindering international cooperation on peaceful uses of nuclear energy."[128] The NSG was formed in 1974 in response to India's nuclear weapon test, which had demonstrated that nuclear materials transferred for peaceful purposes could be used for a nuclear weapons program.

The group follows two sets of voluntary guidelines. The first set governs exports of items designed for nuclear use (including source materials such as plutonium and uranium and nuclear reactors and equipment).[129] This set is known as the "Trigger List" because the export of items on this list triggers application of IAEA safeguards to the recipient facility. The second set governs exports of nuclear-related dual-use equipment and materials and related technology.[130]

Regarding prevention of terrorism, the NSG acknowledges the importance of information sharing, closer cooperation of member states' law enforcement agencies and support of the anti-terrorism work of the IAEA.[131] At the initiative of the United States, the NSG has revised its guidelines to better address the threat of nuclear terrorism.[132]

(4) Wassenaar Arrangement

The Wassenaar Arrangement was formed in 1996 by thirty-three states, most of which are party to the other export control regimes.[133] It is designed to prevent destabilizing accumulations of arms and dual-use technologies by promoting transparency, information sharing and greater responsibility in transfers. Member states apply restrictions to a list of items to "ensure that transfers of arms and dual-use goods and technologies do not contribute to the development or enhancement of military capabilities that undermine international and regional security and stability and are not diverted to support such capabilities."[134] The Wassenaar Arrangement is made up of states that are producers or exporters of arms or industrial equipment and that maintain non-proliferation policies and appropriate national laws.

With respect to terrorism, the Wassenaar Arrangement seeks to prevent the acquisition of conventional arms and dual-use goods and technologies for use by terrorists. To this end, it has developed new means for sharing information and for implementing concrete actions to strengthen export controls over these items. New initiatives to address terrorism include guidelines for the export small arms and light weapons, which the group believes are the preferred weapons of terrorists.[135]

(5) The Zangger Committee

Pursuant to NPT Article III.2, States Parties must subject safeguards to transfers to any non-nuclear weapon State of (a) source or special fissionable material, or (b) equipment or material especially designed or prepared for the processing, use or production of special fissionable material" The 35-member Zangger Committee (ZC), also known as the Nuclear Non-Proliferation Treaty Exporters Committee, is responsible for "harmoniz[ing] implementation" of this provision of the NPT."[136] The ZC maintains a "Trigger List" of (a) source or special fissionable materials, and (b) equipment or materials especially designed or prepared for the

processing, use, or production of special fissionable materials. Export of items on this list trigger a requirement for the application of IAEA safeguards to recipient non-nuclear weapon States.[137] The Trigger List covers items that could contribute to a nuclear explosive program, including plutonium, highly-enriched uranium, reactors, reprocessing and enrichment plants, and equipment and components for such facilities. ZC member states agree that Trigger List items may only be exported if they are 1) not used for nuclear explosives, 2) subject to IAEA safeguards in the recipient non-nuclear weapon state, and 3) not re-exported unless they are subject to safeguards in the new recipient state.

The relative informality of the ZC has enabled it to take the lead on certain nonproliferation issues that would be more difficult to resolve in the Nuclear Suppliers Group (NSG).[138] For example, the Committee recently agreed to add plutonium separation technology to the Trigger List. However, the ZC is also less stringent than the NSG, which requires its members to agree to full scope safeguards.

(6) Assessing the Export Control Regimes

Export controls offer states the ability to proceed with commerce relating to sensitive materials while also protecting them from diversion or misuse. They target proliferation by limiting and regulating the supply of materials that would be available for terrorists or "rogue states."

However, there are several limitations to these regimes as instruments of non-proliferation. They establish a two-tier system of countries that may have and countries that are restricted from having; they only consist of voluntary, political commitments; and it is for each country through its own national legislation and regulations to interpret and implement the guidelines. Because of their voluntary nature, the regimes have no explicit mechanisms to enforce compliance with nonproliferation commitments. No inspection or monitoring systems are in place for member countries. Other concerns, as noted by a report by the United States General Accounting Office, include the rapid pace of technology that requires control lists to be constantly updated and also "secondary proliferation," which is the growing capability of nonmember countries to develop their own sensitive materials, and then sell them outside the regime.[139] Modifying the control lists is a slow task because the regimes operate by consensus, allowing each country a veto.

Export control regimes are an important contribution but in themselves are not sufficient to end proliferation. Ending proliferation requires action on many fronts, including, as noted in *Arms Control Today,* "arms control agreements, multilateral sanctions and incentives, and counterproliferation, all of which are aimed at offering viable alternatives to merely coping with the effects of proliferation."[140]

(D) Other Multilateral Nonproliferation Initiatives

(1) Cooperative Nonproliferation Agreements between the United States and Former Soviet States

The Cooperative Threat Reduction Program, also referred to as the "Nunn-Lugar Program" after the Senators who sponsored its founding legislation, was developed in the early 1990s to assist former Soviet states in safeguarding and destroying large stockpiles of weapons of mass destruction and related infrastructure. The logic behind the program is that these states do not have the money to properly dispose of these materials, or safeguard them from theft or diversion by other states or terrorists. The intelligence that contributed to the creation of these weapons is similarly in need of safeguarding.

Programs have included deactivating warheads, assisting countries with the removal of their nuclear weapons by providing funds and technical expertise, safeguarding chemical stockpiles and biological weapons laboratories and employing former scientists of the Soviet Union so they will not be tempted to sell sensitive information.[141] Total funding is about one billion dollars.[142]

In December 2003, President Bush signed the Nunn-Lugar Program Expansion act, which allows $50 million of Nunn-Lugar funding to be used for countries outside the former Soviet Union. Albania is the first country to receive a pledge of assistance under the expanded Nunn-Lugar Program, which will be used to destroy its chemical weapons stockpile.[143]

The 9/11 Commission has emphasized the importance of the program. Its report stated that "al Qaeda has tried to acquire or make weapons of mass destruction for at least ten years. There is no doubt the United States would be a prime target. Preventing the proliferation of these weapons warrants a maximum effort—by strengthening counterproliferation efforts, expanding the Proliferation Security Initiative, and supporting the Cooperative Threat Reduction program."[144] In a November 2005 report on the status of its recommendations, the Commission assessed progress under the program, stating that it

> has significant accomplishments over the past 14 years in dismantling former Soviet weaponry (40% of ICBMs, 51% of warheads, 64% of strategic bombers and 58% of missile silos), but much remains to be done to secure weapons-grade nuclear materials. The size of the problem still dwarfs the policy response. Approximately half of former Soviet nuclear materials still lack adequate security protection.[145]

The Commission added generally that "[p]reventing terrorists from gaining access to weapons of mass destruction must be elevated above all other problems of national security" and that the president "should develop a comprehensive plan to dramatically accelerate the timetable for securing all nuclear weapons material around the world. . . ."[146]

(2) G-8 Initiatives

In June 2002, the G-8 member states agreed to participate in a "Global Partnership Against the Spread of Weapons and Materials of Mass Destruction." Pursuant to this partnership, the United States agreed to spend $10 billion toward dismantlement efforts over ten years, and the other G-8 nations agreed to collectively spend an additional $10 billion. The Global Partnership is intended to enhance programs in Russia and other former Soviet states, including the following:

- Reducing strategic missiles, bombers, silos and submarines;
- Ending weapons-grade plutonium production;
- Reducing excess weapons-grade plutonium;
- Upgrading storage and transport security for nuclear warheads;
- Upgrading storage security for fissile material;
- Reducing nuclear weapons infrastructure;
- Destroying chemical weapons;
- Eliminating chemical weapons production capability;
- Securing biological pathogens;
- Providing peaceful employment for former weapons scientists;

- Enhancing export controls and border security; and
- Improving safety of civil nuclear reactors.[147]

At the 2004 G-8 Summit, members of the global partnership recommitted to raising $20 billion by 2012 and welcomed the expansion of the Global Partnership to include other donor governments.[148] The most recent progress review at the 2005 G-8 Summit noted "visible progress" with projects to address the priority areas of destruction of chemical weapons, dismantling submarines, disposition of fissile materials and employment of former weapons scientists. The review warned, however, that "more needs to be done to increase the momentum so that the current substantial pledges can be turned into completed projects by 2012, primarily in Russia."[149]

(3) Proliferation Security Initiative

According to the National Strategy to Combat Weapons of Mass Destruction, interdiction is a "critical part of the U.S. strategy to combat WMD and their delivery means."[150] Consistent with this approach, in May 2003, President Bush unveiled a new initiative to develop "direct, practical measures to impede the trafficking in weapons of mass destruction, missiles and related items."[151] This is known as the Proliferation Security Initiative (PSI). It is a global effort by states[152] "which, using their own laws and resources, will coordinate their actions to halt shipments of dangerous technologies to and from states and non-state actors of proliferation concern—at sea, in the air, and on land."[153] The initiative does not specify any one state as its target, although it has generally been characterized as directed at North Korea and possibly Iran.[154] It is also intended to prevent the spread of WMD to terrorists.[155]

In its first stages, PSI participants agreed to share information on suspected proliferation and trafficking, and to conduct joint interdiction training exercises. At a PSI meeting on September 4, 2003, the participants agreed to a set of principles for taking actions in support of interdiction.[156] They are a set of political undertakings that the United States and other PSI participants will disseminate to governments with which they have diplomatic relations in hopes that they will gain widespread support.[157] Under the PSI principles, actions that a state agrees to take include the following: board and search ships flying their flag that are suspected of transporting the subject materials; "seriously consider" giving consent to other states boarding and searching ships flying their flag that are suspected of transporting the subject materials; stop and/or search vessels in their internal waters "that are reasonably suspected of carrying such cargoes to or from states or non-state actors of proliferation concern" and seize such cargoes; and require suspect aircraft that are transiting their airspace to land for inspections and to seize such cargoes.[158] Some sixty nations have agreed informally to cooperate with PSI members on an *ad hoc* basis to intercept "rogue" ships and aircraft in their territorial waters and airspace.[159]

The interdiction principles are limited to instances of interdiction by a state on a vessel flying its own flag, by a state with consent of the state whose flag it flies, or by a state in whose territory the suspect vessel is located.[160]

On June 1, 2005, Croatia became the fourth state—following Liberia, Panama, and the Marshall Islands—to sign a Proliferation Security Initiative Shipboarding Agreement with the United States. The shipboarding agreement signed by the United States and Croatia aims to facilitate cooperation between the two countries to prevent the maritime transfer of proliferation-related shipments by establishing points of contact and procedures to expedite requests to board and search suspect vessels in international waters. If a U.S.- or Croatian-flagged vessel is suspected of carrying proliferation-related cargo, either Party to this agreement

can request the other to confirm the nationality of the ship in question and, if needed, to authorize the boarding, search, and possible detention of the vessel and its cargo.

In a September 2003 press briefing, the State Department explained that questions of permissibility would be answered on a case-by-case basis, and that "we do not intend to proceed with interdictions without a clear national or international authority,"[161] Yet the PSI raises a variety of legal issues relating to the law of the sea. It is a well-established principle of international law that states have jurisdiction over ships flying their flags. However, a state boarding a ship in its territorial waters that is flying another state's flag (without consent of that state) raises issues relating to the right of innocent passage that is recognized as customary law and is codified in the United Nations Convention on the Law of the Sea (UNCLOS).[162] Innocent passage is defined as "not prejudicial to the peace, good order, or security of the coastal State."[163] The list of acts that would be determined as prejudicial to peace, good order or security do not include transporting WMD materials. However, the list of acts prejudicial to the peace does include "any threat or use of force against the sovereignty, territorial integrity or political independence of the coastal State, or in any other manner in violation of the principles of international law embodied in the Charter of the United Nations."[164] The authority to board ships suspected of transporting WMD materials when consent is not given would likely fall under this latter provision.

Interdiction on the high seas also implicates the right to freedom of navigation on the high seas which is recognized as a basic right of all states. A few exceptions to the freedom of navigation exist in UNCLOS, but the search for WMD material is not included. Under customary law as codified in UNCLOS the United States has the authority to board a ship on the high seas when the ship does not display a state's flag (effectively making them pirate ships), or when the state under whose flag the ship sails gives permission to board the ship.[165] Since an important objective of the PSI is to halt WMD trafficking among "rogue" states (which would not give permission to board ships flying their flag), this may place the PSI's objectives in conflict with its members' legal obligations. Attempts have been made to justify the PSI's broader interdiction principles under a customary law rule of anticipatory self-defense; however, this route does not hold much promise as there is insufficient state practice to support the existence of such a rule. The United States may instead pursue the route of modifying current legal obligations by treaty. Treaty-based exceptions to the above rules on interdiction on the high seas have been created for cases of narcotics trafficking[166] and illegal fishing;[167] this may serve as a model for an additional exception based on trafficking of WMD material. Significantly, the United States concluded agreements in 2004 with Panama[168] and Liberia,[169] the two nations with the world's largest shipping registries. The agreements provide procedures for granting consent on short-notice to board ships registered under the signatory nations' flags; the agreement with Liberia allows consent to be presumed if a response to a request is not received within two hours.[170]

Shipping WMD material poses clear risks for proliferation by states and acquisition by non-state actors. The existing legal regime may not provide authority for states to respond to these concerns. Treaty-based modifications to this regime would be of limited effectiveness because they would apply only to signatory states. Another possibility is to pass a Security Council resolution directed against a suspect state, designating a right to board and seize, which would become immediate international law.

PSI has been praised by some as filling in the gaps of the non-proliferation regime (especially for states that are not monitored by the IAEA because they are outside of the NPT), and increasing deterrence and dissuasion.[171] Although many PSI activities are kept secret, a prominent claimed success of the PSI was the September 2003 seizure of cargo in a German ship headed

for Libya. The cargo included parts for centrifuges used to enrich uranium for nuclear weapons programs. The Bush administration credited the seizure as contributing to Libya's decision to give up its nuclear weapons program.[172] However, later reports indicated that the interception resulted from preexisting counterproliferation efforts.[173] Generally, beyond the legal concerns, the potential of the program has also met with some skepticism. For example, former Secretary of Defense William Perry observed, "The administration has suggested that it would interdict such transfers [of products from North Korea's nuclear program]. But a nuclear bomb can be made with a sphere of plutonium the size of a soccer ball. It is wishful thinking to believe we could prevent a package that size from being smuggled out of North Korea."[174]

(E) Assessing the Regimes to prevent Terrorists from Acquiring WMD

The measures described above range from those that are more universal in character and binding under international law (conventions and Security Council resolutions) to those in which the United States and its allies control trade and shipping of WMD-related material and take initiatives to secure dangerous materials and weapons. There are advantages to the more universal approach. The WMD conventions offer global monitoring organizations and processes. As they apply equally among states, they offer incentives for each state to comply, as other states are doing the same. There are valid concerns that these regimes are not able to detect all instances of cheating and that they create a false confidence that by virtue of having signed on to a treaty, a state is cooperating. These concerns do not require the abandonment or downgrading of the existing regimes; the United States may instead decide to improve monitoring and strengthen mechanisms to inspect and investigate allegations of non-compliance, as well as relying on its own means of monitoring and encouraging compliance. On the other hand, the non-universal nonproliferation regimes offer the United States the opportunity to more tightly control outcomes and flexibility in responding to emerging developments, without having to subject its own behavior to international regulation. However, they cause resentment among states which are the targets of, e.g., export controls, and tend to be stopgap in character, serving to slow rather than to stop proliferation. They may best be seen as needed complements to developing global regimes.

V. CONCLUSION

Since the end of World War II, international law has served the United States by internationalizing norms that are at the heart of its political and social structure. An international system has been installed for civil and political rights, women's and children's rights, freedom from torture and slavery, and the accountability of leaders who commit genocide, crimes against humanity, and war crimes. Much of this system has been implemented at the initiative of the United States. The norm that condemns terrorism is in need of similar institutionalization and internationalization.

In pursuit of a norm of repudiation of terrorism, and of capabilities to prevent terrorism, the legal instruments, institutions, initiatives, and arrangements surveyed in this paper—from the anti-terrorism conventions to Security Council resolutions to anti-WMD treaty regimes to the Proliferation Security Initiative—all need vigorous implementation underpinned by the understanding and support of the legal profession and the general public.

NOTES

* **Standing Committee on International Security Affairs Committee Members:** Ajay Ayyappan, John Burroughs, Kenneth P. Carroll, Lloyd Chinn, Yue-Han Chow, Chris Evans, Todd Finger, Shirley

Fingerhood, Miles P. Fischer, Charles Graybow, Richard Hartzman, Nahal Kazemi, Paul Lekas, Donald Leo, Mitchell Mass, Harold S. Nathan, Brolota Shea, Owens, Kenneth C. Payumo, Averill Powers, Alan E. Rabunski, Brigitte Rajacic, Paula G.A. Ryan, Charles Nicholas Rostow, Visuvanathan Rudrakumaran, Aimee Saginaw, Rakesh Sharma, Prof. Margaret D. Stock, Daniel Ulmer (student member), and Linda Wayner.

Subcommittee on Multilateral Instruments to Combat Terrorism: Nicole Deller (chair), John Burroughs, Rakesh Sharma, and Daniel Ulmer (student member).

1. Treaty on the Non-Proliferation of Nuclear Weapons, July 1, 1968, *available at* http://www.iaea.org/Publications/Documents/Infcircs/Others/infcirc140.pdf.

2. HUMAN SECURITY REPORT: WAR AND PEACE IN THE 21ST CENTURY, Human Security Centre, University of British Columbia, Canada 43–44 (2005).

3. U.S. Department of State, *Feith Says Terrorism Makes Palestinian State Less Likely,* April 6, 2002, *available at* http://usinfo.state.gov/regional/nea/summit/text/0426fth.htm.

4. Treaties are agreements among states that are respected as binding agreements under international law. Such agreements may also take the form of "conventions" (a term generally used to agreements open to all states or a large number of states) or "protocols" (a term generally used to describe amendments or additional agreements to existing treaties). The three are generally of equal international legal significance and all are required to be ratified as set forth in Article II of the U.S. Constitution. For a discussion of the various terms used to designate an international agreement *see* United Nations Treaty Collection, *Treaty Reference Guide, available at* http://untreaty.un.org/English/guide.asp. To the extent that an arrangement between or among states is not intended to be binding under international law, this is indicated in the discussion of the arrangement. Examples include export control regimes and the Proliferation Security Initiative.

5. THE 9/11 COMMISSION REPORT: FINAL REPORT OF THE NATIONAL COMMISSION ON TERRORIST ATTACKS UPON THE UNITED STATES 381 (U.S. Government Printing Office, 2004).

6. A list of the states that have signed, ratified or acceded to each of these treaties, along with reservations attached thereto is available from the United Nations Treaty Collection, http://untreaty.un.org/English/Terrorism.asp.

7. Convention on Offenses and Certain Other Acts Committed on Board Aircraft ("Tokyo Convention"), Sept. 14, 1963, 20 U.S.T. 2941, 704 U.N.T.S. 219.

8. Convention for the Suppression of Unlawful Seizure of Aircraft ("Hague Convention"), Dec. 16, 1970, 22 U.S.T. 1641, 860 U.N.T.S. 105.

9. Convention for the Suppression of Unlawful Acts Against the Safety of Civil Aviation ("Montreal Convention"), Sept. 23, 1971, 24 U.S.T. 564, 1975 U.N.T.S. 177.

10. Convention on the Prevention and Punishment of Crimes Against Internationally Protected Persons, Including Diplomatic Agents, Dec. 14, 1973, 28 U.S.T. 1975, 1035 U.N.T.S. 167.

11. International Convention Against the Taking of Hostages, Dec. 17, 1979, T.I.A.S. No. 11081, 1316 U.N.T.S. 206.

12. Convention on the Physical Protection of Nuclear Material, Oct. 26, 1979, T.I.A.S. No. 11,080, 1456 U.N.T.S. 124.

13. IAEA Press Release, July 8, 2005, *available at* http://www.iaea.org/NewsCenter/PressReleases/2005/prn200503.html.

14. Protocol on the Suppression of Unlawful Acts of Violence at Airports Serving International Civil Aviation, supplementary to the Convention for the Suppression of Unlawful Acts Against the Safety of Civil Aviation, Feb. 24, 1988, S. TREATY DOC. NO. 100-19 (1988), 1589 U.N.T.S. 474.

15. Convention for the Suppression of Unlawful Acts Against the Safety of Maritime Navigation, Mar. 10, 1988, S. TREATY DOC. NO. 101-1 (1989), 1678 U.N.T.S. 222.

16. Protocol for the Suppression of Unlawful Acts Against the Safety of Fixed Platforms Located on the Continental Shelf, Mar. 10, 1988, S. TREATY DOC. 101-1 (1989), 1678 U.N.T.S. 304.

17. Convention on the Marking of Plastic Explosives for the Purpose of Identification, Mar. 1, 1991, 30 I.L.M. 726 (entered into force June 21, 1998).

18. International Convention for the Suppression of Terrorist Bombings, Jan. 12, 1998, S. TREATY DOC. 106-6 (1999), 37 I.L.M. 251 (entered into force May 23, 2001).

19. International Convention for the Suppression of the Financing of Terrorism, Jan. 10, 2000, 39 I.L. M. 270 (entered into force April 10, 2002).

20. John F. Murphy, *The Future of Multilateralism and Efforts to Combat International Terrorism,* 25 Colum. J. Transnat'l L. 35, 45 (1986).

21. *Id.*

22. Jennifer Trahan, *Terrorism Conventions: Existing Gaps and Different Approaches,* 8 New Eng. Int'l & Comp. L. Ann. 215, 222–25 (2002).

23. *See* Michael P. Scharf, *Defining Terrorism As the Peace Time Equivalent of War Crimes: A Case of Too Much Convergence Between International Humanitarian Law and International Criminal Law?,* 7 ILSA J. Int'l & Comp. L. 391, 393 (2001), *cited in* Trahan, *supra* note 22 at n. 19.

24. Trahan, *supra* note 22 at 225–26; 229–30.

25. S.C. Res. 1373, U.N. SCOR, 57th Sess. 4385th mtg., U.N. Doc. S/Res/1373 (2001).

26. *Fight against Terrorism Would be long with No Short Cuts, Counter-Terrorism Committee Chairman Tells Security Council,* UN Press Release, Security Council, 4792nd mtg., U.N. Doc SC/7823 (2003).

27. International Terrorism: Multilateral Conventions and Documents 7 (M. Cherif Bassiouni, ed., 2001).

28. Murphy, *supra* note 20 at 92.

29. *See Report of the Ad Hoc Committee established by General Assembly Resolution 5/210 of 17 December 1996,* U.N. GAOR, 57th Sess., Supp. No. 37, Annexes I-III, U.N. Doc. A/57/37 (2002).

30. *See Measures to eliminate international terrorism: Report of the Working Group,* U.N. GAOR 6th Comm., 59th Sess., Annex, Agenda Item 148, p. 4, U.N. Doc. A/C.6/59/L.10 (2004). *See also* Jim Wurst, *U.N. Deadlock Continues on Two Terrorism Treaties*, U.N. Wire, Dec. 10, 2003; Jim Wurst, *Negotiations on Anti-Terrorism Treaties Yield No Progress,* U.N. Wire, February 4, 2002. Like the definition of terrorism, this issue of whether armed forces should be covered is closely related to the Israeli-Palestinian conflict. The Organization of the Islamic Conference has urged that any exclusion from the treaty's provisions for the actions of armed forces should also cover situations of foreign occupation.

31. The goal of achieving a universal definition of terrorism dates back to the League of Nations. The Convention for the Prevention and Punishment of Terrorism included a definition of terrorism, but the treaty never entered into force. *See* Alex Schmidt, *War Crimes Research Symposium: "Terrorism on Trial": Terrorism—The Definitional Problem,* 37 Case W. Res. J. Int'l L. 375, 385 (2005). The UN resumed the attempt to reach a definition after the terrorist attacks at the 1972 Munich Olympics. *Id.* at 386.

32. *See* G.A. Res. 27/3034, U.N. GAOR, 27th Sess., Supp. No. 30, at 119, U.N. Doc. A/RES/27/3034 (1972), *cited in* Malvina Halberstam, *The Evolution of the United Nations Position on Terrorism: From Exempting National Liberation Movements to Criminalizing Terrorism Wherever and by Whomever Committed,* 41 Colum. J. Transnat'l L. 573, 574 (2003).

33. G.A. Res. 40/61, U.N. GAOR, 40th Sess., 108th plen. mtg., para. 1, U.N. Doc A/RES/40/61 (1985), *cited in* Halberstam, *supra* note 32 at 575.

34. *See, e.g.,* In Larger Freedom: Toward Development, Security and Human Rights for All, Report of the Secretary-General ¶ 91 (United Nations 2005); Stephen Stedman, A More Secure World: Our Shared Responsibility, Report of the High-Level Panel on Threats, Challenges and Change ¶ 163 (United Nations 2004).

35. World Summit Outcome, ¶¶ 81, 83.

36. S.C. Res. 1566, U.N. SCOR, 59th Sess., 5053rd mtg., U.N. Doc. S/Res/1566 (2005).

37. Calls for Resolute Action Against Terrorism Tempered in Assembly by Appeals for Caution in Identifying 'Enemy,' U.N. GAOR, 56th Sess., 49th plen. mtg. U.N. Doc. GA/9962 (2001), cited in Aaron J. Noteboom, Terrorism, I Know It When I See It, 81 Or. L. Rev. 553, 565 (2002).

38. Cf. Nicholas Rostow, *Before and After: The Changed UN Response to Terrorism Since September 11th*, 35 Cornell Int'l L.J. 475, 489 (2002), arguing that it is unlikely that consensus will be achieved until the conflicts in the Middle East and over Kashmir are resolved.

39. *See, e.g.,* S.C. Res. 1373.

40. S.C. Res. 1267, U.N. SCOR, 54th Sess., 4051st mtg., U.N. Doc. S/Res/1267 (1999).

41. S.C. Res. 1333, U.N. SCOR, 55th Sess., 4251st mtg., U.N. Doc. S/Res/1333 (2000).

42. S.C. Resolutions 1267 (1999), 1333 (2000), 1390 (2002), 1455 (2003).

43. *'We Must Not Fall Into Complacency' in Fight Against Terrorism, Prime Minister of Spain Tells Council,* United Nations Press Release, Security Council, 4752nd mtg., U.N. Doc. SC/7754 (2003).

44. UN Charter, Art. 25 requires all UN Members to "agree to accept and carry out the decision of the Security Council in accordance with the present Charter."

45. Ilias Bantekas, *The International Law of Terrorist Financing*, 97 AM. J. INT'L L. 315, 326 (2003).

46. Paul Szasz, *The Security Council Starts Legislating,* 96 AM. J. INT'L L. 901, 901 (2002).

47. S.C. Res. 1540, U.N. SCOR, 58th Sess., 4956th mtg., U.N. Doc. S/Res/1540 (2004).

48. S.C. Res. 1566, U.N. SCOR, 59th Sess., 5053rd mtg., U.N. Doc. S/Res/1566 (2004).

49. S.C. Res. 1624, U.N. SCOR, 60th Sess., 5261st mtg., U.N. Doc. S/Res/1624 (2005).

50. For a discussion of the reporting process, *see* Rostow, *supra* note 38 at 483–484 (2002); *see also* the website of the CTC at http://www.un.org/Docs/sc/committees/1373/work.html at 335–336.

51. With respect to financing of terrorism, which is a principal target of Resolution 1373, this first stage goes beyond examining legislation and has already begun looking into states executive machinery to prevent and suppress financing of terrorism. *See* Rosand *infra* note 53 at 336.

52. *See About the CTC: Setting Priorities,* available at http://www.un.org/Docs/sc/committees/1373/priorities.html. The CTC maintains a website containing the status of states' reports and other key documents. *See* http://www.un.org/Docs/sc/committees/1373/.

53. Eric Rosand, *Security Council Resolution 1373, the Counter-Terrorism Committee and the Fight Against Terrorism,* 97 AM. J. INT. L. 333, 336 (2003).

54. *See Directory of Counter-Terrorism Information and Sources of Assistance*. Available at http://www.un.org/Docs/sc/committees/1373/ctc_da/index.html.

55. The Matrix of Assistance Requests is available at http://www.un.org/Docs/sc/committees/1373/ctc_da/matrix.html.

56. UN Press Release, SC/8221, October 19, 2004.

57. UN Doc. S/2004/70. Report by the Chair of the Counter Terrorism Committee on the problems encountered in the implementation of Security Council Resolution 1373 (2001).

58. UN Doc S/2004/124. Proposal for the Revitalization of the Counter-Terrorism Committee.

59. S.C. Res. 1535, U.N. SCOR, 58th Sess., 4936th mtg., U.N. Doc. S/Res/1535 (2004).

60. *See* UN Press Release SC/8041.

61. *See* UN Security Council Presidential Statement, U.N. Doc. S/PRST/2005/64 (2005).

62. *See* http://www.un.org/Docs/sc/committees/1373/procedures.doc and http://www.un.org/Docs/sc/committees/1373/guidelines.doc.

63. David Cortright *et al., An Action Agenda for Enhancing the United Nations Program on Counter-Terrorism,* at 12 (2004), *available at* http://www.ctproject.info/html/report_1.html.

64. *Id.* at 14–21.

65. *See* written statement submitted by Amnesty International, Economic and Social Council, Commission on Human Rights, 59th Sess., Provisional Agenda Item 11, UN Doc. E/CN.4/2003/NGO/183 *available at* http://www.unhchr.ch/Huridocda/Huridoca.nsf/e06a5300f90fa0238025668700518ca4/846e64533954171ec1256d03005ac56f/$FILE/G0311872.pdf; *See also* Sergio Vieira de Mello, The High Commission for Human Rights, Address before the Counter-Terrorism Committee of the Security Council (Oct. 21, 2002) *available at* http://www.un.org/Docs/sc/committees/1373/HC.htm. For analysis of the controversial Security Council practice pursuant to Resolution 1267 and later resolutions of naming individual "terrorists" whose financial assets are frozen absent a quasi-judicial procedure for affected persons to challenge the action, *see* José E. Alvarez, *The Security Council's War on Terrorism: Problems and Policy Options*, in Erica De Wet and André Nollkaemper, eds., Review of the Security Council by Member States 119–145 (2003).

66. World Summit Outcome, *supra* note 35, at ¶ 85.

67. Rome Statute of the International Criminal Court, July 17, 1998, 37 I.L.M. 999 (entered into force July 1, 2002).

68. Ratification status as of December 2004. The ratification status may be found on the website of the Coalition for the International Criminal Court at http://www.iccnow.org.

69. The ICC will also have jurisdiction over the crime of aggression, once the state parties agree to a definition of the crime.

70. In the early stages of drafting the ICC statute, the drafters considered including the crime of terrorism. Its inclusion was ultimately rejected, due to political difficulties, including reaching an agreement on a definition. *See, e.g., Final Act of the United Nations Diplomatic Conference of Plenipotentiaries on the Establishment of an International Criminal Court Done at Rome on 17 July 1998*, U.N. Doc. A/CONF.183/10, Annex I, Resolution E; *see* David Scheffer, *Staying the Course with the International Criminal Court,* 35 Cornell Int. L. J. 47, n. 7 (2001–2002).

71. *See* Article 7 of the Rome Statute for the ICC's definition of crimes against humanity. For support of the argument that terrorist acts may constitute crimes against humanity, *see* Richard J. Goldstone & Janine Simpson, *Evaluating the Role of the International Criminal Court as a Legal Response to Terrorism*, 16 Harv. Hum. Rts. J. 13, 15 (2003); *see also* Scheffer, *supra* note 70.

72. James Podgers, *An Unused Weapon: International Criminal Court Could Play Role in War Against Terrorism, Says New Chief Prosecutor,* ABA Journal eReport, September 19, 2003, *available at* http://www.abajournal.com/ereport.html.

73. *See, e.g.,* Marc Grossman, Under Secretary of State for Political Affairs, Remarks to Center for Strategic and International Studies (May 6, 2002), *available at* http://www.amicc.org/docs/Grossman.pdf.

74. *See, e.g.,* Allison Marston Danner, *Navigating Law and Politics: The Prosecutor of the International Criminal Court and the Independent Counsel,* 55 Stan. L. Rev. 1633, 1646–47, 1655 (2003); Remigius Chibueze, *United States Objection to the International Criminal Court: A Paradox of "Operation Enduring Freedom,"* 9 Ann. Surv. Int'l & Comp. L. 19, 36–46 (2003).

75. William J. Clinton, *Remarks on the Signature of the ICC Treaty* (December 21, 2000). For an analysis of U.S. concerns since the beginning of ICC negotiations, *see* Pam Spees, *The Rome Statute of the International Criminal Court, in* Rule of Power or Rule of Law: An Assessment of U.S. Policies and Actions Regarding Security-Related Treaties (Nicole Deller *et al.* eds., 2002).

76. U.S. Department of State Press Statement, International Criminal Court: Letter to UN Secretary General Kofi Annan (May 6, 2002).

77. 2002 Supplemental Appropriations Act for Further Recovery from and Response to Terrorist Attacks on the United States, Pub. L. No. 107-206, §§ 2001–2015, 116 Stat. 820 (2002) [hereinafter "ASPA"].

78. ASPA § 2007. The ASPA also authorizes the president to use "all means necessary and appropriate" to bring about the release of U.S. and allied personnel from custody of the ICC. ASPA §§ 2008, 2013. Inferring that the language "all means necessary and appropriate" implies military operations, critics have dubbed the law "Hague Invasion Act" after the city in which defendants would be held for prosecution. Steven Mufson & Alan Sipress, *U.N. Funds in Crossfire Over Court; Exemption Sought for U.S. Troops,* Wash. Post, Aug. 16, 2001.

79. Appropriations for foreign operations, export financing and related programs for the fiscal year ending September 30, 2006 and for other purposes, Pub. L. No. 109-102 § 574; Stat. 2172 (2004).

80. ASPA § 2015.

81. 148 Cong. Rec. S 5132 (daily ed. June 6, 2002).

82. Scheffer, *supra* note 70, at 49–50.

83. S.C. Res 1593, U.N. SCOR, 59th Sess. U.N. Doc. S/Res/1593 (2005).

84. Statute for the International Tribunal for the Former Yugoslavia, S. C. Res. 827, U.N. SCOR, 48th Sess. 3217th mtg., U.N. Doc. 5/Res/827 (1993); Statute for the International Tribunal for Rwanda, S.C. Res. 955, U.N. SCOR, 49th Sess., 3453d mtg., U.N. Doc. S/Res/955 (1994).

85. Chapter VII of the UN Charter confers on the Security Council the right to determine the existence of any threat to peace, breach of peace, or act of aggression and decide what measures shall be taken to maintain or restore international peace and security.

86. *See* Anne Marie Slaughter, *Use courts, not combat, to get the bad guys*, Int'l Herald Trib., Nov. 20, 2003; Goldstone & Simpson, *supra* note 71 at 20–21.

87. *See, e.g.,* Anton L. Janik, Jr., *Prosecuting Al Qaeda: America's Human Rights Policy Interests Are Best Served By Trying Terrorists Under International Tribunals,* Denv. J. Int'l L. & Pol'y 498, 521–31 (2002).

88. *See e.g.* U.S. v. Massaoui, No. 01-455-A, (E.D.Va). (federal criminal trial of suspected terrorist); *see also* Detention, Treatment, and Trial of Certain Non-Citizens in the War Against Terrorism, 66 Fed. Reg., (Dep't of Defense, November 13, 2001).

89. Rasul v. Bush, 124 S. Ct. 2686 (2004).

90. Hamdi v. Rumsfeld, 124 S. Ct. 2633 (2004).

91. Hamdan v. Rumsfeld, 165 L.Ed.2d 723 (2006).

92. *Id.* Recent legislation stripped the judiciary of jurisdiction to hear cases regarding Guantanamo detainees except for specific limited appellate jurisdiction and jurisdiction, but the Hamdan case referenced above held that such legislation did not apply to cases pending at enactment. See Detainee Treatment Act of 2005, as included in the Department of Defense Appropriations Act, 2006, Public Law No: 109-148 (2005).

93. *See* Neil A. Lewis, *Military Lawyers Prepare to Speak on Guantanamo,* N.Y. Times, July 11, 2006; Kate Zernike *et al., Administration Prods Congress to Curb the Rights of Detainees*, N.Y. Times, July 13, 2006.

94. Anne Marie Slaughter, *Al Qaeda Should Be Tried Before the World,* N.Y. Times, Nov. 17, 2001.

95. Ruth Wedgwood, *Al Qaeda, Military Commissions and American Self-Defense*, 117 Pol. Sci. Q. 357, 369–73 (2002).

96. *See* Paul R. Williams & Michael P. Scharf, *Prosecute Terrorists on a World Stage,* L.A. Times, Nov. 18, 2001.

97. The White House, National Strategy to Combat Weapons of Mass Destruction 4 (Dec. 2002).

98. *Strengthening Multilateral Nonproliferation Regimes: Hearing before the Subcomm. on International Security, Proliferation and Federal Services of the Senate Comm. on Government Affairs,* 107th Cong. (2002) (statement of Vann H. Van Diepen, Deputy Assistant Secretary of State).

99. Treaty on the Non-Proliferation of Nuclear Weapons, July 1, 1968, 21 UST 483, 729 UNTS 161.

100. India, Pakistan and Israel, never subscribed to this regime. A fourth state, North Korea, announced the withdrawal of its membership in January 2003.

101. The Action Plan is described in *Excerpts from the Introductory Statement by IAEA Director General Dr. Mohamed ElBaradei to the IAEA Board of Governors,* March 18, 2002, *available at* http://www.iaea.org/worldatom/Press/Statements/2002/ebsp2002n001.shtml.

102. *See, e.g., The Physical Protection of Nuclear Material and Nuclear Facilities,* IAEA Doc. INFCIRC/225/Rev. 4 (Corrected) [undated], *available at* http://www.iaea.org/worldatom/Programmes/Protection/inf225rev4/rev4_content.html.

103. Statement by IAEA Director-General Dr. Mohamed ElBaradei, *Nuclear Proliferation and the Potential Threat of Nuclear Terrorism* (Nov. 8, 2004).

104. These initiatives are described in *Nuclear Security—Progress on Measures to Protect Against Nuclear Terror: Report by the Director-General,* IAEA Doc. GOV/INF/2002/11-GC/(46)/14, Attachment 1 at 2-3 (August 12, 2002), *available at* http://www.iaea.org/worldatom/Press/News/PDF/action_plan.pdf.

105. Mohamed ElBaradei, In Search of Security: Finding an Alternative to Nuclear Deterrence, Remarks at the Center for International Security and Cooperation, Stanford University (Nov. 4, 2004), *available at* http://www.iaea.org/NewsCenter/Statements/2004/ebsp2004n012.html.

106. *See* John Burroughs & Elizabeth Shafer, *The Nuclear Nonproliferation Treaty,* in Rule of Power or Rule of Law?, *supra* note 75 at 24–29.

107. 2000 Review Conference of the Parties to the Treaty on the Non-Proliferation of Nuclear Weapons, *Final Document,* May, 2000.

108. See David E. Sanger, *Month of Talks Fails to Bolster Nuclear Treaty,* N. Y. Times, May 28, 2005.

109. Jim Wurst, *Nonproliferation, Disarmament Matters Dropped from U.N. Summit Document,* Global Security Newswire, September 14, 2005.

110. Convention on the Prohibition of the Development, Production and Stockpiling of Bacteriological (Biological) and Toxin Weapons and on Their Destruction, Apr. 10, 1972, Art. 13(2), 26 UST 583, 1015 UNTS 163.

111. Donald Mahley, *Statement by the United States to the Ad Hoc Group of Biological Weapons Convention States Parties,* July 25, 2001, *available at* http://usinfo.state.gov/topical/pol/arms/stories/

01072501.htm. *But see* Donald Mahley's Testimony before a House Subcommittee less than a year prior, wherein he stated that achieving a successful BWC Protocol would be "extraordinarily difficult, but that makes it a worthy challenge." *The Biological Weapons Convention: Status and Implications: Hearing before the Subcomm. on National Security, Veterans Affairs, and International Relations of the Comm. on Government Reform,* 106th Cong. 14 (2003).

112. The proposed measures are set forth in the Fifth Review Conference of the States Parties to the BWC, *Final Document,* 2002, *available at* http://www.opbw.org/rev_cons/5rc/docs/final_dec/BWC-CONF.V-17-(final_doc).pdf. States parties had their most recent meeting to advance these proposals in December, 2004, *available at* http://www.opbw.org/new_process/msp2004_conf.htm.

113. *See, e.g.,* Barbara Hatch Rosenberg, *Allergic Reaction: Washington's Response to the BWC Protocol,* Arms Control Today, July/August 2001.

114. Convention on the Prohibition of the Development, Production, Stockpiling and Use of Chemical Weapons and on their Destruction, Jan 13, 1993, S. Treaty Doc. No. 103-21, 1974 U.N.T.S. 3.

115. For more information on the CWC's contributions to preventing terrorism, *see* Organization for the Prohibition of Chemical Weapons, *Possible Responses to Global Terrorist Threats [undated], available at* http://www.opcw.org/resp/.

116. *See, e.g., Expounding Bush's Approach to U.S. Nuclear Security, An Interview with John R. Bolton,* Arms Control Today, March 2002.

117. As stated above, four states are outside the NPT regime: India, Israel, North Korea and Pakistan. The list of states parties and signatories to the BWC and the CWC may be found at http://www.icrc.org/ihl.

118. George W. Bush, President of the United States, Address before the United Stated General Assembly (Sept. 23, 2003), *available at* http://www.whitehouse.gov/news/releases/2003/09/20030923-4.html#.

119. S.C. Res. 1540, *supra* note 47.

120. See Merav Datan, *Security Council Resolution 1540: WMD and Non-State Trafficking,* Disarmament Diplomacy, April/May 2005.

121. Nuclear Threat Initiative, *Glossary of Terms, available at* http://www.nti.org/b_aboutnti/b_index.html.

122. *The Australia Group: New Measures to Fight the Spread of Chemical and Biological Weapons,* Australia Group Press Release AG/Jun02/Press/7, June 7, 2002. Available at http://projects.sipri.se/cbw/research/AG-press-Jun02.html.

123. Australian Department of Foreign Affairs & Trade, International Security Affairs Division, *The Australia Group, available at* http://www.dfat.gov.au/security/downloads/australian_group.pdf. Includes a list of participants.

124. *See* United States General Accounting Office, *Strategy Needed to Strengthen Multilateral Export Control Regimes,* Report to Congressional Committees, GAO-03-43, October 2002, *available at* http://www.gao.gov/cgi-bin/getrpt?gao-03-43.

125. List of participants can be found at http://www.state.gov/t/np/rls/prsrl/2002/14497.htm.

126. Van Diepen, *supra* note 98. The MTCR only addresses the supply side of missile technology. The United States has also lead the creation of a code of conduct aimed at the demand side, known as the International Code of Conduct against Ballistic Missile Proliferation (ICOC). It is a voluntary "political commitment" aimed at preventing states from developing and stockpiling missile technology. The text may be found at http://projects.sipri.se/expcon/drafticoc.htm. *See also* John Bolton, Remarks at the Launching Conference for the International Code of Conduct Against Ballistic Missile Proliferation, (Nov. 25, 2002), *available at* http://www.state.gov/t/us/rm/15488.htm. A critical review of the ICOC is found at http://www.basicint.org/pubs/Notes/2002international_code.htm.

127. Plenary Meeting of the Missile Technology Control Regime, MTCR Press Release, September, 2003; MTCR Press Release, Plenary meeting of the Missile Technology Control Regime, MTCR Press Release, September 2002. Both documents are available at http://www.mtcr.info.

128. Press Statement, Nuclear Suppliers Group Plenary Meeting, (May 16–17, 2002), *available at* http://www.nsg-online.org/PRESS/2002-03-press-prague.pdf.

129. *See Communication Received from Certain Member States Regarding Guidelines for the Export of Nuclear Material, Equipment and Technology,* IAEA Doc. INFCIRC/254/Rev.5/Part 1 (May 2003), *available at* http://www.nuclearsuppliersgroup.org/PDF/infcirc254r6p1-030516.pdf.

130. See *Communication Received from Certain Member States Regarding Guidelines for the Transfers of Nuclear-Related Dual-Use Equipment, Material, Software and Related Technology*, IAEA Doc. INFCIRC/254/Rev.5/Part 2 (May 2003), *available at* http://www.nuclearsuppliersgroup.org/PDF/infcirc254r5p2-030516.pdf.

131. Press Statement, Nuclear Suppliers Group Plenary Meeting, (May 16–17, 2002).

132. See INFCIRC/254/Rev.5/Part 1, *supra* note 129 and INFCIRC/254/Rev.5/Part 2, *supra* note 129.

133. The list of participants may be found at http://www.wassenaar.org/welcomepage.html.

134. The Wassenaar Arrangement, *Initial Elements,* (July 11–12, 1996), *available at* http://www.wassenaar.org/docs/IE96.html.

135. The Wassenaar Arrangement, *Public Statement for 2002 Plenary,* (Dec. 12, 2002), *available at* http://www.usun-vienna.usia.co.at/wassenaar/public02.html.

136. *See* U.S. Department of State, Bureau of Non-proliferation, Fact Sheet: Zangger Committee, (Sept. 10, 2003); includes a list of member states, *available at* http://www.state.gov/t/np/rls/fs/3054.htm.

137. The Trigger List was first published in September 1974 as IAEA document INFCIRC/209 and has been amended several times since then. The most current form is in *Communication of 15 November 1999 Received from Member States Regarding the Export of Nuclear Material and of Certain Categories of Equipment and Other Material,* IAEA Doc. INFCIRC 209/Rev. 2 (March 2000).

138. *See* U.S. Department of State, Bureau of Non-proliferation, Fact Sheet: Zangger Committee, (Sept. 10, 2003), *available at* http://www.state.gov/t/np/rls/fs/3054.htm.

139. *See* United States General Accounting Office, *Nonproliferation: Strategy Needed to Strengthen Multilateral Export Control Regimes,* (Oct. 2002), *available at* http://www.gao.gov/new.items/d0343.pdf.

140. Michael Beck & Seema Gahlaut, *Creating a New Multilateral Export Control Regime,* Arms Control Today, April 2003.

141. Richard Lugar, *The Next Steps in U.S. Nonproliferation Policy,* Arms Control Today, December 2002.

142. Claire Applegarth, *Modest Hike in Threat Reduction Budget,* Arms Control Today, March 2005.

143. Michael Nguyen, *Albania to Receive Nunn-Lugar Assistance,* Arms Control Today, December 2004.

144. The 9/11 Commission Report: Final Report of the National Commission on Terrorist Attacks Upon the United States 381 (U.S. Government Printing Office, 2004).

145. 9/11 Public Discourse Project: Report on the Status of 9/11 Commission Recommendations, Part III: Foreign Policy, Public Diplomacy, and Nonproliferation 3 (2005).

146. *Id.*

147. The White House, Office of the Press Secretary, *Fact Sheet: G-8 Summit—Preventing the Proliferation of Weapons of Mass Destruction* (June 27, 2002), *available at* http://www.whitehouse.gov/news/releases/2002/06/20020627-7.html. *See also* James C. Kraska, *Averting Nuclear Terrorism: Building a Global Regime of Cooperative Threat Reduction,* 20 Am. U. Int'l L. Rev. 703, 744–56 (2005).

148. G8 Action Plan on Nonproliferation (June, 2004).

149. G8 Global Partnership Annual Report, G8 Senior Group (June 2005).

150. National Strategy to Combat Weapons of Mass Destruction, *supra* note 97.

151. Paul O'Sullivan, *Chairman's Statement: From the Proliferation Security Initiative (PSI) meeting in Brisbane* (July 9–10, 2003), *available at* http://www.dfat.gov.au/globalissues/psi/chair_statement_0603.html.

152. The PSI began with eleven countries as members, which has subsequently increased to fifteen: Australia, Britain, Canada, France, Germany, Italy, Japan, the Netherlands, Norway, Poland, Portugal, Russia, Singapore, Spain, and the United States. In addition, Turkey and Denmark sent representatives to the PSI's December 2003 operational experts meeting. *See* Michael Byers, *Policing the High Seas: The Proliferation Security Initiative,* 98 Am. J. Int'l L. 526, 528 (July 2004).

153. The White House, *'Principles for the Proliferation Security Initiative', Statement by the Press Secretary* (Sept. 4, 2003). "States or non-state actors of proliferation concern" is defined in the Statement

of Interdiction Principles as "those countries or entities that the PSI participants involved establish should be subject to interdiction activities because they are engaged in proliferation. . ." Proliferation Security Initiative, *Statement of Interdiction Principles* (Sept. 4, 2003).

154. *See, e.g.,* Barbara Slavin, *11 nations join plan to stop N. Korean ships; U.S. hopes to put squeeze on Kim,* USA Today, July 23, 2003; Wade Boese, *Countries Draft Guidelines for Intercepting Proliferation,* Arms Control Today, September 2003.

155. President George W. Bush, Remarks by the President to the People of Poland (May 31, 2003).

156. *Statement of Interdiction Principles, supra* note 153.

157. *State Department Background Briefing: The Proliferation Security Initiative,* Federal News Service (Sept. 9, 2003).

158. *Statement of Interdiction Principles, supra* note 153.

159. Byers, *supra* note 152, at 529.

160. Michael Evans, *US plans to seize suspects at will,* The Times (London), July 11, 2003.

161. *State Department Background Briefing, supra* note 157.

162. United Nations Convention on the Law of the Sea, Dec. 10, 1982, 1833 U.N.T.S. 3 (entered into force Nov. 16, 1994) (The U.S. has signed but not ratified the treaty, and accepts its substantive provisions, other than those relating to deep sea bed mining, as binding statements of customary law; Restatement (Third) of the Foreign Relations Law of the United States, pt. V, introductory note, at 5 (1986)).

163. UNCLOS, *supra* note 162, Art. 19.

164. *Id.*

165. *See id.* Art. 20.

166. *See, e.g.,* United Nations Convention Against Illicit Traffic in Narcotic Drugs and Psychotropic Substances (Dec. 20, 1988), 28 ILM 493, U.N. Doc. E/CONF.82/15, *available at* http://www.unodc.org/pdf/convention_1988_en.pdf. In addition, the United States has concluded twenty-three bilateral treaties with Caribbean and Central American states on this subject. For a table of these agreements, *see* http://www.ciponline.org/facts/mar.htm.

167. Agreement for the Implementation of the Provisions of the UN Convention on the Law of the Sea of 10 December 1982, Relating to the Conservation and Management of Straddling Fish Stocks and Highly Migratory Fish Stocks, Art. 21(1), UN Doc. A/CONF.164/37, 34 ILM 1542, at 1563 (1995), *available at* http://www.un.org/Depts/los/convention_agreements/convention_overview_fish_stocks.htm.

168. Amendment to the Supplementary Arrangement Between the Government of the United States of America and the Government of the Republic of Panama to the Arrangement Between the Government of the United States of America and the Government of Panama for Support and Assistance from the United States Coast Guard for the National Maritime Service of the Ministry of Government and Justice, May 12, 2004, *available at* http://www.state.gov/t/np/trty/32858.htm.

169. Agreement Between the Government of the United States of America and the Government of the Republic of Liberia Concerning Cooperation to Suppress the Proliferation of Weapons of Mass Destruction, Their Delivery Systems, and Related Materials by Sea (Feb. 11, 2004), *available at* http://www.state.gov/t/np/trty/32403.htm.

170. *Id.* Art. 4 § 3d.

171. See, e.g., Mark R. Shulman, *The Proliferation Security Initiative and the Evolution of the Law on the Use of Force,* 28 Hous. J. Int'l. L. 771 (2006).

172. Robin Wright, *Ship Incident May Have Swayed Libya; Centrifuges Intercepted in September,* The Washington Post, January 1, 2004.

173. Wade Boese, *Key Interdiction Initiative Claim Misrepresented,* Arms Control Today, July/August 2005.

174. William Perry, *It's Either Nukes or Negotiation,* Wash. Post, July 23, 2003; *see also The Proliferation Security Initiative: An interdiction strategy,* Strategic Comments, August 2003, *available at* http://www.iiss.org/stratcomfree.php?scID=282.

Online Sources

Inter Arma Silent Leges

Press Release, Office of the Press Secretary, President Issues Military Order: Detention, Treatment, and Trial of Certain Non-Citizens in the War against Terrorism (November 13, 2001), *available at* http://www.whitehouse.gov/news/releases/2001/11/20011113-27.html (last accessed August 25, 2006).

Department of Defense, Fact Sheet: Department of Defense Order on Military Commissions (March 21, 2002), *available at* http://www.defenselink.mil/news/Mar2002/d20020321fact.pdf (last accessed on August 25, 2006).

Human Rights Watch, BriefingPaper on U.S. Military Commissions (June 23, 2006), http://hrw.org/backgrounder/usa/gitmo0606/ (last accessed August 25, 2006).

S.J.Res.23, 107th Congress, Authorization for Use of Military Force (January 3, 2001) (enrolled as agreed to or passed by both house and senate), *available at* http://thomas.loc.gov/cgi-bin/query/z?c107:S.J.RES.23.ENR (last accessed August 25, 2006).

Legality and Constitutionality

President George W. Bush, State of the Union Address, Jan. 29, 2002, *available at* http://www.whitehouse.gov/news/releases/2002/01/20020129-11.html (last accessed August 25, 2006).

Human Constitutional Rights, *The War on Iraq: Legal Issues, available at* http://www.hrcr.org/hottopics/Iraq.html (last accessed August 25, 2006).

David M. Ackerman, *Response to Terrorism: Legal Aspects of the Use of Military Force,* Congressional Research Service (September 13, 2001), *available at* http://fpc.state.gov/documents/organization/6217.pdf (last accessed August 24, 2006).

Memorandum, U.S. Department of Justice, Office of Legal Counsel, The President's Constitutional Authority to Conduct Military Operations against Terrorists and Nations Supporting Them (September 25, 2001), http://www.usdoj.gov/olc/warpowers925.htm (last accessed August 25, 2006).

Letter re: UN Charter

U.N. Charter, Chap. 7, art. 51, http://www.un.org/aboutun/charter/ (last accessed August 25, 2006).

S.C. Res. 678, U.N. Doc. S/RES/0678 (1990), *available at* http://www.fas.org/news/un/iraq/sres/sres0678.htm (last accessed August 25, 2006).

U.S. Dept. of State, *White House Background Paper on Iraq: A Decade of Deception and Defiance,* Sept. 12, 2002, available at http://www.fas.org/news/un/iraq/sres/sres0678.htm (last accessed August 25, 2006).

Press Release, Office of the Press Secretary, Joint Resolution to Authorize the Use of United States Armed Forces against Iraq, October 2, 2002, *available at* http://www.whitehouse.gov/news/releases/2002/10/20021002-2.html (last accessed August 25, 2006).

Press Release, Office of the Press Secretary, President's Remarks at the United Nations General Assembly (Sept. 12, 2002), *available at* http://www.whitehouse.gov/news/releases/2002/09/20020912-1.html (last accessed August 25, 2006).

Women and Girls in Afghanistan

Human Rights Watch, *We Want to Live as Humans: Repression of Women and Girls in Western Afghanistan,* Vol. 14, No. 11 (December 2002), http://www.hrw.org/reports/2002/afghnwmn1202/ (last accessed July 10, 2006).

Economic and Social Council, United Nations, Report of the Secretary-General on the situation of women and girls in Afghanistan, E/CN.6/2004/5 (December 19, 2003), *available at* http://daccessdds.un.org/doc/UNDOC/GEN/N03/674/81/PDF/N0367481.pdf?OpenElement (last accessed July 11, 2006).

General Assembly, United Nations, Situation of Women and Girls in Afghanistan, E/CN.6/2003/4 (January 23, 2003), *available at* http://daccessdds.un.org/doc/UNDOC/GEN/N03/556/46/PDF/N0355646.pdf?OpenElement (last accessed July 11, 2006).

Lorne W. Craner, Assistant Secretary, Committee on International Relations, U.S. House of Representatives, Testimony on, *Democracy, Human Rights and Labor Bureau, Department of State,* Before the House International Relations Committee, Subcommittee on Middle East and Central Asia, And the Subcommittee on International Terrorism, Nonproliferation And Human Rights, Afghanistan: Democratization and Human Rights on the Eve of the Constitutional Loya Jirga, November 19, 2003, *available at* http://wwwa.house.gov/international_relations/108/cra111903.htm (last accessed August 25, 2006).

Military Commission Instructions

Department of Defense, Military Commission Order, No. 1, Procedures for Trials by Military Commission of Certain Non-United States Citizens in the War Against Terrorism (March 21, 2002), *available at* http://www.defenselink.mil/news/Mar2002/d20020321ord.pdf (last accessed August 25, 2006).

Ex Parte Milligan, 71 U.S. 2 (1866), *available at* http://www.constitution.org/ussc/071-002a.htm (last accessed August 24, 2006).

Department of Defense, Military Instruction No. 2, Crimes and Elements for Trials by Military Commission (April 30, 2003), *available at* http://www.defenselink.mil/news/May2003/d20030430milcominstno2.pdf (last accessed August 24, 2006).

Press Release, Office of the Press Secretary, *President Issues Military Order: Detention, Treatment, and Trial of Certain Non-Citizens in the War Against Terrorism* (November 13, 2001), *available at* http://www.whitehouse.gov/news/releases/2001/11/20011113-27.html (last accessed August 25, 2006).

Schmitz Letter

Neil A. Lewis, *Tribunals Nearly Ready for Afghanistan Prisoners,* NY Times, April 8, 2003, *available at* http://www.globalpolicy.org/intljustice/general/2003/0408tribunal.htm (last accessed August 25, 2006).

Army Regulation 190-8: Enemy Prisoners of War, Retained Personnel, Civilian Internees, and other Detainees, October 1, 1997, *available at* http://usmilitary.about.com/gi/dynamic/offsite.htm?site=http://www.usapa.army.mil/pdffiles/r190%5F8.pdf (last accessed August 25, 2006).

Geneva Convention (III). Relative to the Treatment of Prisoners of War, Aug. 12, 1949, entered into force Oct. 21, 1950, 6 U.S.T. 3316, 75 U.N.T.S. 135, *available at* http://www.icrc.org/ihl.nsf/

7c4d08d9b287a42141256739003e636b/6fef854a3517b75ac125641e004a9e68 (last accessed August 25, 2006).

Padilla Brief

Padilla v. Rumsfeld, 352 F.3d 695 (2nd Cir. 2003), *available at* http://fl1.findlaw.com/news.findlaw.com/cnn/docs/padilla/padillarums121803opn.pdf (last accessed August 24, 2006).
Rumsfeld v. Padilla, 542 U.S. 426 (2004), *available at* http://caselaw.lp.findlaw.com/scripts/getcase.pl?court=US&vol=000&invol=03-1027#opinion1 (last accessed August 24, 2006).
Human Rights Watch, *Presumption of Guilt: Human Rights Abuses of Post September 11 Detainees,* (August 2002), http://www.hrw.org/reports/2002/us911/ (last accessed August 24, 2006).

Tampering With Animals

An Act to Amend the Agriculture and Markets Law, in Relation to Unlawful Tampering with Animal Activities, S 2996, New York Senate, March 13, 2003, *available at* http://www.animalrights.net/archives/year/2003/000190.html (last accessed July 11, 2006).
American Legislative Exchange Council, *Animal and Ecological Terrorism in America* (2003), *available at* http://www.alec.org/meSWFiles/pdf/AnimalandEcologicalTerrorisminAmerica.pdf (last accessed August 25, 2006).

Padilla Brief and Indefinite Detention Report

Padilla v. Rumsfeld, 542 U.S. 426 (2004), *available at* http://www.supremecourtus.gov/opinions/03pdf/03-1027.pdf#search=%22padilla%20v.%20bush%20supreme%20court%22 (last accessed September 13, 2006).
Hamdan v. Rumsfeld, 548 US ___ (2006), *available at* http://www.law.cornell.edu/supct/html/05-184.ZS.html (last accessed September 13, 2006).

Trial of Saddam Hussein

Law Library of Congress, *Trial of Saddam Hussein,* last modified June 21, 2006, http://www.loc.gov/law/public/saddam/ (last accessed August 25, 2006).
The Iraq Tribunal: Trying Saddam Hussein and Other Top Baath Leaders, Global Policy Forum, http://www.globalpolicy.org/intljustice/iraqindex.htm (last accessed July 14, 2006).
Iraqi Special Tribunal to Try Crimes Against Humanity, Human Constitutional Rights, updated April 9, 2006, *available at* http://www.hrcr.org/hottopics/iraqitribunal.html (last accessed September 13, 2006).
International Covenant on Civil and Political Rights, G.A. Res. 2200A (XXI), UN GAOR, 21st Sess., Supp. No. 16, at 52, UN Doc. A/6316 Dec. 16, 1966, entered into force 23 March 1976, *available at* http://www.ohchr.org/english/law/ccpr.htm (last accessed August 25, 2006).
Universal Declaration of Human Rights, G.A. Res. 217, UN GAOR, 3d Sess., UN Doc. A/810 (1948) art. 5, http://www.unhchr.ch/udhr/lang/eng.htm (last accessed August 25, 2006).

Human Rights Standards

Geneva Convention (III) Relative to the Treatment of Prisoners of War, Aug. 12, 1949, entered into force Oct. 21, 1950, 6 U.S.T. 3316, 75 U.N.T.S. 135, *available at* http://www.icrc.org/ihl.nsf/7c4d08d9b287a42141256739003e636b/6fef854a3517b75ac125641e004a9e68 (last accessed August 25, 2006).
United Nations Convention Against Torture and Other Cruel, Inhuman or Degrading Treatment or Punishment, opened for signature December 10, 1984, G.A. Res. 39/46, 39 UN GAOR Supp. No. 51, UN Doc. A/RES/39/708 (1984), entered into force June 26, 1987, *available at* http://www.ohchr.org/english/law/cat.htm (last accessed August 24, 2006).

Amnesty International, *United States of America: A Safe Haven for Torturers* (2002), *available at* http://www.amnestyusa.org/stoptorture/safehaven.pdf (last accessed August 24, 2006).

Mary Robinson, Statement of the High Commissioner for Human Rights on Detention of Taliban and Al Qaeda Prisoners at U.S. Base in Guantanamo Bay, Cuba (Jan. 16, 2002), *available at* http://www.unhchr.ch/huricane/huricane.nsf/view01/C537C6D4657C7928C1256B43003E7D0B?opendocument (last accessed August 25, 2006).

Dangerous Doctrine

David G. Savage, *Critics Say Terror Probe Bends Immigrations Laws,* LA Times, Sept. 10, 2002, at 17, *available at* http://mediaguidetoislam.sfsu.edu/intheus/pdfs/E_ABS_LATimes.pdf (last accessed August 25, 2006).

Inspector General Criticizes 9/11 Detentions, 13 CQ Researcher No. 37, at 898 (Oct. 24, 2003), *available at* http://www.polisci.umn.edu/courses/fall2003/4303/001/kiosk/USAPatriotAct/CivilLiberties-CQ.pdf (last accessed August 25, 2006).

U.S. Department of Justice, Office of the Inspector General, *The September 11 Detainees: A Review Of The Treatment Of Aliens Held On Immigration Charges In Connection With The Investigation Of The September 11 Attacks 195* (April 2003), http://www.usdoj.gov/oig/special/0306/full.pdf (last accessed August 25, 2006).

Lisa Getter & Jonathan Peterson, *The Nation: Speedier Rate of Deportation Rulings Assailed,* Los Angeles Times, Jan. 5, 2003, at 1, *available at* http://www.usdoj.gov/eoir/press/03/speedierrate.pdf (last accessed August 25, 2006).

Human Rights Watch, *The United States "Disappeared": The CIA's Long-Term "Ghost Detainees"* (Oct. 2004), http://www.hrw.org/backgrounder/usa/us1004/ (last accessed August 25, 2006).

Markey 4674

108th Congress, 2nd Session, HR 4674, introduced June 23, 2004, http://thomas.loc.gov/cgi-bin/query/z?c108:H.R.4674: (last accessed August 25, 2006).

Congressional Budget Office, Foreign Affairs Reform and Restructuring Act of 1998, HR 1757, agreed to March 10, 1998, http://www.cbo.gov/showdoc.cfm?index=490&sequence=0 (last accessed December 21, 2006).

Jane Mayer, *Outsourcing Torture: The Secret History of America's "Extraordinary Rendition" Program,* The New Yorker, Feb. 7, 2005, http://www.newyorker.com/fact/content/?050214fa_fact6 (last accessed August 25, 2006).

Amnesty Int'l., *Below the Radar: Secret Flights to Torture and "Disappear,"* April 5, 2006, *available at* http://web.amnesty.org/library/index/ENGAMR510512006 (last accessed August 25, 2006).

Center For Human Rights and Global Justice, *Congress Must Act to Prevent Mass Transfers to Torture,* June 28, 2005, *available at* http://www.commondreams.org/news2005/0628-22.htm (last accessed August 25, 2006).

Statement Opposing House 9/11 Bill

Laura W. Murphy and Gregory T. Nojeim, *Financial Services: Vote for Privacy, A Letter to the House on the Financial Services Act H.R. 10,* American Civil Liberties Union, July 1, 1999, http://www.aclu.org/privacy/consumer/15153leg19990701.html (last accessed August 25, 2006).

Press Release, Human Rights Watch, *U.S. Proposed Laws Would Lead to Abuse of Immigrants,* April 22, 2004, http://hrw.org/english/docs/2004/04/21/usdom8476.htm (last accessed August 25, 2006).

Executive Office of the President, Office of Management and Budget, *Statement of Administrative Policy: H.R. 10- 9/11 Recommendations Implementation Act,* October 7, 2004, *available at* http://www.whitehouse.gov/omb/legislative/sap/108-2/hr10sap-h.pdf (last accessed August 25, 2006).

New York Civil Liberties Union, *U.S. House 9/11 Bill Includes Anti-Immigrant Provisions,* Oct. 18, 2004, http://www.nyclu.org/hr10_911bill_tp_101804.html (last accessed August 25, 2006).

Position Paper Regarding NLRB

IBM Corp., 341 NLRB No. 148, Jun. 9, 2004, *available at* http://www.nlrb.gov/nlrb/shared_files/decisions/341/341-148.pdf (last accessed August 25, 2006).

Statement of Senator Edward Kennedy on the Immigration Provisions of H.R. 10, AILA InfoNet Doc. No. 04101261, posted Oct. 12, 2004, *available at* http://www.aila.org/content/default.aspx?docid=11594 (last accessed August 25, 2006).

Human Rights First, *H.R. 10: A Threat to Refugees and Torture Victims,* http://www.humanrightsfirst.org/Issues/talk_pts_hr10.htm (last accessed August 25, 2006).

National Labor Relations Act, 29 U.S.C. §§ 151–169, http://www.law.cornell.edu/uscode/29/usc_sup_01_29_10_7_20_II.html (last accessed December 21, 2006).

Torture by Proxy

Amnesty Int'l., *USA: Memorandum to the U.S. Government on the Rights of People in U.S. Custody in Afghanistan and Guantanamo Bay,* (April 2002), *available at* http://web.amnesty.org/library/index/engamr510532002 (last accessed August 25, 2006).

Department of the Army Inspector General, Detainee Operations Inspection (July 2004), *available at* http://www.globalsecurity.org/military/library/report/2004/daig_detainee-ops_21jul2004.pdf (last accessed August 25, 2006).

Hearing on Allegations of Mistreatment of Iraqi prisoners Before the Senate Armed Services Committee, 108th Cong. (May 2004), *available at* http://armed-services.senate.gov/ (last accessed July 17, 2006).

Human Rights Watch, *"Empty Promises:" Diplomatic Assurances No Safeguard against Torture* (April 2004), http://hrw.org/reports/2004/un0404/index.htm (last accessed August 25, 2006).

Press Release, American Civil Liberties Union, *"The Public Should Know Of Our Government's Treatment of Individuals Captured And Held Abroad," Judge Says,* Sept. 15, 2004, *available at* http://www.aclu.org/SafeandFree/SafeandFree.cfm?ID=16465&c=281 (last accessed August 25, 2006).

Gonzales

Press Release, Office of the Press Secretary, *Press Briefing by White House Counsel Judge Alberto Gonzales, DoD General Counsel William Haynes, DoD Deputy General Counsel Daniel Dell'Orto and Army Deputy Chief of Staff for Intelligence General Keith Alexander,* June 22, 2004, *available at* http://www.whitehouse.gov/news/releases/2004/06/20040622-14.html (last accessed August 25, 2006).

Youngstown Sheet & Tube Co. v. Sawyer, 343 U.S. 579 (1952), *available at* http://www.law.cornell.edu/supct/html/historics/USSC_CR_0343_0579_ZS.html (last accessed August 25, 2006).

Department of the Army, Field Manual 34-52, modified Sept. 28, 1992, *available at* http://www.fas.org/irp/doddir/army/fm34-52.pdf (last accessed August 25, 2006).

U.S. Dept. of Justice, Office of Legal Counsel, *Memorandum for Alberto R. Gonzales, Counsel to the President RE: Standards of Conduct for Interrogation under 18 U.S.C. §c 2340-2340A,* Aug. 1, 2002, *available at* http://www.washingtonpost.com/wp-srv/nation/documents/dojinterrogationmemo20020801.pdf (last accessed August 25, 2006).

U.S. Dept. of Justice, Office of Legal Counsel, Memorandum for William J. Haynes II RE: Application of Treaties and Laws to al Qaeda and Taliban Detainees, Jan. 9, 2002, available at http://www.justicescholars.org/pegc/archive/DOJ/20020109_yoomemo.pdf (last accessed August 25, 2006).

Guantanamo Statement

United Nations Convention Against Torture and Other Cruel, Inhuman or Degrading Treatment or Punishment, opened for signature December 10, 1984, G.A. Res. 39/46, 39 UN GAOR Supp. No. 51, at 197, UN Doc. A/RES/39/708 (1984), entered into force June 26, 1987, *available at* http://www.ohchr.org/english/law/cat.htm (last accessed August 25, 2006).

Amnesty International, *Guantanamo: An Icon of Lawlesness* (2005), *available at* http://web.amnesty.org/library/Index/ENGAMR510022005 (last accessed September 13, 2006).

Markey 952

Torture Outsourcing Prevention Act, H.R. 952, 109th Cong. (2005), *available at* http://markey.house.gov/docs/defense/iss_human_rights_bill050217.pdf (last accessed August 25, 2006).

Letter, Morton Skylar, Executive Director, World Organization for Human Rights USA, Mar. 9, 2004, *available at* http://markey.house.gov/docs/defense/iss_human_rights_ltr050309.pdf (last accessed August 25, 2006).

Human Rights Watch, *Empty Promises: Diplomatic Assurances No Safeguard against Torture* (April 2004), http://hrw.org/reports/2004/un0404/ (last accessed August 25, 2006).

Nomination of Haynes

Statement Of Sen. Patrick Leahy, Ranking Member, Judiciary Committee, On The Nomination Of William J. Haynes II To The Fourth Circuit Court Of Appeals, July 11, 2006, *available at* http://leahy.senate.gov/press/200607/071106a.html (last accessed August 25, 2006).

Department of Defense, General Counsel, Memorandum to the Secretary of Defense Regarding Counter-Resistance Techniques, November 27, 2002, *available at* http://www.washingtonpost.com/wp-srv/nation/documents/dodmemos.pdf (last accessed August 25, 2006).

An Injudicious Nominee, N.Y. Times, March 23, 2004, *available at* http://www.nytimes.com/2004/03/23/opinion/23TUE3.html?ex=1395378000&en=de47f2f9a2915150&ei=5007&partner=USERLAND (last accessed December 21, 2006).

Department of Defense, Working Group Report, *Detainee Interrogations in the Global War on Terrorism: Assessments of Legal, Historical, Policy, and Operational Considerations,* Apr. 4, 2003, *available at* http://www.washingtonpost.com/wp-srv/nation/documents/040403dod.pdf (last accessed August 25, 2006).

USA Patriot Act

Department of Justice, Fact Sheet: USA PATRIOT Act Improvement and Reauthorization Act of 2005, Mar. 2, 2006, *available at* http://www.usdoj.gov/opa/pr/2006/March/06_opa_113.html (last accessed August 25, 2006).

American Civil Liberties Union, *ACLU Disappointed with Patriot Act Expansion Bill Approved in Secret; Says "Administrative Subpoenas" Create End-Run Round Constitution,* Jun. 7, 2005, *available at* http://www.aclu.org/safefree/general/17652prs20050607.html (last accessed August 25, 2006).

Congressional Research Service, *USA PATRIOT Act Additional Reauthorization Amendments Act of 2006 (S. 2271)* (Feb. 21, 2006), *available at* http://www.fas.org/sgp/crs/intel/RS22384.pdf (last accessed August 25, 2006).

Hamdan v. Rumsfeld

Hamdan v. Rumsfeld, 344 F. Supp. 2d 152 (D.D.C. 2004), *available at* http://files.findlaw.com/news.findlaw.com/hdocs/docs/tribunals/hamdanrums110804opn.pdf (last accessed August 25, 2006).

Hamdan v. Rumsfeld, 367 U.S. App. D.C. 265 (2005), *available at* http://caselaw.lp.findlaw.com/data2/circs/dc/045393a.pdf (last accessed August 25, 2006).

Hamdan v. Rumsfeld, 126 S. Ct. 622 (2005), *available at* http://www.supremecourtus.gov/opinions/05pdf/05-184.pdf (last accessed August 25, 2006).

International Covenant on Civil and Political Rights, G.A. Res. 2200A (XXI), UN GAOR, 21st Sess., Supp. No. 16, at 52, UN Doc. A/6316 Dec. 16, 1966, entered into force 23 March 1976 *available at* http://www.ohchr.org/english/law/ccpr.htm (last accessed August 25, 2006).

Multilateral Instruments

U.N. Department of Disarmament Affairs, http://disarmament.un.org/ (last accessed December 21, 2006).

Nuclear Non-Proliferation Treaty, http://www.un.org/Depts/dda/WMD/treaty/ (last accessed December 21, 2006).

Organization for the Prohibition of Chemical Weapons, http://www.opcw.org/ (last accessed December 21, 2006).

The Biological and Toxin Weapons Convention Web site, http://www.opbw.org/ (last accessed December 21, 2006).

The U.S. Department of State, Bureau of International Security and Nonproliferation, http://www.state.gov/t/isn/ (last accessed December 21, 2006).

Index

Note on Arabic names: The prefixes "al-" and "el-" have been retained but ignored when the entry is alphabetized, so that al-Zari is listed under Z. "Bin" is treated as a primary element and appears under B.